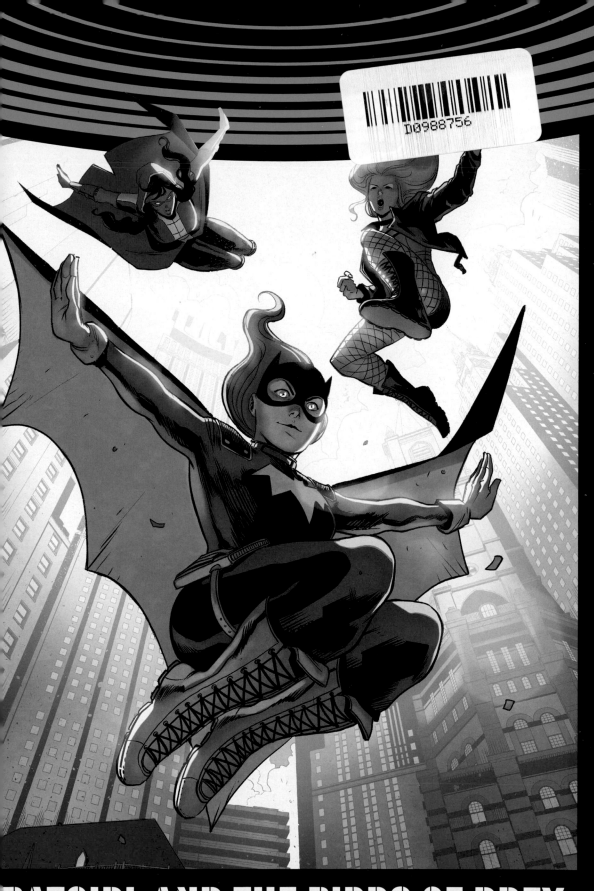

BATGIRL AND THE BIRDS OF PREY
VOL.3 FULL CIRCLE

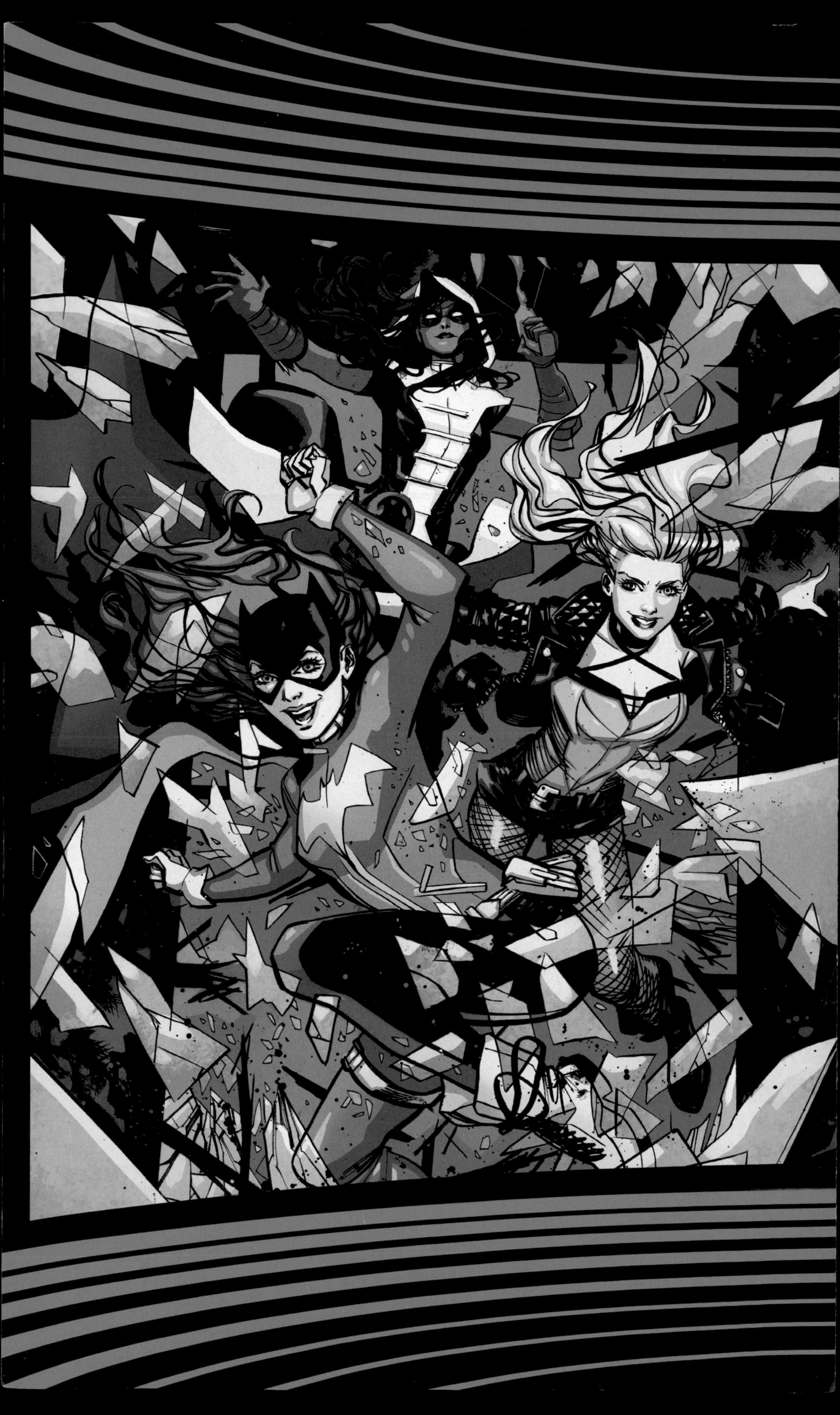

BATGIRL AND THE BIRDS OF PREY
VOL.3 FULL CIRCLE

JULIE BENSON * SHAWNA BENSON
writers

ROGE ANTONIO * MARCIO TAKARA
artists

MARCELO MAIOLO * JORDAN BOYD
colorists

SAIDA TEMOFONTE * JOSH REED
DEZI SIENTY * DERON BENNETT
letterers

TERRY and RACHEL DODSON
collection cover artists

BATMAN created by BOB KANE with BILL FINGER
HUNTRESS created by PAUL LEVITZ, BOB LAYTON and JOE STATON
CALCULATOR created by BOB ROZAKIS and MIKE GRELL

MIKE COTTON KATIE KUBERT Editors – Original Series * **ROB LEVIN** Associate Editor – Original Series
JEB WOODARD Group Editor – Collected Editions * **ERIKA ROTHBERG** Editor – Collected Edition
STEVE COOK Design Director – Books * **SHANNON STEWART** Publication Design

BOB HARRAS Senior VP – Editor-in-Chief, DC Comics
PAT McCALLUM Executive Editor, DC Comics

DIANE NELSON President * **DAN DiDIO** Publisher * **JIM LEE** Publisher * **GEOFF JOHNS** President & Chief Creative Officer
AMIT DESAI Executive VP – Business & Marketing Strategy, Direct to Consumer & Global Franchise Management
SAM ADES Senior VP & General Manager, Digital Services * **BOBBIE CHASE** VP & Executive Editor, Young Reader & Talent Development
MARK CHIARELLO Senior VP – Art, Design & Collected Editions * **JOHN CUNNINGHAM** Senior VP – Sales & Trade Marketing
ANNE DePIES Senior VP – Business Strategy, Finance & Administration * **DON FALLETTI** VP – Manufacturing Operations
LAWRENCE GANEM VP – Editorial Administration & Talent Relations * **ALISON GILL** Senior VP – Manufacturing & Operations
HANK KANALZ Senior VP – Editorial Strategy & Administration * **JAY KOGAN** VP – Legal Affairs * **JACK MAHAN** VP – Business Affairs
NICK J. NAPOLITANO VP – Manufacturing Administration * **EDDIE SCANNELL** VP – Consumer Marketing
COURTNEY SIMMONS Senior VP – Publicity & Communications * **JIM (SKI) SOKOLOWSKI** VP – Comic Book Specialty Sales & Trade Marketing
NANCY SPEARS VP – Mass, Book, Digital Sales & Trade Marketing * **MICHELE R. WELLS** VP – Content Strategy

BATGIRL AND THE BIRDS OF PREY VOL. 3: FULL CIRCLE

Published by DC Comics. Compilation and all new material Copyright © 2018 DC Comics. All Rights Reserved.
Originally published in single magazine form in BATGIRL AND THE BIRDS OF PREY 14-22. Copyright © 2017, 2018 DC Comics. All Rights Reserved.
All characters, their distinctive likenesses and related elements featured in this publication are trademarks of DC Comics.
The stories, characters and incidents featured in this publication are entirely fictional.
DC Comics does not read or accept unsolicited submissions of ideas, stories or artwork.

DC Comics, 2900 West Alameda Ave., Burbank, CA 91505
Printed by LSC Communications, Kendallville, IN, USA. 6/15/18. First Printing.
ISBN: 978-1-4012-7781-9

Library of Congress Cataloging in Publication Data is available.

PEFC Certified

Printed on paper from
sustainably managed
forests, controlled
sources

PEFC/29-31-337   www.pefc.org

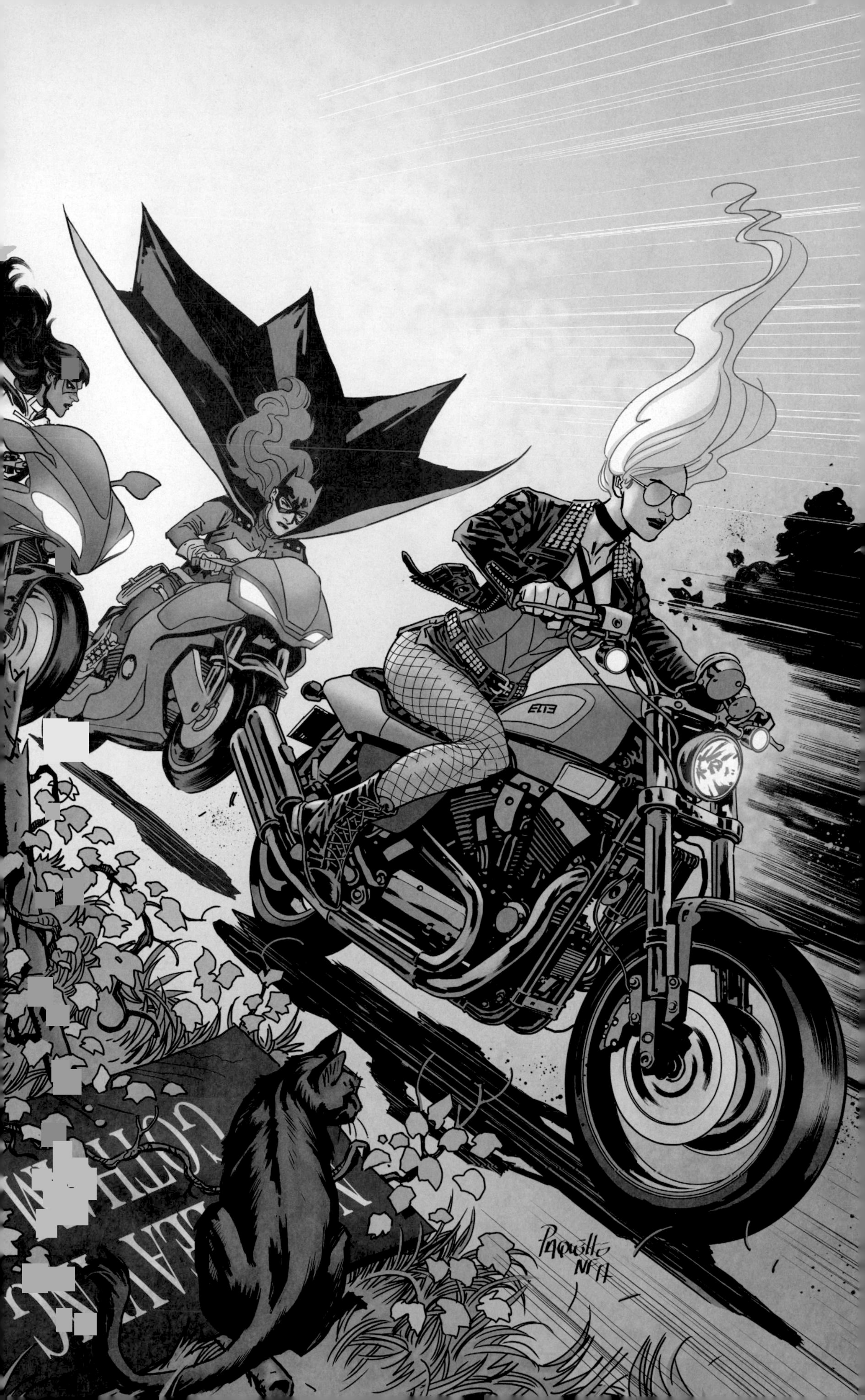

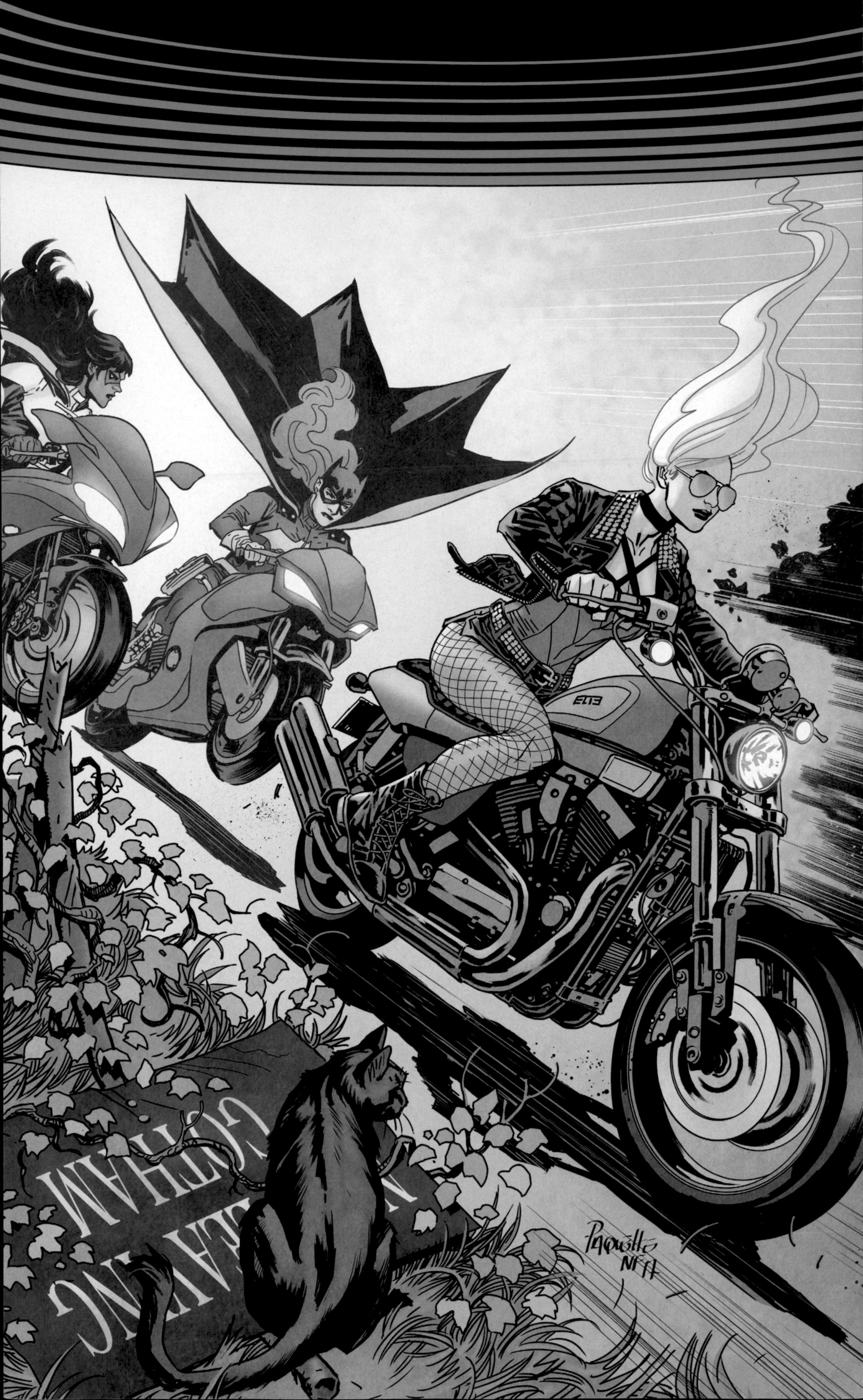
GOTHAM

You are leaving GOTHAM

I TEXTED YOU THE ADDRESS, BARBARA, IN CASE YOU CHANGE YOUR MIND.

I'M SO SORRY, HELENA, BUT WITH GUS GONE AND CALCULATOR IN THE WIND, I FEEL LIKE **SOMEONE** NEEDS TO STAY IN GOTHAM AND HOLD DOWN THE FORT.

BESIDES, YOU'VE GOT DINAH WITH YOU TO HELP CHAPERONE, RIGHT?

SORT OF...

BLYTHE ANN, I CAN'T **BELIEVE** MS. B IS BESTIES WITH THE LEAD SINGER FROM THE BLACK CANARY BAND!

CAN MAYA AND I PUT THIS UP ON CRACKLE-CHAT?

SURE, WHATEVER YOU WANT!

WAIT...

...WHAT'S A CRACKLE-CHAT?

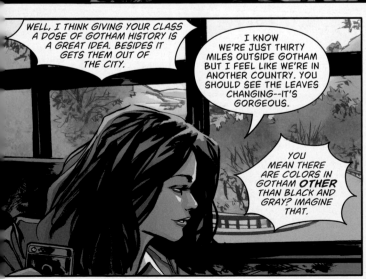

WELL, I THINK GIVING YOUR CLASS A DOSE OF GOTHAM HISTORY IS A GREAT IDEA. BESIDES IT GETS THEM OUT OF THE CITY.

I KNOW WE'RE JUST THIRTY MILES OUTSIDE GOTHAM BUT I FEEL LIKE WE'RE IN ANOTHER COUNTRY. YOU SHOULD SEE THE LEAVES CHANGING--IT'S GORGEOUS.

YOU MEAN THERE ARE COLORS IN GOTHAM **OTHER** THAN BLACK AND GRAY? IMAGINE THAT.

GOTTA GO, I'M GETTING ANOTHER CALL. DON'T GET INTO **TOO** MUCH TROUBLE WITHOUT ME!

WITH DINAH IN TOW? I PROMISE NOTHING.

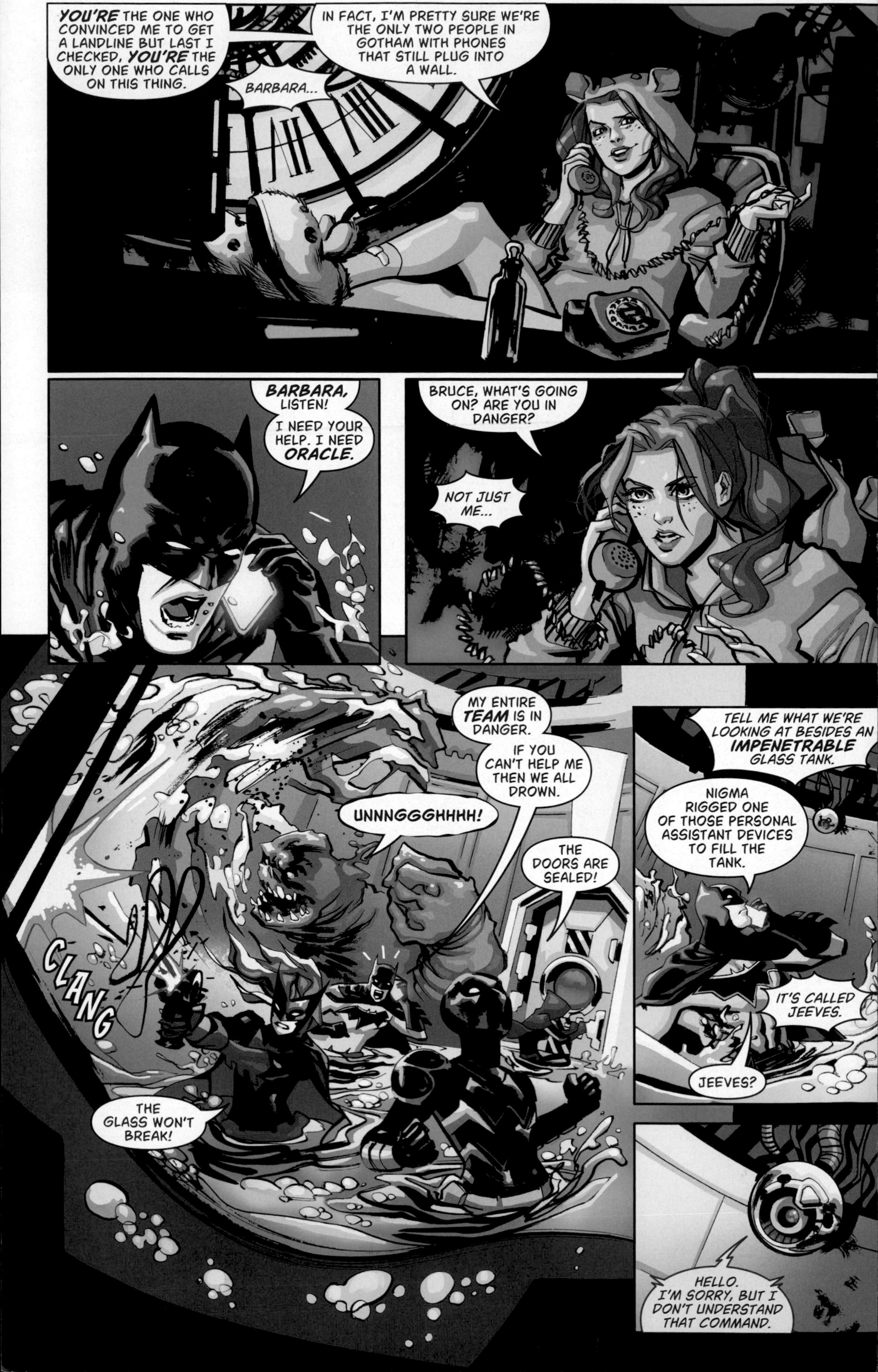
YOU'RE THE ONE WHO CONVINCED ME TO GET A LANDLINE BUT LAST I CHECKED, YOU'RE THE ONLY ONE WHO CALLS ON THIS THING.
IN FACT, I'M PRETTY SURE WE'RE THE ONLY TWO PEOPLE IN GOTHAM WITH PHONES THAT STILL PLUG INTO A WALL.
BARBARA...
BARBARA, LISTEN!
I NEED YOUR HELP. I NEED ORACLE.
BRUCE, WHAT'S GOING ON? ARE YOU IN DANGER?
NOT JUST ME...
MY ENTIRE TEAM IS IN DANGER.
IF YOU CAN'T HELP ME THEN WE ALL DROWN.
UNNNGGGHHHH!
THE DOORS ARE SEALED!
CLANG
THE GLASS WON'T BREAK!
TELL ME WHAT WE'RE LOOKING AT BESIDES AN IMPENETRABLE GLASS TANK.
NIGMA RIGGED ONE OF THOSE PERSONAL ASSISTANT DEVICES TO FILL THE TANK.
IT'S CALLED JEEVES.
JEEVES?
HELLO. I'M SORRY, BUT I DON'T UNDERSTAND THAT COMMAND.

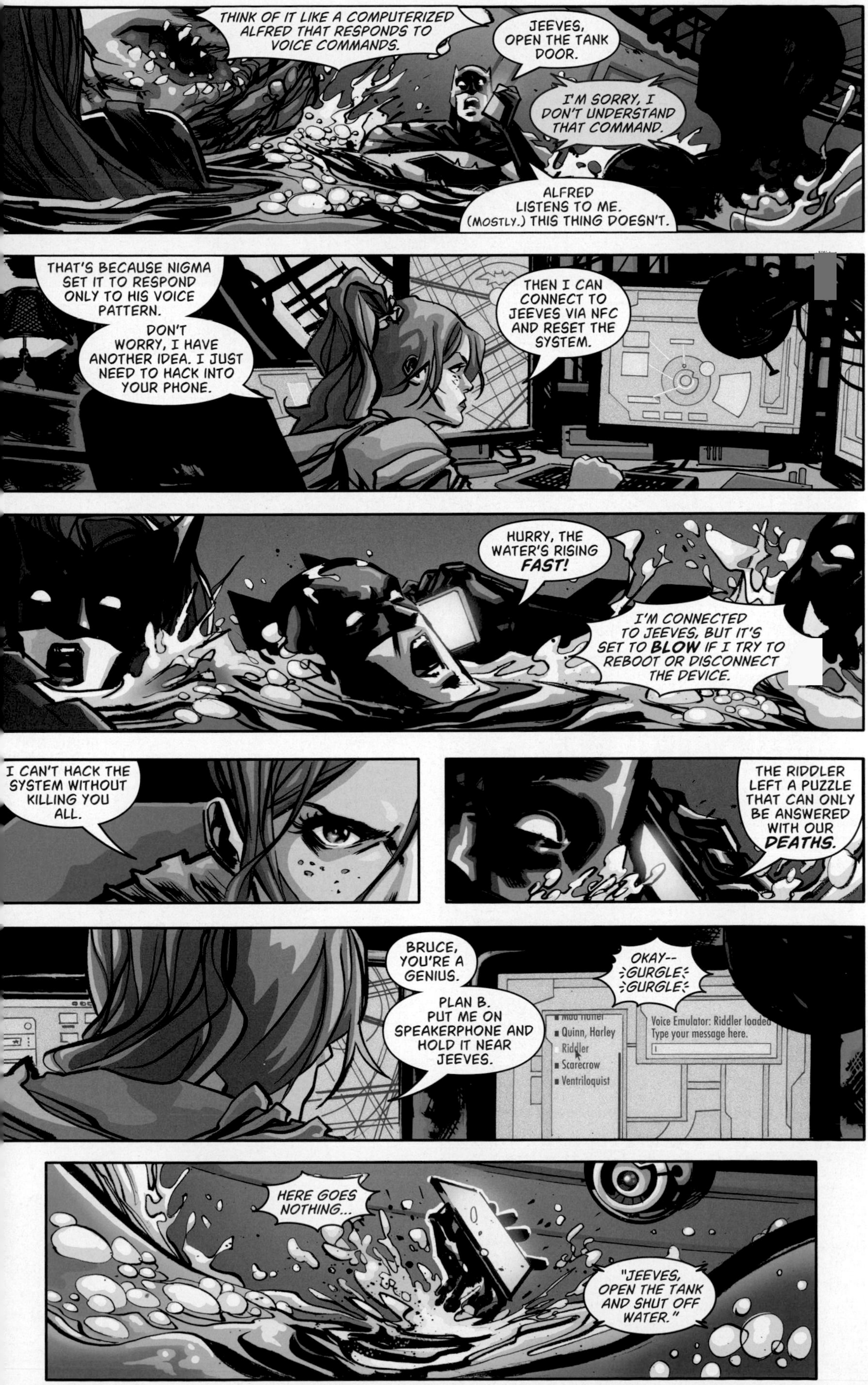
THINK OF IT LIKE A COMPUTERIZED ALFRED THAT RESPONDS TO VOICE COMMANDS.
JEEVES, OPEN THE TANK DOOR.
I'M SORRY, I DON'T UNDERSTAND THAT COMMAND.
ALFRED LISTENS TO ME. (MOSTLY.) THIS THING DOESN'T.
THAT'S BECAUSE NIGMA SET IT TO RESPOND ONLY TO HIS VOICE PATTERN.
DON'T WORRY, I HAVE ANOTHER IDEA. I JUST NEED TO HACK INTO YOUR PHONE.
THEN I CAN CONNECT TO JEEVES VIA NFC AND RESET THE SYSTEM.
HURRY, THE WATER'S RISING FAST!
I'M CONNECTED TO JEEVES, BUT IT'S SET TO BLOW IF I TRY TO REBOOT OR DISCONNECT THE DEVICE.
I CAN'T HACK THE SYSTEM WITHOUT KILLING YOU ALL.
THE RIDDLER LEFT A PUZZLE THAT CAN ONLY BE ANSWERED WITH OUR DEATHS.
BRUCE, YOU'RE A GENIUS.
PLAN B. PUT ME ON SPEAKERPHONE AND HOLD IT NEAR JEEVES.
OKAY-- GURGLE GURGLE
Quinn, Harley
Riddler
Scarecrow
Ventriloquist
Voice Emulator: Riddler loaded
Type your message here.
HERE GOES NOTHING...
"JEEVES, OPEN THE TANK AND SHUT OFF WATER."

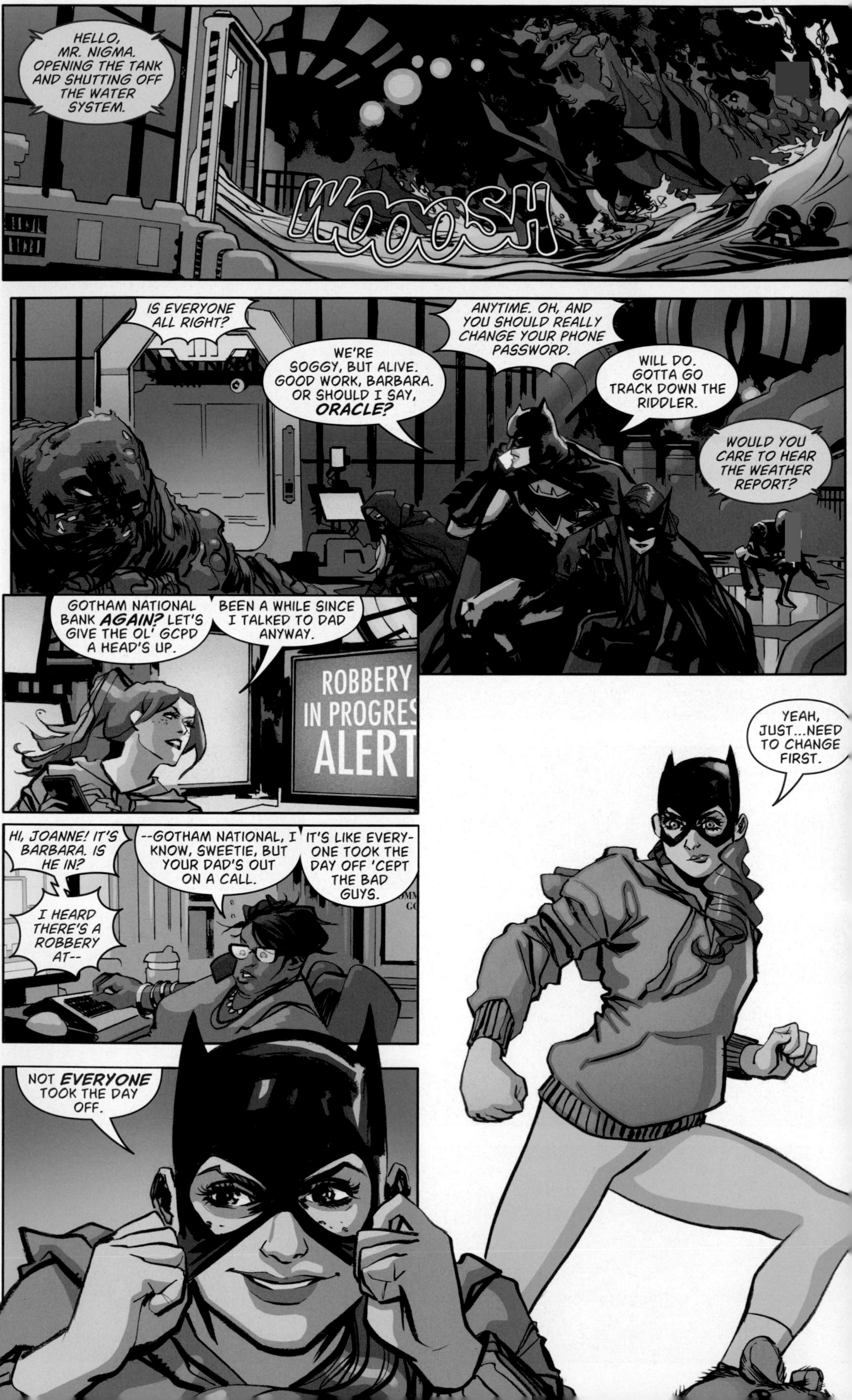
HELLO, MR. NIGMA. OPENING THE TANK AND SHUTTING OFF THE WATER SYSTEM.
WOOOSH
IS EVERYONE ALL RIGHT?
WE'RE SOGGY, BUT ALIVE. GOOD WORK, BARBARA. OR SHOULD I SAY, ORACLE?
ANYTIME. OH, AND YOU SHOULD REALLY CHANGE YOUR PHONE PASSWORD.
WILL DO. GOTTA GO TRACK DOWN THE RIDDLER.
WOULD YOU CARE TO HEAR THE WEATHER REPORT?
GOTHAM NATIONAL BANK AGAIN? LET'S GIVE THE OL' GCPD A HEAD'S UP.
BEEN A WHILE SINCE I TALKED TO DAD ANYWAY.
ROBBERY IN PROGRES
ALERT
HI, JOANNE! IT'S BARBARA. IS HE IN?
I HEARD THERE'S A ROBBERY AT--
--GOTHAM NATIONAL, I KNOW, SWEETIE, BUT YOUR DAD'S OUT ON A CALL.
IT'S LIKE EVERYONE TOOK THE DAY OFF 'CEPT THE BAD GUYS.
NOT EVERYONE TOOK THE DAY OFF.
YEAH, JUST...NEED TO CHANGE FIRST.

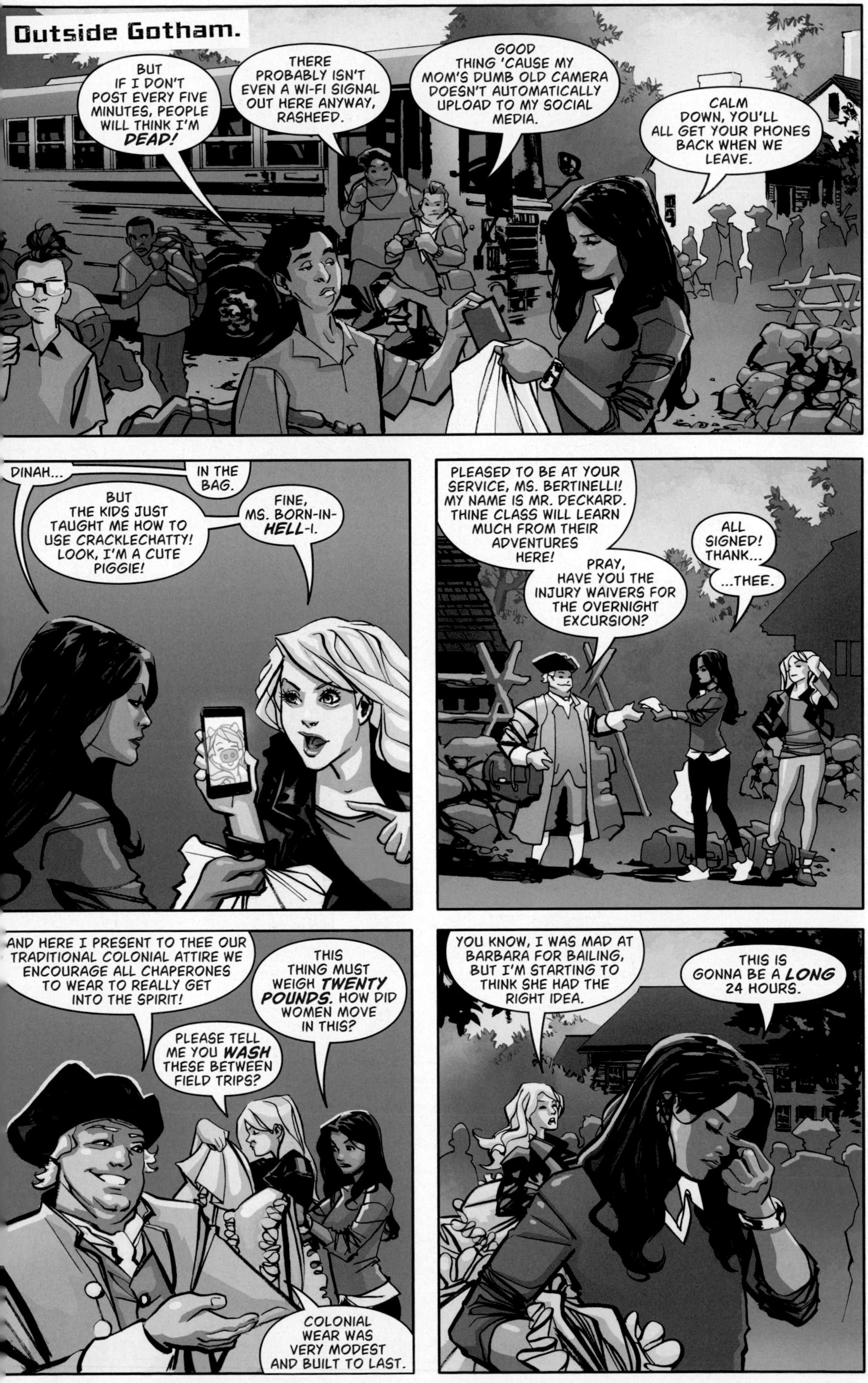
Outside Gotham.
BUT IF I DON'T POST EVERY FIVE MINUTES, PEOPLE WILL THINK I'M DEAD!
THERE PROBABLY ISN'T EVEN A WI-FI SIGNAL OUT HERE ANYWAY, RASHEED.
GOOD THING 'CAUSE MY MOM'S DUMB OLD CAMERA DOESN'T AUTOMATICALLY UPLOAD TO MY SOCIAL MEDIA.
CALM DOWN, YOU'LL ALL GET YOUR PHONES BACK WHEN WE LEAVE.
DINAH...
IN THE BAG.
BUT THE KIDS JUST TAUGHT ME HOW TO USE CRACKLECHATTY! LOOK, I'M A CUTE PIGGIE!
FINE, MS. BORN-IN-HELL-I.
PLEASED TO BE AT YOUR SERVICE, MS. BERTINELLI! MY NAME IS MR. DECKARD. THINE CLASS WILL LEARN MUCH FROM THEIR ADVENTURES HERE!
PRAY, HAVE YOU THE INJURY WAIVERS FOR THE OVERNIGHT EXCURSION?
ALL SIGNED! THANK...
...THEE.
AND HERE I PRESENT TO THEE OUR TRADITIONAL COLONIAL ATTIRE WE ENCOURAGE ALL CHAPERONES TO WEAR TO REALLY GET INTO THE SPIRIT!
THIS THING MUST WEIGH TWENTY POUNDS. HOW DID WOMEN MOVE IN THIS?
PLEASE TELL ME YOU WASH THESE BETWEEN FIELD TRIPS?
COLONIAL WEAR WAS VERY MODEST AND BUILT TO LAST.
YOU KNOW, I WAS MAD AT BARBARA FOR BAILING, BUT I'M STARTING TO THINK SHE HAD THE RIGHT IDEA.
THIS IS GONNA BE A LONG 24 HOURS.

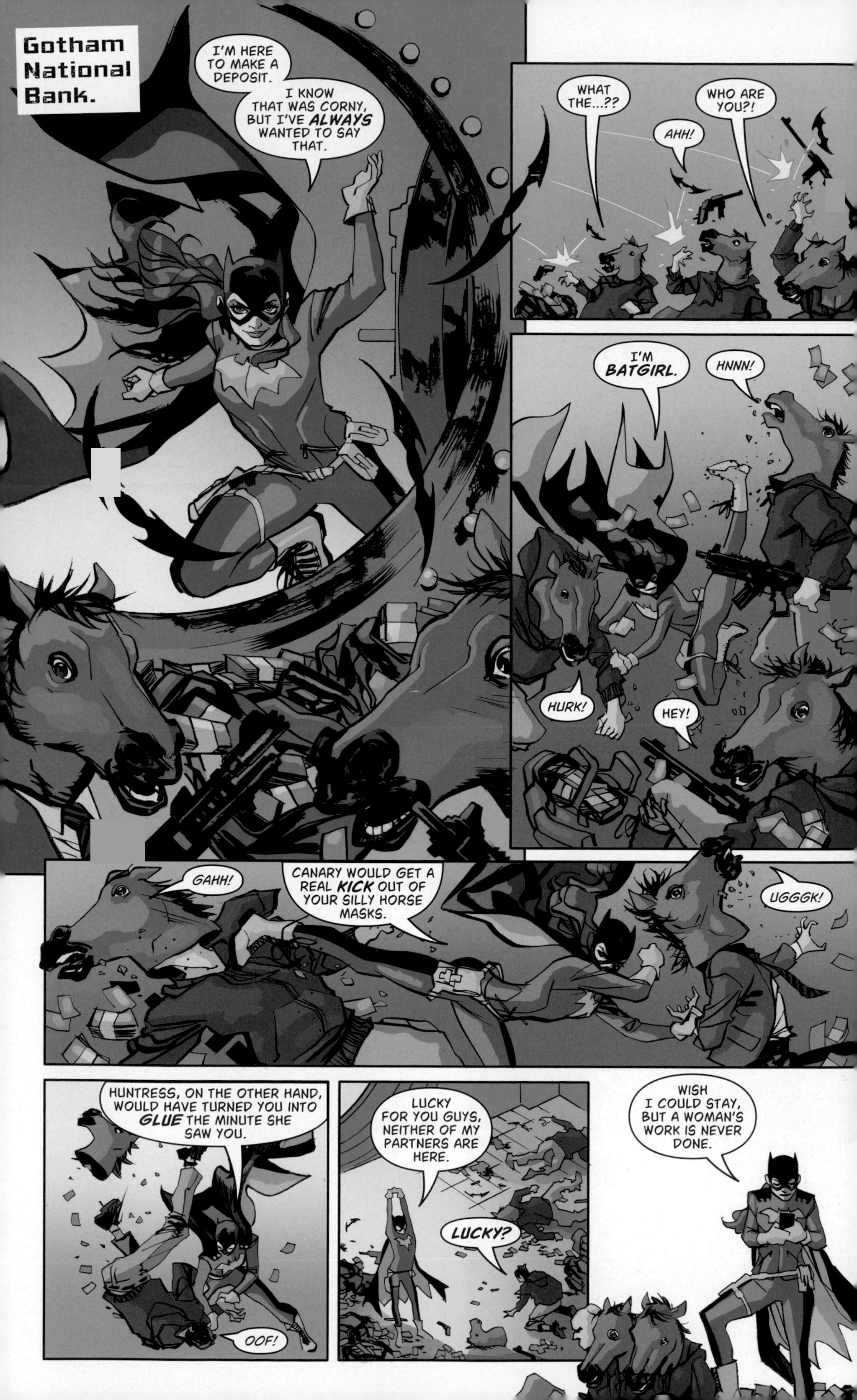
Gotham National Bank.
I'M HERE TO MAKE A DEPOSIT.
I KNOW THAT WAS CORNY, BUT I'VE ALWAYS WANTED TO SAY THAT.
WHAT THE...??
AHH!
WHO ARE YOU?!
I'M BATGIRL.
HNNN!
HURK!
HEY!
GAHH!
CANARY WOULD GET A REAL KICK OUT OF YOUR SILLY HORSE MASKS.
UGGGK!
HUNTRESS, ON THE OTHER HAND, WOULD HAVE TURNED YOU INTO GLUE THE MINUTE SHE SAW YOU.
OOF!
LUCKY FOR YOU GUYS, NEITHER OF MY PARTNERS ARE HERE.
LUCKY?
WISH I COULD STAY, BUT A WOMAN'S WORK IS NEVER DONE.

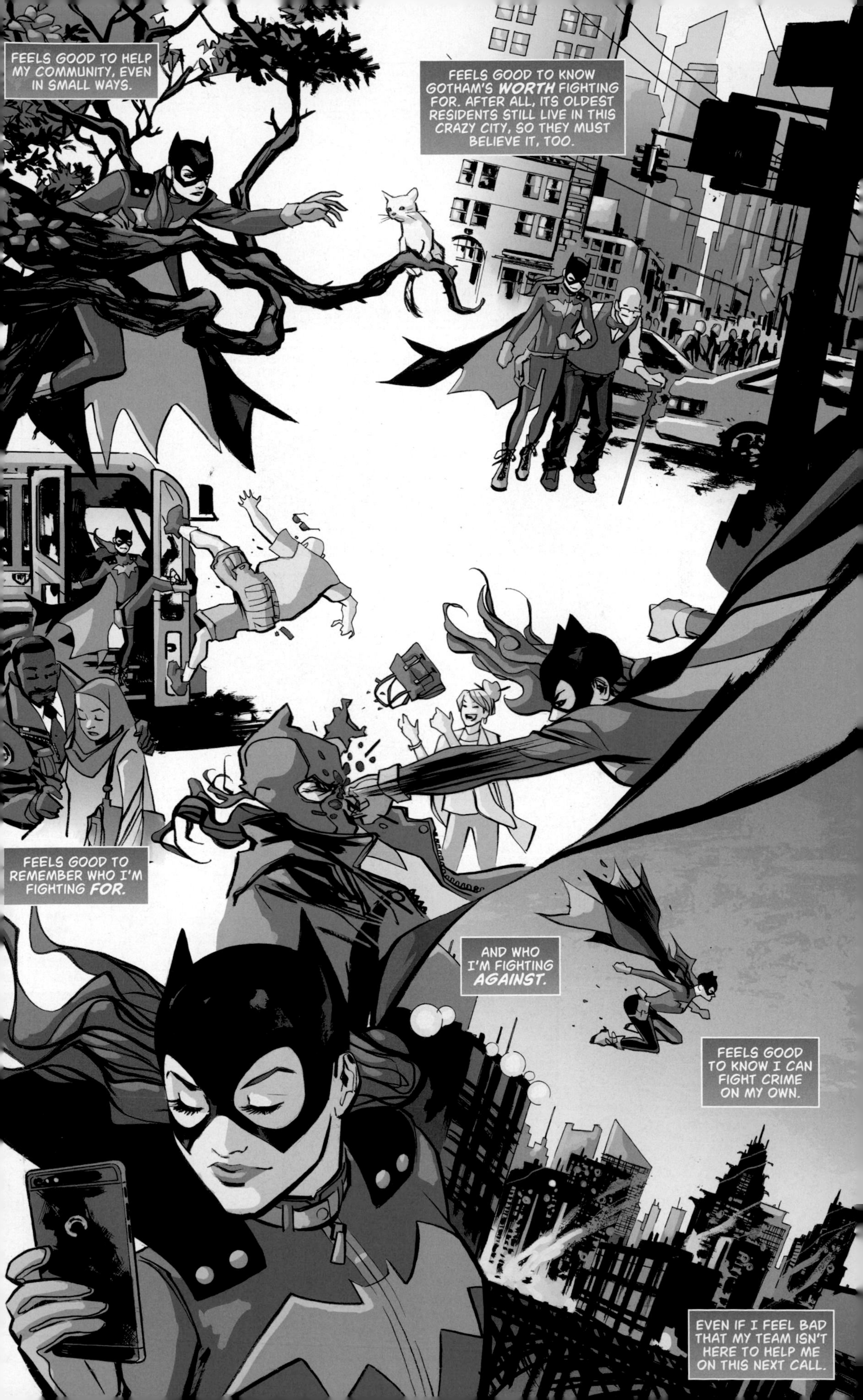
FEELS GOOD TO HELP MY COMMUNITY, EVEN IN SMALL WAYS.
FEELS GOOD TO KNOW GOTHAM'S **WORTH** FIGHTING FOR. AFTER ALL, ITS OLDEST RESIDENTS STILL LIVE IN THIS CRAZY CITY, SO THEY MUST BELIEVE IT, TOO.
FEELS GOOD TO REMEMBER WHO I'M FIGHTING **FOR.**
AND WHO I'M FIGHTING **AGAINST.**
FEELS GOOD TO KNOW I CAN FIGHT CRIME ON MY OWN.
EVEN IF I FEEL BAD THAT MY TEAM ISN'T HERE TO HELP ME ON THIS NEXT CALL.

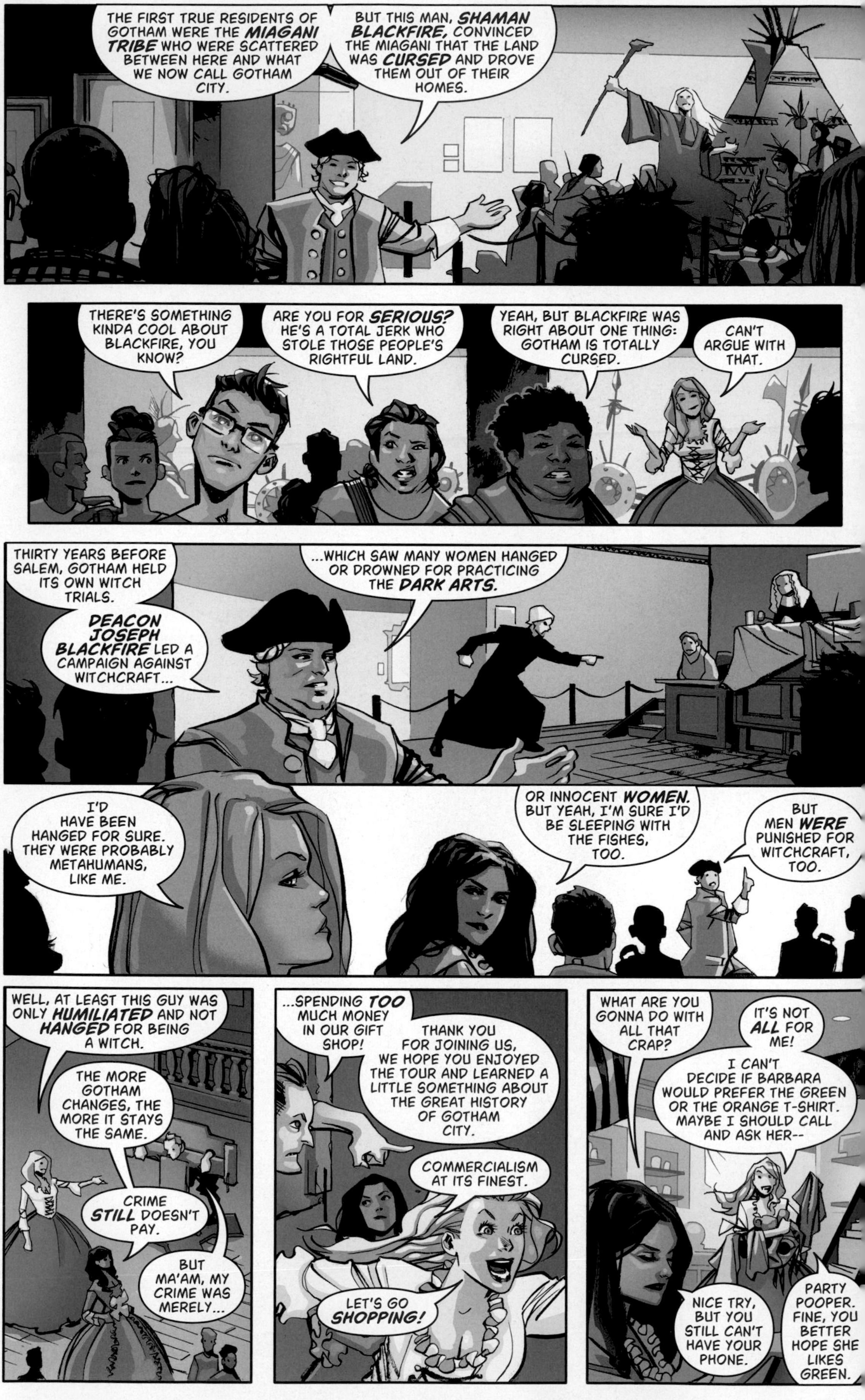
THE FIRST TRUE RESIDENTS OF GOTHAM WERE THE MIAGANI TRIBE WHO WERE SCATTERED BETWEEN HERE AND WHAT WE NOW CALL GOTHAM CITY.
BUT THIS MAN, SHAMAN BLACKFIRE, CONVINCED THE MIAGANI THAT THE LAND WAS CURSED AND DROVE THEM OUT OF THEIR HOMES.
THERE'S SOMETHING KINDA COOL ABOUT BLACKFIRE, YOU KNOW?
ARE YOU FOR SERIOUS? HE'S A TOTAL JERK WHO STOLE THOSE PEOPLE'S RIGHTFUL LAND.
YEAH, BUT BLACKFIRE WAS RIGHT ABOUT ONE THING: GOTHAM IS TOTALLY CURSED.
CAN'T ARGUE WITH THAT.
THIRTY YEARS BEFORE SALEM, GOTHAM HELD ITS OWN WITCH TRIALS.
DEACON JOSEPH BLACKFIRE LED A CAMPAIGN AGAINST WITCHCRAFT...
...WHICH SAW MANY WOMEN HANGED OR DROWNED FOR PRACTICING THE DARK ARTS.
I'D HAVE BEEN HANGED FOR SURE. THEY WERE PROBABLY METAHUMANS, LIKE ME.
OR INNOCENT WOMEN. BUT YEAH, I'M SURE I'D BE SLEEPING WITH THE FISHES, TOO.
BUT MEN WERE PUNISHED FOR WITCHCRAFT, TOO.
WELL, AT LEAST THIS GUY WAS ONLY HUMILIATED AND NOT HANGED FOR BEING A WITCH.
THE MORE GOTHAM CHANGES, THE MORE IT STAYS THE SAME.
CRIME STILL DOESN'T PAY.
BUT MA'AM, MY CRIME WAS MERELY...
...SPENDING TOO MUCH MONEY IN OUR GIFT SHOP!
THANK YOU FOR JOINING US, WE HOPE YOU ENJOYED THE TOUR AND LEARNED A LITTLE SOMETHING ABOUT THE GREAT HISTORY OF GOTHAM CITY.
COMMERCIALISM AT ITS FINEST.
LET'S GO SHOPPING!
WHAT ARE YOU GONNA DO WITH ALL THAT CRAP?
IT'S NOT ALL FOR ME!
I CAN'T DECIDE IF BARBARA WOULD PREFER THE GREEN OR THE ORANGE T-SHIRT. MAYBE I SHOULD CALL AND ASK HER--
NICE TRY, BUT YOU STILL CAN'T HAVE YOUR PHONE.
PARTY POOPER. FINE, YOU BETTER HOPE SHE LIKES GREEN.

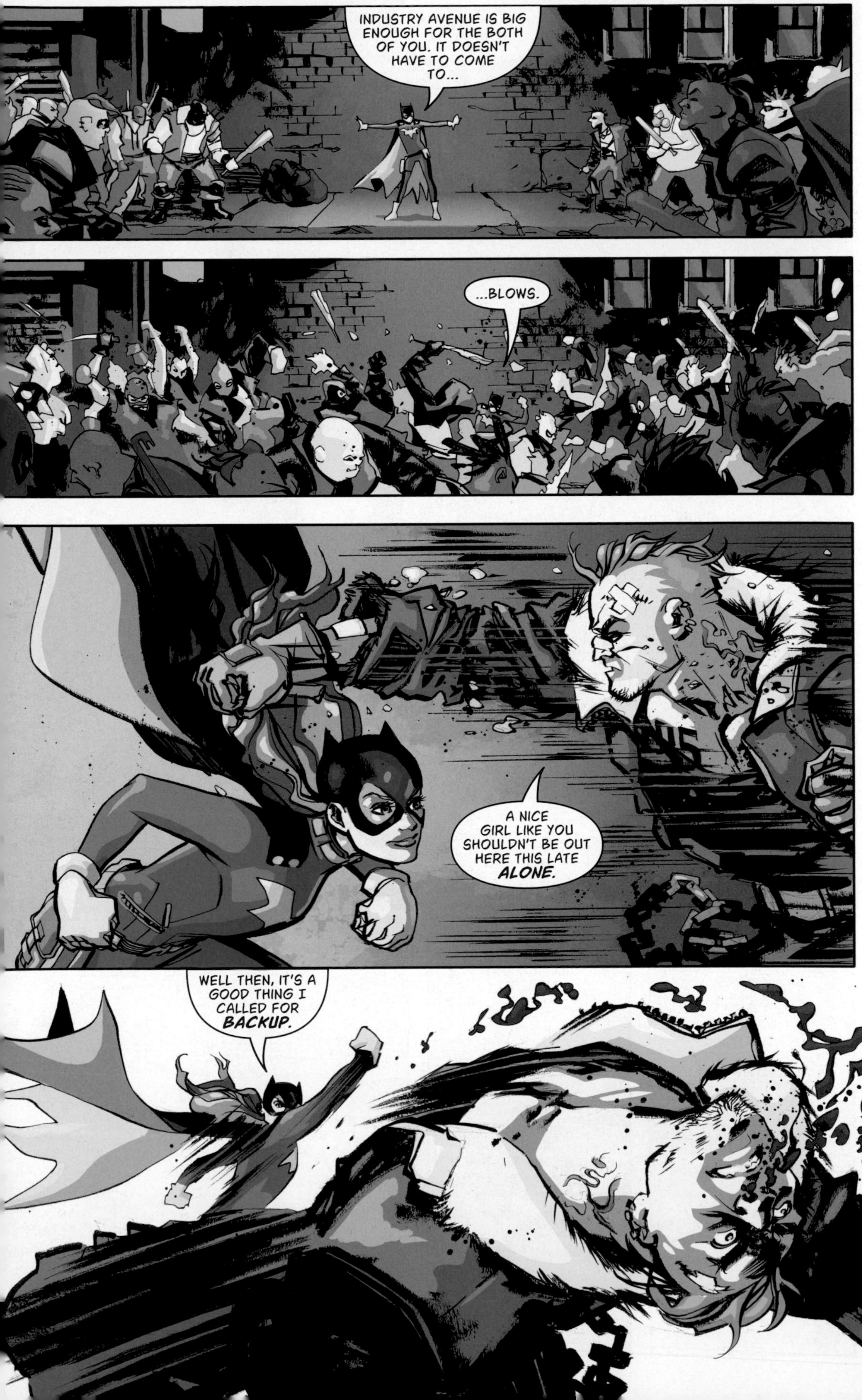
INDUSTRY AVENUE IS BIG ENOUGH FOR THE BOTH OF YOU. IT DOESN'T HAVE TO COME TO...
...BLOWS.
A NICE GIRL LIKE YOU SHOULDN'T BE OUT HERE THIS LATE ALONE.
WELL THEN, IT'S A GOOD THING I CALLED FOR BACKUP.

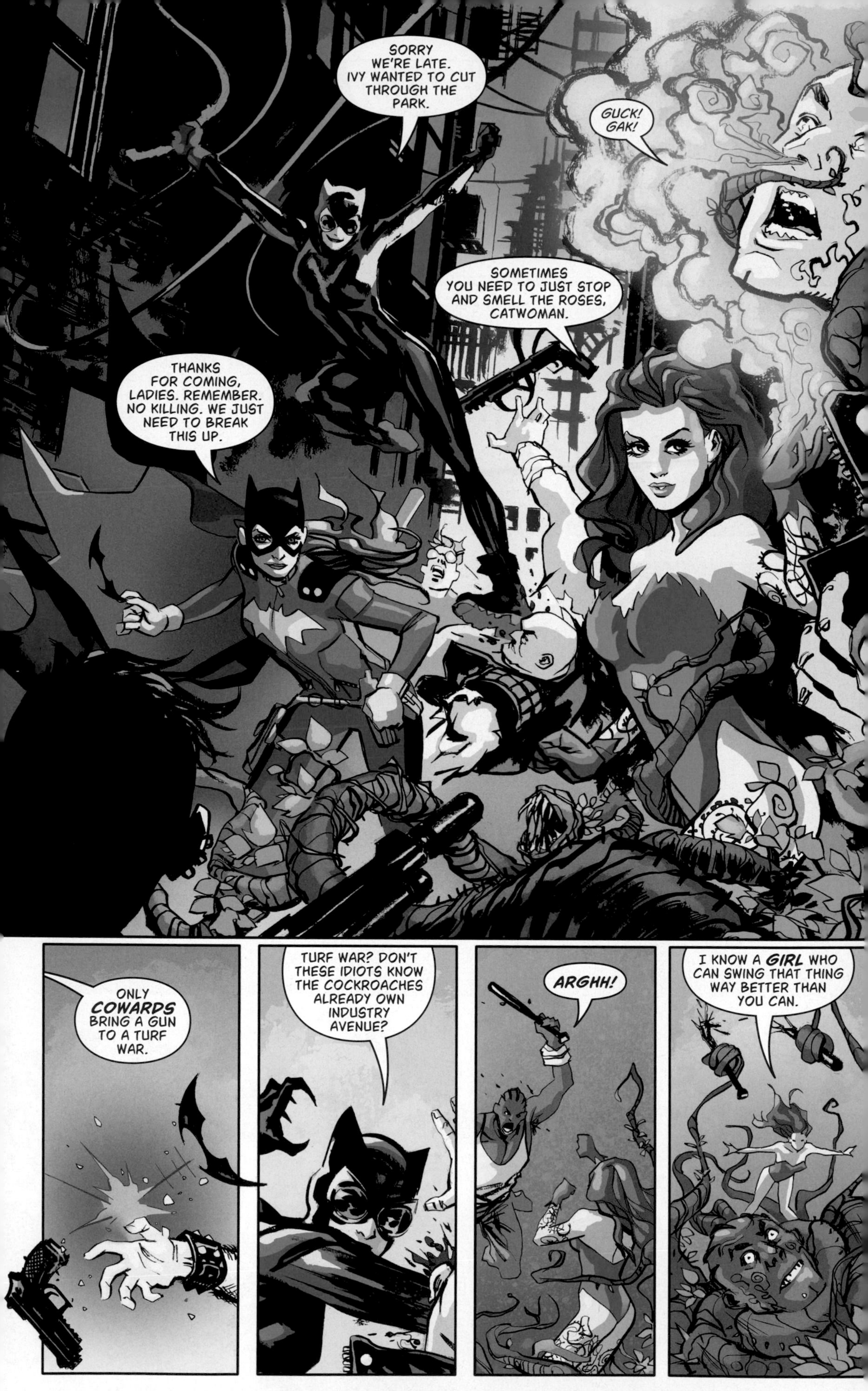
SORRY WE'RE LATE. IVY WANTED TO CUT THROUGH THE PARK.
GUCK! GAK!
SOMETIMES YOU NEED TO JUST STOP AND SMELL THE ROSES, CATWOMAN.
THANKS FOR COMING, LADIES. REMEMBER. NO KILLING. WE JUST NEED TO BREAK THIS UP.
ONLY COWARDS BRING A GUN TO A TURF WAR.
TURF WAR? DON'T THESE IDIOTS KNOW THE COCKROACHES ALREADY OWN INDUSTRY AVENUE?
ARGHH!
I KNOW A GIRL WHO CAN SWING THAT THING WAY BETTER THAN YOU CAN.

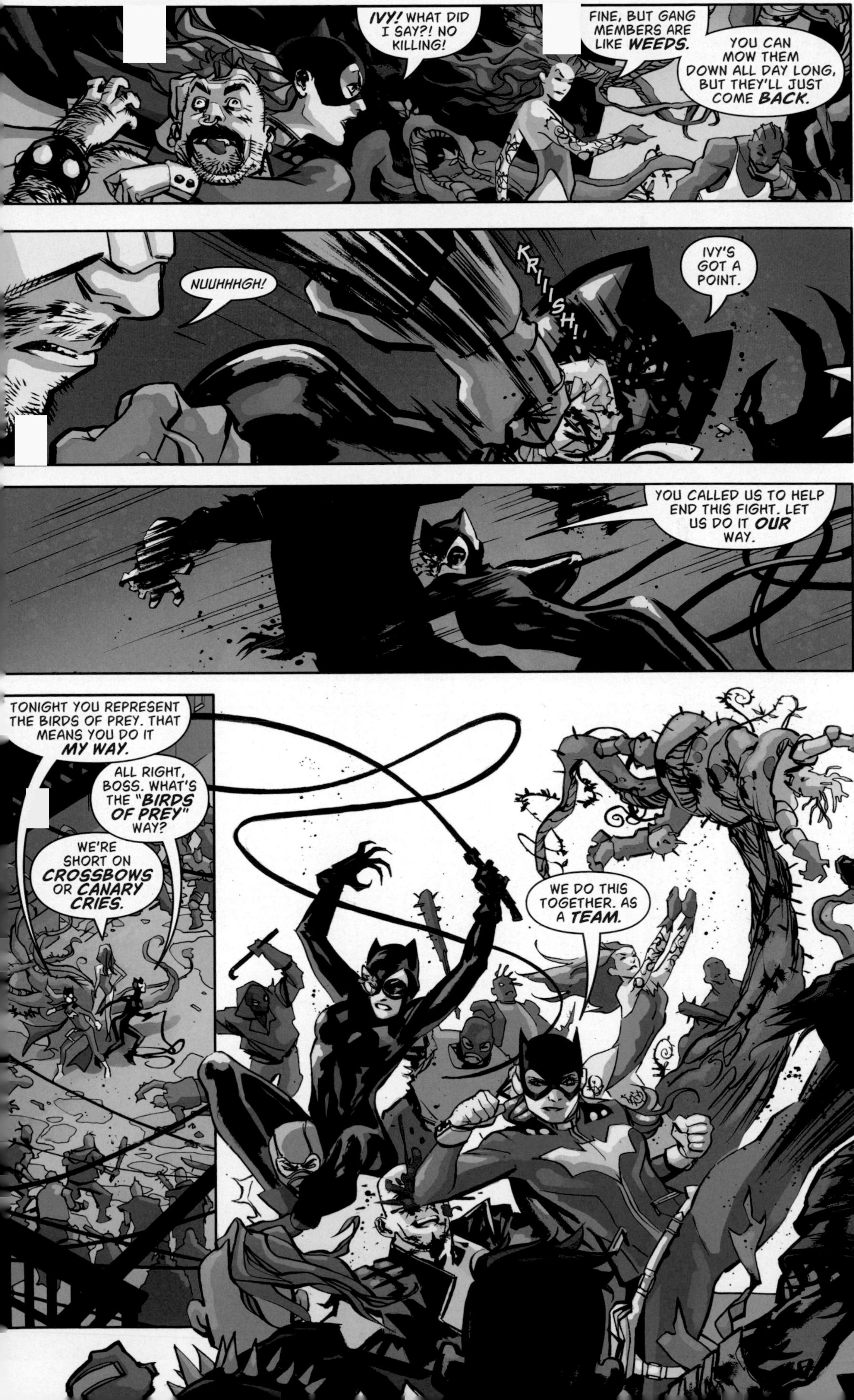
IVY! WHAT DID I SAY?! NO KILLING!
FINE, BUT GANG MEMBERS ARE LIKE WEEDS.
YOU CAN MOW THEM DOWN ALL DAY LONG, BUT THEY'LL JUST COME BACK.
NUUHHHGH!
KRIIISHH!
IVY'S GOT A POINT.
YOU CALLED US TO HELP END THIS FIGHT. LET US DO IT OUR WAY.
TONIGHT YOU REPRESENT THE BIRDS OF PREY. THAT MEANS YOU DO IT MY WAY.
ALL RIGHT, BOSS. WHAT'S THE "BIRDS OF PREY" WAY?
WE'RE SHORT ON CROSSBOWS OR CANARY CRIES.
WE DO THIS TOGETHER. AS A TEAM.

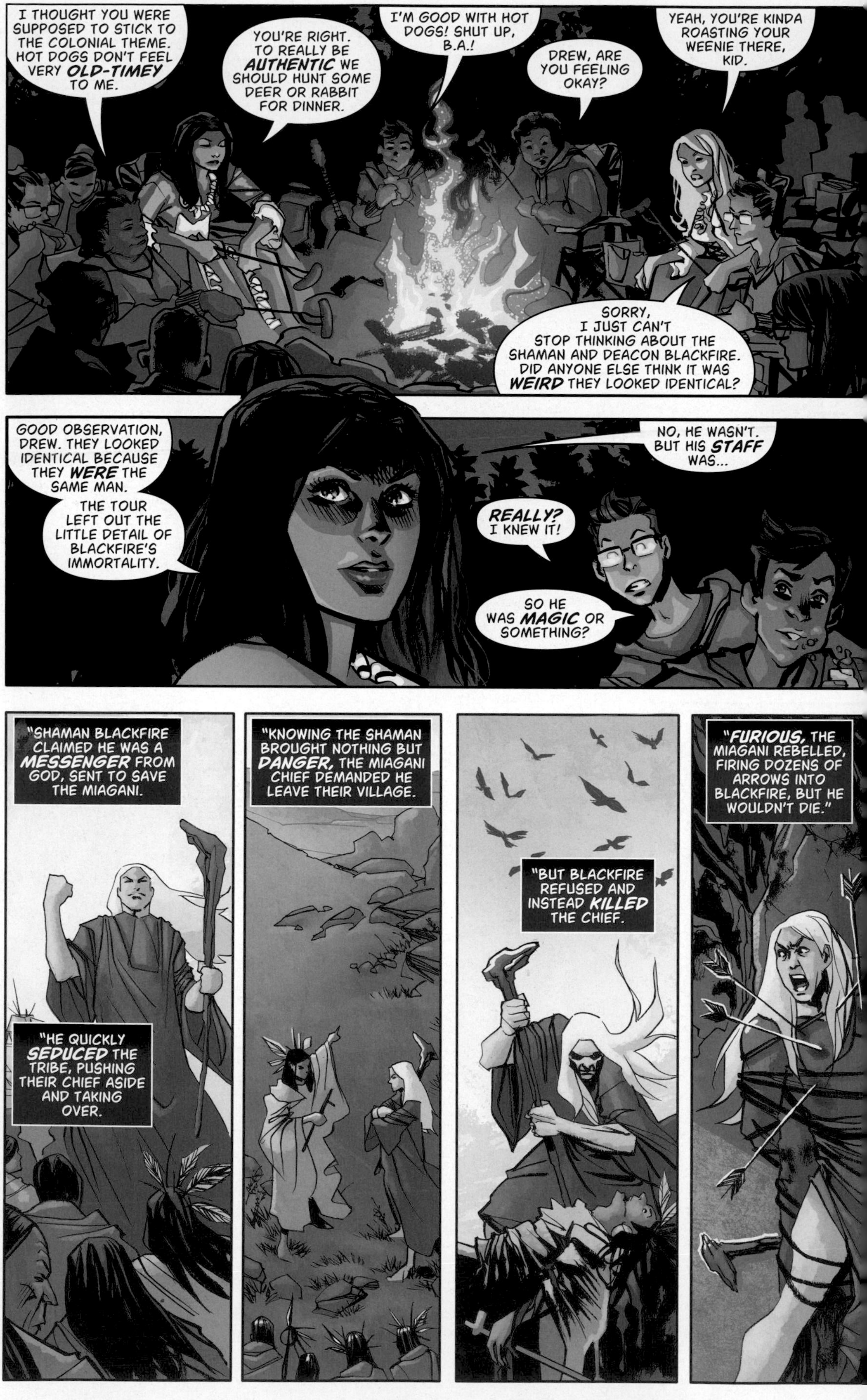
I THOUGHT YOU WERE SUPPOSED TO STICK TO THE COLONIAL THEME. HOT DOGS DON'T FEEL VERY OLD-TIMEY TO ME.
YOU'RE RIGHT. TO REALLY BE AUTHENTIC WE SHOULD HUNT SOME DEER OR RABBIT FOR DINNER.
I'M GOOD WITH HOT DOGS! SHUT UP, B.A.!
DREW, ARE YOU FEELING OKAY?
YEAH, YOU'RE KINDA ROASTING YOUR WEENIE THERE, KID.
SORRY, I JUST CAN'T STOP THINKING ABOUT THE SHAMAN AND DEACON BLACKFIRE. DID ANYONE ELSE THINK IT WAS WEIRD THEY LOOKED IDENTICAL?
GOOD OBSERVATION, DREW. THEY LOOKED IDENTICAL BECAUSE THEY WERE THE SAME MAN.
THE TOUR LEFT OUT THE LITTLE DETAIL OF BLACKFIRE'S IMMORTALITY.
REALLY? I KNEW IT!
SO HE WAS MAGIC OR SOMETHING?
NO, HE WASN'T. BUT HIS STAFF WAS...
"SHAMAN BLACKFIRE CLAIMED HE WAS A MESSENGER FROM GOD, SENT TO SAVE THE MIAGANI.
"HE QUICKLY SEDUCED THE TRIBE, PUSHING THEIR CHIEF ASIDE AND TAKING OVER.
"KNOWING THE SHAMAN BROUGHT NOTHING BUT DANGER, THE MIAGANI CHIEF DEMANDED HE LEAVE THEIR VILLAGE.
"BUT BLACKFIRE REFUSED AND INSTEAD KILLED THE CHIEF.
"FURIOUS, THE MIAGANI REBELLED, FIRING DOZENS OF ARROWS INTO BLACKFIRE, BUT HE WOULDN'T DIE."

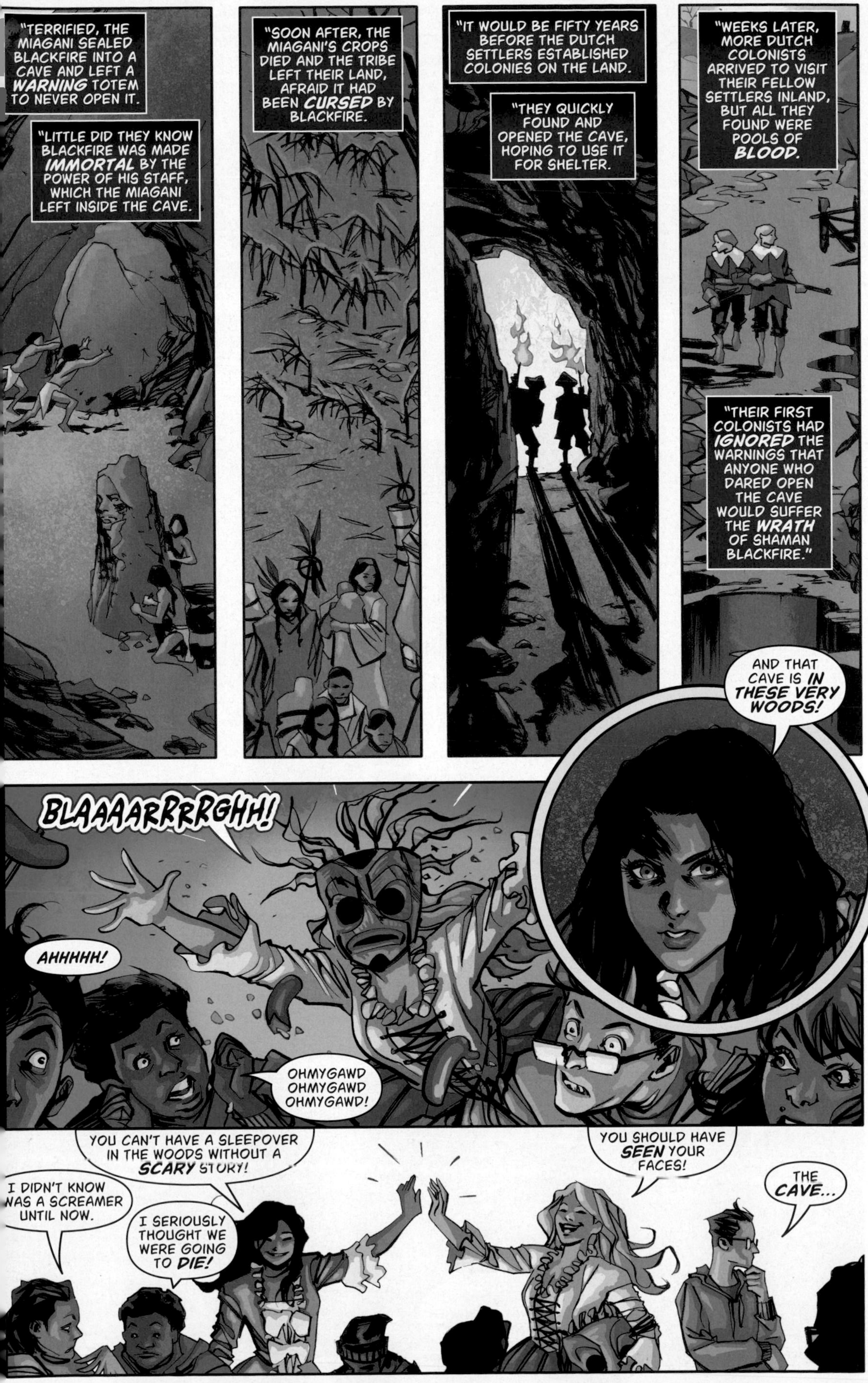
"TERRIFIED, THE MIAGANI SEALED BLACKFIRE INTO A CAVE AND LEFT A WARNING TOTEM TO NEVER OPEN IT.
"LITTLE DID THEY KNOW BLACKFIRE WAS MADE IMMORTAL BY THE POWER OF HIS STAFF, WHICH THE MIAGANI LEFT INSIDE THE CAVE.
"SOON AFTER, THE MIAGANI'S CROPS DIED AND THE TRIBE LEFT THEIR LAND, AFRAID IT HAD BEEN CURSED BY BLACKFIRE.
"IT WOULD BE FIFTY YEARS BEFORE THE DUTCH SETTLERS ESTABLISHED COLONIES ON THE LAND.
"THEY QUICKLY FOUND AND OPENED THE CAVE, HOPING TO USE IT FOR SHELTER.
"WEEKS LATER, MORE DUTCH COLONISTS ARRIVED TO VISIT THEIR FELLOW SETTLERS INLAND, BUT ALL THEY FOUND WERE POOLS OF BLOOD.
"THEIR FIRST COLONISTS HAD IGNORED THE WARNINGS THAT ANYONE WHO DARED OPEN THE CAVE WOULD SUFFER THE WRATH OF SHAMAN BLACKFIRE."
AND THAT CAVE IS IN THESE VERY WOODS!
BLAAAARRRRGHH!
AHHHHH!
OHMYGAWD OHMYGAWD OHMYGAWD!
YOU CAN'T HAVE A SLEEPOVER IN THE WOODS WITHOUT A SCARY STORY!
I DIDN'T KNOW WAS A SCREAMER UNTIL NOW.
I SERIOUSLY THOUGHT WE WERE GOING TO DIE!
YOU SHOULD HAVE SEEN YOUR FACES!
THE CAVE...

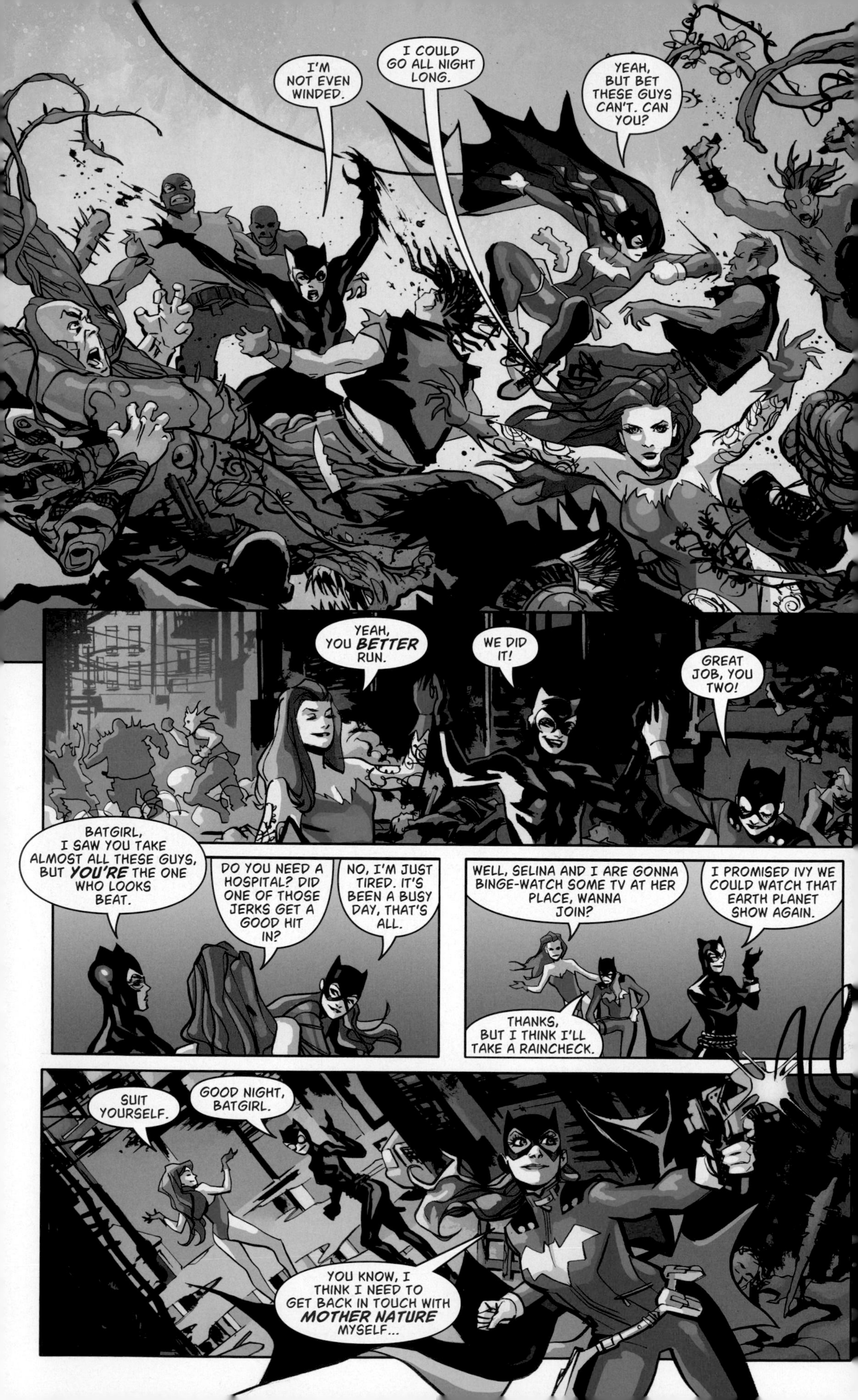
I'M NOT EVEN WINDED.
I COULD GO ALL NIGHT LONG.
YEAH, BUT BET THESE GUYS CAN'T. CAN YOU?
YEAH, YOU BETTER RUN.
WE DID IT!
GREAT JOB, YOU TWO!
BATGIRL, I SAW YOU TAKE ALMOST ALL THESE GUYS, BUT YOU'RE THE ONE WHO LOOKS BEAT.
DO YOU NEED A HOSPITAL? DID ONE OF THOSE JERKS GET A GOOD HIT IN?
NO, I'M JUST TIRED. IT'S BEEN A BUSY DAY, THAT'S ALL.
WELL, SELINA AND I ARE GONNA BINGE-WATCH SOME TV AT HER PLACE, WANNA JOIN?
I PROMISED IVY WE COULD WATCH THAT EARTH PLANET SHOW AGAIN.
THANKS, BUT I THINK I'LL TAKE A RAINCHECK.
SUIT YOURSELF.
GOOD NIGHT, BATGIRL.
YOU KNOW, I THINK I NEED TO GET BACK IN TOUCH WITH MOTHER NATURE MYSELF...

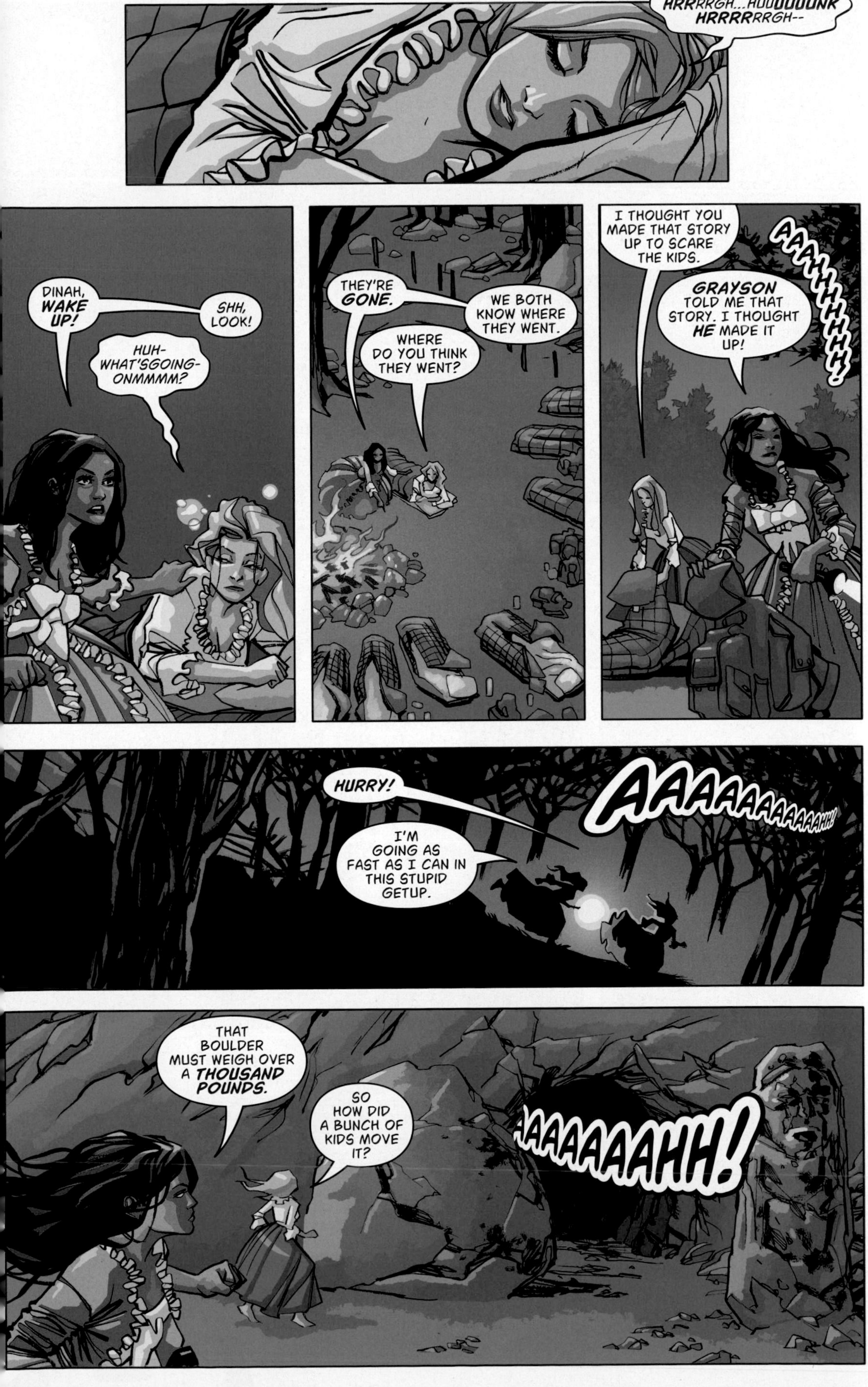
HUUURNK HRRRRGH...HUUUUUUNK HRRRRRRGH--
DINAH, WAKE UP!
SHH, LOOK!
HUH-WHAT'SGOING-ONMMMM?
THEY'RE GONE.
WE BOTH KNOW WHERE THEY WENT.
WHERE DO YOU THINK THEY WENT?
I THOUGHT YOU MADE THAT STORY UP TO SCARE THE KIDS.
GRAYSON TOLD ME THAT STORY. I THOUGHT HE MADE IT UP!
AAAHHHHHH!
HURRY!
I'M GOING AS FAST AS I CAN IN THIS STUPID GETUP.
AAAAAAAAAAAAH!
THAT BOULDER MUST WEIGH OVER A THOUSAND POUNDS.
SO HOW DID A BUNCH OF KIDS MOVE IT?
AAAAAAAAHH!

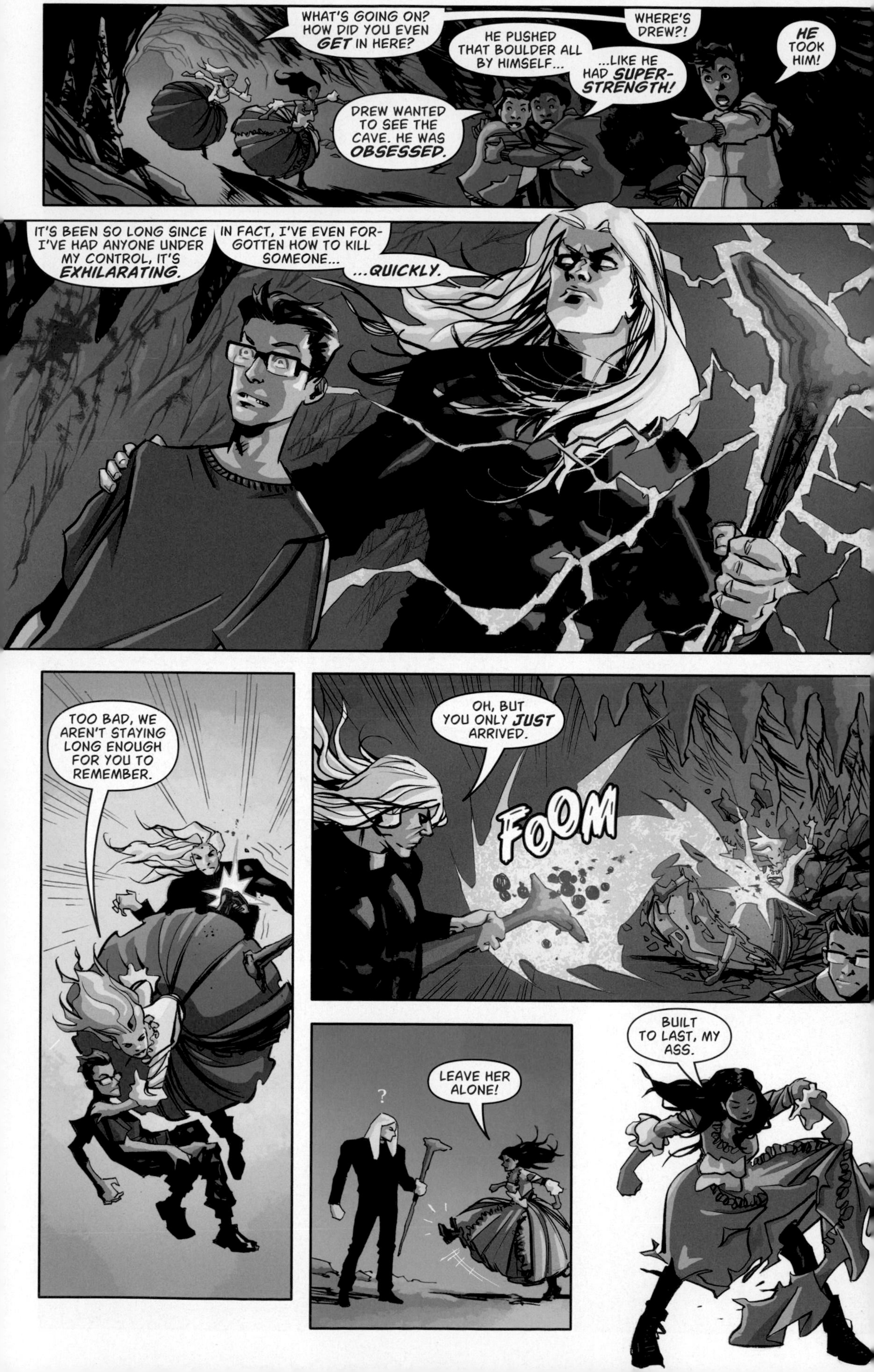

WHAT'S GOING ON? HOW DID YOU EVEN GET IN HERE?
WHERE'S DREW?!
HE PUSHED THAT BOULDER ALL BY HIMSELF...
...LIKE HE HAD SUPER-STRENGTH!
HE TOOK HIM!
DREW WANTED TO SEE THE CAVE. HE WAS OBSESSED.
IT'S BEEN SO LONG SINCE I'VE HAD ANYONE UNDER MY CONTROL, IT'S EXHILARATING.
IN FACT, I'VE EVEN FORGOTTEN HOW TO KILL SOMEONE...
...QUICKLY.
TOO BAD, WE AREN'T STAYING LONG ENOUGH FOR YOU TO REMEMBER.
OH, BUT YOU ONLY JUST ARRIVED.
FOOM
?
LEAVE HER ALONE!
BUILT TO LAST, MY ASS.

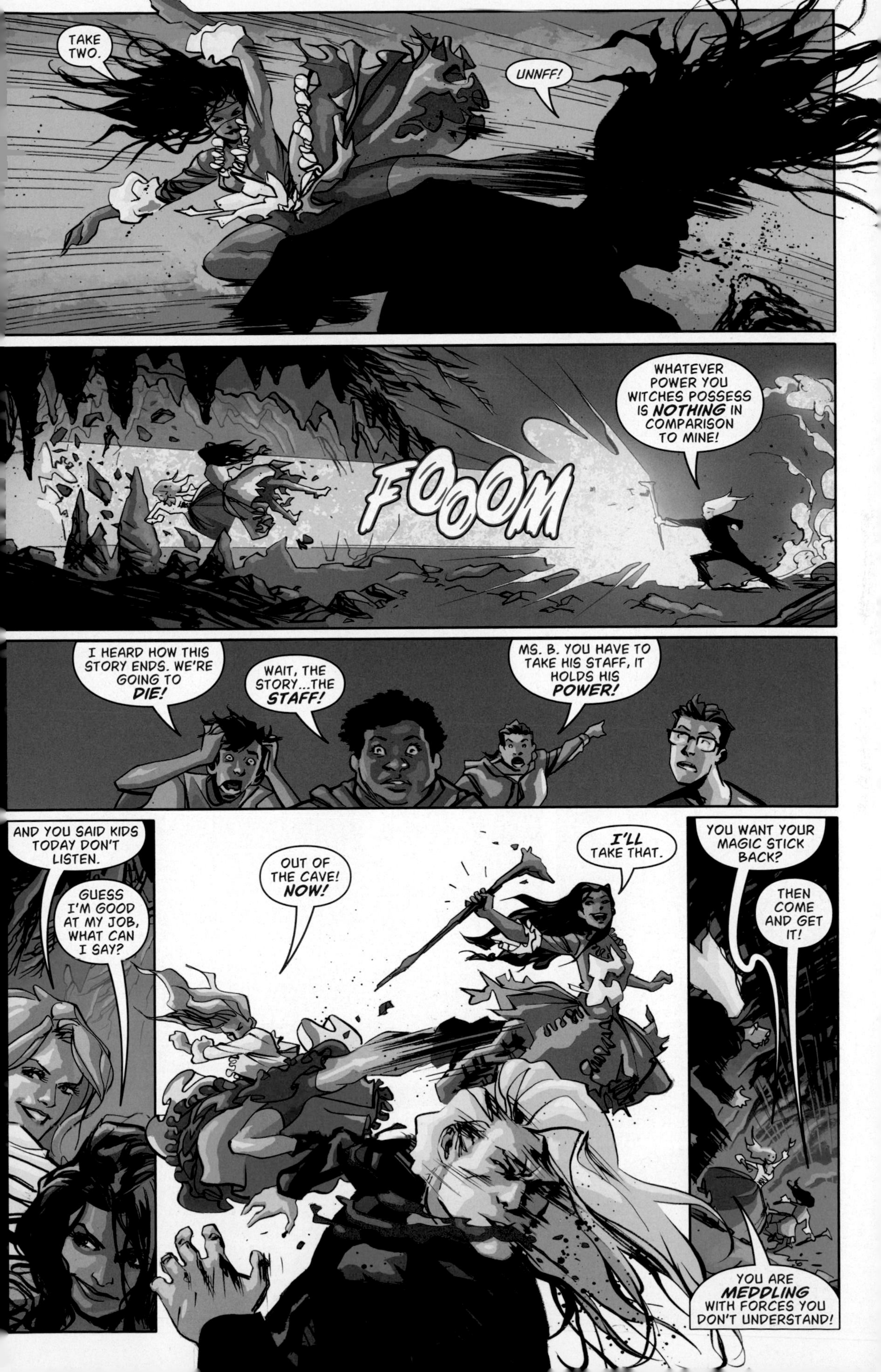
TAKE TWO.
UNNFF!
WHATEVER POWER YOU WITCHES POSSESS IS NOTHING IN COMPARISON TO MINE!
FOOOM
I HEARD HOW THIS STORY ENDS. WE'RE GOING TO DIE!
WAIT, THE STORY...THE STAFF!
MS. B. YOU HAVE TO TAKE HIS STAFF, IT HOLDS HIS POWER!
AND YOU SAID KIDS TODAY DON'T LISTEN.
GUESS I'M GOOD AT MY JOB, WHAT CAN I SAY?
OUT OF THE CAVE! NOW!
I'LL TAKE THAT.
YOU WANT YOUR MAGIC STICK BACK?
THEN COME AND GET IT!
YOU ARE MEDDLING WITH FORCES YOU DON'T UNDERSTAND!

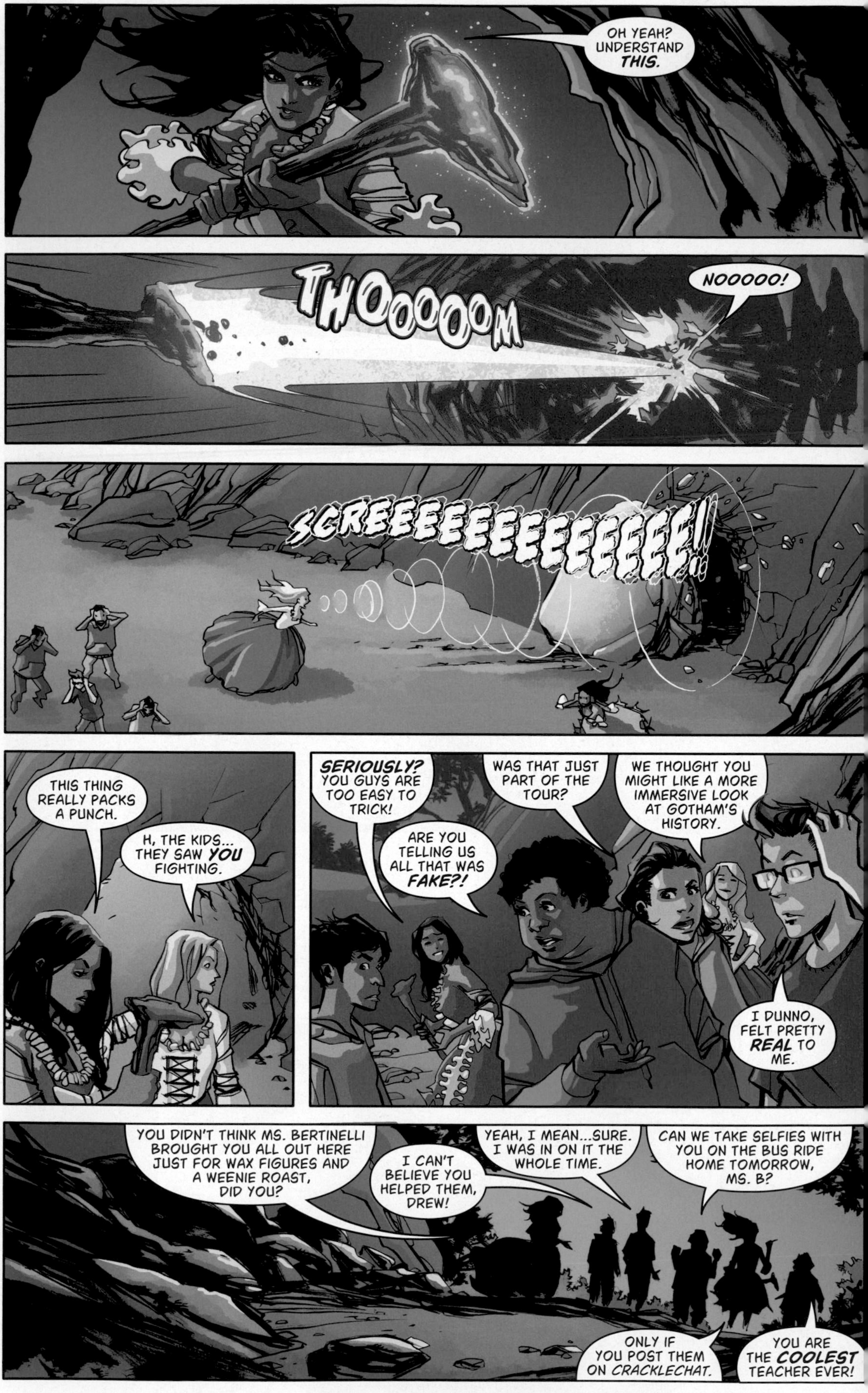
OH YEAH? UNDERSTAND THIS.
THOOOOOM
NOOOOO!
SCREEEEEEEEEEEEEEE!!
THIS THING REALLY PACKS A PUNCH.
H, THE KIDS... THEY SAW YOU FIGHTING.
SERIOUSLY? YOU GUYS ARE TOO EASY TO TRICK!
ARE YOU TELLING US ALL THAT WAS FAKE?!
WAS THAT JUST PART OF THE TOUR?
WE THOUGHT YOU MIGHT LIKE A MORE IMMERSIVE LOOK AT GOTHAM'S HISTORY.
I DUNNO, FELT PRETTY REAL TO ME.
YOU DIDN'T THINK MS. BERTINELLI BROUGHT YOU ALL OUT HERE JUST FOR WAX FIGURES AND A WEENIE ROAST, DID YOU?
I CAN'T BELIEVE YOU HELPED THEM, DREW!
YEAH, I MEAN...SURE. I WAS IN ON IT THE WHOLE TIME.
CAN WE TAKE SELFIES WITH YOU ON THE BUS RIDE HOME TOMORROW, MS. B?
ONLY IF YOU POST THEM ON CRACKLECHAT.
YOU ARE THE COOLEST TEACHER EVER!

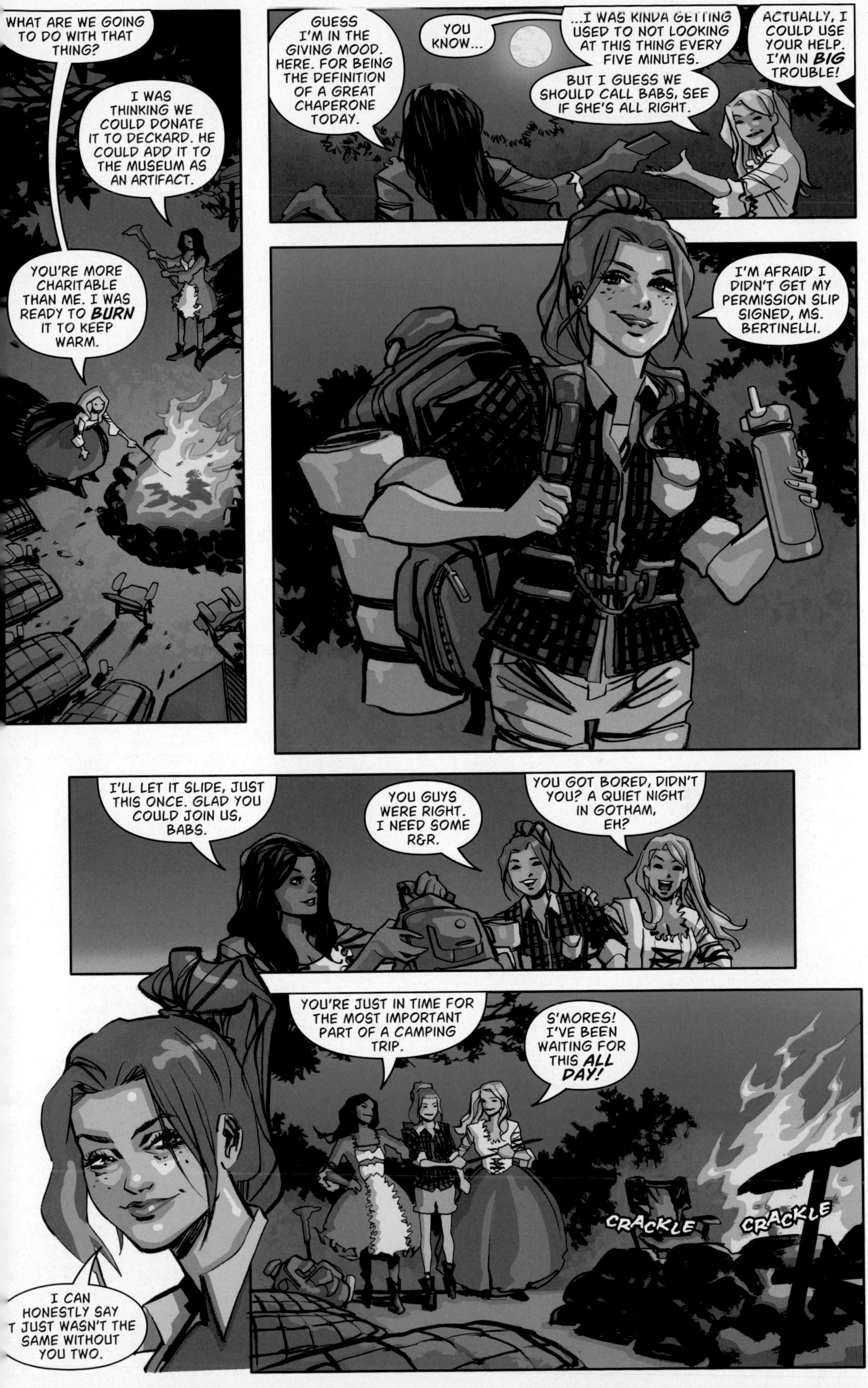
WHAT ARE WE GOING TO DO WITH THAT THING?
I WAS THINKING WE COULD DONATE IT TO DECKARD. HE COULD ADD IT TO THE MUSEUM AS AN ARTIFACT.
YOU'RE MORE CHARITABLE THAN ME. I WAS READY TO BURN IT TO KEEP WARM.
GUESS I'M IN THE GIVING MOOD. HERE. FOR BEING THE DEFINITION OF A GREAT CHAPERONE TODAY.
YOU KNOW...
...I WAS KINDA GETTING USED TO NOT LOOKING AT THIS THING EVERY FIVE MINUTES.
BUT I GUESS WE SHOULD CALL BABS, SEE IF SHE'S ALL RIGHT.
ACTUALLY, I COULD USE YOUR HELP. I'M IN BIG TROUBLE!
I'M AFRAID I DIDN'T GET MY PERMISSION SLIP SIGNED, MS. BERTINELLI.
I'LL LET IT SLIDE, JUST THIS ONCE. GLAD YOU COULD JOIN US, BABS.
YOU GUYS WERE RIGHT. I NEED SOME R&R.
YOU GOT BORED, DIDN'T YOU? A QUIET NIGHT IN GOTHAM, EH?
YOU'RE JUST IN TIME FOR THE MOST IMPORTANT PART OF A CAMPING TRIP.
S'MORES! I'VE BEEN WAITING FOR THIS ALL DAY!
CRACKLE
CRACKLE
I CAN HONESTLY SAY T JUST WASN'T THE SAME WITHOUT YOU TWO.

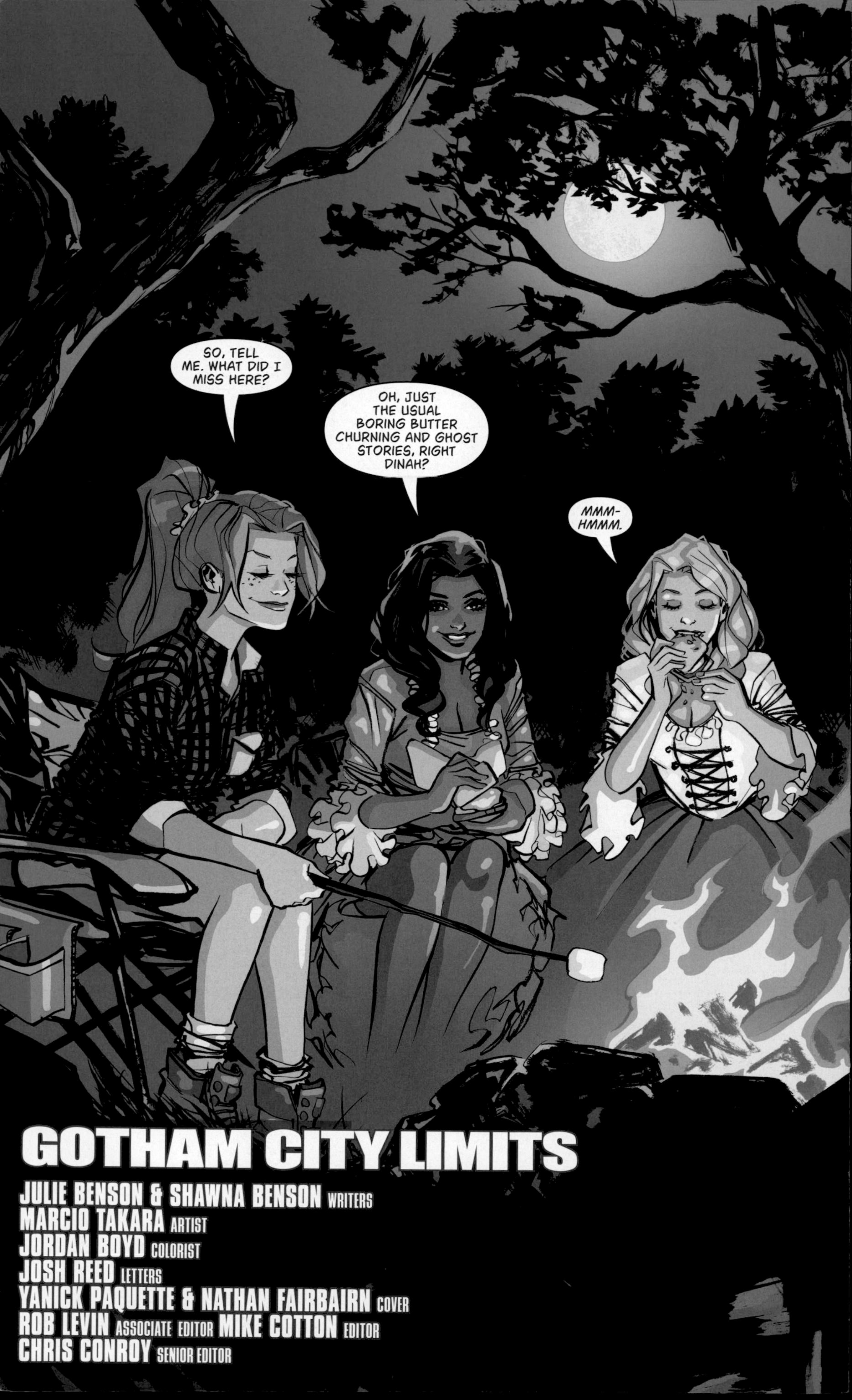
SO, TELL ME. WHAT DID I MISS HERE?
OH, JUST THE USUAL BORING BUTTER CHURNING AND GHOST STORIES, RIGHT DINAH?
MMM-HMMM.

GOTHAM CITY LIMITS

JULIE BENSON & SHAWNA BENSON WRITERS
MARCIO TAKARA ARTIST
JORDAN BOYD COLORIST
JOSH REED LETTERS
YANICK PAQUETTE & NATHAN FAIRBAIRN COVER
ROB LEVIN ASSOCIATE EDITOR MIKE COTTON EDITOR
CHRIS CONROY SENIOR EDITOR

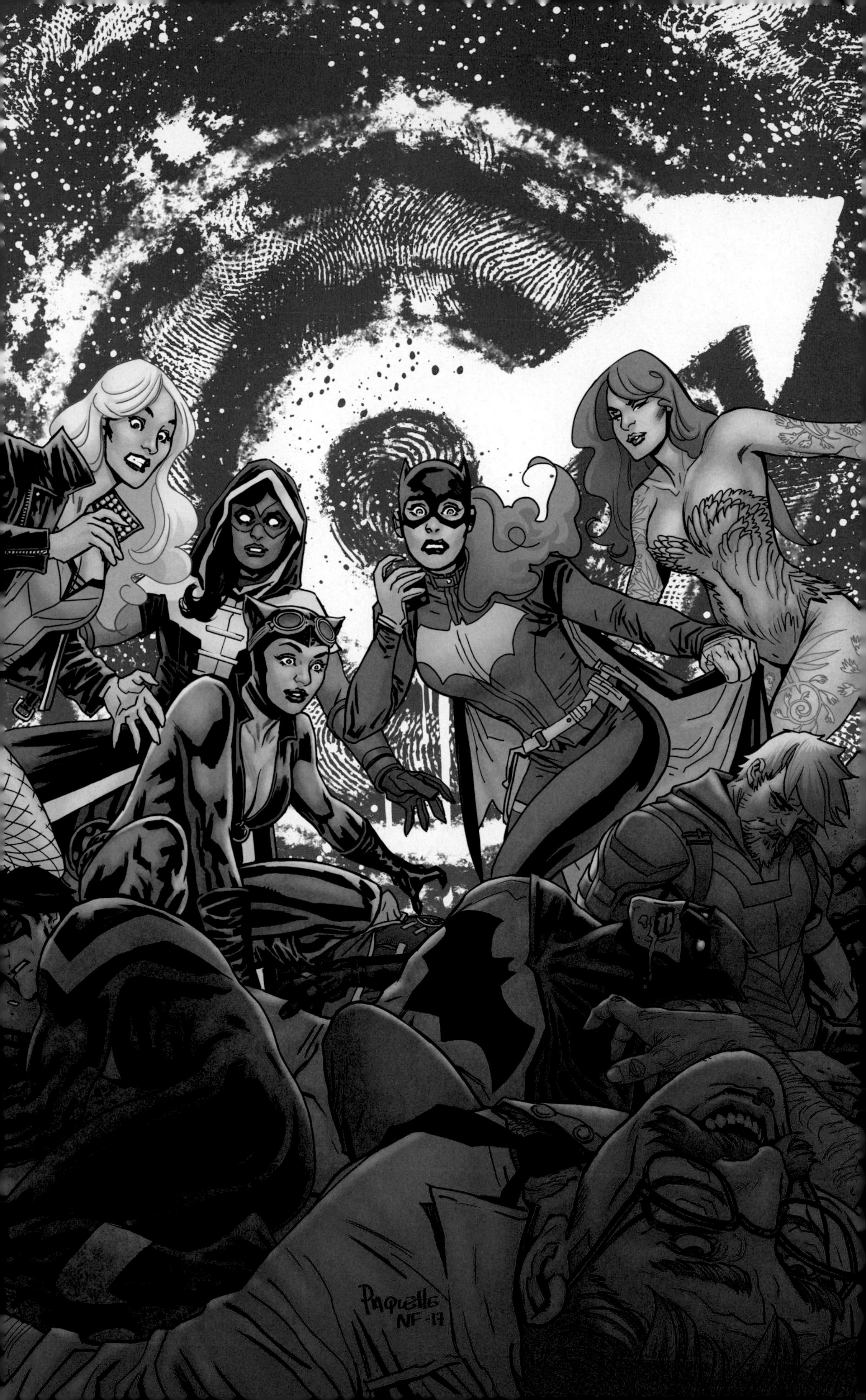

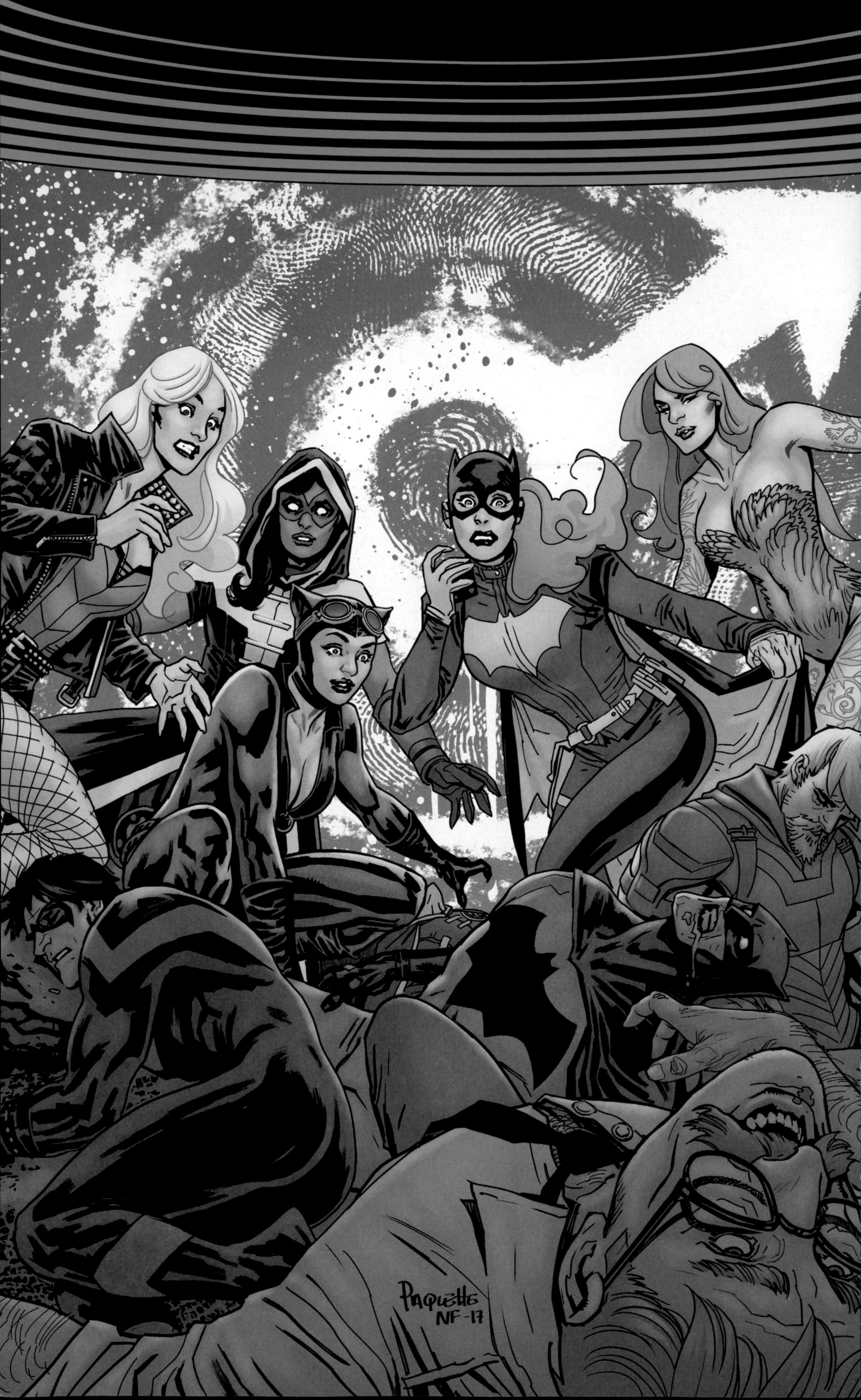
PAQUETTE
NF-17

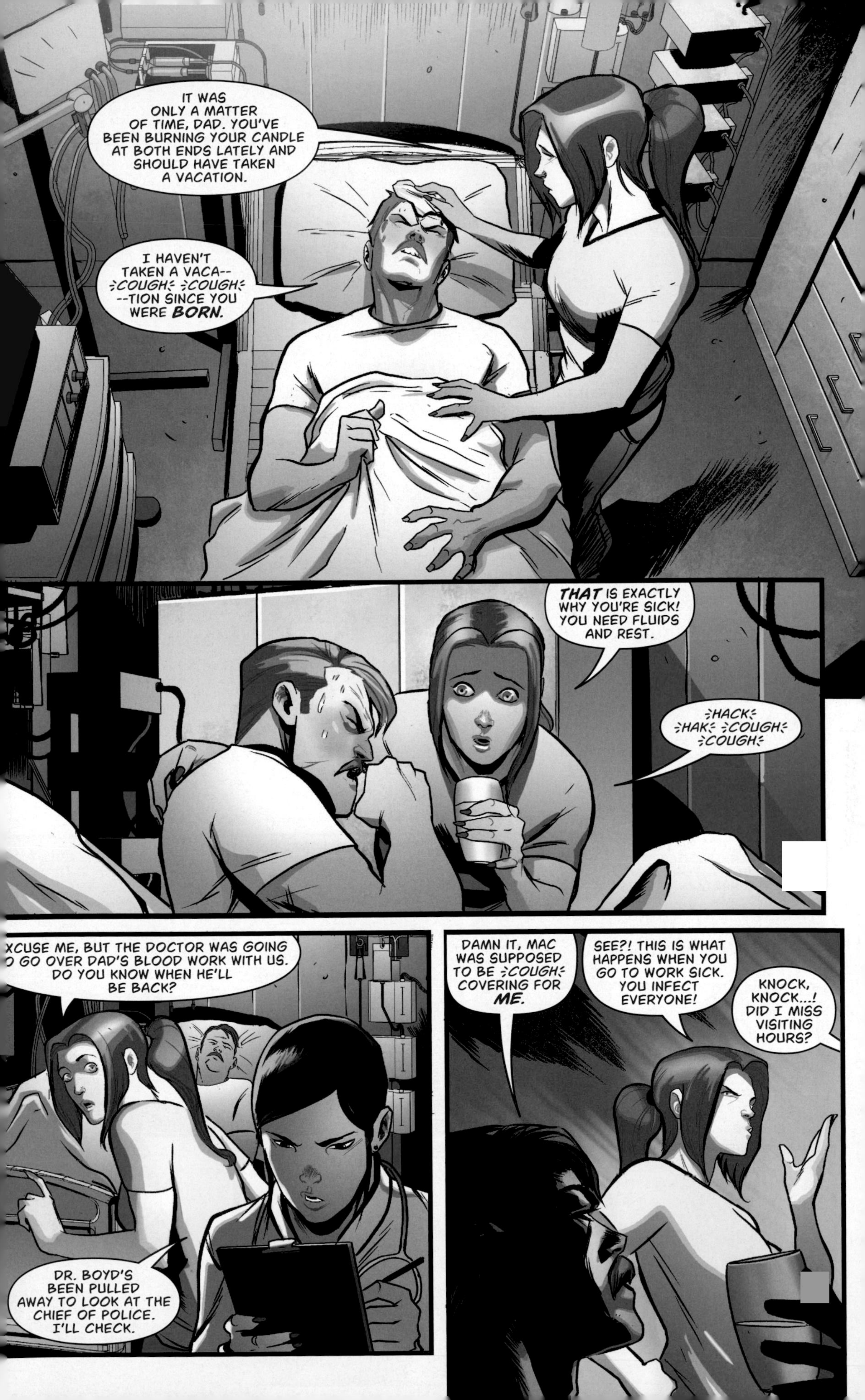
IT WAS ONLY A MATTER OF TIME, DAD. YOU'VE BEEN BURNING YOUR CANDLE AT BOTH ENDS LATELY AND SHOULD HAVE TAKEN A VACATION.
I HAVEN'T TAKEN A VACA-- COUGH COUGH --TION SINCE YOU WERE BORN.
THAT IS EXACTLY WHY YOU'RE SICK! YOU NEED FLUIDS AND REST.
HACK HAK COUGH COUGH
XCUSE ME, BUT THE DOCTOR WAS GOING O GO OVER DAD'S BLOOD WORK WITH US. DO YOU KNOW WHEN HE'LL BE BACK?
DR. BOYD'S BEEN PULLED AWAY TO LOOK AT THE CHIEF OF POLICE. I'LL CHECK.
DAMN IT, MAC WAS SUPPOSED TO BE COUGH COVERING FOR ME.
SEE?! THIS IS WHAT HAPPENS WHEN YOU GO TO WORK SICK. YOU INFECT EVERYONE!
KNOCK, KNOCK...! DID I MISS VISITING HOURS?

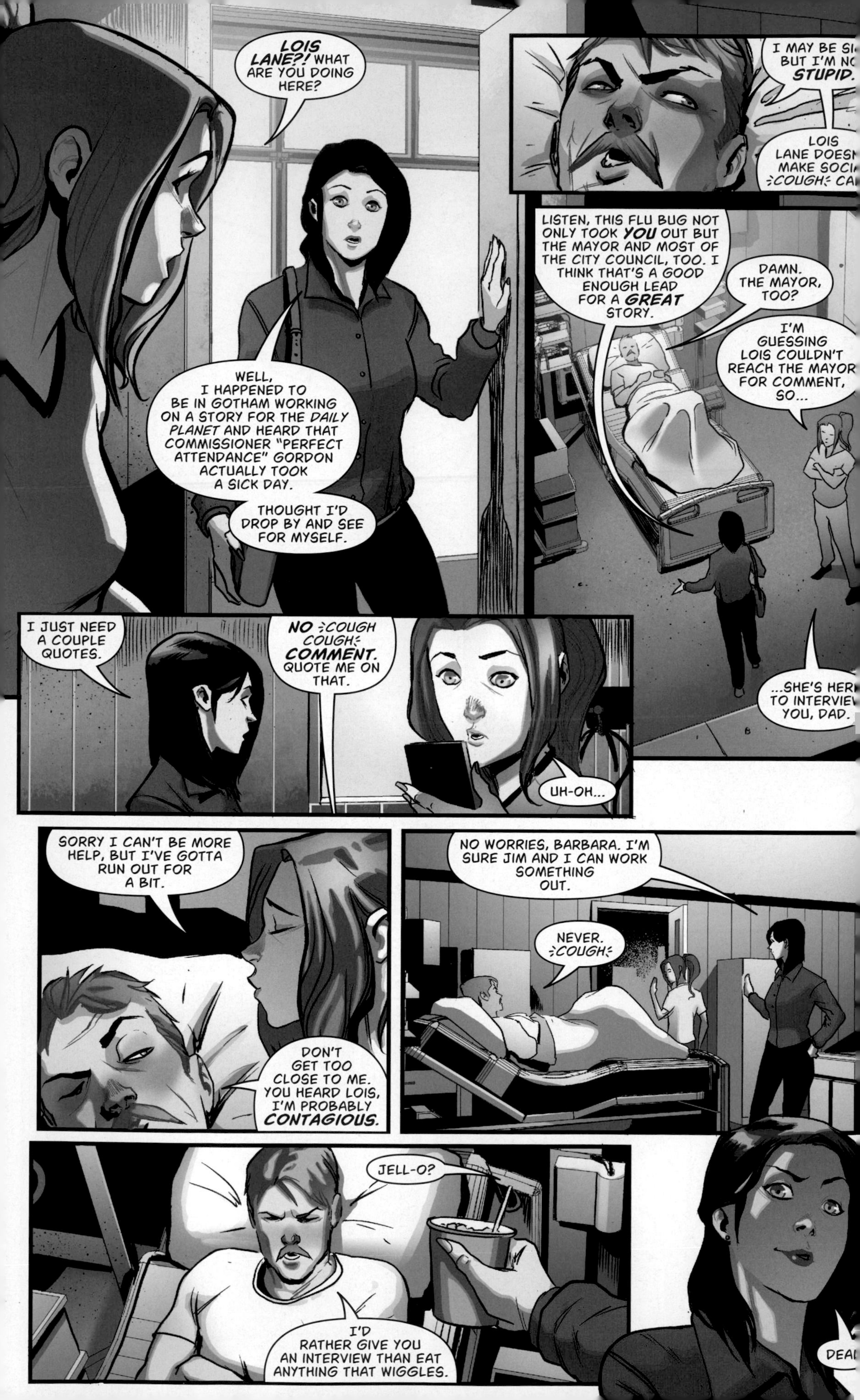
LOIS LANE?! WHAT ARE YOU DOING HERE?
WELL, I HAPPENED TO BE IN GOTHAM WORKING ON A STORY FOR THE *DAILY PLANET* AND HEARD THAT COMMISSIONER "PERFECT ATTENDANCE" GORDON ACTUALLY TOOK A SICK DAY.
THOUGHT I'D DROP BY AND SEE FOR MYSELF.
I MAY BE SI BUT I'M NO **STUPID.**
LOIS LANE DOES MAKE SOCI COUGH CA
LISTEN, THIS FLU BUG NOT ONLY TOOK **YOU** OUT BUT THE MAYOR AND MOST OF THE CITY COUNCIL, TOO. I THINK THAT'S A GOOD ENOUGH LEAD FOR A **GREAT** STORY.
DAMN. THE MAYOR, TOO?
I'M GUESSING LOIS COULDN'T REACH THE MAYOR FOR COMMENT, SO...
...SHE'S HER TO INTERVIE YOU, DAD.
I JUST NEED A COUPLE QUOTES.
NO COUGH COUGH **COMMENT.** QUOTE ME ON THAT.
UH-OH...
SORRY I CAN'T BE MORE HELP, BUT I'VE GOTTA RUN OUT FOR A BIT.
DON'T GET TOO CLOSE TO ME. YOU HEARD LOIS, I'M PROBABLY **CONTAGIOUS.**
NO WORRIES, BARBARA. I'M SURE JIM AND I CAN WORK SOMETHING OUT.
NEVER. COUGH
JELL-O?
I'D RATHER GIVE YOU AN INTERVIEW THAN EAT ANYTHING THAT WIGGLES.
DEA

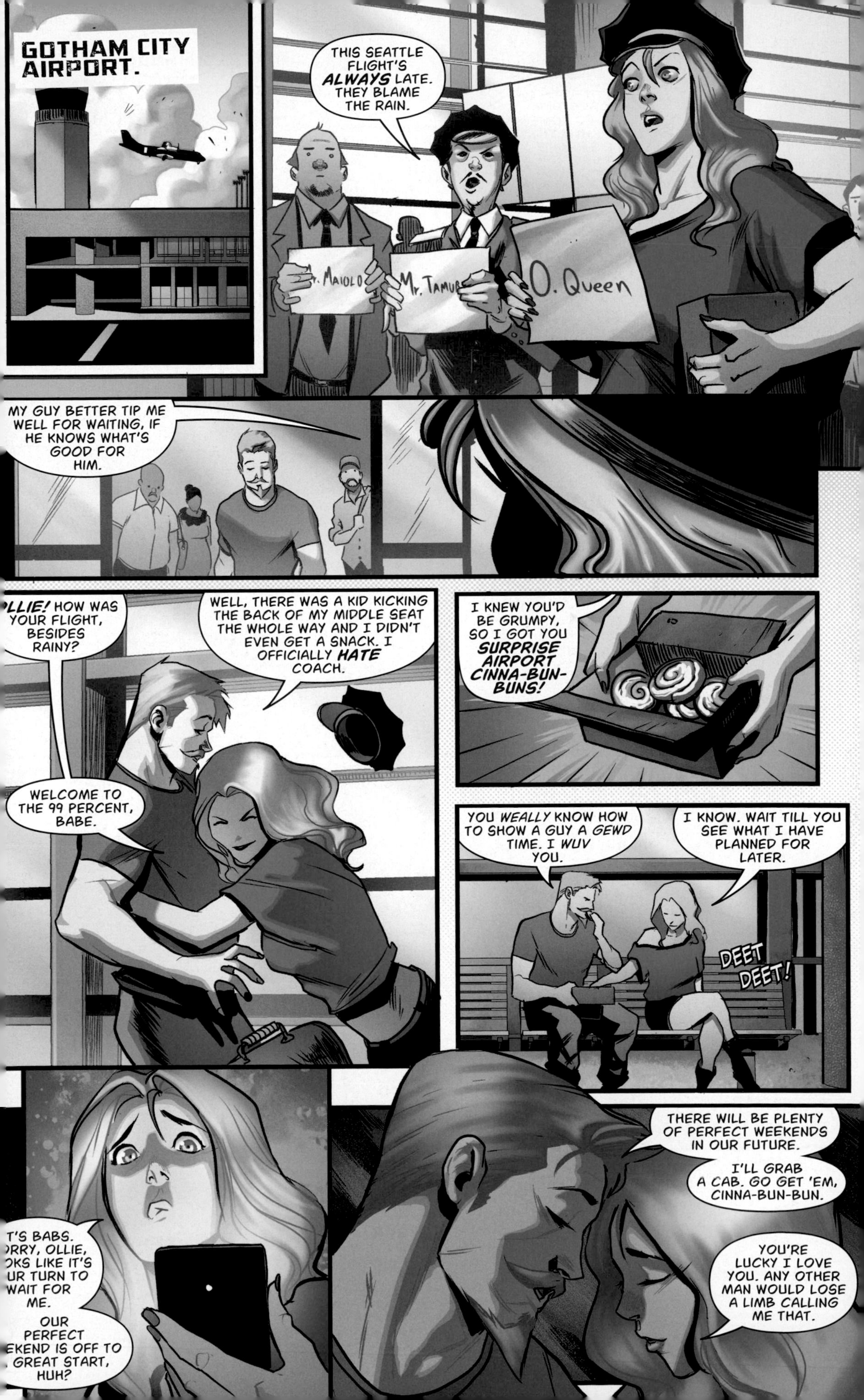
GOTHAM CITY AIRPORT.
THIS SEATTLE FLIGHT'S *ALWAYS* LATE. THEY BLAME THE RAIN.
Mr. MAIOLO
Mr. TAMUR
O. Queen
MY GUY BETTER TIP ME WELL FOR WAITING, IF HE KNOWS WHAT'S GOOD FOR HIM.
LLIE! HOW WAS YOUR FLIGHT, BESIDES RAINY?
WELL, THERE WAS A KID KICKING THE BACK OF MY MIDDLE SEAT THE WHOLE WAY AND I DIDN'T EVEN GET A SNACK. I OFFICIALLY *HATE* COACH.
WELCOME TO THE 99 PERCENT, BABE.
I KNEW YOU'D BE GRUMPY, SO I GOT YOU *SURPRISE AIRPORT CINNA-BUN-BUNS!*
YOU *WEALLY* KNOW HOW TO SHOW A GUY A *GEWD* TIME. I *WUV* YOU.
I KNOW. WAIT TILL YOU SEE WHAT I HAVE PLANNED FOR LATER.
DEET DEET!
T'S BABS. ORRY, OLLIE, OKS LIKE IT'S UR TURN TO WAIT FOR ME.
OUR PERFECT EKEND IS OFF TO GREAT START, HUH?
THERE WILL BE PLENTY OF PERFECT WEEKENDS IN OUR FUTURE.
I'LL GRAB A CAB. GO GET 'EM, CINNA-BUN-BUN.
YOU'RE LUCKY I LOVE YOU. ANY OTHER MAN WOULD LOSE A LIMB CALLING ME THAT.

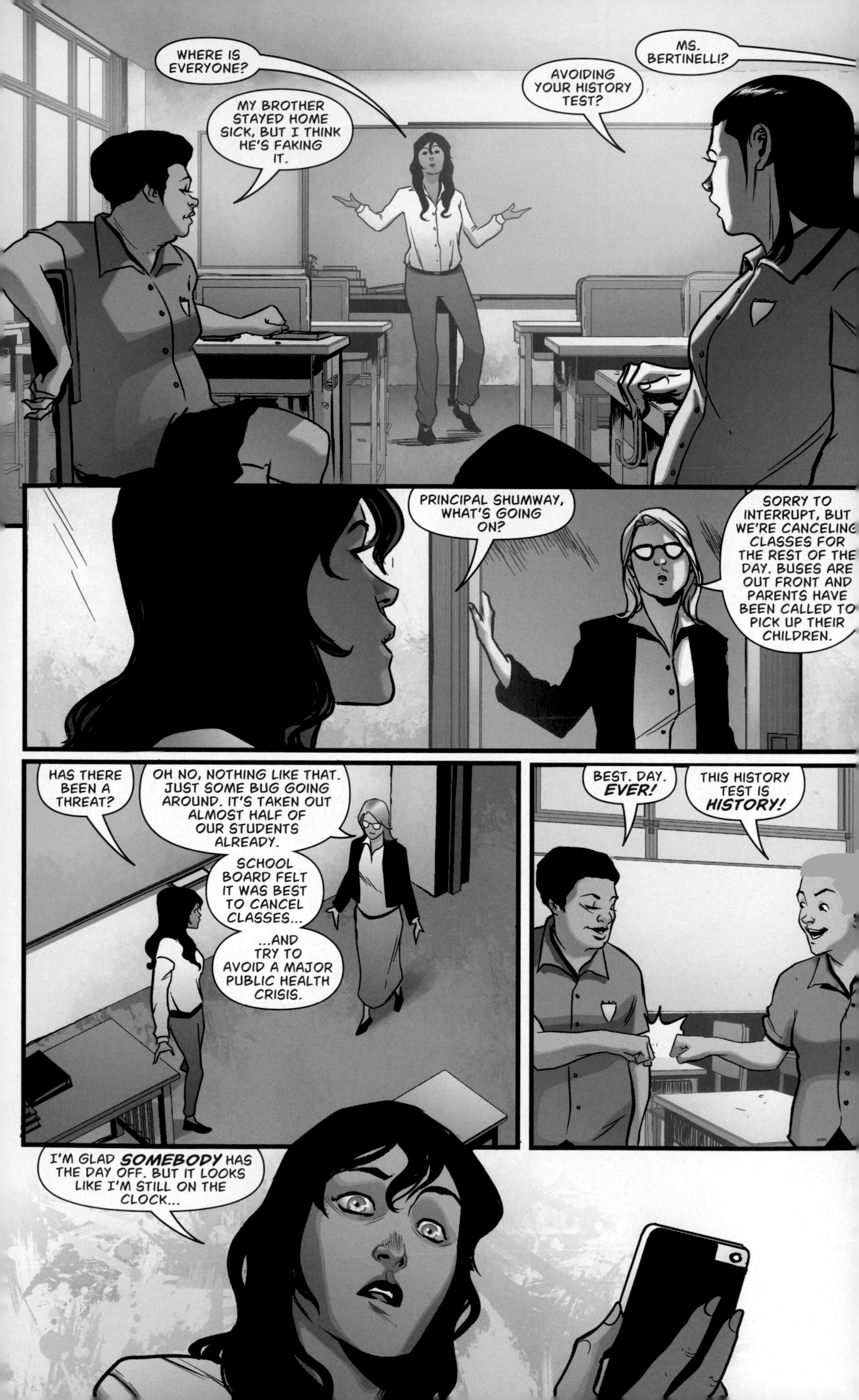
WHERE IS EVERYONE?
MY BROTHER STAYED HOME SICK, BUT I THINK HE'S FAKING IT.
AVOIDING YOUR HISTORY TEST?
MS. BERTINELLI?
PRINCIPAL SHUMWAY, WHAT'S GOING ON?
SORRY TO INTERRUPT, BUT WE'RE CANCELING CLASSES FOR THE REST OF THE DAY. BUSES ARE OUT FRONT AND PARENTS HAVE BEEN CALLED TO PICK UP THEIR CHILDREN.
HAS THERE BEEN A THREAT?
OH NO, NOTHING LIKE THAT. JUST SOME BUG GOING AROUND. IT'S TAKEN OUT ALMOST HALF OF OUR STUDENTS ALREADY.
SCHOOL BOARD FELT IT WAS BEST TO CANCEL CLASSES...
...AND TRY TO AVOID A MAJOR PUBLIC HEALTH CRISIS.
BEST. DAY. *EVER!*
THIS HISTORY TEST IS *HISTORY!*
I'M GLAD *SOMEBODY* HAS THE DAY OFF. BUT IT LOOKS LIKE I'M STILL ON THE CLOCK...

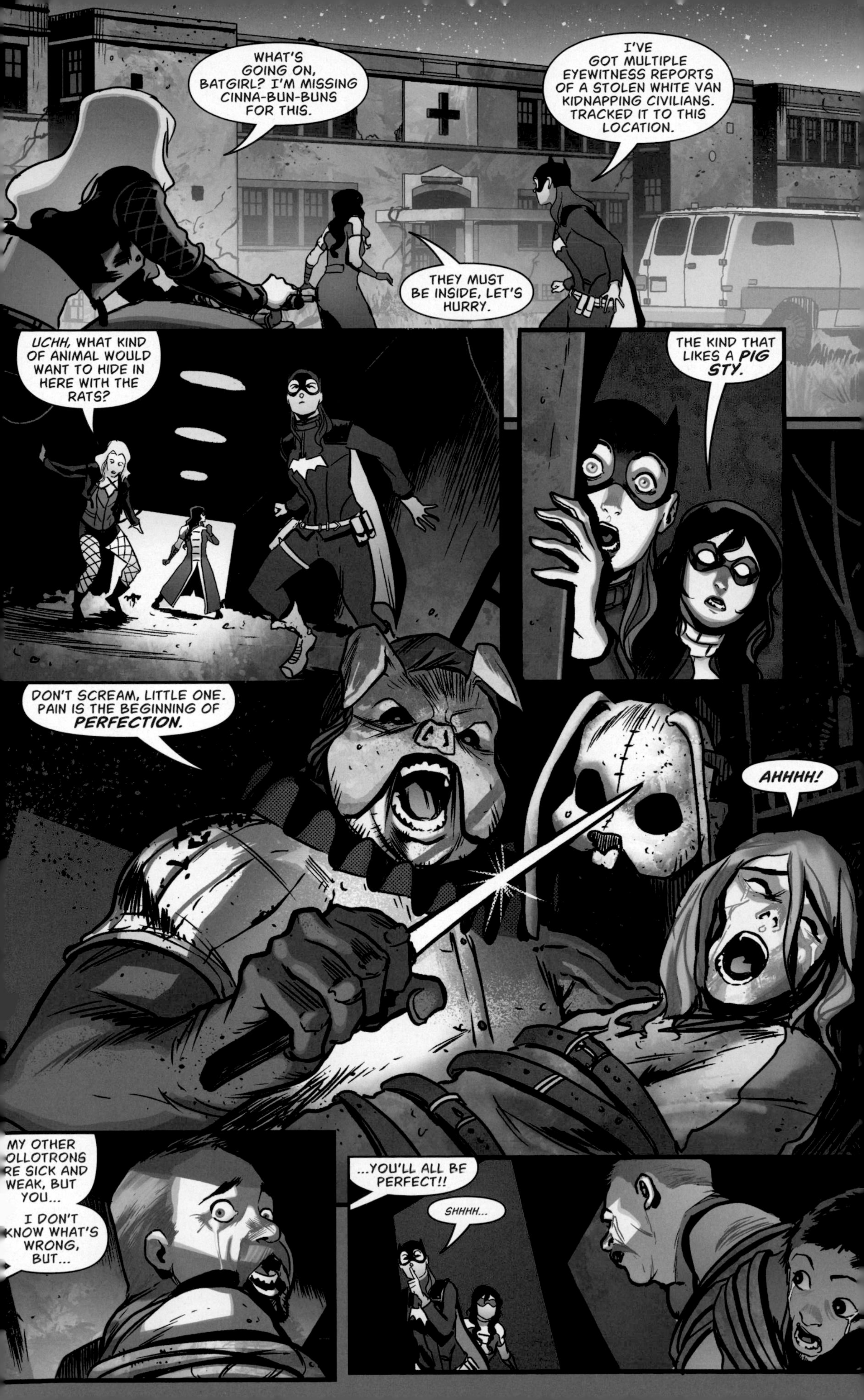
WHAT'S GOING ON, BATGIRL? I'M MISSING CINNA-BUN-BUNS FOR THIS.
I'VE GOT MULTIPLE EYEWITNESS REPORTS OF A STOLEN WHITE VAN KIDNAPPING CIVILIANS. TRACKED IT TO THIS LOCATION.
THEY MUST BE INSIDE, LET'S HURRY.
UCHH, WHAT KIND OF ANIMAL WOULD WANT TO HIDE IN HERE WITH THE RATS?
THE KIND THAT LIKES A PIG STY.
DON'T SCREAM, LITTLE ONE. PAIN IS THE BEGINNING OF PERFECTION.
AHHHH!
MY OTHER OLLOTRONS RE SICK AND WEAK, BUT YOU...
I DON'T KNOW WHAT'S WRONG, BUT...
...YOU'LL ALL BE PERFECT!!
SHHHH...

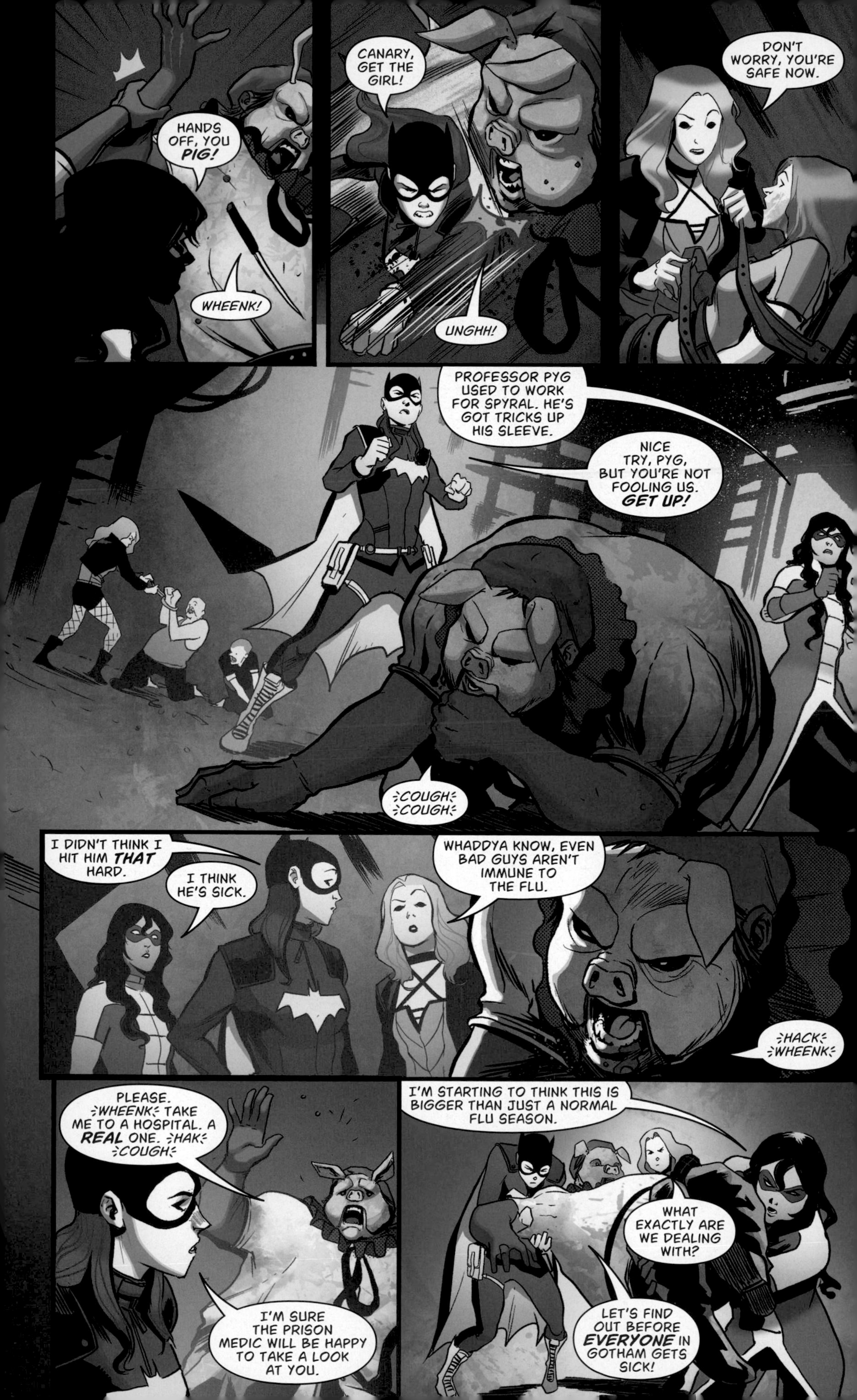
HANDS OFF, YOU PIG!
WHEENK!
CANARY, GET THE GIRL!
UNGHH!
DON'T WORRY, YOU'RE SAFE NOW.
PROFESSOR PYG USED TO WORK FOR SPYRAL. HE'S GOT TRICKS UP HIS SLEEVE.
NICE TRY, PYG, BUT YOU'RE NOT FOOLING US. GET UP!
COUGH COUGH
I DIDN'T THINK I HIT HIM THAT HARD.
I THINK HE'S SICK.
WHADDYA KNOW, EVEN BAD GUYS AREN'T IMMUNE TO THE FLU.
HACK WHEENK
PLEASE. WHEENK TAKE ME TO A HOSPITAL. A REAL ONE. HAK COUGH
I'M SURE THE PRISON MEDIC WILL BE HAPPY TO TAKE A LOOK AT YOU.
I'M STARTING TO THINK THIS IS BIGGER THAN JUST A NORMAL FLU SEASON.
WHAT EXACTLY ARE WE DEALING WITH?
LET'S FIND OUT BEFORE EVERYONE IN GOTHAM GETS SICK!

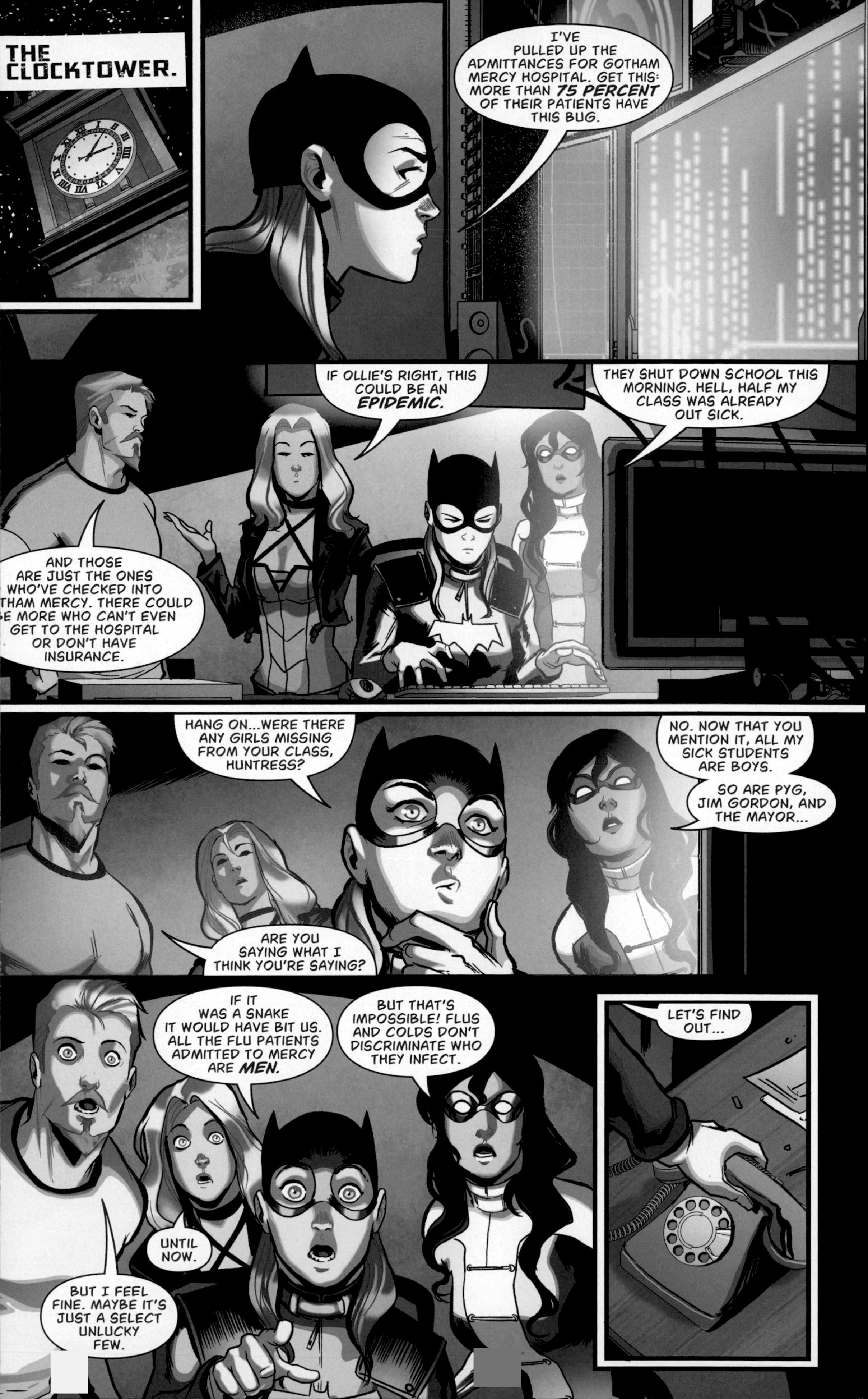
THE CLOCKTOWER.
I'VE PULLED UP THE ADMITTANCES FOR GOTHAM MERCY HOSPITAL. GET THIS: MORE THAN 75 PERCENT OF THEIR PATIENTS HAVE THIS BUG.
IF OLLIE'S RIGHT, THIS COULD BE AN EPIDEMIC.
THEY SHUT DOWN SCHOOL THIS MORNING. HELL, HALF MY CLASS WAS ALREADY OUT SICK.
AND THOSE ARE JUST THE ONES WHO'VE CHECKED INTO THAM MERCY. THERE COULD E MORE WHO CAN'T EVEN GET TO THE HOSPITAL OR DON'T HAVE INSURANCE.
HANG ON...WERE THERE ANY GIRLS MISSING FROM YOUR CLASS, HUNTRESS?
NO. NOW THAT YOU MENTION IT, ALL MY SICK STUDENTS ARE BOYS.
SO ARE PYG, JIM GORDON, AND THE MAYOR...
ARE YOU SAYING WHAT I THINK YOU'RE SAYING?
IF IT WAS A SNAKE IT WOULD HAVE BIT US. ALL THE FLU PATIENTS ADMITTED TO MERCY ARE MEN.
BUT THAT'S IMPOSSIBLE! FLUS AND COLDS DON'T DISCRIMINATE WHO THEY INFECT.
UNTIL NOW.
BUT I FEEL FINE. MAYBE IT'S JUST A SELECT UNLUCKY FEW.
LET'S FIND OUT...

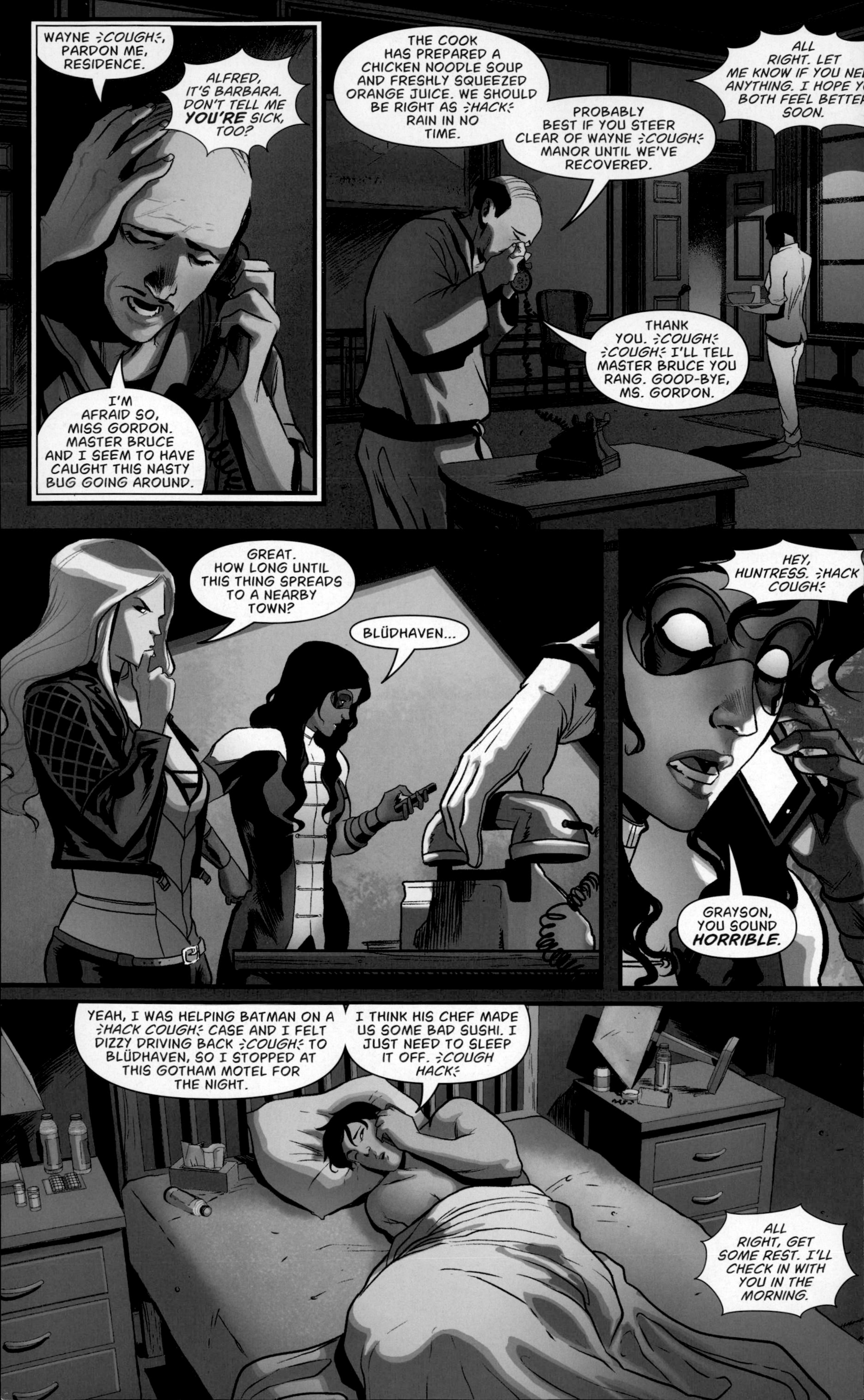
WAYNE COUGH, PARDON ME, RESIDENCE.
ALFRED, IT'S BARBARA. DON'T TELL ME YOU'RE SICK, TOO?
I'M AFRAID SO, MISS GORDON. MASTER BRUCE AND I SEEM TO HAVE CAUGHT THIS NASTY BUG GOING AROUND.
THE COOK HAS PREPARED A CHICKEN NOODLE SOUP AND FRESHLY SQUEEZED ORANGE JUICE. WE SHOULD BE RIGHT AS HACK RAIN IN NO TIME.
PROBABLY BEST IF YOU STEER CLEAR OF WAYNE COUGH MANOR UNTIL WE'VE RECOVERED.
ALL RIGHT. LET ME KNOW IF YOU NE ANYTHING. I HOPE Y BOTH FEEL BETTER SOON.
THANK YOU. COUGH COUGH I'LL TELL MASTER BRUCE YOU RANG. GOOD-BYE, MS. GORDON.
GREAT. HOW LONG UNTIL THIS THING SPREADS TO A NEARBY TOWN?
BLÜDHAVEN...
HEY, HUNTRESS. HACK COUGH
GRAYSON, YOU SOUND HORRIBLE.
YEAH, I WAS HELPING BATMAN ON A HACK COUGH CASE AND I FELT DIZZY DRIVING BACK COUGH TO BLÜDHAVEN, SO I STOPPED AT THIS GOTHAM MOTEL FOR THE NIGHT.
I THINK HIS CHEF MADE US SOME BAD SUSHI. I JUST NEED TO SLEEP IT OFF. COUGH HACK
ALL RIGHT, GET SOME REST. I'LL CHECK IN WITH YOU IN THE MORNING.

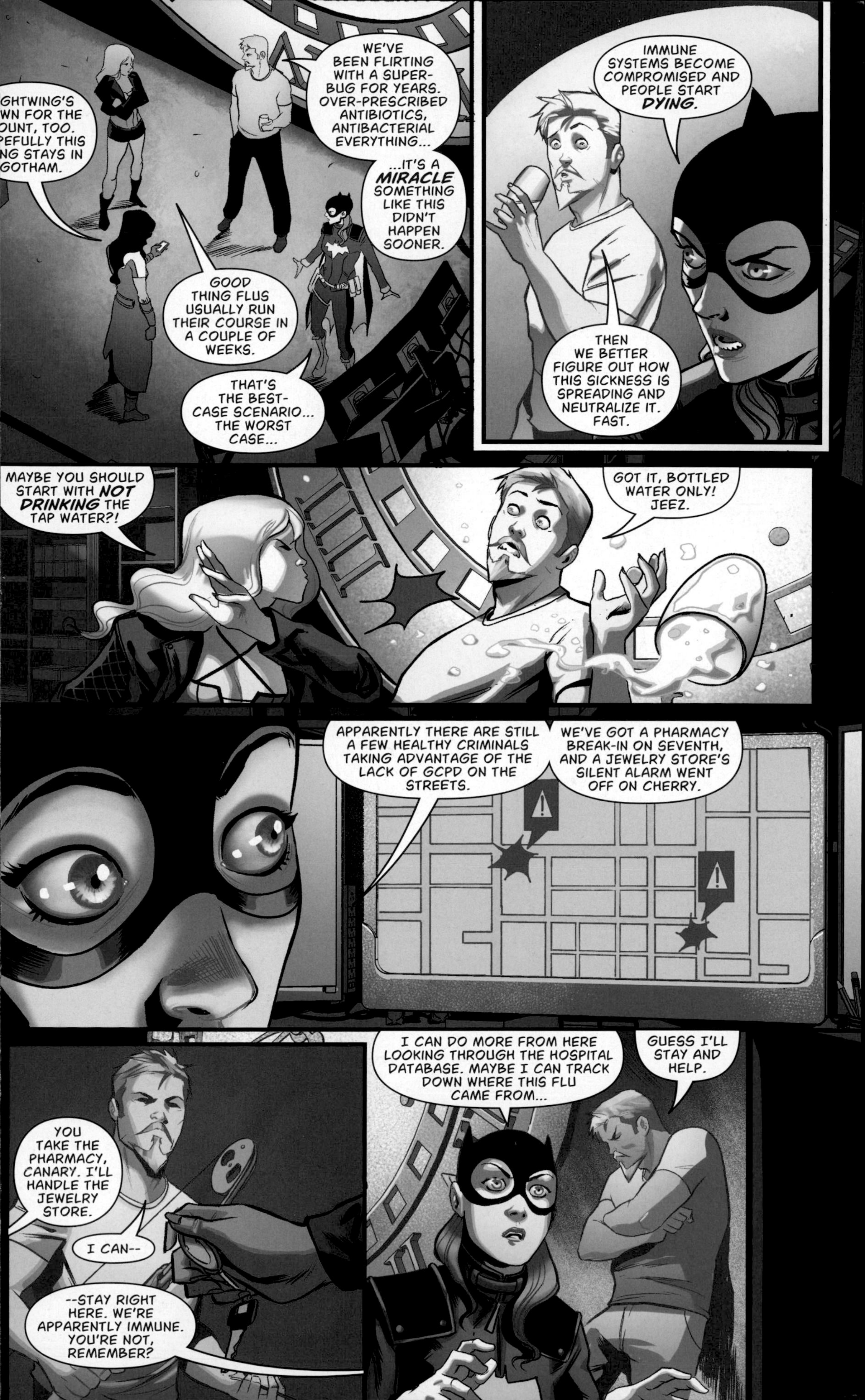
...IGHTWING'S ...WN FOR THE ...OUNT, TOO. ...PEFULLY THIS ...NG STAYS IN GOTHAM.
WE'VE BEEN FLIRTING WITH A SUPER-BUG FOR YEARS. OVER-PRESCRIBED ANTIBIOTICS, ANTIBACTERIAL EVERYTHING...
...IT'S A MIRACLE SOMETHING LIKE THIS DIDN'T HAPPEN SOONER.
GOOD THING FLUS USUALLY RUN THEIR COURSE IN A COUPLE OF WEEKS.
THAT'S THE BEST-CASE SCENARIO... THE WORST CASE...
IMMUNE SYSTEMS BECOME COMPROMISED AND PEOPLE START DYING.
THEN WE BETTER FIGURE OUT HOW THIS SICKNESS IS SPREADING AND NEUTRALIZE IT. FAST.
MAYBE YOU SHOULD START WITH NOT DRINKING THE TAP WATER?!
GOT IT, BOTTLED WATER ONLY! JEEZ.
APPARENTLY THERE ARE STILL A FEW HEALTHY CRIMINALS TAKING ADVANTAGE OF THE LACK OF GCPD ON THE STREETS.
WE'VE GOT A PHARMACY BREAK-IN ON SEVENTH, AND A JEWELRY STORE'S SILENT ALARM WENT OFF ON CHERRY.
YOU TAKE THE PHARMACY, CANARY. I'LL HANDLE THE JEWELRY STORE.
I CAN--
--STAY RIGHT HERE. WE'RE APPARENTLY IMMUNE. YOU'RE NOT, REMEMBER?
I CAN DO MORE FROM HERE LOOKING THROUGH THE HOSPITAL DATABASE. MAYBE I CAN TRACK DOWN WHERE THIS FLU CAME FROM...
GUESS I'LL STAY AND HELP.

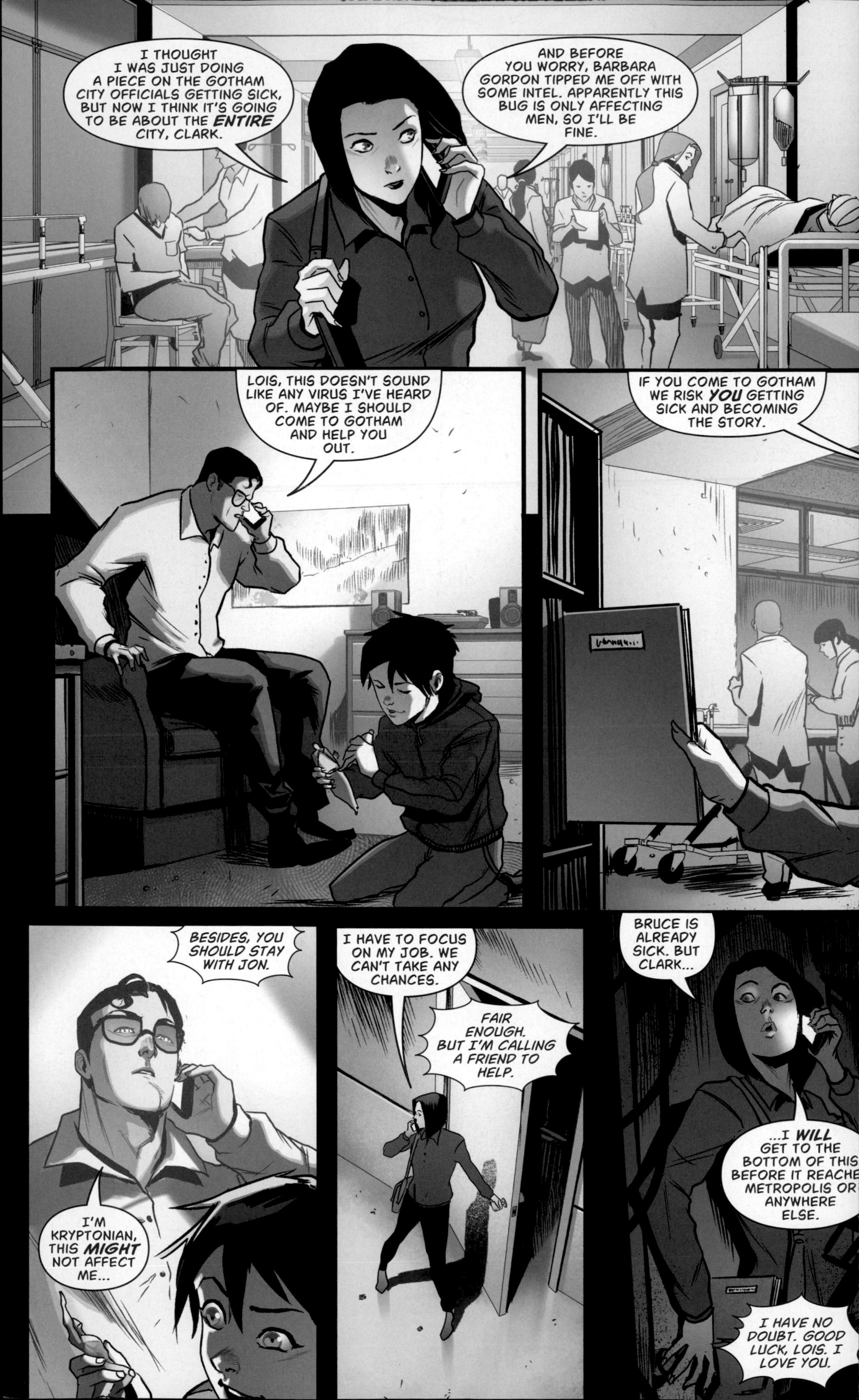
I THOUGHT I WAS JUST DOING A PIECE ON THE GOTHAM CITY OFFICIALS GETTING SICK, BUT NOW I THINK IT'S GOING TO BE ABOUT THE ENTIRE CITY, CLARK.
AND BEFORE YOU WORRY, BARBARA GORDON TIPPED ME OFF WITH SOME INTEL. APPARENTLY THIS BUG IS ONLY AFFECTING MEN, SO I'LL BE FINE.
LOIS, THIS DOESN'T SOUND LIKE ANY VIRUS I'VE HEARD OF. MAYBE I SHOULD COME TO GOTHAM AND HELP YOU OUT.
IF YOU COME TO GOTHAM WE RISK YOU GETTING SICK AND BECOMING THE STORY.
BESIDES, YOU SHOULD STAY WITH JON.
I'M KRYPTONIAN, THIS MIGHT NOT AFFECT ME...
I HAVE TO FOCUS ON MY JOB. WE CAN'T TAKE ANY CHANCES.
FAIR ENOUGH. BUT I'M CALLING A FRIEND TO HELP.
BRUCE IS ALREADY SICK. BUT CLARK...
...I WILL GET TO THE BOTTOM OF THIS BEFORE IT REACHE METROPOLIS OR ANYWHERE ELSE.
I HAVE NO DOUBT. GOOD LUCK, LOIS. I LOVE YOU.

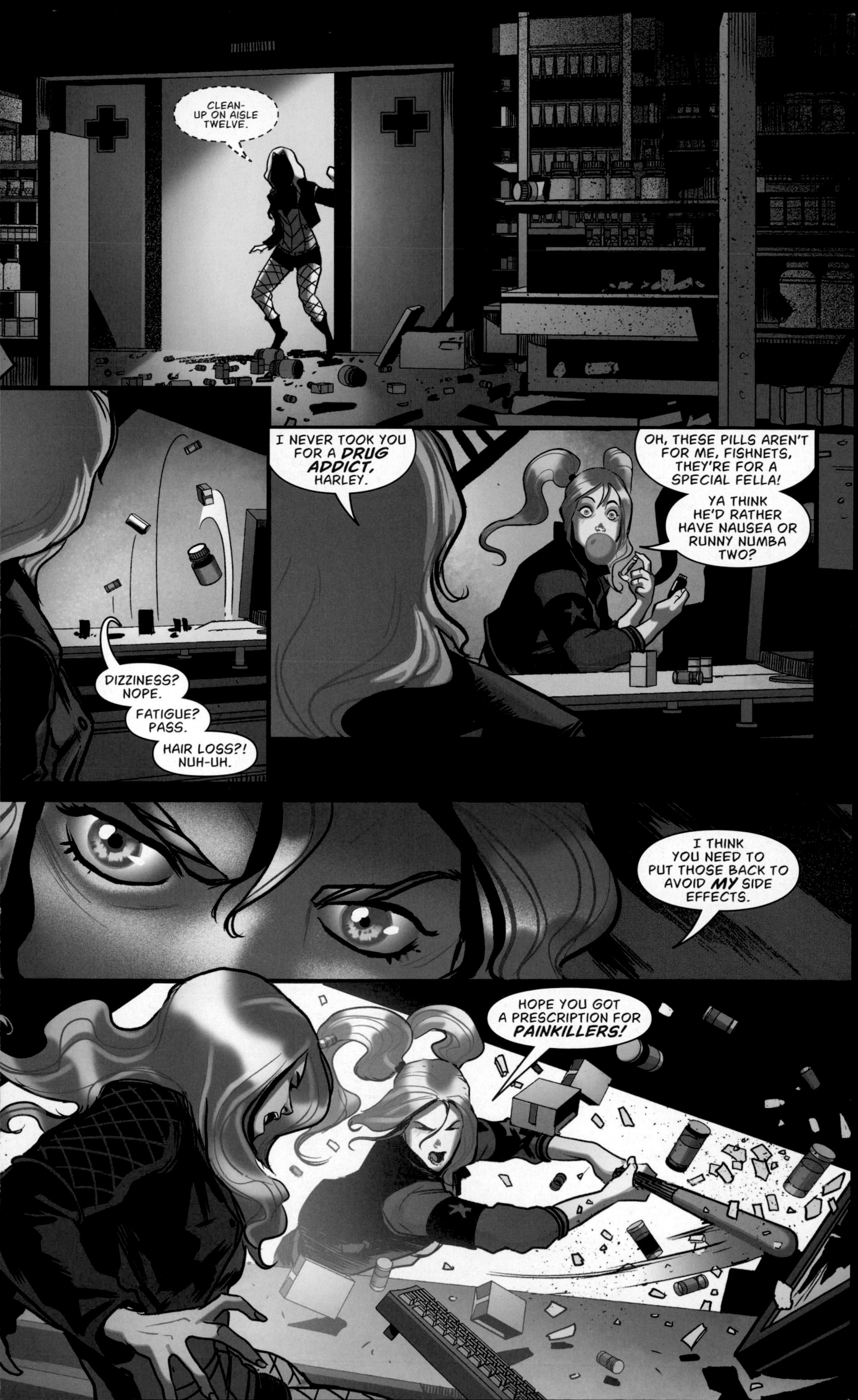
CLEAN-UP ON AISLE TWELVE.
DIZZINESS? NOPE.
FATIGUE? PASS.
HAIR LOSS?! NUH-UH.
I NEVER TOOK YOU FOR A DRUG ADDICT, HARLEY.
OH, THESE PILLS AREN'T FOR ME, FISHNETS, THEY'RE FOR A SPECIAL FELLA!
YA THINK HE'D RATHER HAVE NAUSEA OR RUNNY NUMBA TWO?
I THINK YOU NEED TO PUT THOSE BACK TO AVOID MY SIDE EFFECTS.
HOPE YOU GOT A PRESCRIPTION FOR PAINKILLERS!

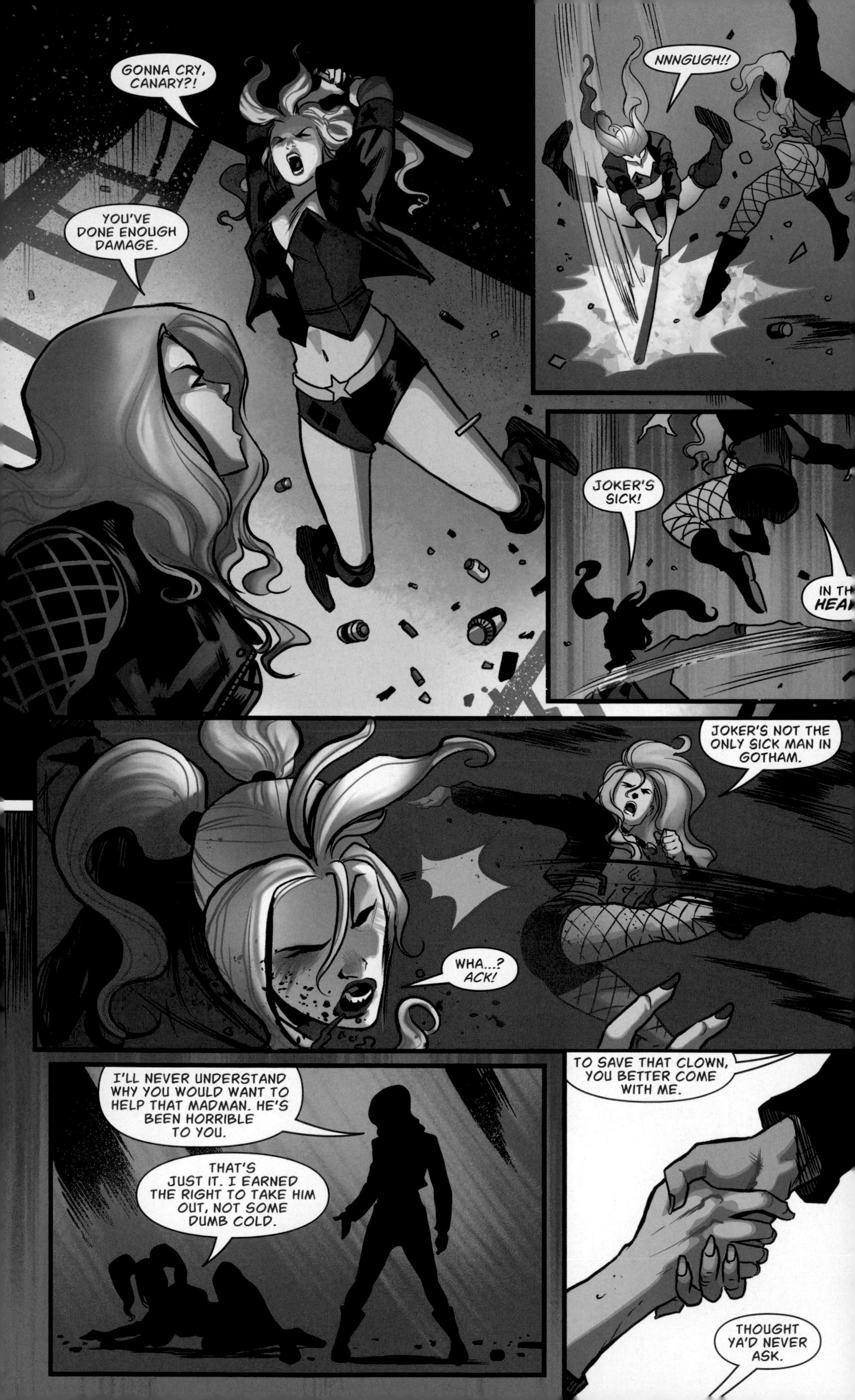
GONNA CRY, CANARY?!
YOU'VE DONE ENOUGH DAMAGE.
NNNGUGH!!
JOKER'S SICK!
IN TH HEA
JOKER'S NOT THE ONLY SICK MAN IN GOTHAM.
WHA...? ACK!
I'LL NEVER UNDERSTAND WHY YOU WOULD WANT TO HELP THAT MADMAN. HE'S BEEN HORRIBLE TO YOU.
THAT'S JUST IT. I EARNED THE RIGHT TO TAKE HIM OUT, NOT SOME DUMB COLD.
TO SAVE THAT CLOWN, YOU BETTER COME WITH ME.
THOUGHT YA'D NEVER ASK.

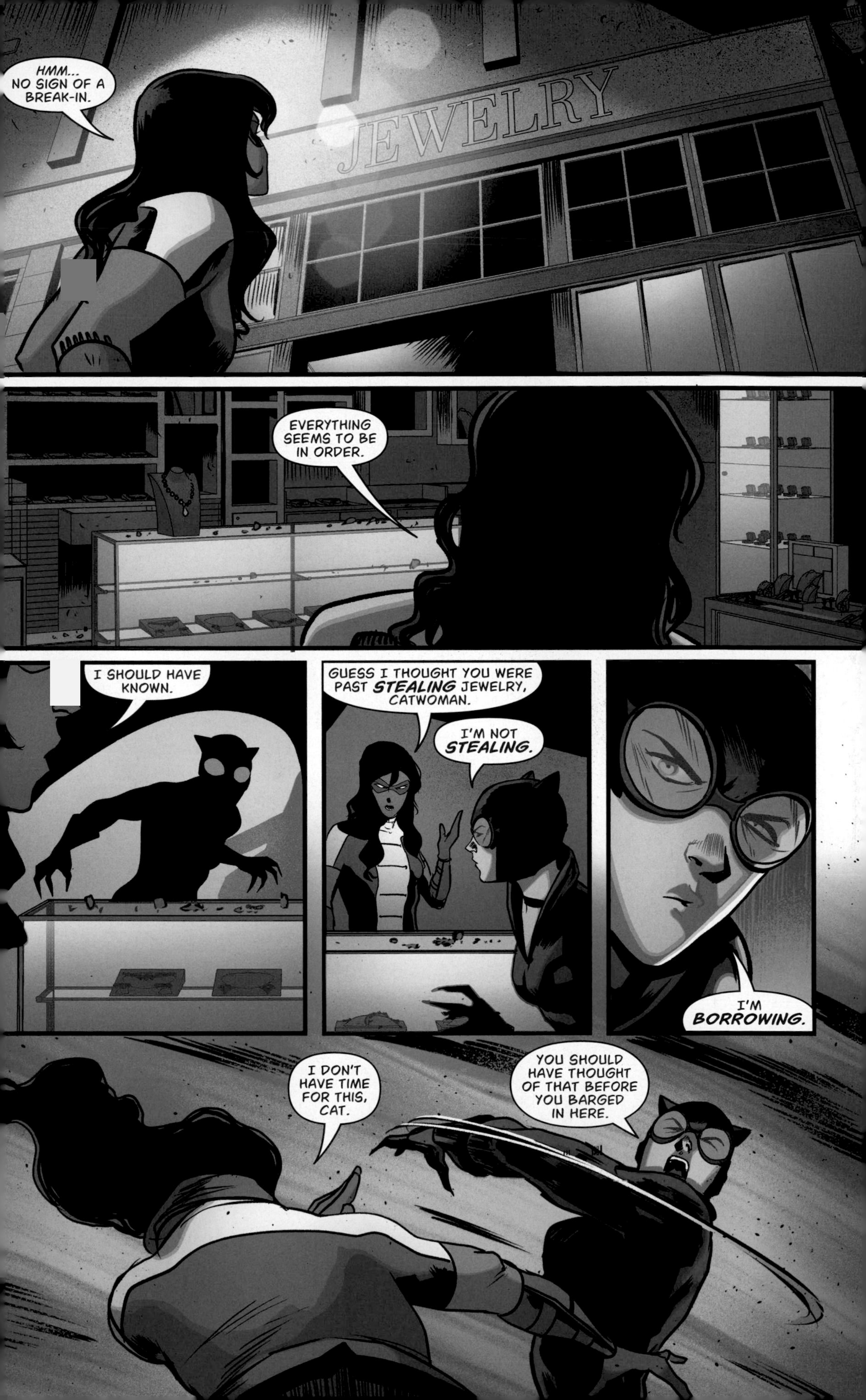
HMM... NO SIGN OF A BREAK-IN.
JEWELRY
EVERYTHING SEEMS TO BE IN ORDER.
I SHOULD HAVE KNOWN.
GUESS I THOUGHT YOU WERE PAST STEALING JEWELRY, CATWOMAN.
I'M NOT STEALING.
I'M BORROWING.
I DON'T HAVE TIME FOR THIS, CAT.
YOU SHOULD HAVE THOUGHT OF THAT BEFORE YOU BARGED IN HERE.

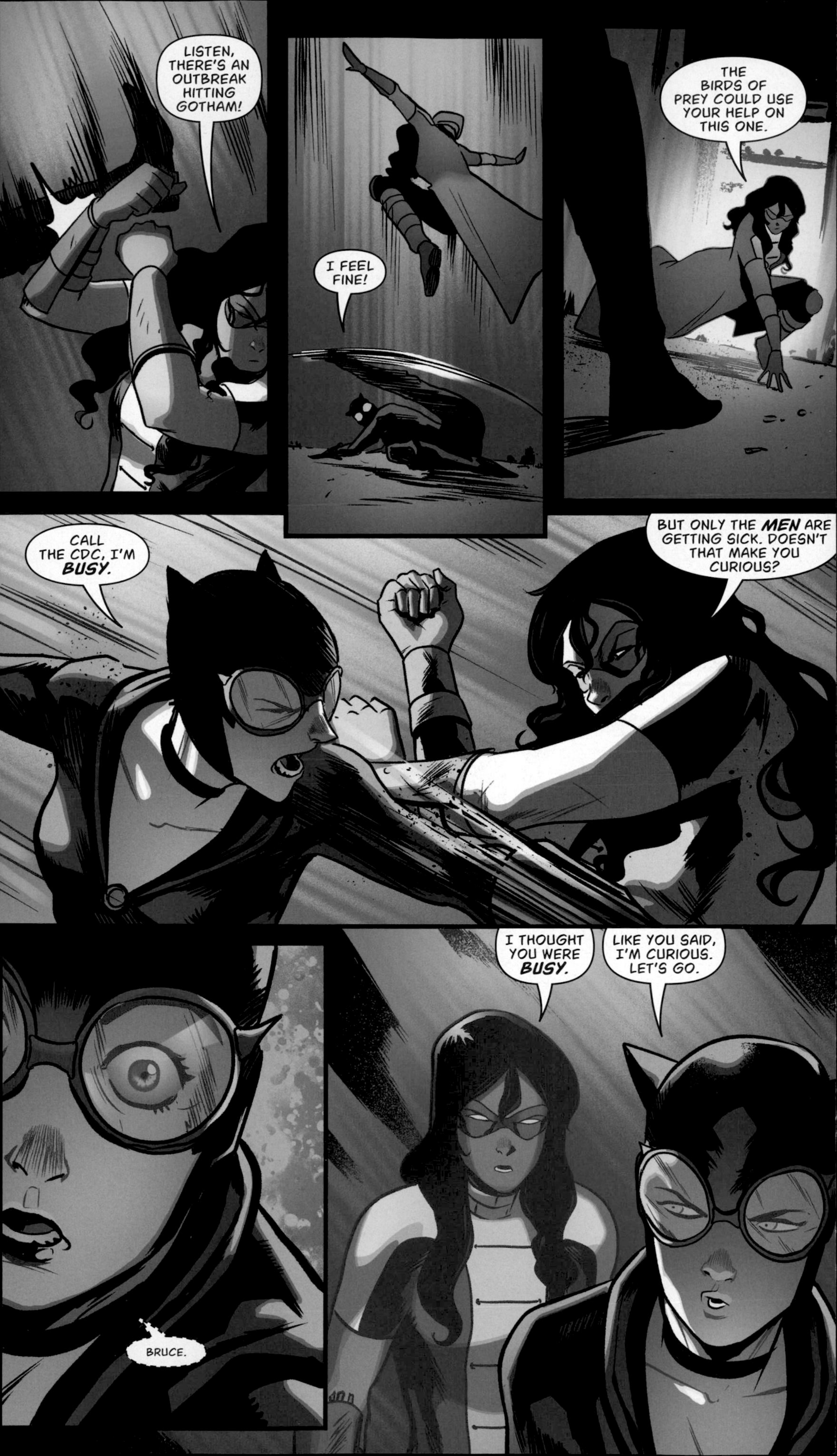
LISTEN, THERE'S AN OUTBREAK HITTING GOTHAM!
I FEEL FINE!
THE BIRDS OF PREY COULD USE YOUR HELP ON THIS ONE.
CALL THE CDC, I'M **BUSY.**
BUT ONLY THE **MEN** ARE GETTING SICK. DOESN'T THAT MAKE YOU CURIOUS?
BRUCE.
I THOUGHT YOU WERE **BUSY.**
LIKE YOU SAID, I'M CURIOUS. LET'S GO.

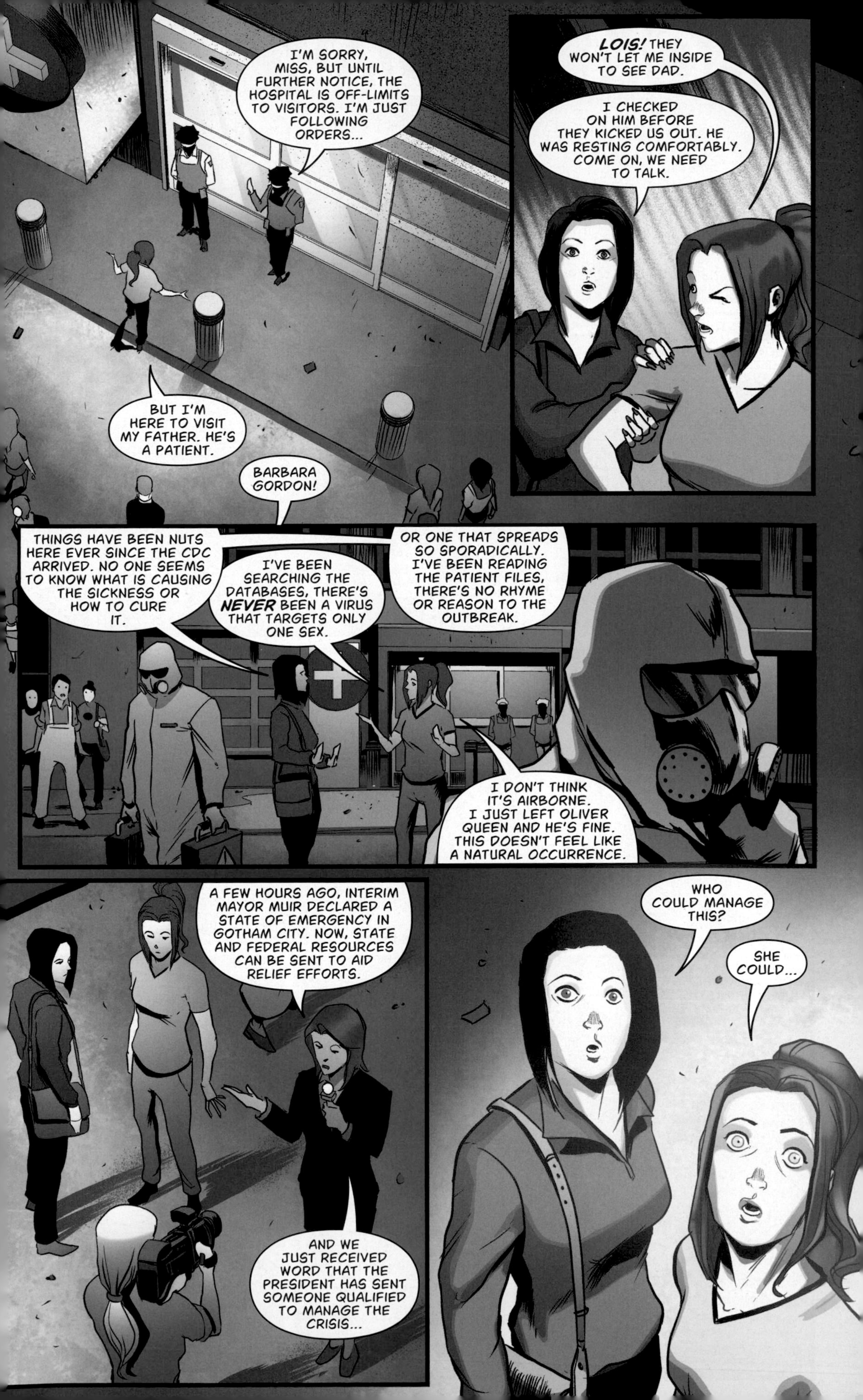
I'M SORRY, MISS, BUT UNTIL FURTHER NOTICE, THE HOSPITAL IS OFF-LIMITS TO VISITORS. I'M JUST FOLLOWING ORDERS...
BUT I'M HERE TO VISIT MY FATHER. HE'S A PATIENT.
BARBARA GORDON!
LOIS! THEY WON'T LET ME INSIDE TO SEE DAD.
I CHECKED ON HIM BEFORE THEY KICKED US OUT. HE WAS RESTING COMFORTABLY. COME ON, WE NEED TO TALK.
THINGS HAVE BEEN NUTS HERE EVER SINCE THE CDC ARRIVED. NO ONE SEEMS TO KNOW WHAT IS CAUSING THE SICKNESS OR HOW TO CURE IT.
I'VE BEEN SEARCHING THE DATABASES, THERE'S NEVER BEEN A VIRUS THAT TARGETS ONLY ONE SEX.
OR ONE THAT SPREADS SO SPORADICALLY. I'VE BEEN READING THE PATIENT FILES, THERE'S NO RHYME OR REASON TO THE OUTBREAK.
I DON'T THINK IT'S AIRBORNE. I JUST LEFT OLIVER QUEEN AND HE'S FINE. THIS DOESN'T FEEL LIKE A NATURAL OCCURRENCE.
A FEW HOURS AGO, INTERIM MAYOR MUIR DECLARED A STATE OF EMERGENCY IN GOTHAM CITY. NOW, STATE AND FEDERAL RESOURCES CAN BE SENT TO AID RELIEF EFFORTS.
AND WE JUST RECEIVED WORD THAT THE PRESIDENT HAS SENT SOMEONE QUALIFIED TO MANAGE THE CRISIS...
WHO COULD MANAGE THIS?
SHE COULD...

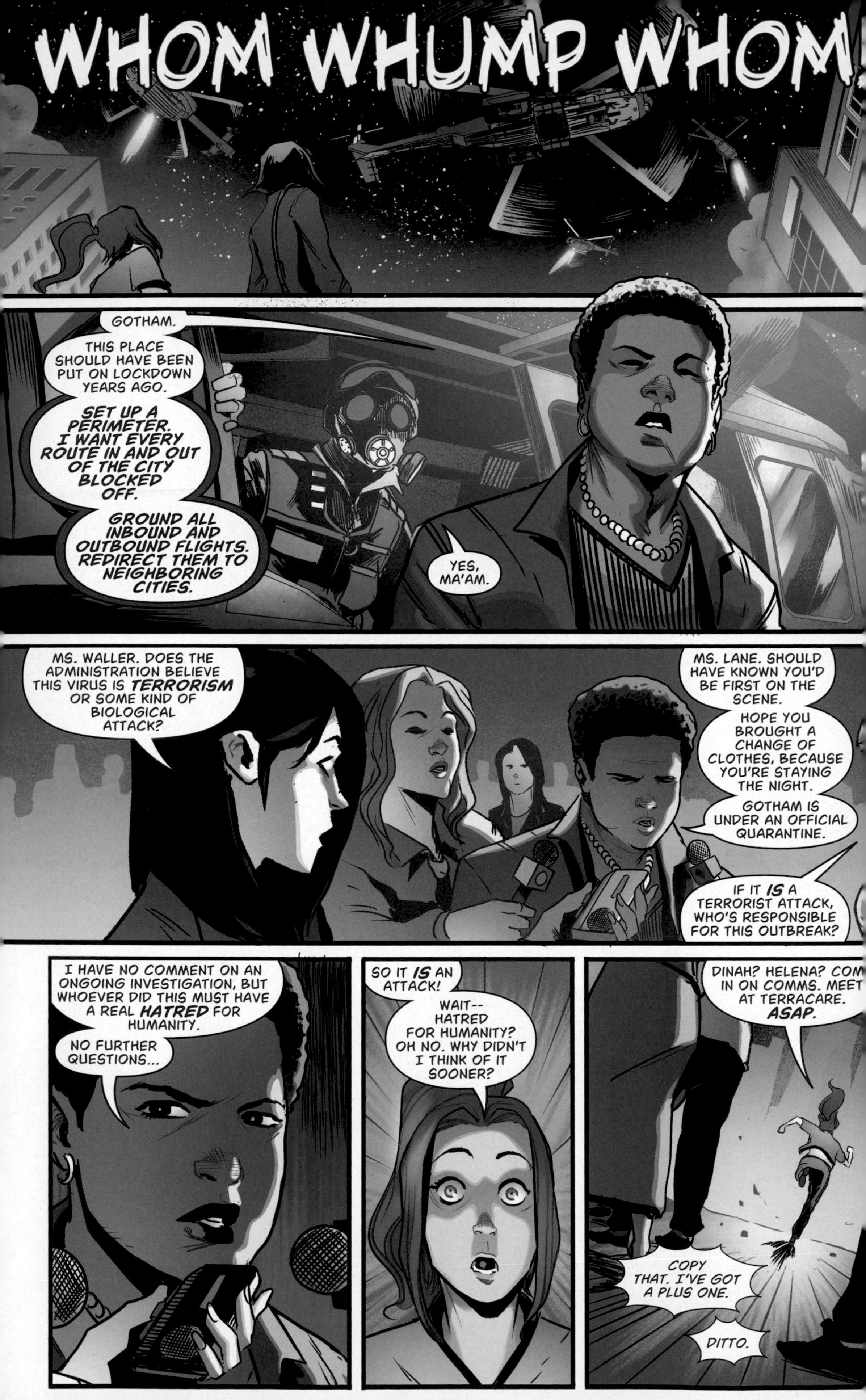
WHOM WHUMP WHOM
GOTHAM.
THIS PLACE SHOULD HAVE BEEN PUT ON LOCKDOWN YEARS AGO.
SET UP A PERIMETER. I WANT EVERY ROUTE IN AND OUT OF THE CITY BLOCKED OFF.
GROUND ALL INBOUND AND OUTBOUND FLIGHTS. REDIRECT THEM TO NEIGHBORING CITIES.
YES, MA'AM.
MS. WALLER. DOES THE ADMINISTRATION BELIEVE THIS VIRUS IS TERRORISM OR SOME KIND OF BIOLOGICAL ATTACK?
MS. LANE. SHOULD HAVE KNOWN YOU'D BE FIRST ON THE SCENE.
HOPE YOU BROUGHT A CHANGE OF CLOTHES, BECAUSE YOU'RE STAYING THE NIGHT.
GOTHAM IS UNDER AN OFFICIAL QUARANTINE.
IF IT IS A TERRORIST ATTACK, WHO'S RESPONSIBLE FOR THIS OUTBREAK?
I HAVE NO COMMENT ON AN ONGOING INVESTIGATION, BUT WHOEVER DID THIS MUST HAVE A REAL HATRED FOR HUMANITY.
NO FURTHER QUESTIONS...
SO IT IS AN ATTACK!
WAIT-- HATRED FOR HUMANITY? OH NO. WHY DIDN'T I THINK OF IT SOONER?
DINAH? HELENA? COM IN ON COMMS. MEET AT TERRACARE. ASAP.
COPY THAT. I'VE GOT A PLUS ONE.
DITTO.

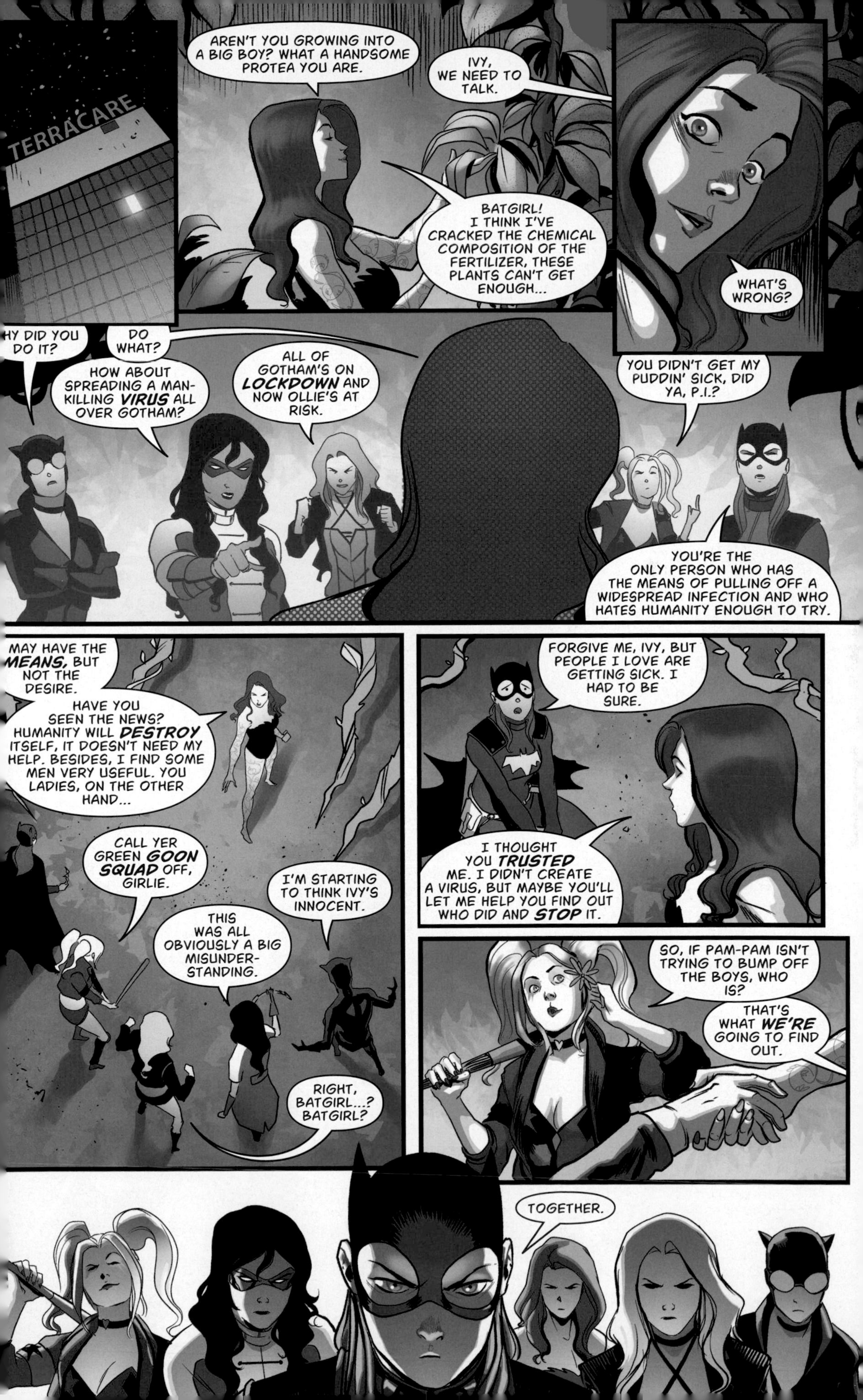
TERRACARE
AREN'T YOU GROWING INTO A BIG BOY? WHAT A HANDSOME PROTEA YOU ARE.
IVY, WE NEED TO TALK.
BATGIRL! I THINK I'VE CRACKED THE CHEMICAL COMPOSITION OF THE FERTILIZER, THESE PLANTS CAN'T GET ENOUGH...
WHAT'S WRONG?
HY DID YOU DO IT?
DO WHAT?
HOW ABOUT SPREADING A MAN-KILLING VIRUS ALL OVER GOTHAM?
ALL OF GOTHAM'S ON LOCKDOWN AND NOW OLLIE'S AT RISK.
YOU DIDN'T GET MY PUDDIN' SICK, DID YA, P.I.?
YOU'RE THE ONLY PERSON WHO HAS THE MEANS OF PULLING OFF A WIDESPREAD INFECTION AND WHO HATES HUMANITY ENOUGH TO TRY.
MAY HAVE THE MEANS, BUT NOT THE DESIRE.
HAVE YOU SEEN THE NEWS? HUMANITY WILL DESTROY ITSELF, IT DOESN'T NEED MY HELP. BESIDES, I FIND SOME MEN VERY USEFUL. YOU LADIES, ON THE OTHER HAND...
CALL YER GREEN GOON SQUAD OFF, GIRLIE.
I'M STARTING TO THINK IVY'S INNOCENT.
THIS WAS ALL OBVIOUSLY A BIG MISUNDER-STANDING.
RIGHT, BATGIRL...? BATGIRL?
FORGIVE ME, IVY, BUT PEOPLE I LOVE ARE GETTING SICK. I HAD TO BE SURE.
I THOUGHT YOU TRUSTED ME. I DIDN'T CREATE A VIRUS, BUT MAYBE YOU'LL LET ME HELP YOU FIND OUT WHO DID AND STOP IT.
SO, IF PAM-PAM ISN'T TRYING TO BUMP OFF THE BOYS, WHO IS?
THAT'S WHAT WE'RE GOING TO FIND OUT.
TOGETHER.

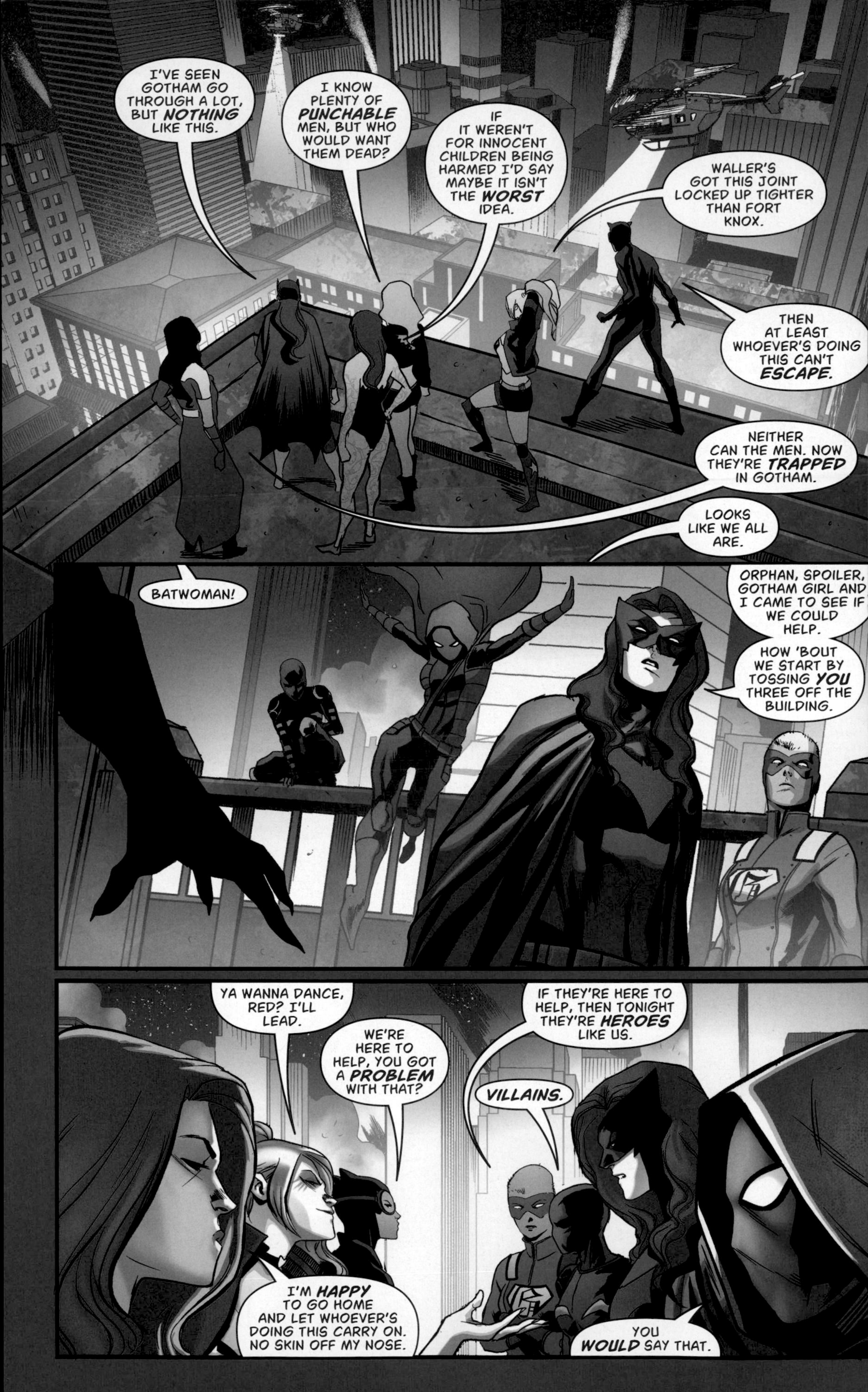

I'VE SEEN GOTHAM GO THROUGH A LOT, BUT NOTHING LIKE THIS.
I KNOW PLENTY OF PUNCHABLE MEN, BUT WHO WOULD WANT THEM DEAD?
IF IT WEREN'T FOR INNOCENT CHILDREN BEING HARMED I'D SAY MAYBE IT ISN'T THE WORST IDEA.
WALLER'S GOT THIS JOINT LOCKED UP TIGHTER THAN FORT KNOX.
THEN AT LEAST WHOEVER'S DOING THIS CAN'T ESCAPE.
NEITHER CAN THE MEN. NOW THEY'RE TRAPPED IN GOTHAM.
LOOKS LIKE WE ALL ARE.
BATWOMAN!
ORPHAN, SPOILER, GOTHAM GIRL AND I CAME TO SEE IF WE COULD HELP.
HOW 'BOUT WE START BY TOSSING YOU THREE OFF THE BUILDING.
YA WANNA DANCE, RED? I'LL LEAD.
WE'RE HERE TO HELP, YOU GOT A PROBLEM WITH THAT?
IF THEY'RE HERE TO HELP, THEN TONIGHT THEY'RE HEROES LIKE US.
VILLAINS.
I'M HAPPY TO GO HOME AND LET WHOEVER'S DOING THIS CARRY ON. NO SKIN OFF MY NOSE.
YOU WOULD SAY THAT.

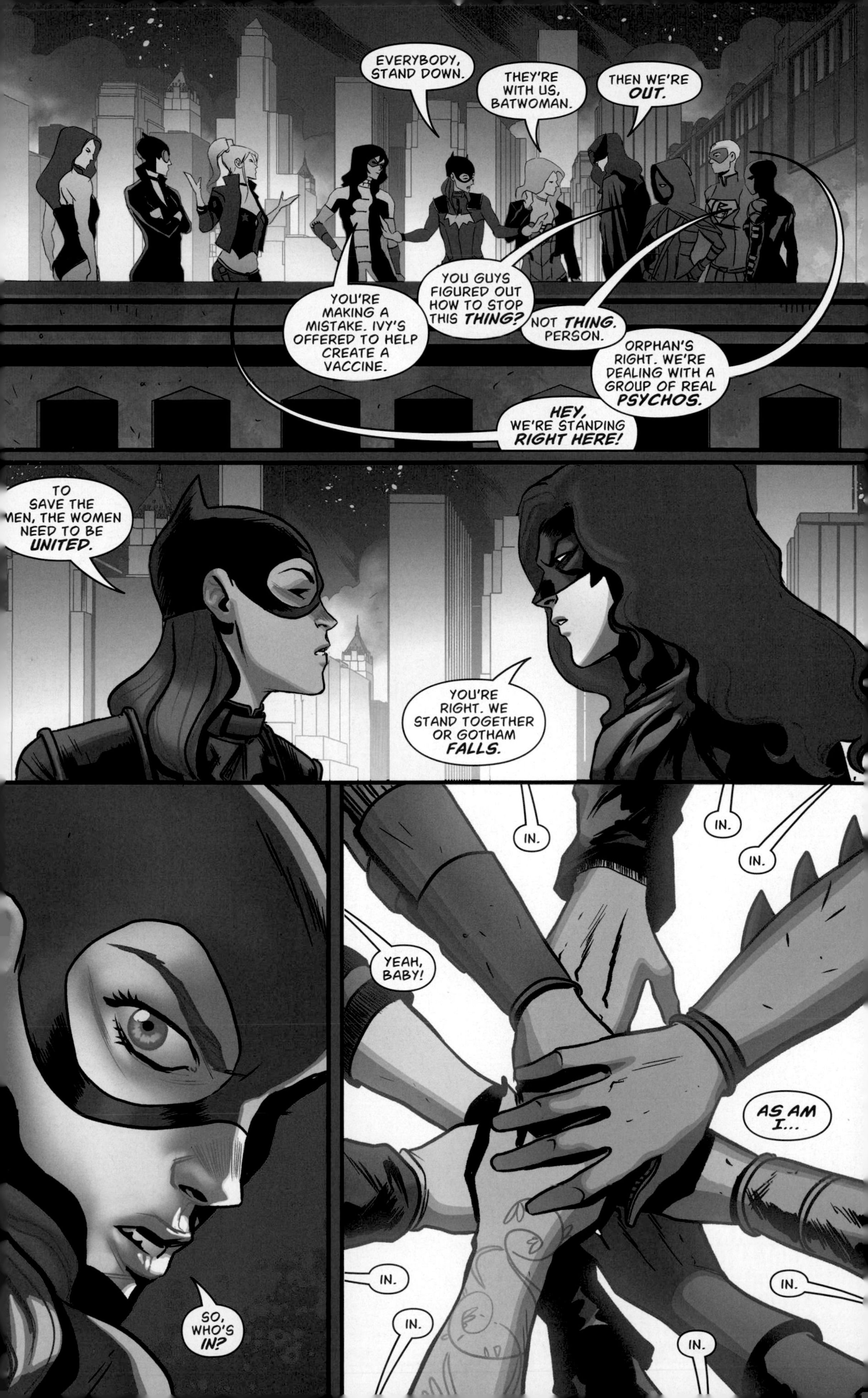

EVERYBODY, STAND DOWN.
THEY'RE WITH US, BATWOMAN.
THEN WE'RE OUT.
YOU'RE MAKING A MISTAKE. IVY'S OFFERED TO HELP CREATE A VACCINE.
YOU GUYS FIGURED OUT HOW TO STOP THIS THING?
NOT THING. PERSON.
ORPHAN'S RIGHT. WE'RE DEALING WITH A GROUP OF REAL PSYCHOS.
HEY, WE'RE STANDING RIGHT HERE!
TO SAVE THE MEN, THE WOMEN NEED TO BE UNITED.
YOU'RE RIGHT. WE STAND TOGETHER OR GOTHAM FALLS.
SO, WHO'S IN?
IN.
IN.
IN.
YEAH, BABY!
AS AM I...
IN.
IN.
IN.
IN.

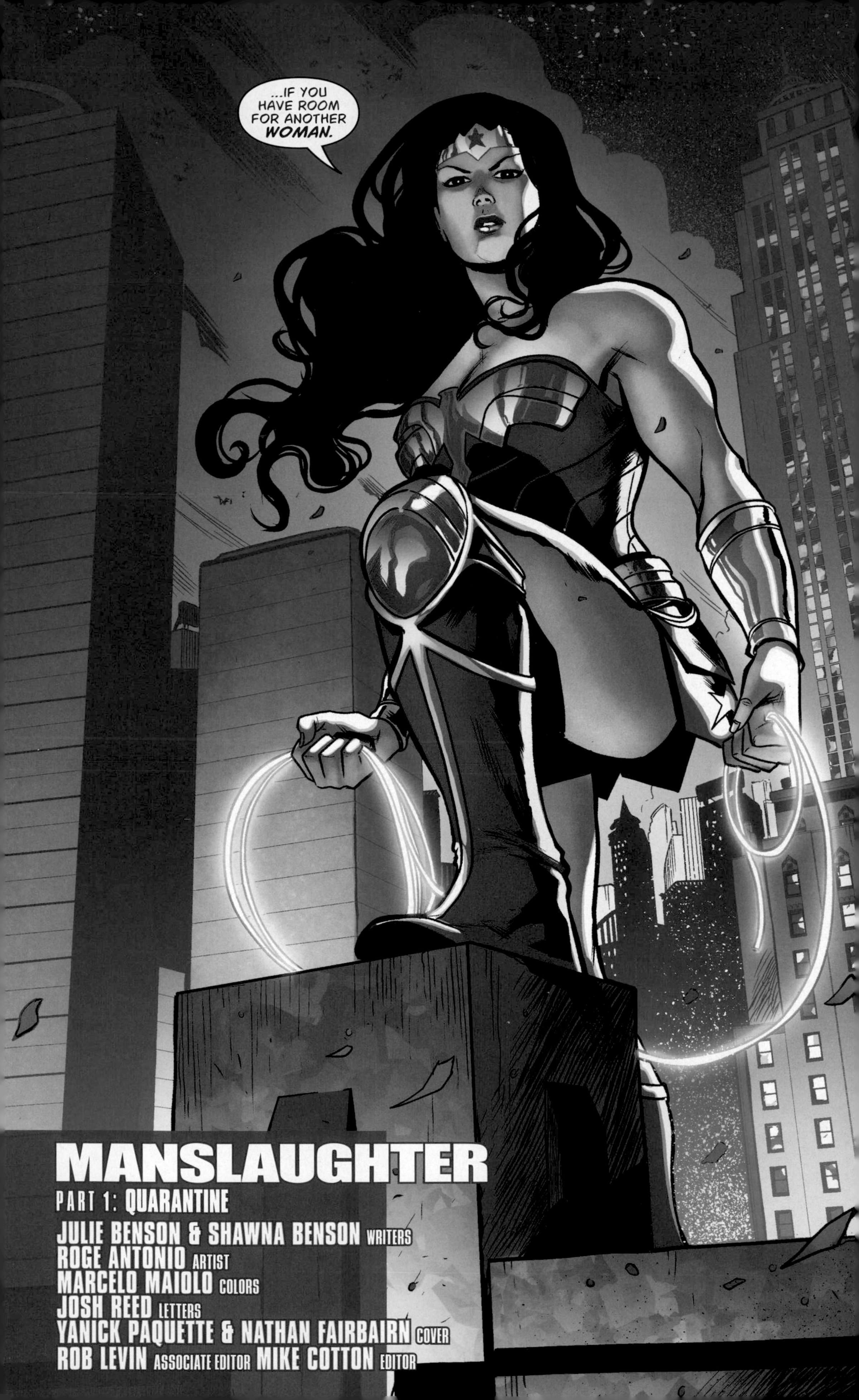
...IF YOU HAVE ROOM FOR ANOTHER WOMAN.
MANSLAUGHTER
PART 1: QUARANTINE
JULIE BENSON & SHAWNA BENSON WRITERS
ROGE ANTONIO ARTIST
MARCELO MAIOLO COLORS
JOSH REED LETTERS
YANICK PAQUETTE & NATHAN FAIRBAIRN COVER
ROB LEVIN ASSOCIATE EDITOR MIKE COTTON EDITOR

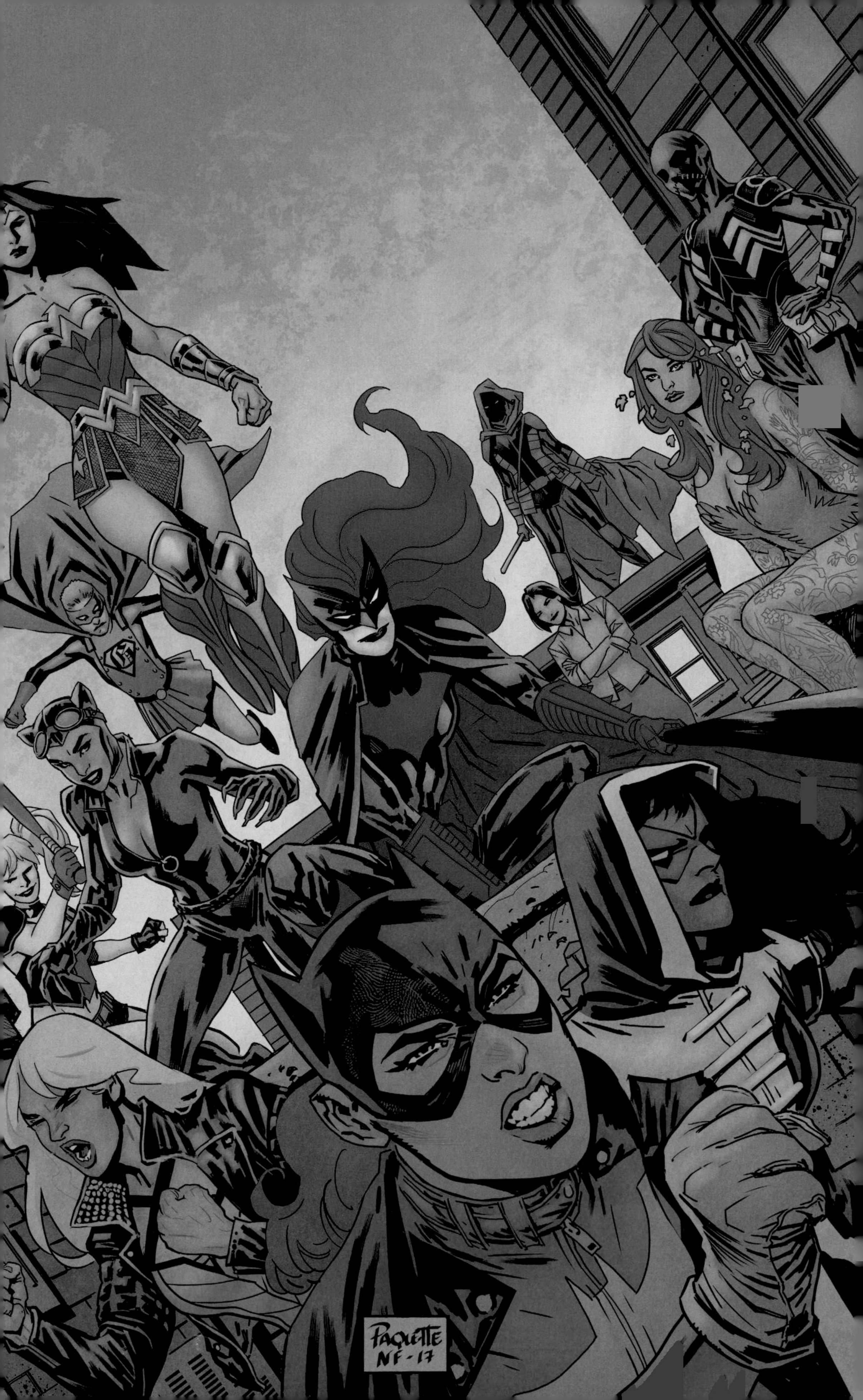
PAQUETTE
NF-17

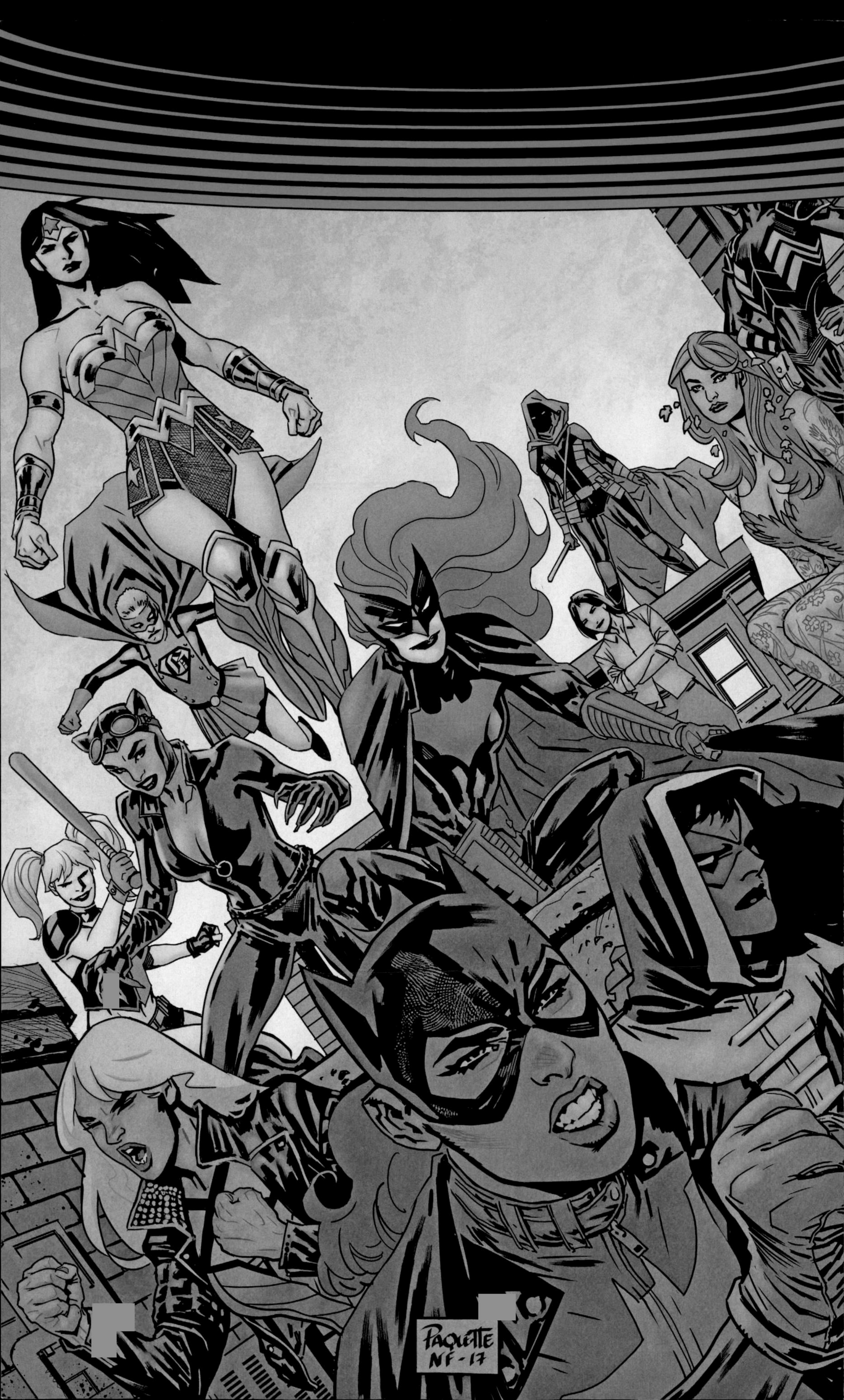
PAQUETTE
NF-17

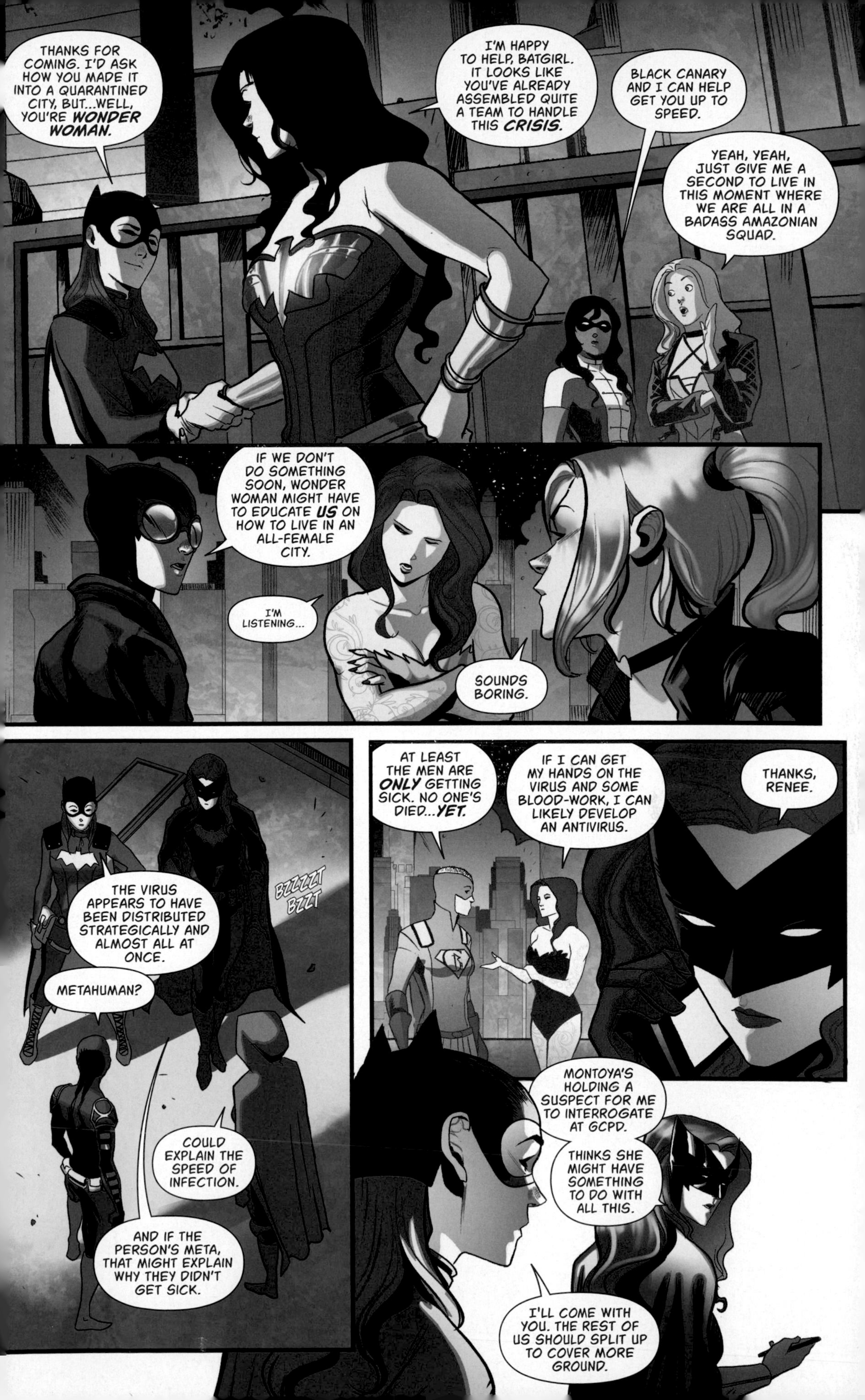
THANKS FOR COMING. I'D ASK HOW YOU MADE IT INTO A QUARANTINED CITY, BUT...WELL, YOU'RE **WONDER WOMAN.**
I'M HAPPY TO HELP, BATGIRL. IT LOOKS LIKE YOU'VE ALREADY ASSEMBLED QUITE A TEAM TO HANDLE THIS **CRISIS.**
BLACK CANARY AND I CAN HELP GET YOU UP TO SPEED.
YEAH, YEAH, JUST GIVE ME A SECOND TO LIVE IN THIS MOMENT WHERE WE ARE ALL IN A BADASS AMAZONIAN SQUAD.
IF WE DON'T DO SOMETHING SOON, WONDER WOMAN MIGHT HAVE TO EDUCATE **US** ON HOW TO LIVE IN AN ALL-FEMALE CITY.
I'M LISTENING...
SOUNDS BORING.
THE VIRUS APPEARS TO HAVE BEEN DISTRIBUTED STRATEGICALLY AND ALMOST ALL AT ONCE.
BZZZZT BZZT
METAHUMAN?
COULD EXPLAIN THE SPEED OF INFECTION.
AND IF THE PERSON'S META, THAT MIGHT EXPLAIN WHY THEY DIDN'T GET SICK.
AT LEAST THE MEN ARE **ONLY** GETTING SICK. NO ONE'S DIED...**YET.**
IF I CAN GET MY HANDS ON THE VIRUS AND SOME BLOOD-WORK, I CAN LIKELY DEVELOP AN ANTIVIRUS.
THANKS, RENEE.
MONTOYA'S HOLDING A SUSPECT FOR ME TO INTERROGATE AT GCPD.
THINKS SHE MIGHT HAVE SOMETHING TO DO WITH ALL THIS.
I'LL COME WITH YOU. THE REST OF US SHOULD SPLIT UP TO COVER MORE GROUND.

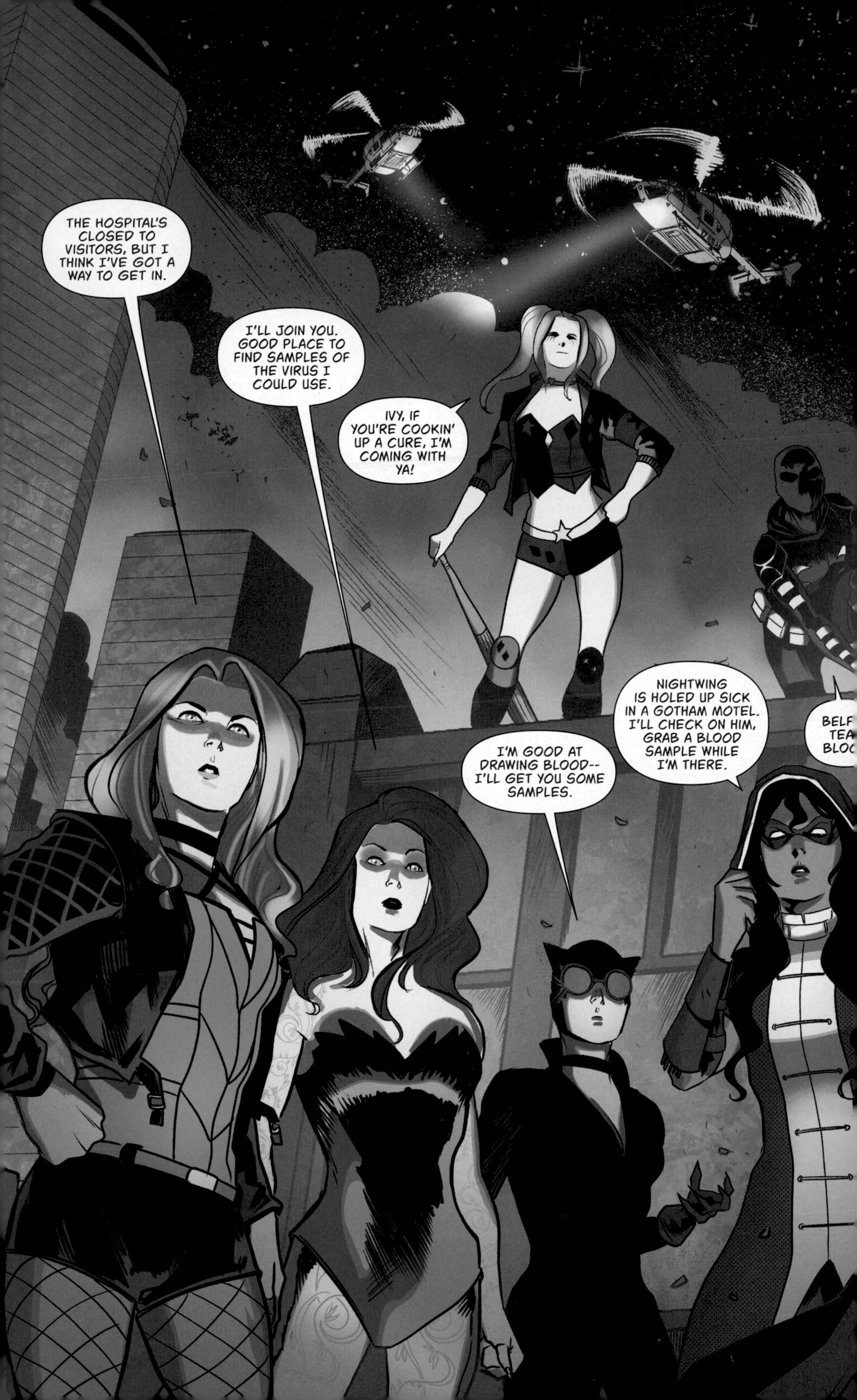
THE HOSPITAL'S CLOSED TO VISITORS, BUT I THINK I'VE GOT A WAY TO GET IN.
I'LL JOIN YOU. GOOD PLACE TO FIND SAMPLES OF THE VIRUS I COULD USE.
IVY, IF YOU'RE COOKIN' UP A CURE, I'M COMING WITH YA!
I'M GOOD AT DRAWING BLOOD-- I'LL GET YOU SOME SAMPLES.
NIGHTWING IS HOLED UP SICK IN A GOTHAM MOTEL. I'LL CHECK ON HIM, GRAB A BLOOD SAMPLE WHILE I'M THERE.

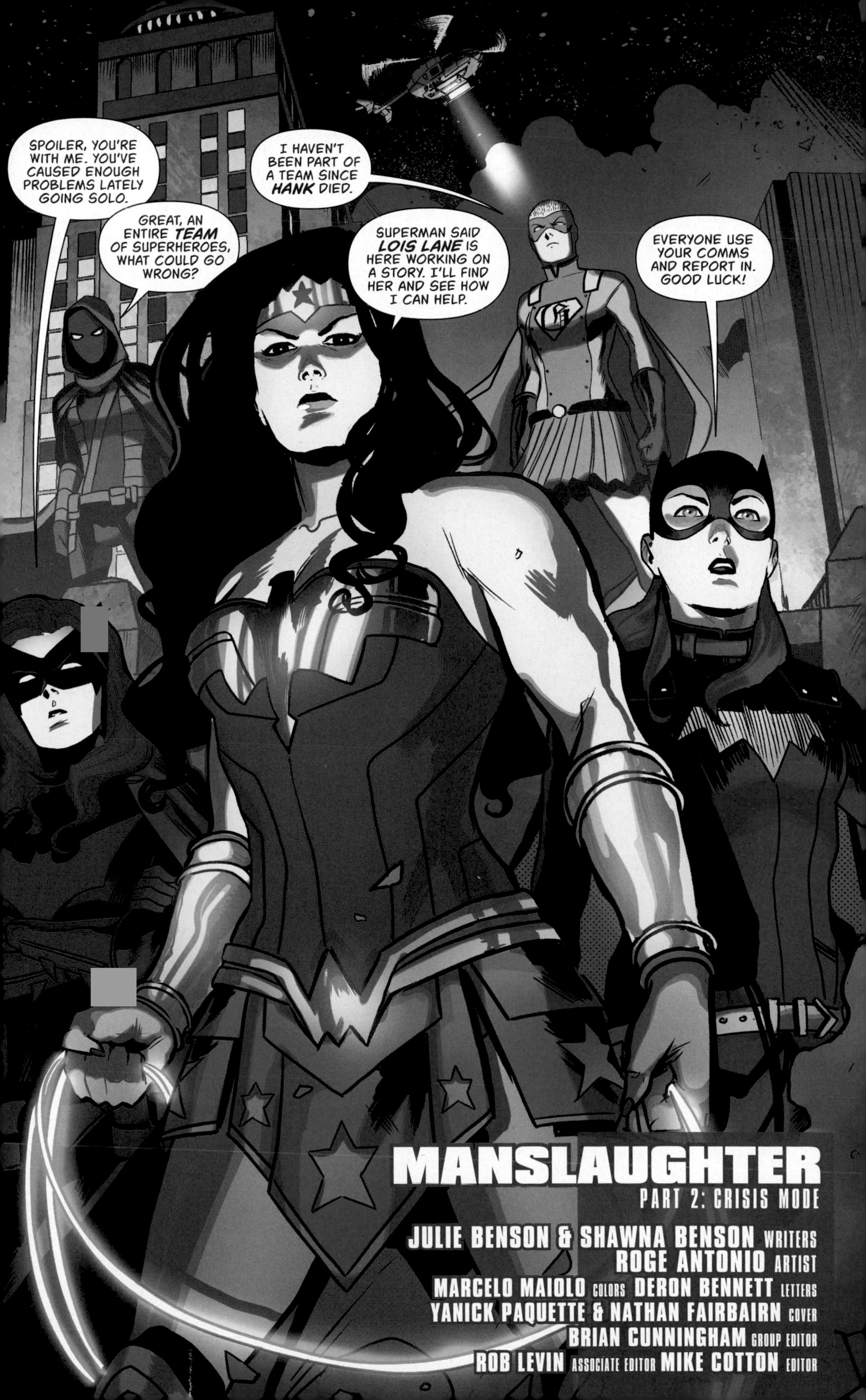
SPOILER, YOU'RE WITH ME. YOU'VE CAUSED ENOUGH PROBLEMS LATELY GOING SOLO.
I HAVEN'T BEEN PART OF A TEAM SINCE **HANK** DIED.
GREAT, AN ENTIRE **TEAM** OF SUPERHEROES, WHAT COULD GO WRONG?
SUPERMAN SAID **LOIS LANE** IS HERE WORKING ON A STORY. I'LL FIND HER AND SEE HOW I CAN HELP.
EVERYONE USE YOUR COMMS AND REPORT IN. GOOD LUCK!
MANSLAUGHTER
PART 2: CRISIS MODE
JULIE BENSON & SHAWNA BENSON WRITERS
ROGE ANTONIO ARTIST
MARCELO MAIOLO COLORS DERON BENNETT LETTERS
YANICK PAQUETTE & NATHAN FAIRBAIRN COVER
BRIAN CUNNINGHAM GROUP EDITOR
ROB LEVIN ASSOCIATE EDITOR MIKE COTTON EDITOR

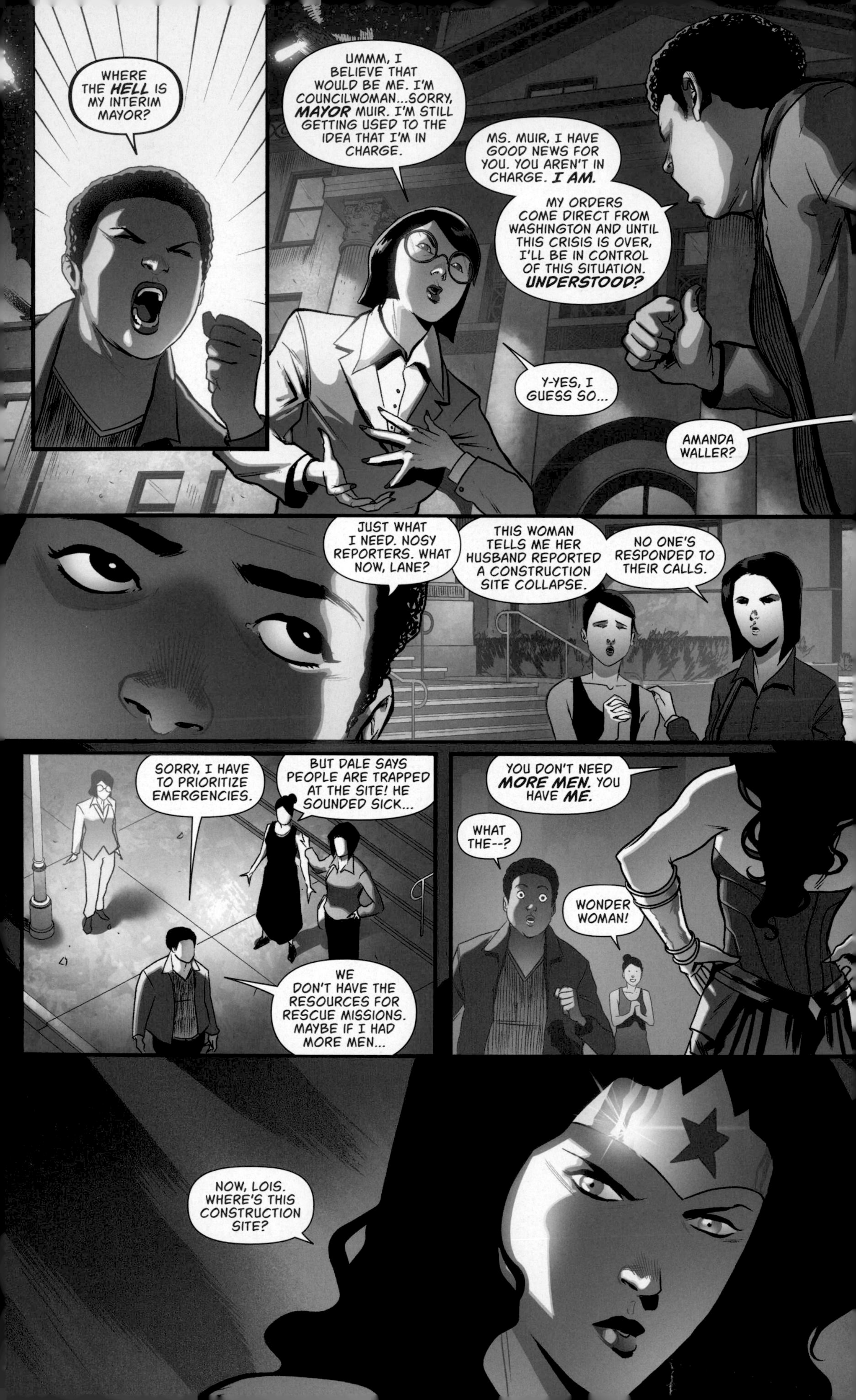
WHERE THE HELL IS MY INTERIM MAYOR?
UMMM, I BELIEVE THAT WOULD BE ME. I'M COUNCILWOMAN...SORRY, MAYOR MUIR. I'M STILL GETTING USED TO THE IDEA THAT I'M IN CHARGE.
MS. MUIR, I HAVE GOOD NEWS FOR YOU. YOU AREN'T IN CHARGE. I AM.
MY ORDERS COME DIRECT FROM WASHINGTON AND UNTIL THIS CRISIS IS OVER, I'LL BE IN CONTROL OF THIS SITUATION. UNDERSTOOD?
Y-YES, I GUESS SO...
AMANDA WALLER?
JUST WHAT I NEED. NOSY REPORTERS. WHAT NOW, LANE?
THIS WOMAN TELLS ME HER HUSBAND REPORTED A CONSTRUCTION SITE COLLAPSE.
NO ONE'S RESPONDED TO THEIR CALLS.
SORRY, I HAVE TO PRIORITIZE EMERGENCIES.
BUT DALE SAYS PEOPLE ARE TRAPPED AT THE SITE! HE SOUNDED SICK...
WE DON'T HAVE THE RESOURCES FOR RESCUE MISSIONS. MAYBE IF I HAD MORE MEN...
YOU DON'T NEED MORE MEN. YOU HAVE ME.
WHAT THE--?
WONDER WOMAN!
NOW, LOIS. WHERE'S THIS CONSTRUCTION SITE?

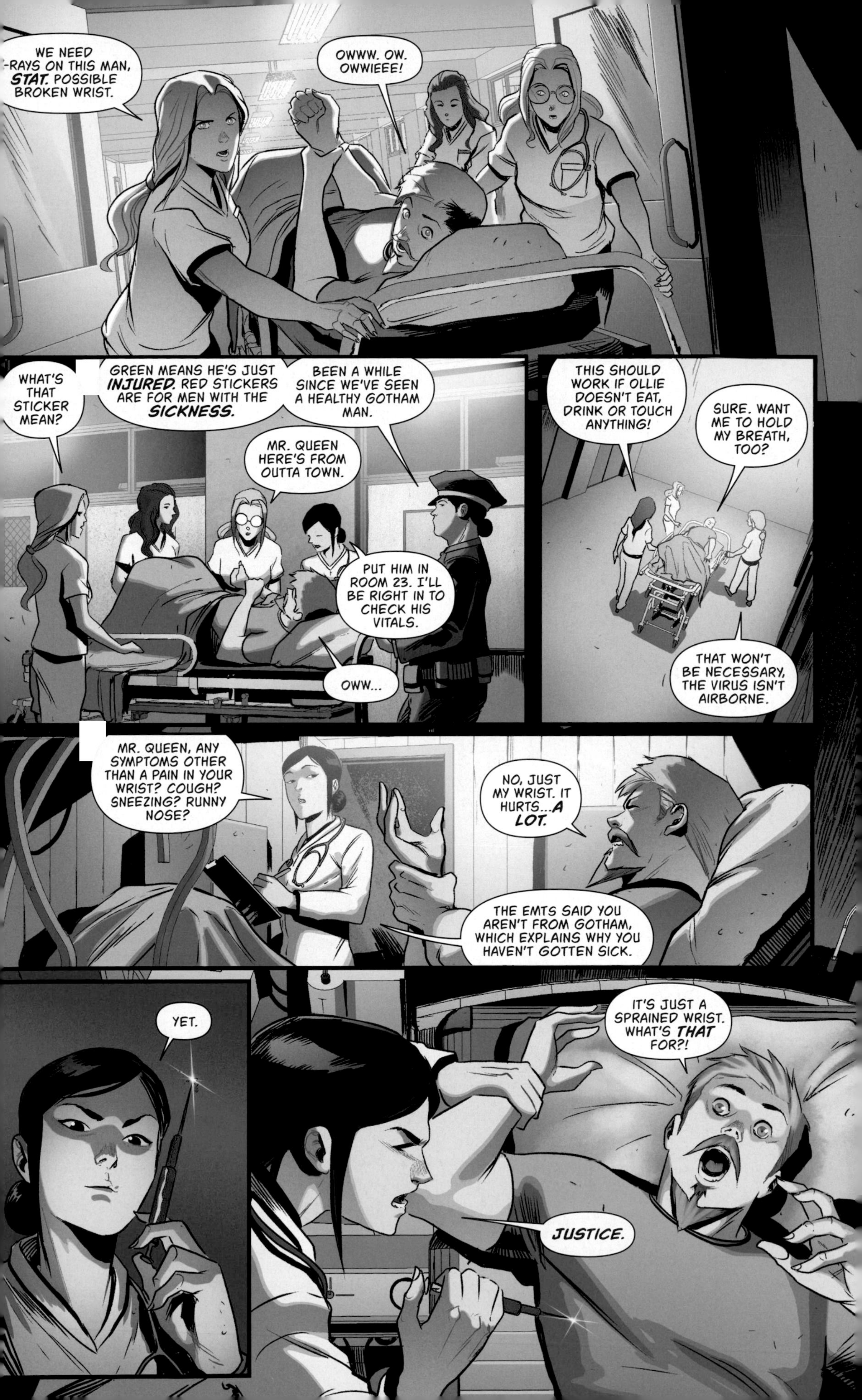
WE NEED X-RAYS ON THIS MAN, STAT. POSSIBLE BROKEN WRIST.
OWWW. OW. OWWIEEE!
WHAT'S THAT STICKER MEAN?
GREEN MEANS HE'S JUST INJURED. RED STICKERS ARE FOR MEN WITH THE SICKNESS.
BEEN A WHILE SINCE WE'VE SEEN A HEALTHY GOTHAM MAN.
MR. QUEEN HERE'S FROM OUTTA TOWN.
PUT HIM IN ROOM 23. I'LL BE RIGHT IN TO CHECK HIS VITALS.
OWW...
THIS SHOULD WORK IF OLLIE DOESN'T EAT, DRINK OR TOUCH ANYTHING!
SURE. WANT ME TO HOLD MY BREATH, TOO?
THAT WON'T BE NECESSARY, THE VIRUS ISN'T AIRBORNE.
MR. QUEEN, ANY SYMPTOMS OTHER THAN A PAIN IN YOUR WRIST? COUGH? SNEEZING? RUNNY NOSE?
NO, JUST MY WRIST. IT HURTS...A LOT.
THE EMTS SAID YOU AREN'T FROM GOTHAM, WHICH EXPLAINS WHY YOU HAVEN'T GOTTEN SICK.
YET.
IT'S JUST A SPRAINED WRIST. WHAT'S THAT FOR?!
JUSTICE.

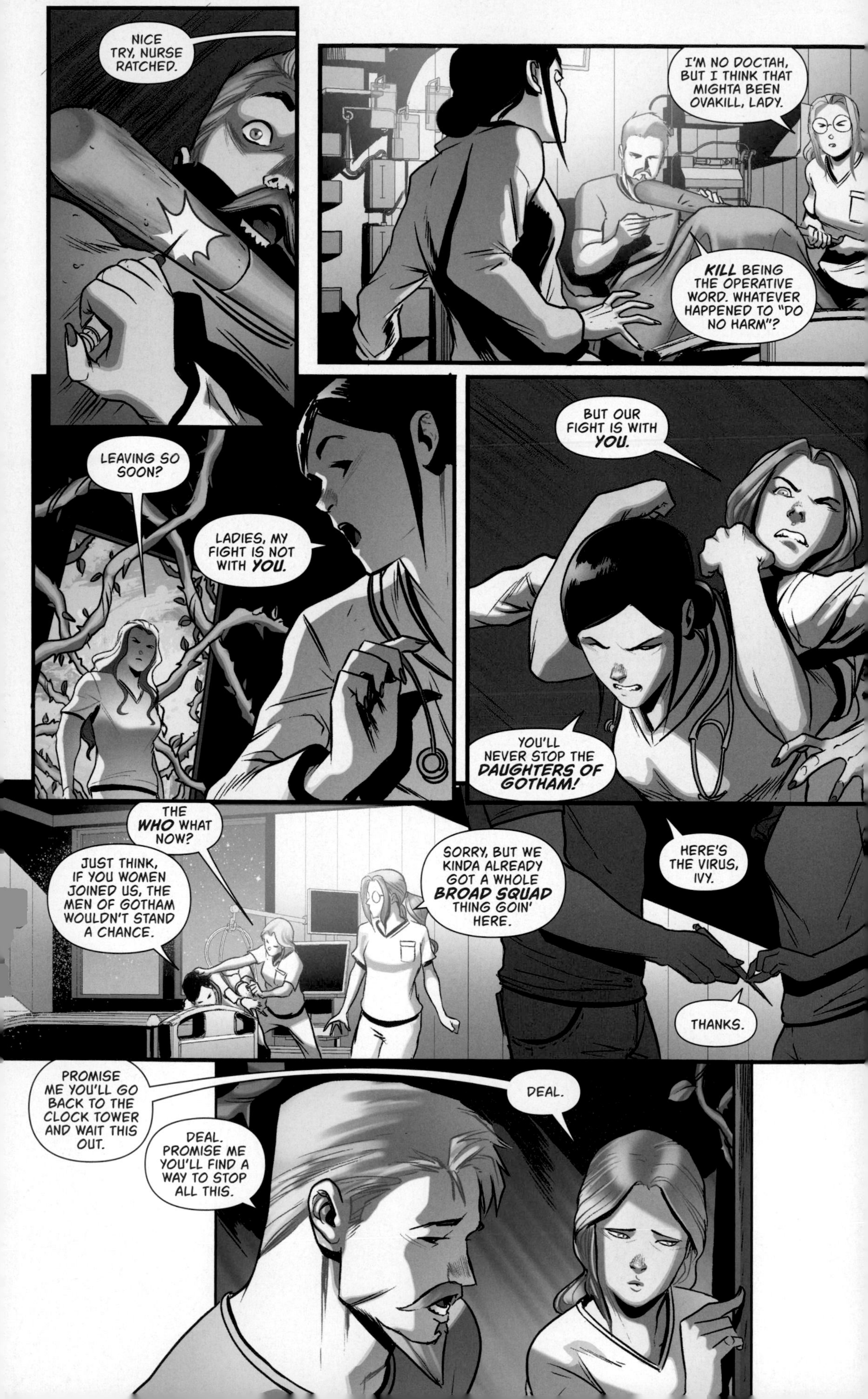
NICE TRY, NURSE RATCHED.
I'M NO DOCTAH, BUT I THINK THAT MIGHTA BEEN OVAKILL, LADY.
KILL BEING THE OPERATIVE WORD. WHATEVER HAPPENED TO "DO NO HARM"?
LEAVING SO SOON?
LADIES, MY FIGHT IS NOT WITH YOU.
BUT OUR FIGHT IS WITH YOU.
YOU'LL NEVER STOP THE DAUGHTERS OF GOTHAM!
THE WHO WHAT NOW?
JUST THINK, IF YOU WOMEN JOINED US, THE MEN OF GOTHAM WOULDN'T STAND A CHANCE.
SORRY, BUT WE KINDA ALREADY GOT A WHOLE BROAD SQUAD THING GOIN' HERE.
HERE'S THE VIRUS, IVY.
THANKS.
PROMISE ME YOU'LL GO BACK TO THE CLOCK TOWER AND WAIT THIS OUT.
DEAL. PROMISE ME YOU'LL FIND A WAY TO STOP ALL THIS.
DEAL.

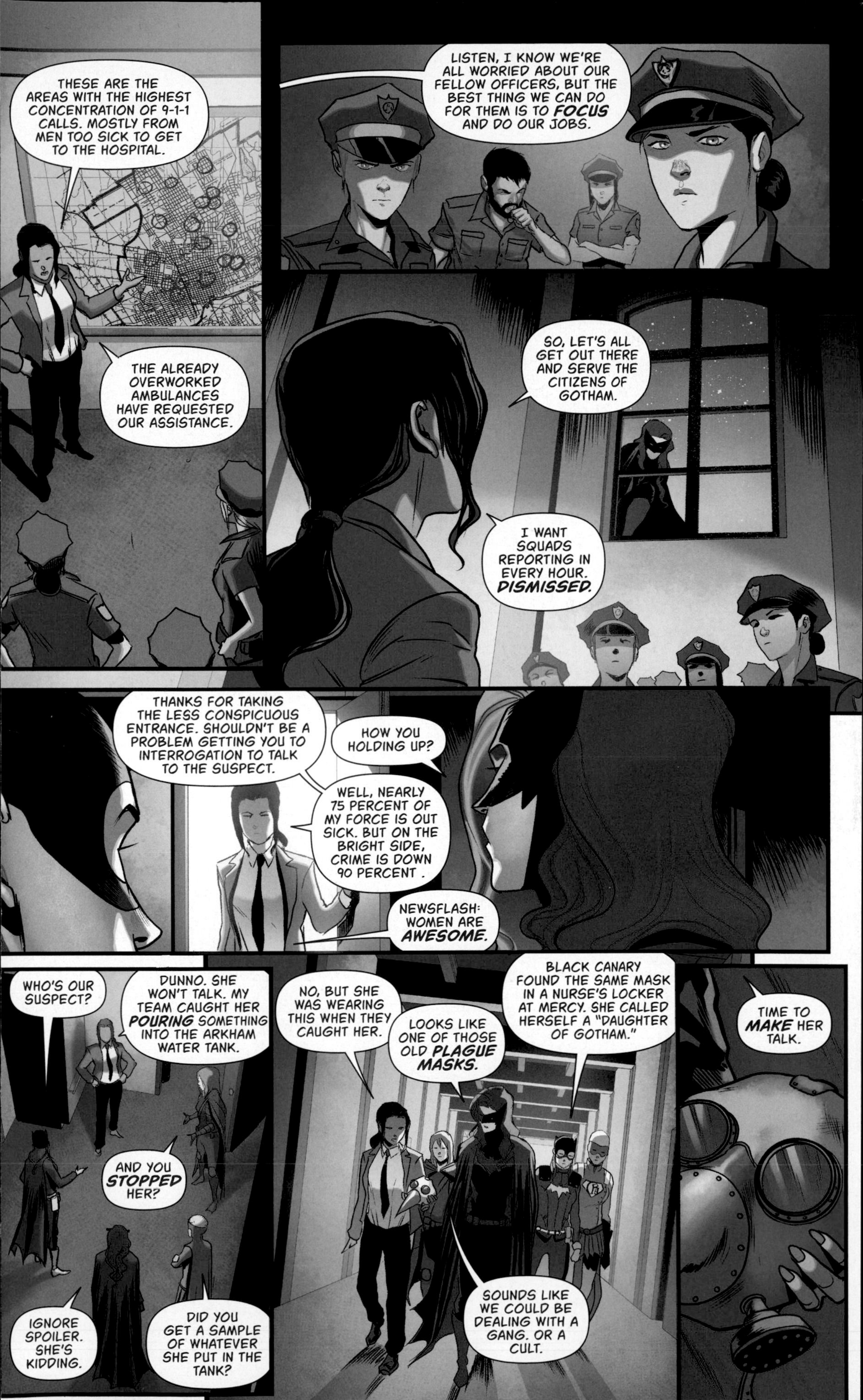
THESE ARE THE AREAS WITH THE HIGHEST CONCENTRATION OF 9-1-1 CALLS. MOSTLY FROM MEN TOO SICK TO GET TO THE HOSPITAL.
THE ALREADY OVERWORKED AMBULANCES HAVE REQUESTED OUR ASSISTANCE.
LISTEN, I KNOW WE'RE ALL WORRIED ABOUT OUR FELLOW OFFICERS, BUT THE BEST THING WE CAN DO FOR THEM IS TO FOCUS AND DO OUR JOBS.
SO, LET'S ALL GET OUT THERE AND SERVE THE CITIZENS OF GOTHAM.
I WANT SQUADS REPORTING IN EVERY HOUR. DISMISSED.
THANKS FOR TAKING THE LESS CONSPICUOUS ENTRANCE. SHOULDN'T BE A PROBLEM GETTING YOU TO INTERROGATION TO TALK TO THE SUSPECT.
HOW YOU HOLDING UP?
WELL, NEARLY 75 PERCENT OF MY FORCE IS OUT SICK. BUT ON THE BRIGHT SIDE, CRIME IS DOWN 90 PERCENT .
NEWSFLASH: WOMEN ARE AWESOME.
WHO'S OUR SUSPECT?
DUNNO. SHE WON'T TALK. MY TEAM CAUGHT HER POURING SOMETHING INTO THE ARKHAM WATER TANK.
AND YOU STOPPED HER?
IGNORE SPOILER. SHE'S KIDDING.
DID YOU GET A SAMPLE OF WHATEVER SHE PUT IN THE TANK?
NO, BUT SHE WAS WEARING THIS WHEN THEY CAUGHT HER.
LOOKS LIKE ONE OF THOSE OLD PLAGUE MASKS.
BLACK CANARY FOUND THE SAME MASK IN A NURSE'S LOCKER AT MERCY. SHE CALLED HERSELF A "DAUGHTER OF GOTHAM."
SOUNDS LIKE WE COULD BE DEALING WITH A GANG. OR A CULT.
TIME TO MAKE HER TALK.

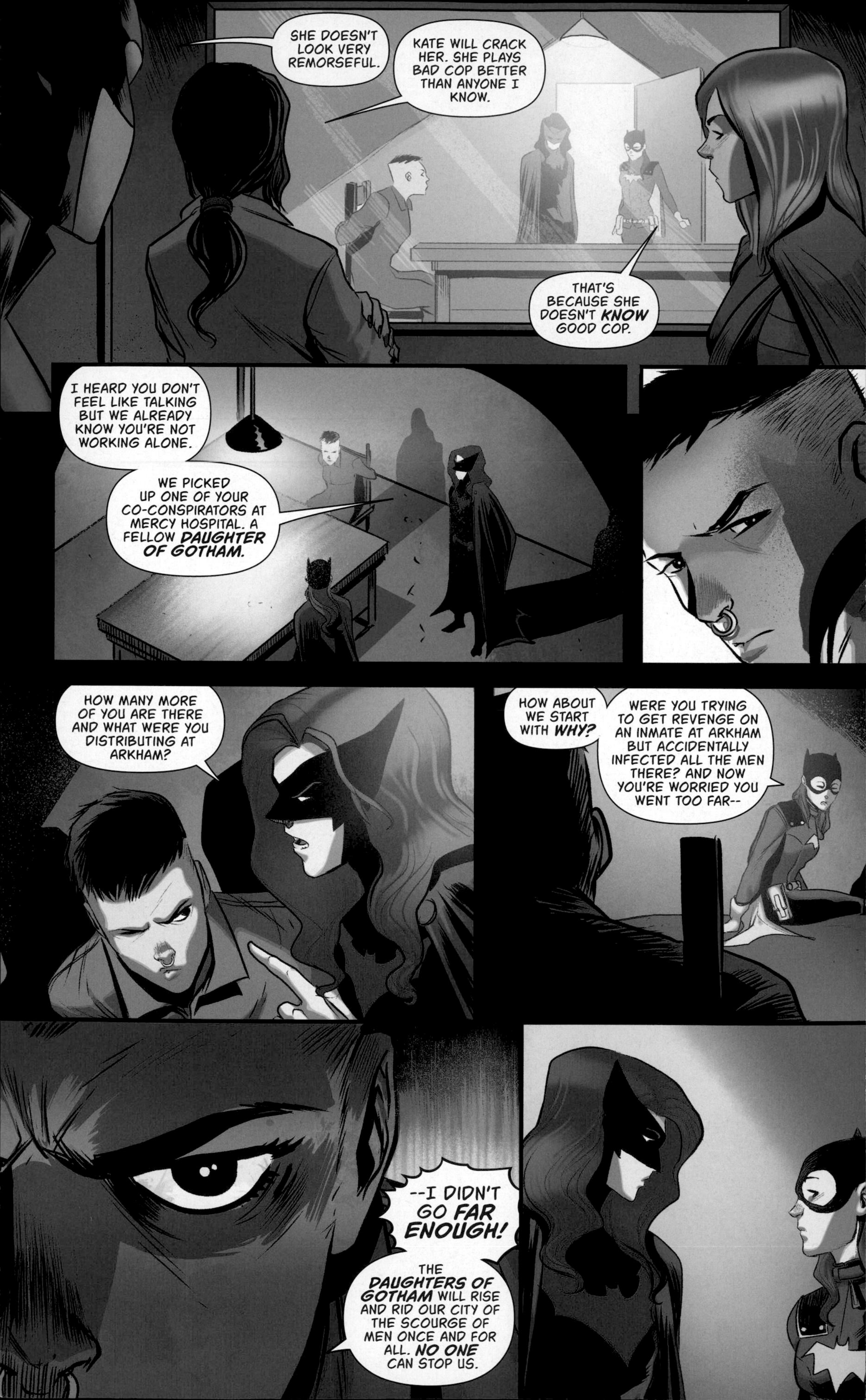
SHE DOESN'T LOOK VERY REMORSEFUL.
KATE WILL CRACK HER. SHE PLAYS BAD COP BETTER THAN ANYONE I KNOW.
THAT'S BECAUSE SHE DOESN'T KNOW GOOD COP.
I HEARD YOU DON'T FEEL LIKE TALKING BUT WE ALREADY KNOW YOU'RE NOT WORKING ALONE.
WE PICKED UP ONE OF YOUR CO-CONSPIRATORS AT MERCY HOSPITAL. A FELLOW DAUGHTER OF GOTHAM.
HOW MANY MORE OF YOU ARE THERE AND WHAT WERE YOU DISTRIBUTING AT ARKHAM?
HOW ABOUT WE START WITH WHY?
WERE YOU TRYING TO GET REVENGE ON AN INMATE AT ARKHAM BUT ACCIDENTALLY INFECTED ALL THE MEN THERE? AND NOW YOU'RE WORRIED YOU WENT TOO FAR--
--I DIDN'T GO FAR ENOUGH!
THE DAUGHTERS OF GOTHAM WILL RISE AND RID OUR CITY OF THE SCOURGE OF MEN ONCE AND FOR ALL. NO ONE CAN STOP US.

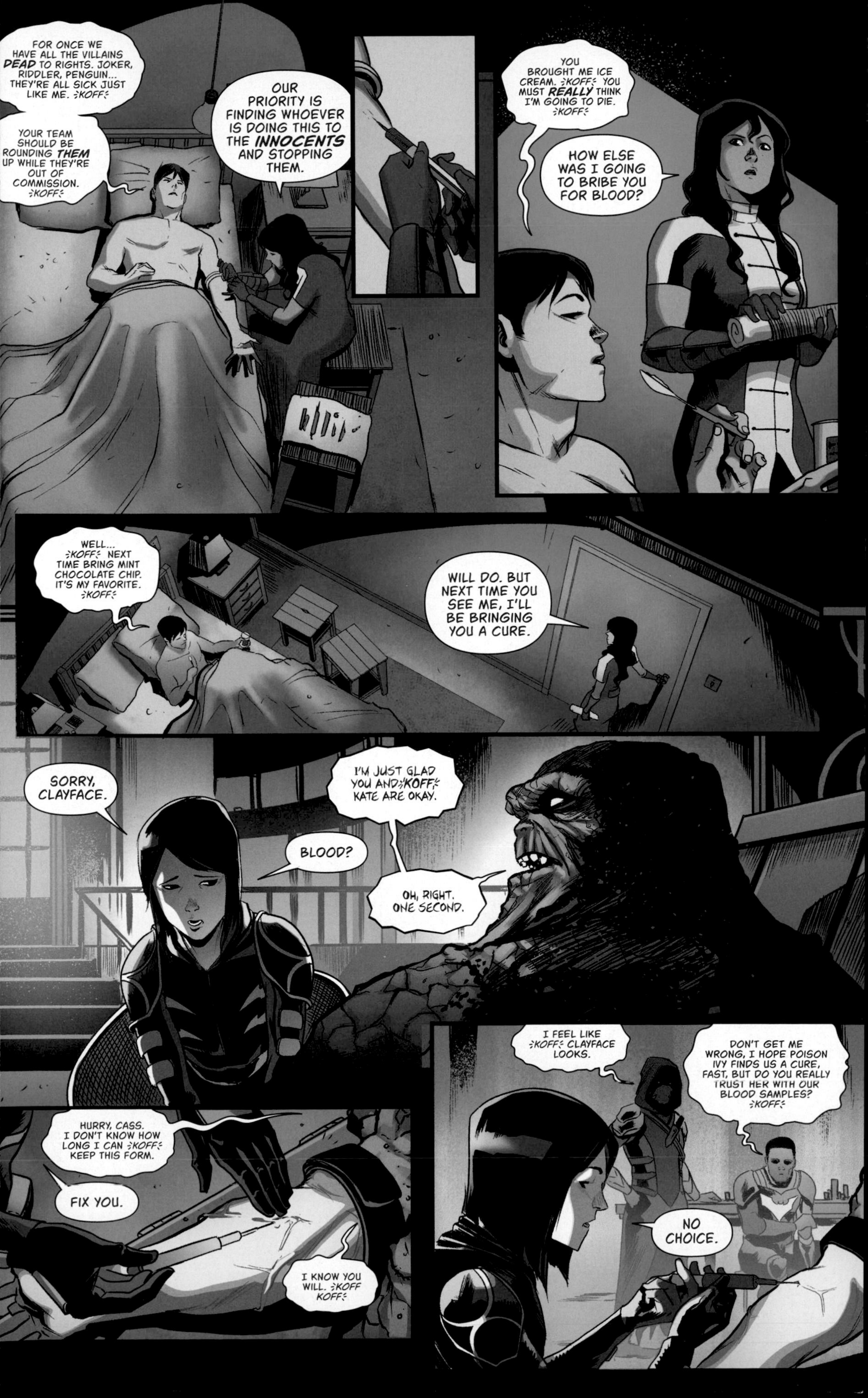
FOR ONCE WE HAVE ALL THE VILLAINS DEAD TO RIGHTS. JOKER, RIDDLER, PENGUIN... THEY'RE ALL SICK JUST LIKE ME. KOFF
YOUR TEAM SHOULD BE ROUNDING THEM UP WHILE THEY'RE OUT OF COMMISSION. KOFF
OUR PRIORITY IS FINDING WHOEVER IS DOING THIS TO THE INNOCENTS AND STOPPING THEM.
YOU BROUGHT ME ICE CREAM. KOFF YOU MUST REALLY THINK I'M GOING TO DIE. KOFF
HOW ELSE WAS I GOING TO BRIBE YOU FOR BLOOD?
WELL... KOFF NEXT TIME BRING MINT CHOCOLATE CHIP. IT'S MY FAVORITE. KOFF
WILL DO. BUT NEXT TIME YOU SEE ME, I'LL BE BRINGING YOU A CURE.
SORRY, CLAYFACE.
I'M JUST GLAD YOU AND KOFF KATE ARE OKAY.
BLOOD?
OH, RIGHT. ONE SECOND.
HURRY, CASS. I DON'T KNOW HOW LONG I CAN KOFF KEEP THIS FORM.
FIX YOU.
I KNOW YOU WILL. KOFF KOFF
I FEEL LIKE KOFF CLAYFACE LOOKS.
DON'T GET ME WRONG, I HOPE POISON IVY FINDS US A CURE, FAST, BUT DO YOU REALLY TRUST HER WITH OUR BLOOD SAMPLES? KOFF
NO CHOICE.

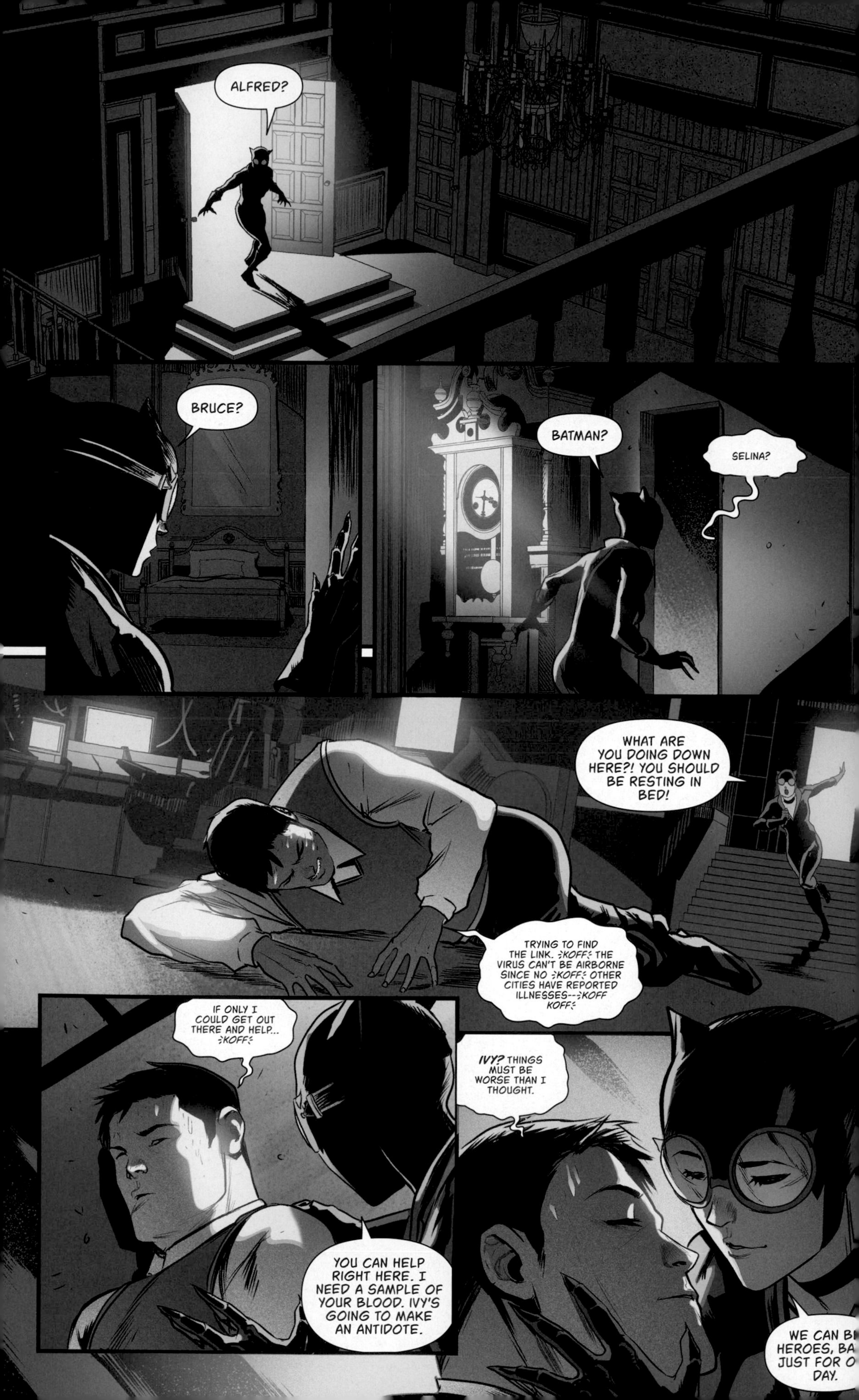

ALFRED?
BRUCE?
BATMAN?
SELINA?
WHAT ARE YOU DOING DOWN HERE?! YOU SHOULD BE RESTING IN BED!
TRYING TO FIND THE LINK. KOFF THE VIRUS CAN'T BE AIRBORNE SINCE NO KOFF OTHER CITIES HAVE REPORTED ILLNESSES-- KOFF KOFF
IF ONLY I COULD GET OUT THERE AND HELP... KOFF
YOU CAN HELP RIGHT HERE. I NEED A SAMPLE OF YOUR BLOOD. IVY'S GOING TO MAKE AN ANTIDOTE.
IVY? THINGS MUST BE WORSE THAN I THOUGHT.
WE CAN B
HEROES, BA
JUST FOR O
DAY.

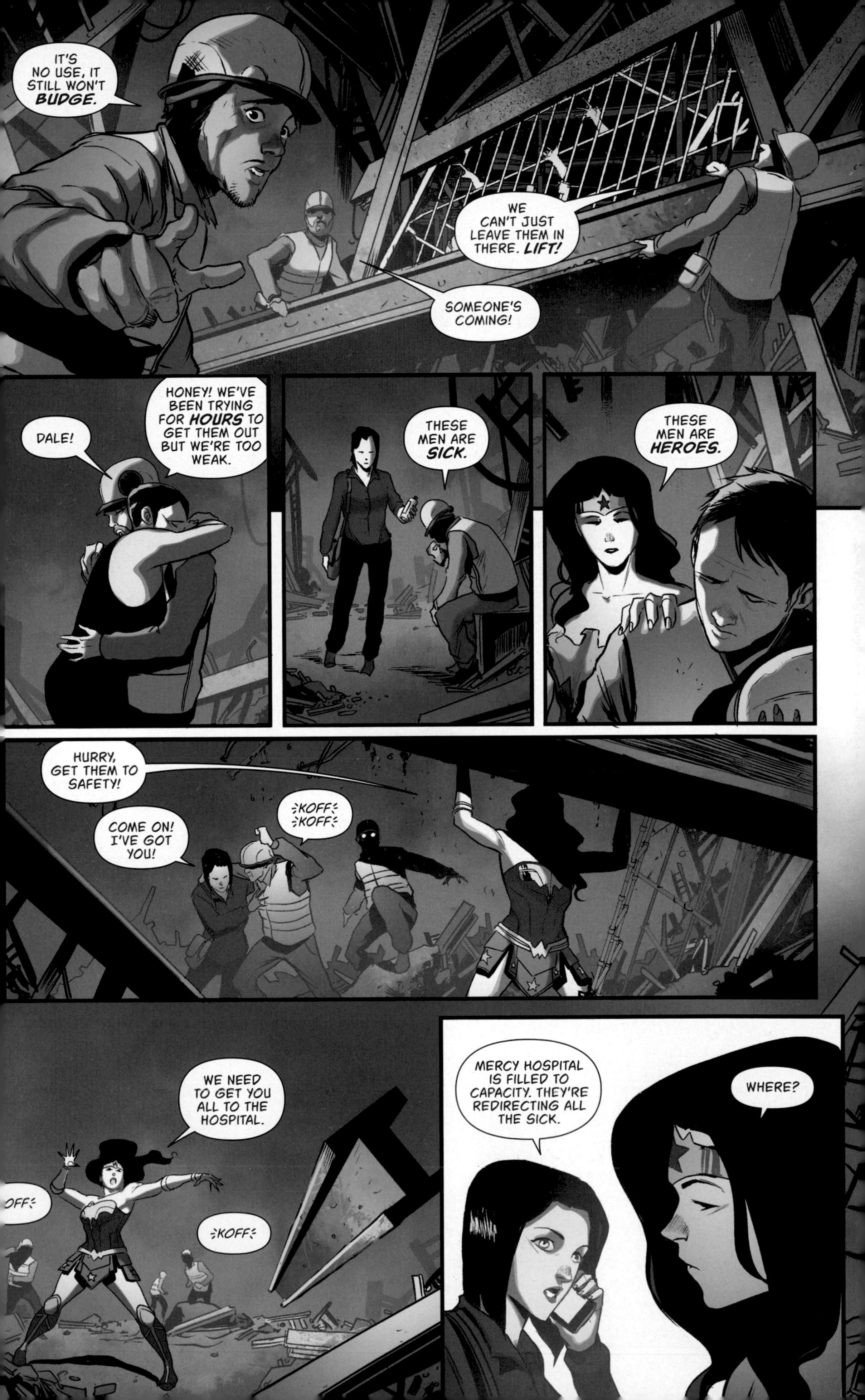
IT'S NO USE, IT STILL WON'T BUDGE.
WE CAN'T JUST LEAVE THEM IN THERE. LIFT!
SOMEONE'S COMING!
DALE!
HONEY! WE'VE BEEN TRYING FOR HOURS TO GET THEM OUT BUT WE'RE TOO WEAK.
THESE MEN ARE SICK.
THESE MEN ARE HEROES.
HURRY, GET THEM TO SAFETY!
COME ON! I'VE GOT YOU!
KOFF KOFF
WE NEED TO GET YOU ALL TO THE HOSPITAL.
KOFF
MERCY HOSPITAL IS FILLED TO CAPACITY. THEY'RE REDIRECTING ALL THE SICK.
WHERE?

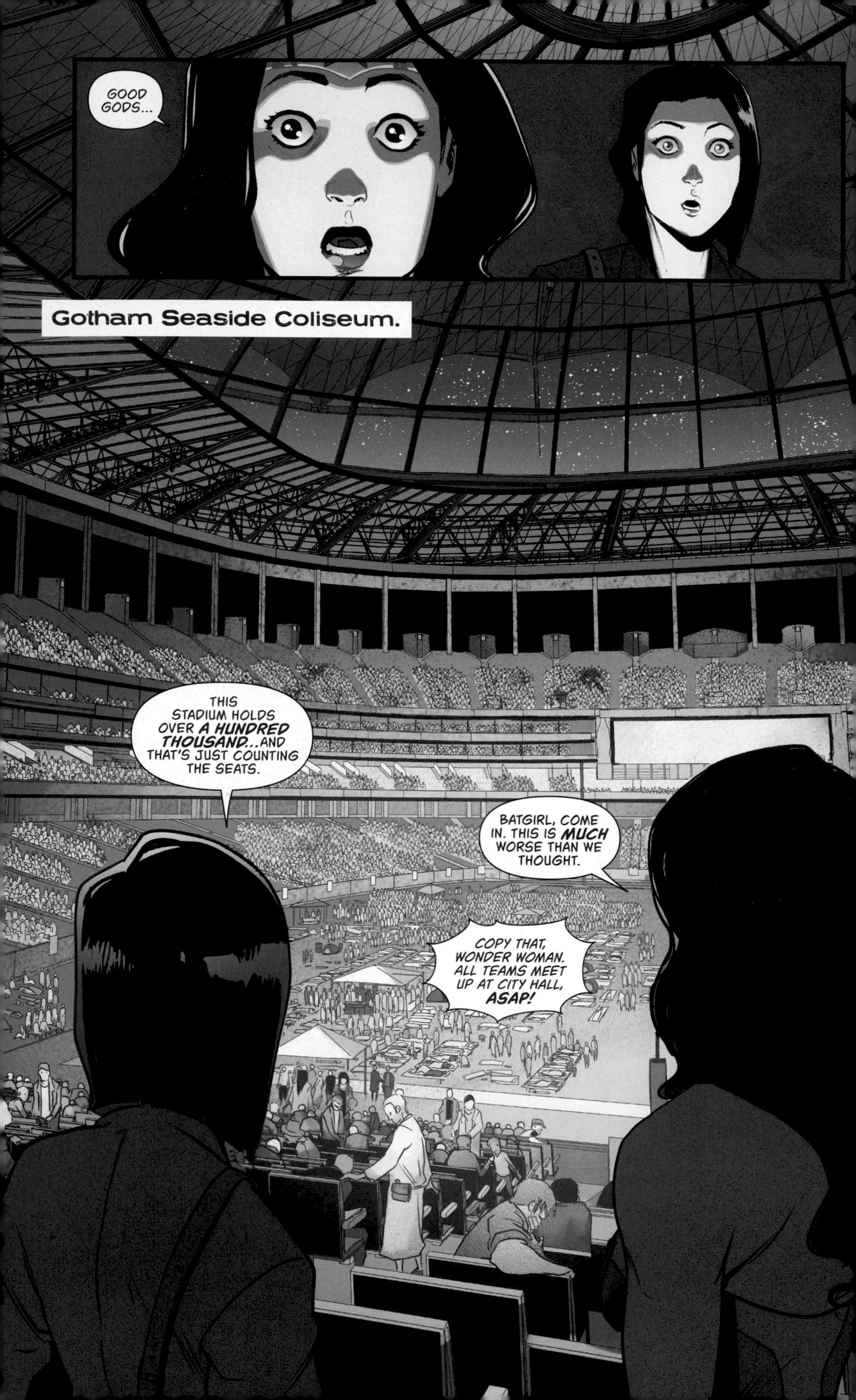
GOOD GODS...
Gotham Seaside Coliseum.
THIS STADIUM HOLDS OVER A HUNDRED THOUSAND...AND THAT'S JUST COUNTING THE SEATS.
BATGIRL, COME IN. THIS IS MUCH WORSE THAN WE THOUGHT.
COPY THAT, WONDER WOMAN. ALL TEAMS MEET UP AT CITY HALL, ASAP!

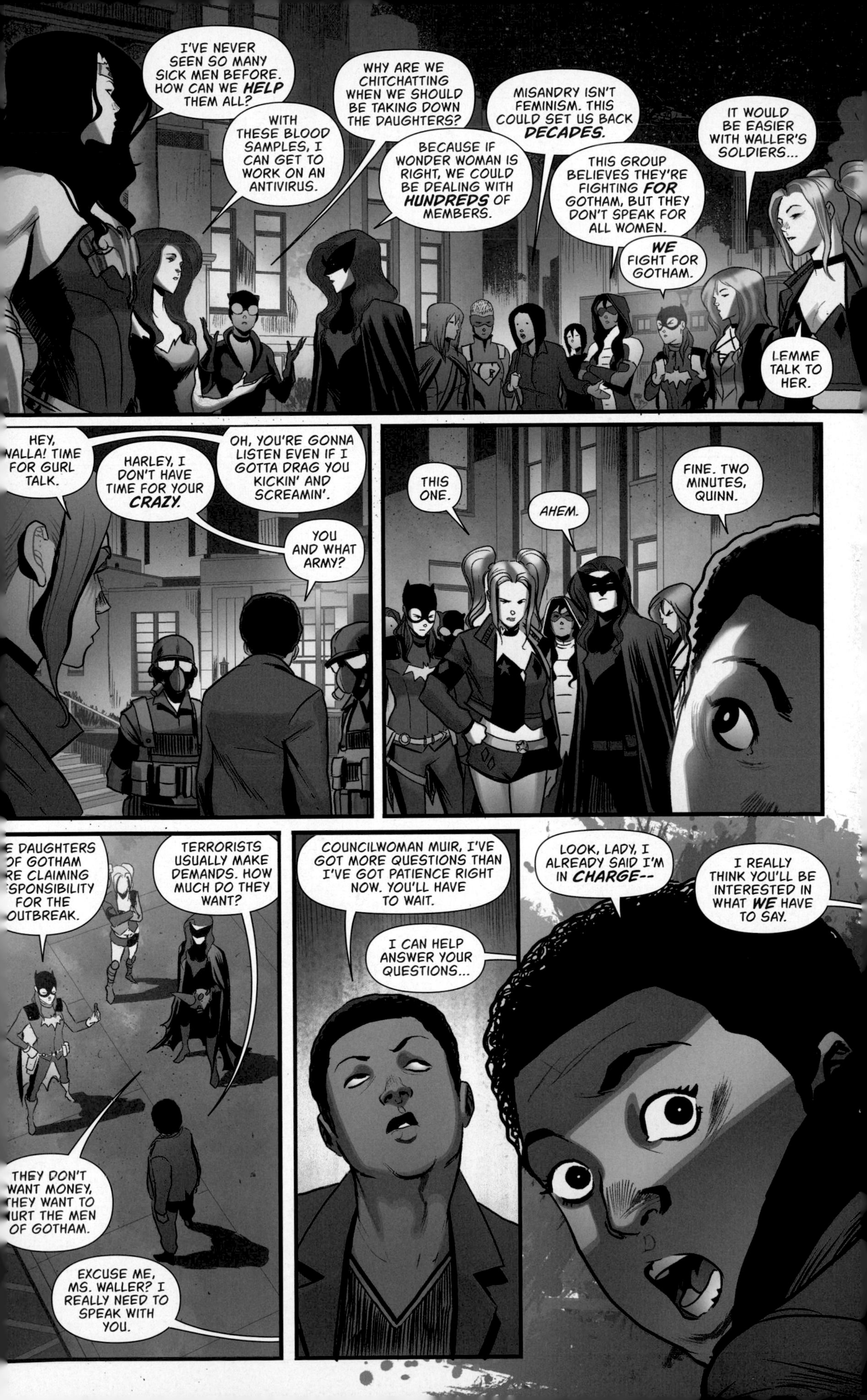

I'VE NEVER SEEN SO MANY SICK MEN BEFORE. HOW CAN WE HELP THEM ALL?
WITH THESE BLOOD SAMPLES, I CAN GET TO WORK ON AN ANTIVIRUS.
WHY ARE WE CHITCHATTING WHEN WE SHOULD BE TAKING DOWN THE DAUGHTERS?
BECAUSE IF WONDER WOMAN IS RIGHT, WE COULD BE DEALING WITH HUNDREDS OF MEMBERS.
MISANDRY ISN'T FEMINISM. THIS COULD SET US BACK DECADES.
THIS GROUP BELIEVES THEY'RE FIGHTING FOR GOTHAM, BUT THEY DON'T SPEAK FOR ALL WOMEN.
WE FIGHT FOR GOTHAM.
IT WOULD BE EASIER WITH WALLER'S SOLDIERS...
LEMME TALK TO HER.
HEY, ALLA! TIME FOR GURL TALK.
HARLEY, I DON'T HAVE TIME FOR YOUR CRAZY.
OH, YOU'RE GONNA LISTEN EVEN IF I GOTTA DRAG YOU KICKIN' AND SCREAMIN'.
YOU AND WHAT ARMY?
THIS ONE.
AHEM.
FINE. TWO MINUTES, QUINN.
E DAUGHTERS OF GOTHAM RE CLAIMING ESPONSIBILITY FOR THE OUTBREAK.
TERRORISTS USUALLY MAKE DEMANDS. HOW MUCH DO THEY WANT?
THEY DON'T WANT MONEY, THEY WANT TO URT THE MEN OF GOTHAM.
EXCUSE ME, MS. WALLER? I REALLY NEED TO SPEAK WITH YOU.
COUNCILWOMAN MUIR, I'VE GOT MORE QUESTIONS THAN I'VE GOT PATIENCE RIGHT NOW. YOU'LL HAVE TO WAIT.
I CAN HELP ANSWER YOUR QUESTIONS...
LOOK, LADY, I ALREADY SAID I'M IN CHARGE--
I REALLY THINK YOU'LL BE INTERESTED IN WHAT WE HAVE TO SAY.

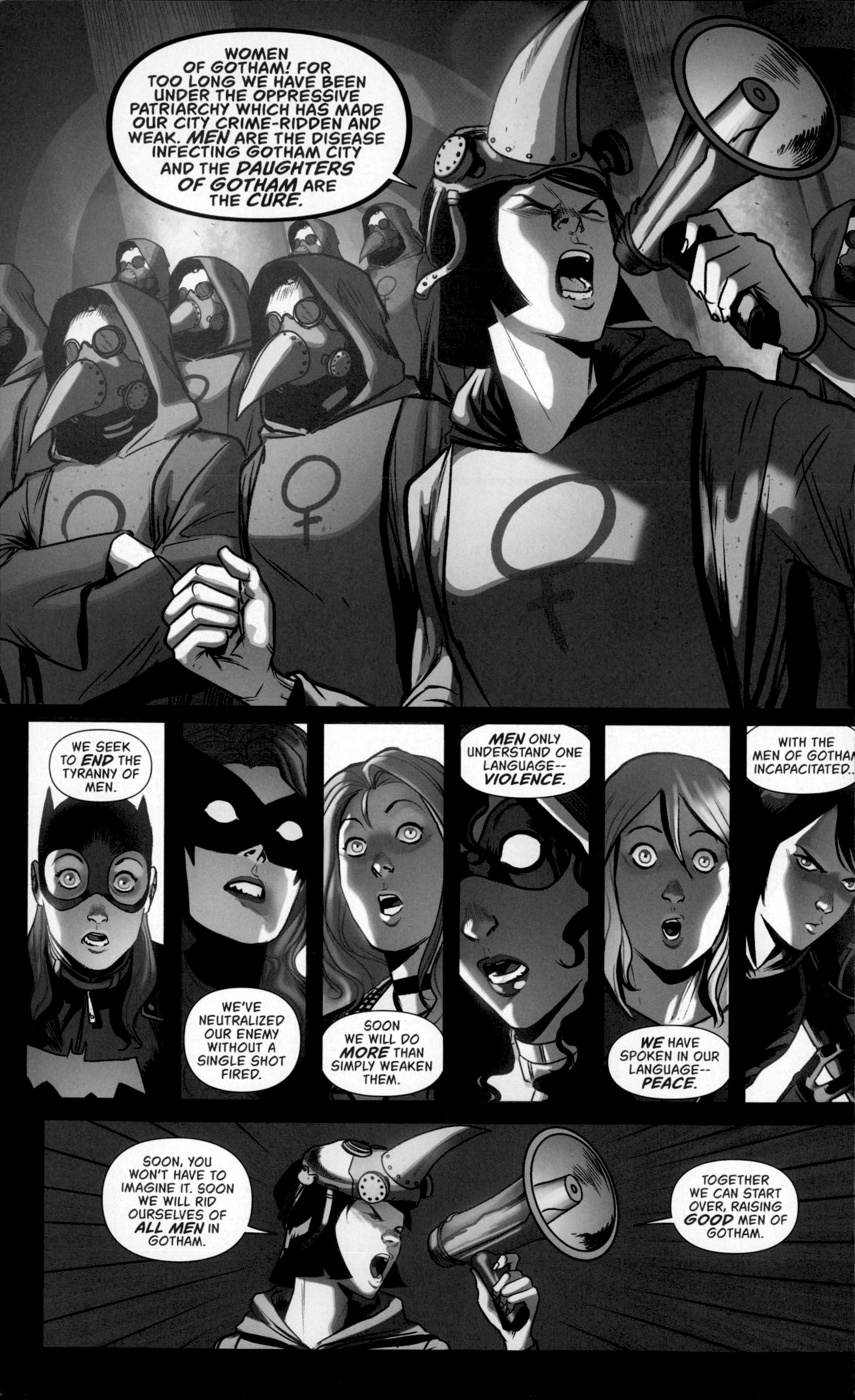
WOMEN OF GOTHAM! FOR TOO LONG WE HAVE BEEN UNDER THE OPPRESSIVE PATRIARCHY WHICH HAS MADE OUR CITY CRIME-RIDDEN AND WEAK. MEN ARE THE DISEASE INFECTING GOTHAM CITY AND THE DAUGHTERS OF GOTHAM ARE THE CURE.
WE SEEK TO END THE TYRANNY OF MEN.
WE'VE NEUTRALIZED OUR ENEMY WITHOUT A SINGLE SHOT FIRED.
SOON WE WILL DO MORE THAN SIMPLY WEAKEN THEM.
MEN ONLY UNDERSTAND ONE LANGUAGE-- VIOLENCE.
WE HAVE SPOKEN IN OUR LANGUAGE-- PEACE.
WITH THE MEN OF GOTHAM INCAPACITATED...
SOON, YOU WON'T HAVE TO IMAGINE IT. SOON WE WILL RID OURSELVES OF ALL MEN IN GOTHAM.
TOGETHER WE CAN START OVER, RAISING GOOD MEN OF GOTHAM.

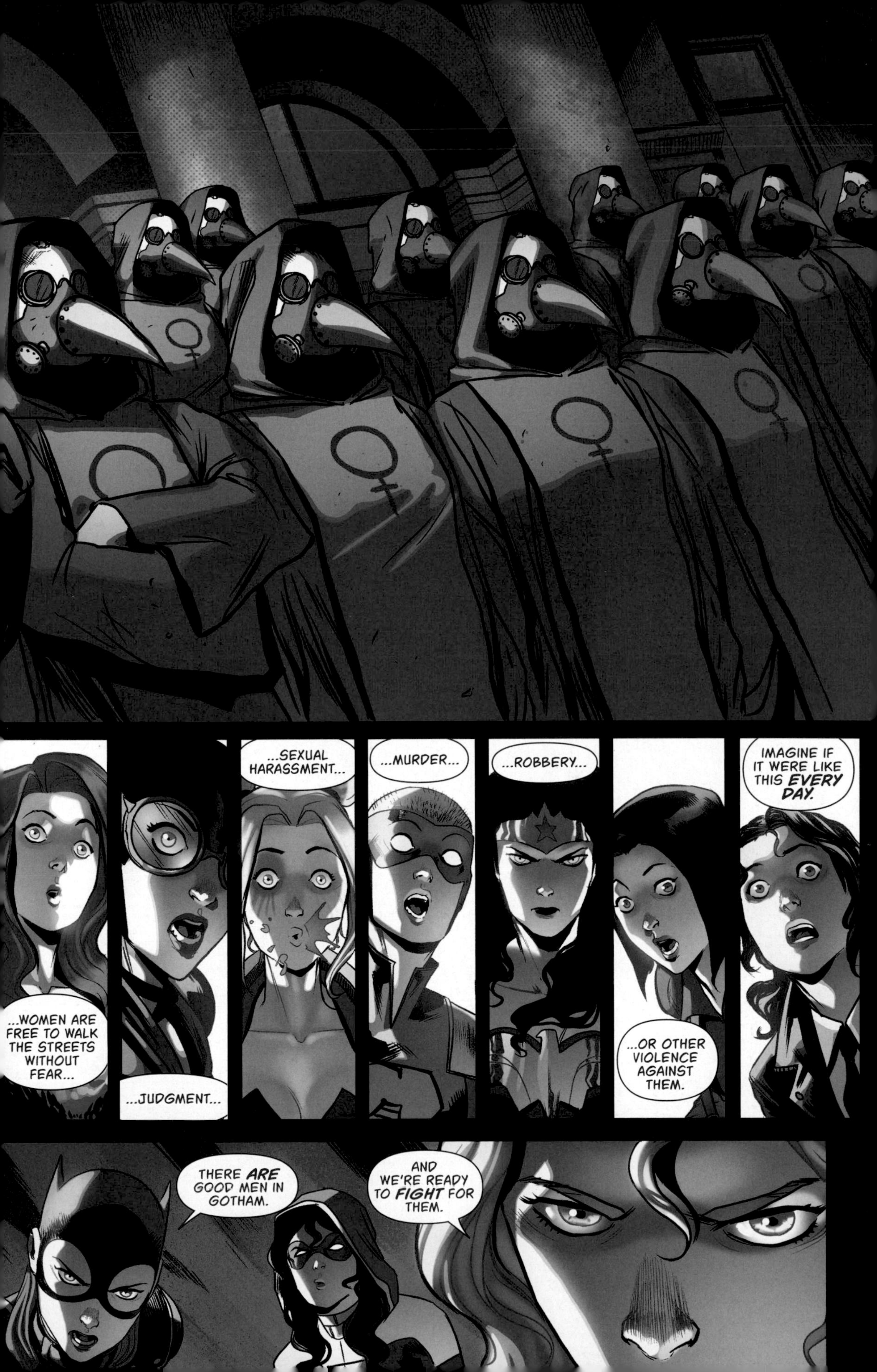
...WOMEN ARE FREE TO WALK THE STREETS WITHOUT FEAR...
...JUDGMENT...
...SEXUAL HARASSMENT...
...MURDER...
...ROBBERY...
...OR OTHER VIOLENCE AGAINST THEM.
IMAGINE IF IT WERE LIKE THIS EVERY DAY.
THERE ARE GOOD MEN IN GOTHAM.
AND WE'RE READY TO FIGHT FOR THEM.

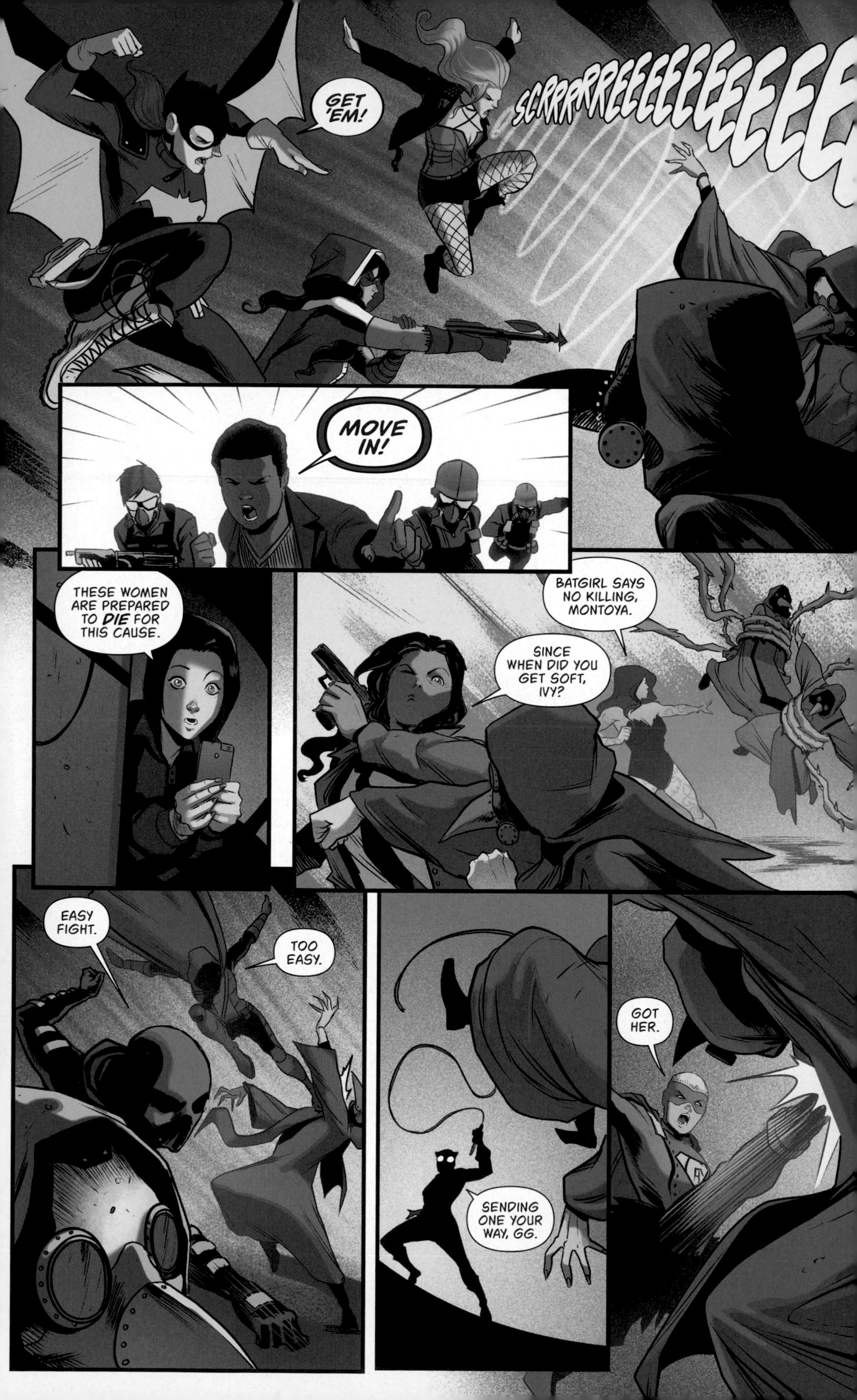
GET 'EM!
SCRRRRREEEEEEEEEEEE
MOVE IN!
THESE WOMEN ARE PREPARED TO DIE FOR THIS CAUSE.
BATGIRL SAYS NO KILLING, MONTOYA.
SINCE WHEN DID YOU GET SOFT, IVY?
EASY FIGHT.
TOO EASY.
SENDING ONE YOUR WAY, GG.
GOT HER.

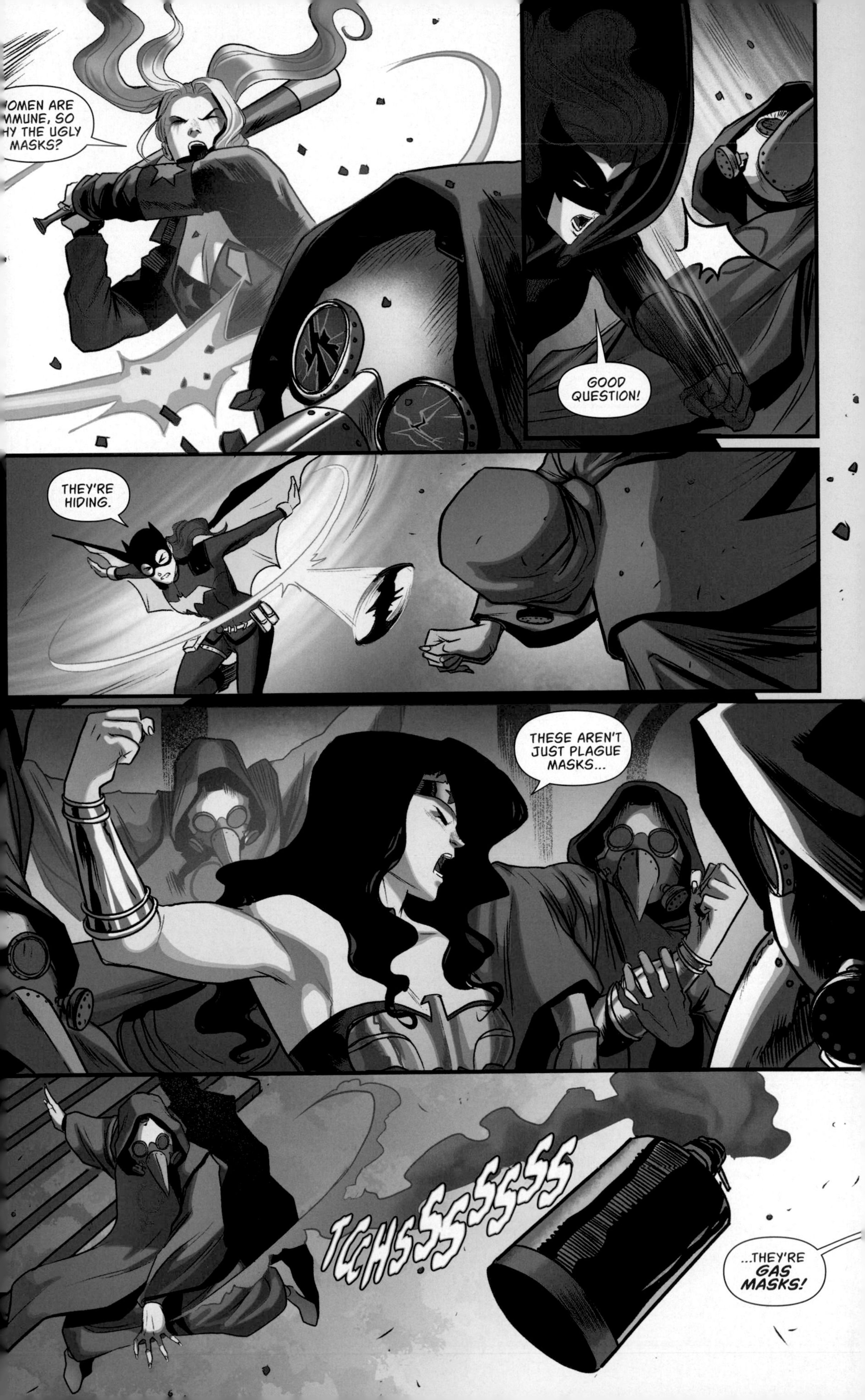
OMEN ARE MMUNE, SO HY THE UGLY MASKS?
GOOD QUESTION!
THEY'RE HIDING.
THESE AREN'T JUST PLAGUE MASKS...
TCHSSSSSSSS
...THEY'RE GAS MASKS!

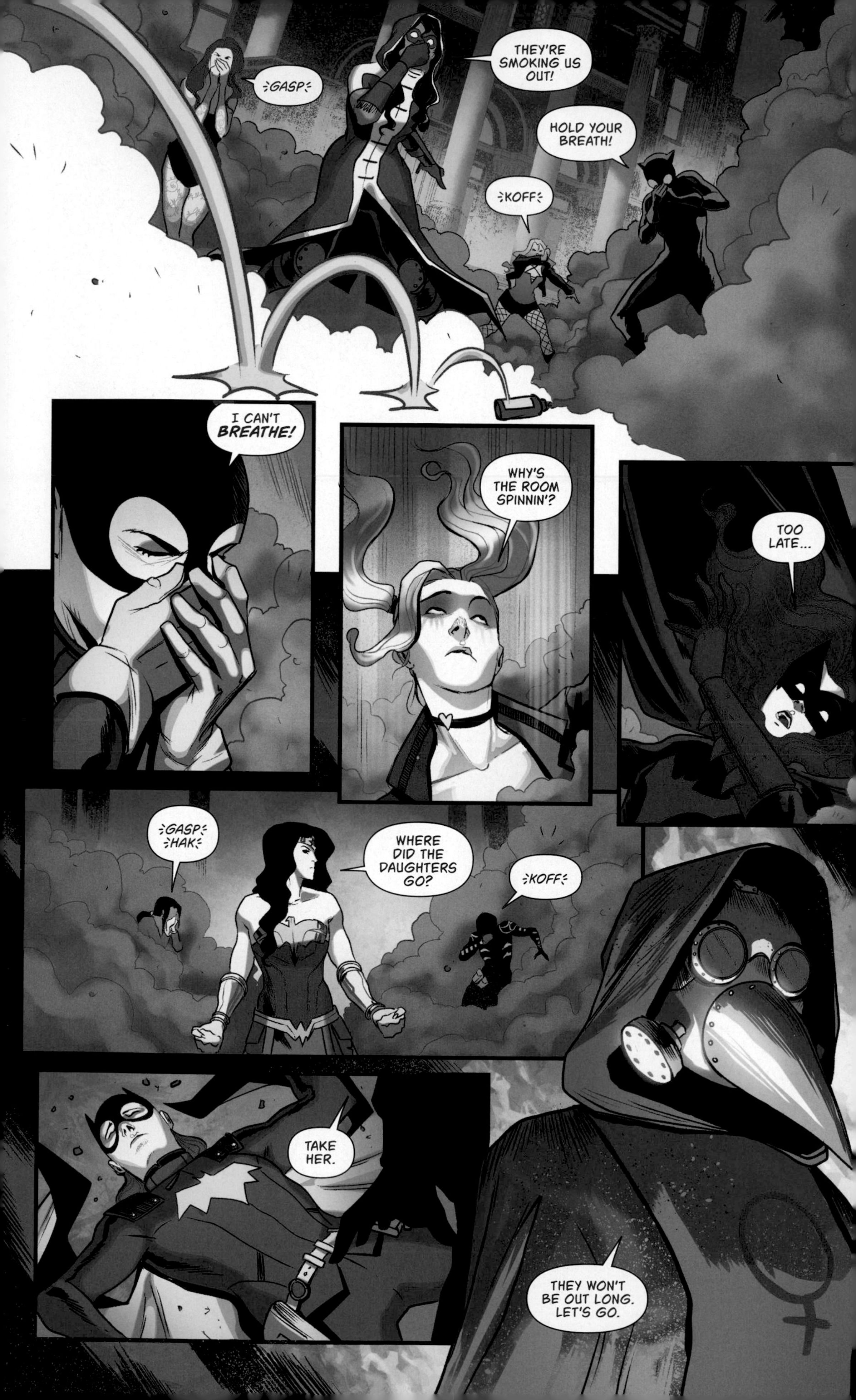

GASP
THEY'RE SMOKING US OUT!
HOLD YOUR BREATH!
KOFF
I CAN'T BREATHE!
WHY'S THE ROOM SPINNIN'?
TOO LATE...
GASP HAK
WHERE DID THE DAUGHTERS GO?
KOFF
TAKE HER.
THEY WON'T BE OUT LONG. LET'S GO.

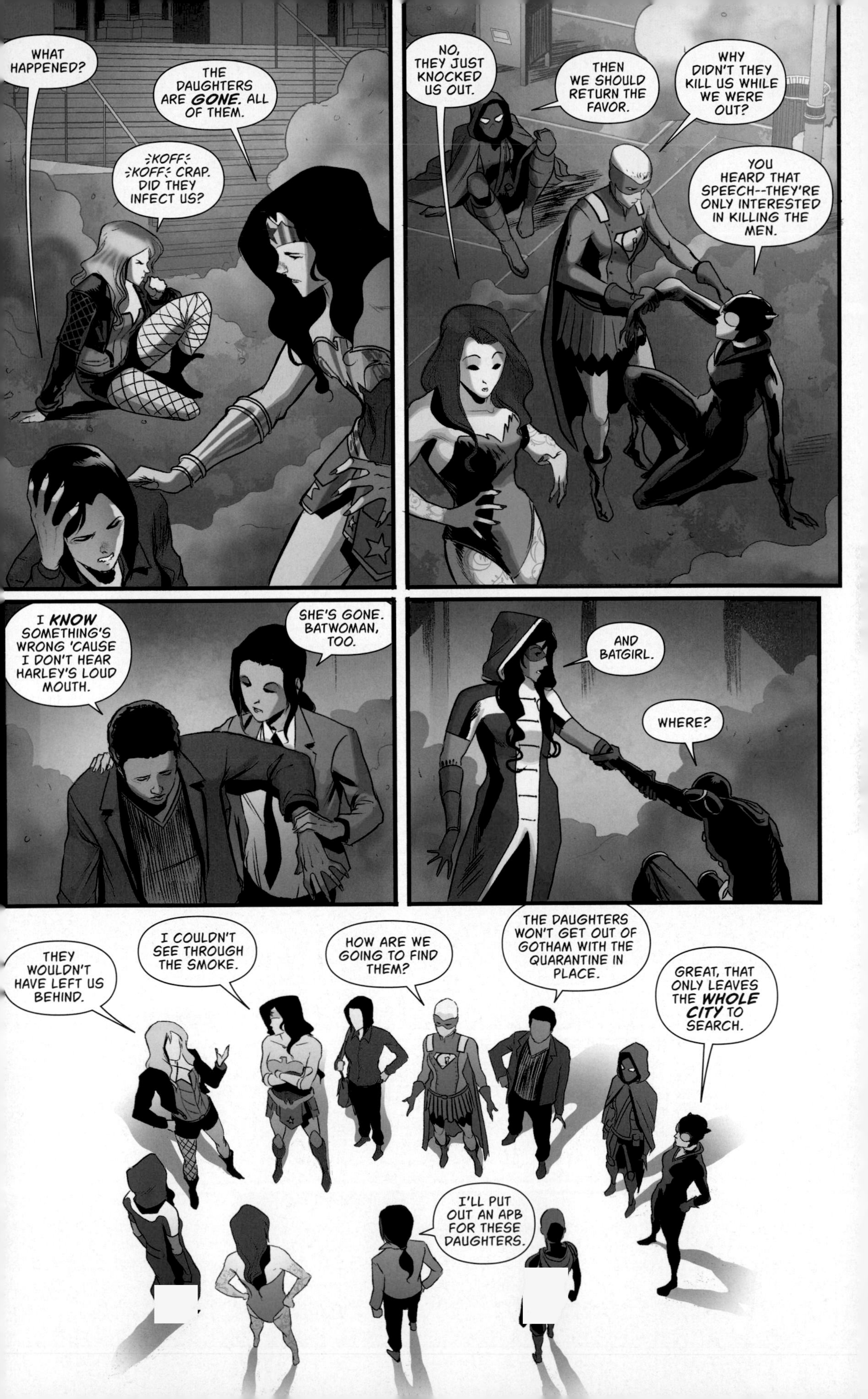
WHAT HAPPENED?
THE DAUGHTERS ARE GONE. ALL OF THEM.
KOFF KOFF CRAP. DID THEY INFECT US?
NO, THEY JUST KNOCKED US OUT.
THEN WE SHOULD RETURN THE FAVOR.
WHY DIDN'T THEY KILL US WHILE WE WERE OUT?
YOU HEARD THAT SPEECH--THEY'RE ONLY INTERESTED IN KILLING THE MEN.
I KNOW SOMETHING'S WRONG 'CAUSE I DON'T HEAR HARLEY'S LOUD MOUTH.
SHE'S GONE. BATWOMAN, TOO.
AND BATGIRL.
WHERE?
THEY WOULDN'T HAVE LEFT US BEHIND.
I COULDN'T SEE THROUGH THE SMOKE.
HOW ARE WE GOING TO FIND THEM?
THE DAUGHTERS WON'T GET OUT OF GOTHAM WITH THE QUARANTINE IN PLACE.
GREAT, THAT ONLY LEAVES THE WHOLE CITY TO SEARCH.
I'LL PUT OUT AN APB FOR THESE DAUGHTERS.

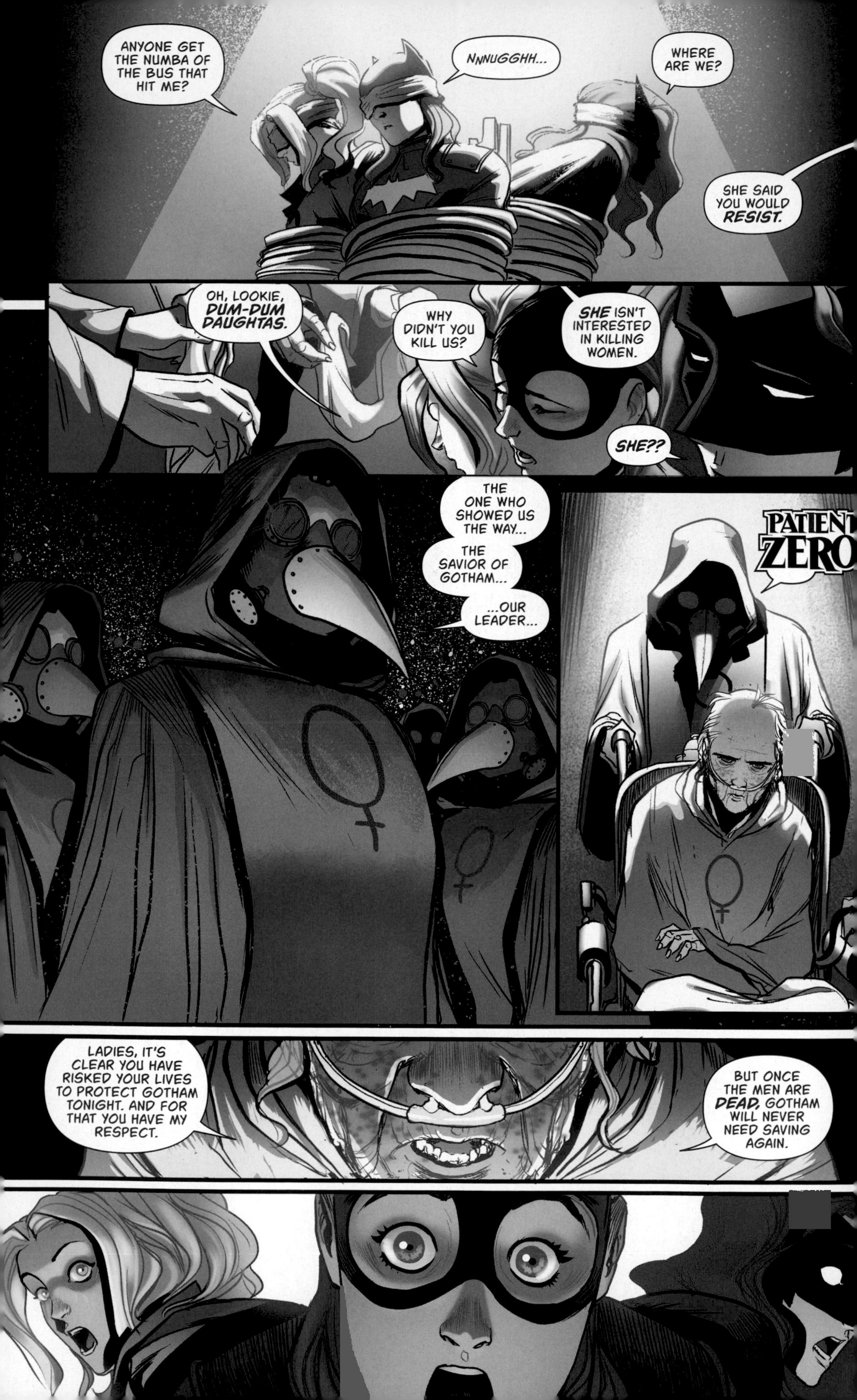
ANYONE GET THE NUMBA OF THE BUS THAT HIT ME?
NNNUGGHH...
WHERE ARE WE?
SHE SAID YOU WOULD RESIST.
OH, LOOKIE, DUM-DUM DAUGHTAS.
WHY DIDN'T YOU KILL US?
SHE ISN'T INTERESTED IN KILLING WOMEN.
SHE??
THE ONE WHO SHOWED US THE WAY...
THE SAVIOR OF GOTHAM...
...OUR LEADER...
PATIENT ZERO
LADIES, IT'S CLEAR YOU HAVE RISKED YOUR LIVES TO PROTECT GOTHAM TONIGHT. AND FOR THAT YOU HAVE MY RESPECT.
BUT ONCE THE MEN ARE DEAD, GOTHAM WILL NEVER NEED SAVING AGAIN.

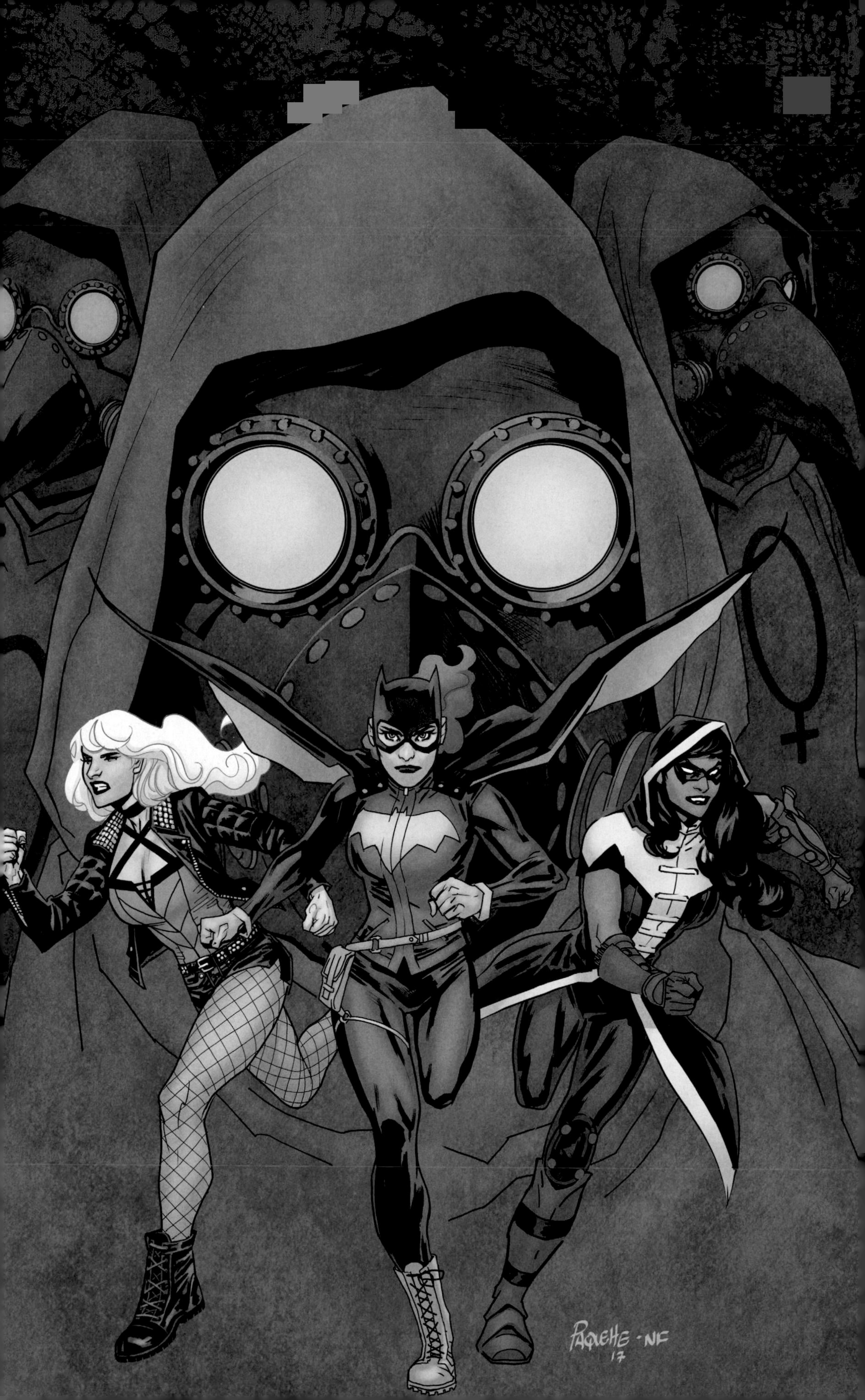

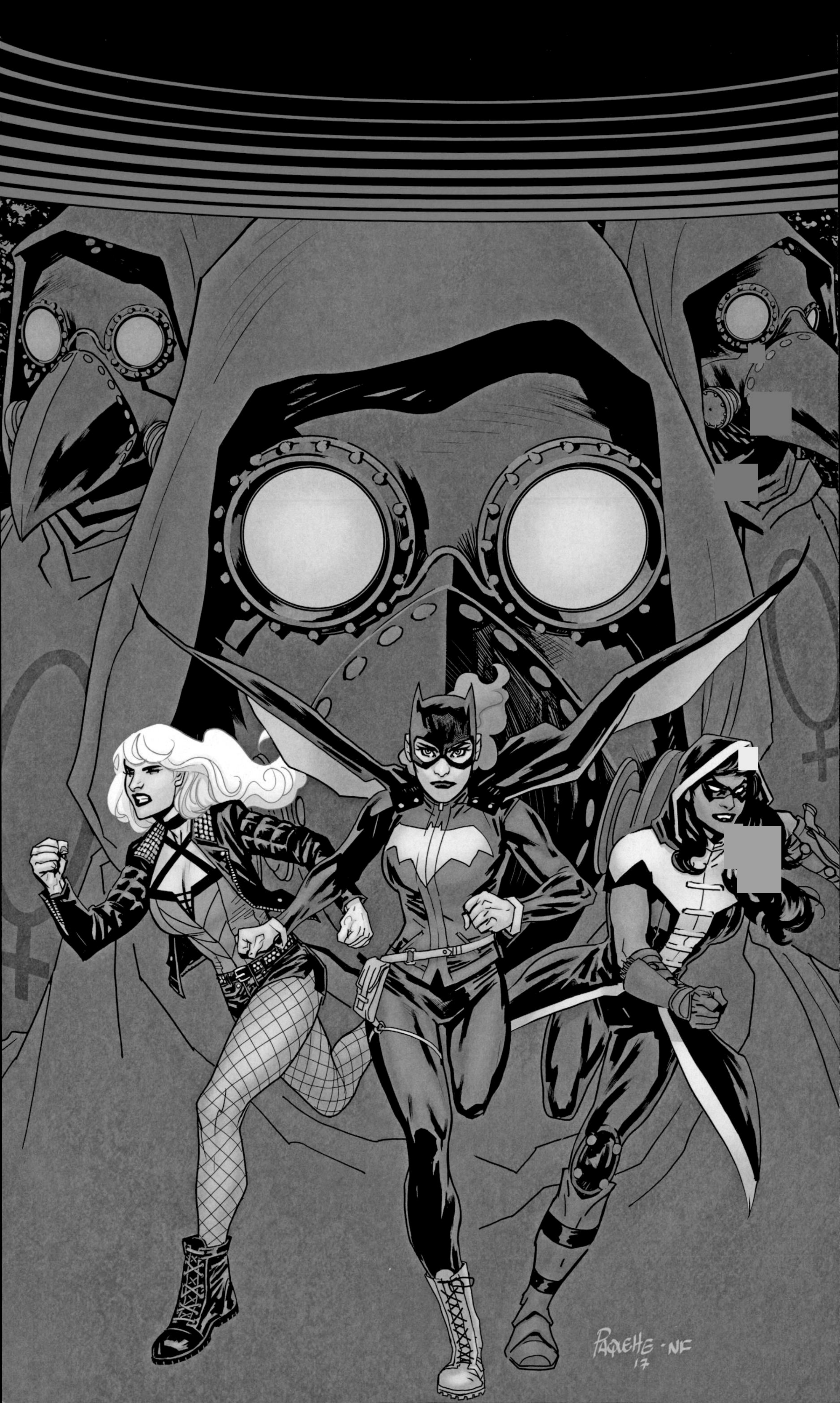

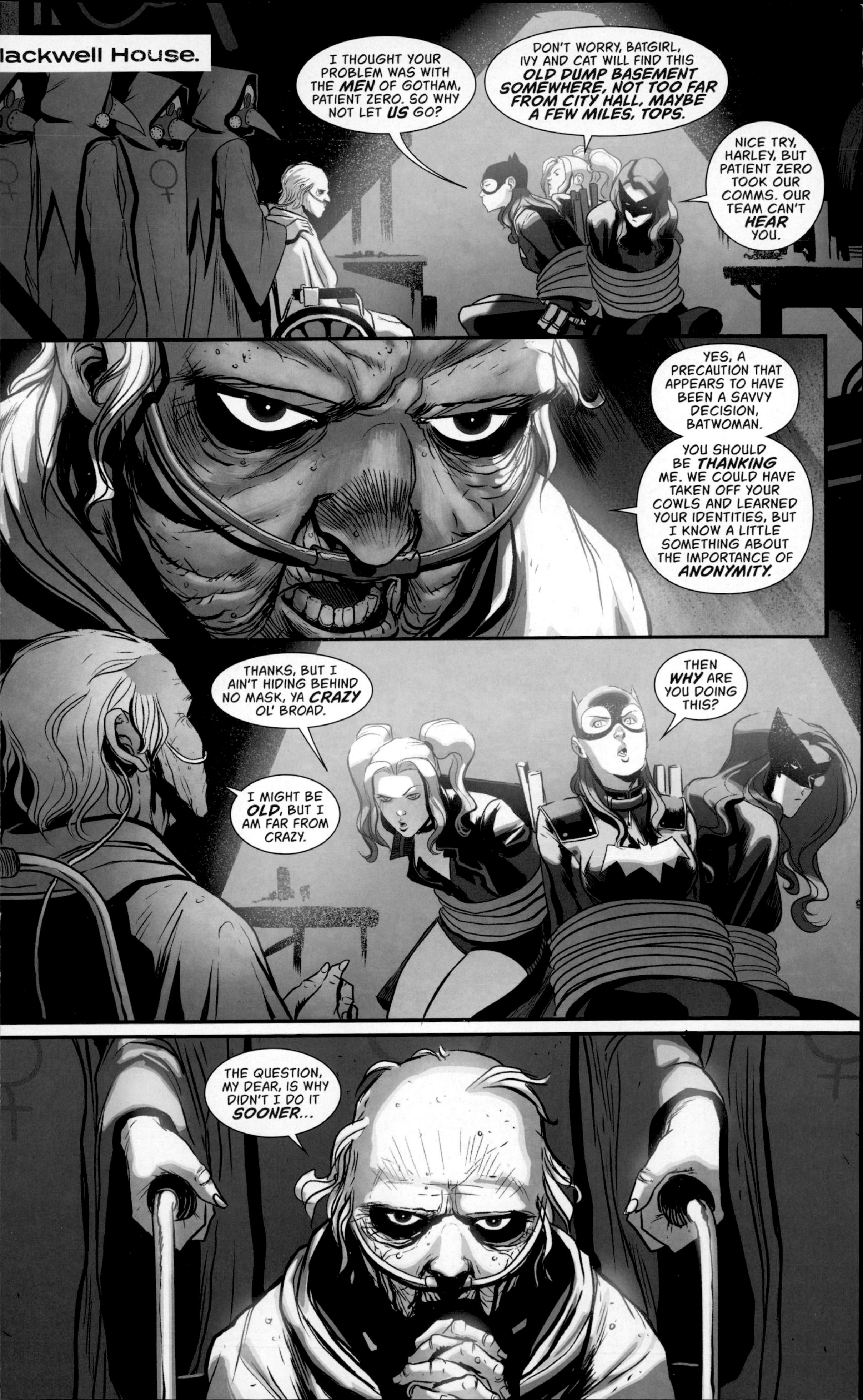
lackwell House.
I THOUGHT YOUR PROBLEM WAS WITH THE MEN OF GOTHAM, PATIENT ZERO. SO WHY NOT LET US GO?
DON'T WORRY, BATGIRL, IVY AND CAT WILL FIND THIS OLD DUMP BASEMENT SOMEWHERE, NOT TOO FAR FROM CITY HALL, MAYBE A FEW MILES, TOPS.
NICE TRY, HARLEY, BUT PATIENT ZERO TOOK OUR COMMS. OUR TEAM CAN'T HEAR YOU.
YES, A PRECAUTION THAT APPEARS TO HAVE BEEN A SAVVY DECISION, BATWOMAN.
YOU SHOULD BE THANKING ME. WE COULD HAVE TAKEN OFF YOUR COWLS AND LEARNED YOUR IDENTITIES, BUT I KNOW A LITTLE SOMETHING ABOUT THE IMPORTANCE OF ANONYMITY.
THANKS, BUT I AIN'T HIDING BEHIND NO MASK, YA CRAZY OL' BROAD.
THEN WHY ARE YOU DOING THIS?
I MIGHT BE OLD, BUT I AM FAR FROM CRAZY.
THE QUESTION, MY DEAR, IS WHY DIDN'T I DO IT SOONER...

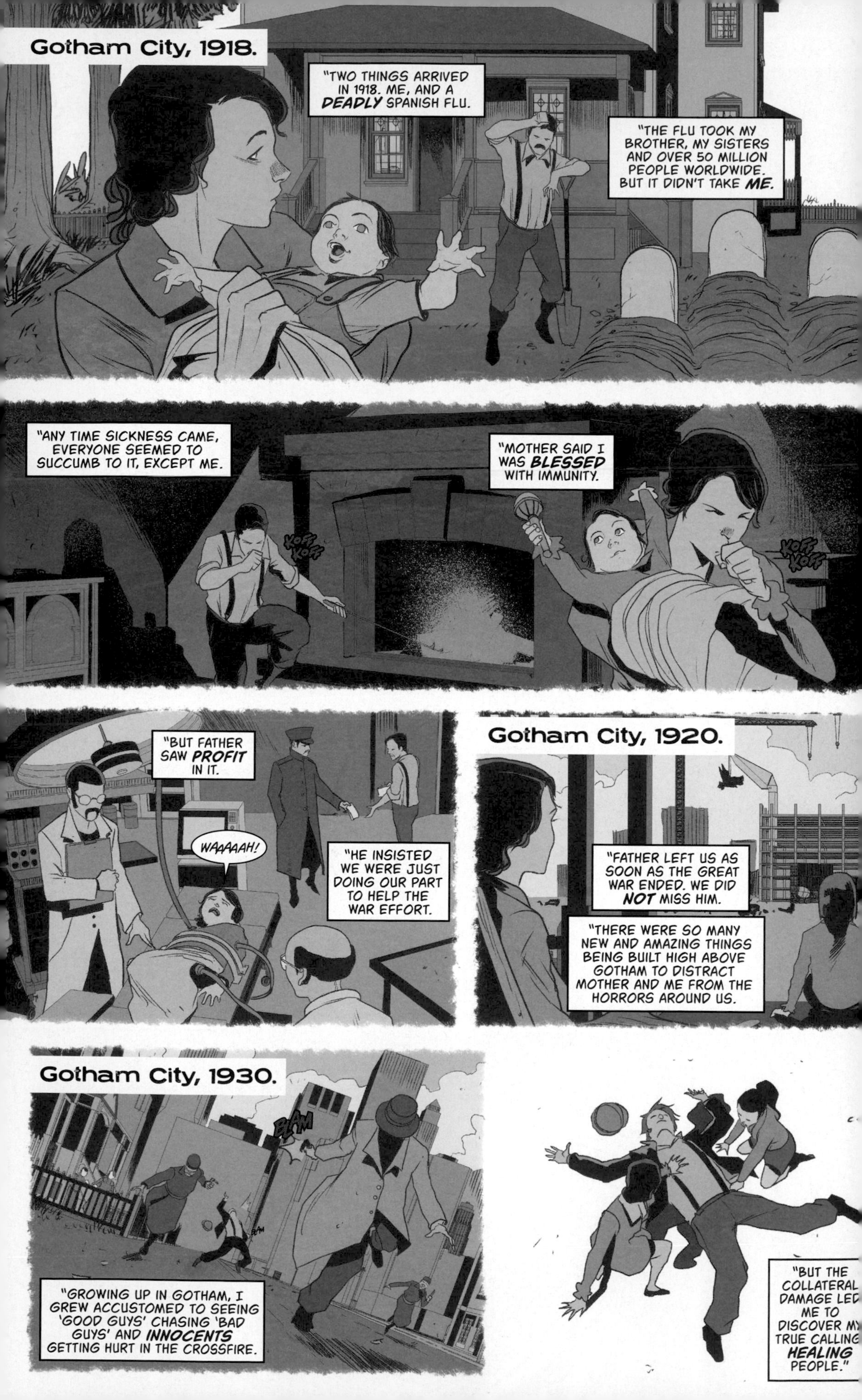
Gotham City, 1918.
"TWO THINGS ARRIVED IN 1918. ME, AND A DEADLY SPANISH FLU.
"THE FLU TOOK MY BROTHER, MY SISTERS AND OVER 50 MILLION PEOPLE WORLDWIDE. BUT IT DIDN'T TAKE ME.
"ANY TIME SICKNESS CAME, EVERYONE SEEMED TO SUCCUMB TO IT, EXCEPT ME.
KOFF KOFF
"MOTHER SAID I WAS BLESSED WITH IMMUNITY.
KOFF KOFF
"BUT FATHER SAW PROFIT IN IT.
WAAAAAH!
"HE INSISTED WE WERE JUST DOING OUR PART TO HELP THE WAR EFFORT.
Gotham City, 1920.
"FATHER LEFT US AS SOON AS THE GREAT WAR ENDED. WE DID NOT MISS HIM.
"THERE WERE SO MANY NEW AND AMAZING THINGS BEING BUILT HIGH ABOVE GOTHAM TO DISTRACT MOTHER AND ME FROM THE HORRORS AROUND US.
Gotham City, 1930.
BLAM
BLAM
"GROWING UP IN GOTHAM, I GREW ACCUSTOMED TO SEEING 'GOOD GUYS' CHASING 'BAD GUYS' AND INNOCENTS GETTING HURT IN THE CROSSFIRE.
"BUT THE COLLATERAL DAMAGE LED ME TO DISCOVER MY TRUE CALLING: HEALING PEOPLE."

Gotham City, 1941.

"WE SENT OUR **BEST** MEN TO WORLD WAR TWO, AND AS A RESULT, THE **WORST** WERE LEFT BEHIND.

"THIS TIME, I HELPED THE WAR EFFORT BY **STUDYING** MY OWN IMMUNITY.

"I HOPED TO FIND CURES FOR THE MEN ON THE FIELD SUFFERING ALL MANNER OF DISEASES.

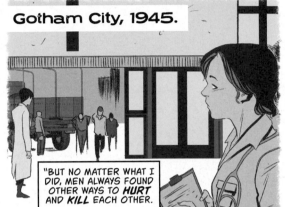

Gotham City, 1945.

"BUT NO MATTER WHAT I DID, MEN ALWAYS FOUND OTHER WAYS TO **HURT** AND **KILL** EACH OTHER.

Gotham City, 2016.

KPA-KOOOMMMM

"DECADES WENT BY AND I WATCHED THE BATTLES IN GOTHAM GET **DARKER**...

"...AND **DARKER**.

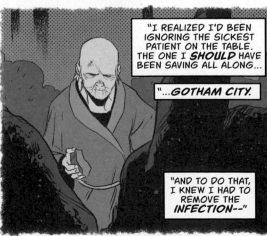

"I REALIZED I'D BEEN IGNORING THE SICKEST PATIENT ON THE TABLE. THE ONE I **SHOULD** HAVE BEEN SAVING ALL ALONG...

"...GOTHAM CITY.

"AND TO DO THAT, I KNEW I HAD TO REMOVE THE **INFECTION**--"

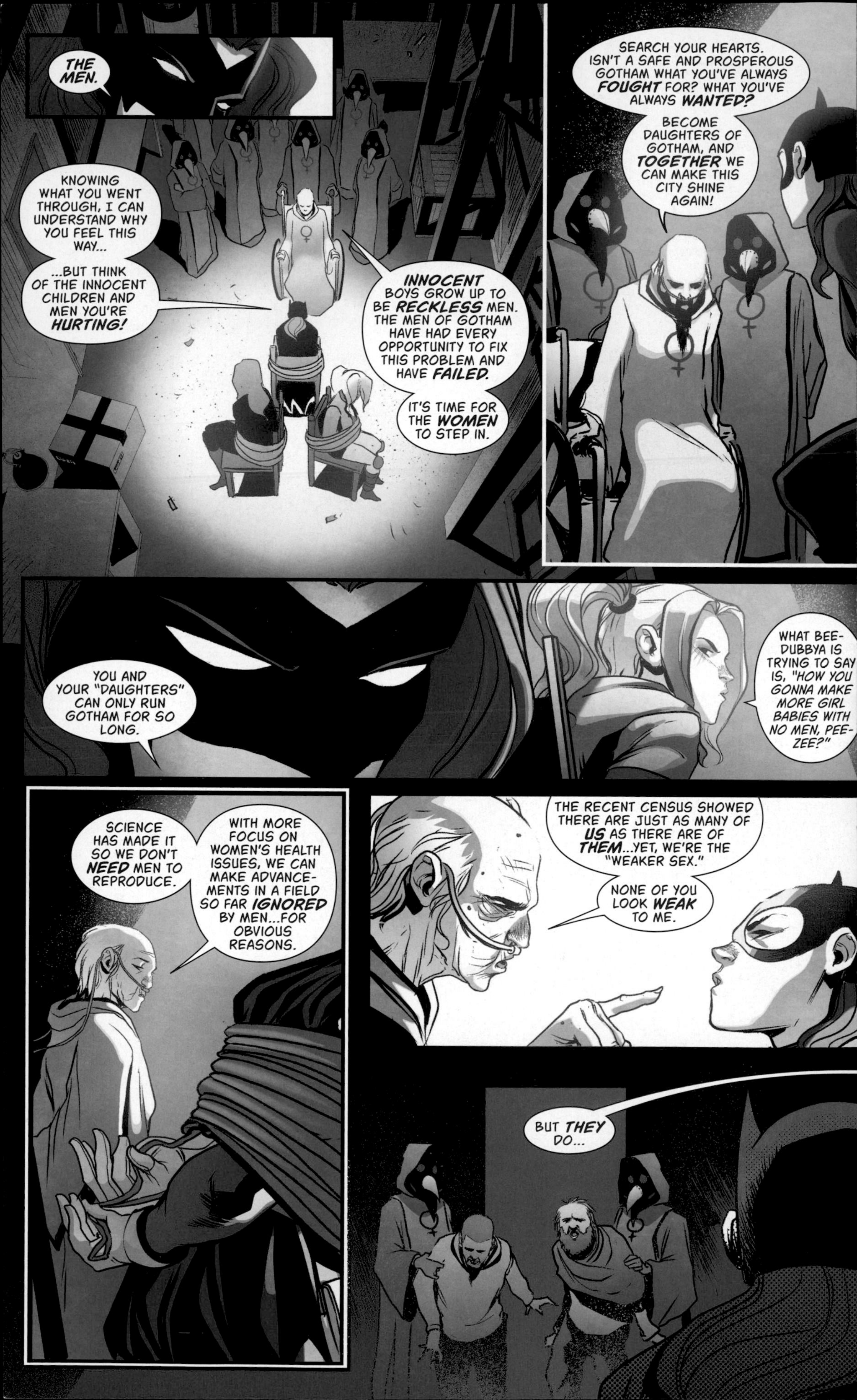
THE MEN.
KNOWING WHAT YOU WENT THROUGH, I CAN UNDERSTAND WHY YOU FEEL THIS WAY...
...BUT THINK OF THE INNOCENT CHILDREN AND MEN YOU'RE HURTING!
INNOCENT BOYS GROW UP TO BE RECKLESS MEN. THE MEN OF GOTHAM HAVE HAD EVERY OPPORTUNITY TO FIX THIS PROBLEM AND HAVE FAILED.
IT'S TIME FOR THE WOMEN TO STEP IN.
SEARCH YOUR HEARTS. ISN'T A SAFE AND PROSPEROUS GOTHAM WHAT YOU'VE ALWAYS FOUGHT FOR? WHAT YOU'VE ALWAYS WANTED?
BECOME DAUGHTERS OF GOTHAM, AND TOGETHER WE CAN MAKE THIS CITY SHINE AGAIN!
YOU AND YOUR "DAUGHTERS" CAN ONLY RUN GOTHAM FOR SO LONG.
WHAT BEE-DUBBYA IS TRYING TO SAY IS, "HOW YOU GONNA MAKE MORE GIRL BABIES WITH NO MEN, PEE-ZEE?"
SCIENCE HAS MADE IT SO WE DON'T NEED MEN TO REPRODUCE.
WITH MORE FOCUS ON WOMEN'S HEALTH ISSUES, WE CAN MAKE ADVANCE-MENTS IN A FIELD SO FAR IGNORED BY MEN...FOR OBVIOUS REASONS.
THE RECENT CENSUS SHOWED THERE ARE JUST AS MANY OF US AS THERE ARE OF THEM...YET, WE'RE THE "WEAKER SEX."
NONE OF YOU LOOK WEAK TO ME.
BUT THEY DO...

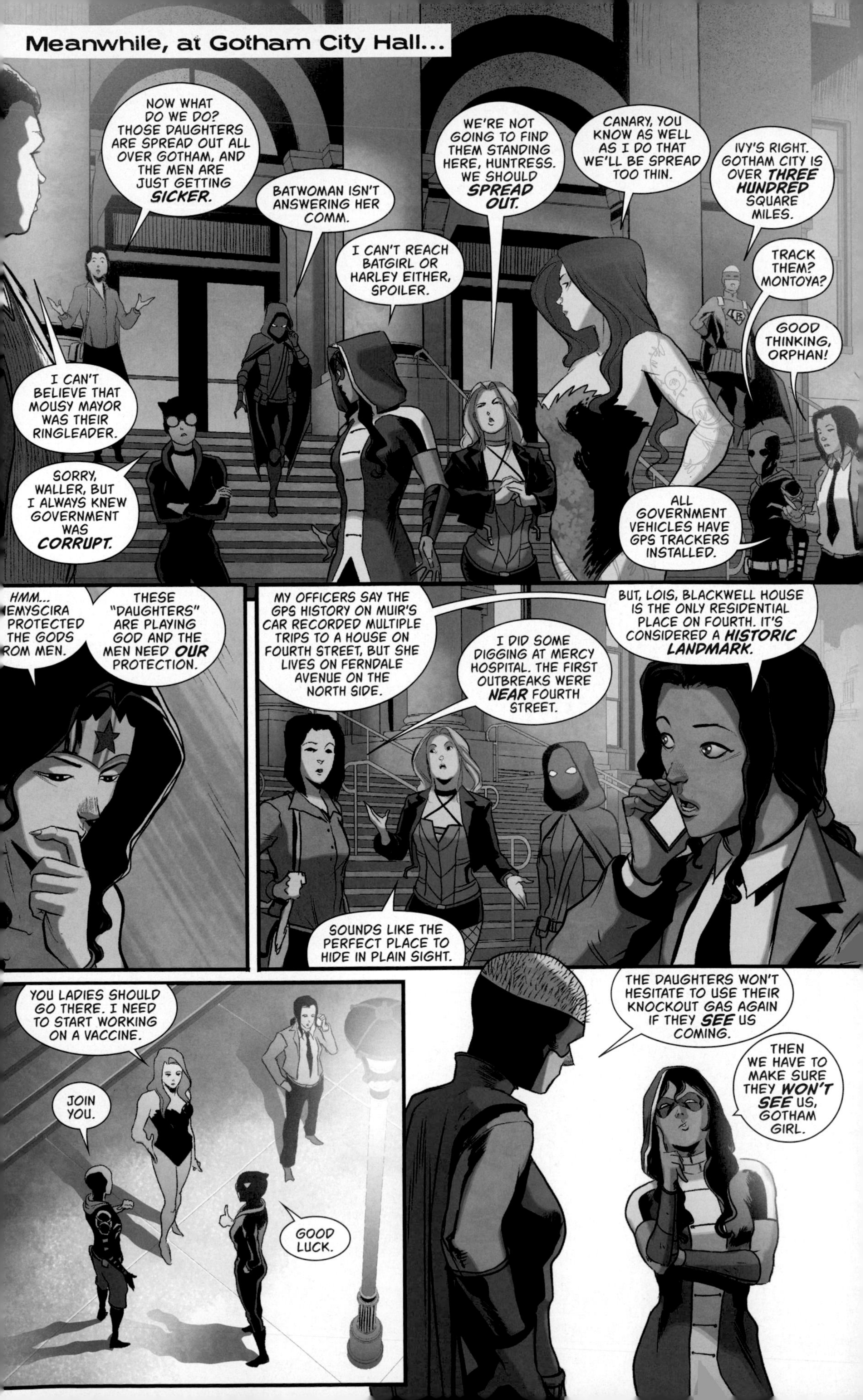
Meanwhile, at Gotham City Hall...
NOW WHAT DO WE DO? THOSE DAUGHTERS ARE SPREAD OUT ALL OVER GOTHAM, AND THE MEN ARE JUST GETTING SICKER.
BATWOMAN ISN'T ANSWERING HER COMM.
I CAN'T REACH BATGIRL OR HARLEY EITHER, SPOILER.
WE'RE NOT GOING TO FIND THEM STANDING HERE, HUNTRESS. WE SHOULD SPREAD OUT.
CANARY, YOU KNOW AS WELL AS I DO THAT WE'LL BE SPREAD TOO THIN.
IVY'S RIGHT. GOTHAM CITY IS OVER THREE HUNDRED SQUARE MILES.
TRACK THEM? MONTOYA?
GOOD THINKING, ORPHAN!
I CAN'T BELIEVE THAT MOUSY MAYOR WAS THEIR RINGLEADER.
SORRY, WALLER, BUT I ALWAYS KNEW GOVERNMENT WAS CORRUPT.
ALL GOVERNMENT VEHICLES HAVE GPS TRACKERS INSTALLED.
HMM... EMYSCIRA PROTECTED THE GODS ROM MEN.
THESE "DAUGHTERS" ARE PLAYING GOD AND THE MEN NEED OUR PROTECTION.
MY OFFICERS SAY THE GPS HISTORY ON MUIR'S CAR RECORDED MULTIPLE TRIPS TO A HOUSE ON FOURTH STREET, BUT SHE LIVES ON FERNDALE AVENUE ON THE NORTH SIDE.
I DID SOME DIGGING AT MERCY HOSPITAL. THE FIRST OUTBREAKS WERE NEAR FOURTH STREET.
BUT, LOIS, BLACKWELL HOUSE IS THE ONLY RESIDENTIAL PLACE ON FOURTH. IT'S CONSIDERED A HISTORIC LANDMARK.
SOUNDS LIKE THE PERFECT PLACE TO HIDE IN PLAIN SIGHT.
YOU LADIES SHOULD GO THERE. I NEED TO START WORKING ON A VACCINE.
JOIN YOU.
GOOD LUCK.
THE DAUGHTERS WON'T HESITATE TO USE THEIR KNOCKOUT GAS AGAIN IF THEY SEE US COMING.
THEN WE HAVE TO MAKE SURE THEY WON'T SEE US, GOTHAM GIRL.

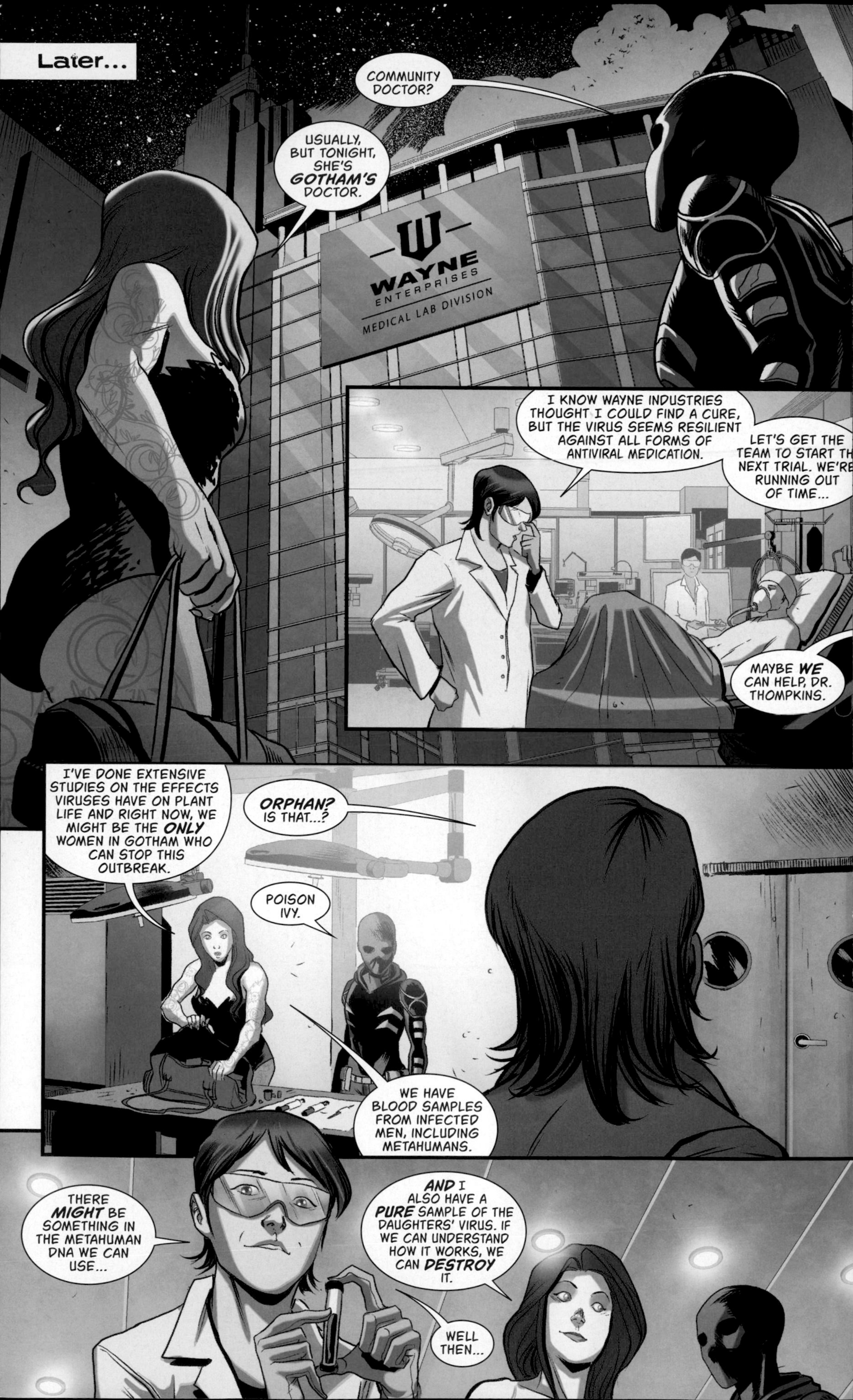
Later...
COMMUNITY DOCTOR?
USUALLY, BUT TONIGHT, SHE'S GOTHAM'S DOCTOR.
WAYNE ENTERPRISES MEDICAL LAB DIVISION
I KNOW WAYNE INDUSTRIES THOUGHT I COULD FIND A CURE, BUT THE VIRUS SEEMS RESILIENT AGAINST ALL FORMS OF ANTIVIRAL MEDICATION.
LET'S GET THE TEAM TO START TH NEXT TRIAL. WE'RE RUNNING OUT OF TIME...
MAYBE WE CAN HELP, DR. THOMPKINS.
I'VE DONE EXTENSIVE STUDIES ON THE EFFECTS VIRUSES HAVE ON PLANT LIFE AND RIGHT NOW, WE MIGHT BE THE ONLY WOMEN IN GOTHAM WHO CAN STOP THIS OUTBREAK.
ORPHAN? IS THAT...?
POISON IVY.
WE HAVE BLOOD SAMPLES FROM INFECTED MEN, INCLUDING METAHUMANS.
THERE MIGHT BE SOMETHING IN THE METAHUMAN DNA WE CAN USE...
AND I ALSO HAVE A PURE SAMPLE OF THE DAUGHTERS' VIRUS. IF WE CAN UNDERSTAND HOW IT WORKS, WE CAN DESTROY IT.
WELL THEN...

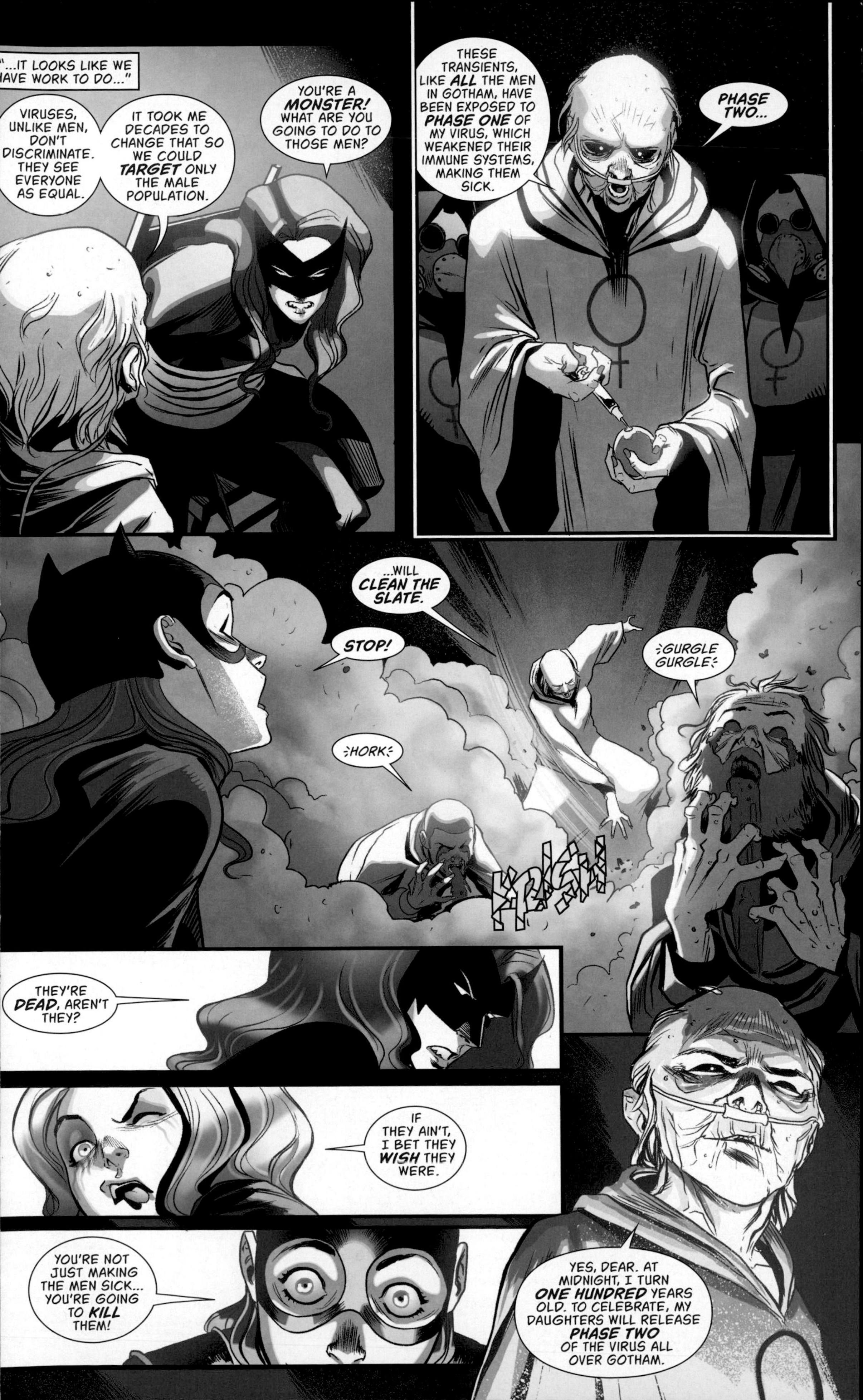
"...IT LOOKS LIKE WE
HAVE WORK TO DO..."
VIRUSES, UNLIKE MEN, DON'T DISCRIMINATE. THEY SEE EVERYONE AS EQUAL.
IT TOOK ME DECADES TO CHANGE THAT SO WE COULD TARGET ONLY THE MALE POPULATION.
YOU'RE A MONSTER! WHAT ARE YOU GOING TO DO TO THOSE MEN?
THESE TRANSIENTS, LIKE ALL THE MEN IN GOTHAM, HAVE BEEN EXPOSED TO PHASE ONE OF MY VIRUS, WHICH WEAKENED THEIR IMMUNE SYSTEMS, MAKING THEM SICK.
PHASE TWO...
...WILL CLEAN THE SLATE.
STOP!
GURGLE GURGLE
HORK
KRASH!
THEY'RE DEAD, AREN'T THEY?
IF THEY AIN'T, I BET THEY WISH THEY WERE.
YOU'RE NOT JUST MAKING THE MEN SICK... YOU'RE GOING TO KILL THEM!
YES, DEAR. AT MIDNIGHT, I TURN ONE HUNDRED YEARS OLD. TO CELEBRATE, MY DAUGHTERS WILL RELEASE PHASE TWO OF THE VIRUS ALL OVER GOTHAM.

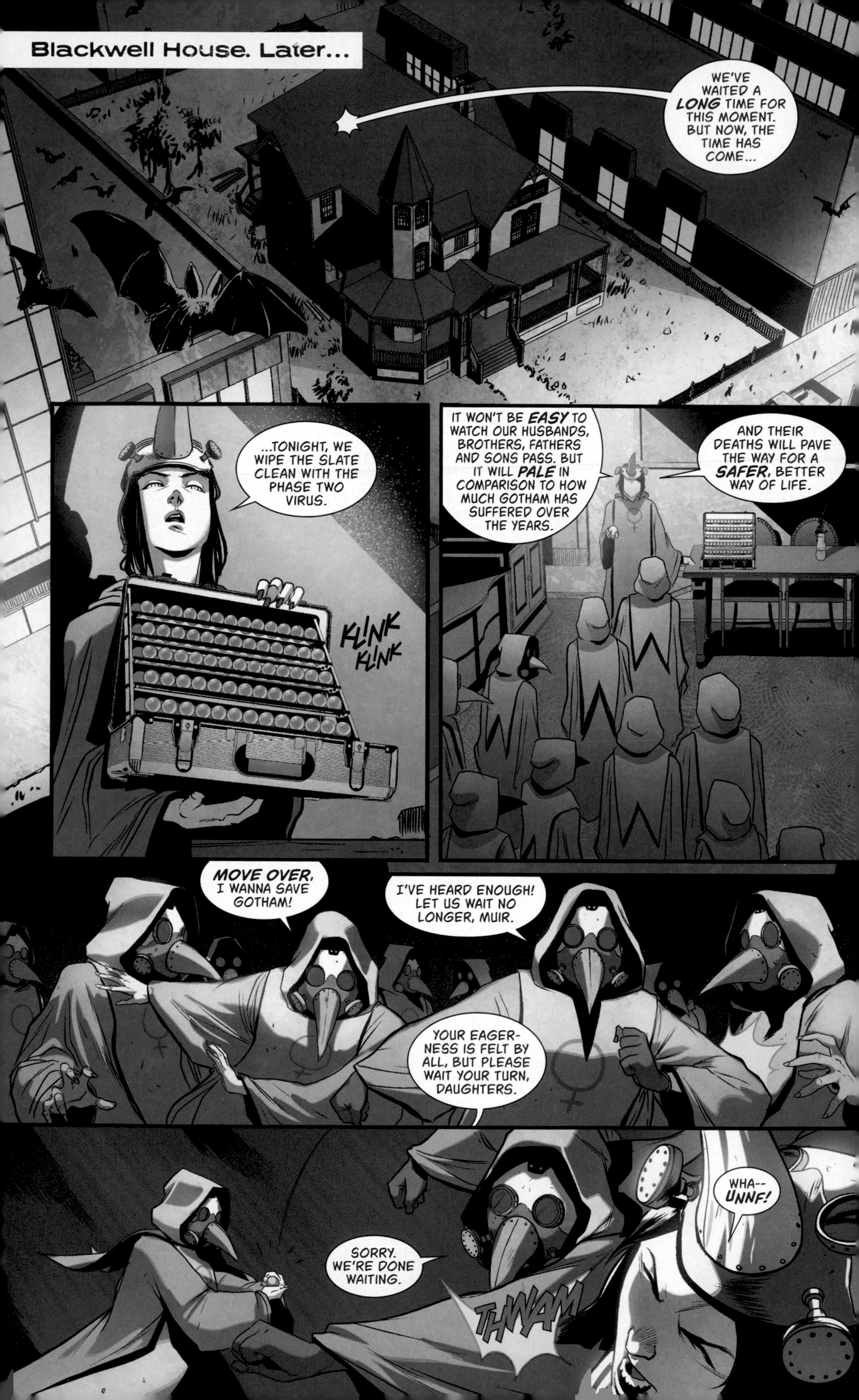
Blackwell House. Later...
WE'VE WAITED A LONG TIME FOR THIS MOMENT. BUT NOW, THE TIME HAS COME...
...TONIGHT, WE WIPE THE SLATE CLEAN WITH THE PHASE TWO VIRUS.
KLINK KLINK
IT WON'T BE EASY TO WATCH OUR HUSBANDS, BROTHERS, FATHERS AND SONS PASS. BUT IT WILL PALE IN COMPARISON TO HOW MUCH GOTHAM HAS SUFFERED OVER THE YEARS.
AND THEIR DEATHS WILL PAVE THE WAY FOR A SAFER, BETTER WAY OF LIFE.
MOVE OVER, I WANNA SAVE GOTHAM!
I'VE HEARD ENOUGH! LET US WAIT NO LONGER, MUIR.
YOUR EAGER-NESS IS FELT BY ALL, BUT PLEASE WAIT YOUR TURN, DAUGHTERS.
WHA-- UNNF!
SORRY. WE'RE DONE WAITING.
THWAM

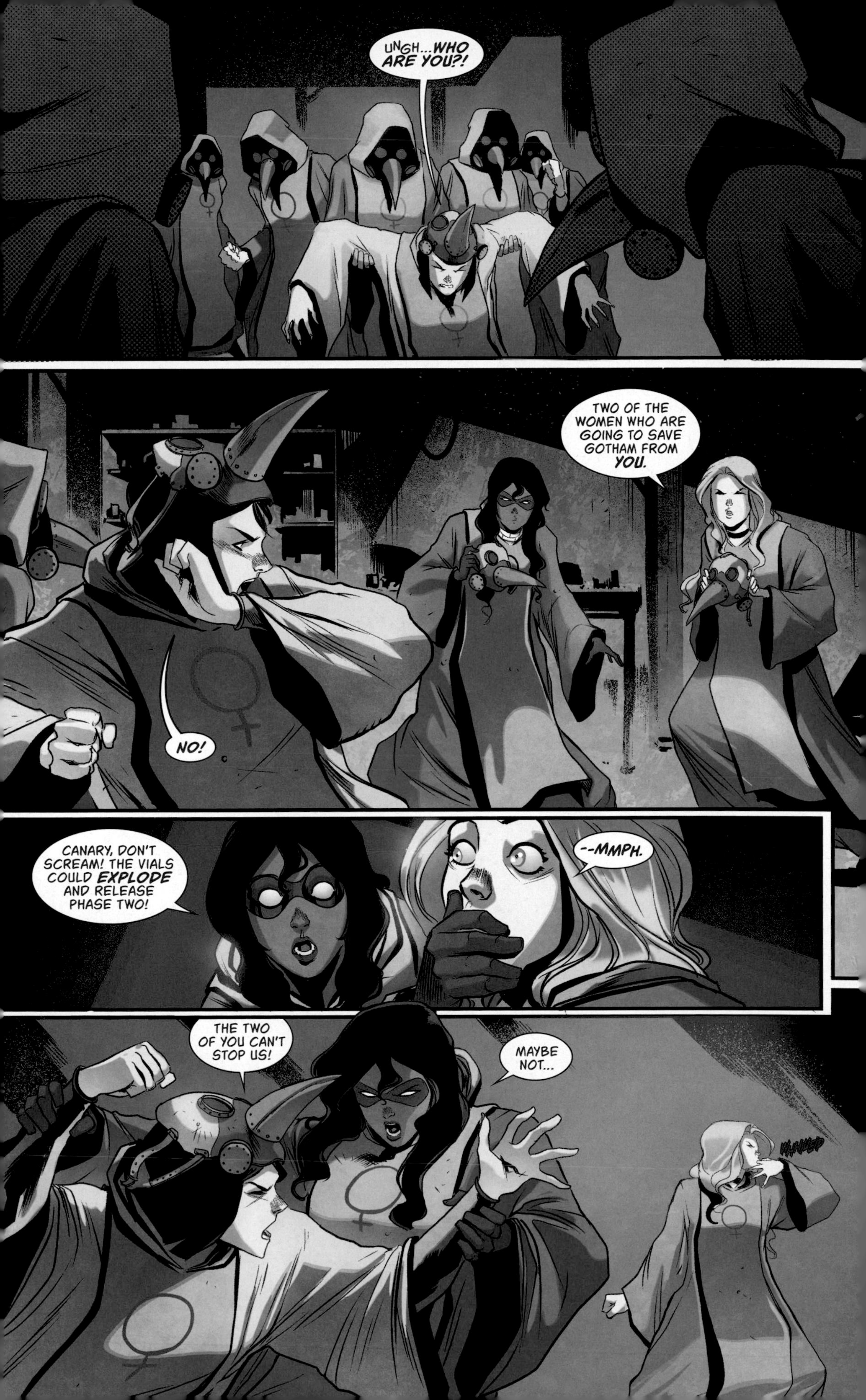
UNGH...WHO ARE YOU?!
TWO OF THE WOMEN WHO ARE GOING TO SAVE GOTHAM FROM YOU.
NO!
CANARY, DON'T SCREAM! THE VIALS COULD EXPLODE AND RELEASE PHASE TWO!
--MMPH.
THE TWO OF YOU CAN'T STOP US!
MAYBE NOT...

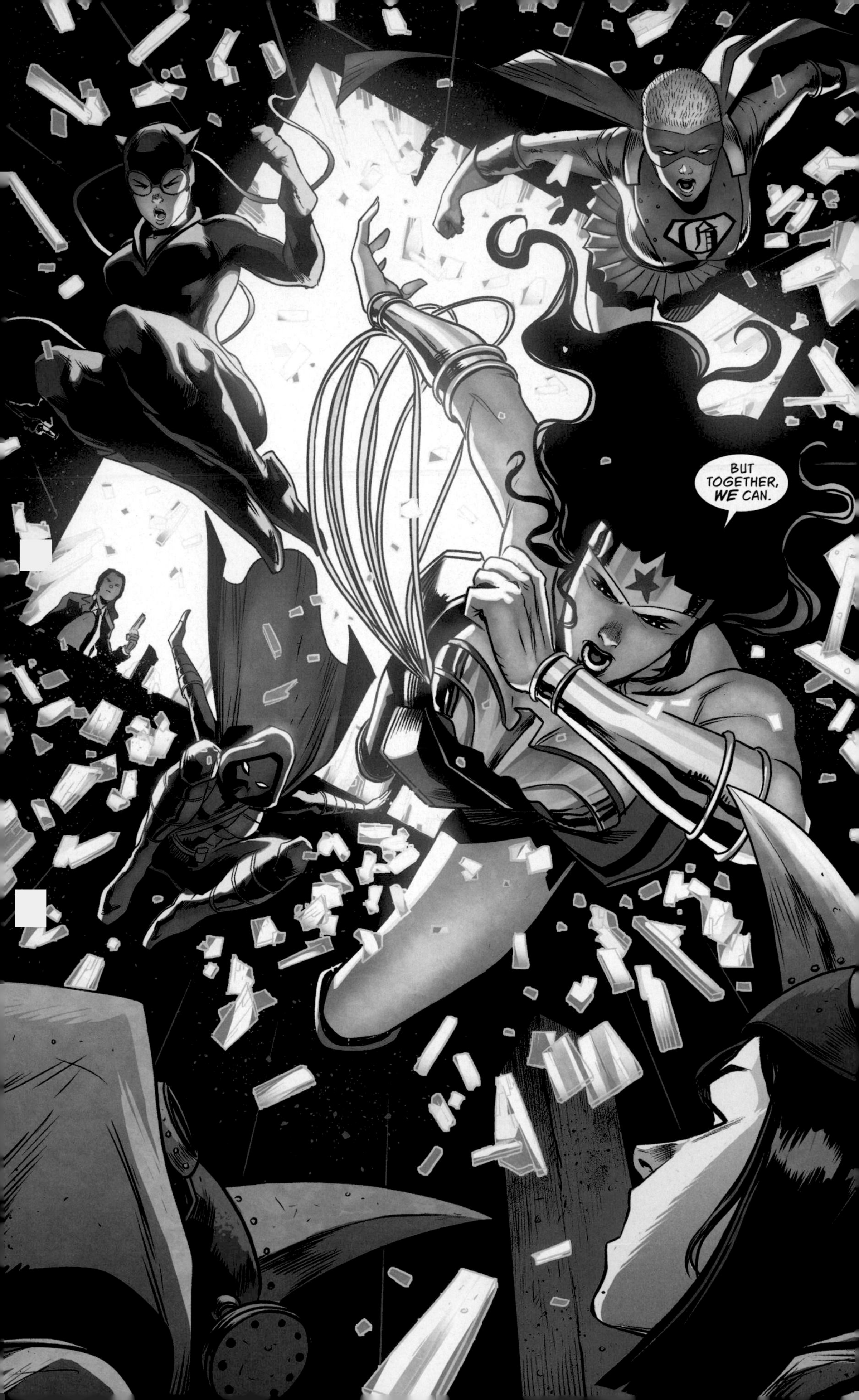
BUT TOGETHER, WE CAN.

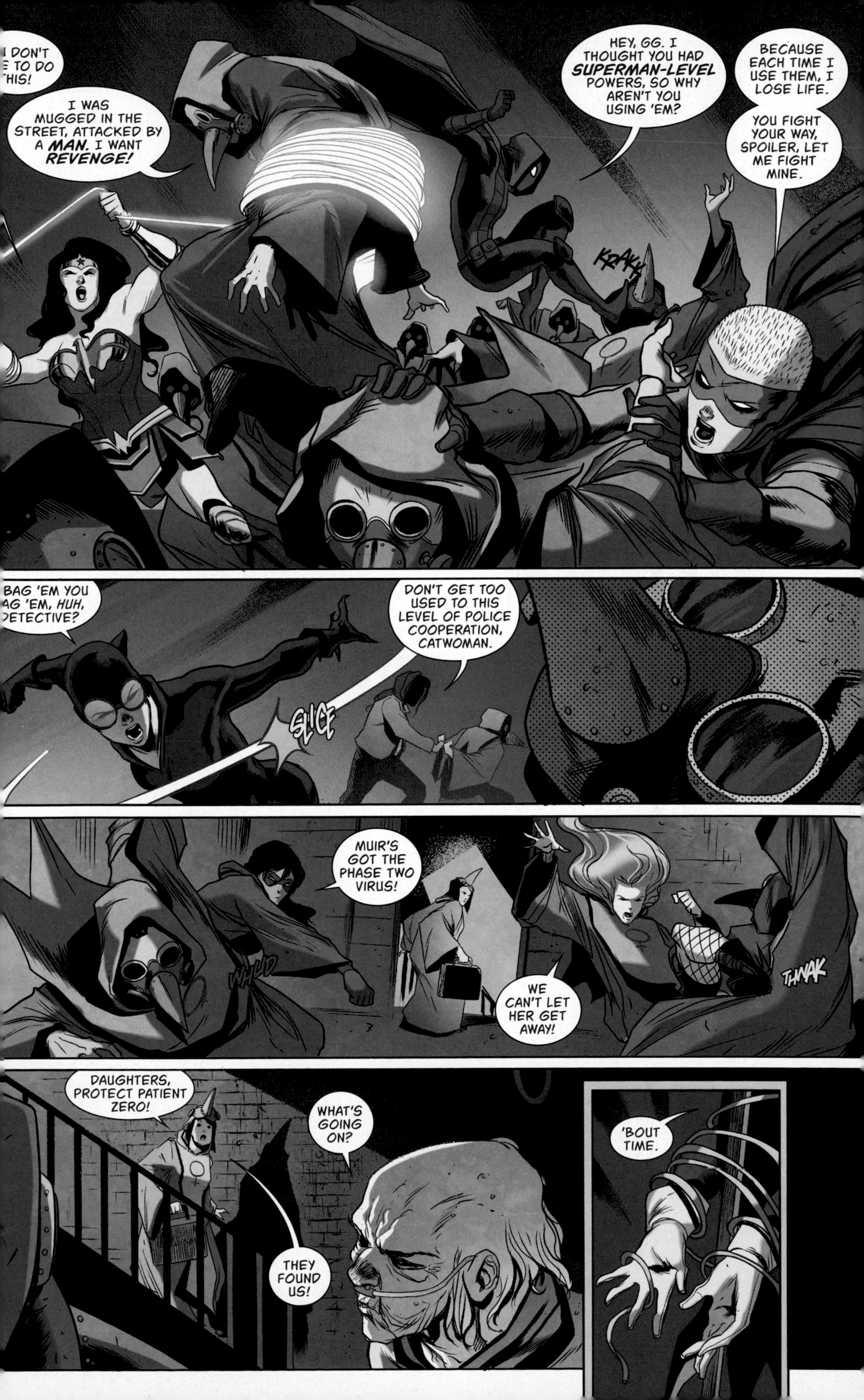

DON'T E TO DO THIS!
I WAS MUGGED IN THE STREET, ATTACKED BY A **MAN**. I WANT **REVENGE!**
HEY, GG. I THOUGHT YOU HAD **SUPERMAN-LEVEL** POWERS, SO WHY AREN'T YOU USING 'EM?
BECAUSE EACH TIME I USE THEM, I LOSE LIFE.
YOU FIGHT YOUR WAY, SPOILER, LET ME FIGHT MINE.
KRAKK
BAG 'EM YOU AG 'EM, *HUH*, ETECTIVE?
DON'T GET TOO USED TO THIS LEVEL OF POLICE COOPERATION, CATWOMAN.
SLICE
MUIR'S GOT THE PHASE TWO VIRUS!
WHUD
WE CAN'T LET HER GET AWAY!
THWAK
DAUGHTERS, PROTECT PATIENT ZERO!
WHAT'S GOING ON?
THEY FOUND US!
'BOUT TIME.

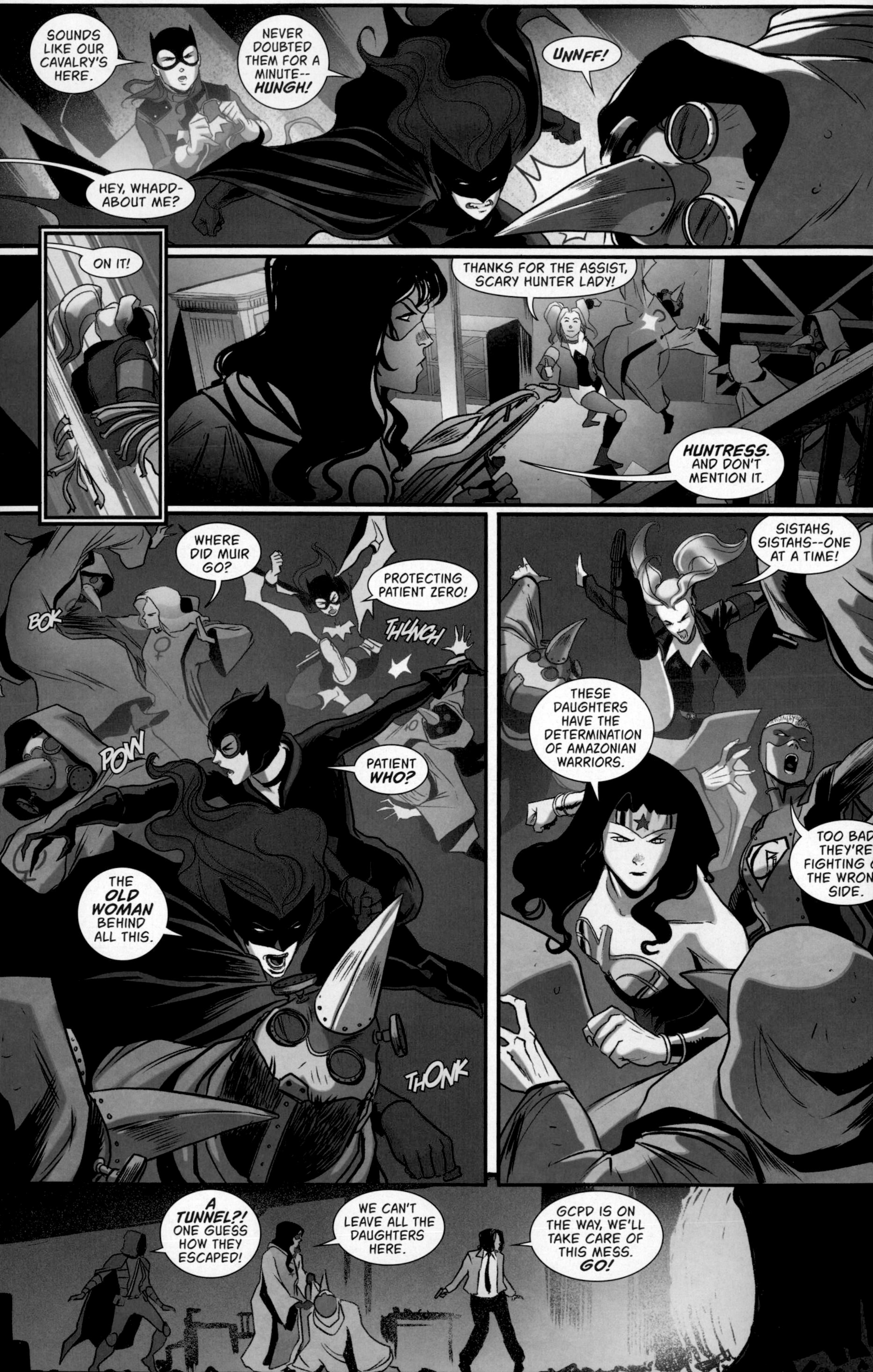

SOUNDS LIKE OUR CAVALRY'S HERE.
NEVER DOUBTED THEM FOR A MINUTE-- **HUNGH!**
UNNFF!
HEY, WHADD-ABOUT ME?
ON IT!
THANKS FOR THE ASSIST, SCARY HUNTER LADY!
HUNTRESS. AND DON'T MENTION IT.
WHERE DID MUIR GO?
PROTECTING PATIENT ZERO!
BOK
THUNCH
POW
PATIENT **WHO?**
THE **OLD WOMAN** BEHIND ALL THIS.
THONK
SISTAHS, SISTAHS--ONE AT A TIME!
THESE DAUGHTERS HAVE THE DETERMINATION OF AMAZONIAN WARRIORS.
TOO BAD THEY'RE FIGHTING O THE WRON SIDE.
A TUNNEL?! ONE GUESS HOW THEY ESCAPED!
WE CAN'T LEAVE ALL THE DAUGHTERS HERE.
GCPD IS ON THE WAY, WE'LL TAKE CARE OF THIS MESS. **GO!**

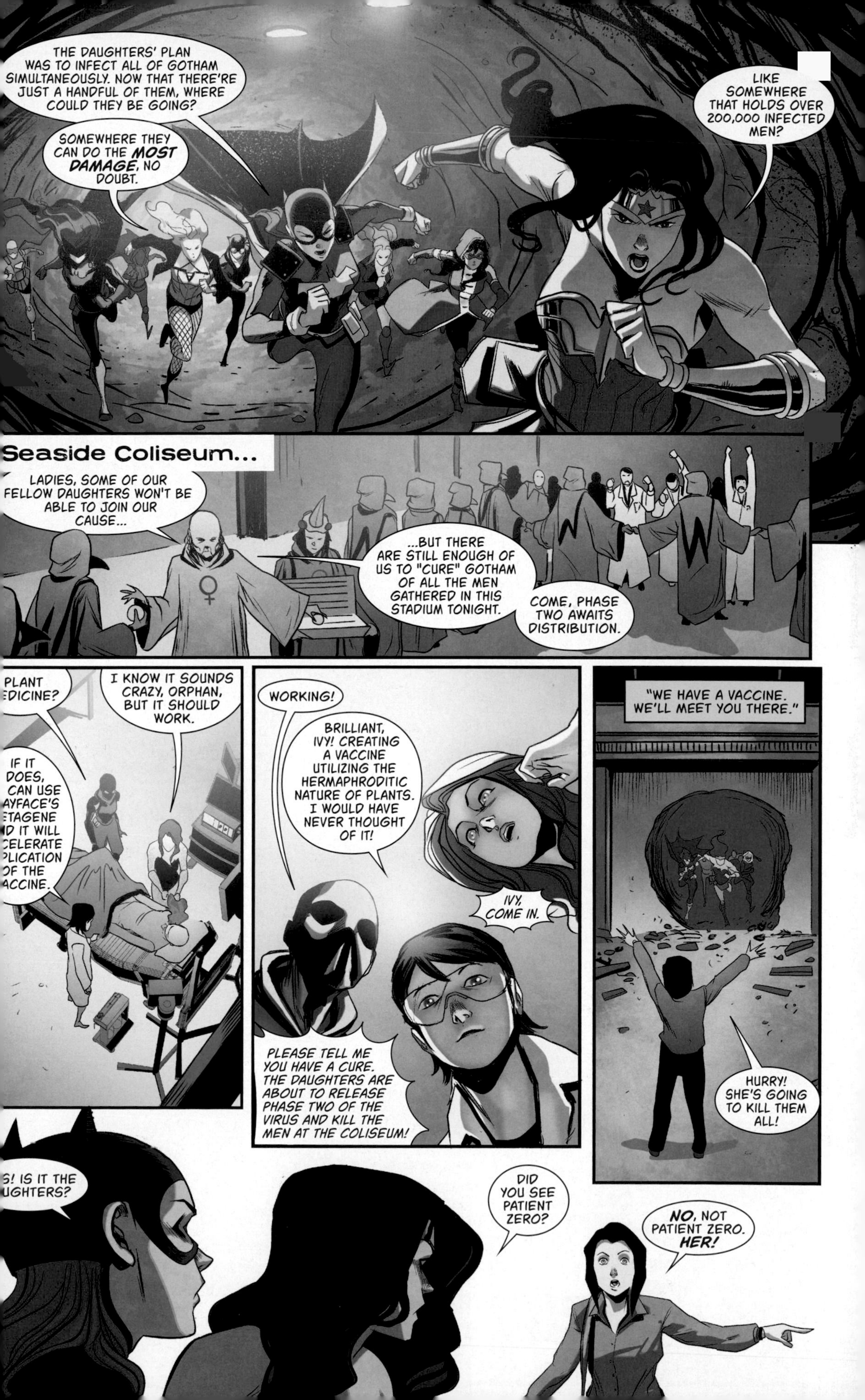

THE DAUGHTERS' PLAN WAS TO INFECT ALL OF GOTHAM SIMULTANEOUSLY. NOW THAT THERE'RE JUST A HANDFUL OF THEM, WHERE COULD THEY BE GOING?
SOMEWHERE THEY CAN DO THE MOST DAMAGE, NO DOUBT.
LIKE SOMEWHERE THAT HOLDS OVER 200,000 INFECTED MEN?
Seaside Coliseum...
LADIES, SOME OF OUR FELLOW DAUGHTERS WON'T BE ABLE TO JOIN OUR CAUSE...
...BUT THERE ARE STILL ENOUGH OF US TO "CURE" GOTHAM OF ALL THE MEN GATHERED IN THIS STADIUM TONIGHT.
COME, PHASE TWO AWAITS DISTRIBUTION.
PLANT EDICINE?
I KNOW IT SOUNDS CRAZY, ORPHAN, BUT IT SHOULD WORK.
IF IT DOES, CAN USE AYFACE'S ETAGENE D IT WILL CELERATE PLICATION OF THE ACCINE.
WORKING!
BRILLIANT, IVY! CREATING A VACCINE UTILIZING THE HERMAPHRODITIC NATURE OF PLANTS. I WOULD HAVE NEVER THOUGHT OF IT!
IVY, COME IN.
PLEASE TELL ME YOU HAVE A CURE. THE DAUGHTERS ARE ABOUT TO RELEASE PHASE TWO OF THE VIRUS AND KILL THE MEN AT THE COLISEUM!
"WE HAVE A VACCINE. WE'LL MEET YOU THERE."
HURRY! SHE'S GOING TO KILL THEM ALL!
S! IS IT THE UGHTERS?
DID YOU SEE PATIENT ZERO?
NO, NOT PATIENT ZERO. HER!

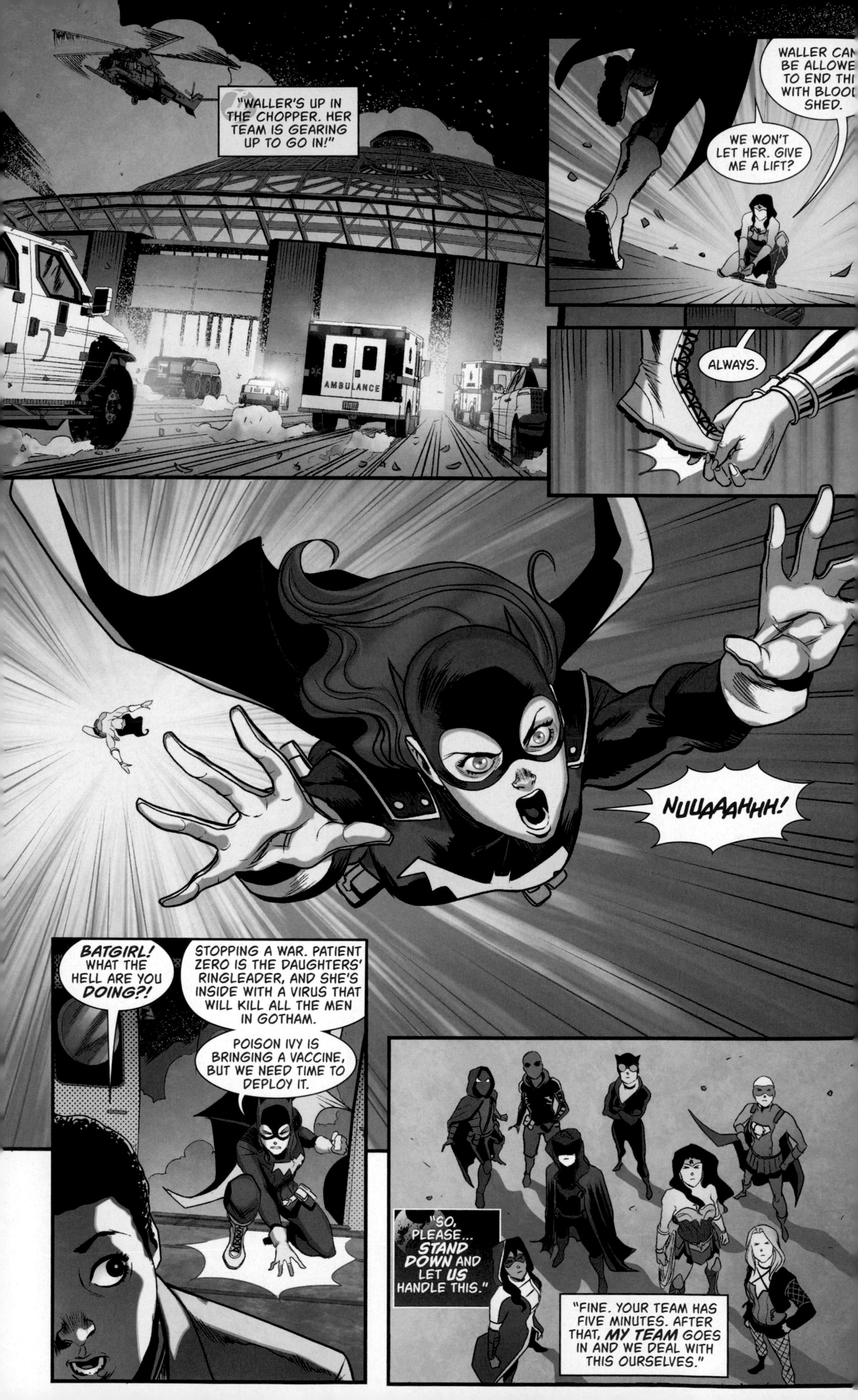
"WALLER'S UP IN THE CHOPPER. HER TEAM IS GEARING UP TO GO IN!"
WALLER CAN BE ALLOWE TO END THI WITH BLOOD SHED.
WE WON'T LET HER. GIVE ME A LIFT?
ALWAYS.
NUUAAAHHH!
BATGIRL! WHAT THE HELL ARE YOU DOING?!
STOPPING A WAR. PATIENT ZERO IS THE DAUGHTERS' RINGLEADER, AND SHE'S INSIDE WITH A VIRUS THAT WILL KILL ALL THE MEN IN GOTHAM.
POISON IVY IS BRINGING A VACCINE, BUT WE NEED TIME TO DEPLOY IT.
"SO, PLEASE... STAND DOWN AND LET US HANDLE THIS."
"FINE. YOUR TEAM HAS FIVE MINUTES. AFTER THAT, MY TEAM GOES IN AND WE DEAL WITH THIS OURSELVES."

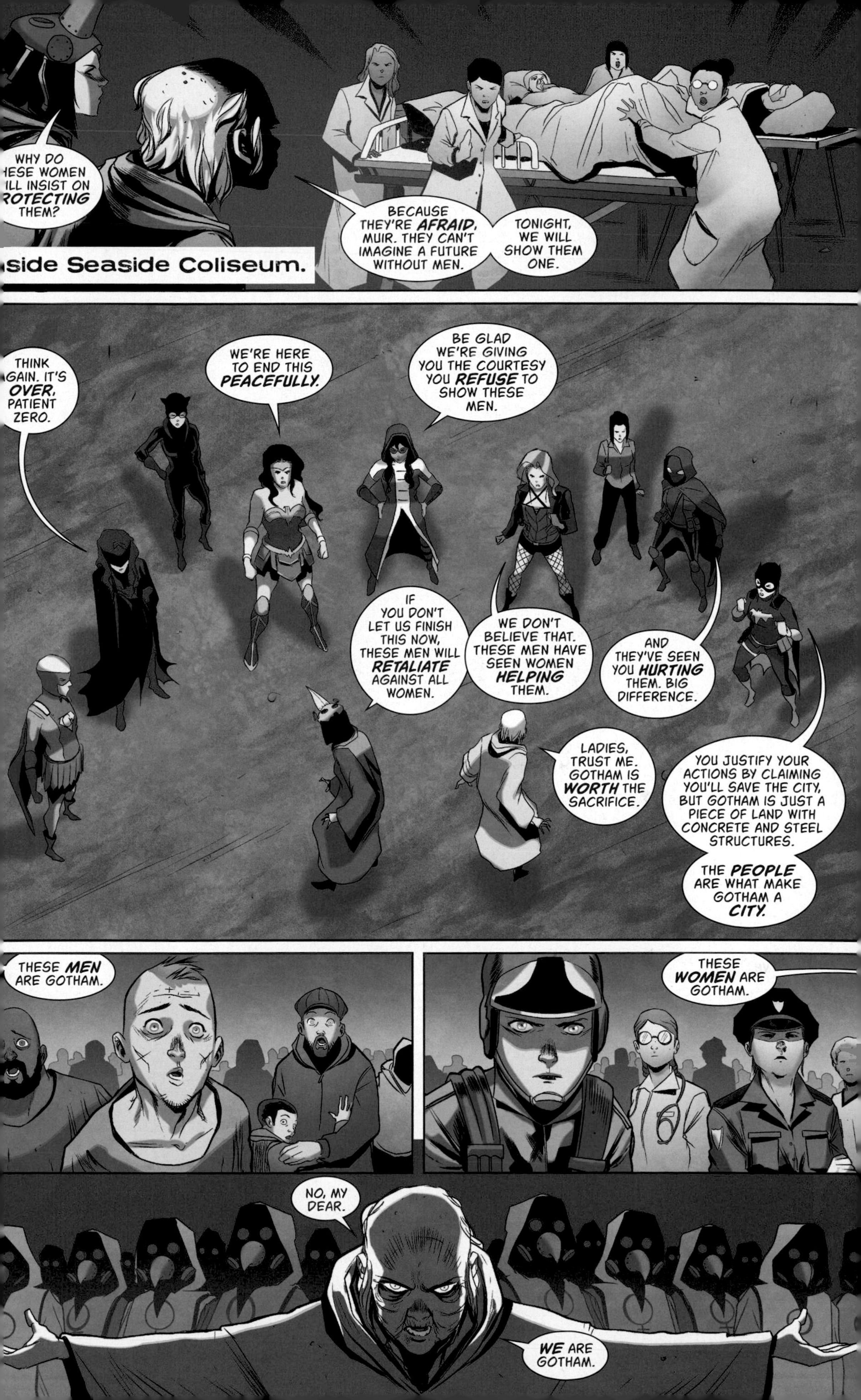

WHY DO
HESE WOMEN
ILL INSIST ON
ROTECTING
THEM?
side Seaside Coliseum.
BECAUSE THEY'RE AFRAID, MUIR. THEY CAN'T IMAGINE A FUTURE WITHOUT MEN.
TONIGHT, WE WILL SHOW THEM ONE.
THINK
GAIN. IT'S
OVER,
PATIENT
ZERO.
WE'RE HERE TO END THIS PEACEFULLY.
BE GLAD WE'RE GIVING YOU THE COURTESY YOU REFUSE TO SHOW THESE MEN.
IF YOU DON'T LET US FINISH THIS NOW, THESE MEN WILL RETALIATE AGAINST ALL WOMEN.
WE DON'T BELIEVE THAT. THESE MEN HAVE SEEN WOMEN HELPING THEM.
AND THEY'VE SEEN YOU HURTING THEM. BIG DIFFERENCE.
LADIES, TRUST ME. GOTHAM IS WORTH THE SACRIFICE.
YOU JUSTIFY YOUR ACTIONS BY CLAIMING YOU'LL SAVE THE CITY, BUT GOTHAM IS JUST A PIECE OF LAND WITH CONCRETE AND STEEL STRUCTURES.
THE PEOPLE ARE WHAT MAKE GOTHAM A CITY.
THESE MEN ARE GOTHAM.
THESE WOMEN ARE GOTHAM.
NO, MY DEAR.
WE ARE GOTHAM.

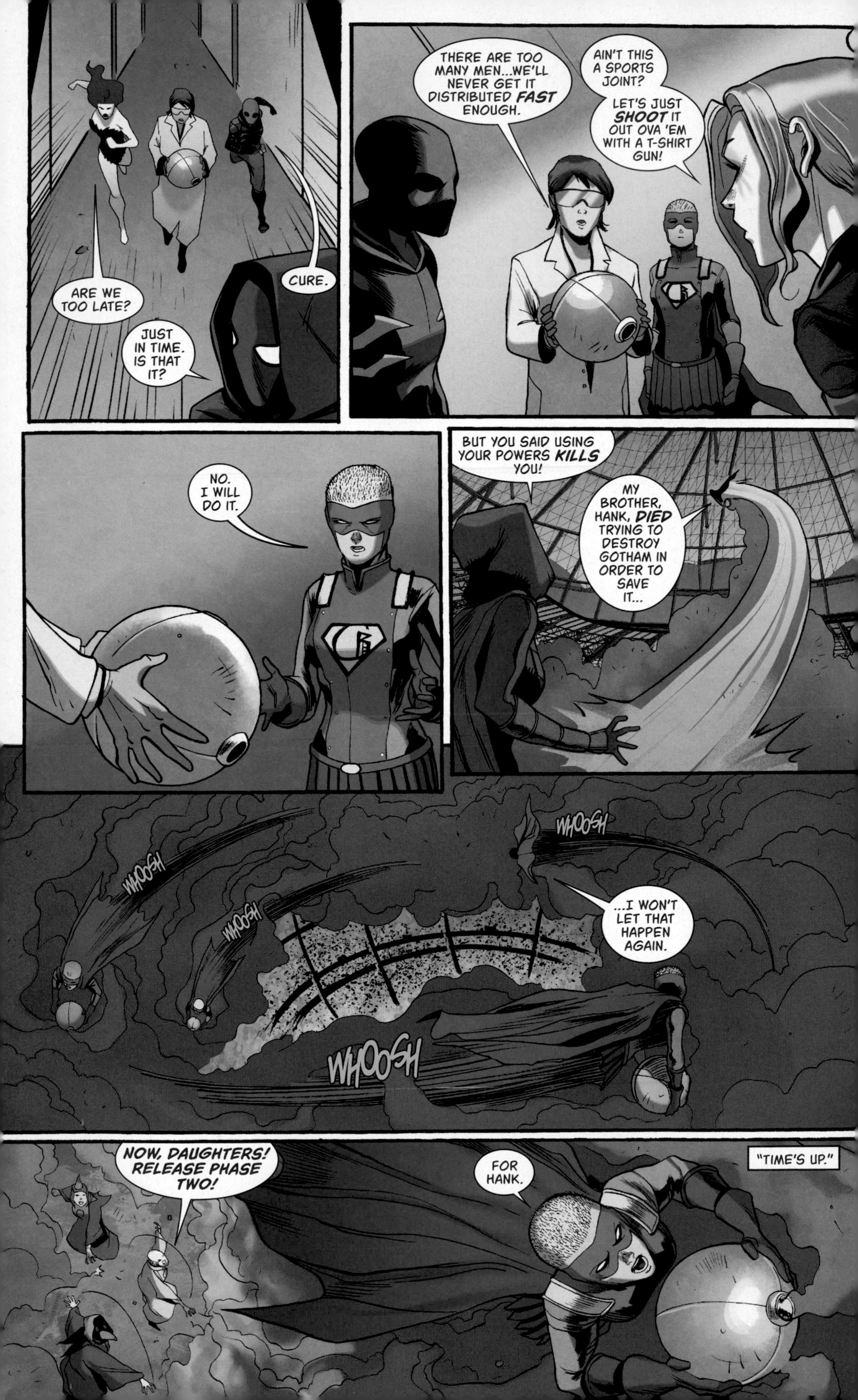

ARE WE TOO LATE?
JUST IN TIME. IS THAT IT?
CURE.
THERE ARE TOO MANY MEN...WE'LL NEVER GET IT DISTRIBUTED **FAST** ENOUGH.
AIN'T THIS A SPORTS JOINT?
LET'S JUST **SHOOT** IT OUT OVA 'EM WITH A T-SHIRT GUN!
NO. I WILL DO IT.
BUT YOU SAID USING YOUR POWERS **KILLS** YOU!
MY BROTHER, HANK, **DIED** TRYING TO DESTROY GOTHAM IN ORDER TO SAVE IT...
WHOOSH
WHOOSH
WHOOSH
...I WON'T LET THAT HAPPEN AGAIN.
WHOOSH
NOW, DAUGHTERS! RELEASE PHASE TWO!
FOR HANK.
"TIME'S UP."

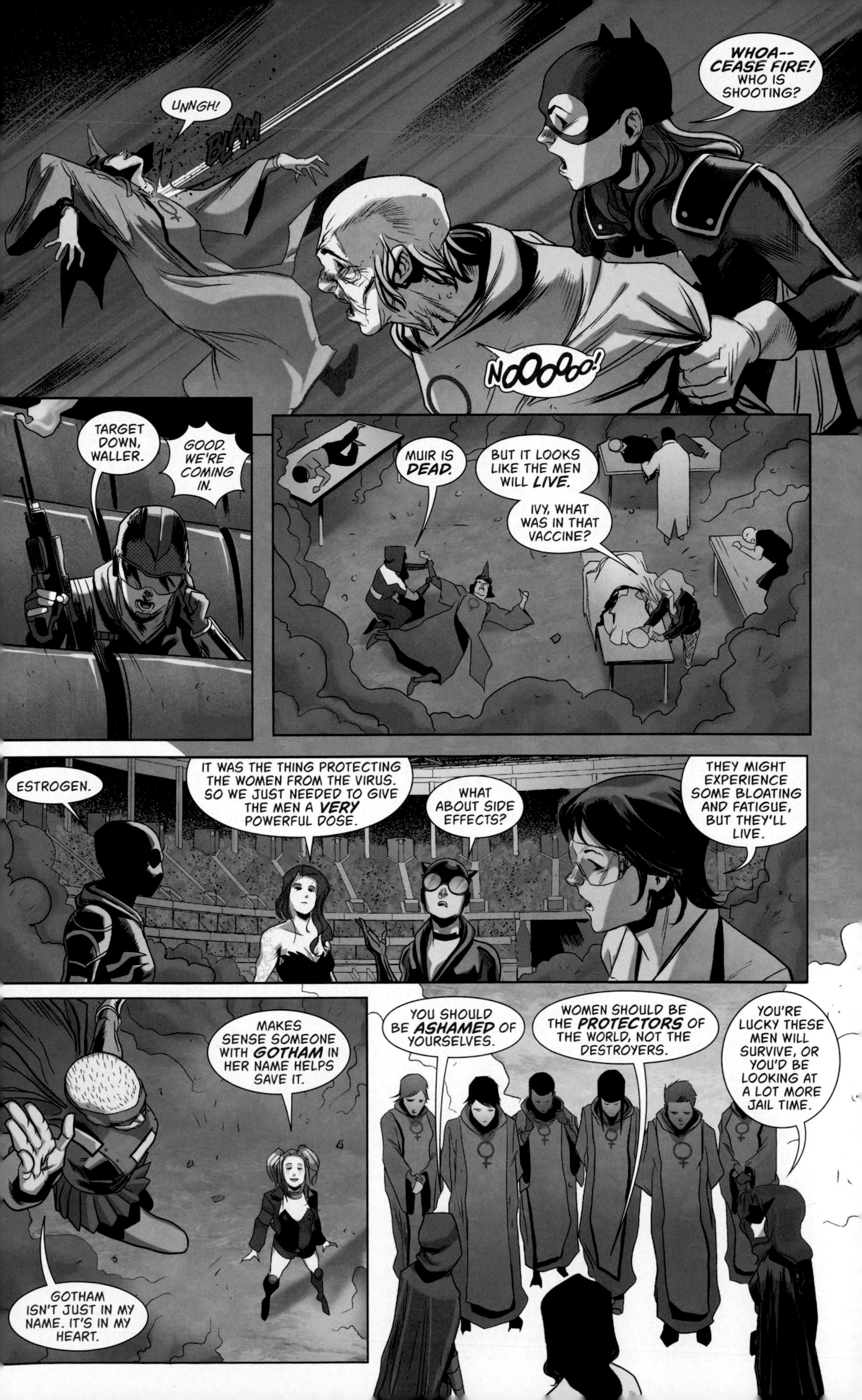
UNNGH!
BLAM
WHOA-- CEASE FIRE! WHO IS SHOOTING?
NOOOOOO!
TARGET DOWN, WALLER.
GOOD. WE'RE COMING IN.
MUIR IS DEAD.
BUT IT LOOKS LIKE THE MEN WILL LIVE.
IVY, WHAT WAS IN THAT VACCINE?
ESTROGEN.
IT WAS THE THING PROTECTING THE WOMEN FROM THE VIRUS. SO WE JUST NEEDED TO GIVE THE MEN A VERY POWERFUL DOSE.
WHAT ABOUT SIDE EFFECTS?
THEY MIGHT EXPERIENCE SOME BLOATING AND FATIGUE, BUT THEY'LL LIVE.
MAKES SENSE SOMEONE WITH GOTHAM IN HER NAME HELPS SAVE IT.
GOTHAM ISN'T JUST IN MY NAME. IT'S IN MY HEART.
YOU SHOULD BE ASHAMED OF YOURSELVES.
WOMEN SHOULD BE THE PROTECTORS OF THE WORLD, NOT THE DESTROYERS.
YOU'RE LUCKY THESE MEN WILL SURVIVE, OR YOU'D BE LOOKING AT A LOT MORE JAIL TIME.

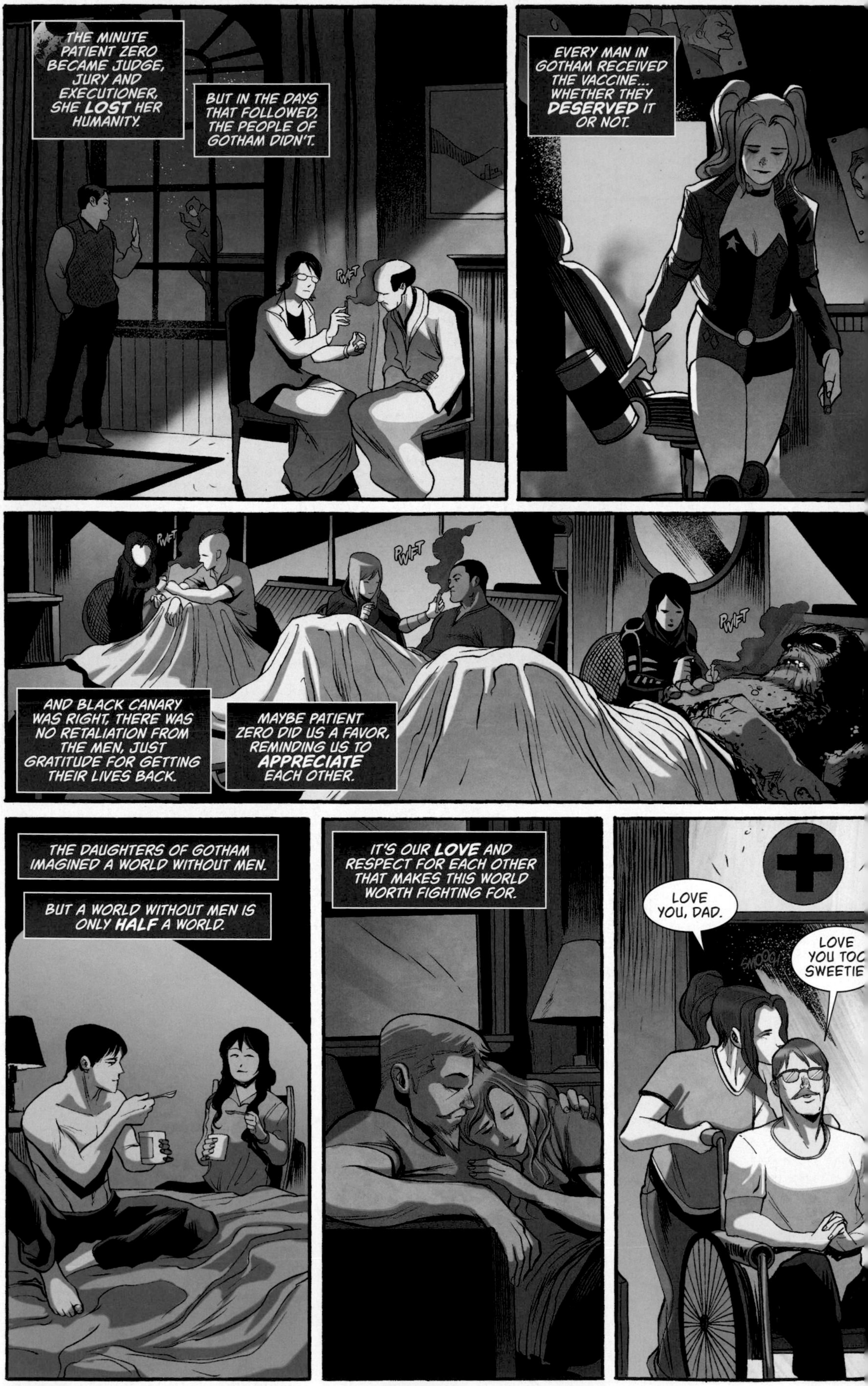

THE MINUTE PATIENT ZERO BECAME JUDGE, JURY AND EXECUTIONER, SHE LOST HER HUMANITY.
BUT IN THE DAYS THAT FOLLOWED, THE PEOPLE OF GOTHAM DIDN'T.
PWFT
EVERY MAN IN GOTHAM RECEIVED THE VACCINE... WHETHER THEY DESERVED IT OR NOT.
PWFT
PWFT
PWFT
AND BLACK CANARY WAS RIGHT, THERE WAS NO RETALIATION FROM THE MEN, JUST GRATITUDE FOR GETTING THEIR LIVES BACK.
MAYBE PATIENT ZERO DID US A FAVOR, REMINDING US TO APPRECIATE EACH OTHER.
THE DAUGHTERS OF GOTHAM IMAGINED A WORLD WITHOUT MEN.
BUT A WORLD WITHOUT MEN IS ONLY HALF A WORLD.
IT'S OUR LOVE AND RESPECT FOR EACH OTHER THAT MAKES THIS WORLD WORTH FIGHTING FOR.
LOVE YOU, DAD.
LOVE YOU TOO SWEETIE

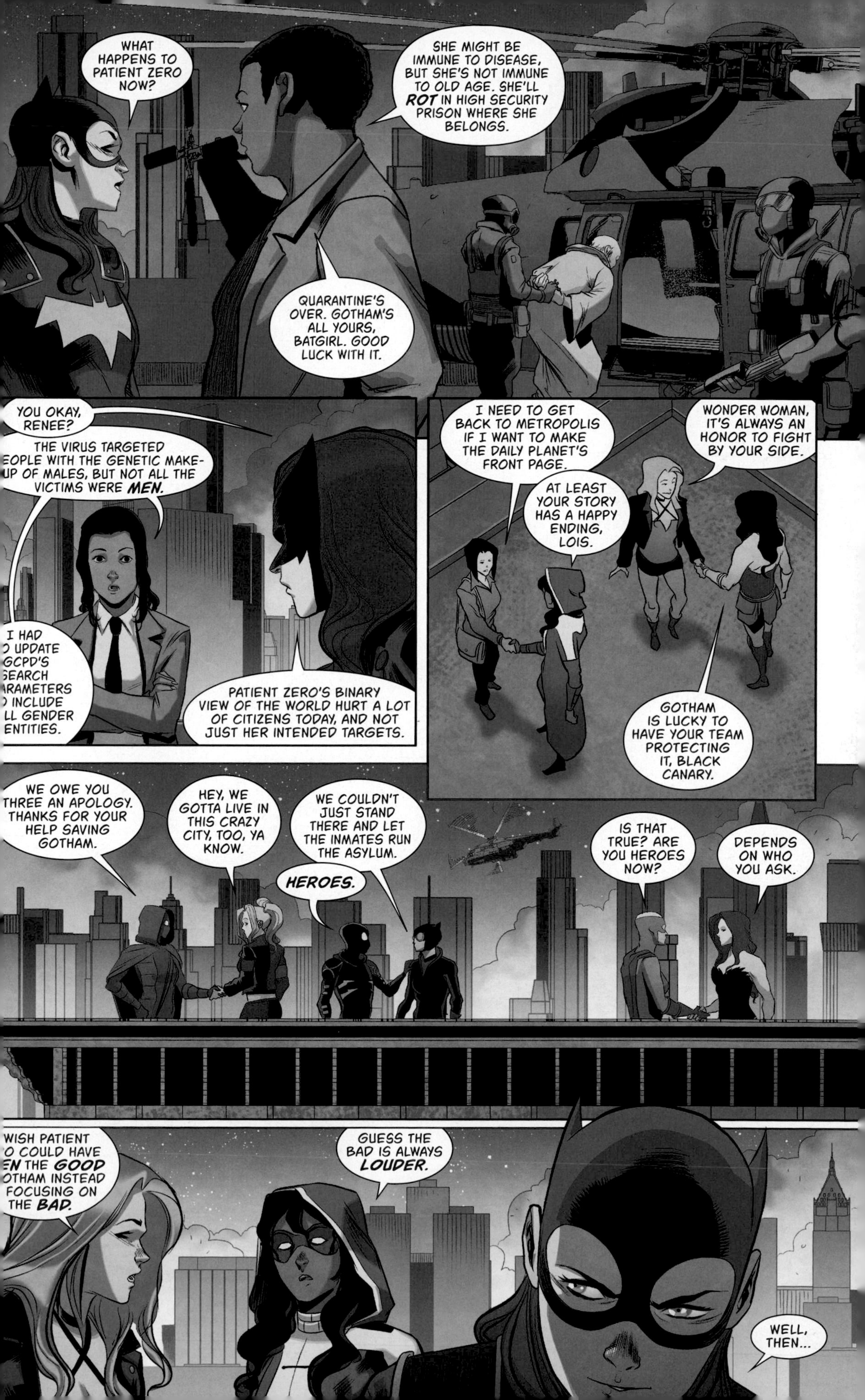
WHAT HAPPENS TO PATIENT ZERO NOW?
SHE MIGHT BE IMMUNE TO DISEASE, BUT SHE'S NOT IMMUNE TO OLD AGE. SHE'LL ROT IN HIGH SECURITY PRISON WHERE SHE BELONGS.
QUARANTINE'S OVER. GOTHAM'S ALL YOURS, BATGIRL. GOOD LUCK WITH IT.
YOU OKAY, RENEE?
THE VIRUS TARGETED EOPLE WITH THE GENETIC MAKE-UP OF MALES, BUT NOT ALL THE VICTIMS WERE MEN.
I HAD O UPDATE GCPD'S SEARCH ARAMETERS O INCLUDE LL GENDER ENTITIES.
PATIENT ZERO'S BINARY VIEW OF THE WORLD HURT A LOT OF CITIZENS TODAY, AND NOT JUST HER INTENDED TARGETS.
I NEED TO GET BACK TO METROPOLIS IF I WANT TO MAKE THE DAILY PLANET'S FRONT PAGE.
AT LEAST YOUR STORY HAS A HAPPY ENDING, LOIS.
WONDER WOMAN, IT'S ALWAYS AN HONOR TO FIGHT BY YOUR SIDE.
GOTHAM IS LUCKY TO HAVE YOUR TEAM PROTECTING IT, BLACK CANARY.
WE OWE YOU THREE AN APOLOGY. THANKS FOR YOUR HELP SAVING GOTHAM.
HEY, WE GOTTA LIVE IN THIS CRAZY CITY, TOO, YA KNOW.
WE COULDN'T JUST STAND THERE AND LET THE INMATES RUN THE ASYLUM.
HEROES.
IS THAT TRUE? ARE YOU HEROES NOW?
DEPENDS ON WHO YOU ASK.
WISH PATIENT O COULD HAVE EN THE GOOD OTHAM INSTEAD FOCUSING ON THE BAD.
GUESS THE BAD IS ALWAYS LOUDER.
WELL, THEN...

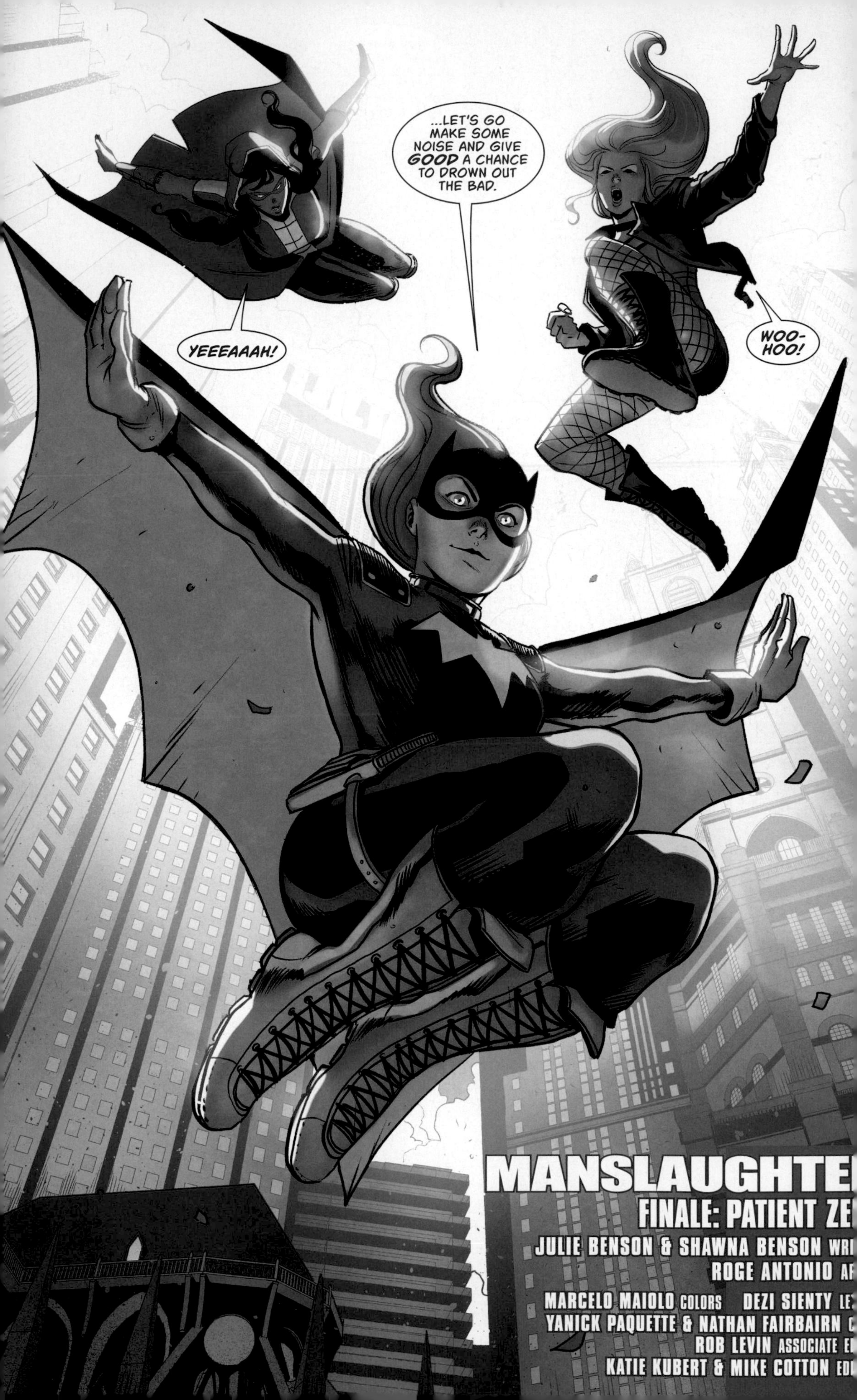
...LET'S GO MAKE SOME NOISE AND GIVE GOOD A CHANCE TO DROWN OUT THE BAD.
YEEEAAAH!
WOO-HOO!
FINALE:
JULIE BENSON & SHAWNA BENSON
ROGE ANTONIO
MARCELO MAIOLO COLORS DEZI SIENTY
YANICK PAQUETTE & NATHAN FAIRBAIRN
ROB LEVIN ASSOCIATE
KATIE KUBERT & MIKE COTTON

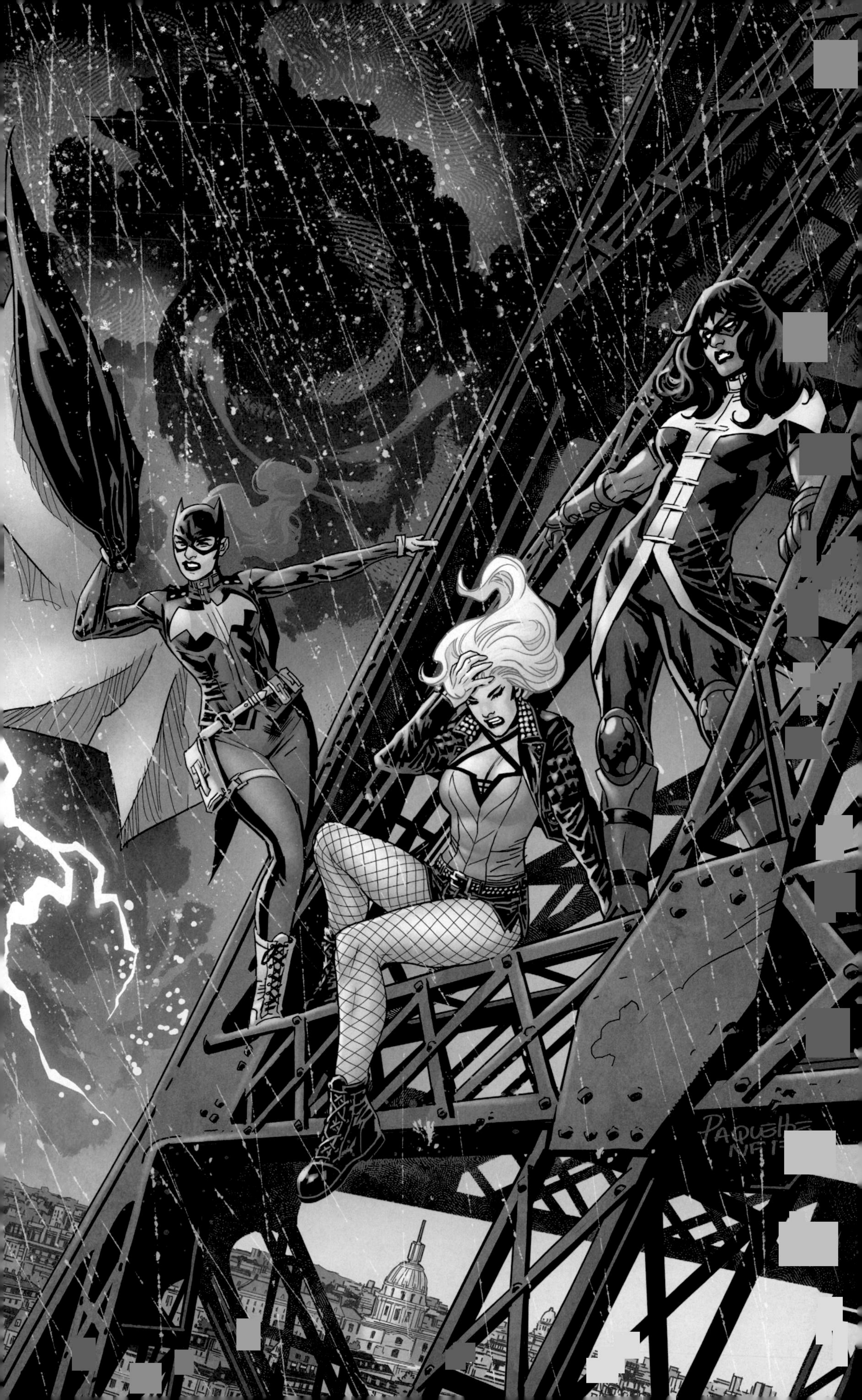

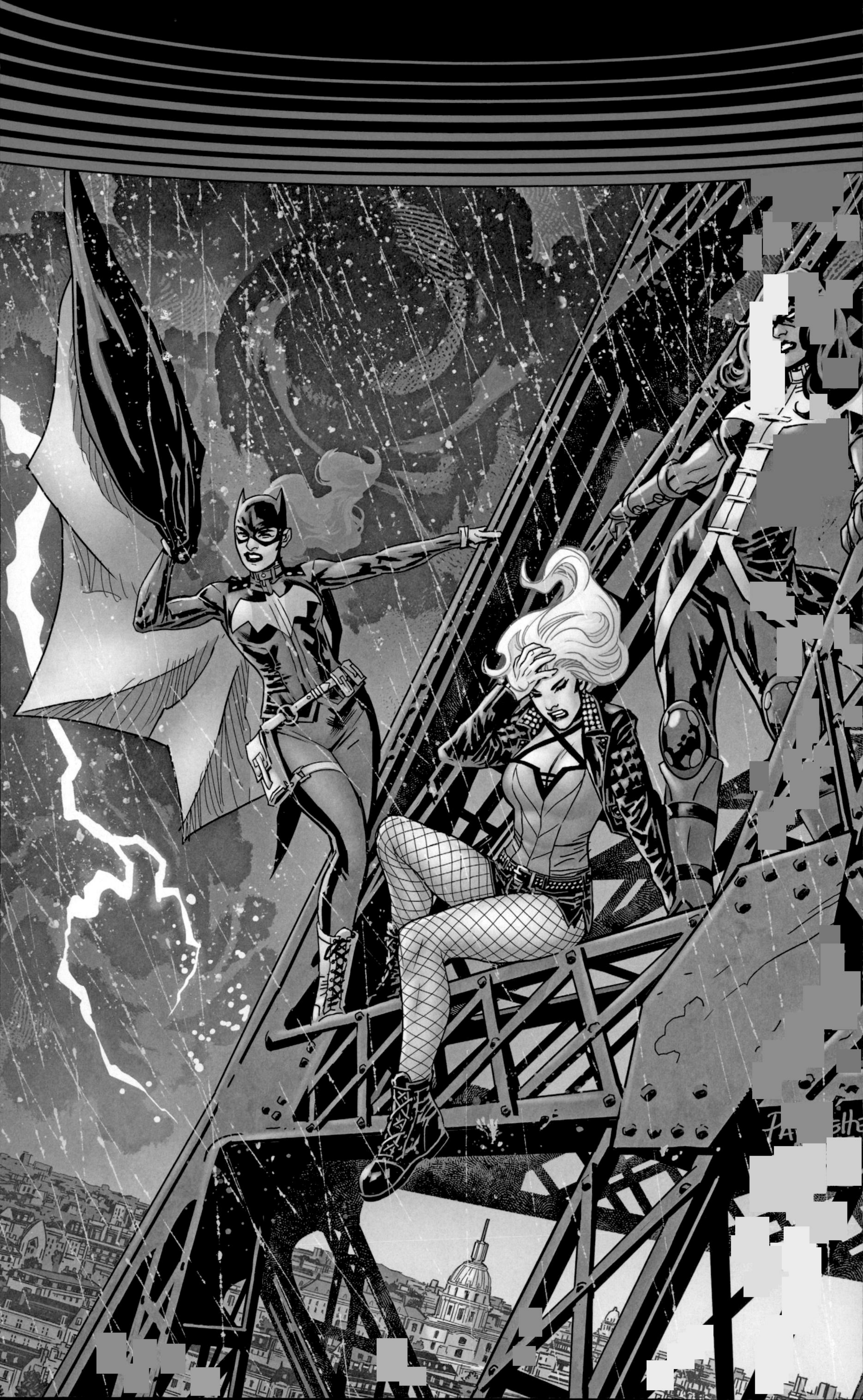

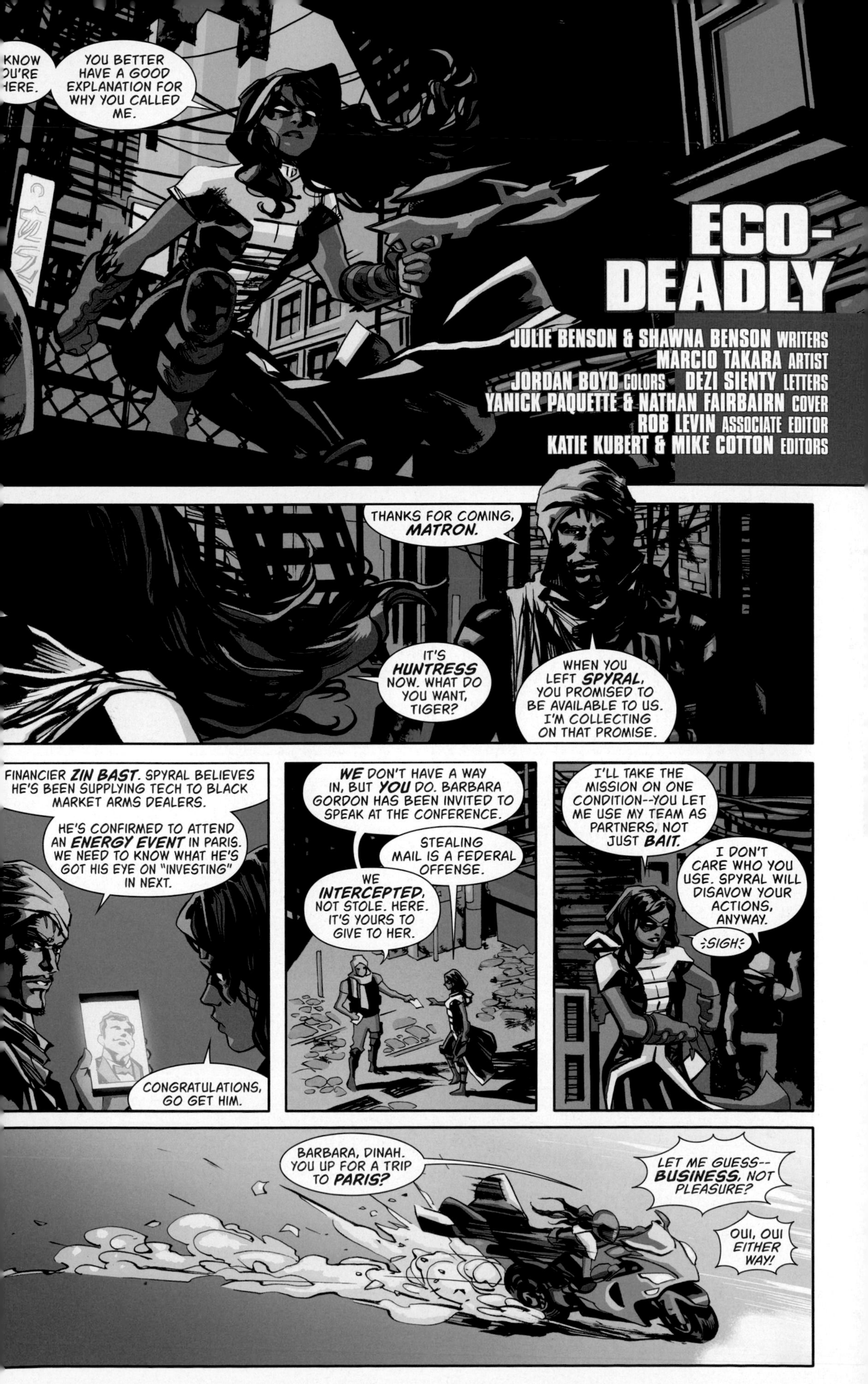
KNOW
OU'RE
HERE.
YOU BETTER HAVE A GOOD EXPLANATION FOR WHY YOU CALLED ME.
ECO-DEADLY
JULIE BENSON & SHAWNA BENSON WRITERS
MARCIO TAKARA ARTIST
JORDAN BOYD COLORS DEZI SIENTY LETTERS
YANICK PAQUETTE & NATHAN FAIRBAIRN COVER
ROB LEVIN ASSOCIATE EDITOR
KATIE KUBERT & MIKE COTTON EDITORS
THANKS FOR COMING, MATRON.
IT'S HUNTRESS NOW. WHAT DO YOU WANT, TIGER?
WHEN YOU LEFT SPYRAL, YOU PROMISED TO BE AVAILABLE TO US. I'M COLLECTING ON THAT PROMISE.
FINANCIER ZIN BAST. SPYRAL BELIEVES HE'S BEEN SUPPLYING TECH TO BLACK MARKET ARMS DEALERS.
HE'S CONFIRMED TO ATTEND AN ENERGY EVENT IN PARIS. WE NEED TO KNOW WHAT HE'S GOT HIS EYE ON "INVESTING" IN NEXT.
CONGRATULATIONS, GO GET HIM.
WE DON'T HAVE A WAY IN, BUT YOU DO. BARBARA GORDON HAS BEEN INVITED TO SPEAK AT THE CONFERENCE.
STEALING MAIL IS A FEDERAL OFFENSE.
WE INTERCEPTED, NOT STOLE. HERE. IT'S YOURS TO GIVE TO HER.
I'LL TAKE THE MISSION ON ONE CONDITION--YOU LET ME USE MY TEAM AS PARTNERS, NOT JUST BAIT.
I DON'T CARE WHO YOU USE. SPYRAL WILL DISAVOW YOUR ACTIONS, ANYWAY.
SIGH
BARBARA, DINAH. YOU UP FOR A TRIP TO PARIS?
LET ME GUESS--BUSINESS, NOT PLEASURE?
OUI, OUI EITHER WAY!

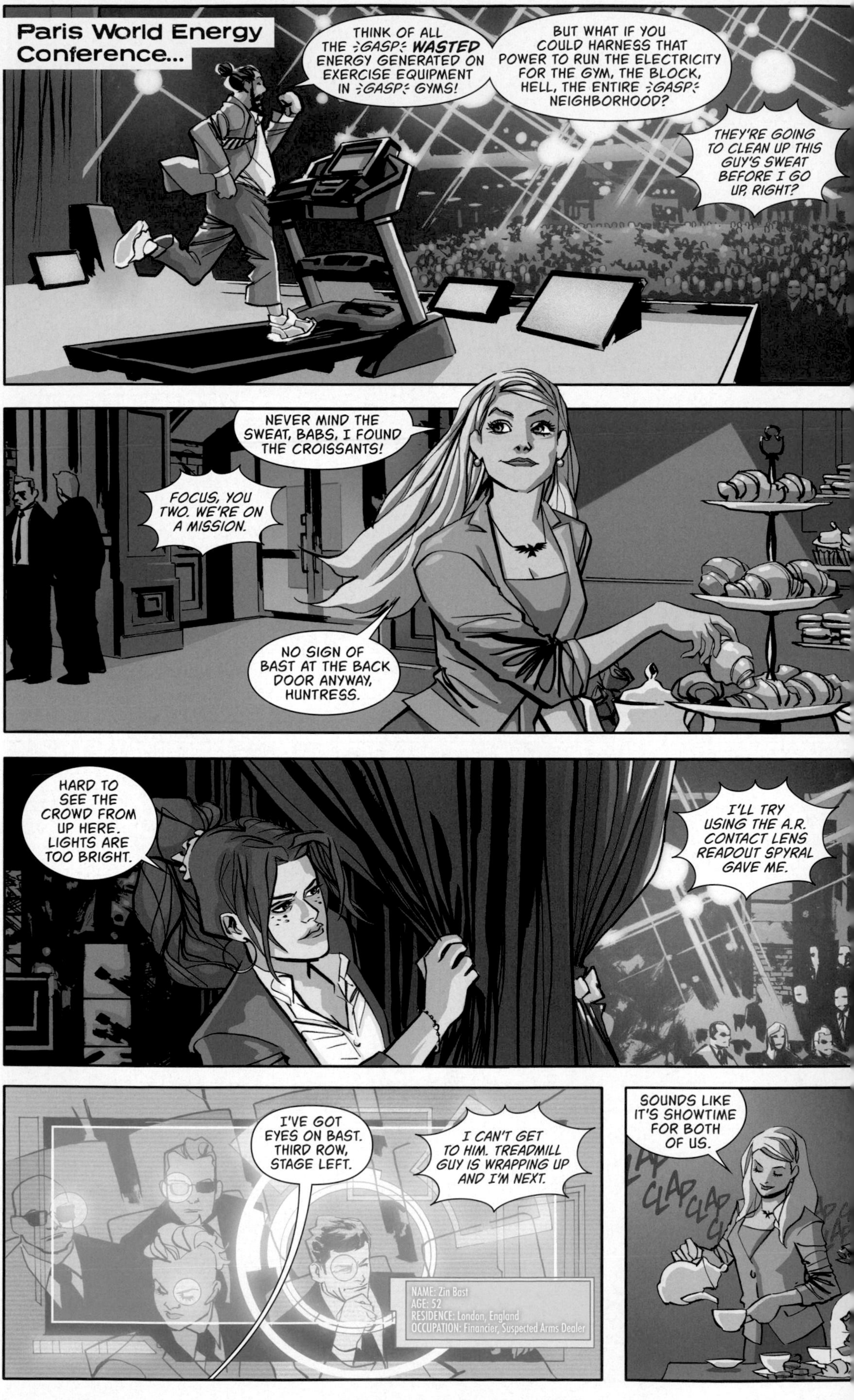
Paris World Energy Conference...
THINK OF ALL THE *GASP* WASTED ENERGY GENERATED ON EXERCISE EQUIPMENT IN *GASP* GYMS!
BUT WHAT IF YOU COULD HARNESS THAT POWER TO RUN THE ELECTRICITY FOR THE GYM, THE BLOCK, HELL, THE ENTIRE *GASP* NEIGHBORHOOD?
THEY'RE GOING TO CLEAN UP THIS GUY'S SWEAT BEFORE I GO UP, RIGHT?
NEVER MIND THE SWEAT, BABS, I FOUND THE CROISSANTS!
FOCUS, YOU TWO. WE'RE ON A MISSION.
NO SIGN OF BAST AT THE BACK DOOR ANYWAY, HUNTRESS.
HARD TO SEE THE CROWD FROM UP HERE. LIGHTS ARE TOO BRIGHT.
I'LL TRY USING THE A.R. CONTACT LENS READOUT SPYRAL GAVE ME.
I'VE GOT EYES ON BAST. THIRD ROW, STAGE LEFT.
I CAN'T GET TO HIM. TREADMILL GUY IS WRAPPING UP AND I'M NEXT.
NAME: Zin Bast
AGE: 52
RESIDENCE: London, England
OCCUPATION: Financier, Suspected Arms Dealer
SOUNDS LIKE IT'S SHOWTIME FOR BOTH OF US.
CLAP CLAP CLAP

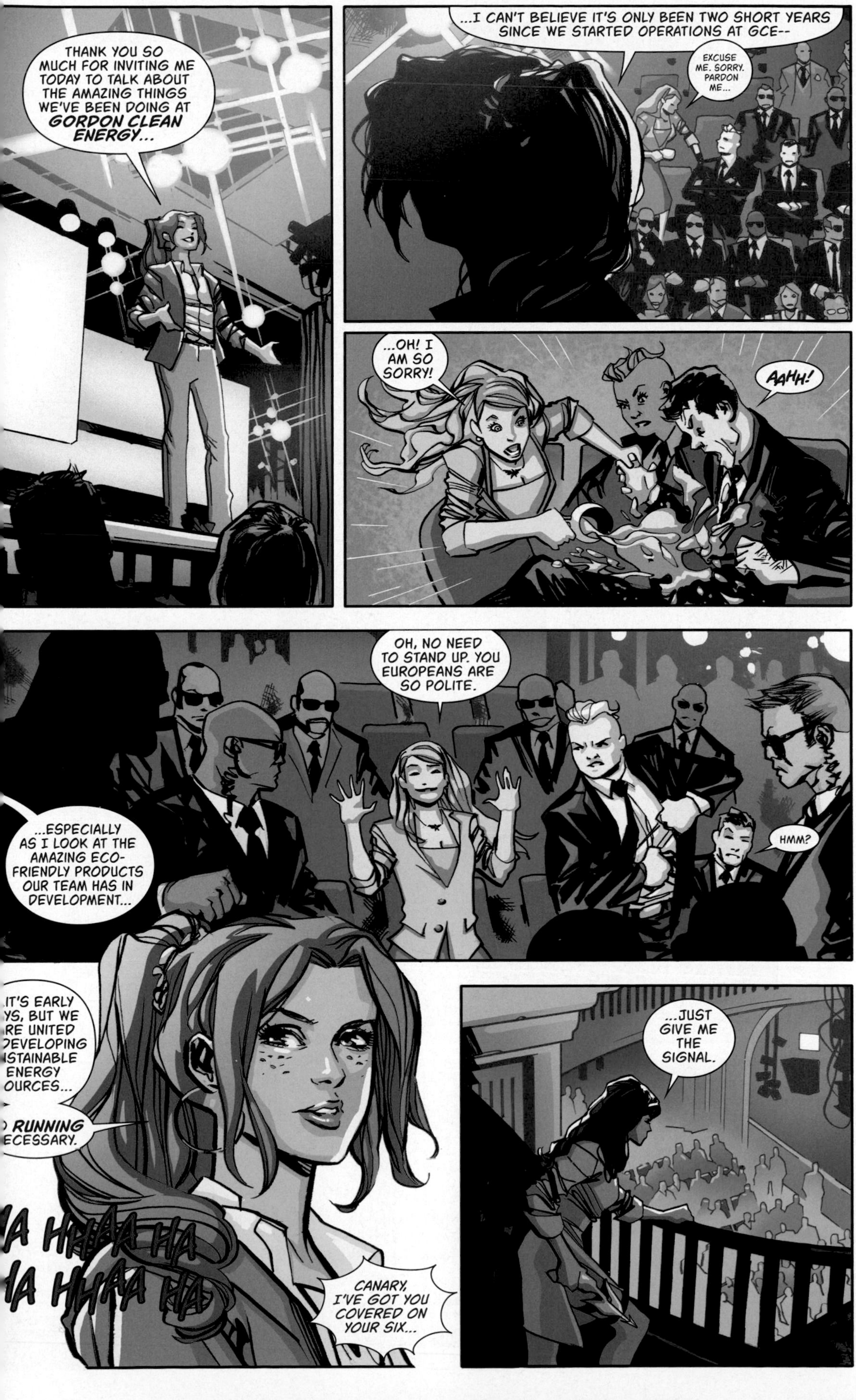
THANK YOU SO MUCH FOR INVITING ME TODAY TO TALK ABOUT THE AMAZING THINGS WE'VE BEEN DOING AT GORDON CLEAN ENERGY...
...I CAN'T BELIEVE IT'S ONLY BEEN TWO SHORT YEARS SINCE WE STARTED OPERATIONS AT GCE--
EXCUSE ME. SORRY. PARDON ME...
...OH! I AM SO SORRY!
AAHH!
OH, NO NEED TO STAND UP. YOU EUROPEANS ARE SO POLITE.
...ESPECIALLY AS I LOOK AT THE AMAZING ECO-FRIENDLY PRODUCTS OUR TEAM HAS IN DEVELOPMENT...
HMM?
IT'S EARLY
YS, BUT WE
RE UNITED
DEVELOPING
ISTAINABLE
ENERGY
OURCES...
RUNNING
ECESSARY.
HA HHAA HA
HA HHAA HA
CANARY, I'VE GOT YOU COVERED ON YOUR SIX...
...JUST GIVE ME THE SIGNAL.

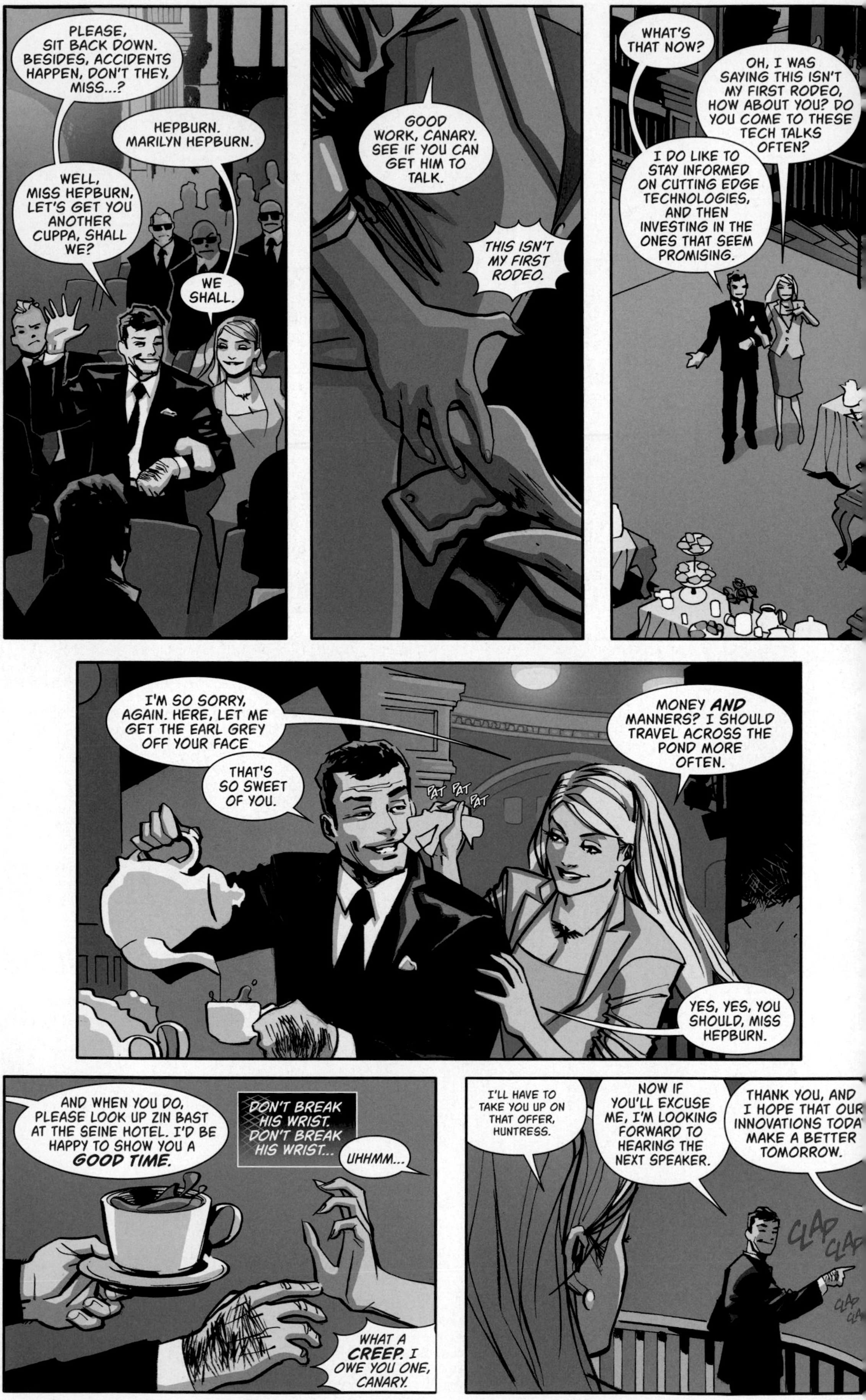
PLEASE, SIT BACK DOWN. BESIDES, ACCIDENTS HAPPEN, DON'T THEY, MISS...?
HEPBURN. MARILYN HEPBURN.
WELL, MISS HEPBURN, LET'S GET YOU ANOTHER CUPPA, SHALL WE?
WE SHALL.
GOOD WORK, CANARY. SEE IF YOU CAN GET HIM TO TALK.
THIS ISN'T MY FIRST RODEO.
WHAT'S THAT NOW?
OH, I WAS SAYING THIS ISN'T MY FIRST RODEO, HOW ABOUT YOU? DO YOU COME TO THESE TECH TALKS OFTEN?
I DO LIKE TO STAY INFORMED ON CUTTING EDGE TECHNOLOGIES, AND THEN INVESTING IN THE ONES THAT SEEM PROMISING.
I'M SO SORRY, AGAIN. HERE, LET ME GET THE EARL GREY OFF YOUR FACE
THAT'S SO SWEET OF YOU.
PAT PAT PAT
MONEY AND MANNERS? I SHOULD TRAVEL ACROSS THE POND MORE OFTEN.
YES, YES, YOU SHOULD, MISS HEPBURN.
AND WHEN YOU DO, PLEASE LOOK UP ZIN BAST AT THE SEINE HOTEL. I'D BE HAPPY TO SHOW YOU A GOOD TIME.
DON'T BREAK HIS WRIST. DON'T BREAK HIS WRIST...
UHHMM...
WHAT A CREEP. I OWE YOU ONE, CANARY.
I'LL HAVE TO TAKE YOU UP ON THAT OFFER, HUNTRESS.
NOW IF YOU'LL EXCUSE ME, I'M LOOKING FORWARD TO HEARING THE NEXT SPEAKER.
THANK YOU, AND I HOPE THAT OUR INNOVATIONS TODA MAKE A BETTER TOMORROW.
CLAP CLAP
CLAP CLA

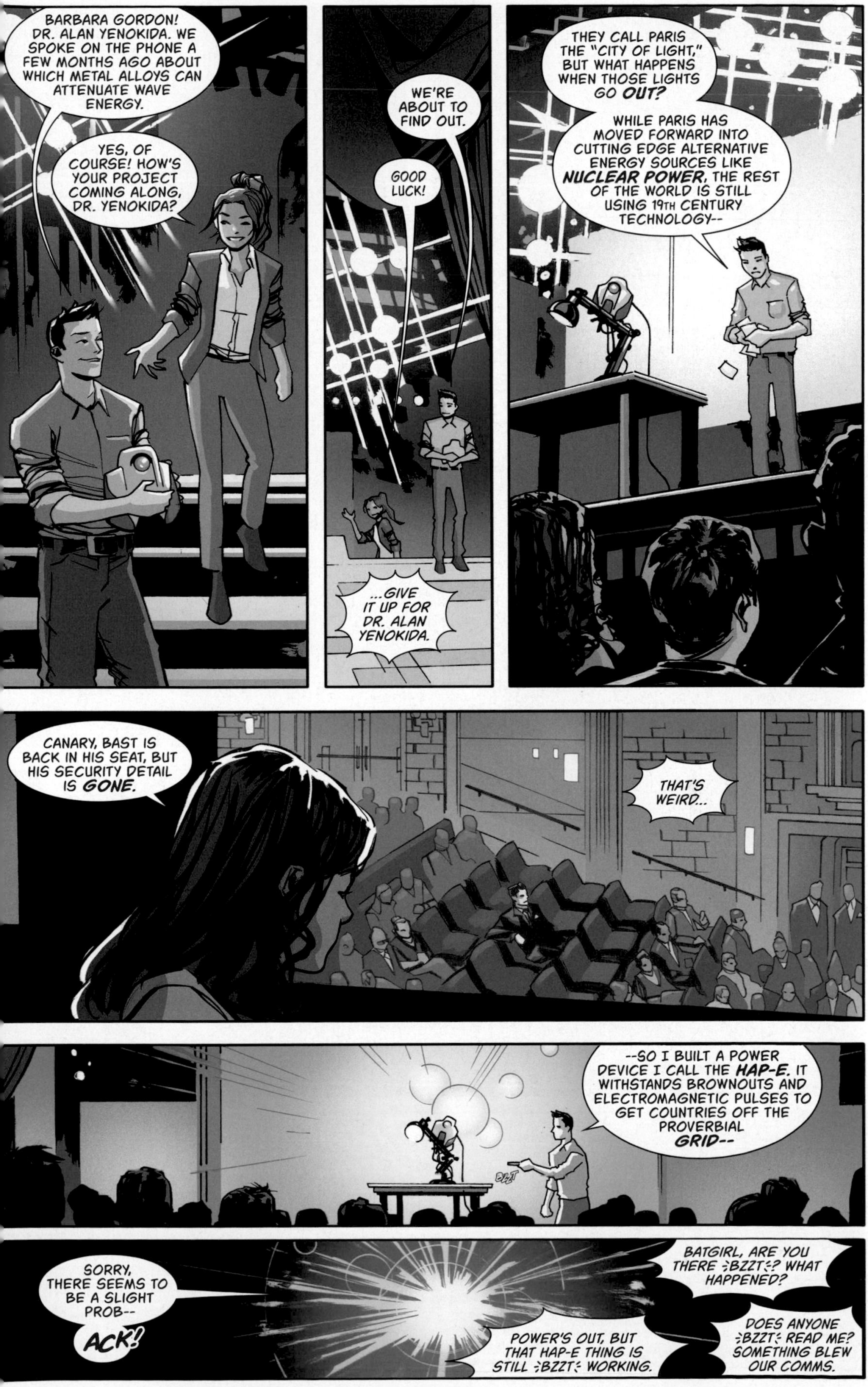
BARBARA GORDON! DR. ALAN YENOKIDA. WE SPOKE ON THE PHONE A FEW MONTHS AGO ABOUT WHICH METAL ALLOYS CAN ATTENUATE WAVE ENERGY.
YES, OF COURSE! HOW'S YOUR PROJECT COMING ALONG, DR. YENOKIDA?
WE'RE ABOUT TO FIND OUT.
GOOD LUCK!
...GIVE IT UP FOR DR. ALAN YENOKIDA.
THEY CALL PARIS THE "CITY OF LIGHT," BUT WHAT HAPPENS WHEN THOSE LIGHTS GO OUT?
WHILE PARIS HAS MOVED FORWARD INTO CUTTING EDGE ALTERNATIVE ENERGY SOURCES LIKE NUCLEAR POWER, THE REST OF THE WORLD IS STILL USING 19TH CENTURY TECHNOLOGY--
CANARY, BAST IS BACK IN HIS SEAT, BUT HIS SECURITY DETAIL IS GONE.
THAT'S WEIRD...
--SO I BUILT A POWER DEVICE I CALL THE HAP-E. IT WITHSTANDS BROWNOUTS AND ELECTROMAGNETIC PULSES TO GET COUNTRIES OFF THE PROVERBIAL GRID--
BZZT
SORRY, THERE SEEMS TO BE A SLIGHT PROB--
ACK!
BATGIRL, ARE YOU THERE BZZT? WHAT HAPPENED?
POWER'S OUT, BUT THAT HAP-E THING IS STILL BZZT WORKING.
DOES ANYONE BZZT READ ME? SOMETHING BLEW OUR COMMS.

DR. YENOKIDA'S **GONE!** AND SO IS HIS HAP-E THING.

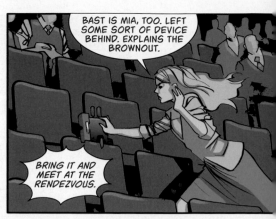

BAST IS MIA, TOO. LEFT SOME SORT OF DEVICE BEHIND. EXPLAINS THE BROWNOUT.

BRING IT AND MEET AT THE RENDEZVOUS.

GEE, IF ONLY WE HAD SOMETHING **MORE** CONSPICUOUS ON A **SPY MISSION.**

NOW WHERE'S THE FUN IN THAT?

LET'S ROLL!

THIS IS AN EMP DEVICE. DR. YENOKIDA CLAIMED HIS INVENTION COULD WITHSTAND ANY SORT OF ENERGY SURGE. APPARENTLY, BAST WANTED TO TEST HAP-E OUT **BEFORE** HE STOLE IT.

BUT WHY? A BATTERY ISN'T A VERY GOOD WEAPON.

NO, BUT HAP-E COULD **POWER** A WEAPON.

CANARY WAS ABLE TO PLACE A TRACKER ON BAST. HE'S HEADING TO THE SEINE HOTEL.

GOOD THING THAT CREEP HIT ON ME AFTER ALL.

I'LL GET US A ROOM NUMBER.

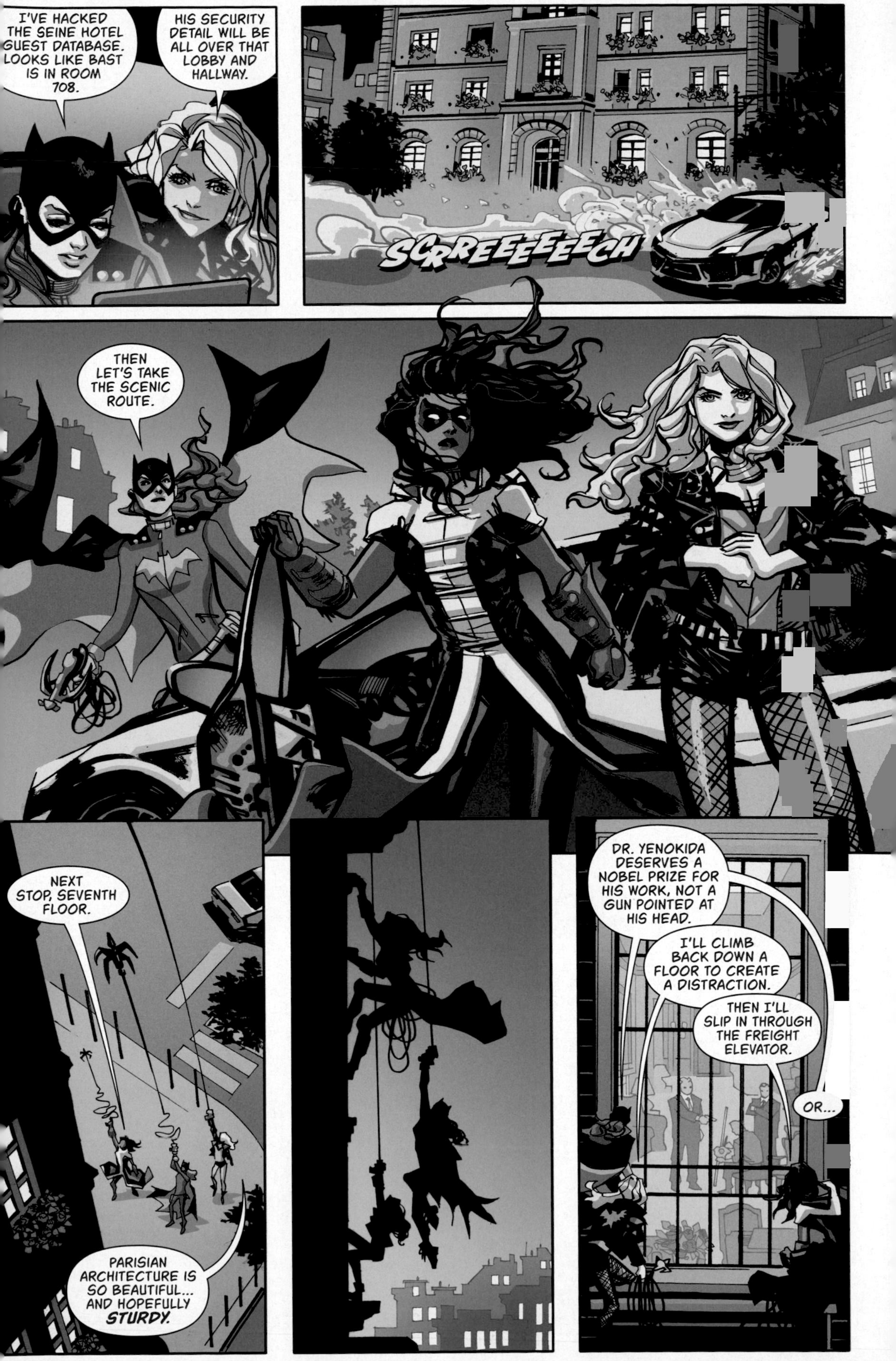
I'VE HACKED THE SEINE HOTEL GUEST DATABASE. LOOKS LIKE BAST IS IN ROOM 708.
HIS SECURITY DETAIL WILL BE ALL OVER THAT LOBBY AND HALLWAY.
SCRREEEEEEECH
THEN LET'S TAKE THE SCENIC ROUTE.
NEXT STOP, SEVENTH FLOOR.
PARISIAN ARCHITECTURE IS SO BEAUTIFUL... AND HOPEFULLY STURDY.
DR. YENOKIDA DESERVES A NOBEL PRIZE FOR HIS WORK, NOT A GUN POINTED AT HIS HEAD.
I'LL CLIMB BACK DOWN A FLOOR TO CREATE A DISTRACTION.
THEN I'LL SLIP IN THROUGH THE FREIGHT ELEVATOR.
OR...

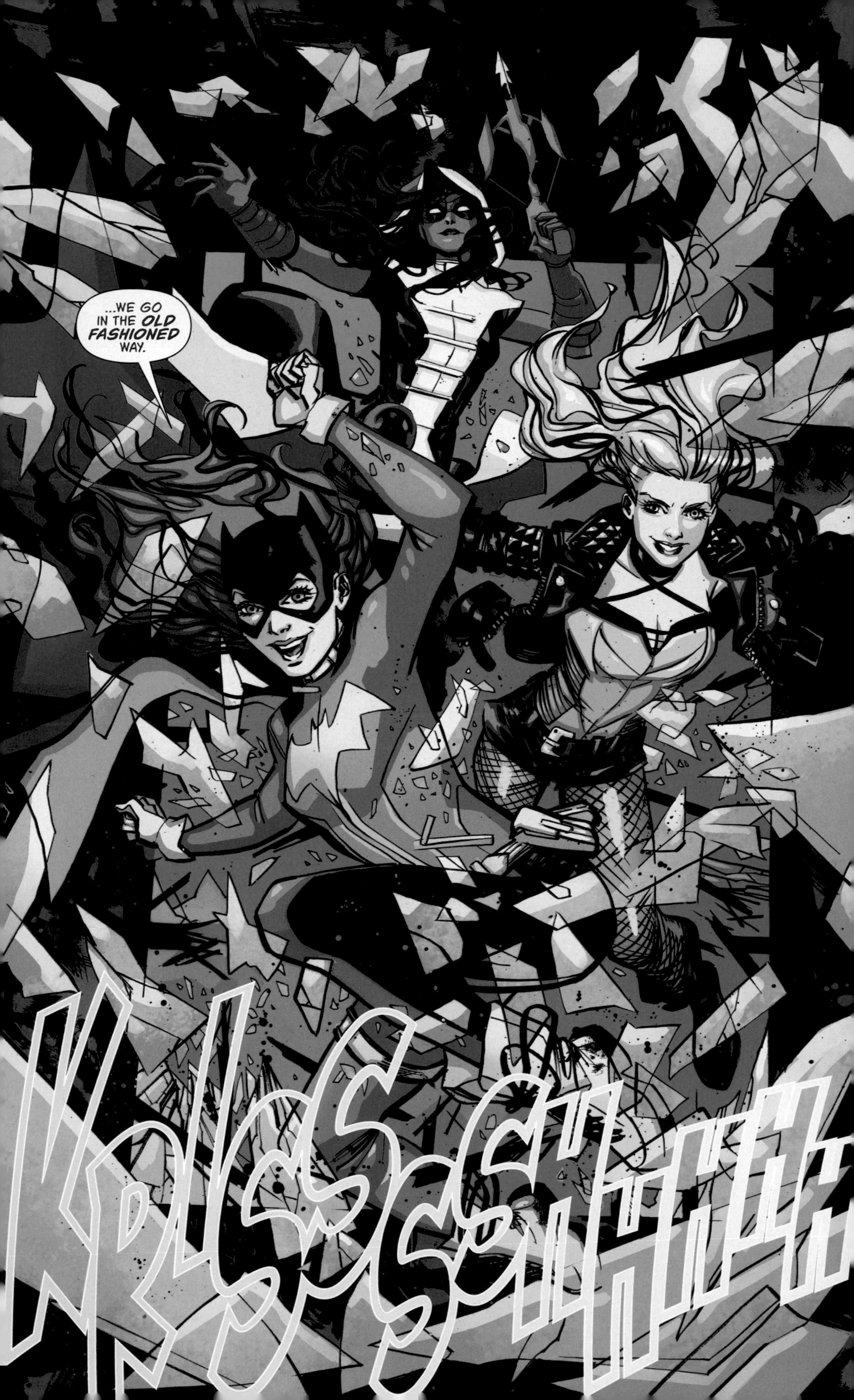
...WE GO IN THE OLD FASHIONED WAY.

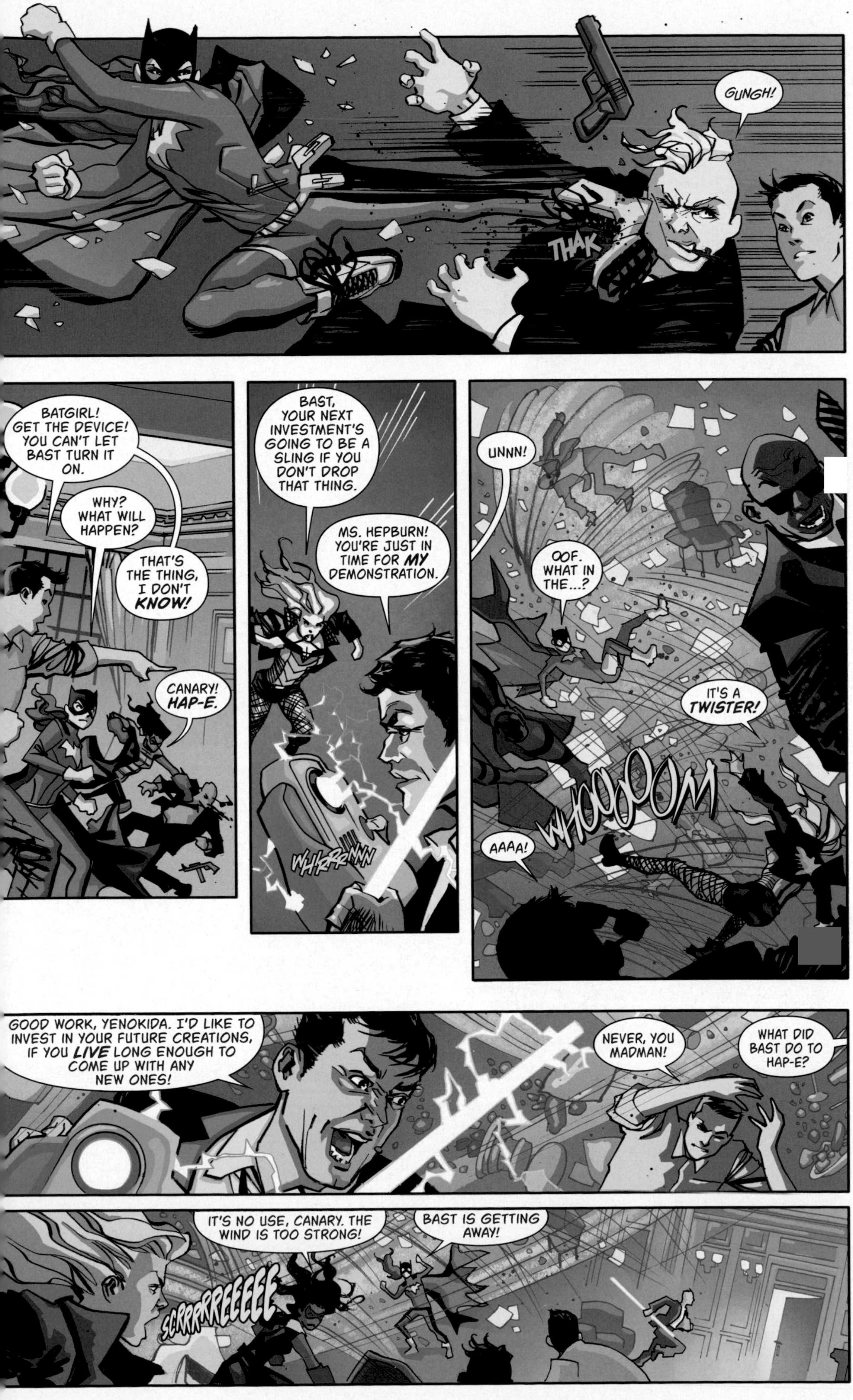
GUNGH!
THAK
BATGIRL! GET THE DEVICE! YOU CAN'T LET BAST TURN IT ON.
WHY? WHAT WILL HAPPEN?
THAT'S THE THING, I DON'T KNOW!
CANARY! HAP-E.
BAST, YOUR NEXT INVESTMENT'S GOING TO BE A SLING IF YOU DON'T DROP THAT THING.
MS. HEPBURN! YOU'RE JUST IN TIME FOR MY DEMONSTRATION.
WHIRRRNNN
UNNN!
OOF. WHAT IN THE...?
IT'S A TWISTER!
WHOOOOOM
AAAA!
GOOD WORK, YENOKIDA. I'D LIKE TO INVEST IN YOUR FUTURE CREATIONS, IF YOU LIVE LONG ENOUGH TO COME UP WITH ANY NEW ONES!
NEVER, YOU MADMAN!
WHAT DID BAST DO TO HAP-E?
IT'S NO USE, CANARY. THE WIND IS TOO STRONG!
BAST IS GETTING AWAY!
SCRRRRREEEEEE

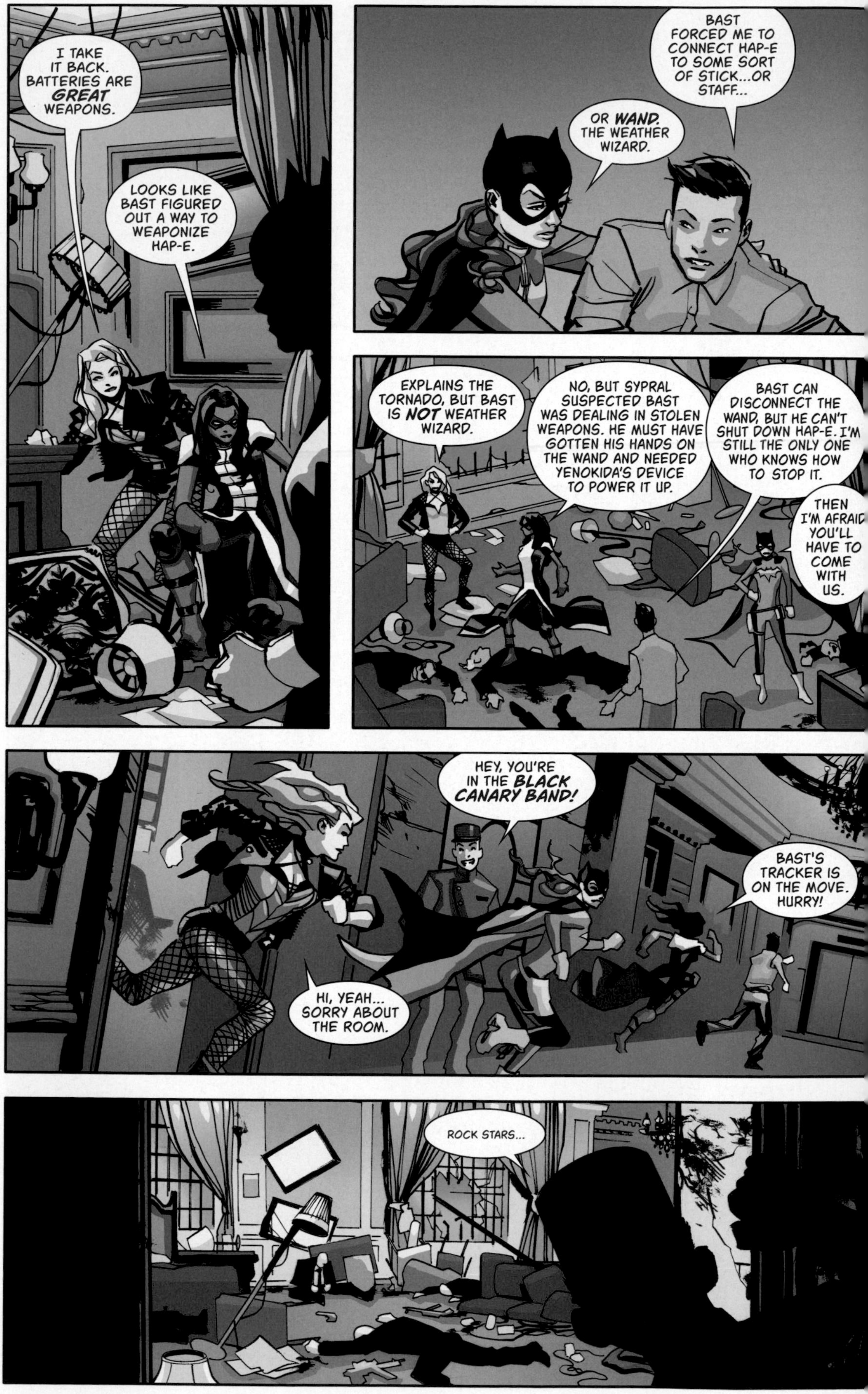
I TAKE IT BACK. BATTERIES ARE GREAT WEAPONS.
LOOKS LIKE BAST FIGURED OUT A WAY TO WEAPONIZE HAP-E.
BAST FORCED ME TO CONNECT HAP-E TO SOME SORT OF STICK...OR STAFF...
OR WAND. THE WEATHER WIZARD.
EXPLAINS THE TORNADO, BUT BAST IS NOT WEATHER WIZARD.
NO, BUT SYPRAL SUSPECTED BAST WAS DEALING IN STOLEN WEAPONS. HE MUST HAVE GOTTEN HIS HANDS ON THE WAND AND NEEDED YENOKIDA'S DEVICE TO POWER IT UP.
BAST CAN DISCONNECT THE WAND, BUT HE CAN'T SHUT DOWN HAP-E. I'M STILL THE ONLY ONE WHO KNOWS HOW TO STOP IT.
THEN I'M AFRAID YOU'LL HAVE TO COME WITH US.
HEY, YOU'RE IN THE BLACK CANARY BAND!
HI, YEAH... SORRY ABOUT THE ROOM.
BAST'S TRACKER IS ON THE MOVE. HURRY!
ROCK STARS...

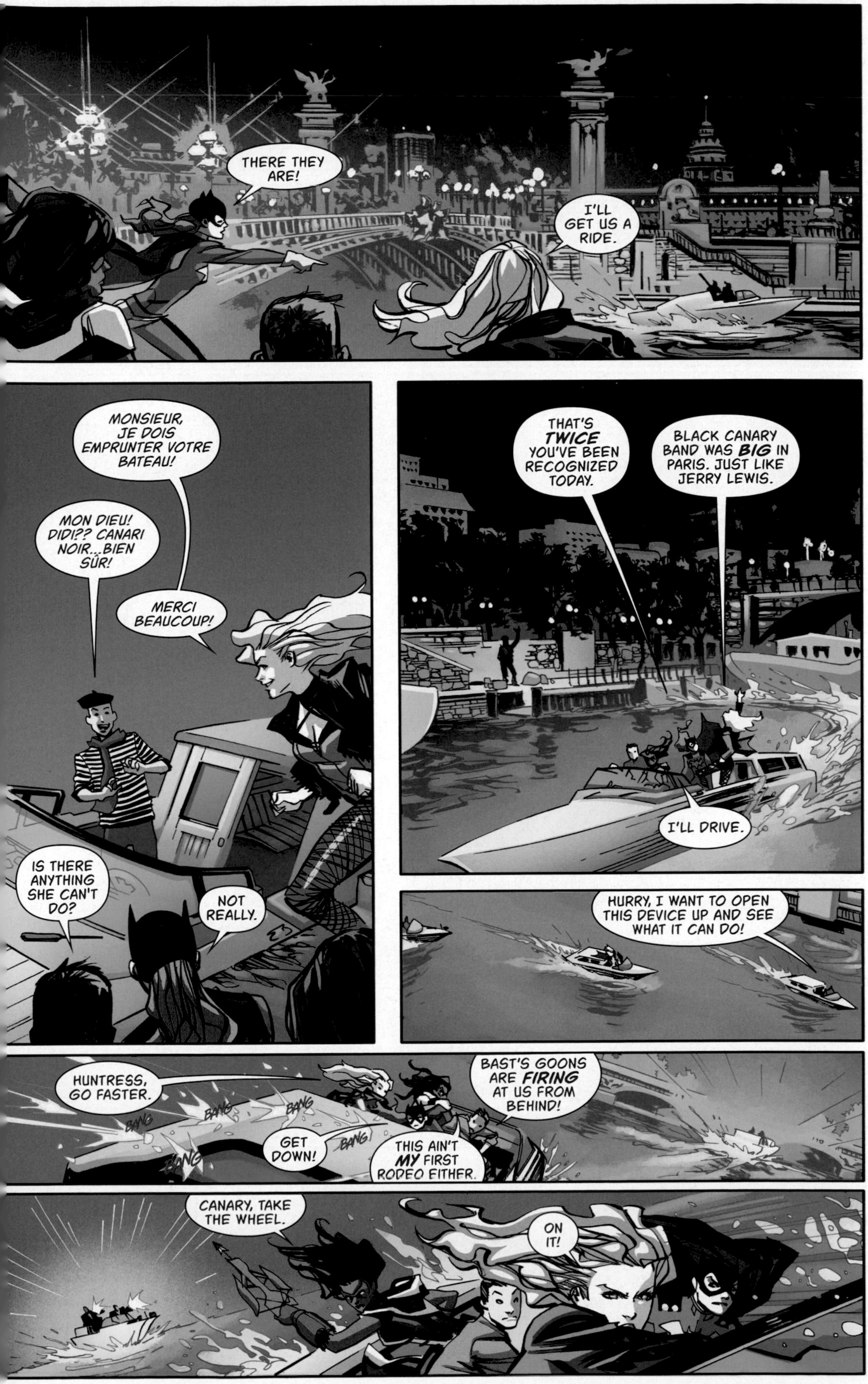
THERE THEY ARE!
I'LL GET US A RIDE.
MONSIEUR, JE DOIS EMPRUNTER VOTRE BATEAU!
MON DIEU! DIDI?? CANARI NOIR...BIEN SÛR!
MERCI BEAUCOUP!
IS THERE ANYTHING SHE CAN'T DO?
NOT REALLY.
THAT'S TWICE YOU'VE BEEN RECOGNIZED TODAY.
BLACK CANARY BAND WAS BIG IN PARIS. JUST LIKE JERRY LEWIS.
I'LL DRIVE.
HURRY, I WANT TO OPEN THIS DEVICE UP AND SEE WHAT IT CAN DO!
HUNTRESS, GO FASTER.
BANG
BANG
BANG
BAST'S GOONS ARE FIRING AT US FROM BEHIND!
GET DOWN!
BANG
THIS AIN'T MY FIRST RODEO EITHER.
CANARY, TAKE THE WHEEL.
ON IT!

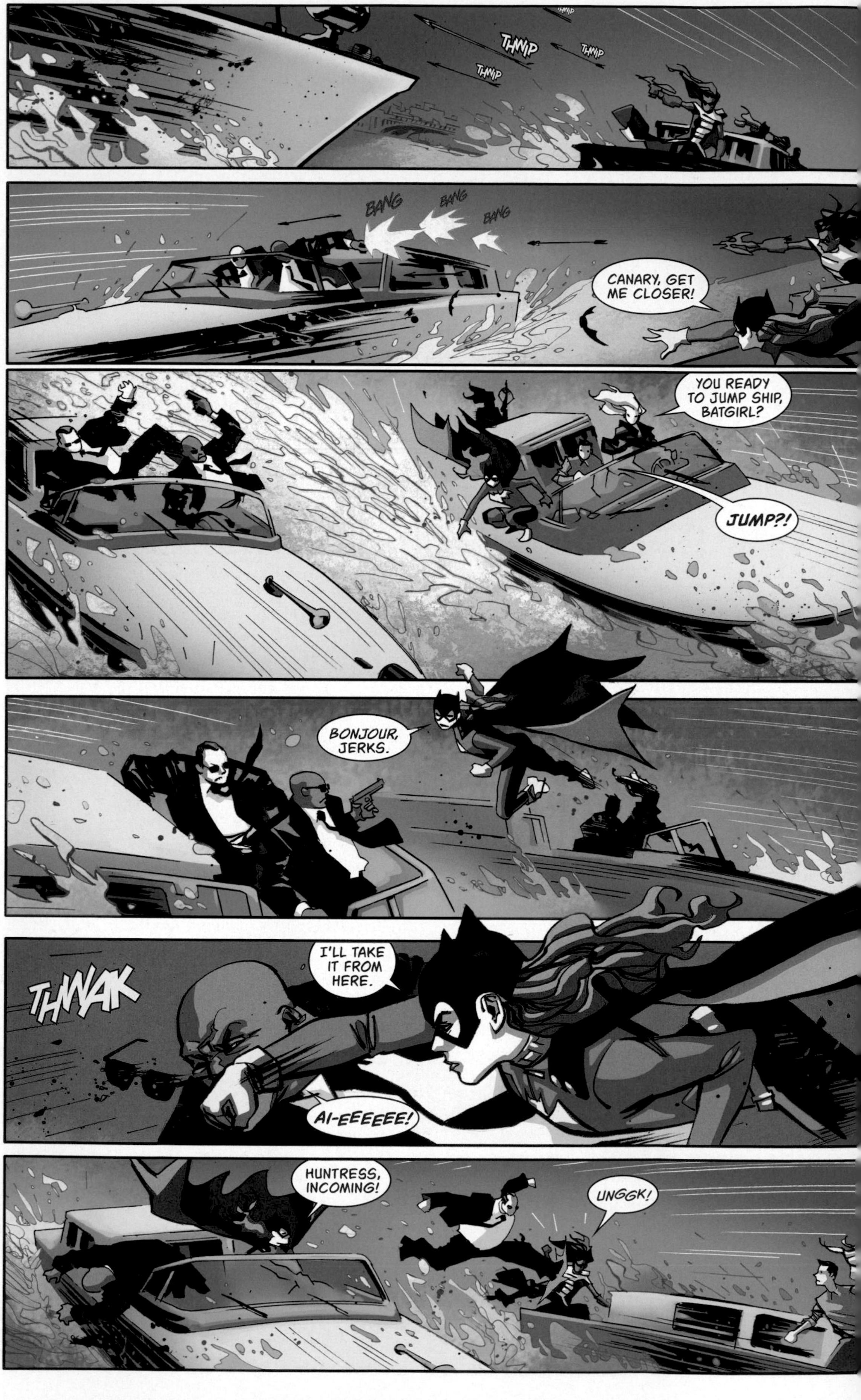
THWIP
THWIP
THWIP
THWIP
BANG
BANG
BANG
CANARY, GET ME CLOSER!
YOU READY TO JUMP SHIP, BATGIRL?
JUMP?!
BONJOUR, JERKS.
THWAK
I'LL TAKE IT FROM HERE.
AI-EEEEEE!
HUNTRESS, INCOMING!
UNGGK!

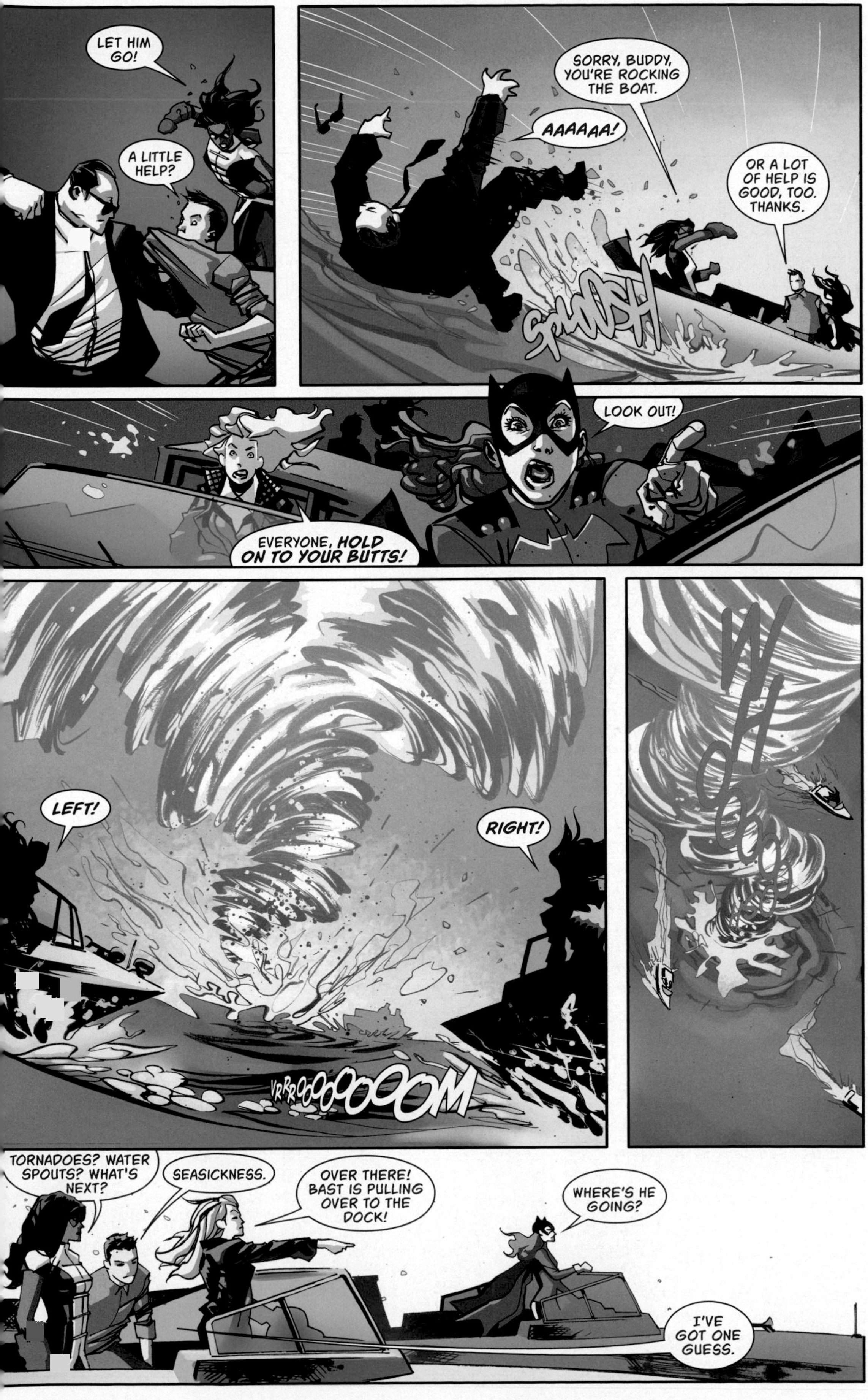
LET HIM GO!
A LITTLE HELP?
SORRY, BUDDY, YOU'RE ROCKING THE BOAT.
AAAAAA!
SPLOOSH
OR A LOT OF HELP IS GOOD, TOO. THANKS.
LOOK OUT!
EVERYONE, HOLD ON TO YOUR BUTTS!
LEFT!
RIGHT!
VRRROOOOOOOOM
WHOOOOOOO
TORNADOES? WATER SPOUTS? WHAT'S NEXT?
SEASICKNESS.
OVER THERE! BAST IS PULLING OVER TO THE DOCK!
WHERE'S HE GOING?
I'VE GOT ONE GUESS.

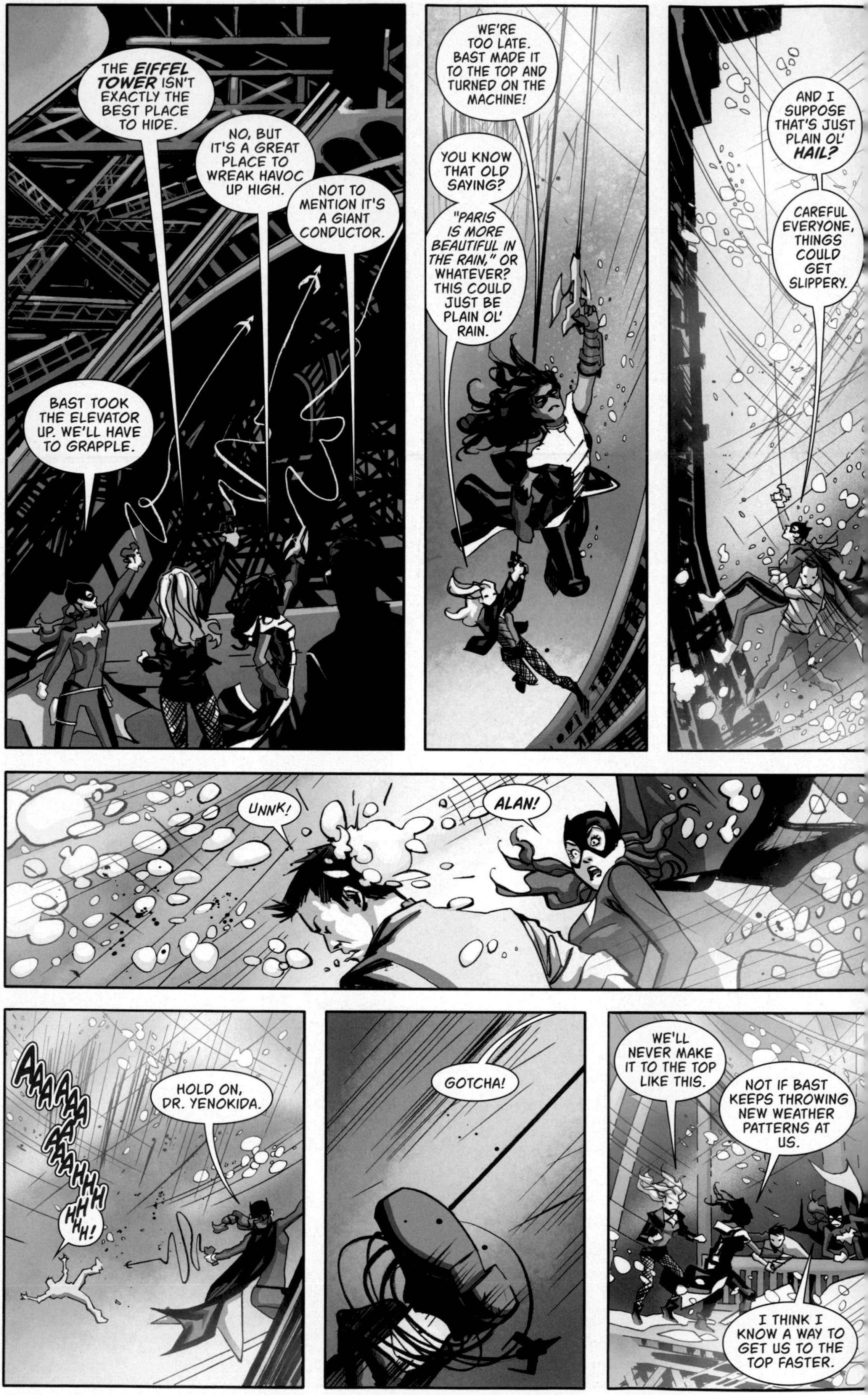
THE **EIFFEL TOWER** ISN'T EXACTLY THE BEST PLACE TO HIDE.
NO, BUT IT'S A GREAT PLACE TO WREAK HAVOC UP HIGH.
NOT TO MENTION IT'S A GIANT CONDUCTOR.
BAST TOOK THE ELEVATOR UP. WE'LL HAVE TO GRAPPLE.
WE'RE TOO LATE. BAST MADE IT TO THE TOP AND TURNED ON THE MACHINE!
YOU KNOW THAT OLD SAYING?
"PARIS IS MORE BEAUTIFUL IN THE RAIN," OR WHATEVER? THIS COULD JUST BE PLAIN OL' RAIN.
AND I SUPPOSE THAT'S JUST PLAIN OL' **HAIL?**
CAREFUL EVERYONE, THINGS COULD GET SLIPPERY.
UNNK!
ALAN!
AAAAAAAAAAAAAHHHHHHH!
HOLD ON, DR. YENOKIDA.
GOTCHA!
WE'LL NEVER MAKE IT TO THE TOP LIKE THIS.
NOT IF BAST KEEPS THROWING NEW WEATHER PATTERNS AT US.
I THINK I KNOW A WAY TO GET US TO THE TOP FASTER.

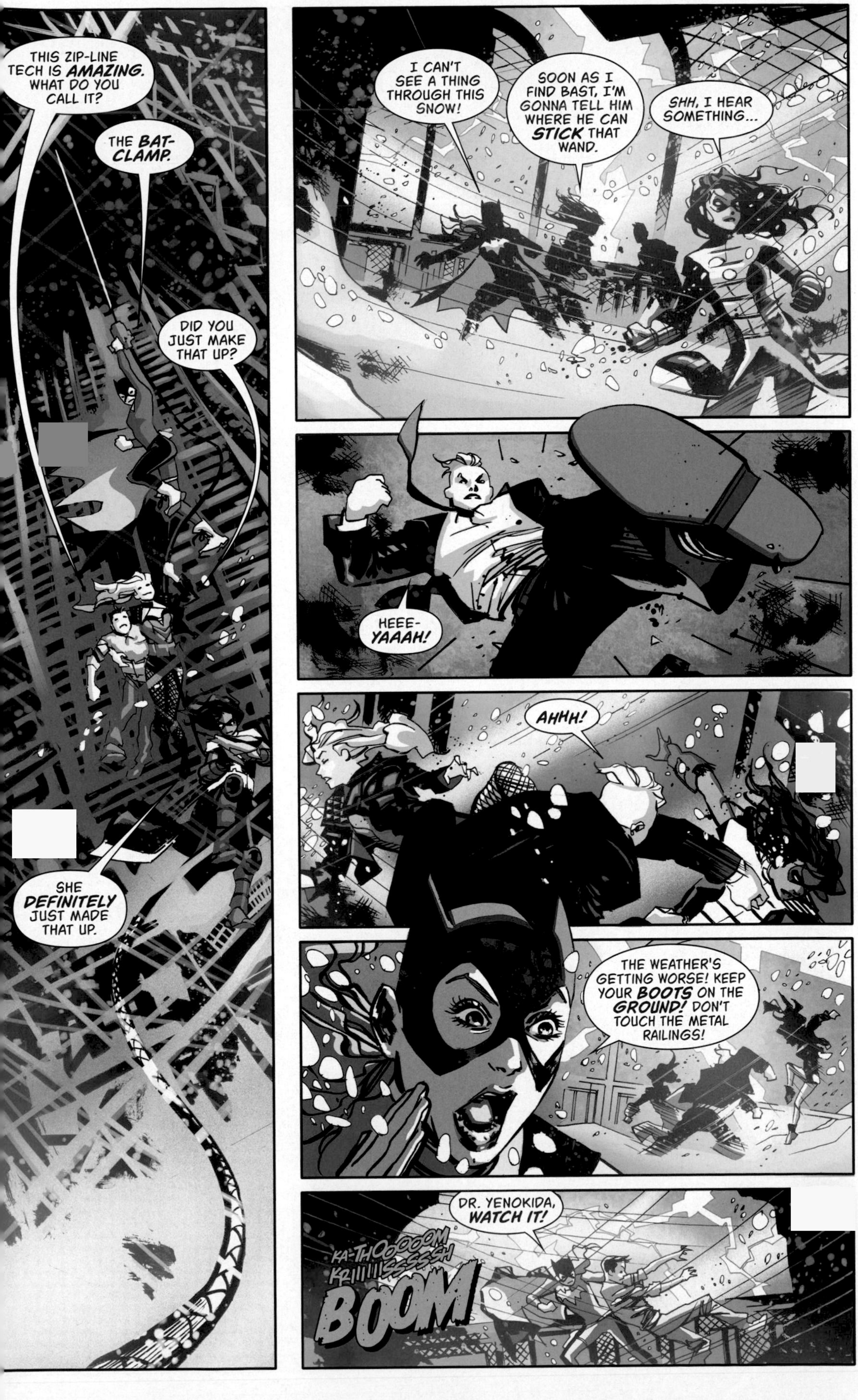
THIS ZIP-LINE TECH IS AMAZING. WHAT DO YOU CALL IT?
THE BAT-CLAMP.
DID YOU JUST MAKE THAT UP?
SHE DEFINITELY JUST MADE THAT UP.
I CAN'T SEE A THING THROUGH THIS SNOW!
SOON AS I FIND BAST, I'M GONNA TELL HIM WHERE HE CAN STICK THAT WAND.
SHH, I HEAR SOMETHING...
HEEE-YAAAH!
AHHH!
THE WEATHER'S GETTING WORSE! KEEP YOUR BOOTS ON THE GROUND! DON'T TOUCH THE METAL RAILINGS!
DR. YENOKIDA, WATCH IT!
KA-THOOOOOM
KRIIIIIISSSSSH
BOOM

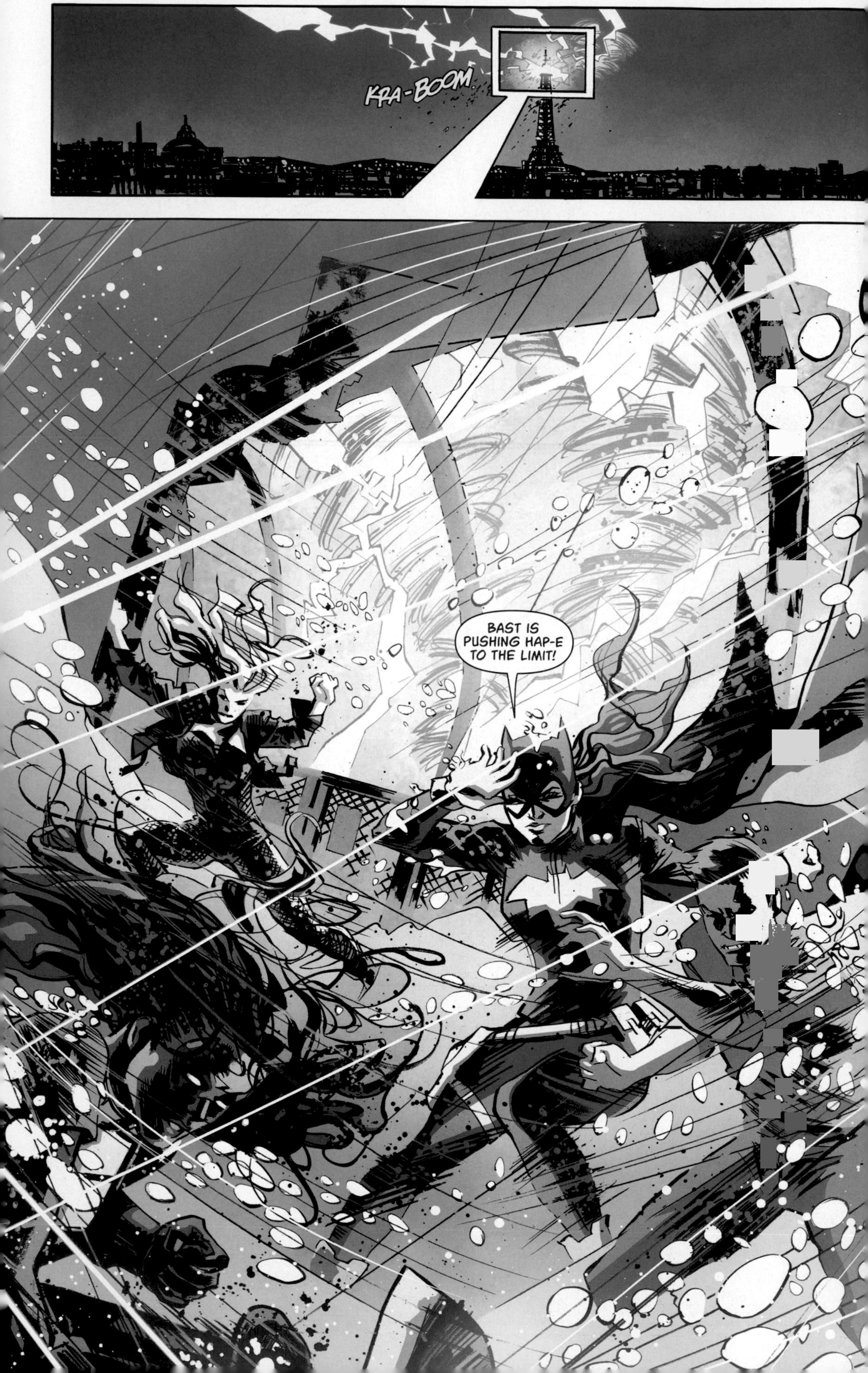
KRA-BOOM
BAST IS PUSHING HAP-E TO THE LIMIT!

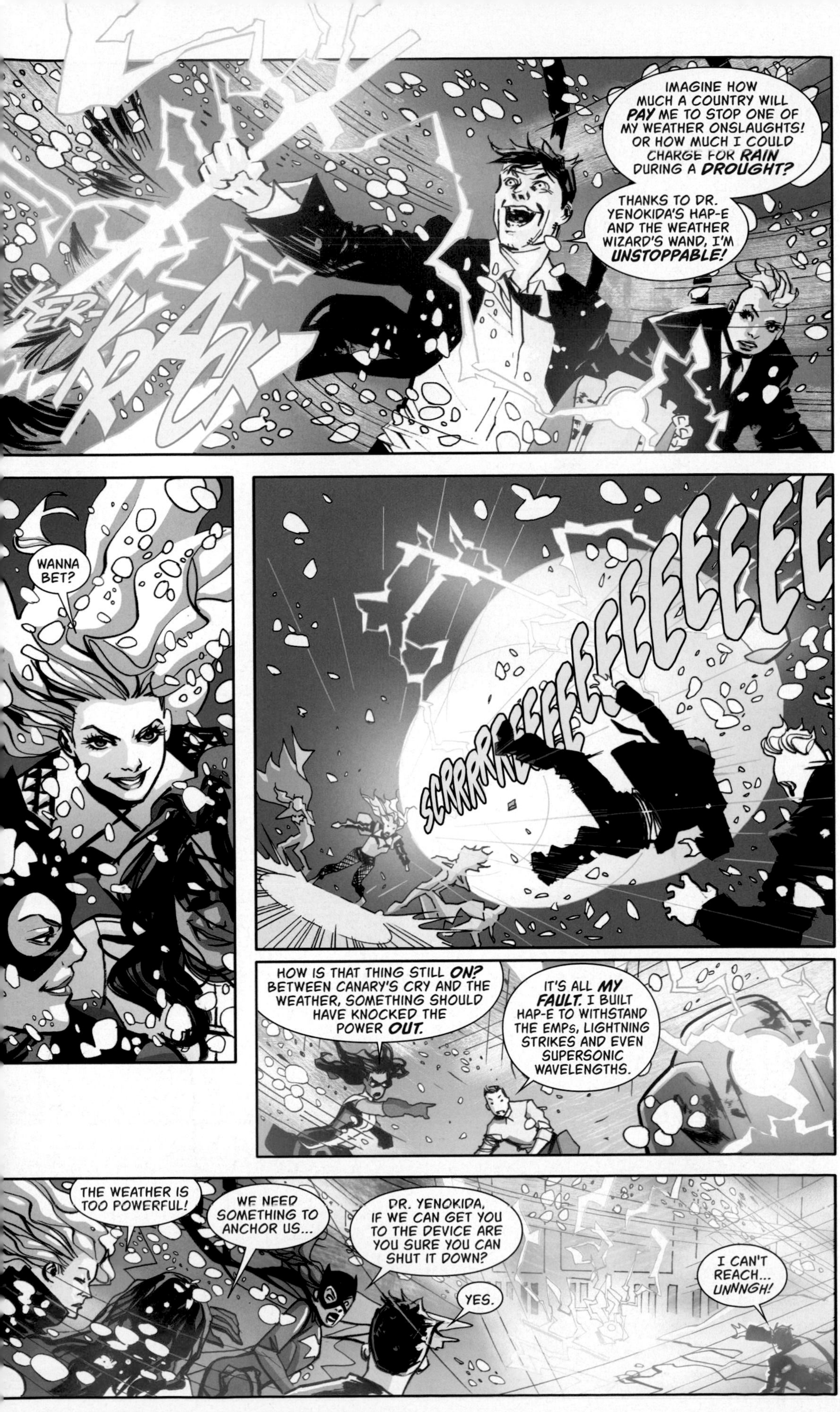
KER-KRACK
IMAGINE HOW MUCH A COUNTRY WILL PAY ME TO STOP ONE OF MY WEATHER ONSLAUGHTS! OR HOW MUCH I COULD CHARGE FOR RAIN DURING A DROUGHT?
THANKS TO DR. YENOKIDA'S HAP-E AND THE WEATHER WIZARD'S WAND, I'M UNSTOPPABLE!
WANNA BET?
SCRRRREEEEEEEEEEEEEE
HOW IS THAT THING STILL ON? BETWEEN CANARY'S CRY AND THE WEATHER, SOMETHING SHOULD HAVE KNOCKED THE POWER OUT.
IT'S ALL MY FAULT. I BUILT HAP-E TO WITHSTAND THE EMPs, LIGHTNING STRIKES AND EVEN SUPERSONIC WAVELENGTHS.
THE WEATHER IS TOO POWERFUL!
WE NEED SOMETHING TO ANCHOR US...
DR. YENOKIDA, IF WE CAN GET YOU TO THE DEVICE ARE YOU SURE YOU CAN SHUT IT DOWN?
YES.
I CAN'T REACH... UNNNGH!

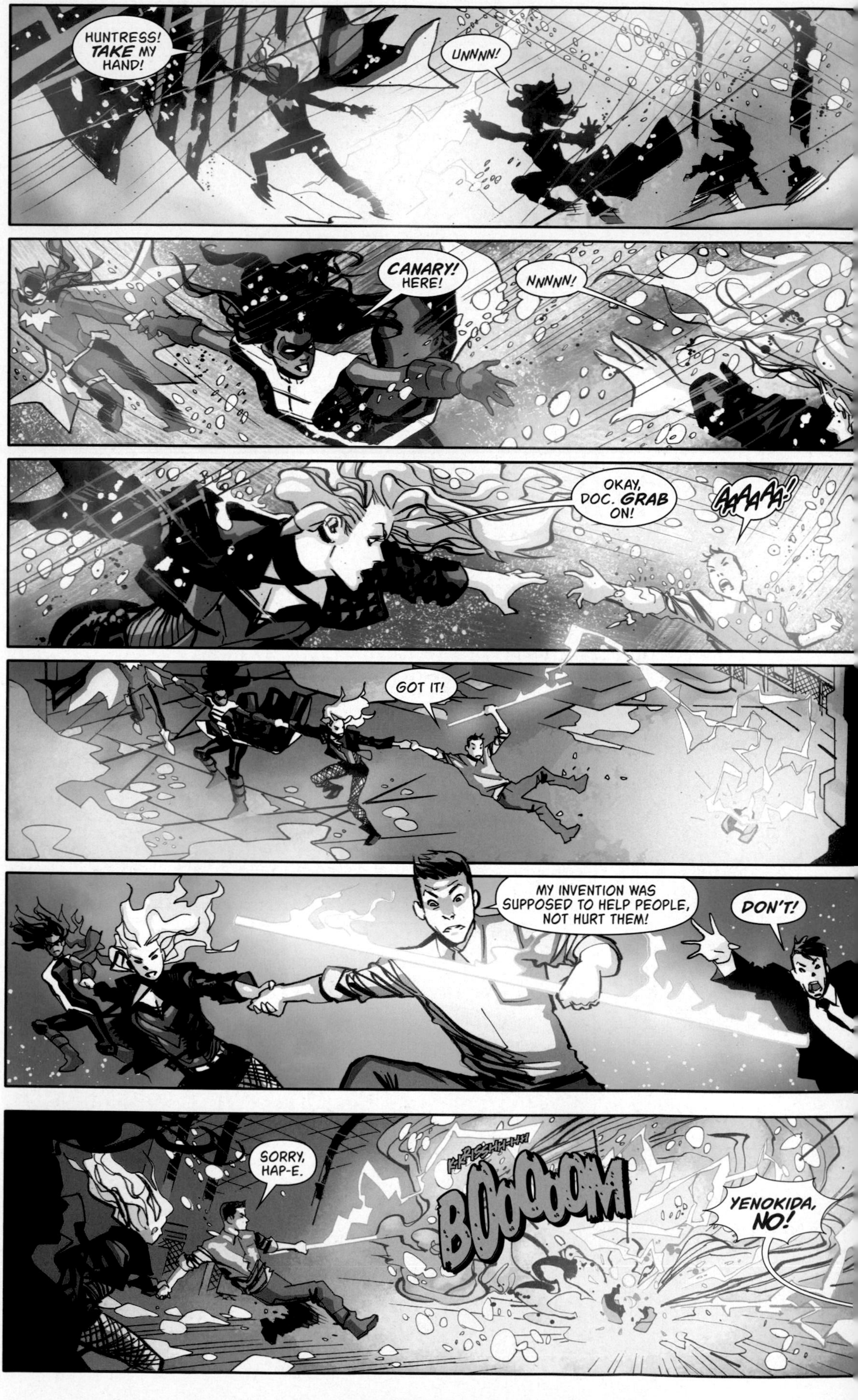
HUNTRESS! TAKE MY HAND!
UNNNN!
CANARY! HERE!
NNNNN!
OKAY, DOC. GRAB ON!
AAAAAA!
GOT IT!
MY INVENTION WAS SUPPOSED TO HELP PEOPLE, NOT HURT THEM!
DON'T!
SORRY, HAP-E.
KRASSHHHH
BOOOOOM
YENOKIDA, NO!

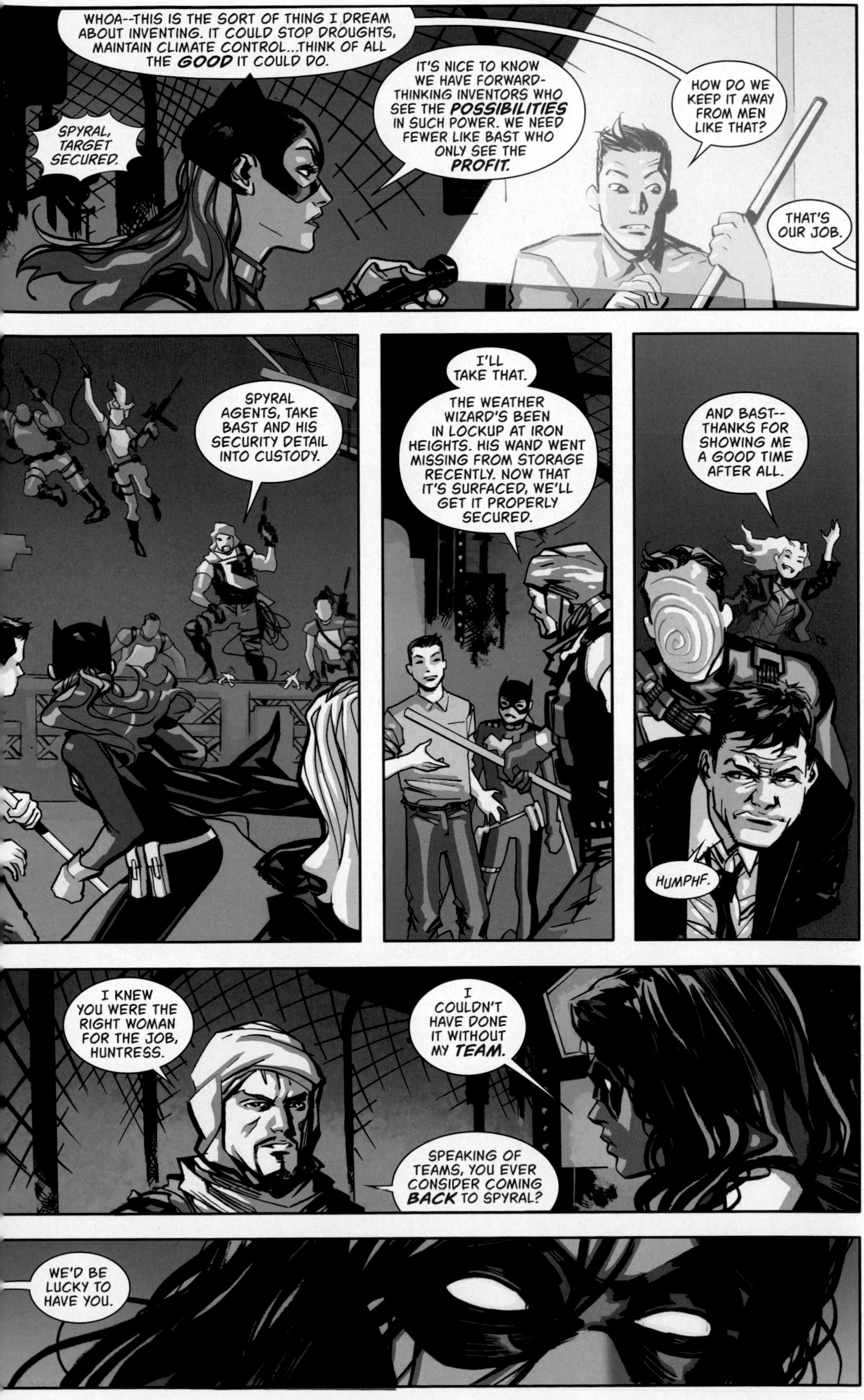
WHOA--THIS IS THE SORT OF THING I DREAM ABOUT INVENTING. IT COULD STOP DROUGHTS, MAINTAIN CLIMATE CONTROL...THINK OF ALL THE GOOD IT COULD DO.
SPYRAL, TARGET SECURED.
IT'S NICE TO KNOW WE HAVE FORWARD-THINKING INVENTORS WHO SEE THE POSSIBILITIES IN SUCH POWER. WE NEED FEWER LIKE BAST WHO ONLY SEE THE PROFIT.
HOW DO WE KEEP IT AWAY FROM MEN LIKE THAT?
THAT'S OUR JOB.
SPYRAL AGENTS, TAKE BAST AND HIS SECURITY DETAIL INTO CUSTODY.
I'LL TAKE THAT.
THE WEATHER WIZARD'S BEEN IN LOCKUP AT IRON HEIGHTS. HIS WAND WENT MISSING FROM STORAGE RECENTLY. NOW THAT IT'S SURFACED, WE'LL GET IT PROPERLY SECURED.
AND BAST-- THANKS FOR SHOWING ME A GOOD TIME AFTER ALL.
HUMPHF.
I KNEW YOU WERE THE RIGHT WOMAN FOR THE JOB, HUNTRESS.
I COULDN'T HAVE DONE IT WITHOUT MY TEAM.
SPEAKING OF TEAMS, YOU EVER CONSIDER COMING BACK TO SPYRAL?
WE'D BE LUCKY TO HAVE YOU.

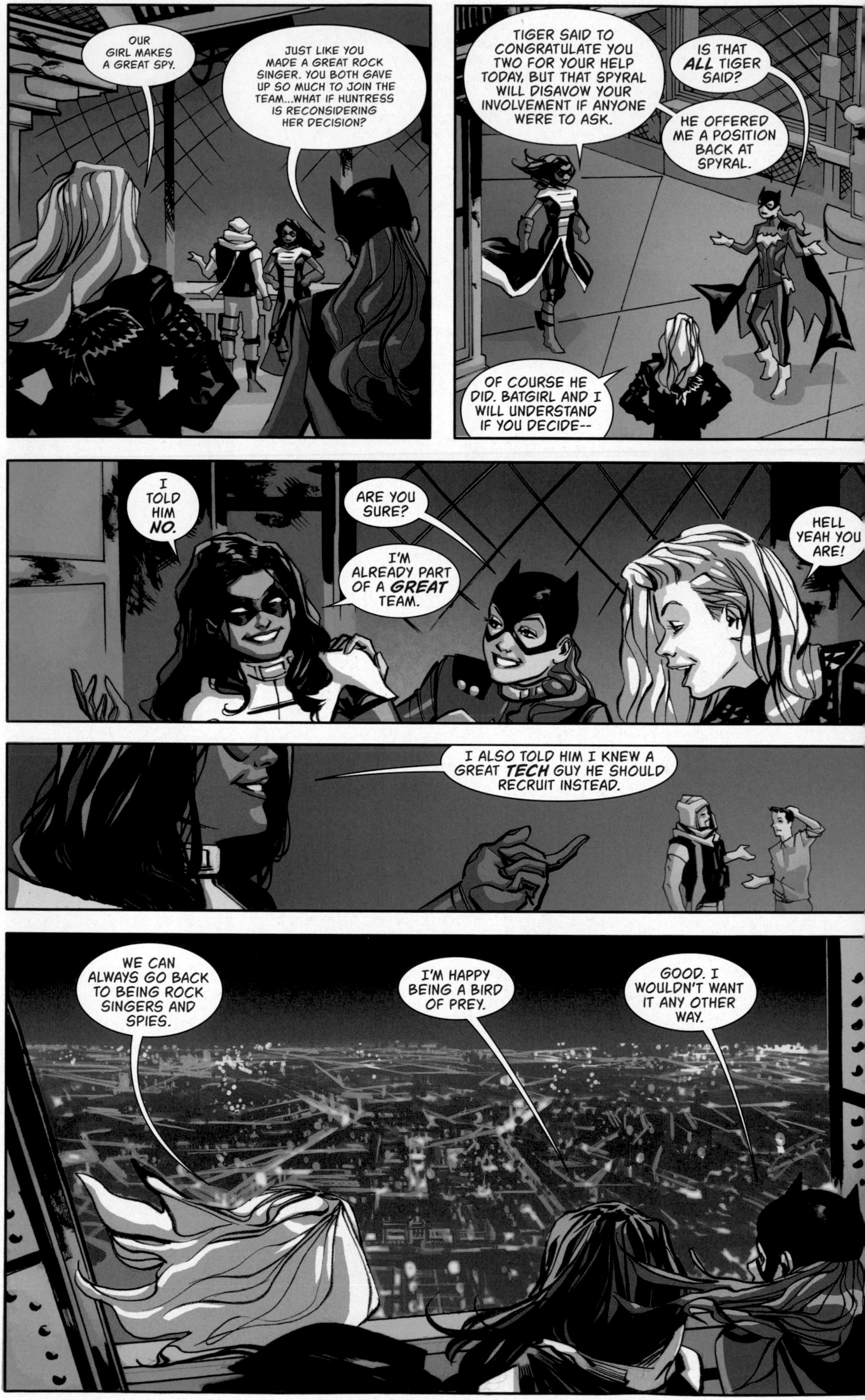
OUR GIRL MAKES A GREAT SPY.
JUST LIKE YOU MADE A GREAT ROCK SINGER. YOU BOTH GAVE UP SO MUCH TO JOIN THE TEAM...WHAT IF HUNTRESS IS RECONSIDERING HER DECISION?
TIGER SAID TO CONGRATULATE YOU TWO FOR YOUR HELP TODAY, BUT THAT SPYRAL WILL DISAVOW YOUR INVOLVEMENT IF ANYONE WERE TO ASK.
IS THAT ALL TIGER SAID?
HE OFFERED ME A POSITION BACK AT SPYRAL.
OF COURSE HE DID. BATGIRL AND I WILL UNDERSTAND IF YOU DECIDE--
I TOLD HIM NO.
ARE YOU SURE?
I'M ALREADY PART OF A GREAT TEAM.
HELL YEAH YOU ARE!
I ALSO TOLD HIM I KNEW A GREAT TECH GUY HE SHOULD RECRUIT INSTEAD.
WE CAN ALWAYS GO BACK TO BEING ROCK SINGERS AND SPIES.
I'M HAPPY BEING A BIRD OF PREY.
GOOD. I WOULDN'T WANT IT ANY OTHER WAY.

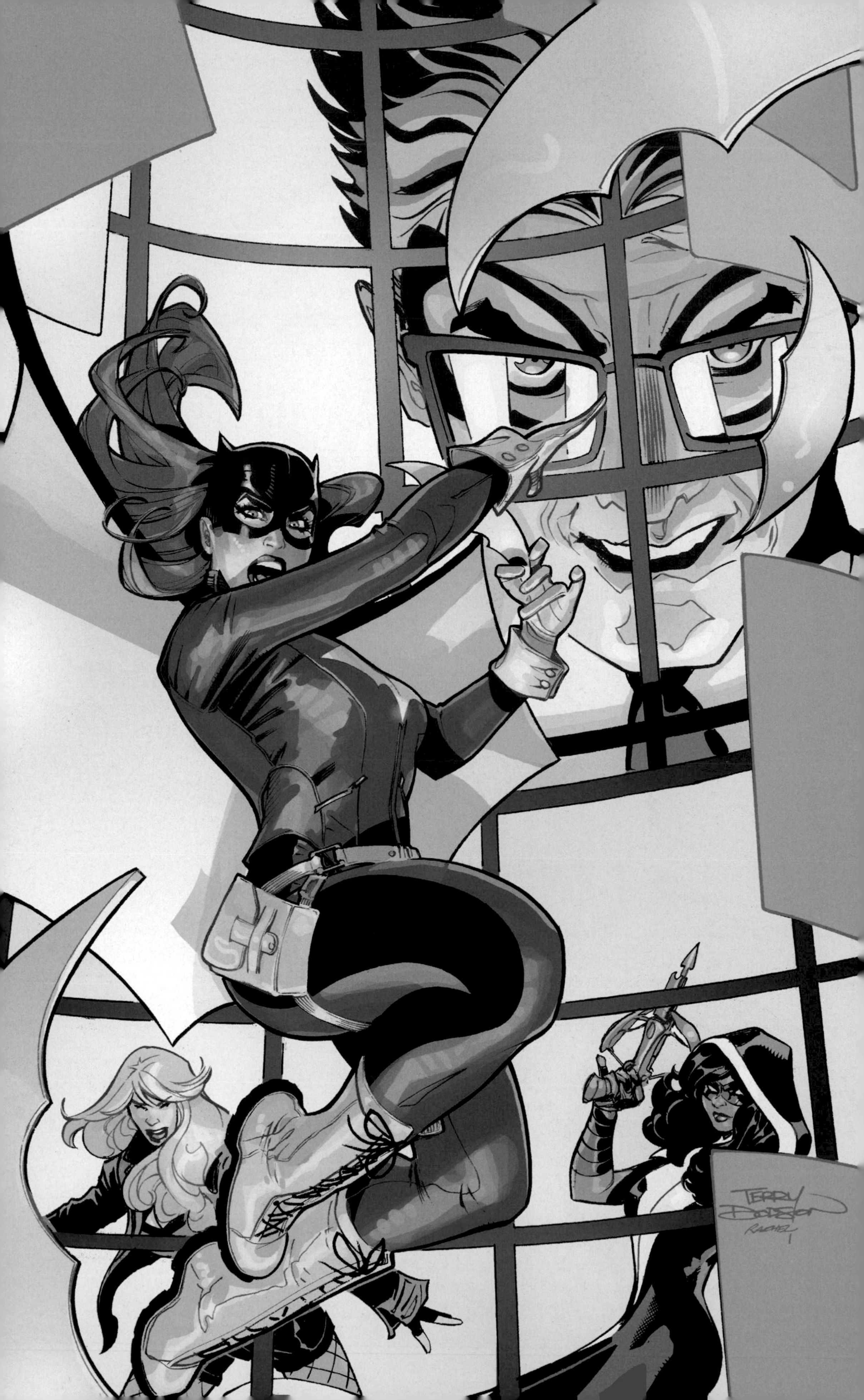
TERRY DODSON
RACHEL

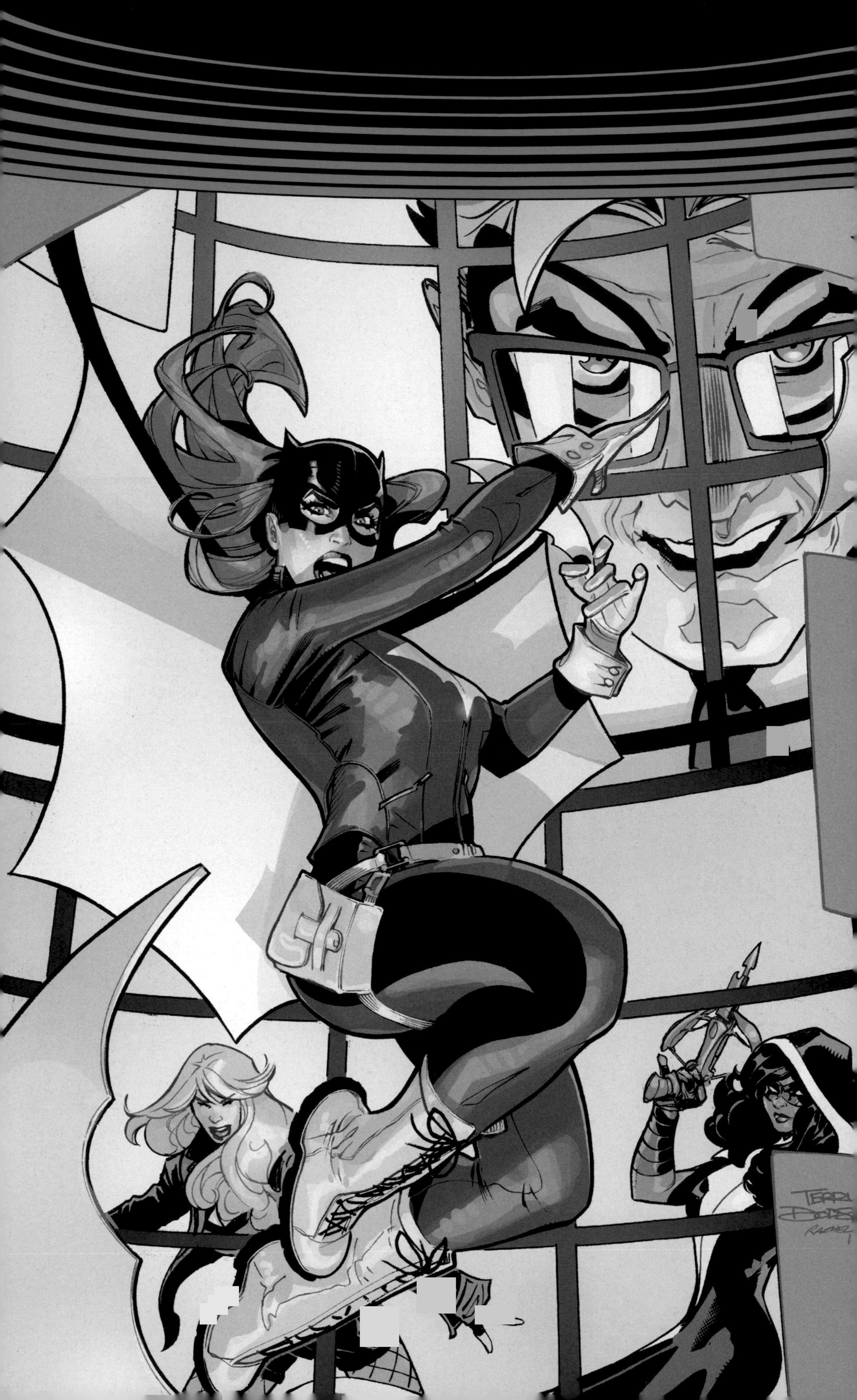

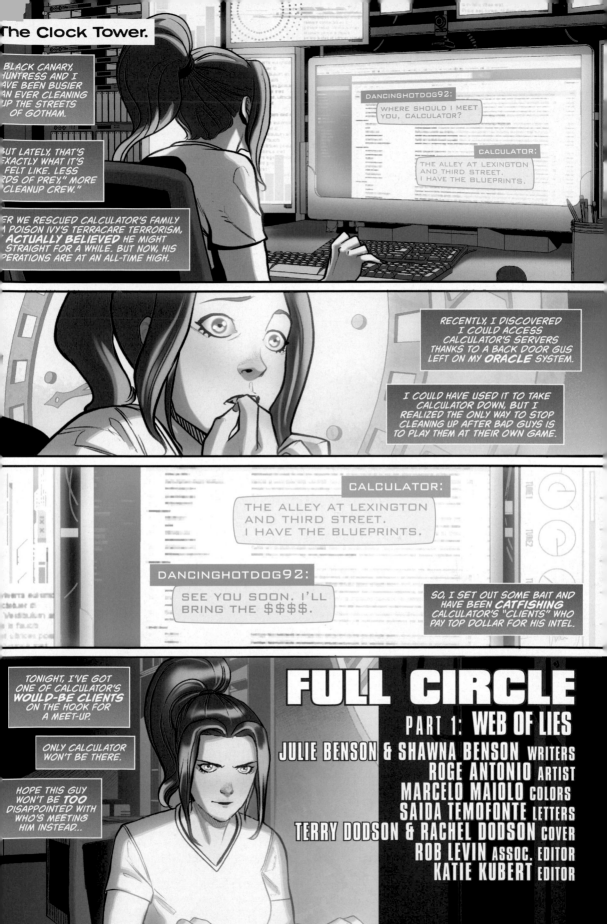

BLACK CANARY, HUNTRESS AND I HAVE BEEN BUSIER THAN EVER CLEANING UP THE STREETS OF GOTHAM.

BUT LATELY, THAT'S EXACTLY WHAT IT'S FELT LIKE. LESS "BIRDS OF PREY." MORE "CLEANUP CREW."

AFTER WE RESCUED CALCULATOR'S FAMILY FROM POISON IVY'S TERRACARE TERRORISM, I ACTUALLY BELIEVED HE MIGHT GO STRAIGHT FOR A WHILE. BUT NOW, HIS OPERATIONS ARE AT AN ALL-TIME HIGH.

DANCINGHOTDOG92:
WHERE SHOULD I MEET YOU, CALCULATOR?

CALCULATOR:
THE ALLEY AT LEXINGTON AND THIRD STREET. I HAVE THE BLUEPRINTS.

RECENTLY, I DISCOVERED I COULD ACCESS CALCULATOR'S SERVERS THANKS TO A BACK DOOR GUS LEFT ON MY ORACLE SYSTEM.

I COULD HAVE USED IT TO TAKE CALCULATOR DOWN, BUT I REALIZED THE ONLY WAY TO STOP CLEANING UP AFTER BAD GUYS IS TO PLAY THEM AT THEIR OWN GAME.

CALCULATOR:
THE ALLEY AT LEXINGTON AND THIRD STREET. I HAVE THE BLUEPRINTS.

DANCINGHOTDOG92:
SEE YOU SOON. I'LL BRING THE $$$$.

SO, I SET OUT SOME BAIT AND HAVE BEEN CATFISHING CALCULATOR'S "CLIENTS" WHO PAY TOP DOLLAR FOR HIS INTEL.

TONIGHT, I'VE GOT ONE OF CALCULATOR'S WOULD-BE CLIENTS ON THE HOOK FOR A MEET-UP.

ONLY CALCULATOR WON'T BE THERE.

HOPE THIS GUY WON'T BE TOO DISAPPOINTED WITH WHO'S MEETING HIM INSTEAD...

FULL CIRCLE
PART 1: WEB OF LIES

JULIE BENSON & SHAWNA BENSON WRITERS
ROGE ANTONIO ARTIST
MARCELO MAIOLO COLORS
SAIDA TEMOFONTE LETTERS
TERRY DODSON & RACHEL DODSON COVER
ROB LEVIN ASSOC. EDITOR
KATIE KUBERT EDITOR

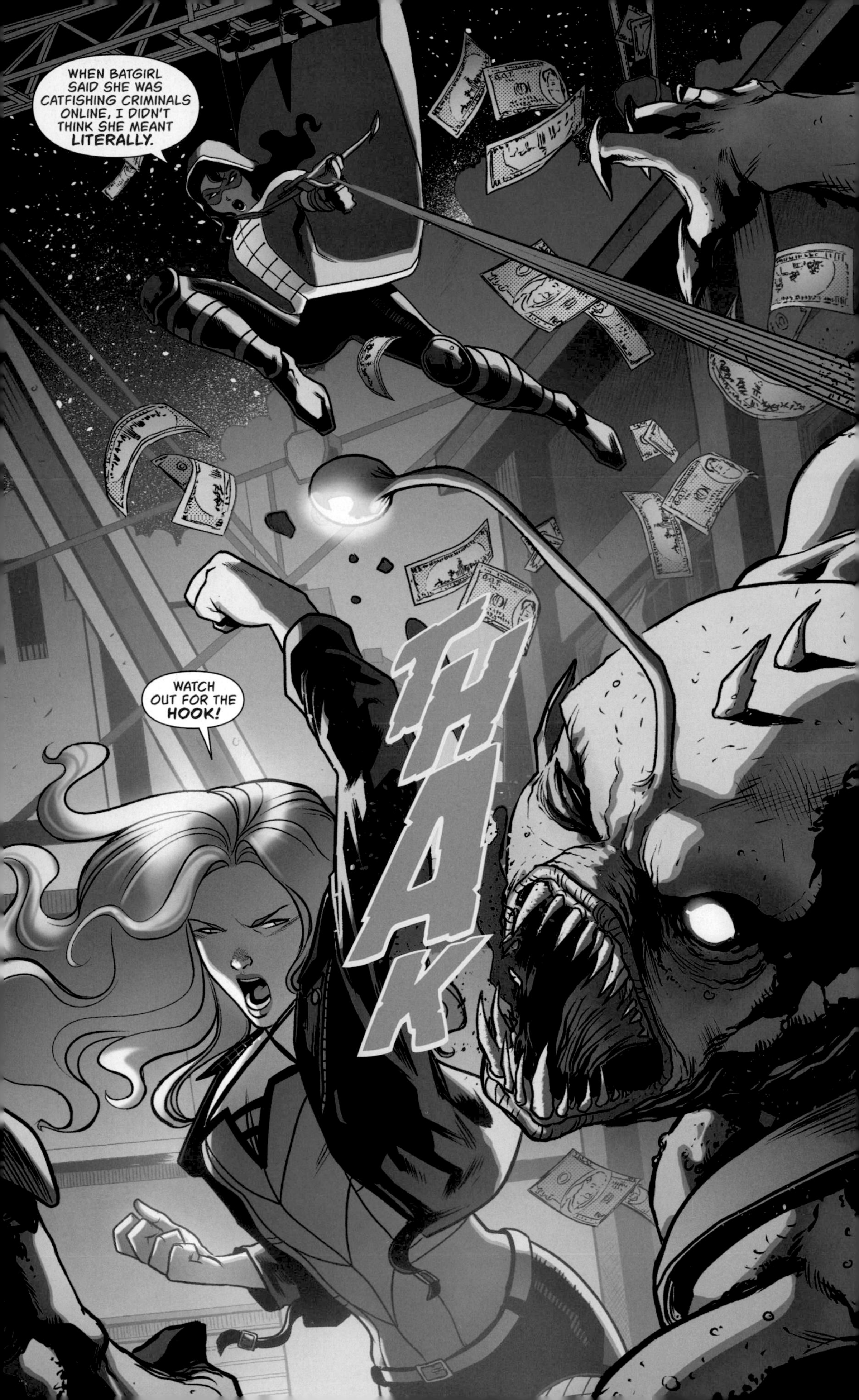
WHEN BATGIRL SAID SHE WAS CATFISHING CRIMINALS ONLINE, I DIDN'T THINK SHE MEANT **LITERALLY.**
WATCH OUT FOR THE **HOOK!**
THAK

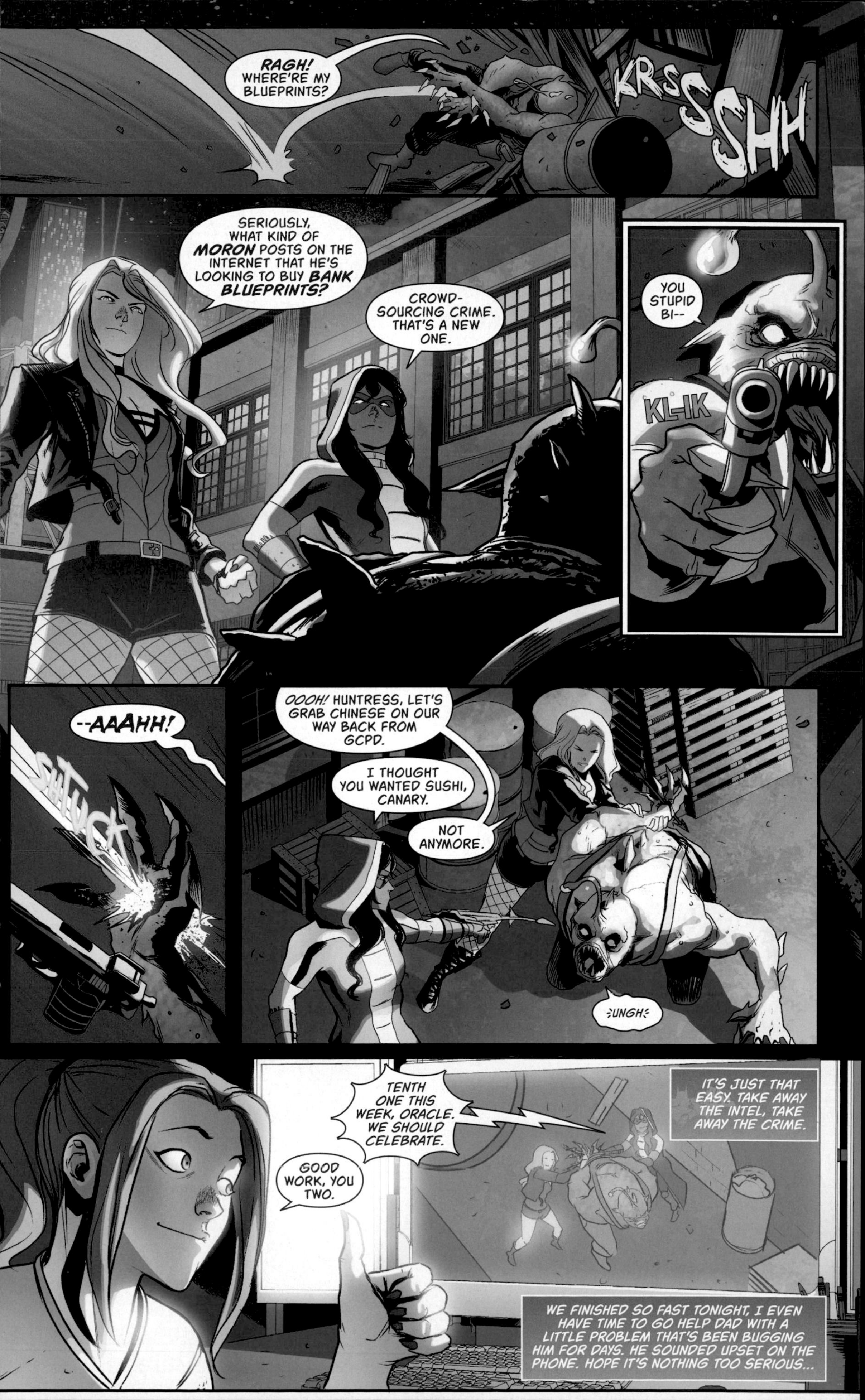

RAGH! WHERE'RE MY BLUEPRINTS?
KRSSSHH
SERIOUSLY, WHAT KIND OF MORON POSTS ON THE INTERNET THAT HE'S LOOKING TO BUY BANK BLUEPRINTS?
CROWD-SOURCING CRIME. THAT'S A NEW ONE.
YOU STUPID BI--
KL-IK
--AAAHH!
SHTUCK
OOOH! HUNTRESS, LET'S GRAB CHINESE ON OUR WAY BACK FROM GCPD.
I THOUGHT YOU WANTED SUSHI, CANARY.
NOT ANYMORE.
UNGH
TENTH ONE THIS WEEK, ORACLE. WE SHOULD CELEBRATE.
GOOD WORK, YOU TWO.
IT'S JUST THAT EASY. TAKE AWAY THE INTEL, TAKE AWAY THE CRIME.
WE FINISHED SO FAST TONIGHT, I EVEN HAVE TIME TO GO HELP DAD WITH A LITTLE PROBLEM THAT'S BEEN BUGGING HIM FOR DAYS. HE SOUNDED UPSET ON THE PHONE. HOPE IT'S NOTHING TOO SERIOUS...

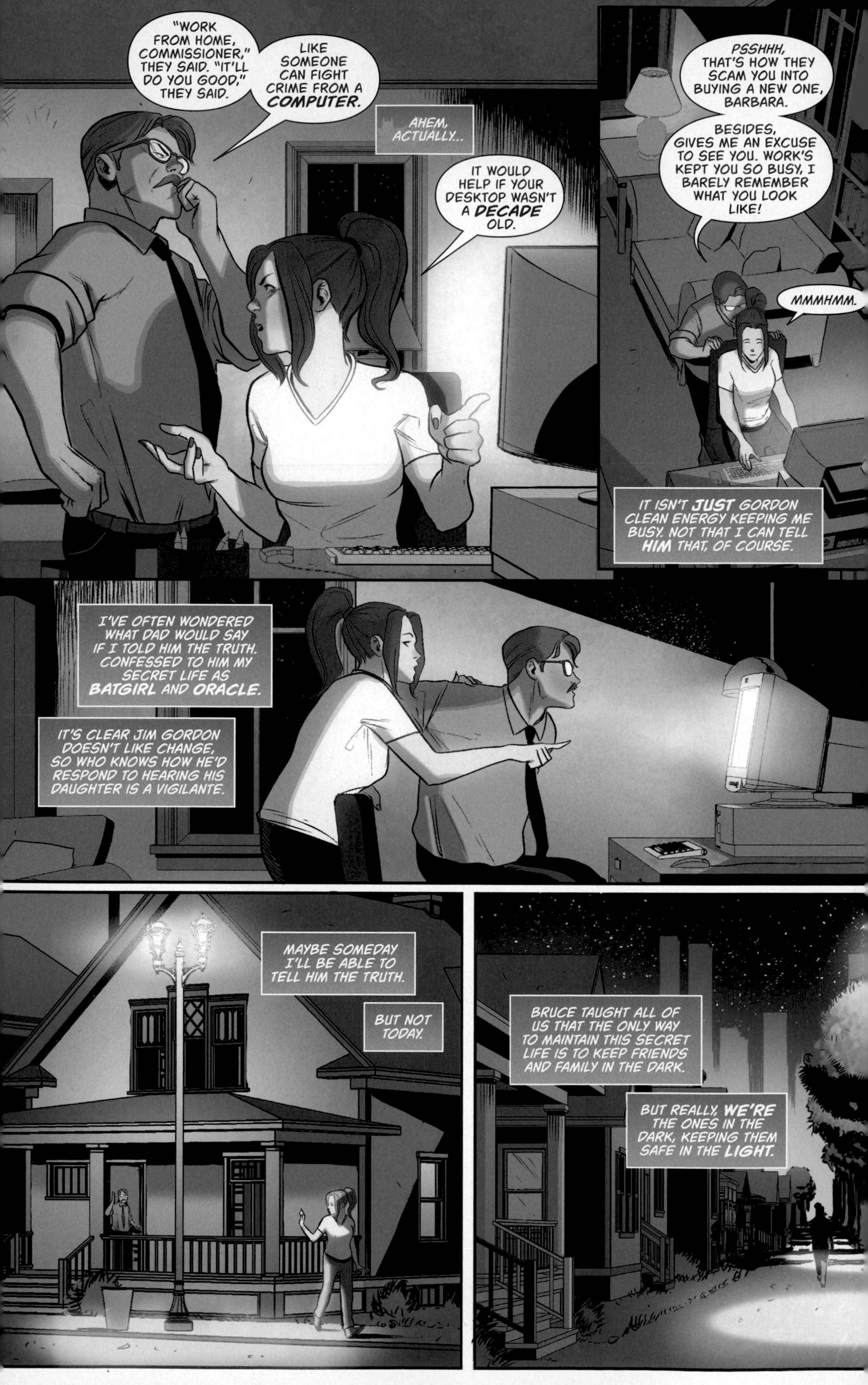

"WORK FROM HOME, COMMISSIONER," THEY SAID. "IT'LL DO YOU GOOD," THEY SAID.
LIKE SOMEONE CAN FIGHT CRIME FROM A COMPUTER.
AHEM, ACTUALLY...
IT WOULD HELP IF YOUR DESKTOP WASN'T A DECADE OLD.
PSSHHH, THAT'S HOW THEY SCAM YOU INTO BUYING A NEW ONE, BARBARA.
BESIDES, GIVES ME AN EXCUSE TO SEE YOU. WORK'S KEPT YOU SO BUSY, I BARELY REMEMBER WHAT YOU LOOK LIKE!
MMMHMM.
IT ISN'T JUST GORDON CLEAN ENERGY KEEPING ME BUSY. NOT THAT I CAN TELL HIM THAT, OF COURSE.
I'VE OFTEN WONDERED WHAT DAD WOULD SAY IF I TOLD HIM THE TRUTH. CONFESSED TO HIM MY SECRET LIFE AS BATGIRL AND ORACLE.
IT'S CLEAR JIM GORDON DOESN'T LIKE CHANGE, SO WHO KNOWS HOW HE'D RESPOND TO HEARING HIS DAUGHTER IS A VIGILANTE.
MAYBE SOMEDAY I'LL BE ABLE TO TELL HIM THE TRUTH.
BUT NOT TODAY.
BRUCE TAUGHT ALL OF US THAT THE ONLY WAY TO MAINTAIN THIS SECRET LIFE IS TO KEEP FRIENDS AND FAMILY IN THE DARK.
BUT REALLY, WE'RE THE ONES IN THE DARK, KEEPING THEM SAFE IN THE LIGHT.

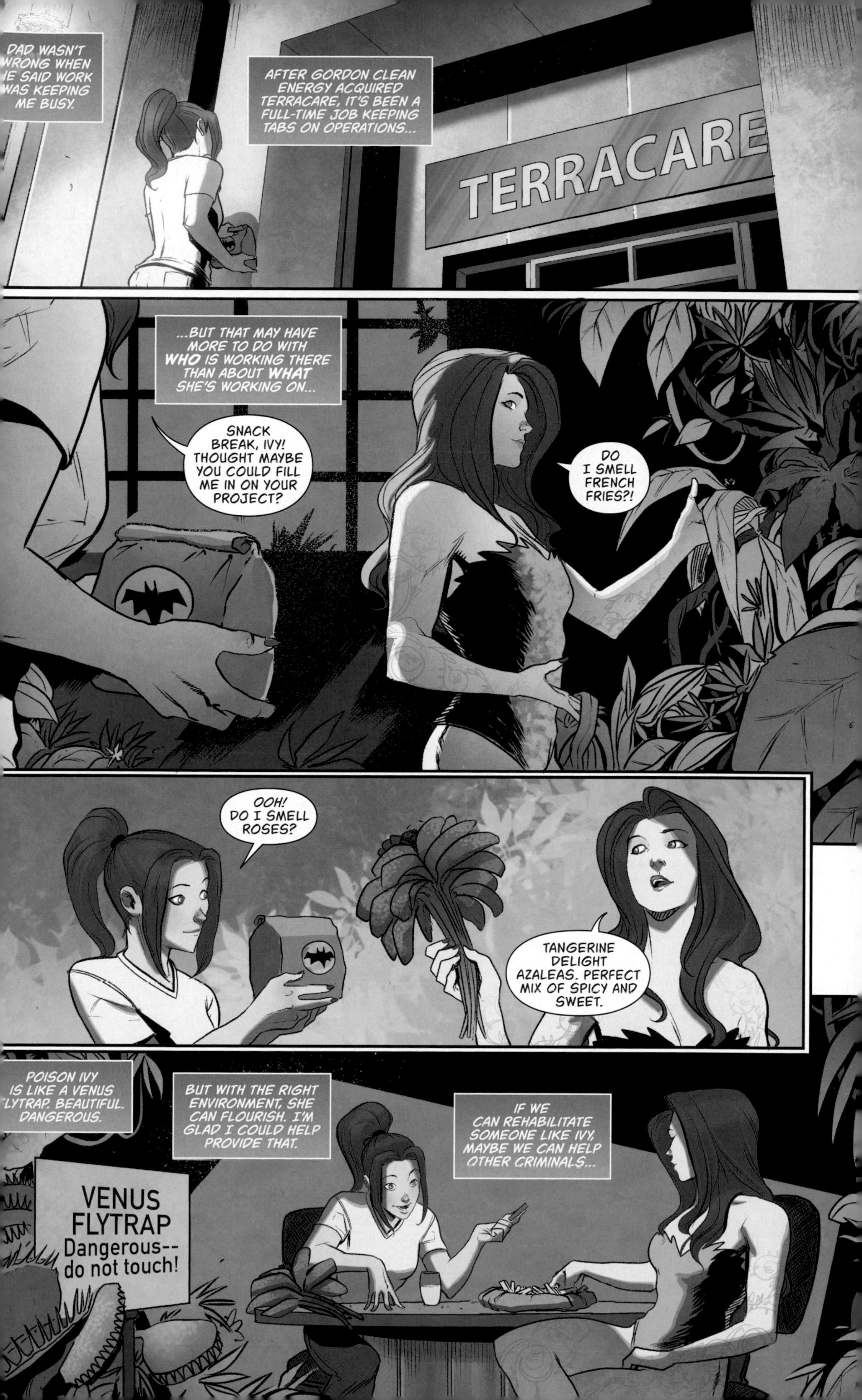
DAD WASN'T WRONG WHEN HE SAID WORK WAS KEEPING ME BUSY.
AFTER GORDON CLEAN ENERGY ACQUIRED TERRACARE, IT'S BEEN A FULL-TIME JOB KEEPING TABS ON OPERATIONS...
TERRACARE
...BUT THAT MAY HAVE MORE TO DO WITH WHO IS WORKING THERE THAN ABOUT WHAT SHE'S WORKING ON...
SNACK BREAK, IVY! THOUGHT MAYBE YOU COULD FILL ME IN ON YOUR PROJECT?
DO I SMELL FRENCH FRIES?!
OOH! DO I SMELL ROSES?
TANGERINE DELIGHT AZALEAS. PERFECT MIX OF SPICY AND SWEET.
POISON IVY IS LIKE A VENUS FLYTRAP. BEAUTIFUL. DANGEROUS.
BUT WITH THE RIGHT ENVIRONMENT, SHE CAN FLOURISH. I'M GLAD I COULD HELP PROVIDE THAT.
IF WE CAN REHABILITATE SOMEONE LIKE IVY, MAYBE WE CAN HELP OTHER CRIMINALS...
VENUS FLYTRAP Dangerous-- do not touch!

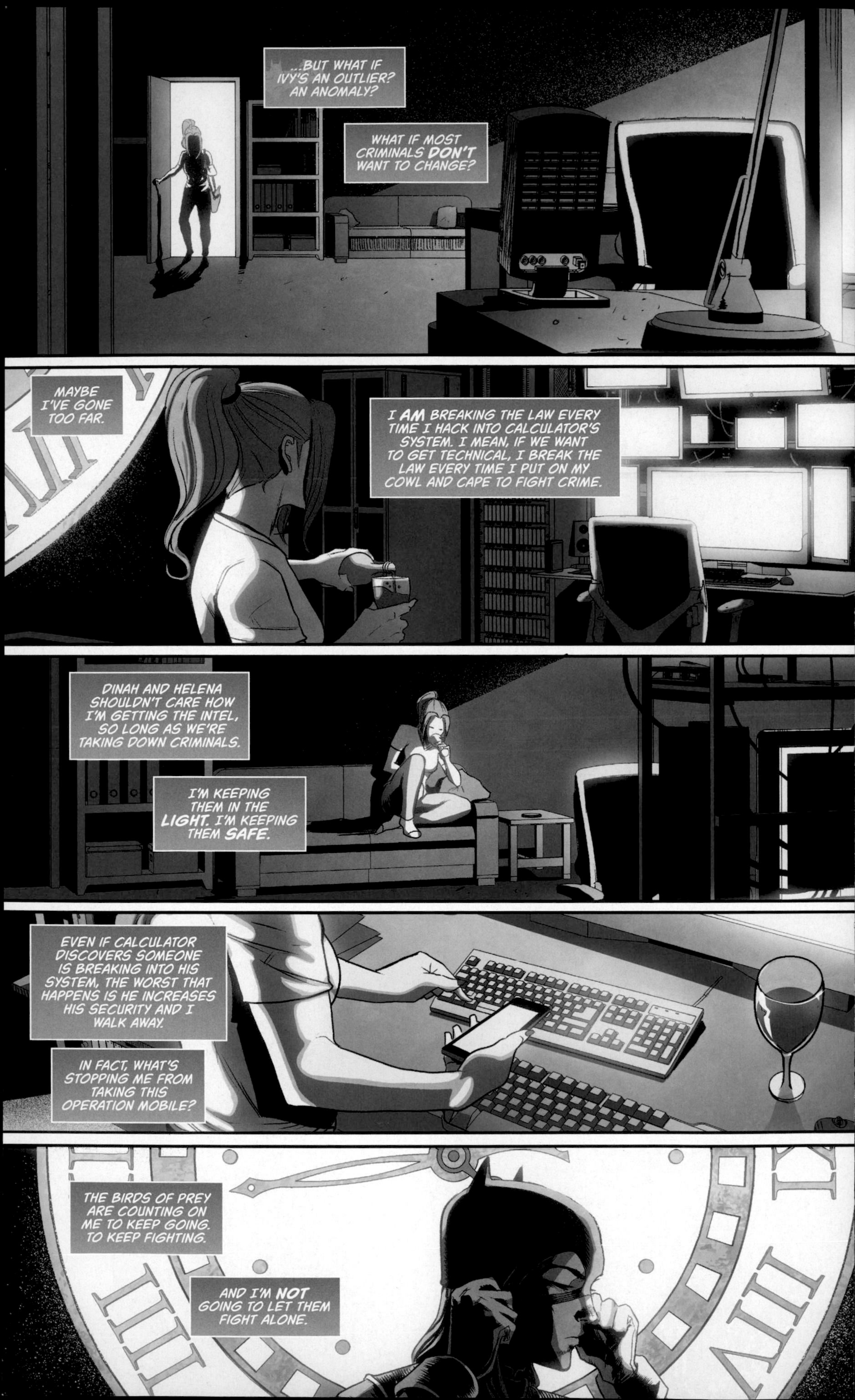
...BUT WHAT IF IVY'S AN OUTLIER? AN ANOMALY?
WHAT IF MOST CRIMINALS DON'T WANT TO CHANGE?
MAYBE I'VE GONE TOO FAR.
I AM BREAKING THE LAW EVERY TIME I HACK INTO CALCULATOR'S SYSTEM. I MEAN, IF WE WANT TO GET TECHNICAL, I BREAK THE LAW EVERY TIME I PUT ON MY COWL AND CAPE TO FIGHT CRIME.
DINAH AND HELENA SHOULDN'T CARE HOW I'M GETTING THE INTEL, SO LONG AS WE'RE TAKING DOWN CRIMINALS.
I'M KEEPING THEM IN THE LIGHT. I'M KEEPING THEM SAFE.
EVEN IF CALCULATOR DISCOVERS SOMEONE IS BREAKING INTO HIS SYSTEM, THE WORST THAT HAPPENS IS HE INCREASES HIS SECURITY AND I WALK AWAY.
IN FACT, WHAT'S STOPPING ME FROM TAKING THIS OPERATION MOBILE?
THE BIRDS OF PREY ARE COUNTING ON ME TO KEEP GOING. TO KEEP FIGHTING.
AND I'M NOT GOING TO LET THEM FIGHT ALONE.

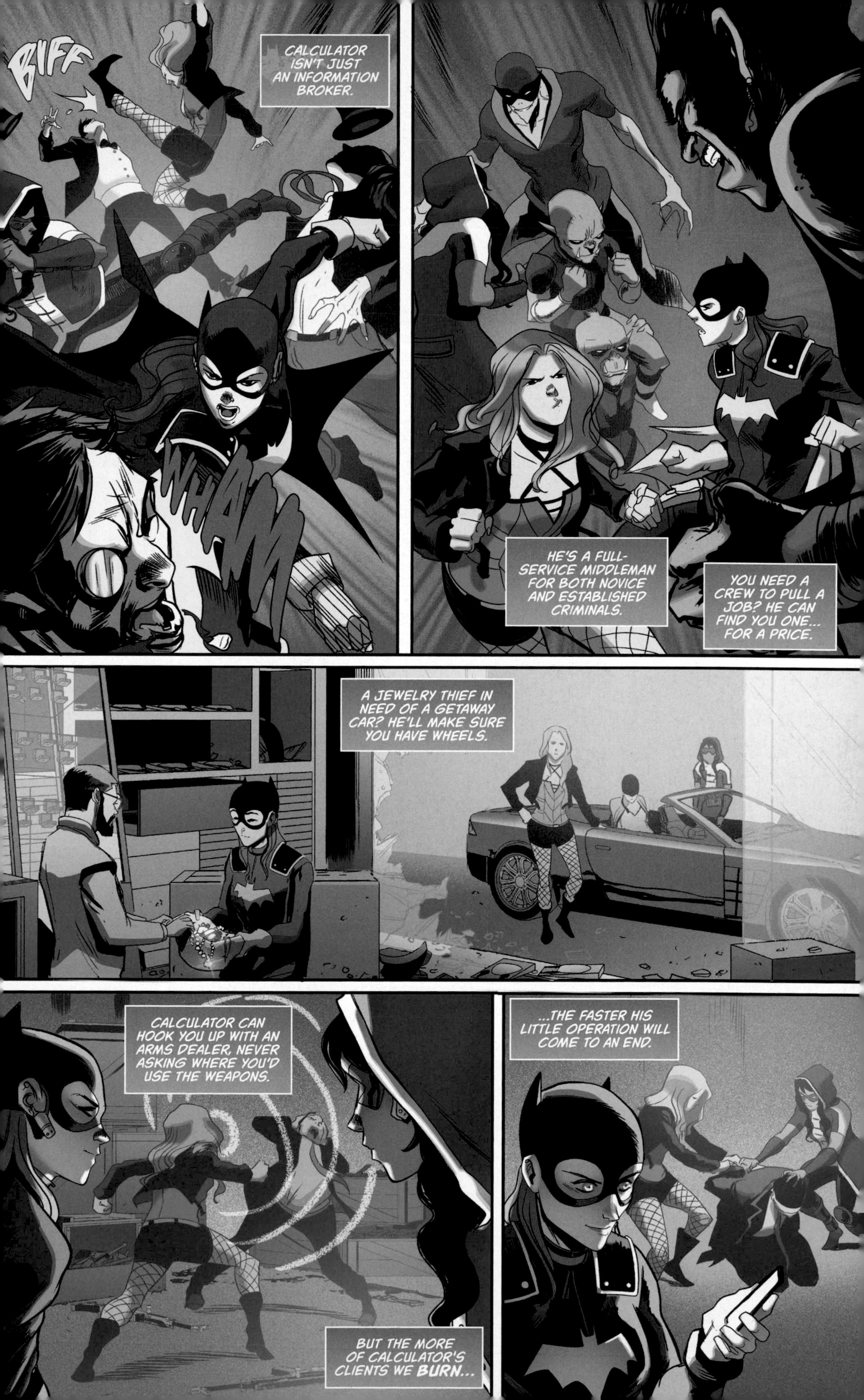
BIFF
CALCULATOR ISN'T JUST AN INFORMATION BROKER.
WHAM
HE'S A FULL-SERVICE MIDDLEMAN FOR BOTH NOVICE AND ESTABLISHED CRIMINALS.
YOU NEED A CREW TO PULL A JOB? HE CAN FIND YOU ONE... FOR A PRICE.
A JEWELRY THIEF IN NEED OF A GETAWAY CAR? HE'LL MAKE SURE YOU HAVE WHEELS.
CALCULATOR CAN HOOK YOU UP WITH AN ARMS DEALER, NEVER ASKING WHERE YOU'D USE THE WEAPONS.
BUT THE MORE OF CALCULATOR'S CLIENTS WE BURN...
...THE FASTER HIS LITTLE OPERATION WILL COME TO AN END.

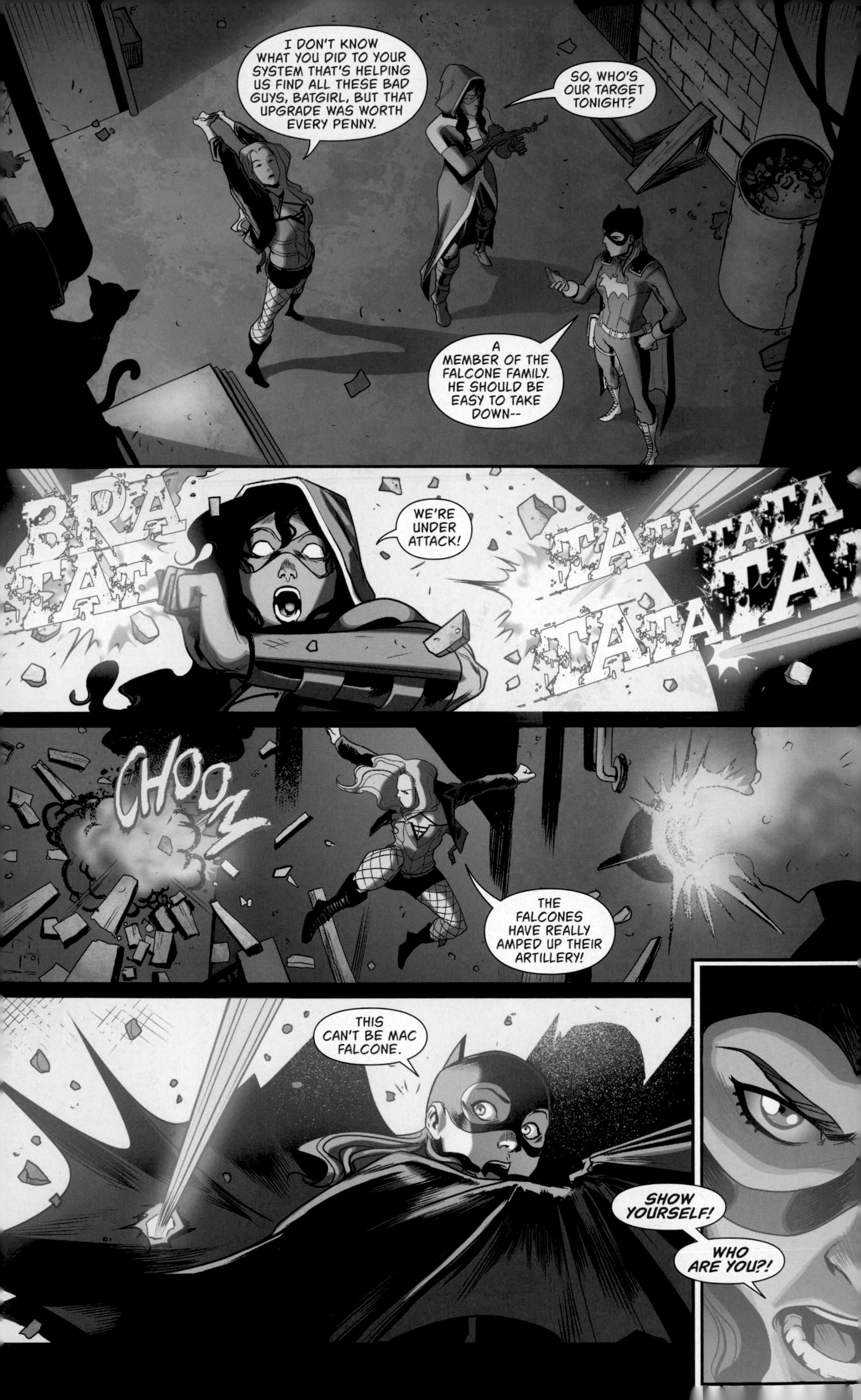
I DON'T KNOW WHAT YOU DID TO YOUR SYSTEM THAT'S HELPING US FIND ALL THESE BAD GUYS, BATGIRL, BUT THAT UPGRADE WAS WORTH EVERY PENNY.
SO, WHO'S OUR TARGET TONIGHT?
A MEMBER OF THE FALCONE FAMILY. HE SHOULD BE EASY TO TAKE DOWN--
BRATAT
WE'RE UNDER ATTACK!
TATATATATATATA
CHOOM
THE FALCONES HAVE REALLY AMPED UP THEIR ARTILLERY!
THIS CAN'T BE MAC FALCONE.
SHOW YOURSELF!
WHO ARE YOU?!

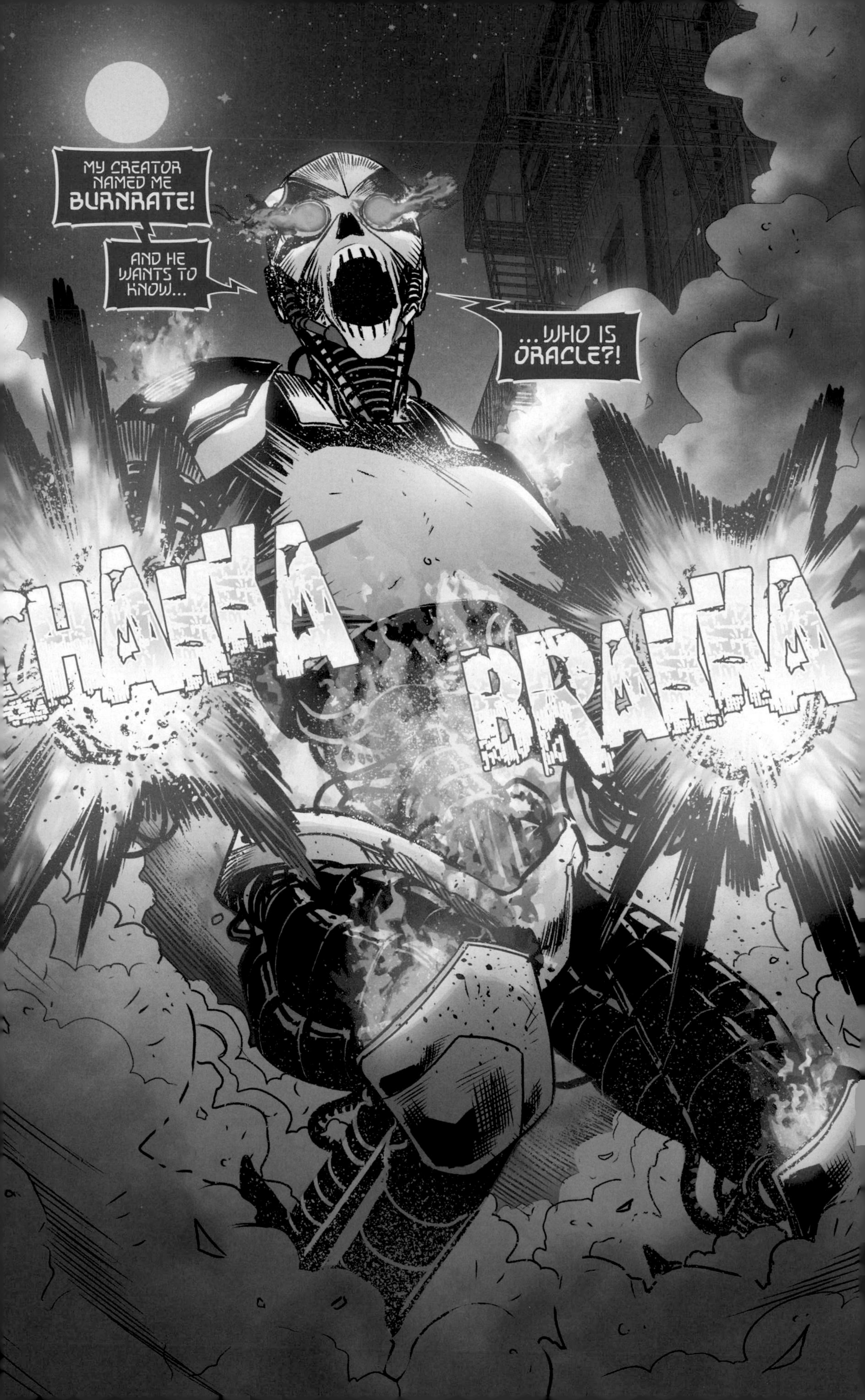
MY CREATOR NAMED ME BURNRATE!
AND HE WANTS TO KNOW...
...WHO IS ORACLE?!
CHAKKA
BRAKKA

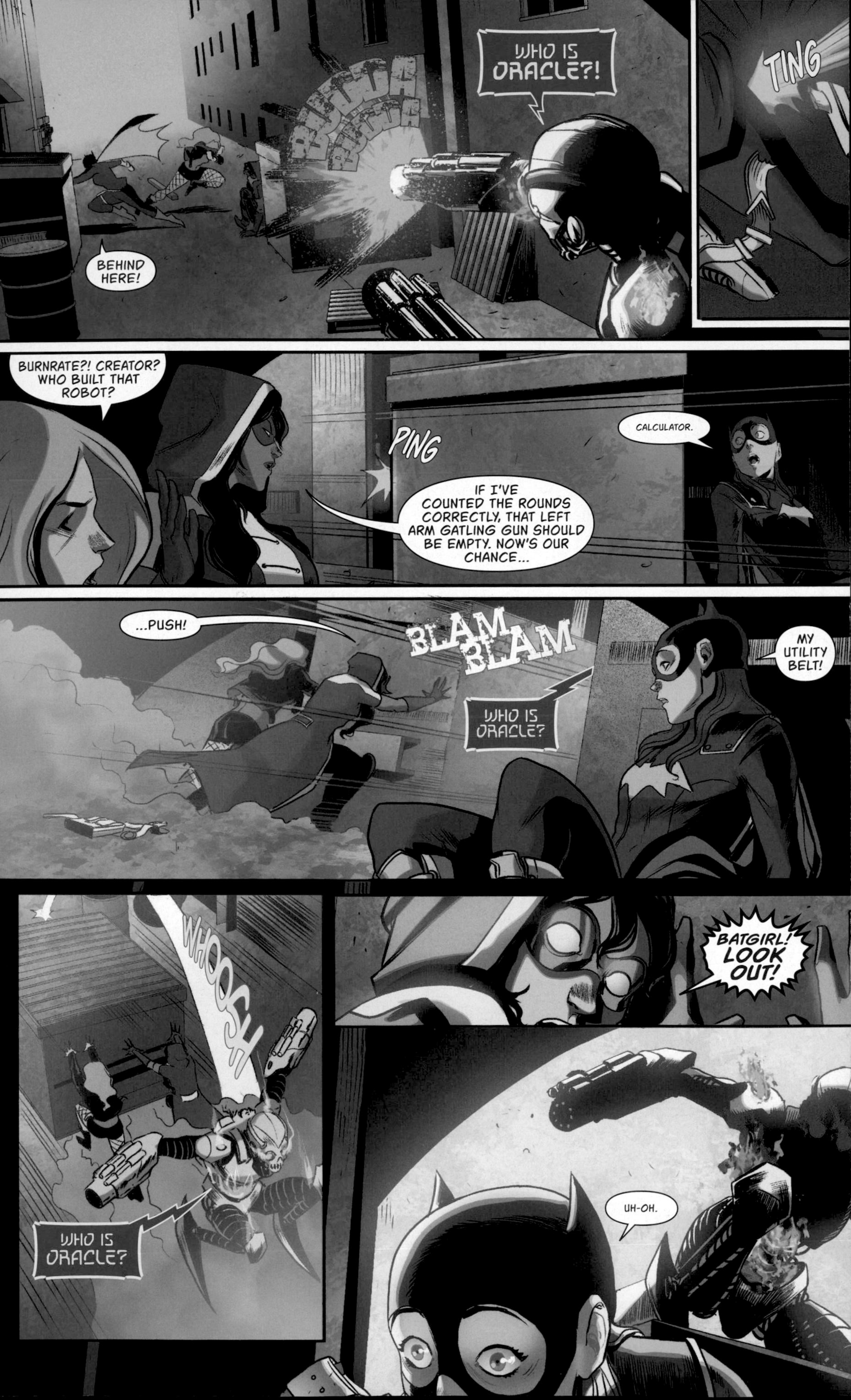
BEHIND HERE!
BUDDA BUDDA BUDDA
WHO IS ORACLE?!
TING
BURNRATE?! CREATOR? WHO BUILT THAT ROBOT?
PING
IF I'VE COUNTED THE ROUNDS CORRECTLY, THAT LEFT ARM GATLING GUN SHOULD BE EMPTY. NOW'S OUR CHANCE...
CALCULATOR.
...PUSH!
BLAM BLAM
WHO IS ORACLE?
MY UTILITY BELT!
WHOOSH
WHO IS ORACLE?
BATGIRL! LOOK OUT!
UH-OH.

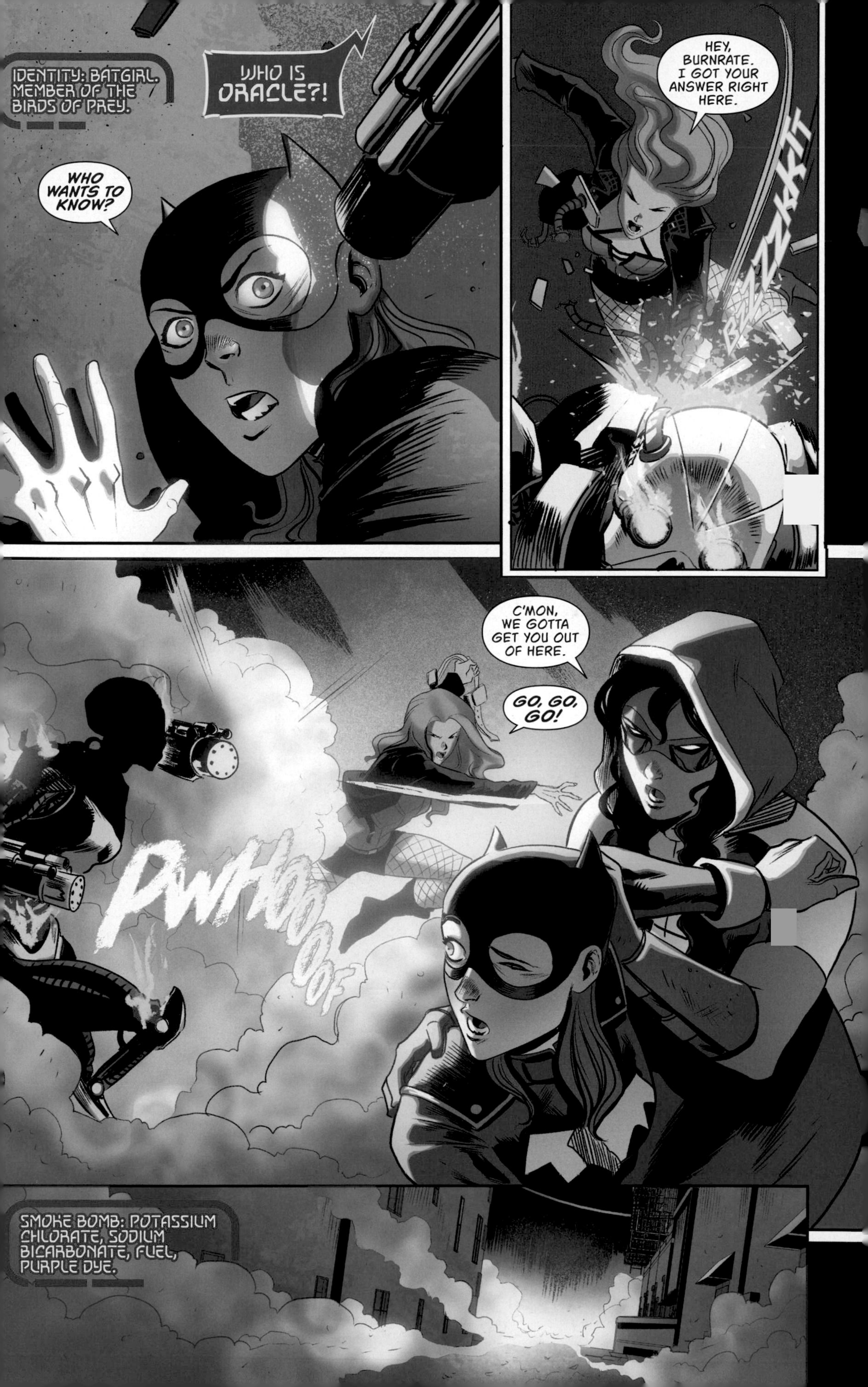
IDENTITY: BATGIRL. MEMBER OF THE BIRDS OF PREY.
WHO IS ORACLE?!
WHO WANTS TO KNOW?
HEY, BURNRATE. I GOT YOUR ANSWER RIGHT HERE.
BZZZKKTT
C'MON, WE GOTTA GET YOU OUT OF HERE.
GO, GO, GO!
PWHOOOOOF
SMOKE BOMB: POTASSIUM CHLORATE, SODIUM BICARBONATE, FUEL, PURPLE DYE.

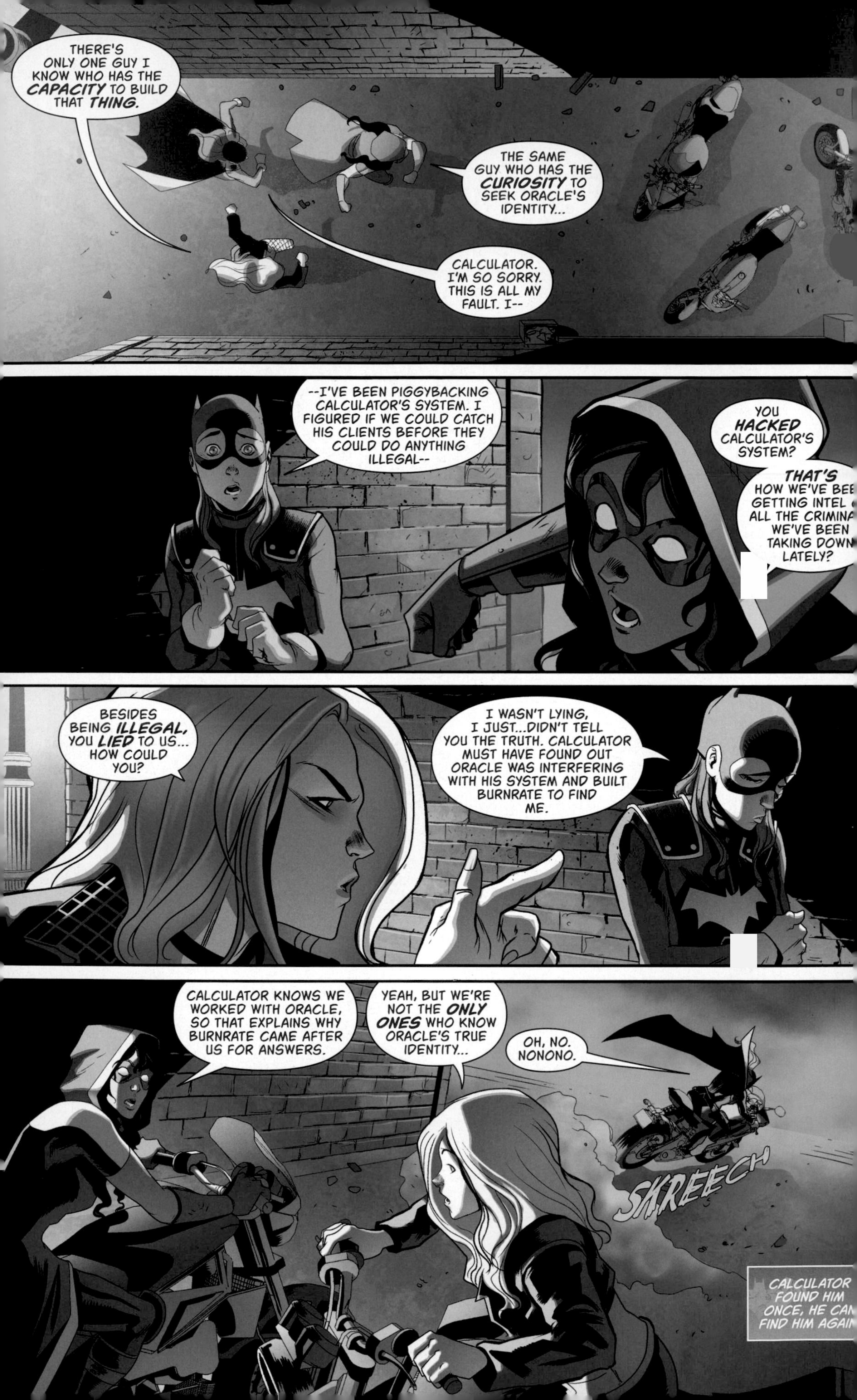
THERE'S ONLY ONE GUY I KNOW WHO HAS THE CAPACITY TO BUILD THAT THING.
THE SAME GUY WHO HAS THE CURIOSITY TO SEEK ORACLE'S IDENTITY...
CALCULATOR. I'M SO SORRY. THIS IS ALL MY FAULT. I--
--I'VE BEEN PIGGYBACKING CALCULATOR'S SYSTEM. I FIGURED IF WE COULD CATCH HIS CLIENTS BEFORE THEY COULD DO ANYTHING ILLEGAL--
YOU HACKED CALCULATOR'S SYSTEM?
THAT'S HOW WE'VE BEE GETTING INTEL ALL THE CRIMINA WE'VE BEEN TAKING DOWN LATELY?
BESIDES BEING ILLEGAL, YOU LIED TO US... HOW COULD YOU?
I WASN'T LYING, I JUST...DIDN'T TELL YOU THE TRUTH. CALCULATOR MUST HAVE FOUND OUT ORACLE WAS INTERFERING WITH HIS SYSTEM AND BUILT BURNRATE TO FIND ME.
CALCULATOR KNOWS WE WORKED WITH ORACLE, SO THAT EXPLAINS WHY BURNRATE CAME AFTER US FOR ANSWERS.
YEAH, BUT WE'RE NOT THE ONLY ONES WHO KNOW ORACLE'S TRUE IDENTITY...
OH, NO. NONONO.
SKREECH
CALCULATOR FOUND HIM ONCE, HE CAN FIND HIM AGAIN

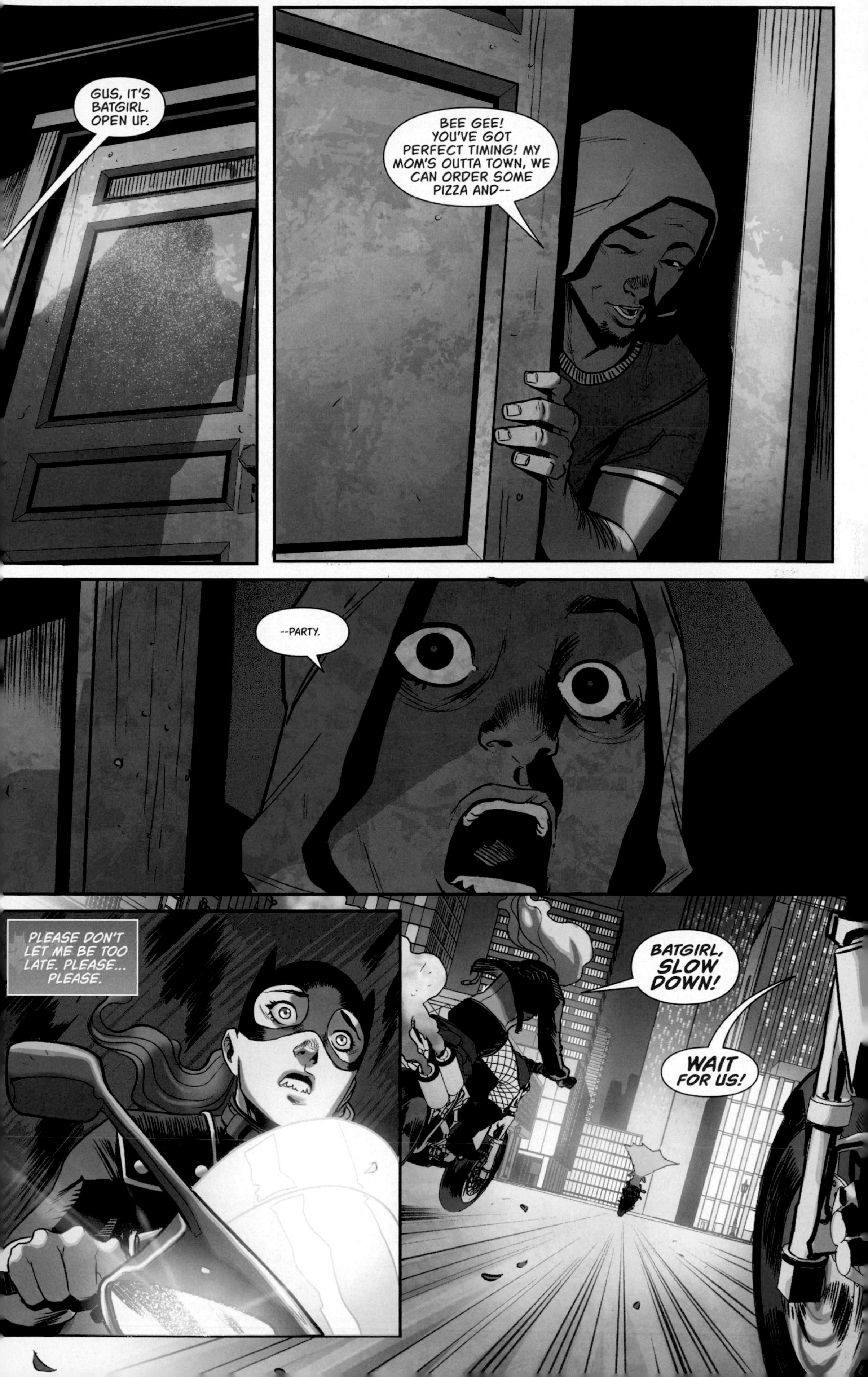
GUS, IT'S BATGIRL. OPEN UP.
BEE GEE! YOU'VE GOT PERFECT TIMING! MY MOM'S OUTTA TOWN, WE CAN ORDER SOME PIZZA AND--
--PARTY.
PLEASE DON'T LET ME BE TOO LATE. PLEASE... PLEASE.
BATGIRL, SLOW DOWN!
WAIT FOR US!

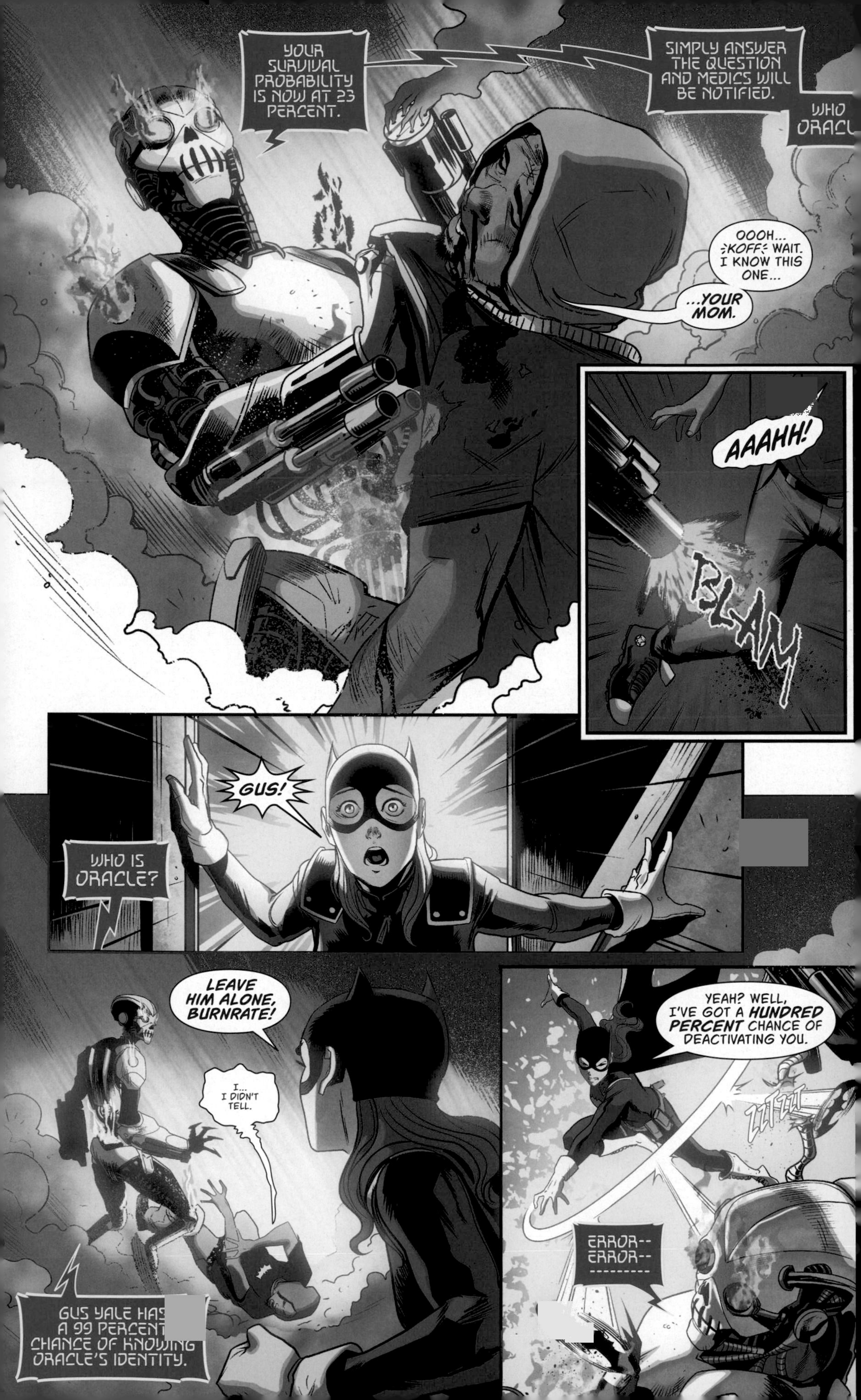
YOUR SURVIVAL PROBABILITY IS NOW AT 23 PERCENT.
SIMPLY ANSWER THE QUESTION AND MEDICS WILL BE NOTIFIED.
WHO ORACL
OOOH... *KOFF* WAIT. I KNOW THIS ONE...
...YOUR MOM.
AAAHH!
BLAM
GUS!
WHO IS ORACLE?
LEAVE HIM ALONE, BURNRATE!
I... I DIDN'T TELL.
GUS YALE HAS A 99 PERCENT CHANCE OF KNOWING ORACLE'S IDENTITY.
YEAH? WELL, I'VE GOT A HUNDRED PERCENT CHANCE OF DEACTIVATING YOU.
ERROR-- ERROR-- --------

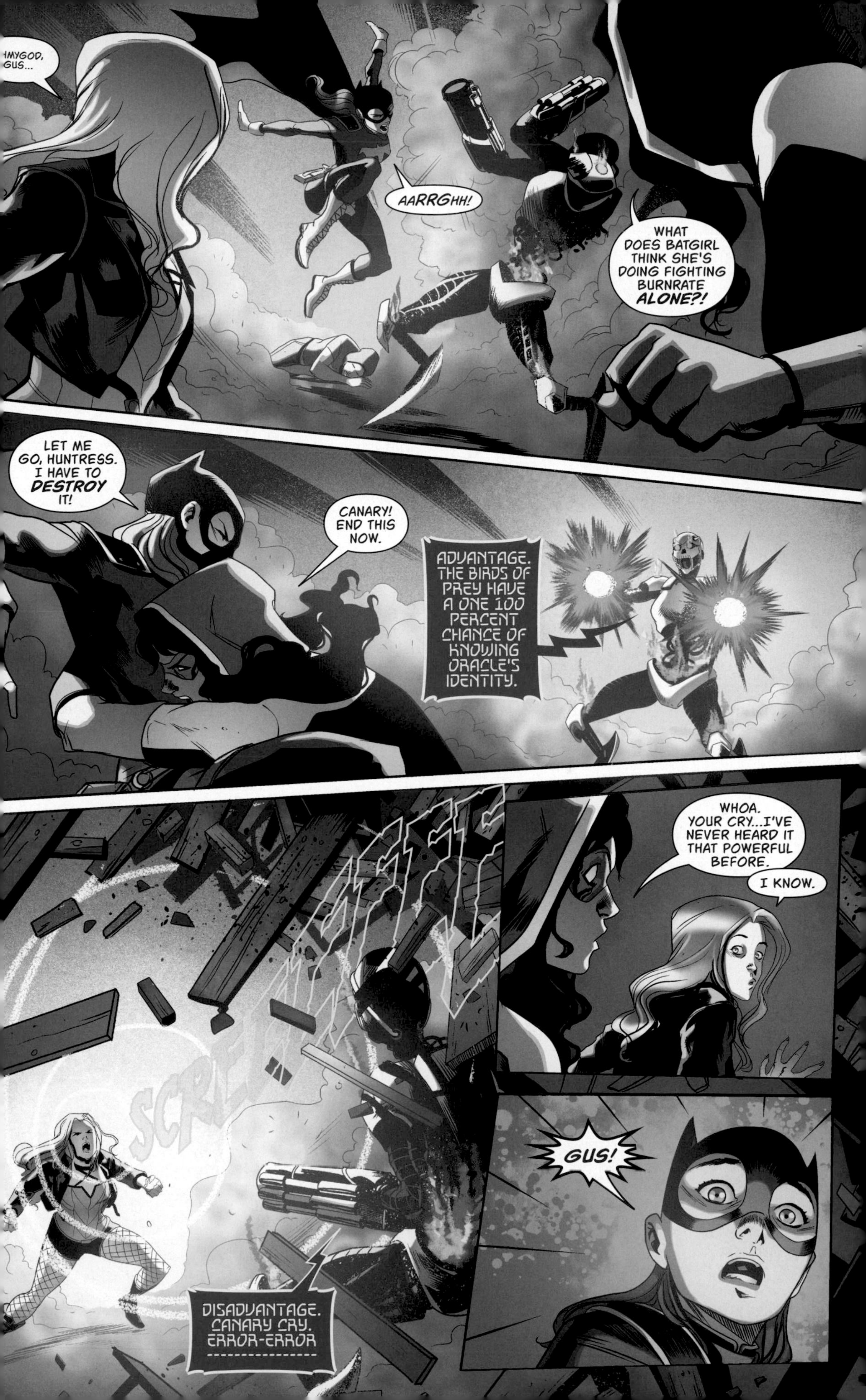

HMYGOD, GUS...
AARRGHH!
WHAT DOES BATGIRL THINK SHE'S DOING FIGHTING BURNRATE ALONE?!
LET ME GO, HUNTRESS. I HAVE TO DESTROY IT!
CANARY! END THIS NOW.
ADVANTAGE. THE BIRDS OF PREY HAVE A ONE 100 PERCENT CHANCE OF KNOWING ORACLE'S IDENTITY.
WHOA. YOUR CRY...I'VE NEVER HEARD IT THAT POWERFUL BEFORE.
I KNOW.
GUS!
DISADVANTAGE. CANARY CRY. ERROR-ERROR

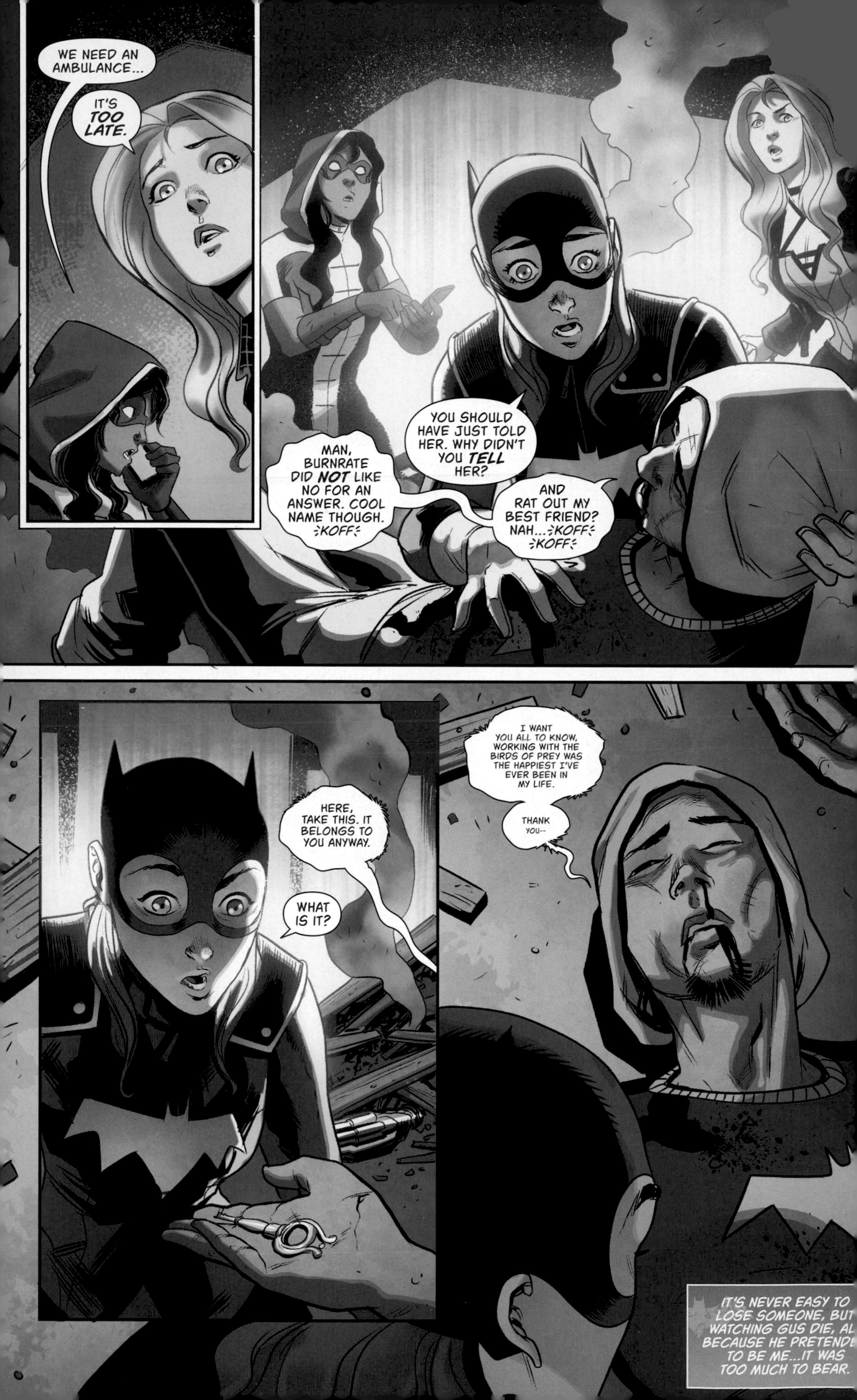
WE NEED AN AMBULANCE...
IT'S TOO LATE.
YOU SHOULD HAVE JUST TOLD HER. WHY DIDN'T YOU TELL HER?
MAN, BURNRATE DID NOT LIKE NO FOR AN ANSWER. COOL NAME THOUGH. KOFF
AND RAT OUT MY BEST FRIEND? NAH... KOFF KOFF
HERE, TAKE THIS. IT BELONGS TO YOU ANYWAY.
WHAT IS IT?
I WANT YOU ALL TO KNOW, WORKING WITH THE BIRDS OF PREY WAS THE HAPPIEST I'VE EVER BEEN IN MY LIFE.
THANK YOU--
IT'S NEVER EASY TO LOSE SOMEONE, BUT WATCHING GUS DIE, ALL BECAUSE HE PRETENDED TO BE ME...IT WAS TOO MUCH TO BEAR.

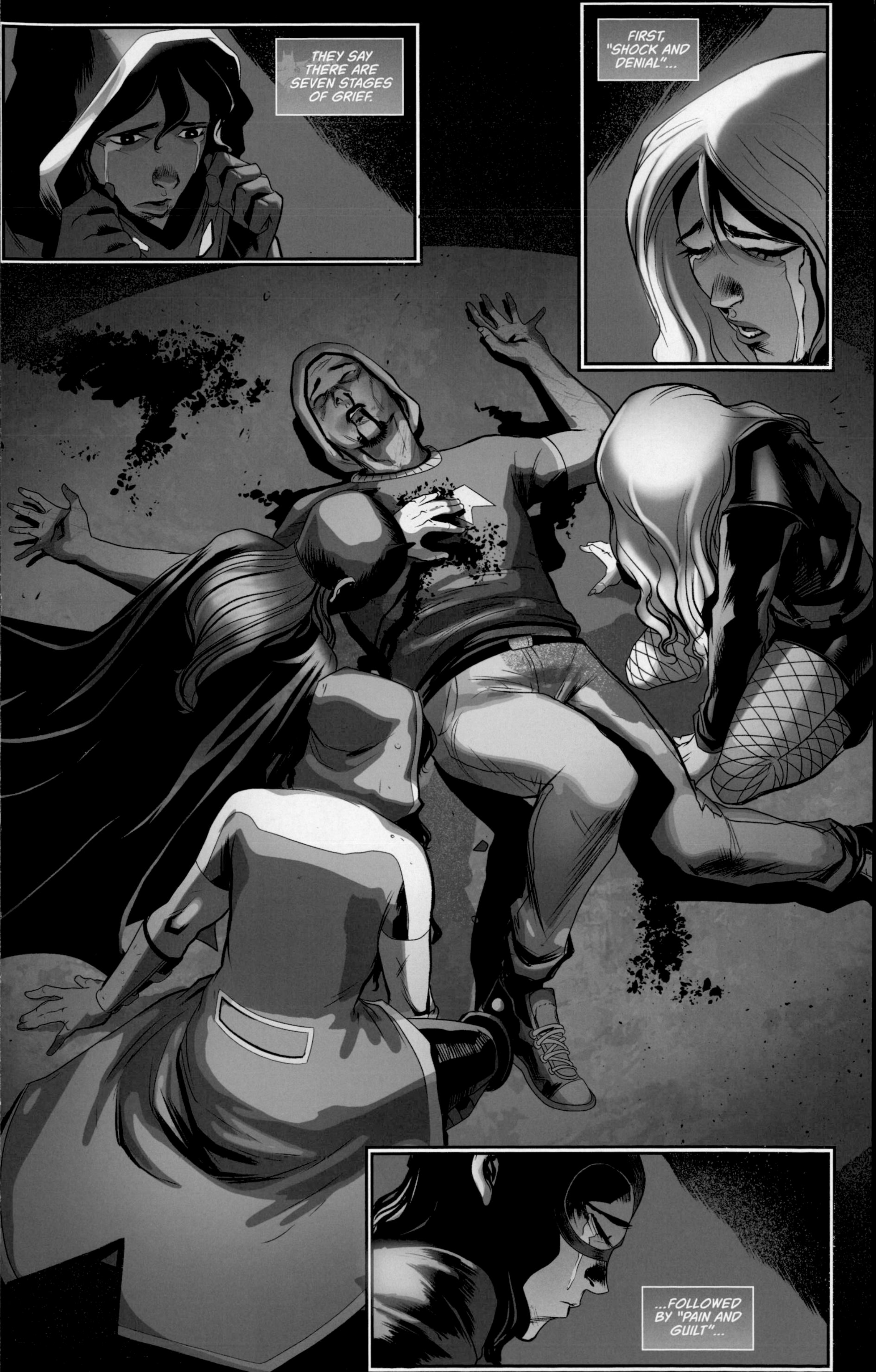
THEY SAY THERE ARE SEVEN STAGES OF GRIEF.
FIRST, "SHOCK AND DENIAL"...
...FOLLOWED BY "PAIN AND GUILT"...

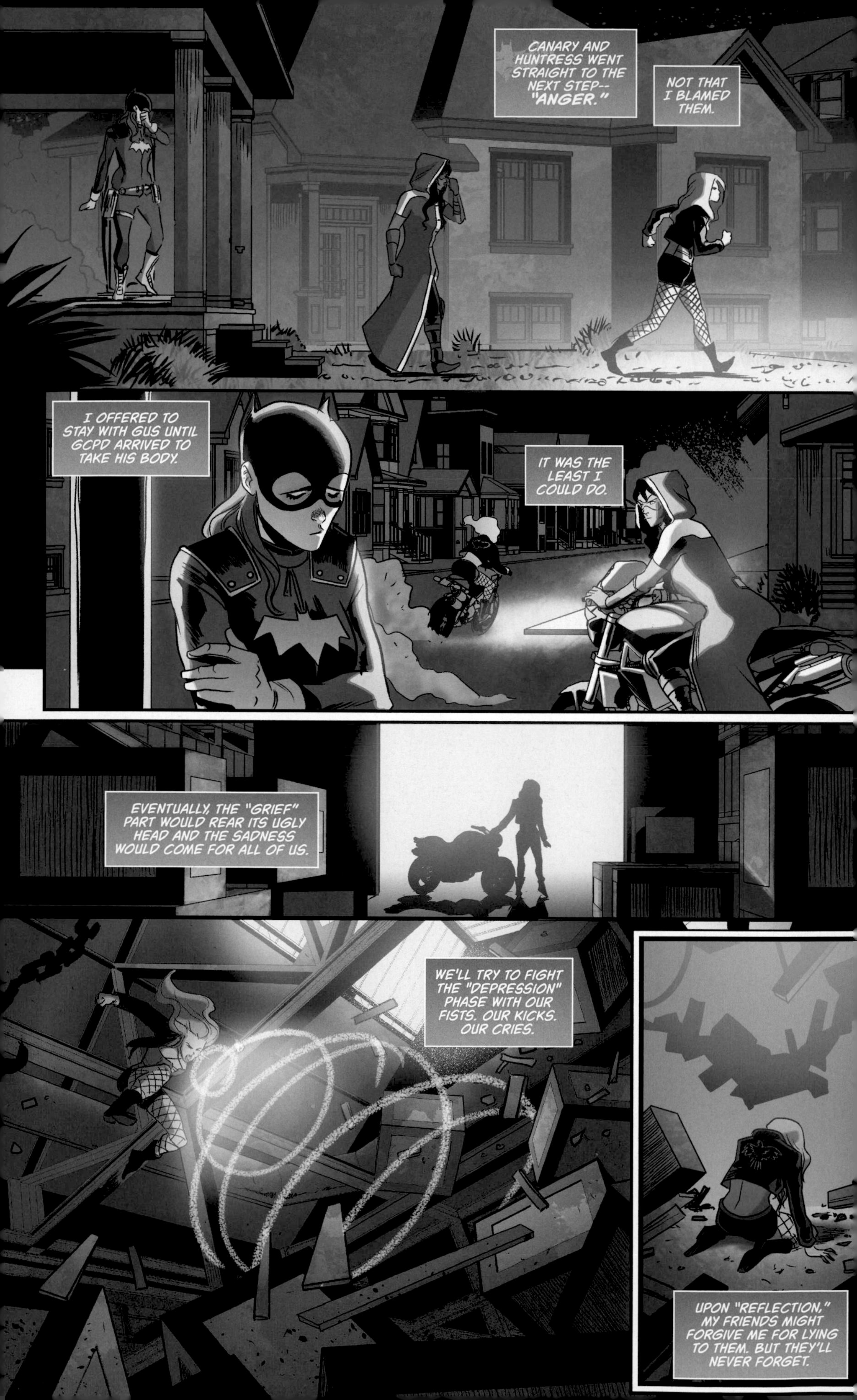
CANARY AND HUNTRESS WENT STRAIGHT TO THE NEXT STEP-- "ANGER."
NOT THAT I BLAMED THEM.
I OFFERED TO STAY WITH GUS UNTIL GCPD ARRIVED TO TAKE HIS BODY.
IT WAS THE LEAST I COULD DO.
EVENTUALLY, THE "GRIEF" PART WOULD REAR ITS UGLY HEAD AND THE SADNESS WOULD COME FOR ALL OF US.
WE'LL TRY TO FIGHT THE "DEPRESSION" PHASE WITH OUR FISTS. OUR KICKS. OUR CRIES.
UPON "REFLECTION," MY FRIENDS MIGHT FORGIVE ME FOR LYING TO THEM. BUT THEY'LL NEVER FORGET.

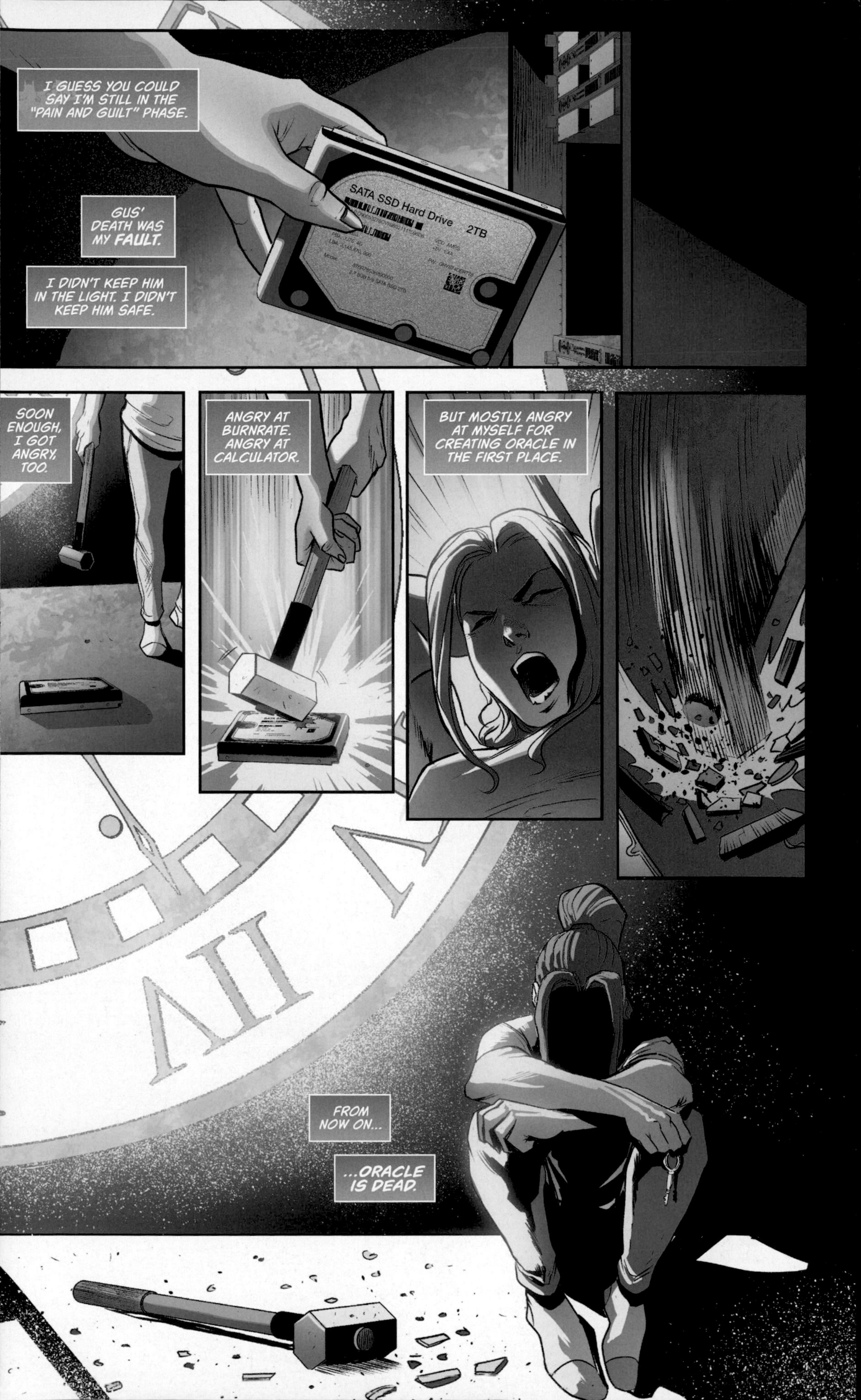
I GUESS YOU COULD SAY I'M STILL IN THE "PAIN AND GUILT" PHASE.
SATA SSD Hard Drive 2TB
GUS' DEATH WAS MY FAULT.
I DIDN'T KEEP HIM IN THE LIGHT. I DIDN'T KEEP HIM SAFE.
SOON ENOUGH, I GOT ANGRY, TOO.
ANGRY AT BURNRATE. ANGRY AT CALCULATOR.
BUT MOSTLY, ANGRY AT MYSELF FOR CREATING ORACLE IN THE FIRST PLACE.
FROM NOW ON...
...ORACLE IS DEAD.

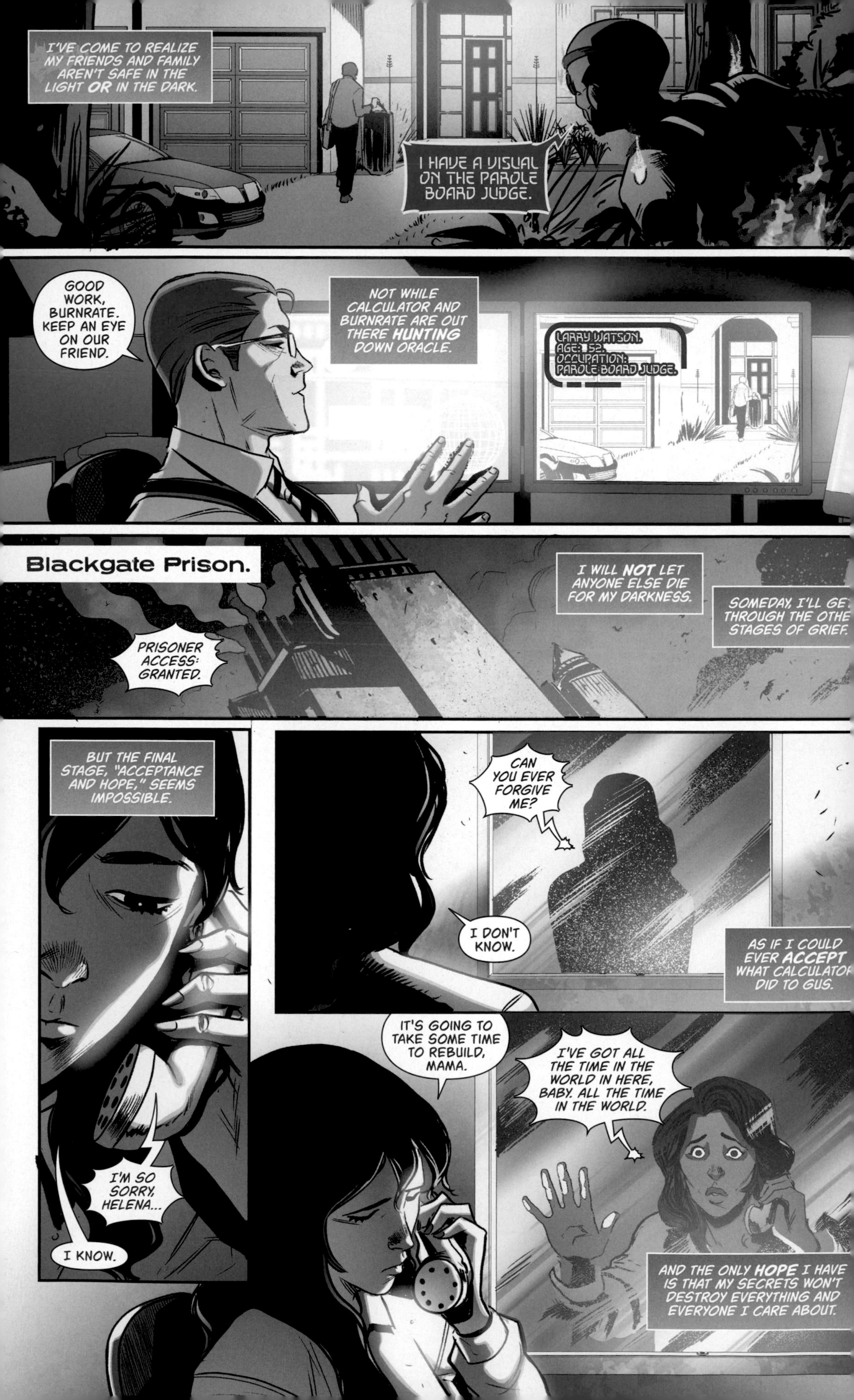

I'VE COME TO REALIZE MY FRIENDS AND FAMILY AREN'T SAFE IN THE LIGHT OR IN THE DARK.
I HAVE A VISUAL ON THE PAROLE BOARD JUDGE.
GOOD WORK, BURNRATE. KEEP AN EYE ON OUR FRIEND.
NOT WHILE CALCULATOR AND BURNRATE ARE OUT THERE HUNTING DOWN ORACLE.
LARRY WATSON. AGE: 52. OCCUPATION: PAROLE BOARD JUDGE.
Blackgate Prison.
PRISONER ACCESS: GRANTED.
I WILL NOT LET ANYONE ELSE DIE FOR MY DARKNESS.
SOMEDAY, I'LL GET THROUGH THE OTHER STAGES OF GRIEF.
BUT THE FINAL STAGE, "ACCEPTANCE AND HOPE," SEEMS IMPOSSIBLE.
CAN YOU EVER FORGIVE ME?
I DON'T KNOW.
AS IF I COULD EVER ACCEPT WHAT CALCULATOR DID TO GUS.
I'M SO SORRY, HELENA...
I KNOW.
IT'S GOING TO TAKE SOME TIME TO REBUILD, MAMA.
I'VE GOT ALL THE TIME IN THE WORLD IN HERE, BABY. ALL THE TIME IN THE WORLD.
AND THE ONLY HOPE I HAVE IS THAT MY SECRETS WON'T DESTROY EVERYTHING AND EVERYONE I CARE ABOUT.

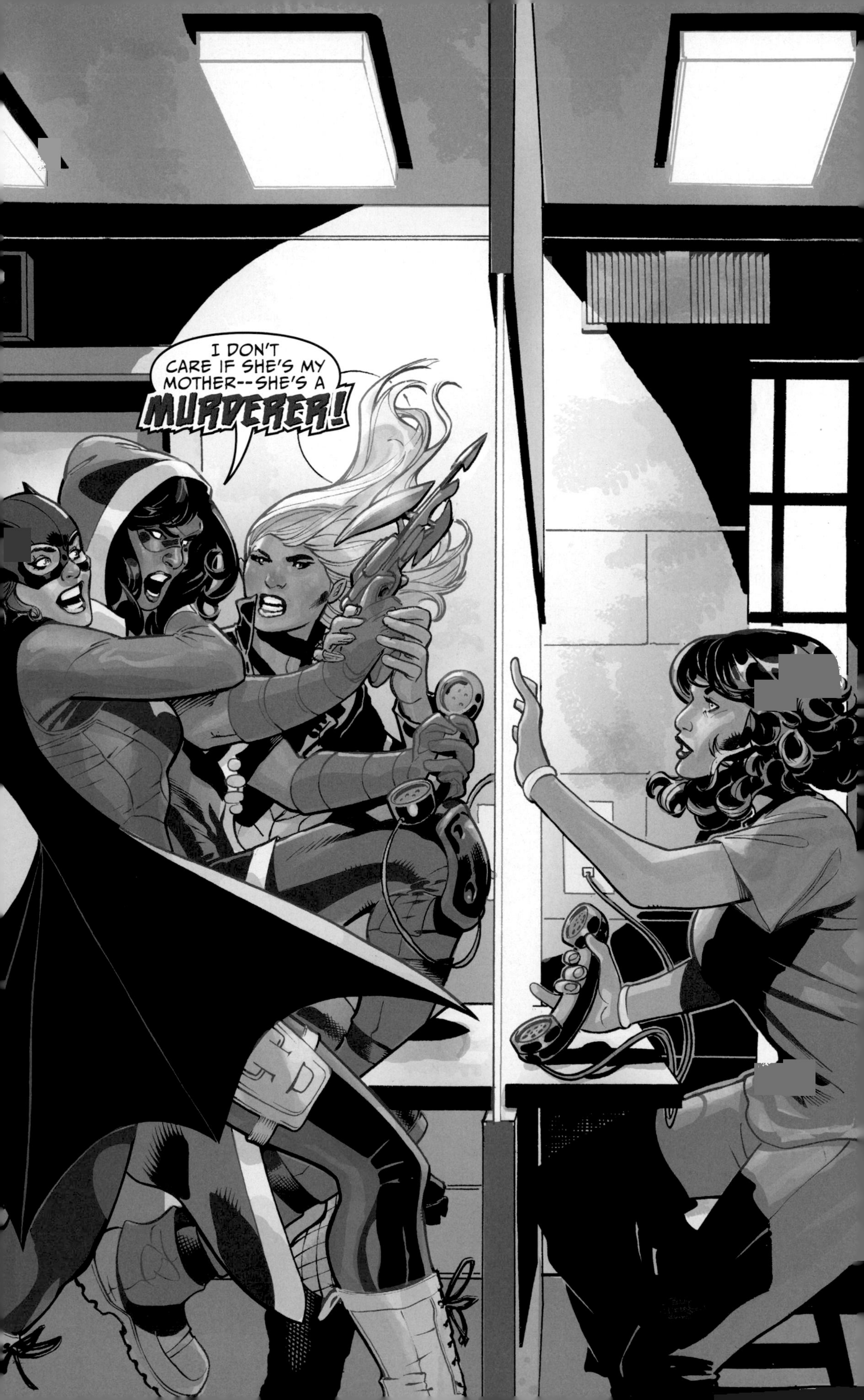
I DON'T CARE IF SHE'S MY MOTHER--SHE'S A MURDERER!

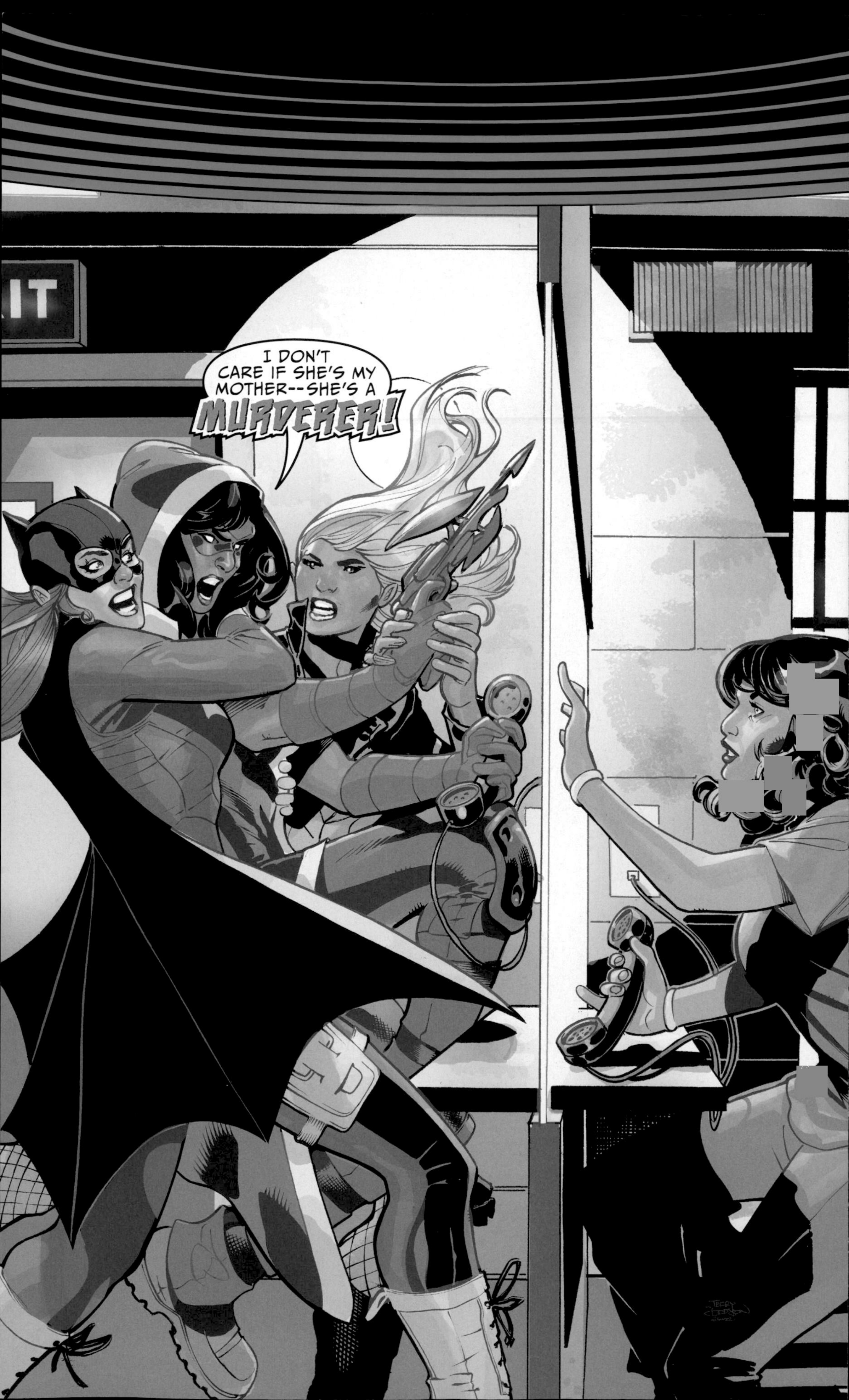
IT
I DON'T CARE IF SHE'S MY MOTHER--SHE'S A MURDERER!

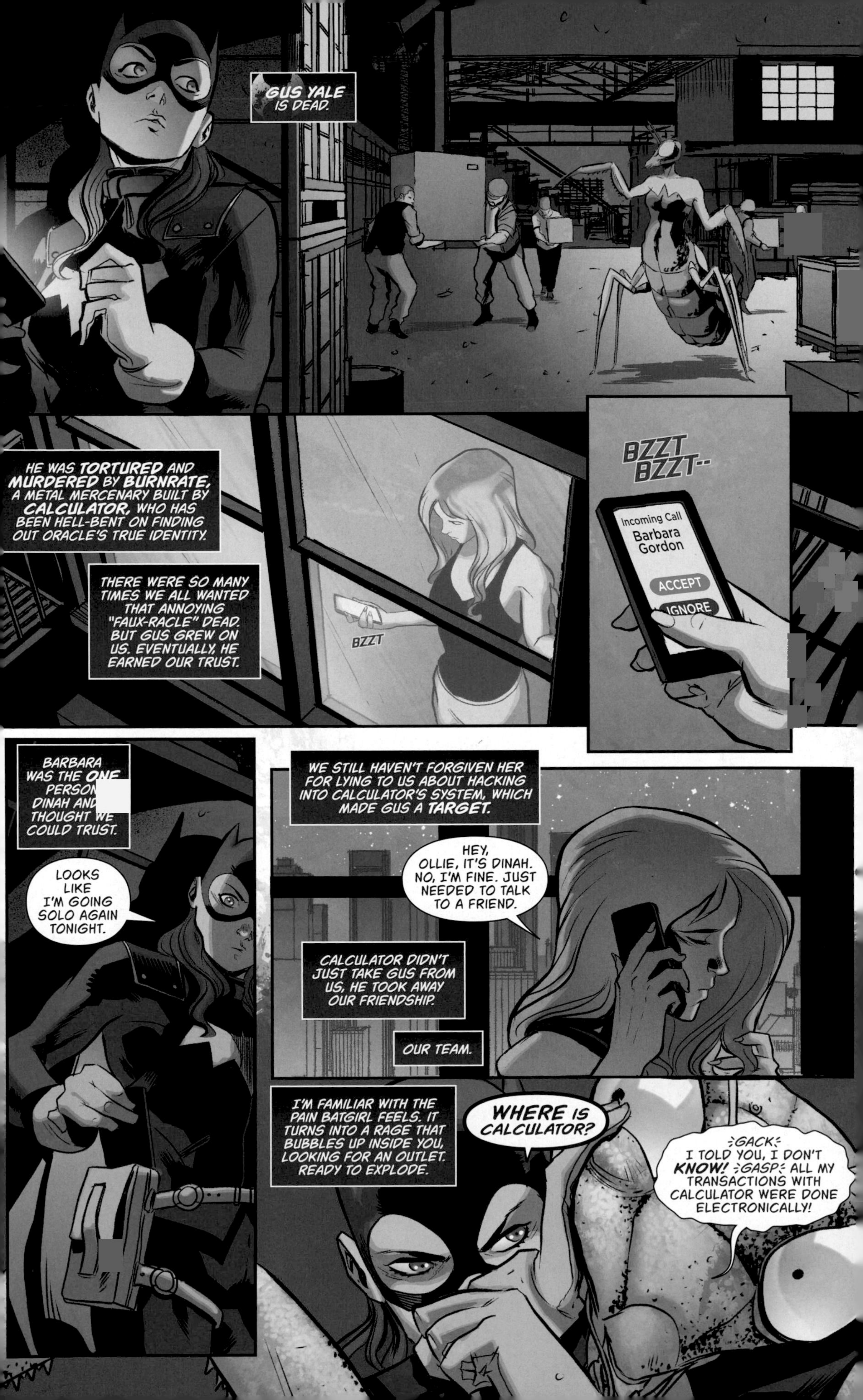
GUS YALE IS DEAD.
HE WAS TORTURED AND MURDERED BY BURNRATE, A METAL MERCENARY BUILT BY CALCULATOR, WHO HAS BEEN HELL-BENT ON FINDING OUT ORACLE'S TRUE IDENTITY.
THERE WERE SO MANY TIMES WE ALL WANTED THAT ANNOYING "FAUX-RACLE" DEAD. BUT GUS GREW ON US. EVENTUALLY, HE EARNED OUR TRUST.
BZZT
BZZT BZZT--
Incoming Call
Barbara Gordon
ACCEPT
IGNORE
BARBARA WAS THE ONE PERSON DINAH AND THOUGHT WE COULD TRUST.
LOOKS LIKE I'M GOING SOLO AGAIN TONIGHT.
WE STILL HAVEN'T FORGIVEN HER FOR LYING TO US ABOUT HACKING INTO CALCULATOR'S SYSTEM, WHICH MADE GUS A TARGET.
HEY, OLLIE, IT'S DINAH. NO, I'M FINE. JUST NEEDED TO TALK TO A FRIEND.
CALCULATOR DIDN'T JUST TAKE GUS FROM US, HE TOOK AWAY OUR FRIENDSHIP.
OUR TEAM.
I'M FAMILIAR WITH THE PAIN BATGIRL FEELS. IT TURNS INTO A RAGE THAT BUBBLES UP INSIDE YOU, LOOKING FOR AN OUTLET. READY TO EXPLODE.
WHERE IS CALCULATOR?
GACK I TOLD YOU, I DON'T KNOW! GASP ALL MY TRANSACTIONS WITH CALCULATOR WERE DONE ELECTRONICALLY!

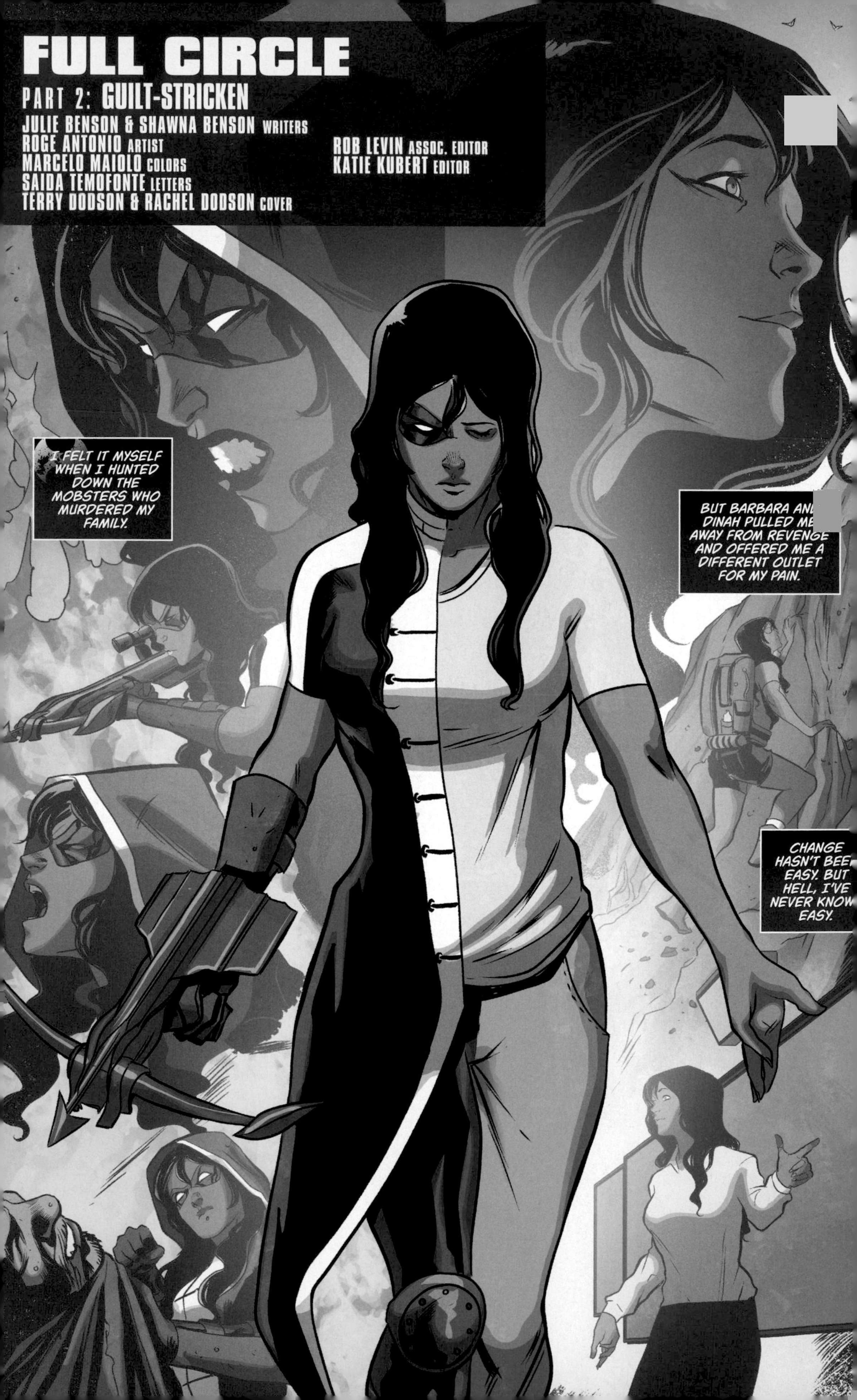

FULL CIRCLE
PART 2: GUILT-STRICKEN
JULIE BENSON & SHAWNA BENSON WRITERS
ROGE ANTONIO ARTIST
MARCELO MAIOLO COLORS
SAIDA TEMOFONTE LETTERS
TERRY DODSON & RACHEL DODSON COVER
ROB LEVIN ASSOC. EDITOR
KATIE KUBERT EDITOR
I FELT IT MYSELF WHEN I HUNTED DOWN THE MOBSTERS WHO MURDERED MY FAMILY.
BUT BARBARA AN DINAH PULLED ME AWAY FROM REVENGE AND OFFERED ME A DIFFERENT OUTLET FOR MY PAIN.
CHANGE HASN'T BEE EASY. BUT HELL, I'VE NEVER KNOW EASY.

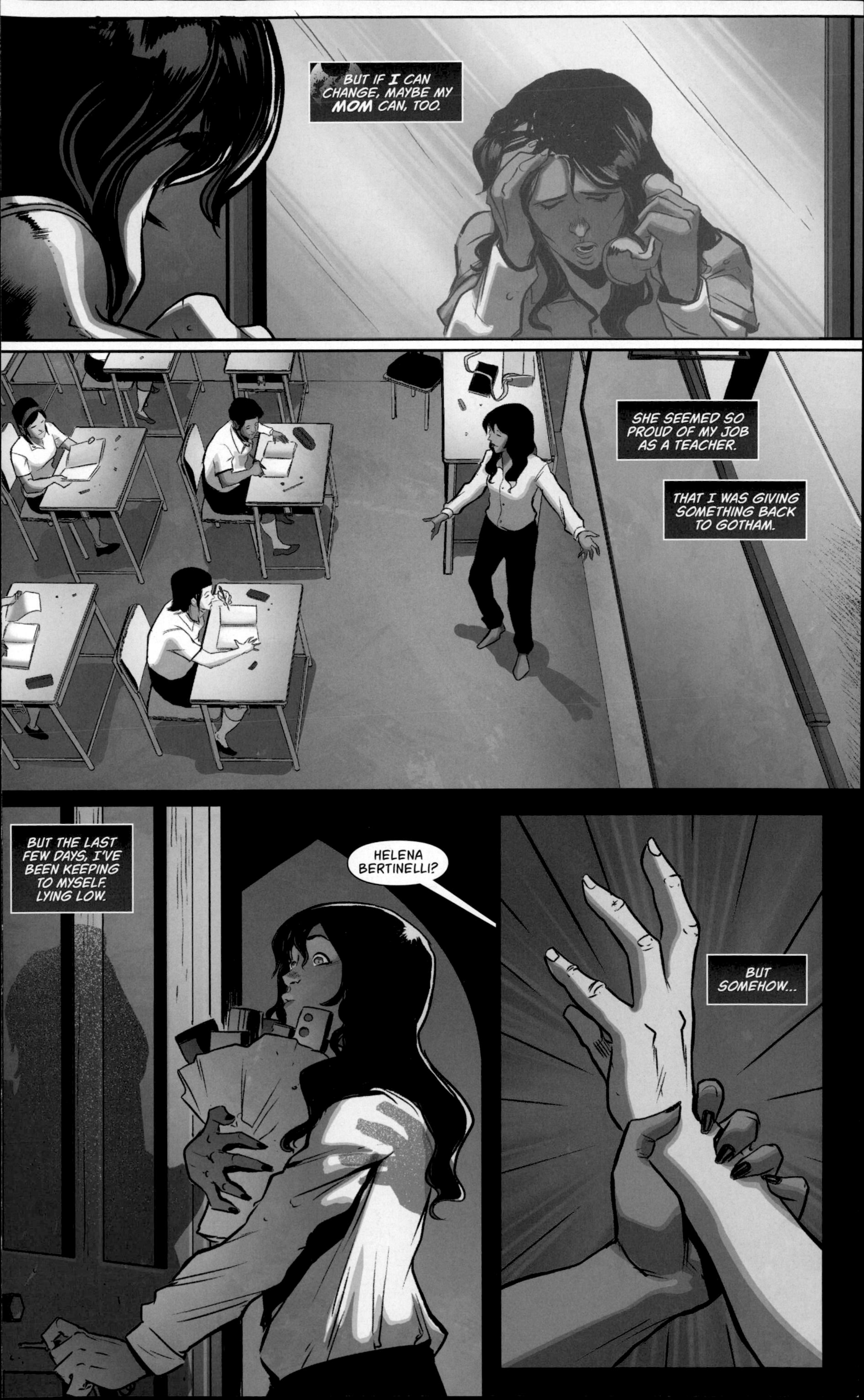
BUT IF I CAN CHANGE, MAYBE MY MOM CAN, TOO.
SHE SEEMED SO PROUD OF MY JOB AS A TEACHER.
THAT I WAS GIVING SOMETHING BACK TO GOTHAM.
BUT THE LAST FEW DAYS, I'VE BEEN KEEPING TO MYSELF. LYING LOW.
HELENA BERTINELLI?
BUT SOMEHOW...

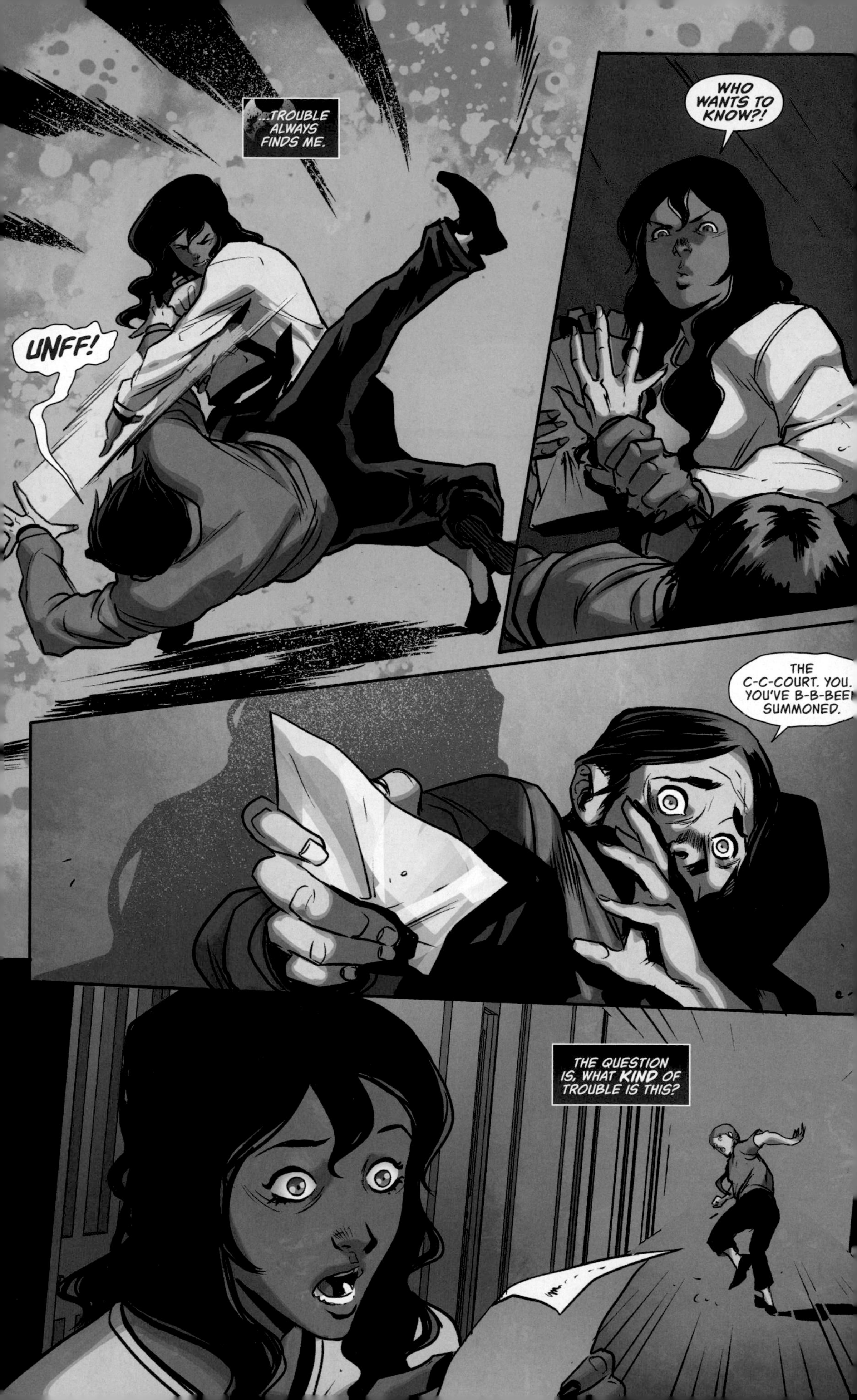
...TROUBLE ALWAYS FINDS ME.
UNFF!
WHO WANTS TO KNOW?!
THE C-C-COURT. YOU. YOU'VE B-B-BEEN SUMMONED.
THE QUESTION IS, WHAT KIND OF TROUBLE IS THIS?

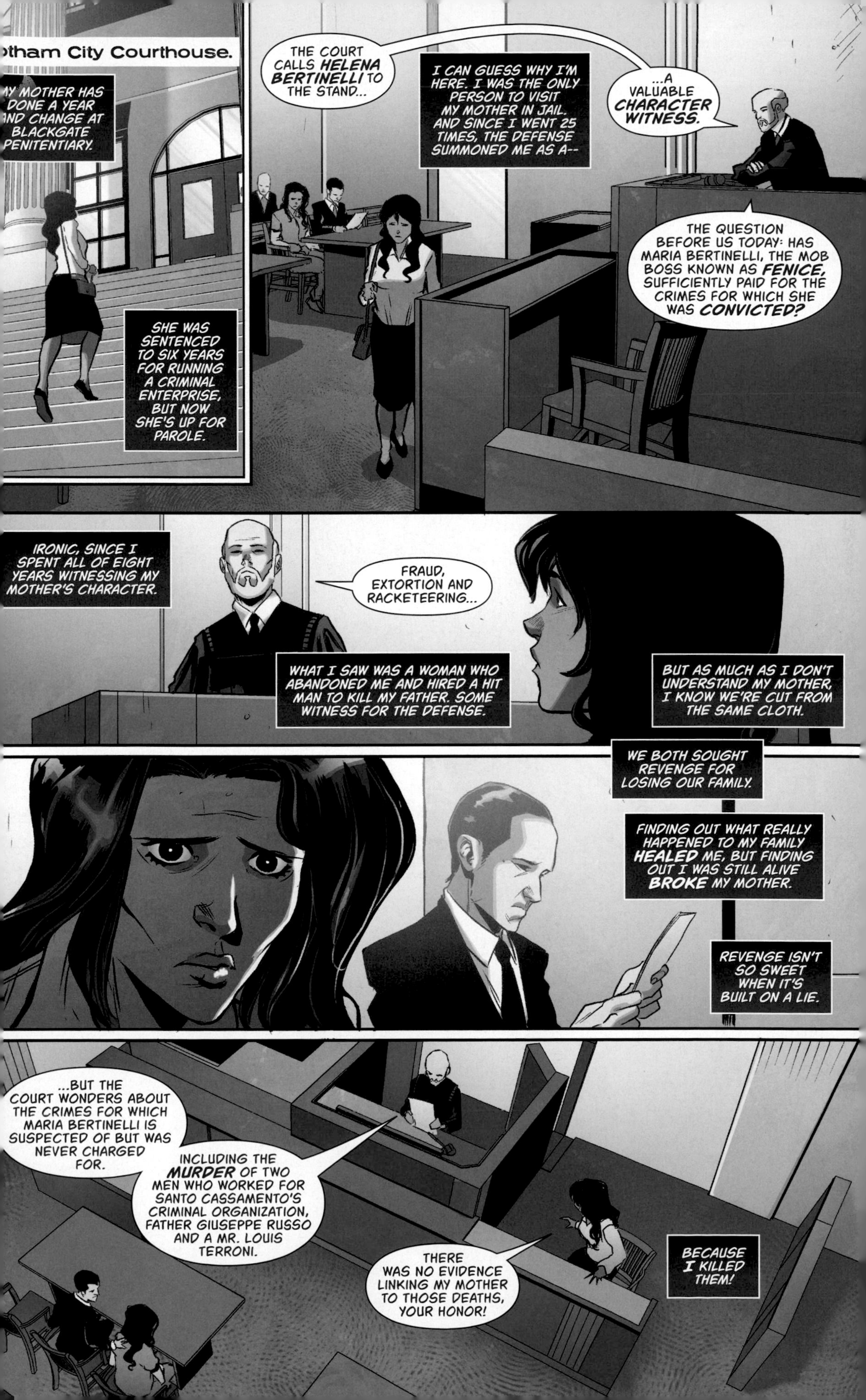

otham City Courthouse.
MY MOTHER HAS DONE A YEAR AND CHANGE AT BLACKGATE PENITENTIARY.
SHE WAS SENTENCED TO SIX YEARS FOR RUNNING A CRIMINAL ENTERPRISE, BUT NOW SHE'S UP FOR PAROLE.
THE COURT CALLS HELENA BERTINELLI TO THE STAND...
I CAN GUESS WHY I'M HERE. I WAS THE ONLY PERSON TO VISIT MY MOTHER IN JAIL. AND SINCE I WENT 25 TIMES, THE DEFENSE SUMMONED ME AS A--
...A VALUABLE CHARACTER WITNESS.
THE QUESTION BEFORE US TODAY: HAS MARIA BERTINELLI, THE MOB BOSS KNOWN AS FENICE, SUFFICIENTLY PAID FOR THE CRIMES FOR WHICH SHE WAS CONVICTED?
IRONIC, SINCE I SPENT ALL OF EIGHT YEARS WITNESSING MY MOTHER'S CHARACTER.
FRAUD, EXTORTION AND RACKETEERING...
WHAT I SAW WAS A WOMAN WHO ABANDONED ME AND HIRED A HIT MAN TO KILL MY FATHER. SOME WITNESS FOR THE DEFENSE.
BUT AS MUCH AS I DON'T UNDERSTAND MY MOTHER, I KNOW WE'RE CUT FROM THE SAME CLOTH.
WE BOTH SOUGHT REVENGE FOR LOSING OUR FAMILY.
FINDING OUT WHAT REALLY HAPPENED TO MY FAMILY HEALED ME, BUT FINDING OUT I WAS STILL ALIVE BROKE MY MOTHER.
REVENGE ISN'T SO SWEET WHEN IT'S BUILT ON A LIE.
...BUT THE COURT WONDERS ABOUT THE CRIMES FOR WHICH MARIA BERTINELLI IS SUSPECTED OF BUT WAS NEVER CHARGED FOR.
INCLUDING THE MURDER OF TWO MEN WHO WORKED FOR SANTO CASSAMENTO'S CRIMINAL ORGANIZATION, FATHER GIUSEPPE RUSSO AND A MR. LOUIS TERRONI.
THERE WAS NO EVIDENCE LINKING MY MOTHER TO THOSE DEATHS, YOUR HONOR!
BECAUSE I KILLED THEM!

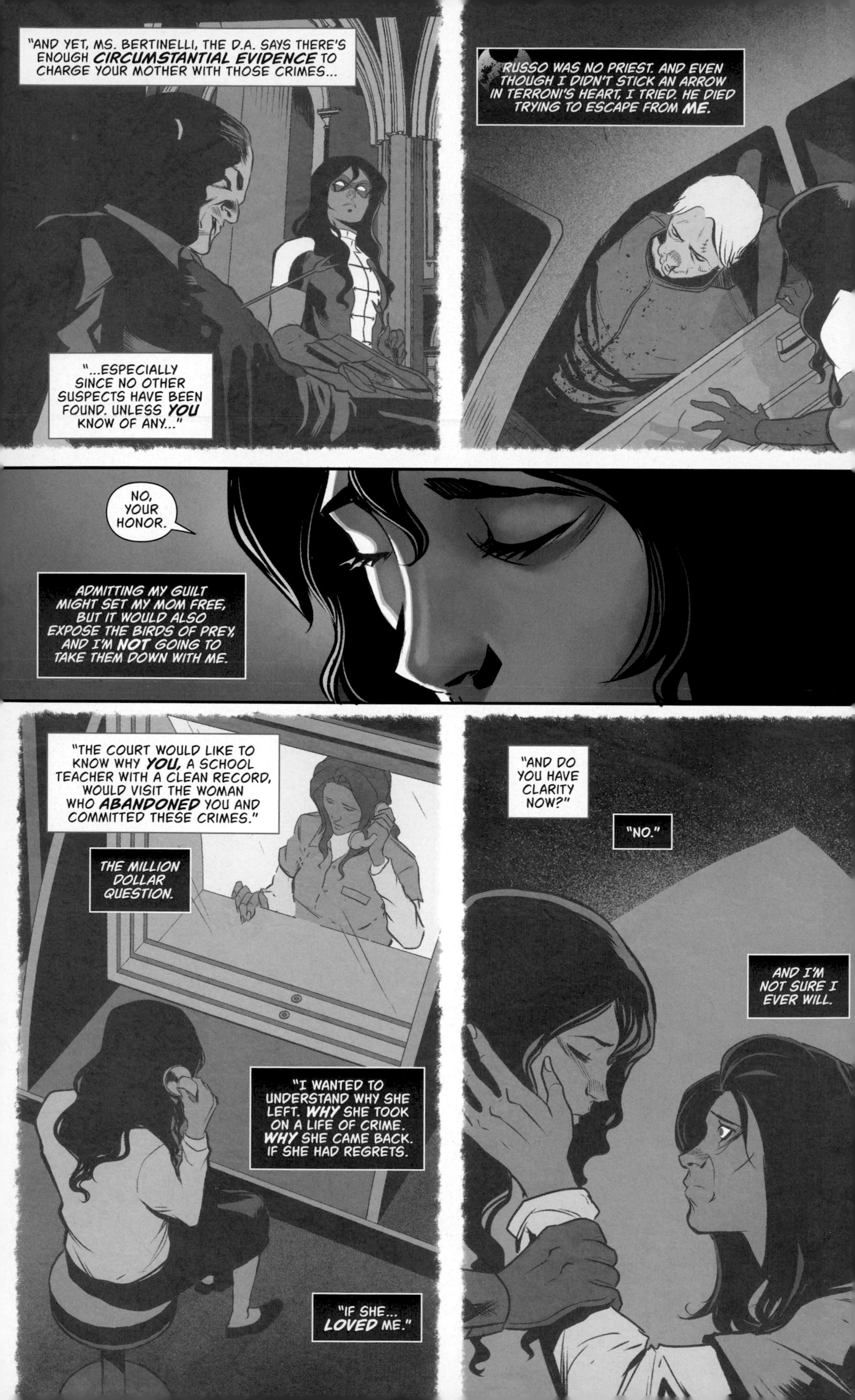

"AND YET, MS. BERTINELLI, THE D.A. SAYS THERE'S ENOUGH CIRCUMSTANTIAL EVIDENCE TO CHARGE YOUR MOTHER WITH THOSE CRIMES...
"...ESPECIALLY SINCE NO OTHER SUSPECTS HAVE BEEN FOUND. UNLESS YOU KNOW OF ANY..."
RUSSO WAS NO PRIEST. AND EVEN THOUGH I DIDN'T STICK AN ARROW IN TERRONI'S HEART, I TRIED. HE DIED TRYING TO ESCAPE FROM ME.
NO, YOUR HONOR.
ADMITTING MY GUILT MIGHT SET MY MOM FREE, BUT IT WOULD ALSO EXPOSE THE BIRDS OF PREY, AND I'M NOT GOING TO TAKE THEM DOWN WITH ME.
"THE COURT WOULD LIKE TO KNOW WHY YOU, A SCHOOL TEACHER WITH A CLEAN RECORD, WOULD VISIT THE WOMAN WHO ABANDONED YOU AND COMMITTED THESE CRIMES."
THE MILLION DOLLAR QUESTION.
"I WANTED TO UNDERSTAND WHY SHE LEFT. WHY SHE TOOK ON A LIFE OF CRIME. WHY SHE CAME BACK. IF SHE HAD REGRETS.
"IF SHE... LOVED ME."
"AND DO YOU HAVE CLARITY NOW?"
"NO."
AND I'M NOT SURE I EVER WILL.

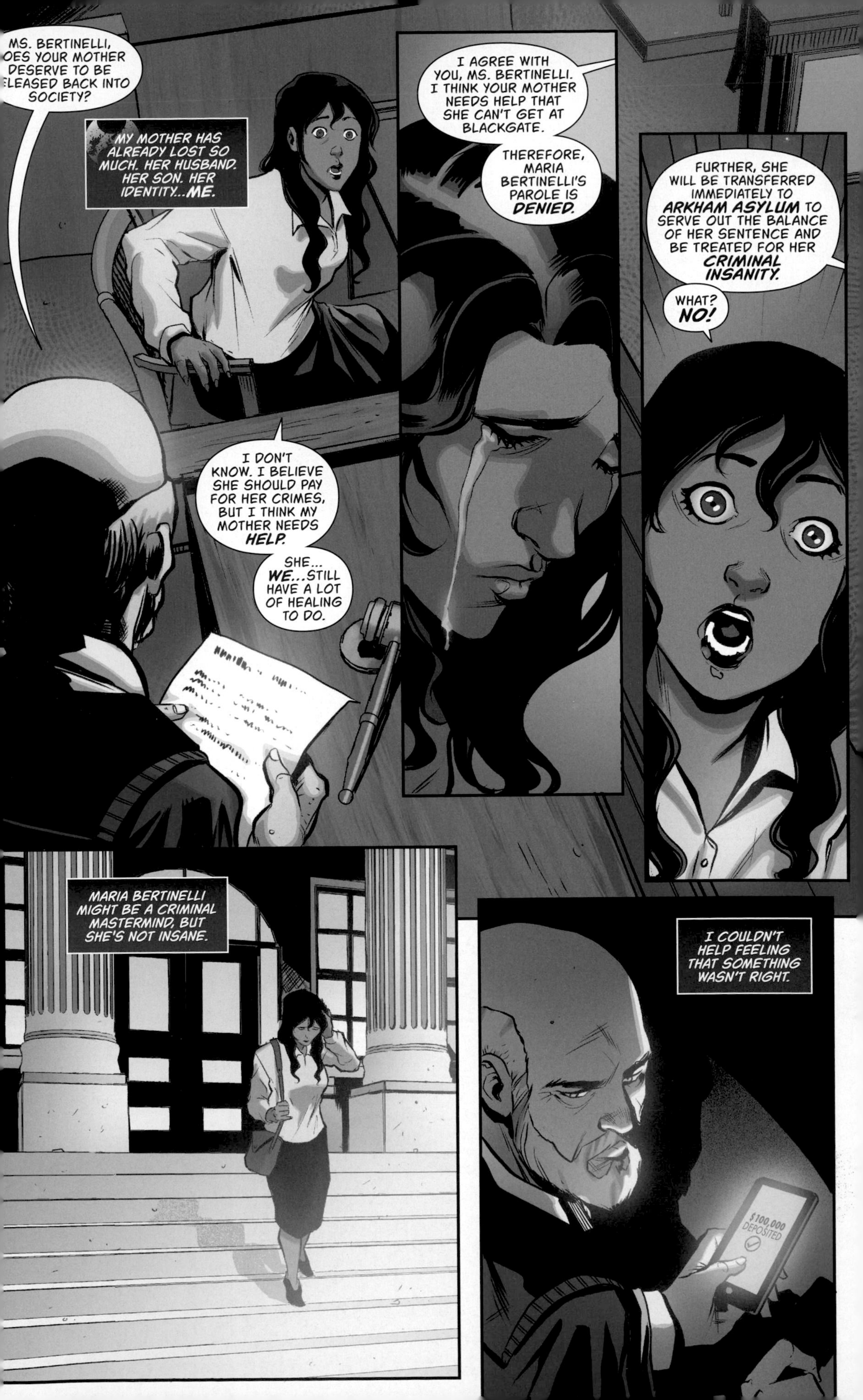
MS. BERTINELLI, OES YOUR MOTHER DESERVE TO BE ELEASED BACK INTO SOCIETY?
MY MOTHER HAS ALREADY LOST SO MUCH. HER HUSBAND. HER SON. HER IDENTITY...ME.
I DON'T KNOW. I BELIEVE SHE SHOULD PAY FOR HER CRIMES, BUT I THINK MY MOTHER NEEDS HELP.
SHE... WE...STILL HAVE A LOT OF HEALING TO DO.
I AGREE WITH YOU, MS. BERTINELLI. I THINK YOUR MOTHER NEEDS HELP THAT SHE CAN'T GET AT BLACKGATE.
THEREFORE, MARIA BERTINELLI'S PAROLE IS DENIED.
FURTHER, SHE WILL BE TRANSFERRED IMMEDIATELY TO ARKHAM ASYLUM TO SERVE OUT THE BALANCE OF HER SENTENCE AND BE TREATED FOR HER CRIMINAL INSANITY.
WHAT? NO!
MARIA BERTINELLI MIGHT BE A CRIMINAL MASTERMIND, BUT SHE'S NOT INSANE.
I COULDN'T HELP FEELING THAT SOMETHING WASN'T RIGHT.
$100,000 DEPOSITED

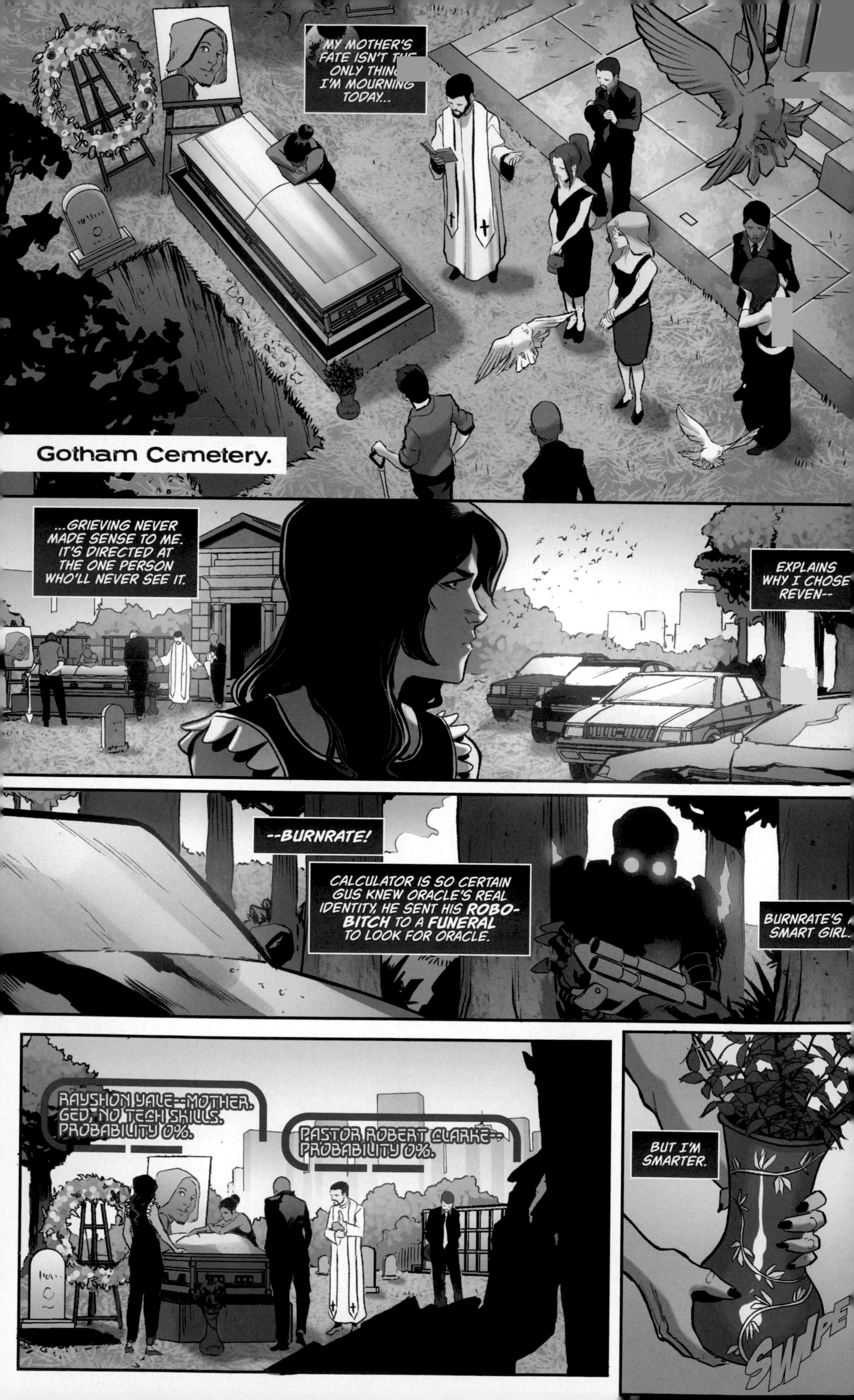
MY MOTHER'S FATE ISN'T TH ONLY THIN I'M MOURNIN TODAY...
Gotham Cemetery.
...GRIEVING NEVER MADE SENSE TO ME. IT'S DIRECTED AT THE ONE PERSON WHO'LL NEVER SEE IT.
EXPLAINS WHY I CHOSE REVEN--
--BURNRATE!
CALCULATOR IS SO CERTAIN GUS KNEW ORACLE'S REAL IDENTITY, HE SENT HIS ROBO-BITCH TO A FUNERAL TO LOOK FOR ORACLE.
BURNRATE'S SMART GIRL.
RAYSHON YALE--MOTHER. GED, NO TECH SKILLS. PROBABILITY 0%.
PASTOR ROBERT CLARKE--PROBABILITY 0%.
BUT I'M SMARTER.
SWIPE

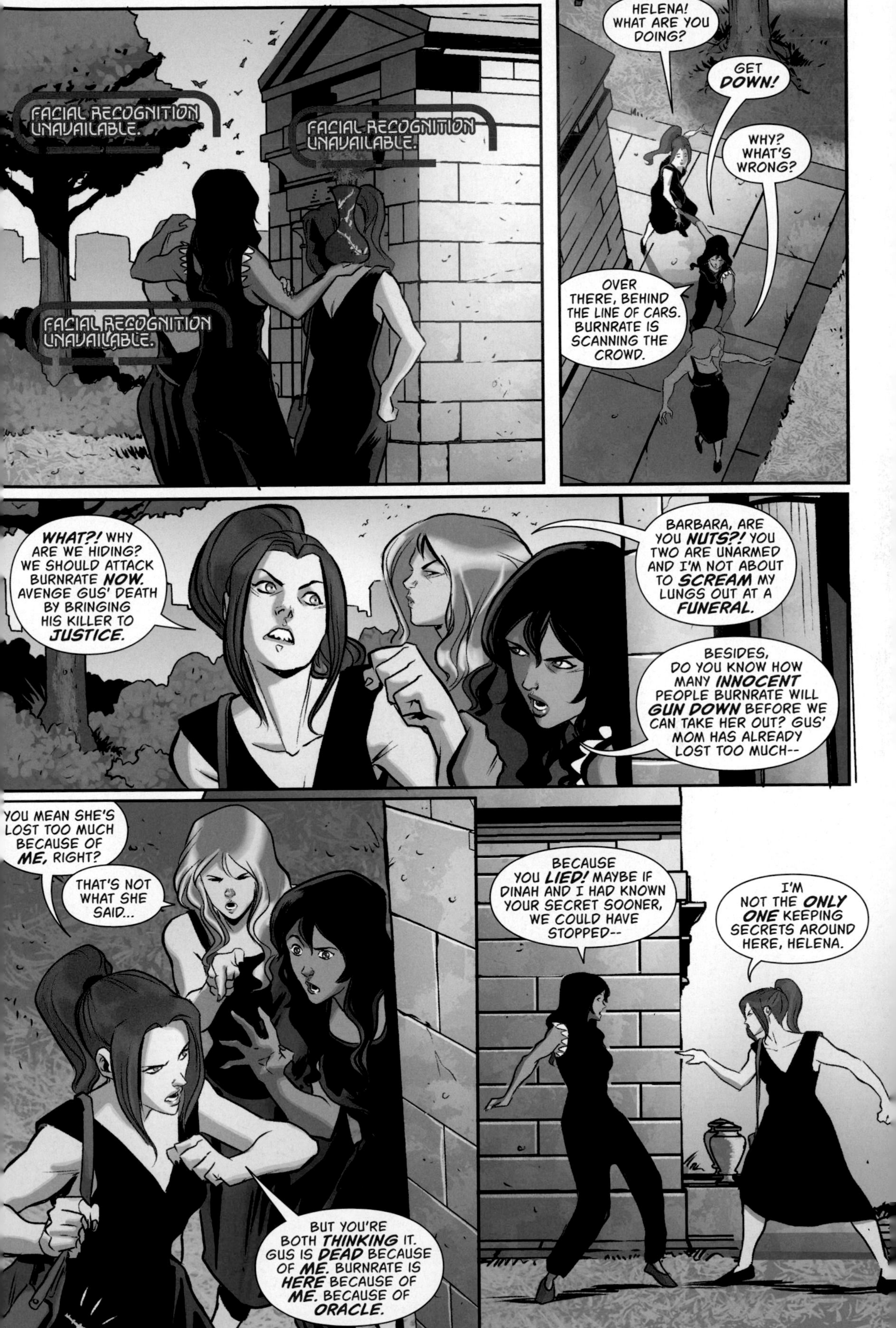
FACIAL RECOGNITION UNAVAILABLE.
FACIAL RECOGNITION UNAVAILABLE.
FACIAL RECOGNITION UNAVAILABLE.
HELENA! WHAT ARE YOU DOING?
GET DOWN!
WHY? WHAT'S WRONG?
OVER THERE, BEHIND THE LINE OF CARS. BURNRATE IS SCANNING THE CROWD.
WHAT?! WHY ARE WE HIDING? WE SHOULD ATTACK BURNRATE NOW. AVENGE GUS' DEATH BY BRINGING HIS KILLER TO JUSTICE.
BARBARA, ARE YOU NUTS?! YOU TWO ARE UNARMED AND I'M NOT ABOUT TO SCREAM MY LUNGS OUT AT A FUNERAL.
BESIDES, DO YOU KNOW HOW MANY INNOCENT PEOPLE BURNRATE WILL GUN DOWN BEFORE WE CAN TAKE HER OUT? GUS' MOM HAS ALREADY LOST TOO MUCH--
YOU MEAN SHE'S LOST TOO MUCH BECAUSE OF ME, RIGHT?
THAT'S NOT WHAT SHE SAID...
BUT YOU'RE BOTH THINKING IT. GUS IS DEAD BECAUSE OF ME. BURNRATE IS HERE BECAUSE OF ME. BECAUSE OF ORACLE.
BECAUSE YOU LIED! MAYBE IF DINAH AND I HAD KNOWN YOUR SECRET SOONER, WE COULD HAVE STOPPED--
I'M NOT THE ONLY ONE KEEPING SECRETS AROUND HERE, HELENA.

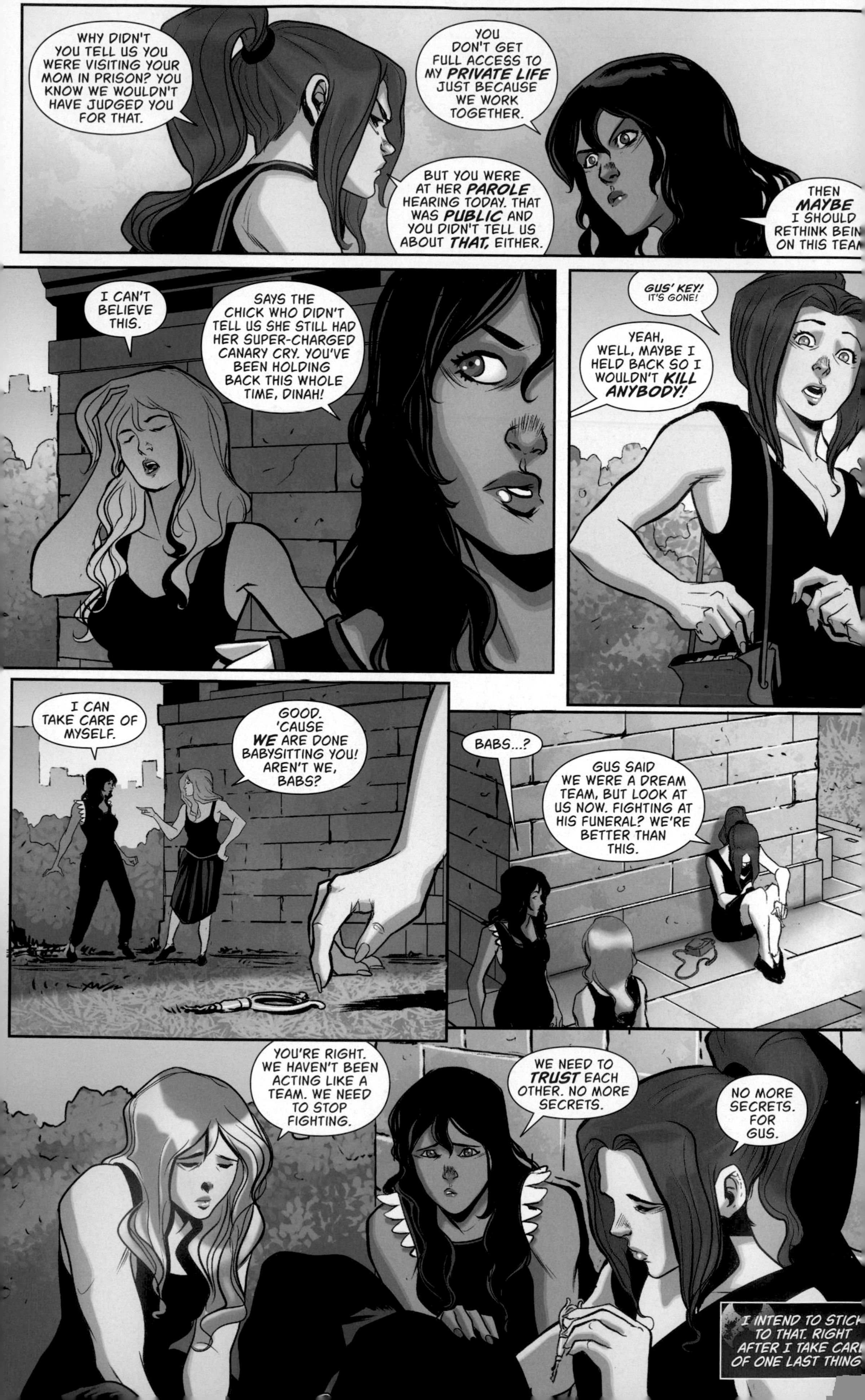
WHY DIDN'T YOU TELL US YOU WERE VISITING YOUR MOM IN PRISON? YOU KNOW WE WOULDN'T HAVE JUDGED YOU FOR THAT.
YOU DON'T GET FULL ACCESS TO MY PRIVATE LIFE JUST BECAUSE WE WORK TOGETHER.
BUT YOU WERE AT HER PAROLE HEARING TODAY. THAT WAS PUBLIC AND YOU DIDN'T TELL US ABOUT THAT, EITHER.
THEN MAYBE I SHOULD RETHINK BEIN ON THIS TEAM
I CAN'T BELIEVE THIS.
SAYS THE CHICK WHO DIDN'T TELL US SHE STILL HAD HER SUPER-CHARGED CANARY CRY. YOU'VE BEEN HOLDING BACK THIS WHOLE TIME, DINAH!
GUS' KEY! IT'S GONE!
YEAH, WELL, MAYBE I HELD BACK SO I WOULDN'T KILL ANYBODY!
I CAN TAKE CARE OF MYSELF.
GOOD. 'CAUSE WE ARE DONE BABYSITTING YOU! AREN'T WE, BABS?
BABS...?
GUS SAID WE WERE A DREAM TEAM, BUT LOOK AT US NOW. FIGHTING AT HIS FUNERAL? WE'RE BETTER THAN THIS.
YOU'RE RIGHT. WE HAVEN'T BEEN ACTING LIKE A TEAM. WE NEED TO STOP FIGHTING.
WE NEED TO TRUST EACH OTHER. NO MORE SECRETS.
NO MORE SECRETS. FOR GUS.
I INTEND TO STICK TO THAT. RIGHT AFTER I TAKE CARE OF ONE LAST THING.

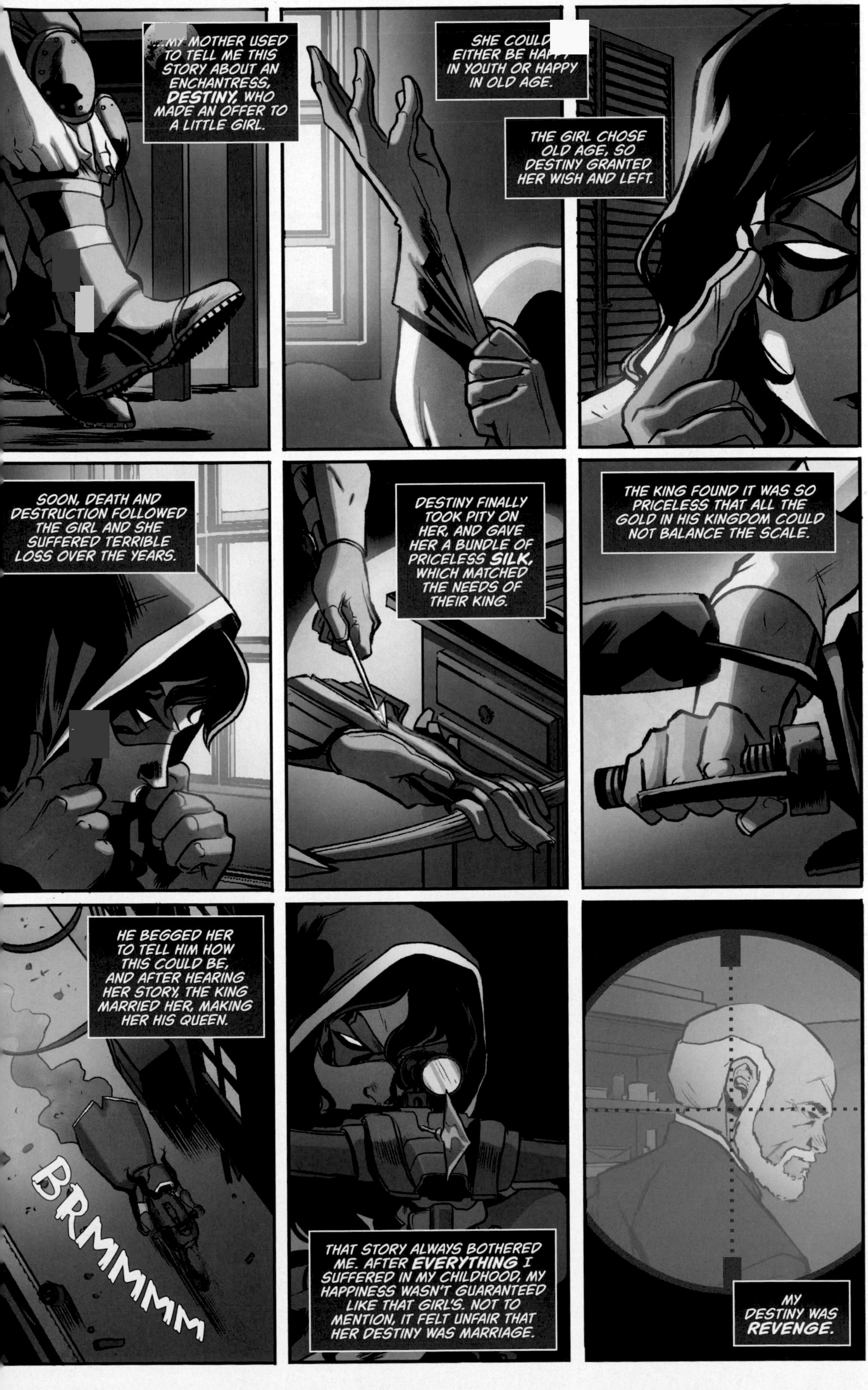

...MY MOTHER USED TO TELL ME THIS STORY ABOUT AN ENCHANTRESS, **DESTINY,** WHO MADE AN OFFER TO A LITTLE GIRL.
SHE COULD EITHER BE HAP IN YOUTH OR HAPPY IN OLD AGE.
THE GIRL CHOSE OLD AGE, SO DESTINY GRANTED HER WISH AND LEFT.
SOON, DEATH AND DESTRUCTION FOLLOWED THE GIRL AND SHE SUFFERED TERRIBLE LOSS OVER THE YEARS.
DESTINY FINALLY TOOK PITY ON HER, AND GAVE HER A BUNDLE OF PRICELESS **SILK,** WHICH MATCHED THE NEEDS OF THEIR KING.
THE KING FOUND IT WAS SO PRICELESS THAT ALL THE GOLD IN HIS KINGDOM COULD NOT BALANCE THE SCALE.
HE BEGGED HER TO TELL HIM HOW THIS COULD BE, AND AFTER HEARING HER STORY, THE KING MARRIED HER, MAKING HER HIS QUEEN.
BRMMMMM
THAT STORY ALWAYS BOTHERED ME. AFTER **EVERYTHING** I SUFFERED IN MY CHILDHOOD, MY HAPPINESS WASN'T GUARANTEED LIKE THAT GIRL'S. NOT TO MENTION, IT FELT UNFAIR THAT HER DESTINY WAS MARRIAGE.
MY DESTINY WAS **REVENGE.**

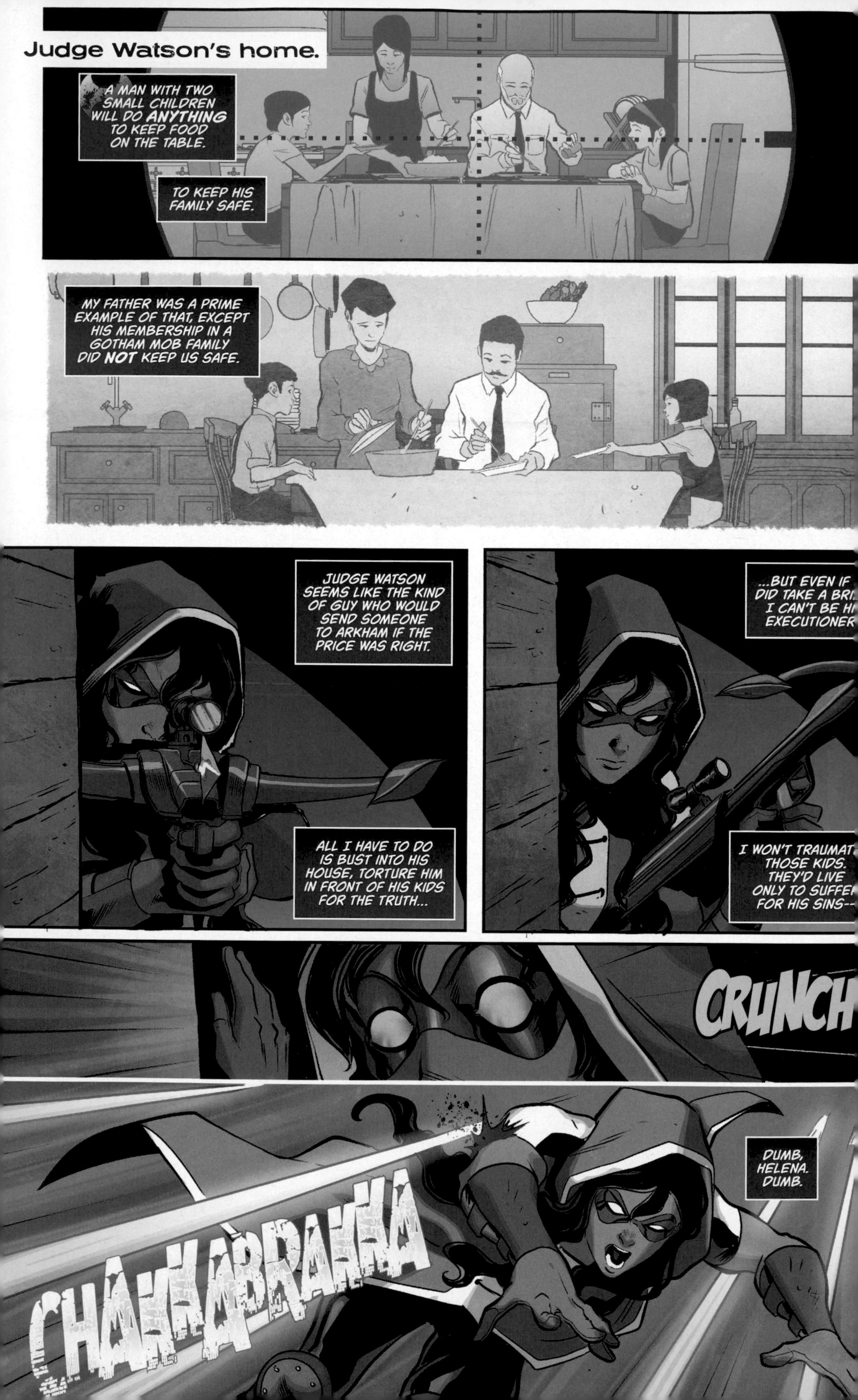
Judge Watson's home.
A MAN WITH TWO SMALL CHILDREN WILL DO ANYTHING TO KEEP FOOD ON THE TABLE.
TO KEEP HIS FAMILY SAFE.
MY FATHER WAS A PRIME EXAMPLE OF THAT, EXCEPT HIS MEMBERSHIP IN A GOTHAM MOB FAMILY DID NOT KEEP US SAFE.
JUDGE WATSON SEEMS LIKE THE KIND OF GUY WHO WOULD SEND SOMEONE TO ARKHAM IF THE PRICE WAS RIGHT.
ALL I HAVE TO DO IS BUST INTO HIS HOUSE, TORTURE HIM IN FRONT OF HIS KIDS FOR THE TRUTH...
...BUT EVEN IF DID TAKE A BRI I CAN'T BE HI EXECUTIONER
I WON'T TRAUMAT THOSE KIDS. THEY'D LIVE ONLY TO SUFFE FOR HIS SINS--
CRUNCH
DUMB, HELENA. DUMB.
CHAKKABRAKKA

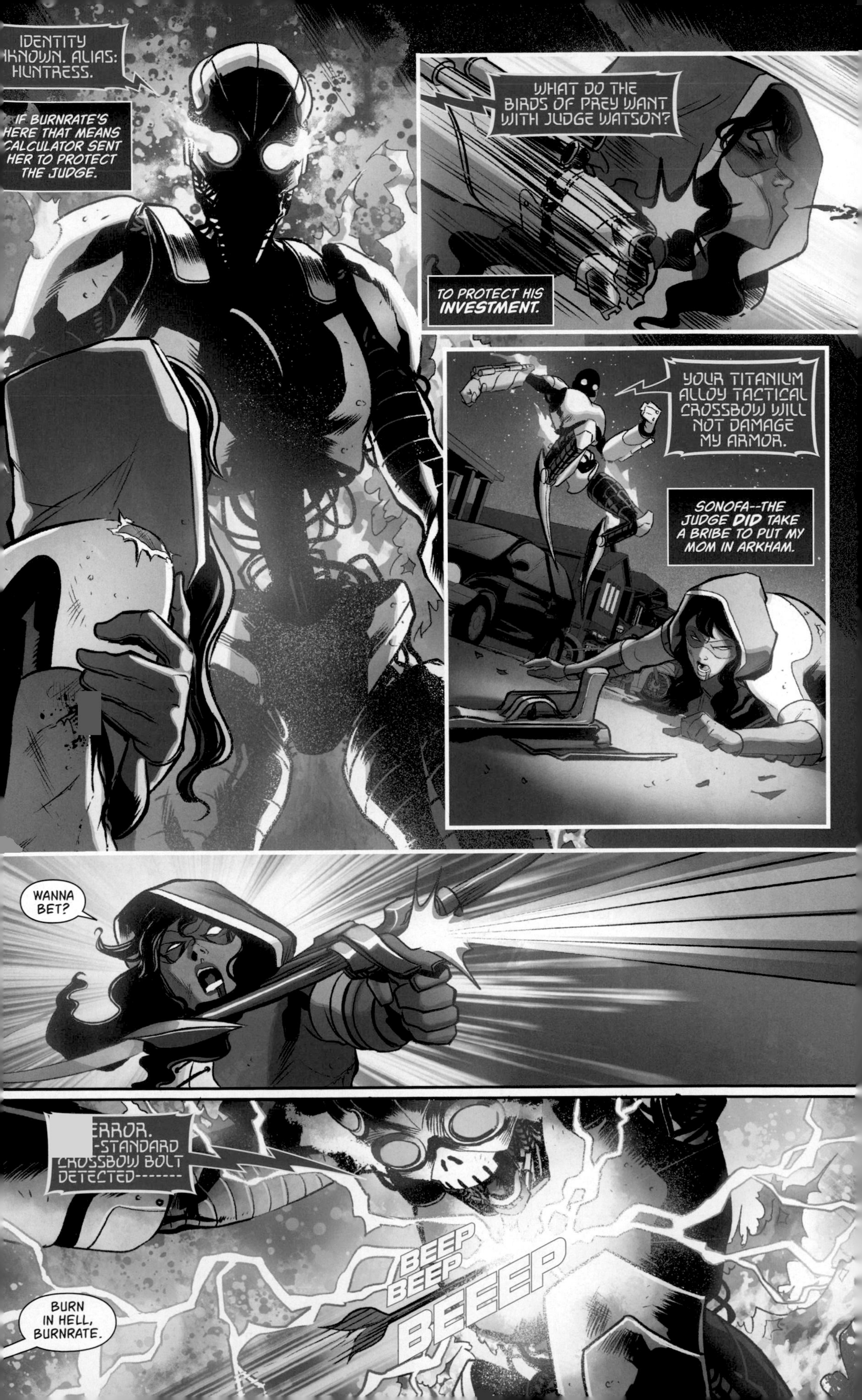
IDENTITY UNKNOWN. ALIAS: HUNTRESS.
IF BURNRATE'S HERE THAT MEANS CALCULATOR SENT HER TO PROTECT THE JUDGE.
WHAT DO THE BIRDS OF PREY WANT WITH JUDGE WATSON?
TO PROTECT HIS INVESTMENT.
YOUR TITANIUM ALLOY TACTICAL CROSSBOW WILL NOT DAMAGE MY ARMOR.
SONOFA--THE JUDGE DID TAKE A BRIBE TO PUT MY MOM IN ARKHAM.
WANNA BET?
ERROR. -STANDARD CROSSBOW BOLT DETECTED-------
BEEP BEEP BEEEEP
BURN IN HELL, BURNRATE.

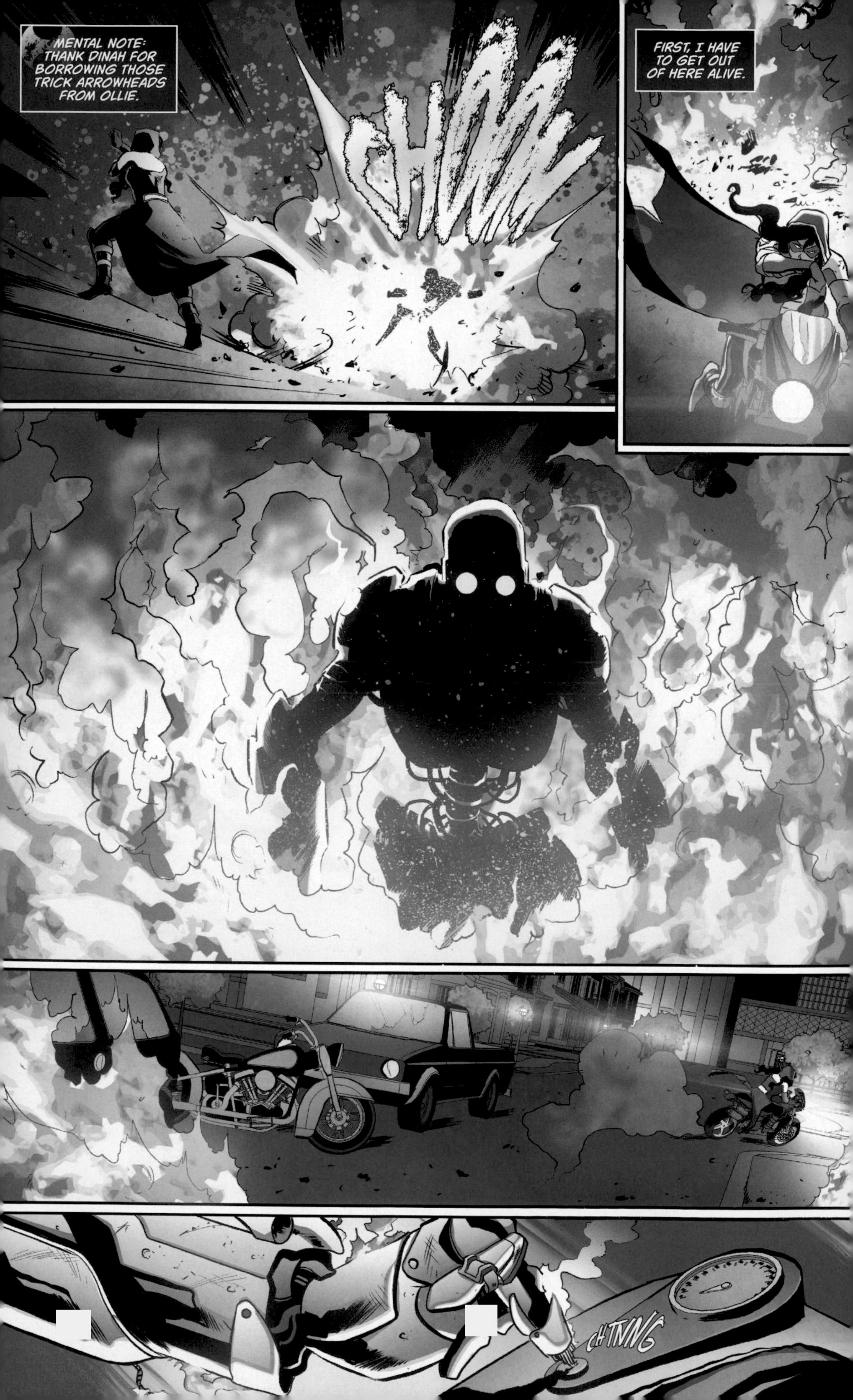
MENTAL NOTE: THANK DINAH FOR BORROWING THOSE TRICK ARROWHEADS FROM OLLIE.
CHOOM
FIRST, I HAVE TO GET OUT OF HERE ALIVE.
CHTNNG

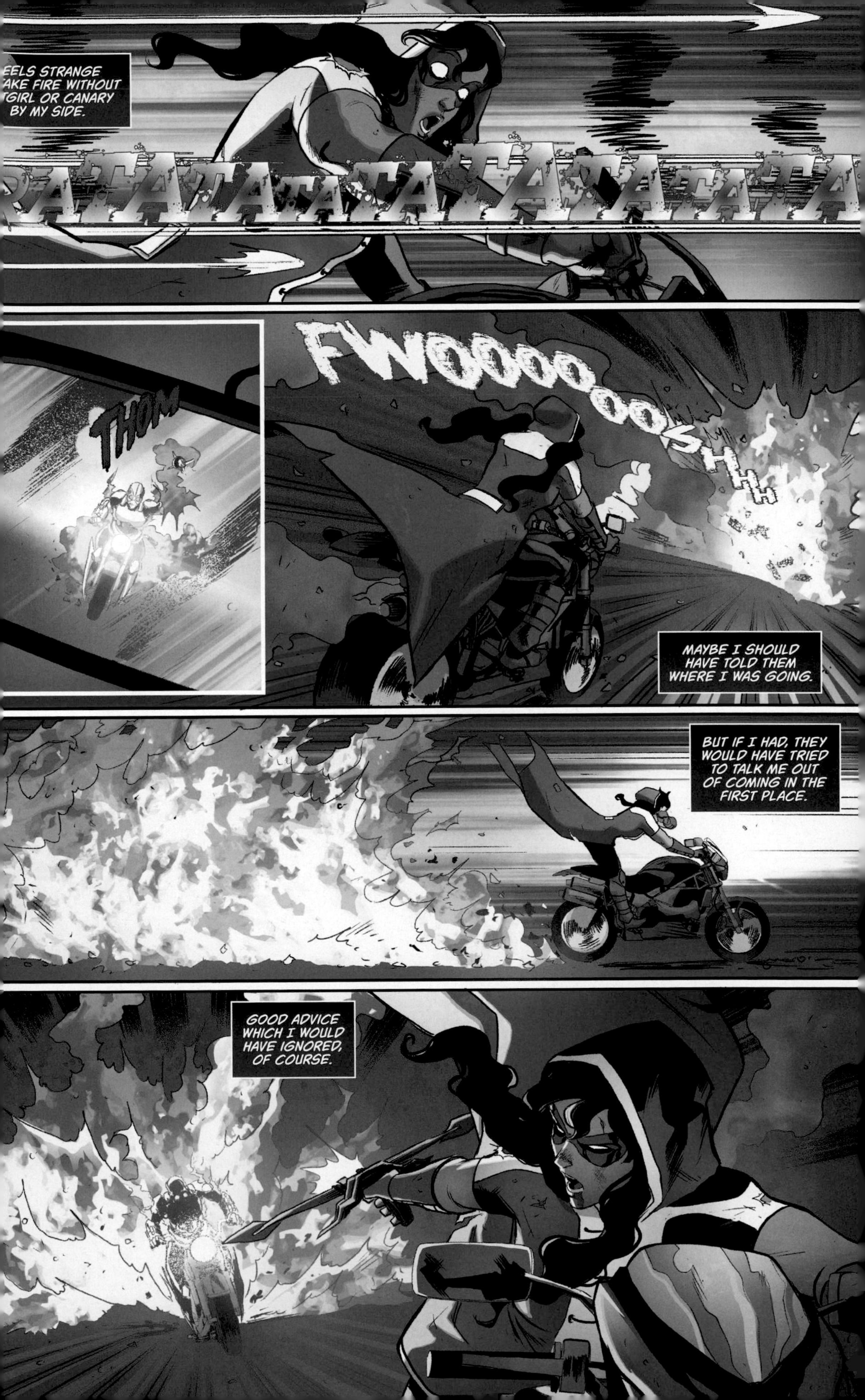
EELS STRANGE
AKE FIRE WITHOUT
TGIRL OR CANARY
BY MY SIDE.
RATATATATATATATA
THOM
FWOOOOOOOSHH
MAYBE I SHOULD
HAVE TOLD THEM
WHERE I WAS GOING.
BUT IF I HAD, THEY
WOULD HAVE TRIED
TO TALK ME OUT
OF COMING IN THE
FIRST PLACE.
GOOD ADVICE
WHICH I WOULD
HAVE IGNORED,
OF COURSE.

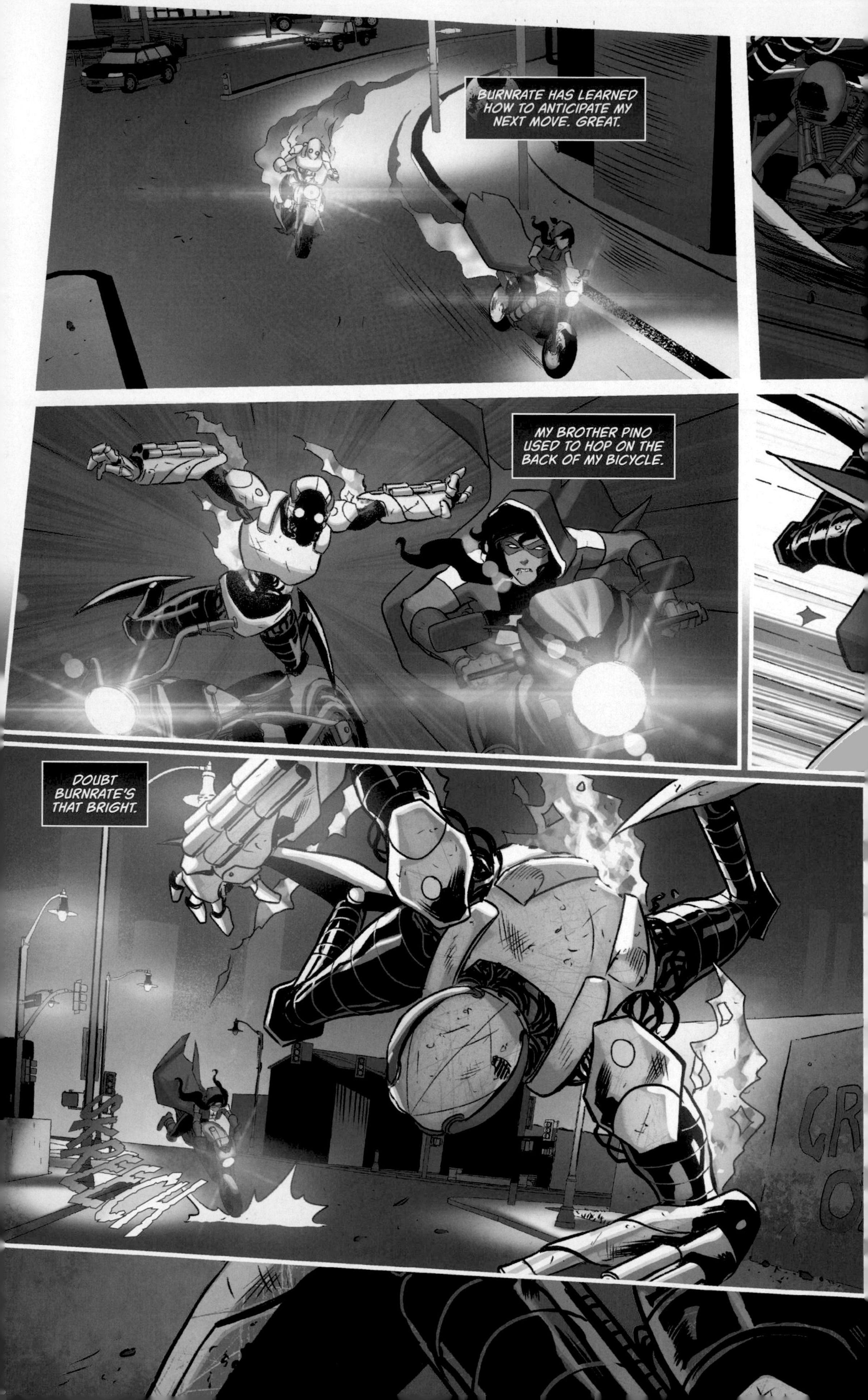
BURNRATE HAS LEARNED HOW TO ANTICIPATE MY NEXT MOVE. GREAT.
MY BROTHER PINO USED TO HOP ON THE BACK OF MY BICYCLE.
DOUBT BURNRATE'S THAT BRIGHT.

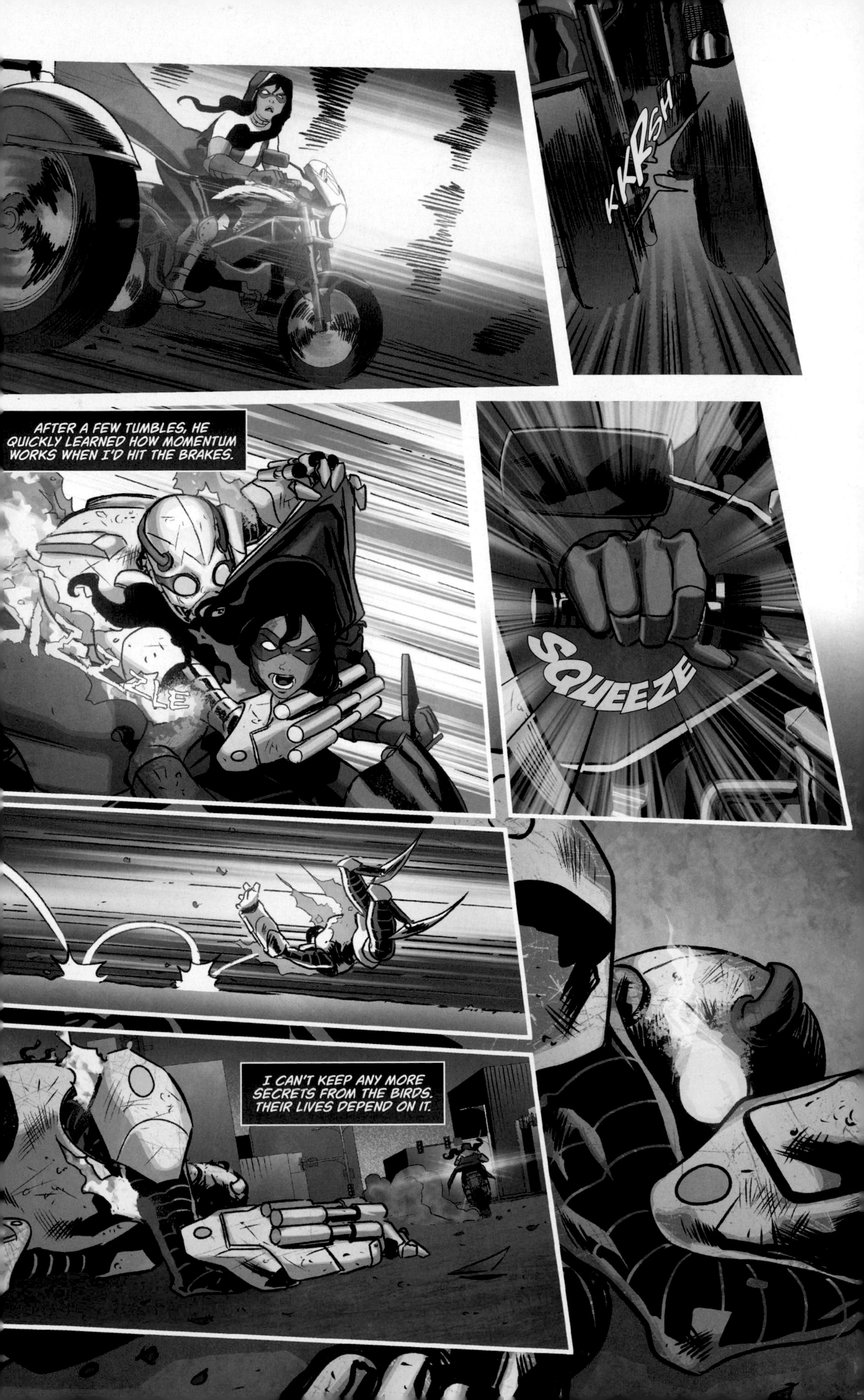
KKRSH
AFTER A FEW TUMBLES, HE QUICKLY LEARNED HOW MOMENTUM WORKS WHEN I'D HIT THE BRAKES.
SQUEEZE
I CAN'T KEEP ANY MORE SECRETS FROM THE BIRDS. THEIR LIVES DEPEND ON IT.

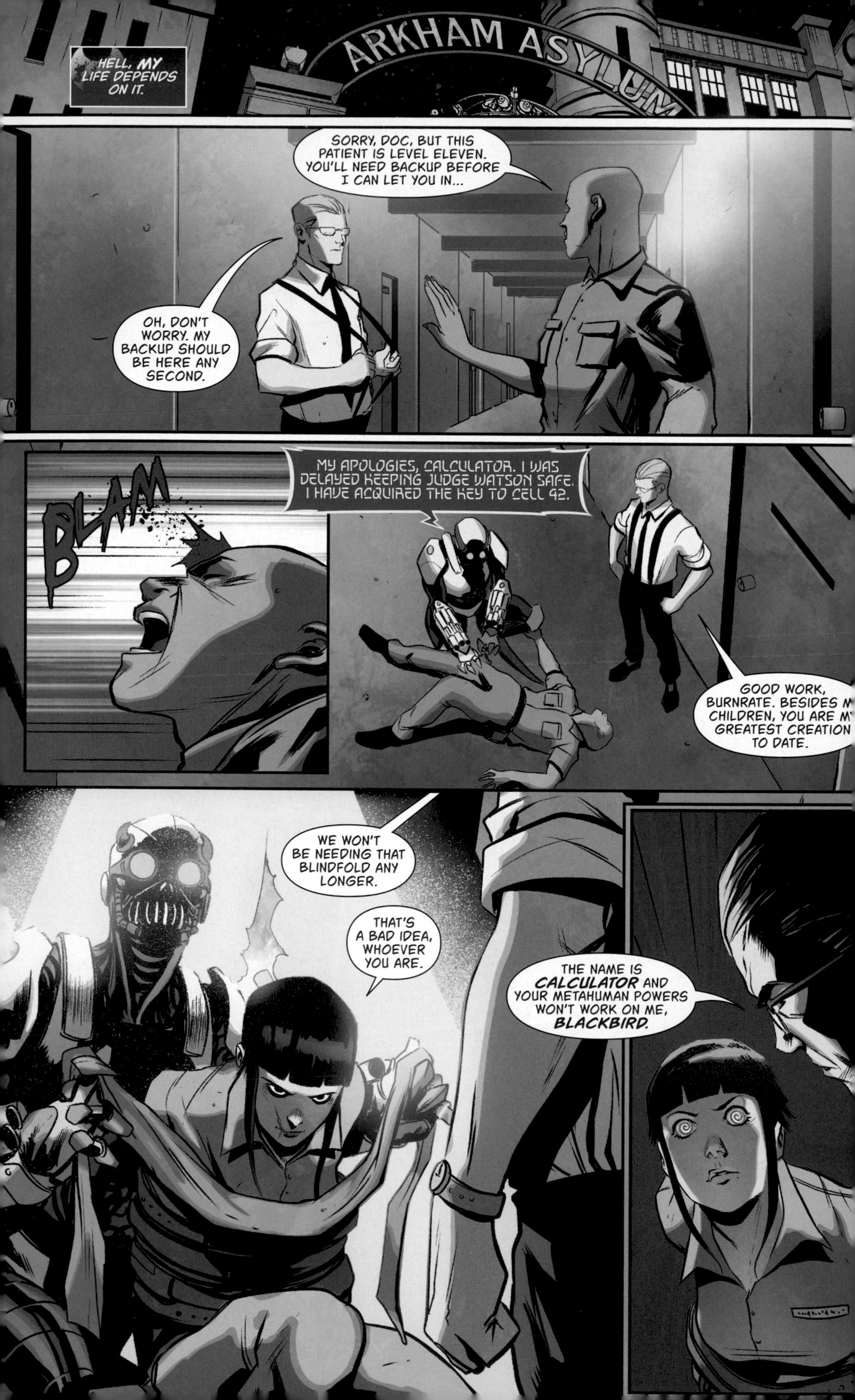
HELL, MY LIFE DEPENDS ON IT.
ARKHAM ASYLUM
SORRY, DOC, BUT THIS PATIENT IS LEVEL ELEVEN. YOU'LL NEED BACKUP BEFORE I CAN LET YOU IN...
OH, DON'T WORRY. MY BACKUP SHOULD BE HERE ANY SECOND.
BLAM
MY APOLOGIES, CALCULATOR. I WAS DELAYED KEEPING JUDGE WATSON SAFE. I HAVE ACQUIRED THE KEY TO CELL 42.
GOOD WORK, BURNRATE. BESIDES MY CHILDREN, YOU ARE MY GREATEST CREATION TO DATE.
WE WON'T BE NEEDING THAT BLINDFOLD ANY LONGER.
THAT'S A BAD IDEA, WHOEVER YOU ARE.
THE NAME IS CALCULATOR AND YOUR METAHUMAN POWERS WON'T WORK ON ME, BLACKBIRD.

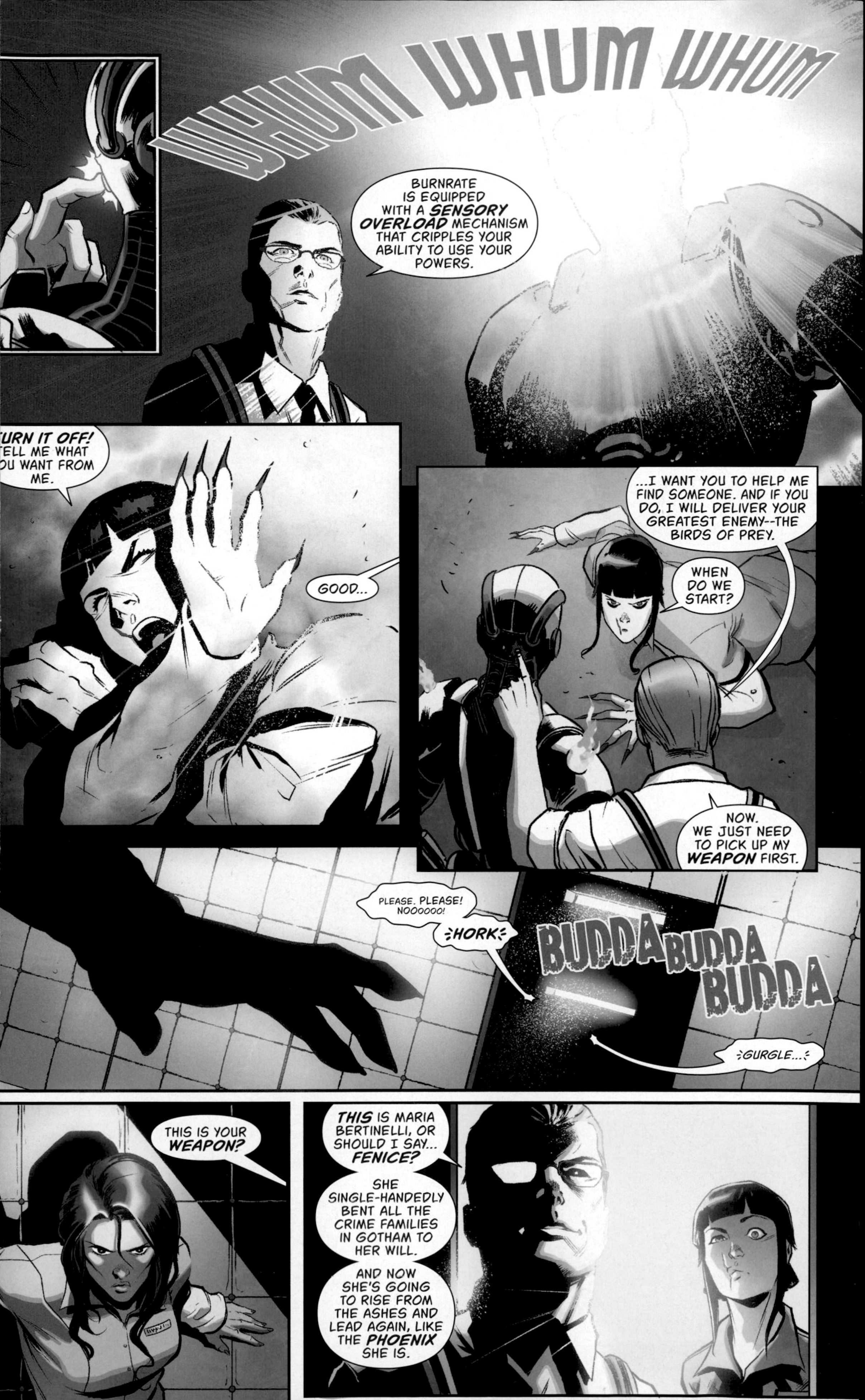
WHUM WHUM WHUM
BURNRATE IS EQUIPPED WITH A SENSORY OVERLOAD MECHANISM THAT CRIPPLES YOUR ABILITY TO USE YOUR POWERS.
TURN IT OFF! TELL ME WHAT YOU WANT FROM ME.
GOOD...
...I WANT YOU TO HELP ME FIND SOMEONE. AND IF YOU DO, I WILL DELIVER YOUR GREATEST ENEMY--THE BIRDS OF PREY.
WHEN DO WE START?
NOW. WE JUST NEED TO PICK UP MY WEAPON FIRST.
PLEASE. PLEASE! NOOOOOO!
HORK
BUDDA BUDDA BUDDA
GURGLE...
THIS IS YOUR WEAPON?
THIS IS MARIA BERTINELLI, OR SHOULD I SAY... FENICE?
SHE SINGLE-HANDEDLY BENT ALL THE CRIME FAMILIES IN GOTHAM TO HER WILL.
AND NOW SHE'S GOING TO RISE FROM THE ASHES AND LEAD AGAIN, LIKE THE PHOENIX SHE IS.

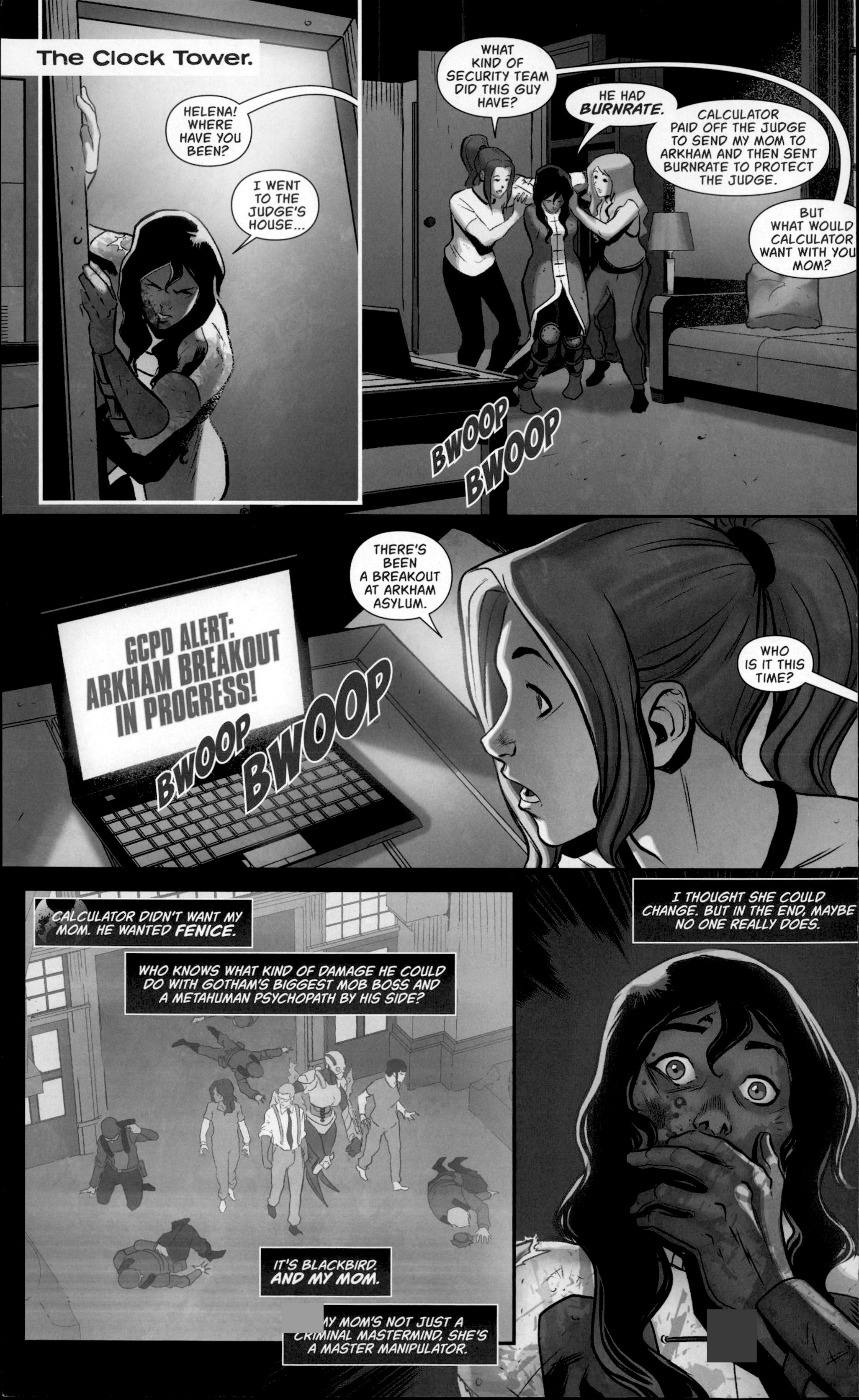
The Clock Tower.
HELENA! WHERE HAVE YOU BEEN?
I WENT TO THE JUDGE'S HOUSE...
WHAT KIND OF SECURITY TEAM DID THIS GUY HAVE?
HE HAD BURNRATE.
CALCULATOR PAID OFF THE JUDGE TO SEND MY MOM TO ARKHAM AND THEN SENT BURNRATE TO PROTECT THE JUDGE.
BUT WHAT WOULD CALCULATOR WANT WITH YOU MOM?
BWOOP BWOOP
THERE'S BEEN A BREAKOUT AT ARKHAM ASYLUM.
GCPD ALERT: ARKHAM BREAKOUT IN PROGRESS!
BWOOP BWOOP
WHO IS IT THIS TIME?
CALCULATOR DIDN'T WANT MY MOM. HE WANTED FENICE.
WHO KNOWS WHAT KIND OF DAMAGE HE COULD DO WITH GOTHAM'S BIGGEST MOB BOSS AND A METAHUMAN PSYCHOPATH BY HIS SIDE?
IT'S BLACKBIRD. AND MY MOM.
MY MOM'S NOT JUST A CRIMINAL MASTERMIND, SHE'S A MASTER MANIPULATOR.
I THOUGHT SHE COULD CHANGE. BUT IN THE END, MAYBE NO ONE REALLY DOES.

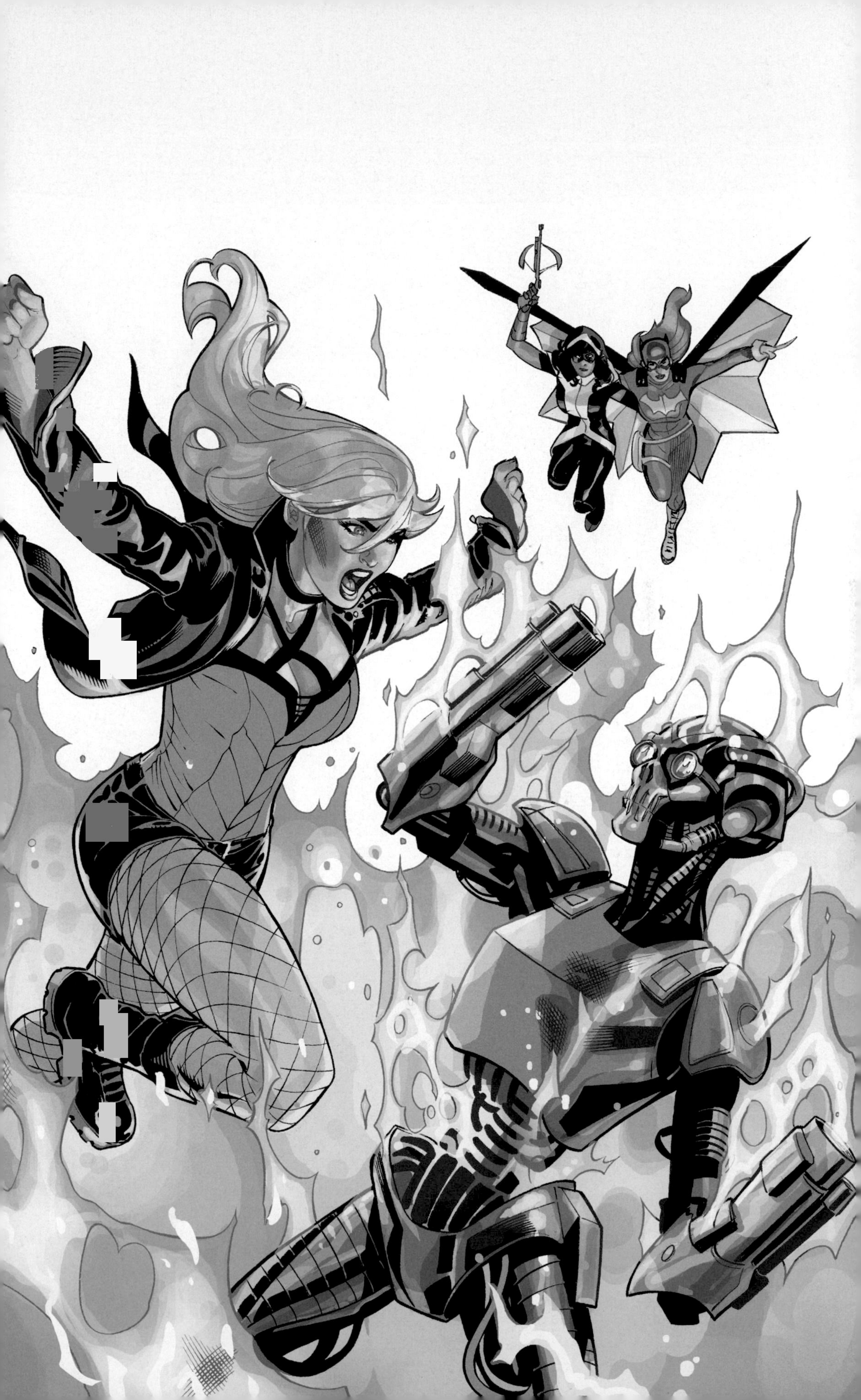

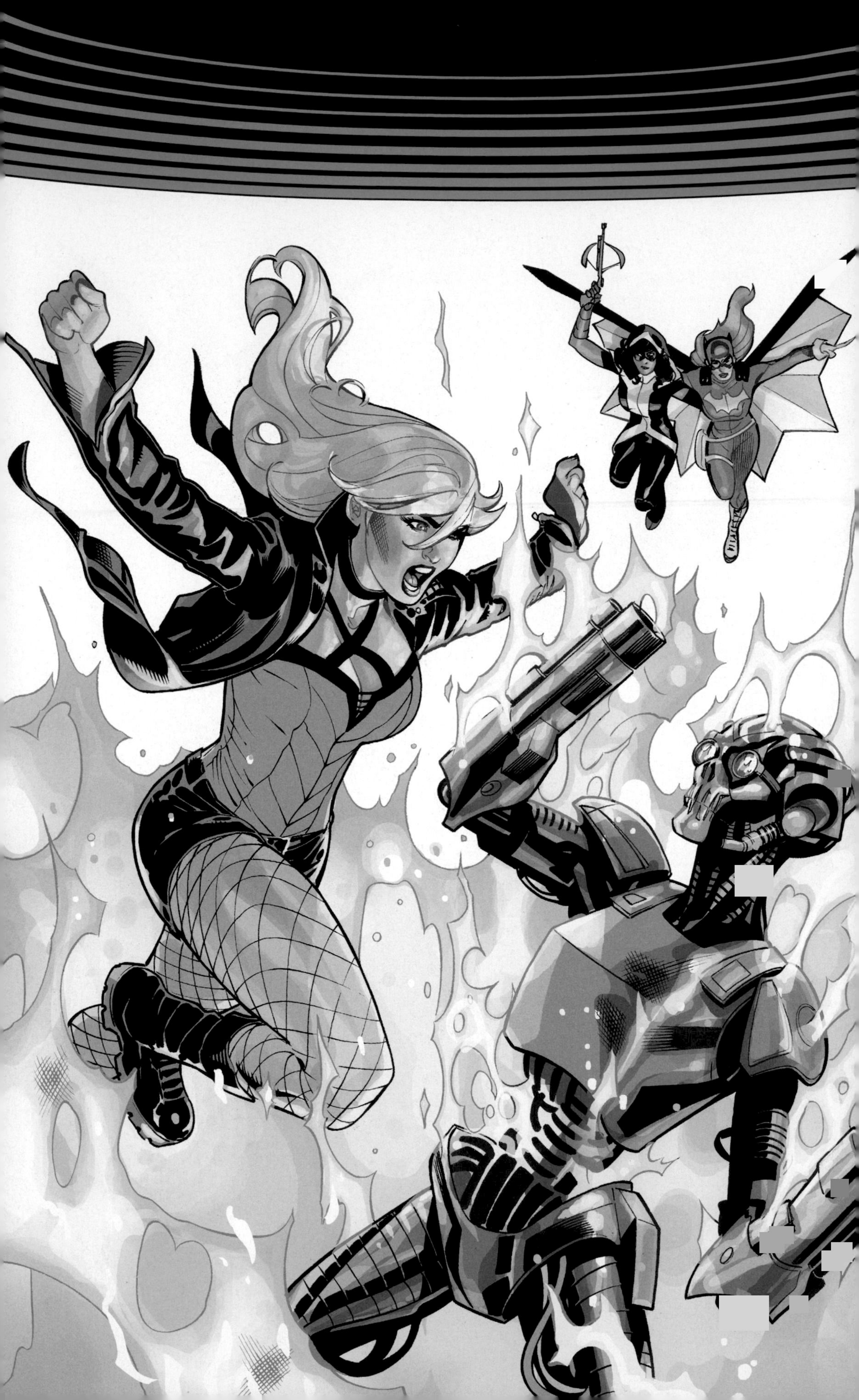

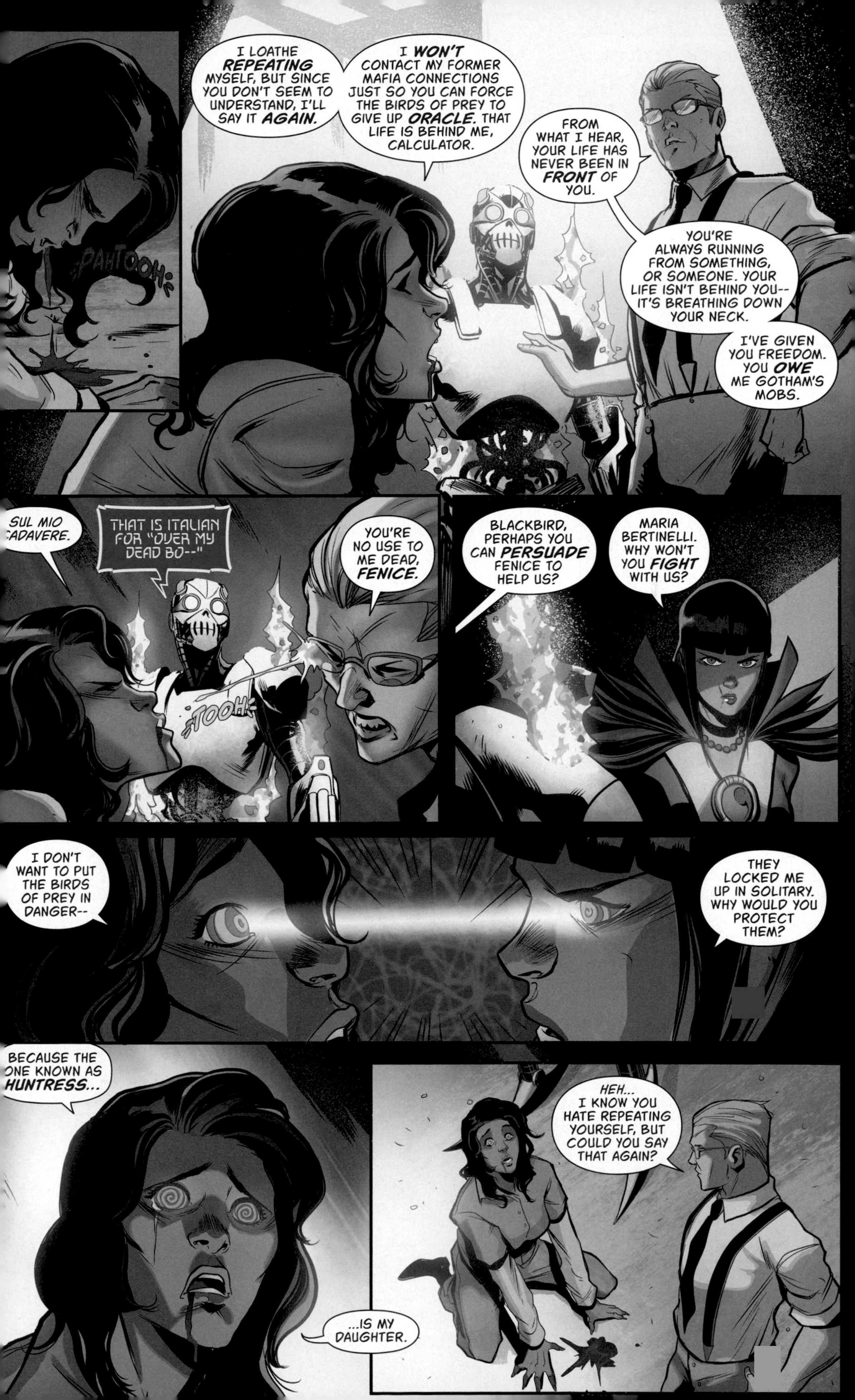
PAHTOOH
I LOATHE REPEATING MYSELF, BUT SINCE YOU DON'T SEEM TO UNDERSTAND, I'LL SAY IT AGAIN.
I WON'T CONTACT MY FORMER MAFIA CONNECTIONS JUST SO YOU CAN FORCE THE BIRDS OF PREY TO GIVE UP ORACLE. THAT LIFE IS BEHIND ME, CALCULATOR.
FROM WHAT I HEAR, YOUR LIFE HAS NEVER BEEN IN FRONT OF YOU.
YOU'RE ALWAYS RUNNING FROM SOMETHING, OR SOMEONE. YOUR LIFE ISN'T BEHIND YOU-- IT'S BREATHING DOWN YOUR NECK.
I'VE GIVEN YOU FREEDOM. YOU OWE ME GOTHAM'S MOBS.
SUL MIO CADAVERE.
THAT IS ITALIAN FOR "OVER MY DEAD BO--"
TOOH
YOU'RE NO USE TO ME DEAD, FENICE.
BLACKBIRD, PERHAPS YOU CAN PERSUADE FENICE TO HELP US?
MARIA BERTINELLI. WHY WON'T YOU FIGHT WITH US?
I DON'T WANT TO PUT THE BIRDS OF PREY IN DANGER--
THEY LOCKED ME UP IN SOLITARY. WHY WOULD YOU PROTECT THEM?
BECAUSE THE ONE KNOWN AS HUNTRESS...
...IS MY DAUGHTER.
HEH... I KNOW YOU HATE REPEATING YOURSELF, BUT COULD YOU SAY THAT AGAIN?

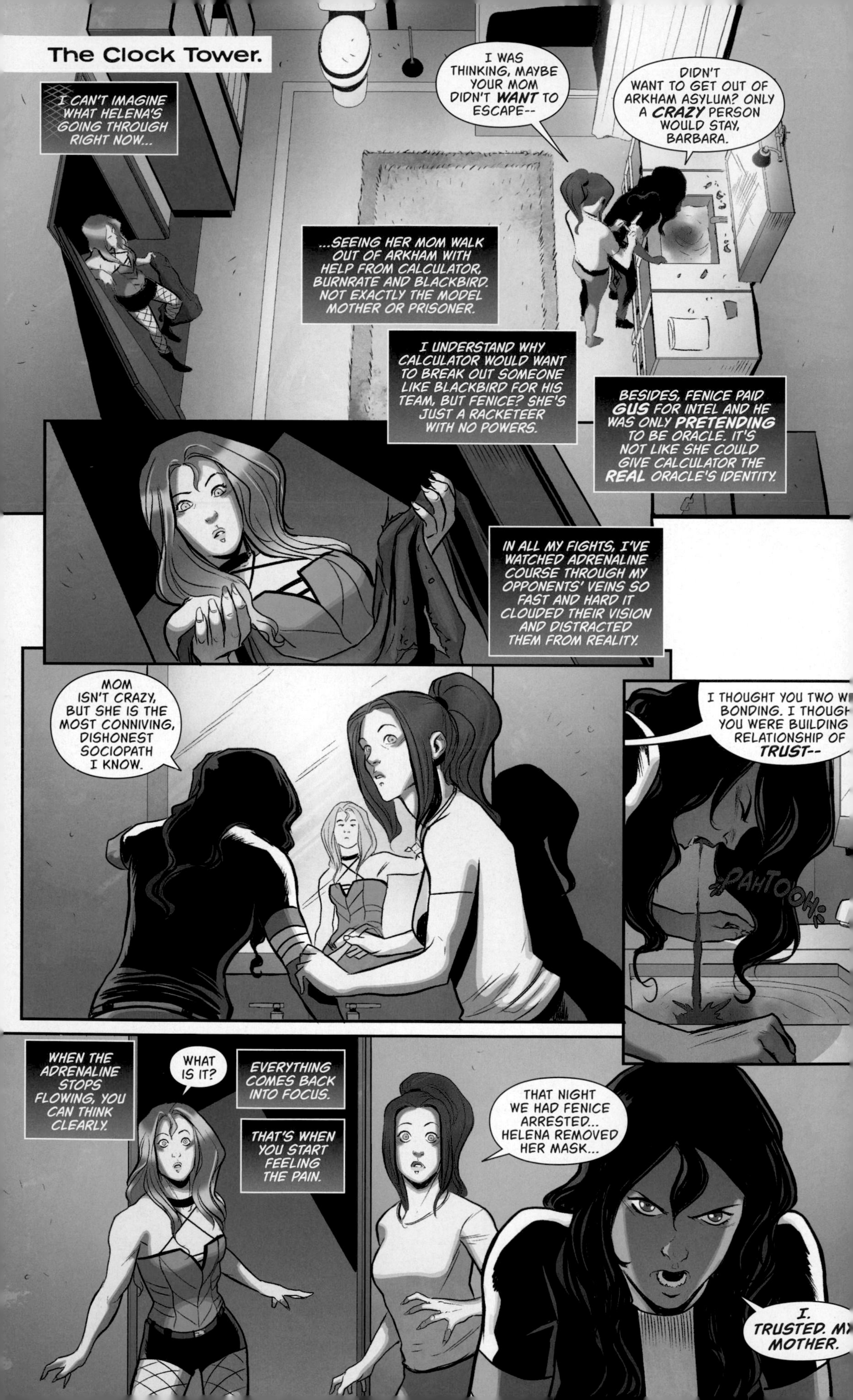

The Clock Tower.
I CAN'T IMAGINE WHAT HELENA'S GOING THROUGH RIGHT NOW...
I WAS THINKING, MAYBE YOUR MOM DIDN'T WANT TO ESCAPE--
DIDN'T WANT TO GET OUT OF ARKHAM ASYLUM? ONLY A CRAZY PERSON WOULD STAY, BARBARA.
...SEEING HER MOM WALK OUT OF ARKHAM WITH HELP FROM CALCULATOR, BURNRATE AND BLACKBIRD. NOT EXACTLY THE MODEL MOTHER OR PRISONER.
I UNDERSTAND WHY CALCULATOR WOULD WANT TO BREAK OUT SOMEONE LIKE BLACKBIRD FOR HIS TEAM, BUT FENICE? SHE'S JUST A RACKETEER WITH NO POWERS.
BESIDES, FENICE PAID GUS FOR INTEL AND HE WAS ONLY PRETENDING TO BE ORACLE. IT'S NOT LIKE SHE COULD GIVE CALCULATOR THE REAL ORACLE'S IDENTITY.
IN ALL MY FIGHTS, I'VE WATCHED ADRENALINE COURSE THROUGH MY OPPONENTS' VEINS SO FAST AND HARD IT CLOUDED THEIR VISION AND DISTRACTED THEM FROM REALITY.
MOM ISN'T CRAZY, BUT SHE IS THE MOST CONNIVING, DISHONEST SOCIOPATH I KNOW.
I THOUGHT YOU TWO W BONDING. I THOUG YOU WERE BUILDING RELATIONSHIP OF TRUST--
PAHTOOH
WHEN THE ADRENALINE STOPS FLOWING, YOU CAN THINK CLEARLY.
WHAT IS IT?
EVERYTHING COMES BACK INTO FOCUS.
THAT'S WHEN YOU START FEELING THE PAIN.
THAT NIGHT WE HAD FENICE ARRESTED... HELENA REMOVED HER MASK...
I. TRUSTED. MY MOTHER.

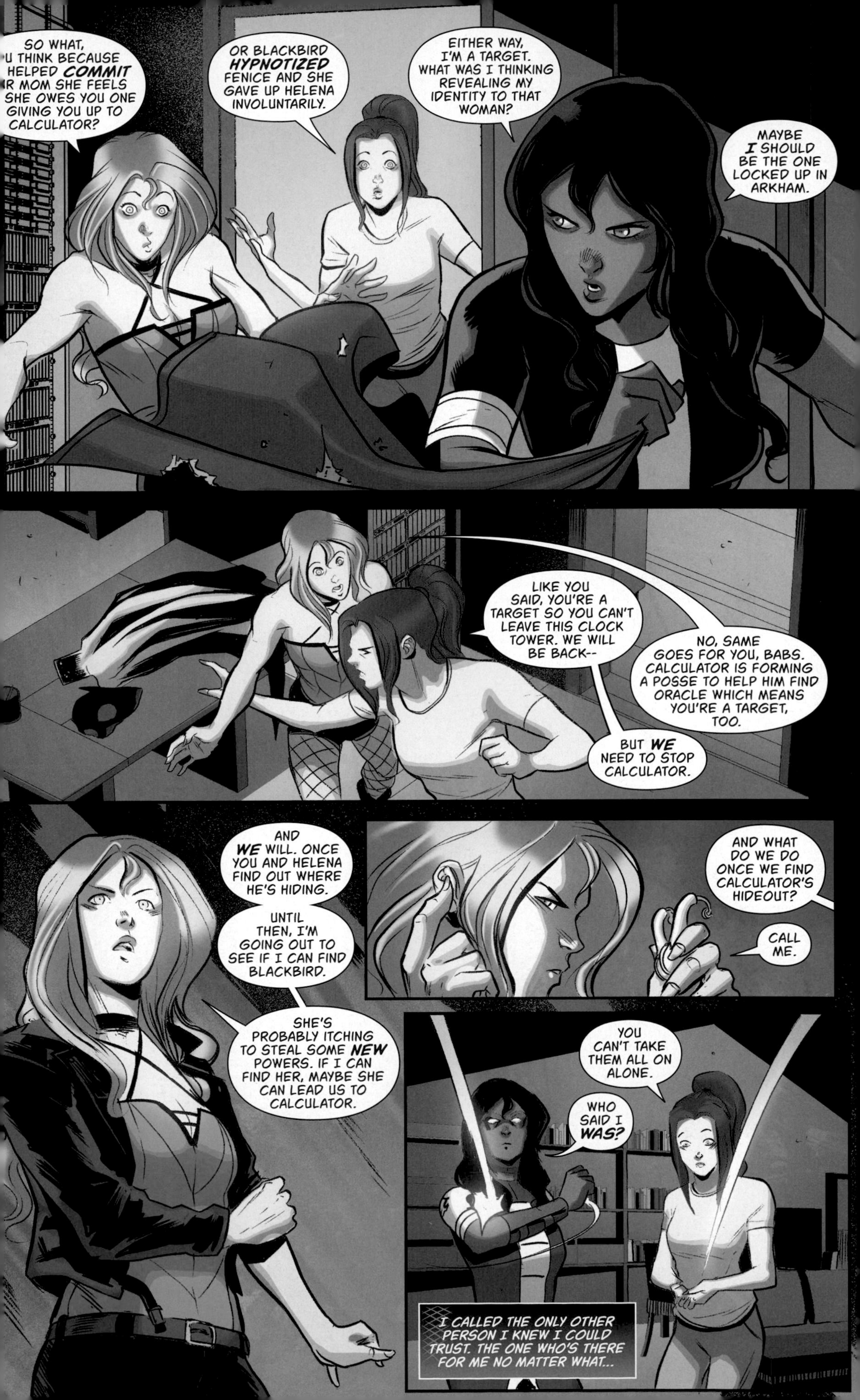
SO WHAT, ...U THINK BECAUSE ... HELPED COMMIT ...R MOM SHE FEELS SHE OWES YOU ONE GIVING YOU UP TO CALCULATOR?
OR BLACKBIRD HYPNOTIZED FENICE AND SHE GAVE UP HELENA INVOLUNTARILY.
EITHER WAY, I'M A TARGET. WHAT WAS I THINKING REVEALING MY IDENTITY TO THAT WOMAN?
MAYBE I SHOULD BE THE ONE LOCKED UP IN ARKHAM.
LIKE YOU SAID, YOU'RE A TARGET SO YOU CAN'T LEAVE THIS CLOCK TOWER. WE WILL BE BACK--
NO, SAME GOES FOR YOU, BABS. CALCULATOR IS FORMING A POSSE TO HELP HIM FIND ORACLE WHICH MEANS YOU'RE A TARGET, TOO.
BUT WE NEED TO STOP CALCULATOR.
AND WE WILL. ONCE YOU AND HELENA FIND OUT WHERE HE'S HIDING.
UNTIL THEN, I'M GOING OUT TO SEE IF I CAN FIND BLACKBIRD.
SHE'S PROBABLY ITCHING TO STEAL SOME NEW POWERS. IF I CAN FIND HER, MAYBE SHE CAN LEAD US TO CALCULATOR.
AND WHAT DO WE DO ONCE WE FIND CALCULATOR'S HIDEOUT?
CALL ME.
YOU CAN'T TAKE THEM ALL ON ALONE.
WHO SAID I WAS?
I CALLED THE ONLY OTHER PERSON I KNEW I COULD TRUST. THE ONE WHO'S THERE FOR ME NO MATTER WHAT...

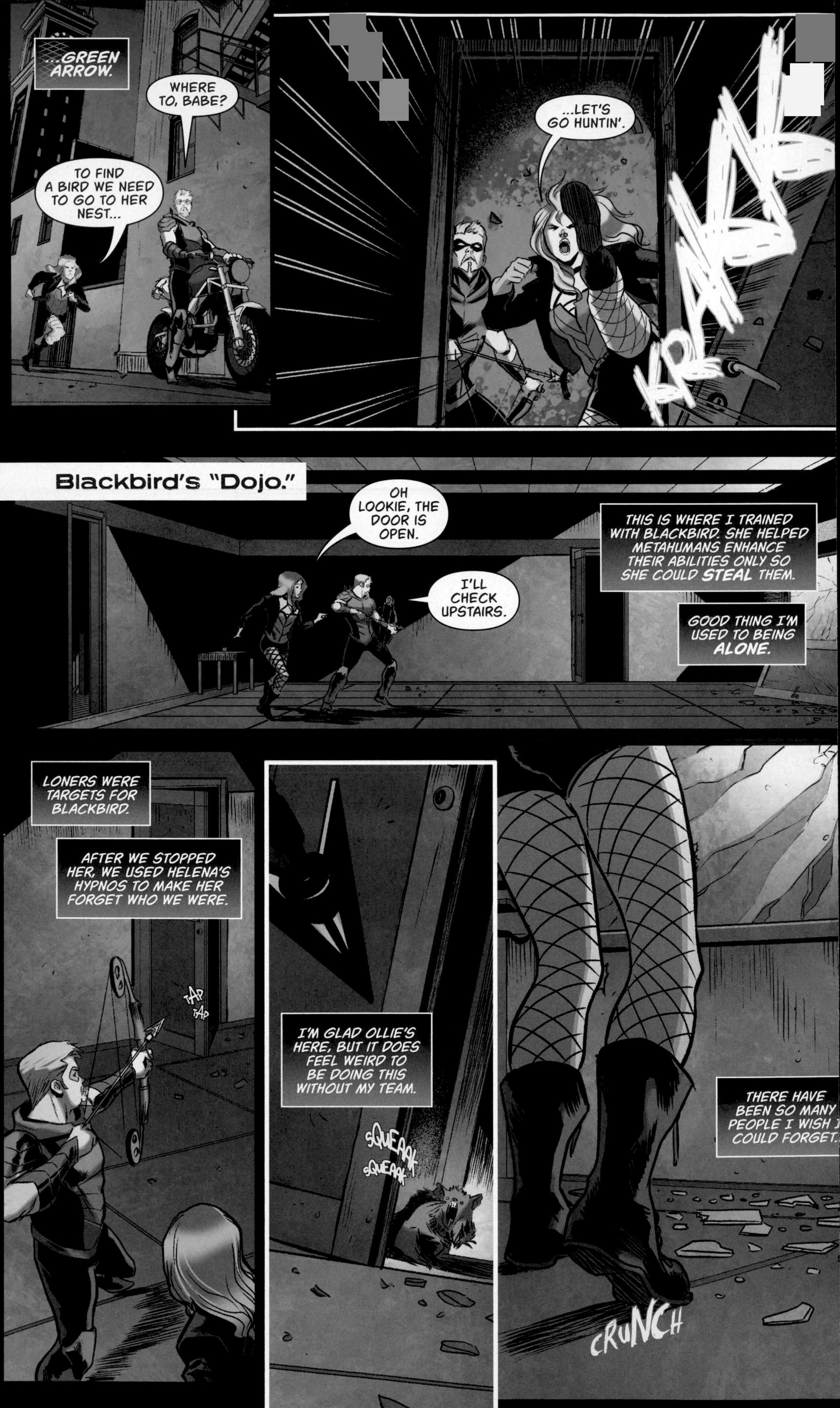

...GREEN ARROW.
WHERE TO, BABE?
TO FIND A BIRD WE NEED TO GO TO HER NEST...
...LET'S GO HUNTIN'.
KRAKS
Blackbird's "Dojo."
OH LOOKIE, THE DOOR IS OPEN.
I'LL CHECK UPSTAIRS.
THIS IS WHERE I TRAINED WITH BLACKBIRD. SHE HELPED METAHUMANS ENHANCE THEIR ABILITIES ONLY SO SHE COULD STEAL THEM.
GOOD THING I'M USED TO BEING ALONE.
LONERS WERE TARGETS FOR BLACKBIRD.
AFTER WE STOPPED HER, WE USED HELENA'S HYPNOS TO MAKE HER FORGET WHO WE WERE.
TAP TAP
I'M GLAD OLLIE'S HERE, BUT IT DOES FEEL WEIRD TO BE DOING THIS WITHOUT MY TEAM.
SQUEAAK SQUEAAK
THERE HAVE BEEN SO MANY PEOPLE I WISH I COULD FORGET.
CRUNCH

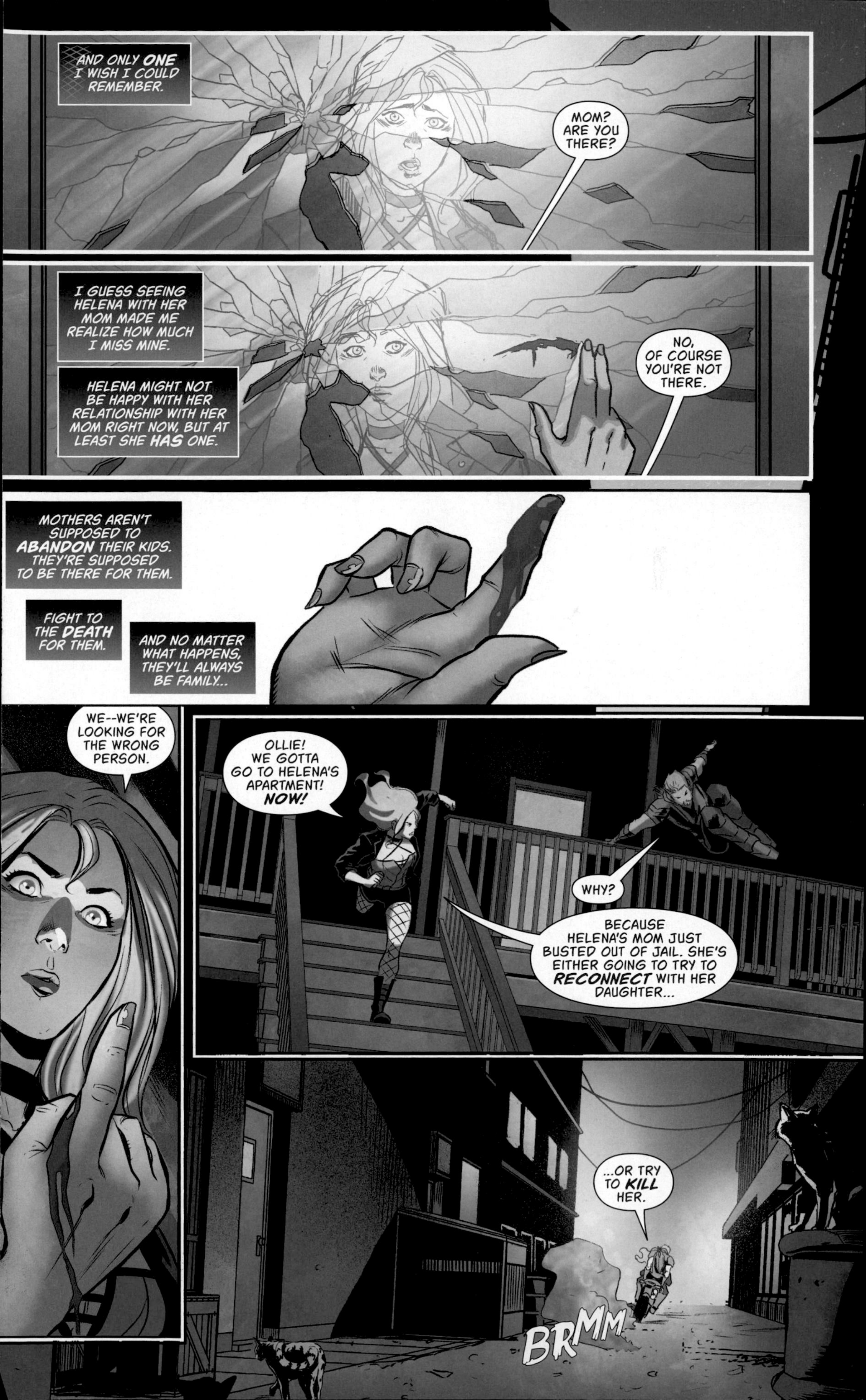
AND ONLY ONE I WISH I COULD REMEMBER.
MOM? ARE YOU THERE?
I GUESS SEEING HELENA WITH HER MOM MADE ME REALIZE HOW MUCH I MISS MINE.
HELENA MIGHT NOT BE HAPPY WITH HER RELATIONSHIP WITH HER MOM RIGHT NOW, BUT AT LEAST SHE HAS ONE.
NO, OF COURSE YOU'RE NOT THERE.
MOTHERS AREN'T SUPPOSED TO ABANDON THEIR KIDS. THEY'RE SUPPOSED TO BE THERE FOR THEM.
FIGHT TO THE DEATH FOR THEM.
AND NO MATTER WHAT HAPPENS, THEY'LL ALWAYS BE FAMILY...
WE--WE'RE LOOKING FOR THE WRONG PERSON.
OLLIE! WE GOTTA GO TO HELENA'S APARTMENT! NOW!
WHY?
BECAUSE HELENA'S MOM JUST BUSTED OUT OF JAIL. SHE'S EITHER GOING TO TRY TO RECONNECT WITH HER DAUGHTER...
...OR TRY TO KILL HER.
BRMM

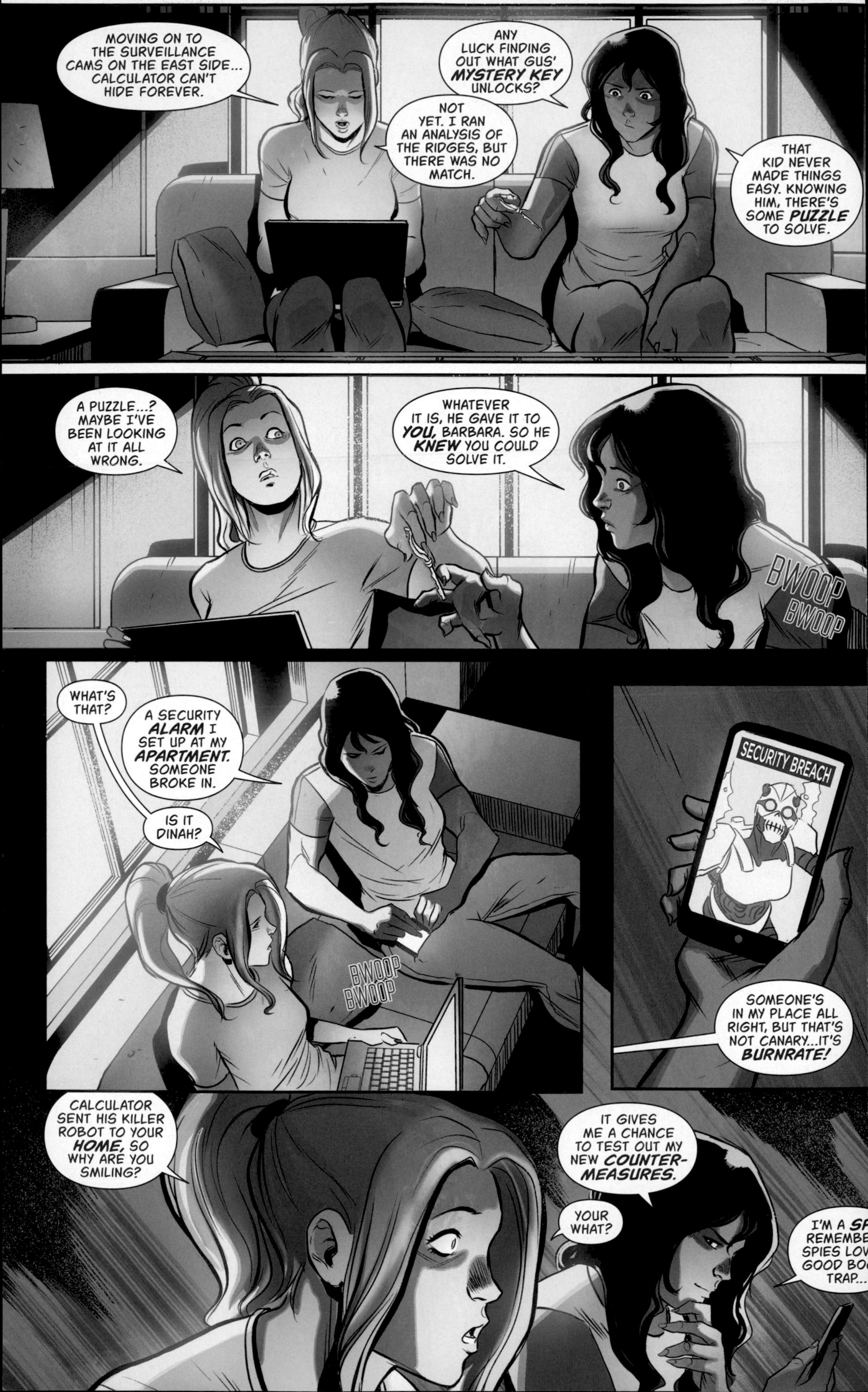
MOVING ON TO THE SURVEILLANCE CAMS ON THE EAST SIDE... CALCULATOR CAN'T HIDE FOREVER.
ANY LUCK FINDING OUT WHAT GUS' MYSTERY KEY UNLOCKS?
NOT YET. I RAN AN ANALYSIS OF THE RIDGES, BUT THERE WAS NO MATCH.
THAT KID NEVER MADE THINGS EASY. KNOWING HIM, THERE'S SOME PUZZLE TO SOLVE.
A PUZZLE...? MAYBE I'VE BEEN LOOKING AT IT ALL WRONG.
WHATEVER IT IS, HE GAVE IT TO YOU, BARBARA. SO HE KNEW YOU COULD SOLVE IT.
BWOOP BWOOP
WHAT'S THAT?
A SECURITY ALARM I SET UP AT MY APARTMENT. SOMEONE BROKE IN.
IS IT DINAH?
BWOOP BWOOP
SECURITY BREACH
SOMEONE'S IN MY PLACE ALL RIGHT, BUT THAT'S NOT CANARY...IT'S BURNRATE!
CALCULATOR SENT HIS KILLER ROBOT TO YOUR HOME, SO WHY ARE YOU SMILING?
IT GIVES ME A CHANCE TO TEST OUT MY NEW COUNTER-MEASURES.
YOUR WHAT?

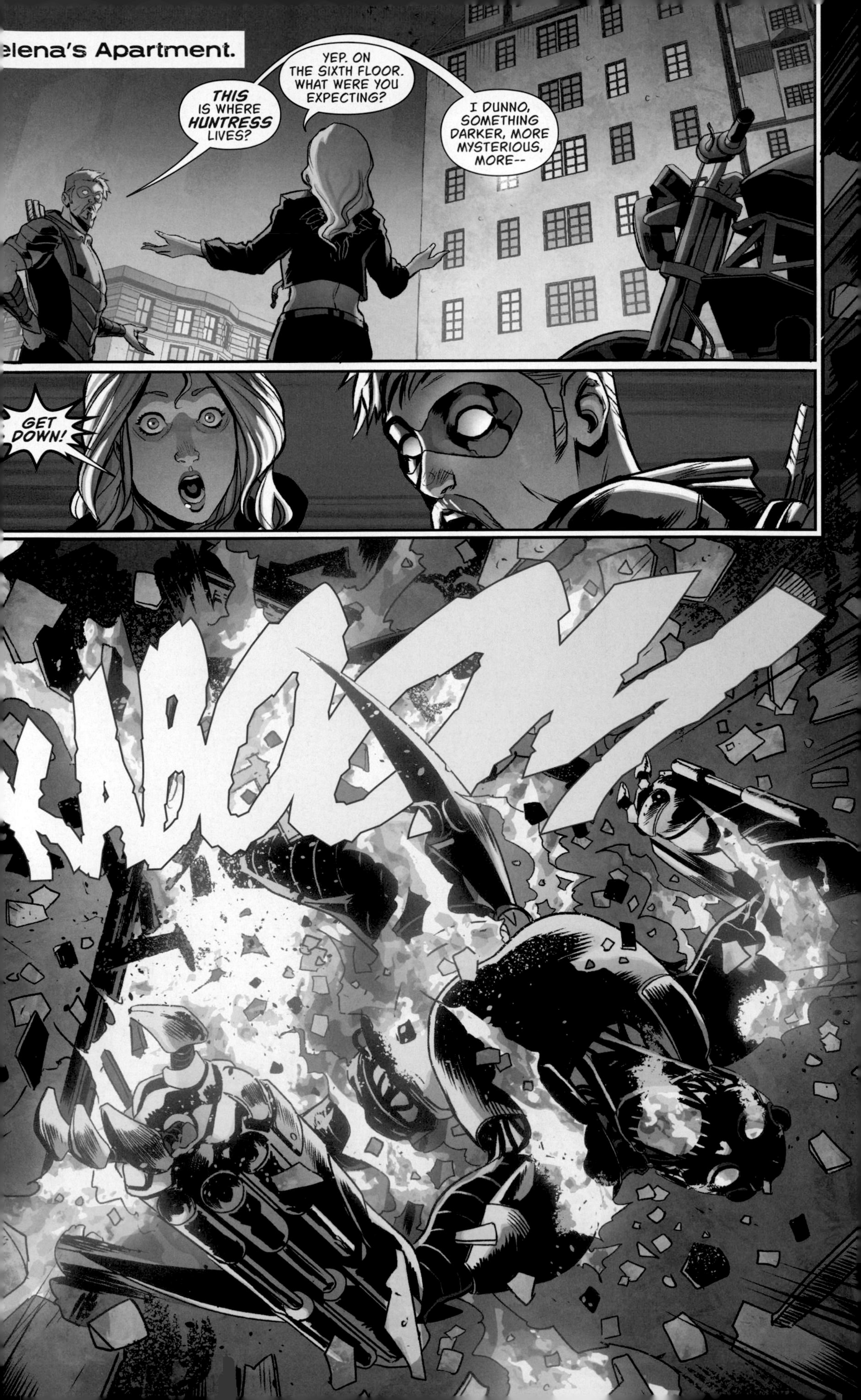
elena's Apartment.
THIS IS WHERE HUNTRESS LIVES?
YEP. ON THE SIXTH FLOOR. WHAT WERE YOU EXPECTING?
I DUNNO, SOMETHING DARKER, MORE MYSTERIOUS, MORE--
GET DOWN!
KABOOM!

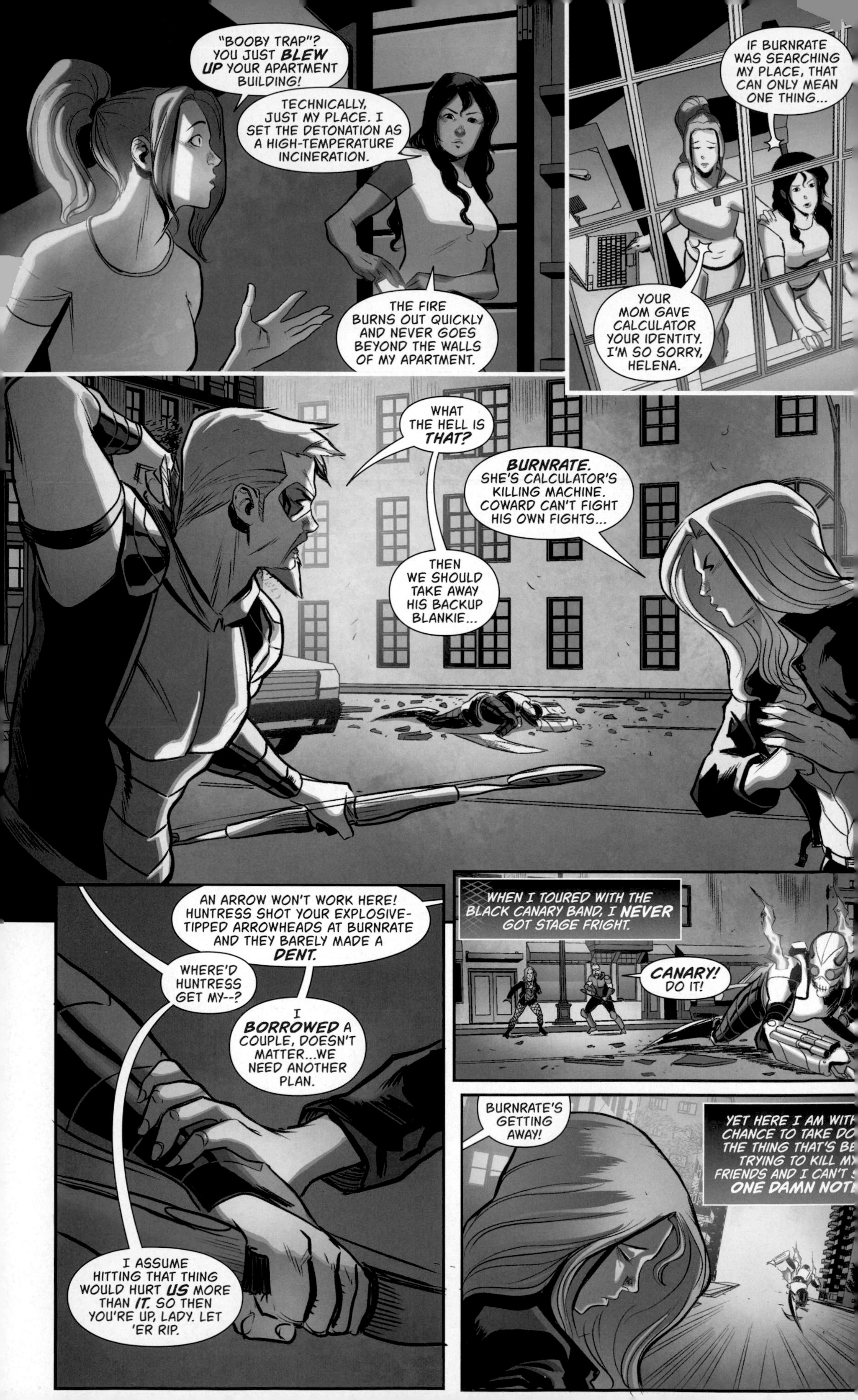
"BOOBY TRAP"? YOU JUST BLEW UP YOUR APARTMENT BUILDING!
TECHNICALLY, JUST MY PLACE. I SET THE DETONATION AS A HIGH-TEMPERATURE INCINERATION.
THE FIRE BURNS OUT QUICKLY AND NEVER GOES BEYOND THE WALLS OF MY APARTMENT.
IF BURNRATE WAS SEARCHING MY PLACE, THAT CAN ONLY MEAN ONE THING...
YOUR MOM GAVE CALCULATOR YOUR IDENTITY. I'M SO SORRY, HELENA.
WHAT THE HELL IS THAT?
BURNRATE. SHE'S CALCULATOR'S KILLING MACHINE. COWARD CAN'T FIGHT HIS OWN FIGHTS...
THEN WE SHOULD TAKE AWAY HIS BACKUP BLANKIE...
AN ARROW WON'T WORK HERE! HUNTRESS SHOT YOUR EXPLOSIVE-TIPPED ARROWHEADS AT BURNRATE AND THEY BARELY MADE A DENT.
WHERE'D HUNTRESS GET MY--?
I BORROWED A COUPLE, DOESN'T MATTER...WE NEED ANOTHER PLAN.
I ASSUME HITTING THAT THING WOULD HURT US MORE THAN IT. SO THEN YOU'RE UP, LADY. LET 'ER RIP.
WHEN I TOURED WITH THE BLACK CANARY BAND, I NEVER GOT STAGE FRIGHT.
CANARY! DO IT!
BURNRATE'S GETTING AWAY!
YET HERE I AM WITH CHANCE TO TAKE DO THE THING THAT'S BE TRYING TO KILL MY FRIENDS AND I CAN'T ONE DAMN NOT

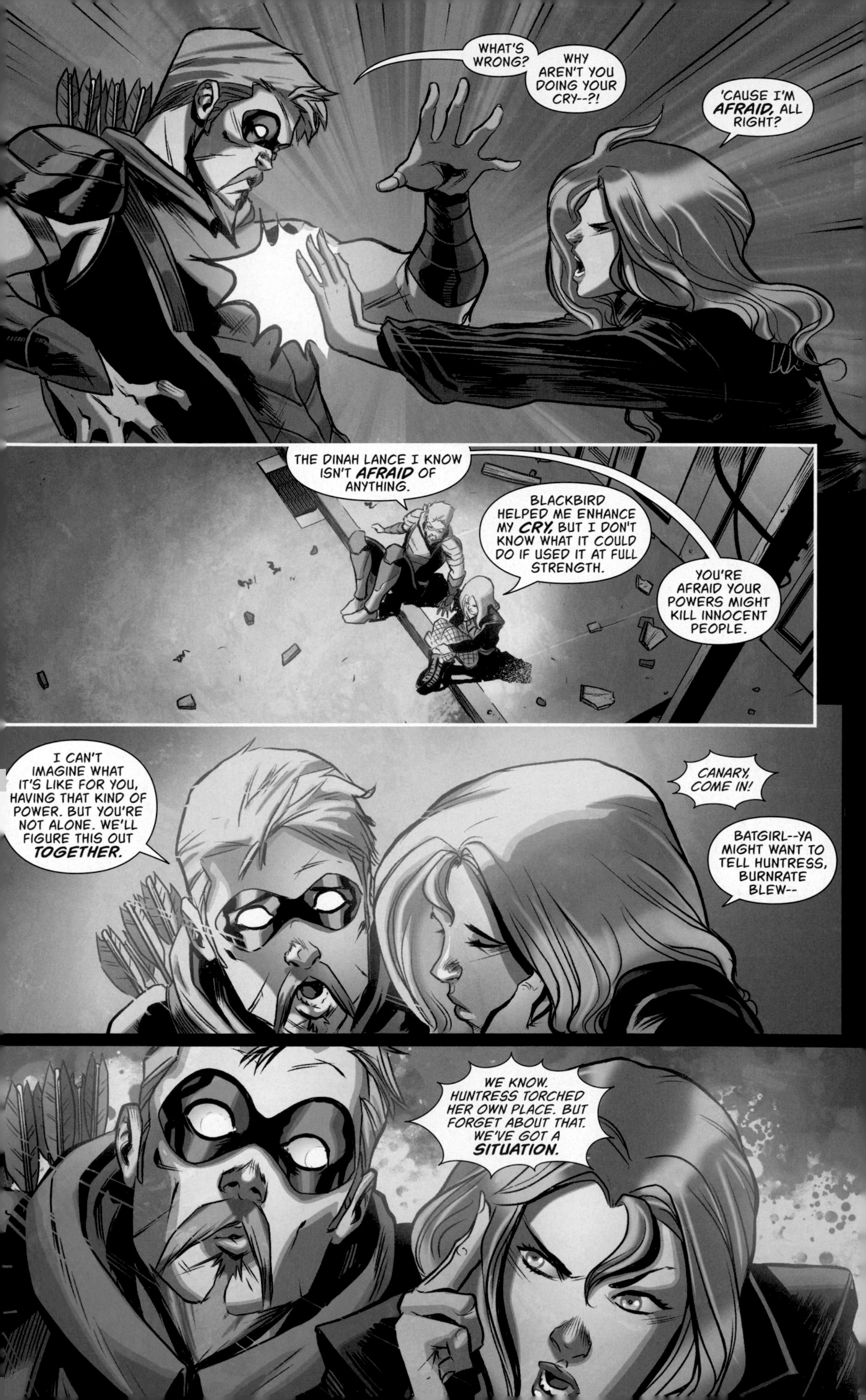
WHAT'S WRONG?
WHY AREN'T YOU DOING YOUR CRY--?!
'CAUSE I'M AFRAID, ALL RIGHT?
THE DINAH LANCE I KNOW ISN'T AFRAID OF ANYTHING.
BLACKBIRD HELPED ME ENHANCE MY CRY, BUT I DON'T KNOW WHAT IT COULD DO IF USED IT AT FULL STRENGTH.
YOU'RE AFRAID YOUR POWERS MIGHT KILL INNOCENT PEOPLE.
I CAN'T IMAGINE WHAT IT'S LIKE FOR YOU, HAVING THAT KIND OF POWER. BUT YOU'RE NOT ALONE. WE'LL FIGURE THIS OUT TOGETHER.
CANARY, COME IN!
BATGIRL--YA MIGHT WANT TO TELL HUNTRESS, BURNRATE BLEW--
WE KNOW. HUNTRESS TORCHED HER OWN PLACE. BUT FORGET ABOUT THAT. WE'VE GOT A SITUATION.

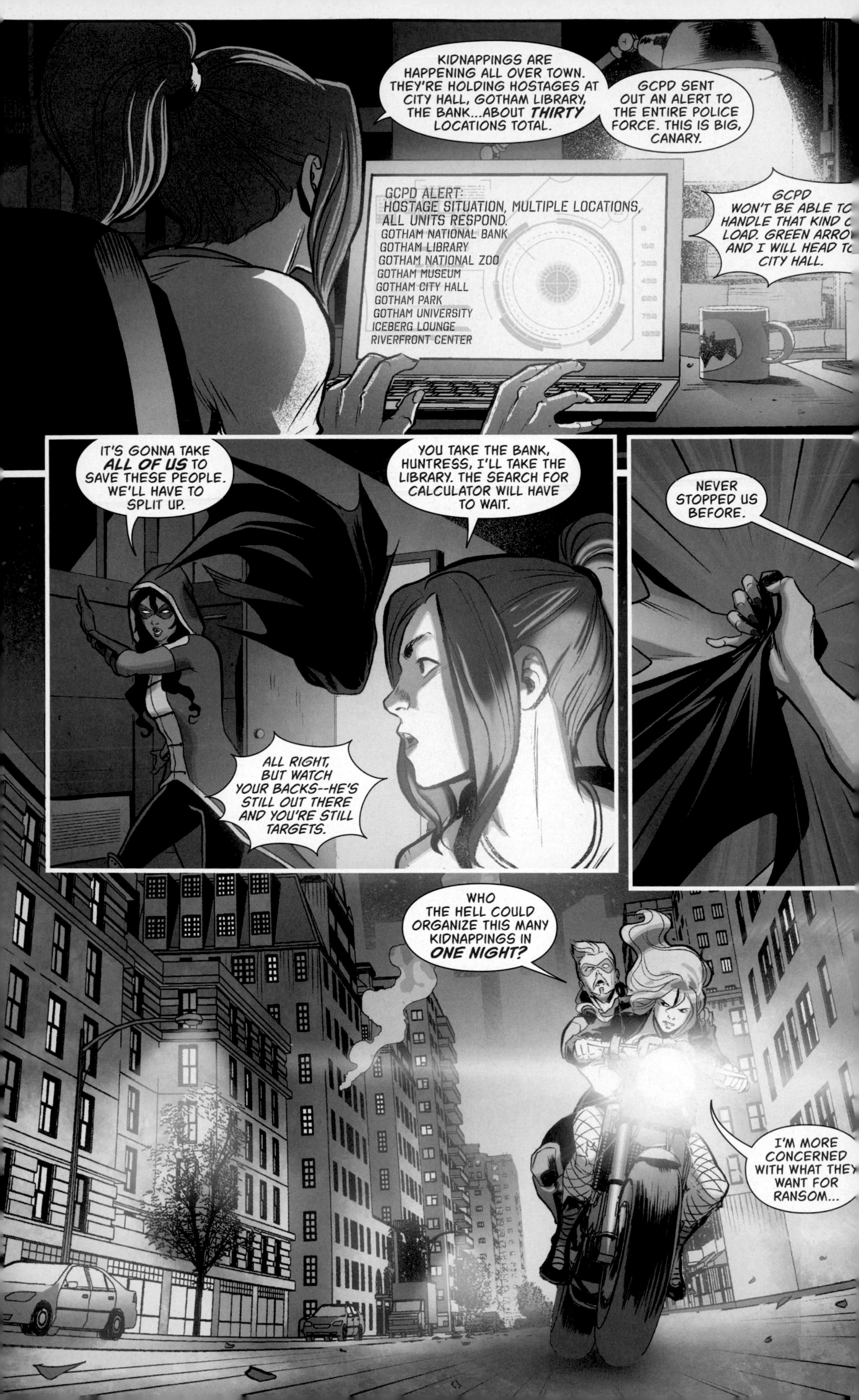
KIDNAPPINGS ARE HAPPENING ALL OVER TOWN. THEY'RE HOLDING HOSTAGES AT CITY HALL, GOTHAM LIBRARY, THE BANK...ABOUT THIRTY LOCATIONS TOTAL.
GCPD SENT OUT AN ALERT TO THE ENTIRE POLICE FORCE. THIS IS BIG, CANARY.
GCPD ALERT:
HOSTAGE SITUATION, MULTIPLE LOCATIONS,
ALL UNITS RESPOND.
GOTHAM NATIONAL BANK
GOTHAM LIBRARY
GOTHAM NATIONAL ZOO
GOTHAM MUSEUM
GOTHAM CITY HALL
GOTHAM PARK
GOTHAM UNIVERSITY
ICEBERG LOUNGE
RIVERFRONT CENTER
GCPD WON'T BE ABLE TO HANDLE THAT KIND O LOAD. GREEN ARRO AND I WILL HEAD TO CITY HALL.
IT'S GONNA TAKE ALL OF US TO SAVE THESE PEOPLE. WE'LL HAVE TO SPLIT UP.
YOU TAKE THE BANK, HUNTRESS, I'LL TAKE THE LIBRARY. THE SEARCH FOR CALCULATOR WILL HAVE TO WAIT.
NEVER STOPPED US BEFORE.
ALL RIGHT, BUT WATCH YOUR BACKS--HE'S STILL OUT THERE AND YOU'RE STILL TARGETS.
WHO THE HELL COULD ORGANIZE THIS MANY KIDNAPPINGS IN ONE NIGHT?
I'M MORE CONCERNED WITH WHAT THE WANT FOR RANSOM...

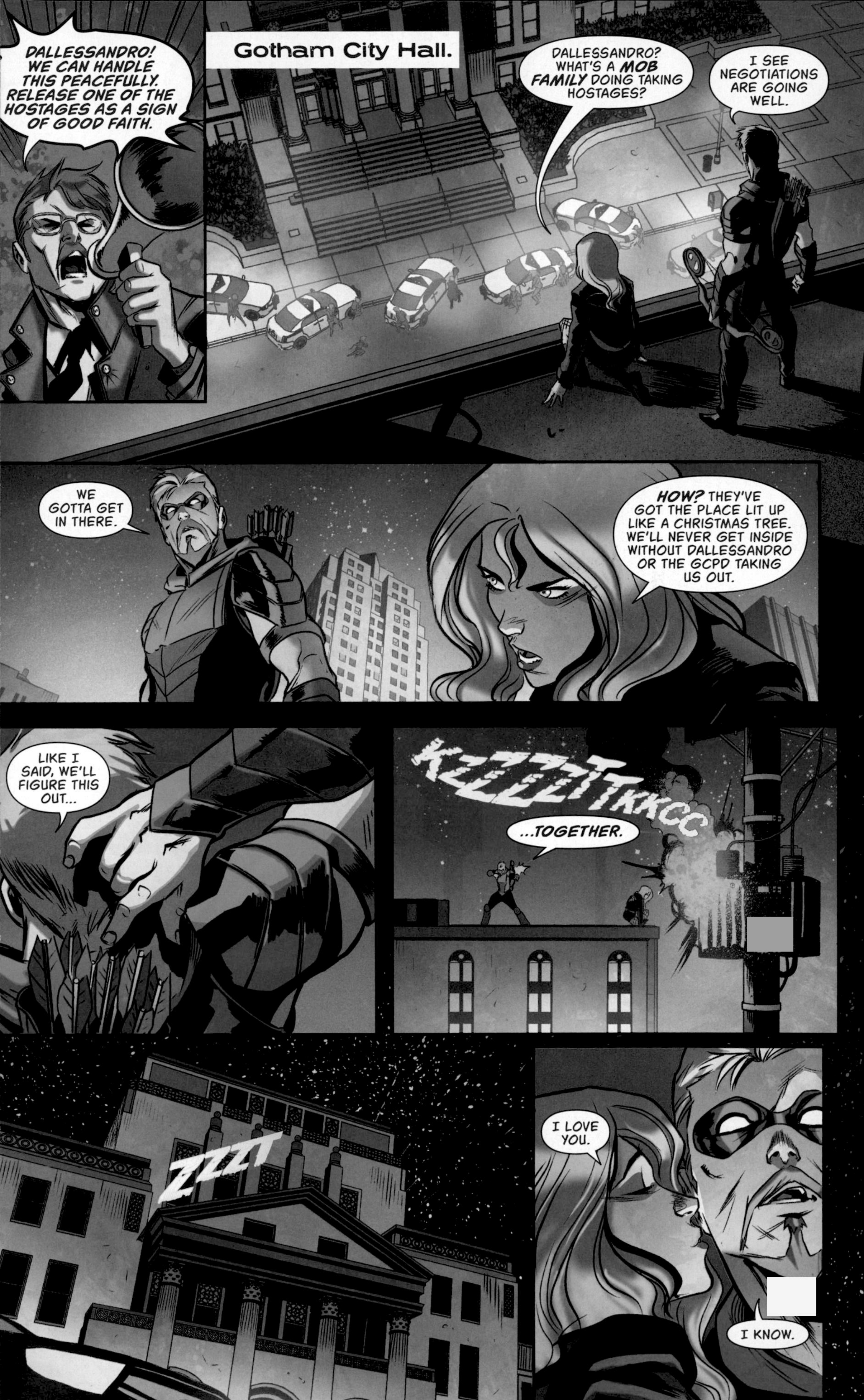
DALLESSANDRO! WE CAN HANDLE THIS PEACEFULLY. RELEASE ONE OF THE HOSTAGES AS A SIGN OF GOOD FAITH.
Gotham City Hall.
DALLESSANDRO? WHAT'S A MOB FAMILY DOING TAKING HOSTAGES?
I SEE NEGOTIATIONS ARE GOING WELL.
WE GOTTA GET IN THERE.
HOW? THEY'VE GOT THE PLACE LIT UP LIKE A CHRISTMAS TREE. WE'LL NEVER GET INSIDE WITHOUT DALLESSANDRO OR THE GCPD TAKING US OUT.
LIKE I SAID, WE'LL FIGURE THIS OUT...
KZZZZTKKCC
...TOGETHER.
ZZZT
I LOVE YOU.
I KNOW.

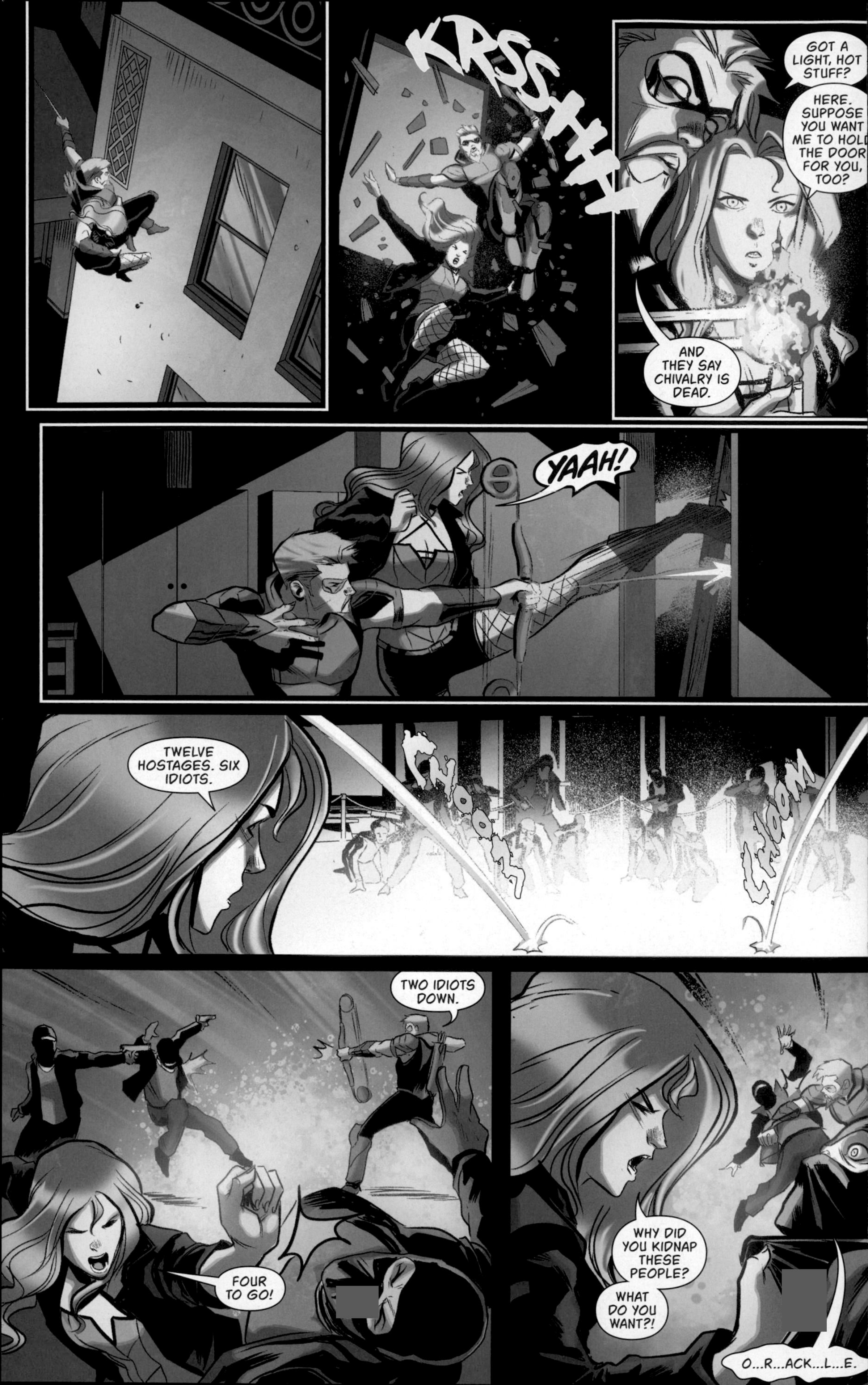
KRSSHHH
GOT A LIGHT, HOT STUFF?
HERE. SUPPOSE YOU WANT ME TO HOLD THE DOOR FOR YOU, TOO?
AND THEY SAY CHIVALRY IS DEAD.
YAAH!
TWELVE HOSTAGES. SIX IDIOTS.
CHOOM
TWO IDIOTS DOWN.
FOUR TO GO!
WHY DID YOU KIDNAP THESE PEOPLE?
WHAT DO YOU WANT?!
O...R...ACK...L...E.

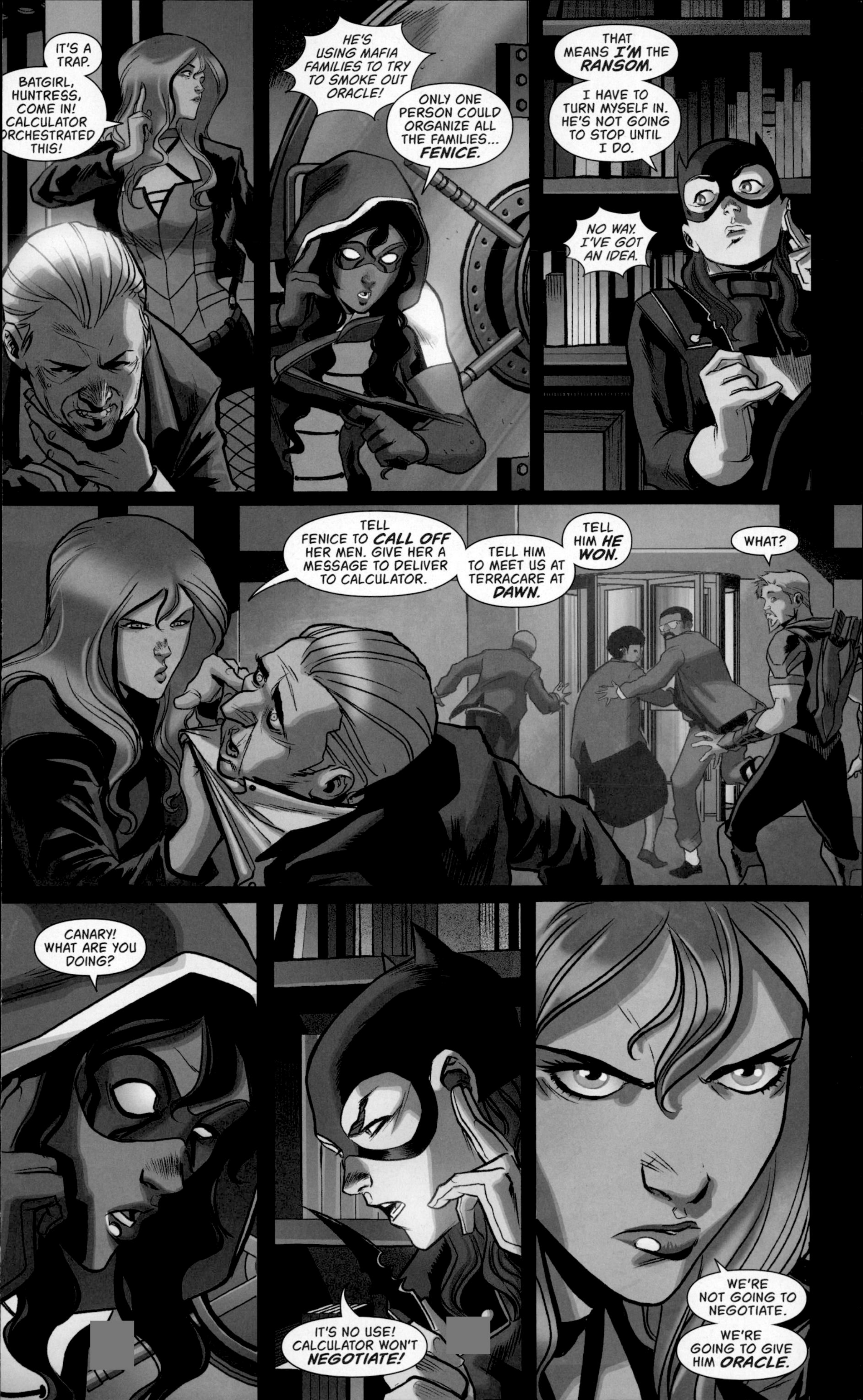

IT'S A TRAP.
BATGIRL, HUNTRESS, COME IN! CALCULATOR ORCHESTRATED THIS!
HE'S USING MAFIA FAMILIES TO TRY TO SMOKE OUT ORACLE!
ONLY ONE PERSON COULD ORGANIZE ALL THE FAMILIES... FENICE.
THAT MEANS I'M THE RANSOM.
I HAVE TO TURN MYSELF IN. HE'S NOT GOING TO STOP UNTIL I DO.
NO WAY. I'VE GOT AN IDEA.
TELL FENICE TO CALL OFF HER MEN. GIVE HER A MESSAGE TO DELIVER TO CALCULATOR.
TELL HIM TO MEET US AT TERRACARE AT DAWN.
TELL HIM HE WON.
WHAT?
CANARY! WHAT ARE YOU DOING?
IT'S NO USE! CALCULATOR WON'T NEGOTIATE!
WE'RE NOT GOING TO NEGOTIATE.
WE'RE GOING TO GIVE HIM ORACLE.

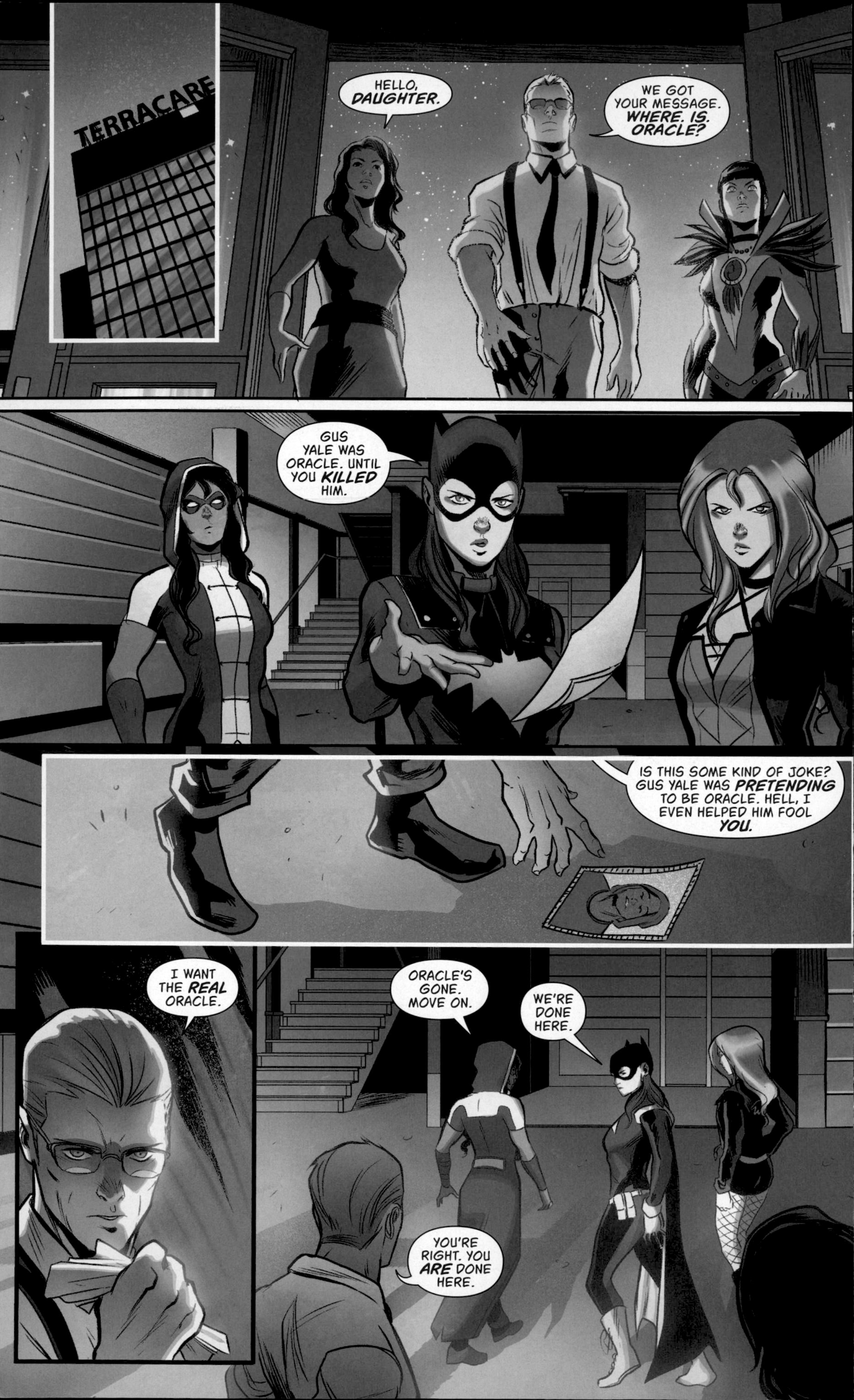
TERRACARE
HELLO, DAUGHTER.
WE GOT YOUR MESSAGE. WHERE. IS. ORACLE?
GUS YALE WAS ORACLE. UNTIL YOU KILLED HIM.
IS THIS SOME KIND OF JOKE? GUS YALE WAS PRETENDING TO BE ORACLE. HELL, I EVEN HELPED HIM FOOL YOU.
I WANT THE REAL ORACLE.
ORACLE'S GONE. MOVE ON.
WE'RE DONE HERE.
YOU'RE RIGHT. YOU ARE DONE HERE.

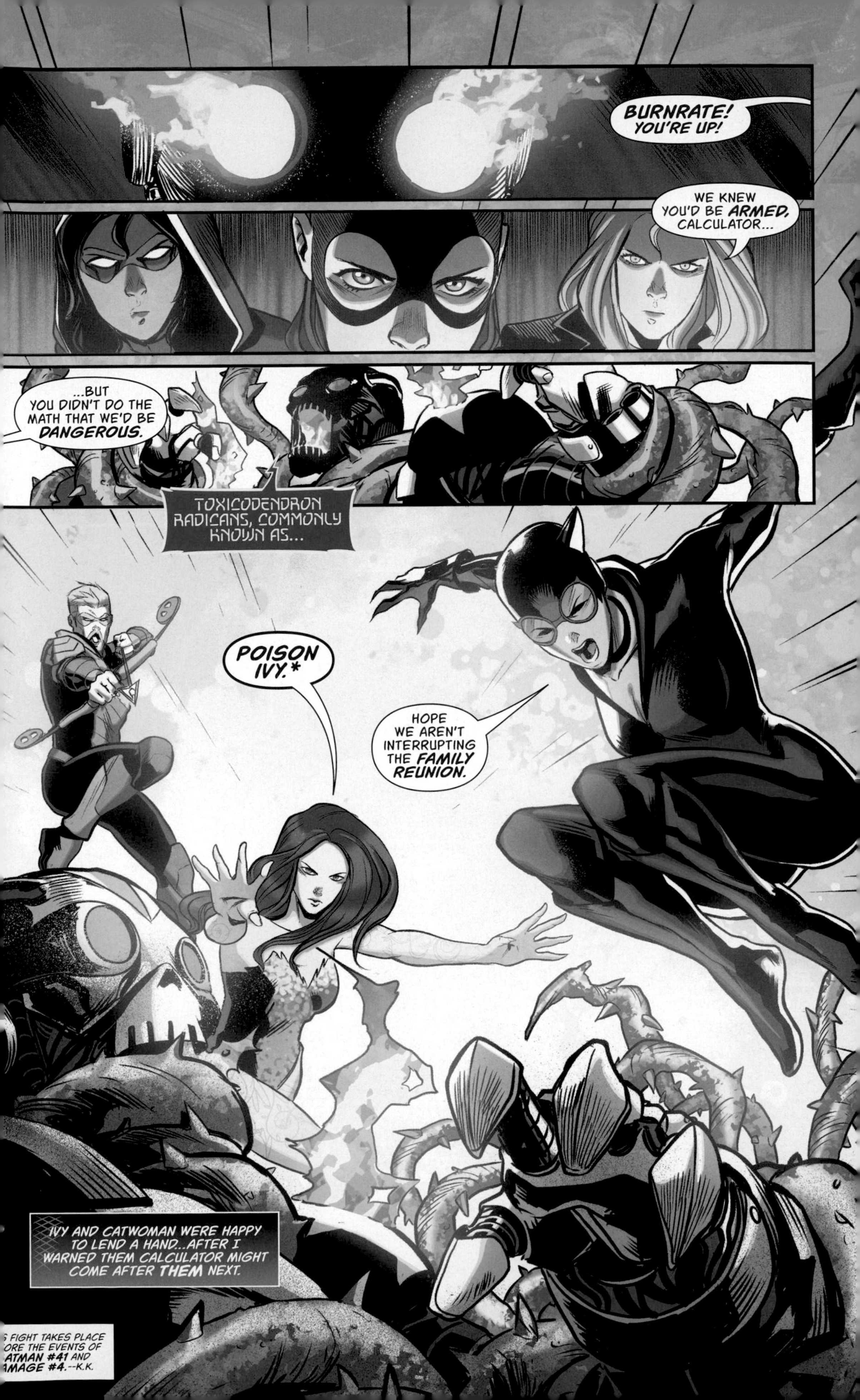
BURNRATE! YOU'RE UP!
WE KNEW YOU'D BE ARMED, CALCULATOR...
...BUT YOU DIDN'T DO THE MATH THAT WE'D BE DANGEROUS.
TOXICODENDRON RADICANS, COMMONLY KNOWN AS...
POISON IVY.*
HOPE WE AREN'T INTERRUPTING THE FAMILY REUNION.
IVY AND CATWOMAN WERE HAPPY TO LEND A HAND...AFTER I WARNED THEM CALCULATOR MIGHT COME AFTER THEM NEXT.
S FIGHT TAKES PLACE ORE THE EVENTS OF ATMAN #41 AND AMAGE #4.--K.K.

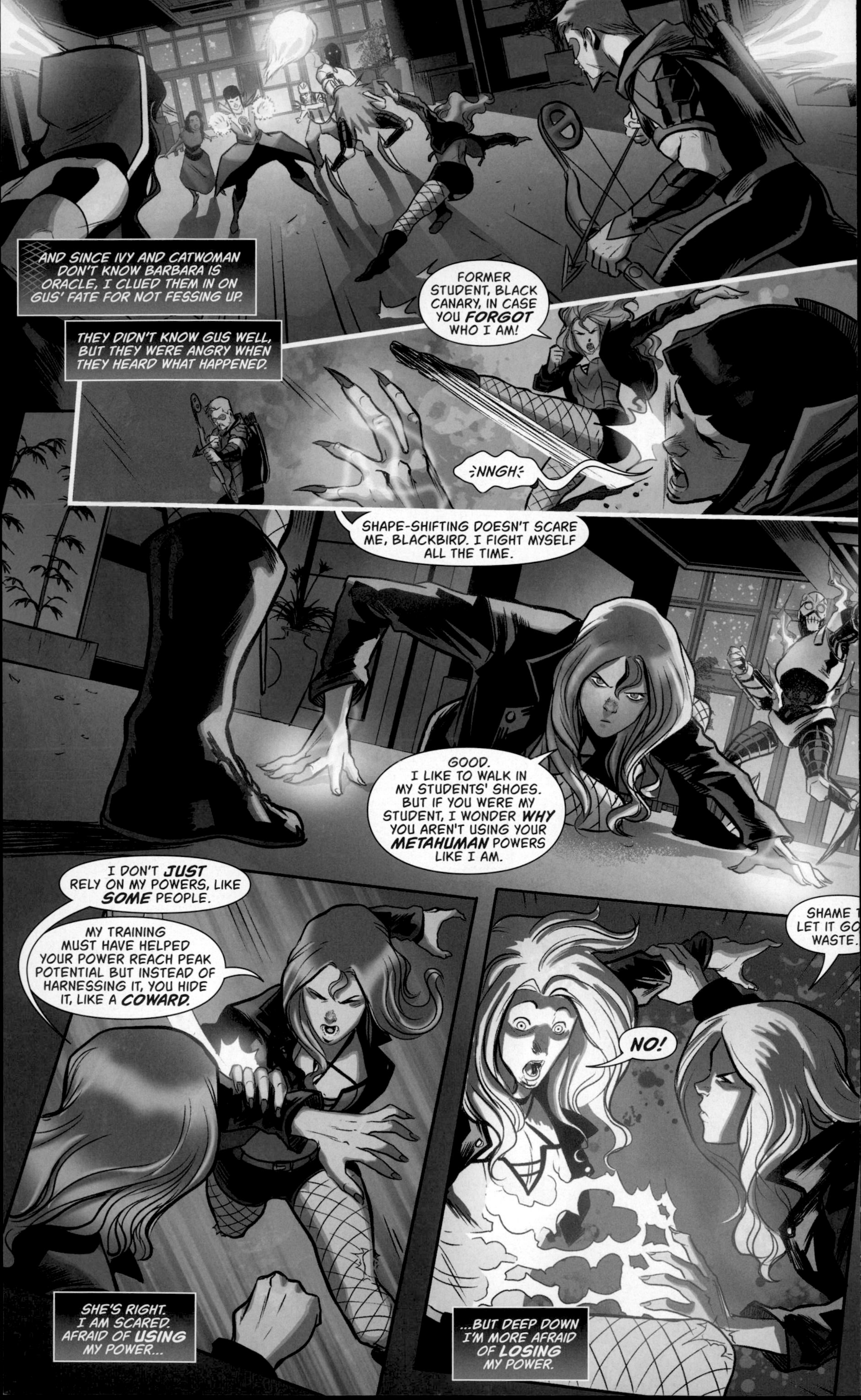
AND SINCE IVY AND CATWOMAN DON'T KNOW BARBARA IS ORACLE, I CLUED THEM IN ON GUS' FATE FOR NOT FESSING UP.
THEY DIDN'T KNOW GUS WELL, BUT THEY WERE ANGRY WHEN THEY HEARD WHAT HAPPENED.
FORMER STUDENT, BLACK CANARY, IN CASE YOU FORGOT WHO I AM!
NNGH
SHAPE-SHIFTING DOESN'T SCARE ME, BLACKBIRD. I FIGHT MYSELF ALL THE TIME.
GOOD. I LIKE TO WALK IN MY STUDENTS' SHOES. BUT IF YOU WERE MY STUDENT, I WONDER WHY YOU AREN'T USING YOUR METAHUMAN POWERS LIKE I AM.
I DON'T JUST RELY ON MY POWERS, LIKE SOME PEOPLE.
MY TRAINING MUST HAVE HELPED YOUR POWER REACH PEAK POTENTIAL BUT INSTEAD OF HARNESSING IT, YOU HIDE IT, LIKE A COWARD.
SHE'S RIGHT. I AM SCARED. AFRAID OF USING MY POWER...
SHAME LET IT GO WASTE.
NO!
...BUT DEEP DOWN I'M MORE AFRAID OF LOSING MY POWER.

THUNK

GET AWAY FROM HER!

AH!

ARE YOU OKAY, CANARY?

I'M ALL RIGHT. LET'S GO HELP THE OTHERS.

OH HELL NO. YOU'RE AREN'T RUNNING OUT ON ME AGAIN, MOM!

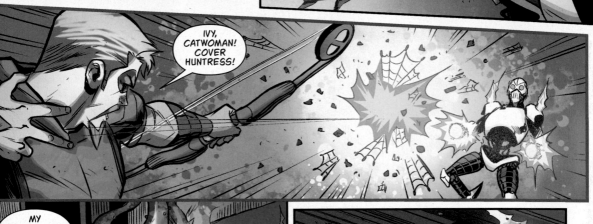

IVY, CATWOMAN! COVER HUNTRESS!

MY VINES WON'T LAST AGAINST BURNRATE'S FIREPOWER! CAT?

WORKING ON IT...

KRAK

...BITCH BROKE MY NAIL.

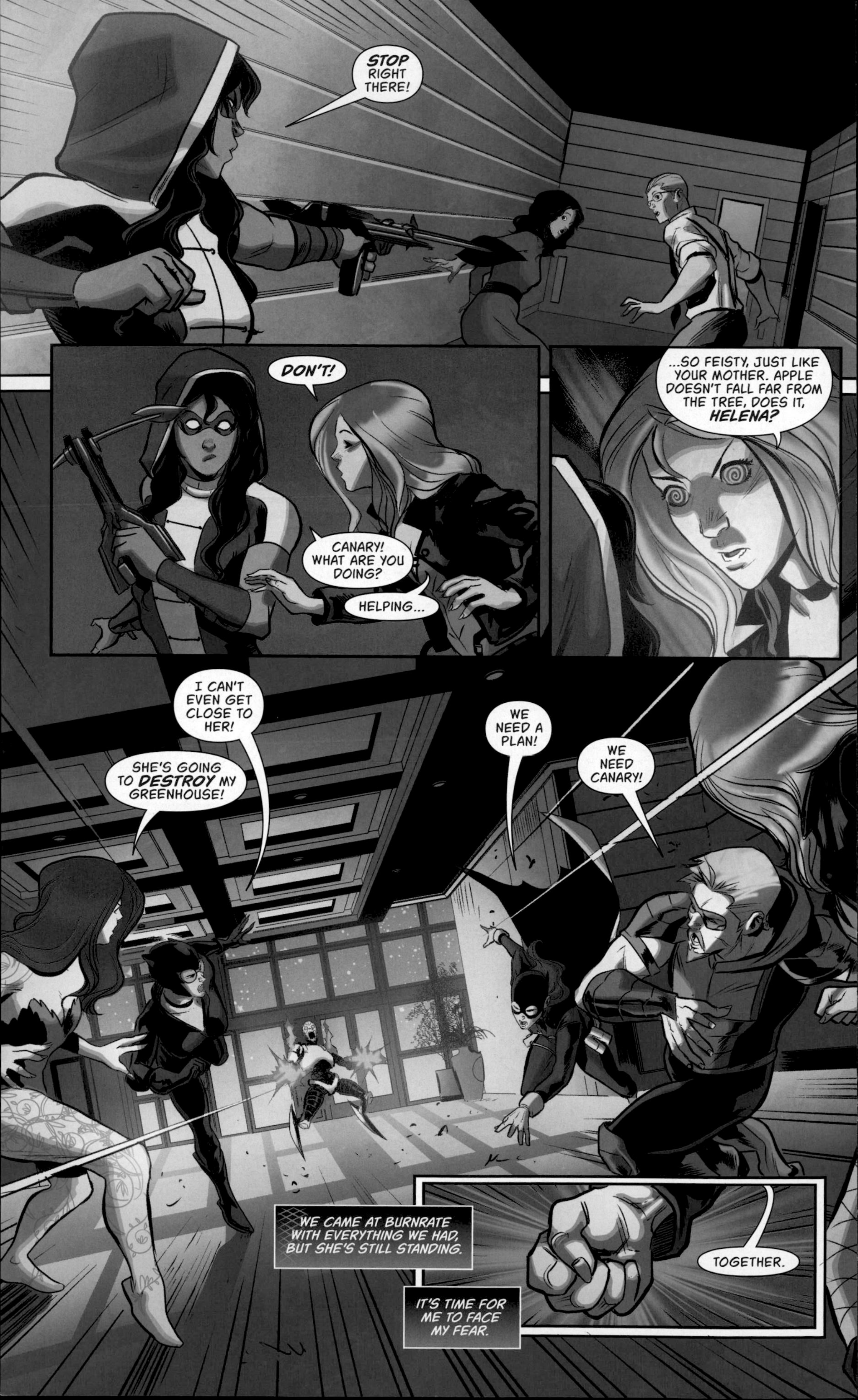
STOP RIGHT THERE!
DON'T!
CANARY! WHAT ARE YOU DOING?
HELPING...
...SO FEISTY, JUST LIKE YOUR MOTHER. APPLE DOESN'T FALL FAR FROM THE TREE, DOES IT, HELENA?
I CAN'T EVEN GET CLOSE TO HER!
SHE'S GOING TO DESTROY MY GREENHOUSE!
WE NEED A PLAN!
WE NEED CANARY!
WE CAME AT BURNRATE WITH EVERYTHING WE HAD, BUT SHE'S STILL STANDING.
IT'S TIME FOR ME TO FACE MY FEAR.
TOGETHER.

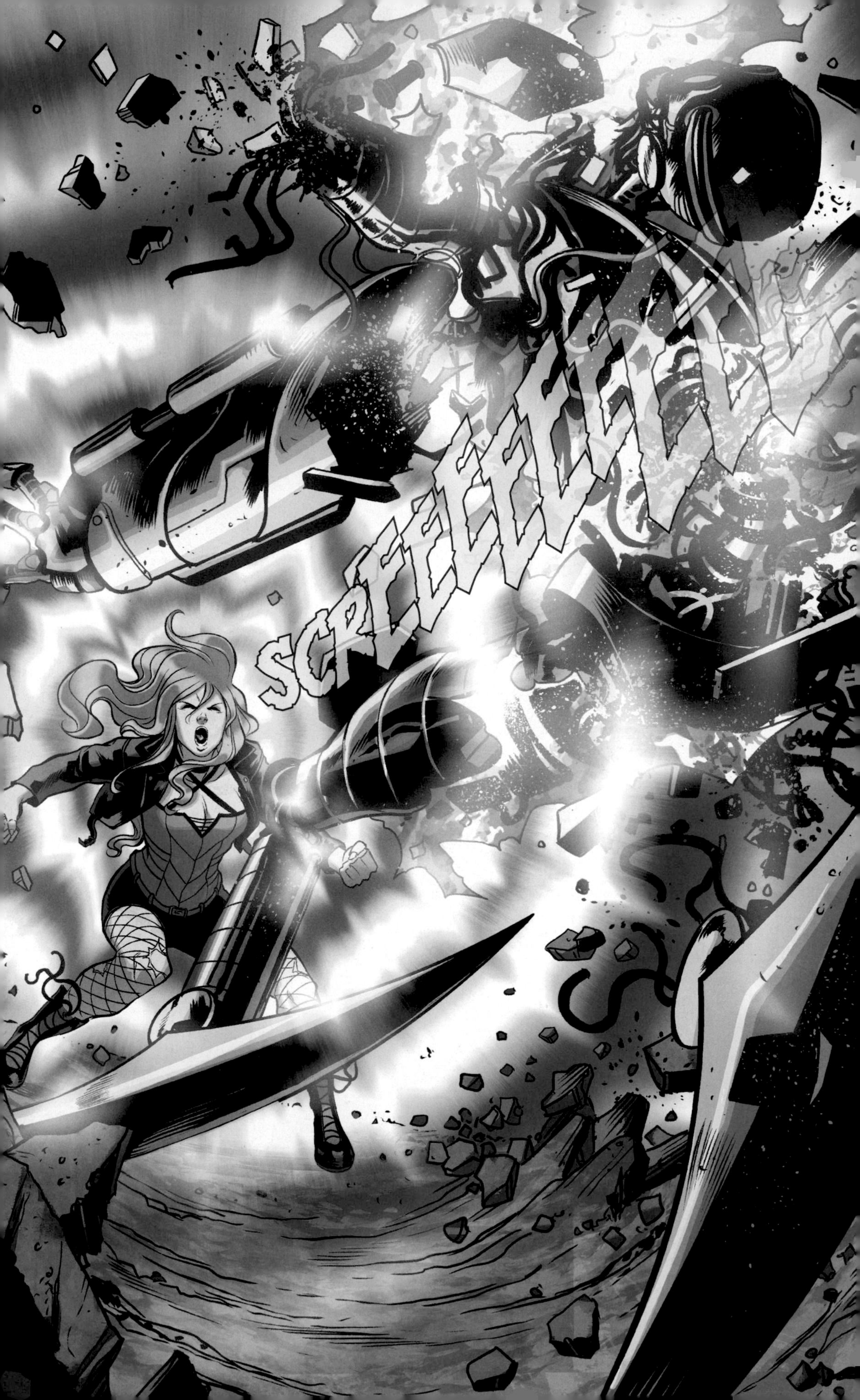
SCREEEEEEE

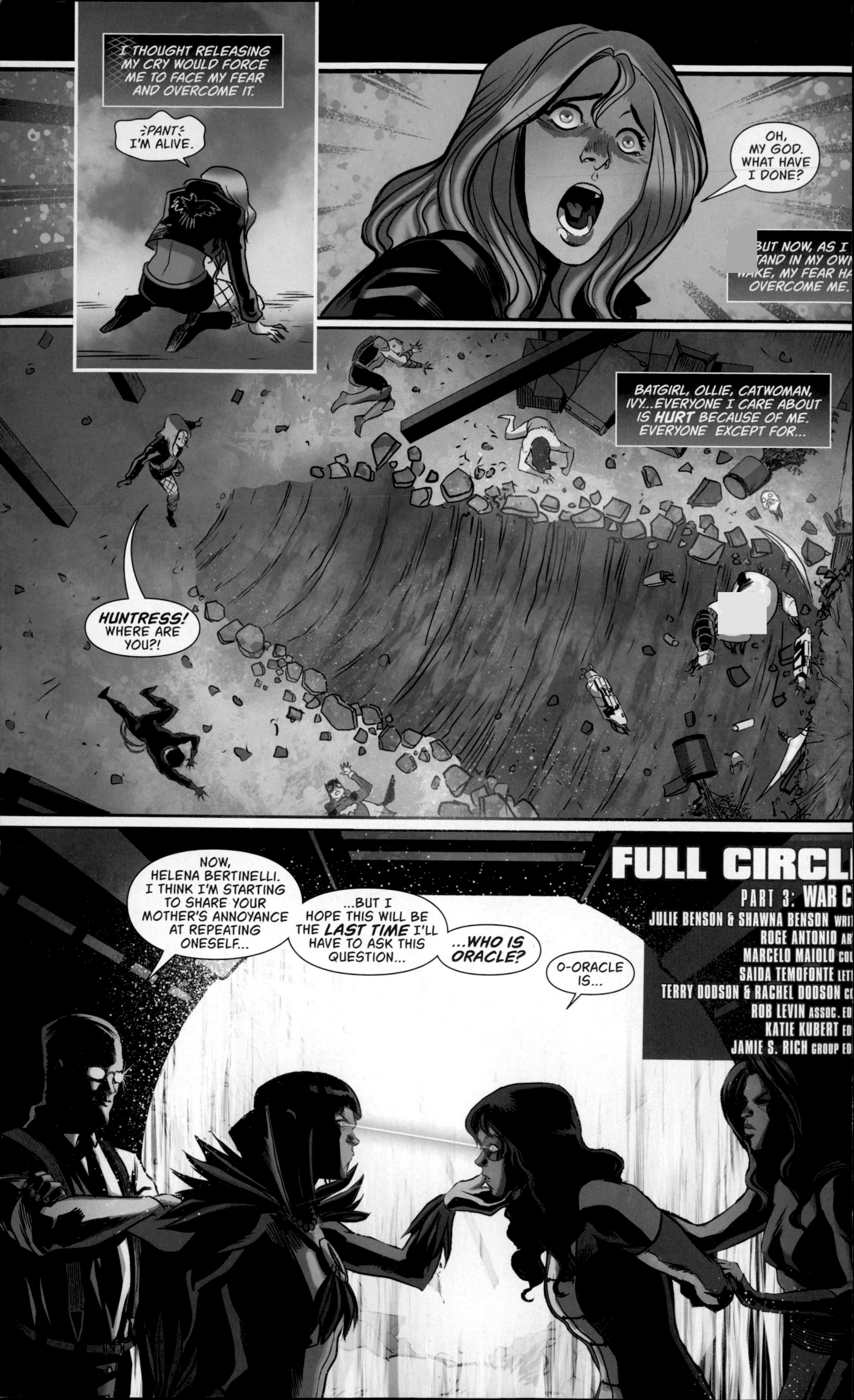

I THOUGHT RELEASING MY CRY WOULD FORCE ME TO FACE MY FEAR AND OVERCOME IT.
PANT I'M ALIVE.
OH, MY GOD. WHAT HAVE I DONE?
BUT NOW, AS I TAND IN MY OWN WAKE, MY FEAR HA OVERCOME ME.
BATGIRL, OLLIE, CATWOMAN, IVY...EVERYONE I CARE ABOUT IS HURT BECAUSE OF ME. EVERYONE EXCEPT FOR...
HUNTRESS! WHERE ARE YOU?!
FULL CIRCL
PART 3: WAR C
JULIE BENSON & SHAWNA BENSON WRIT
ROGE ANTONIO AR
MARCELO MAIOLO COL
SAIDA TEMOFONTE LET
TERRY DODSON & RACHEL DODSON CO
ROB LEVIN ASSOC. ED
KATIE KUBERT ED
JAMIE S. RICH GROUP ED
NOW, HELENA BERTINELLI. I THINK I'M STARTING TO SHARE YOUR MOTHER'S ANNOYANCE AT REPEATING ONESELF...
...BUT I HOPE THIS WILL BE THE LAST TIME I'LL HAVE TO ASK THIS QUESTION...
...WHO IS ORACLE?
O-ORACLE IS...

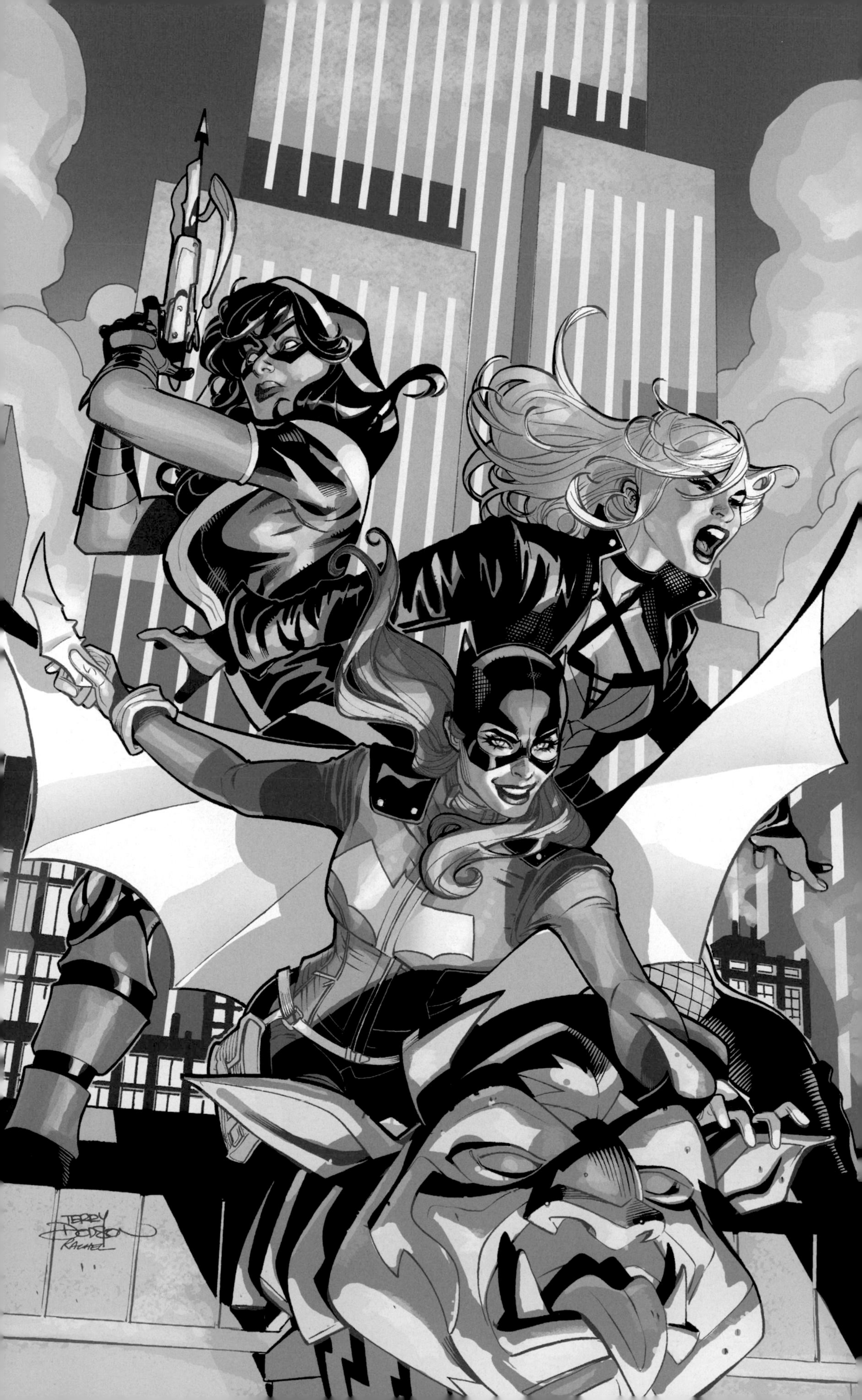
TERRY DODSON
RACHEL

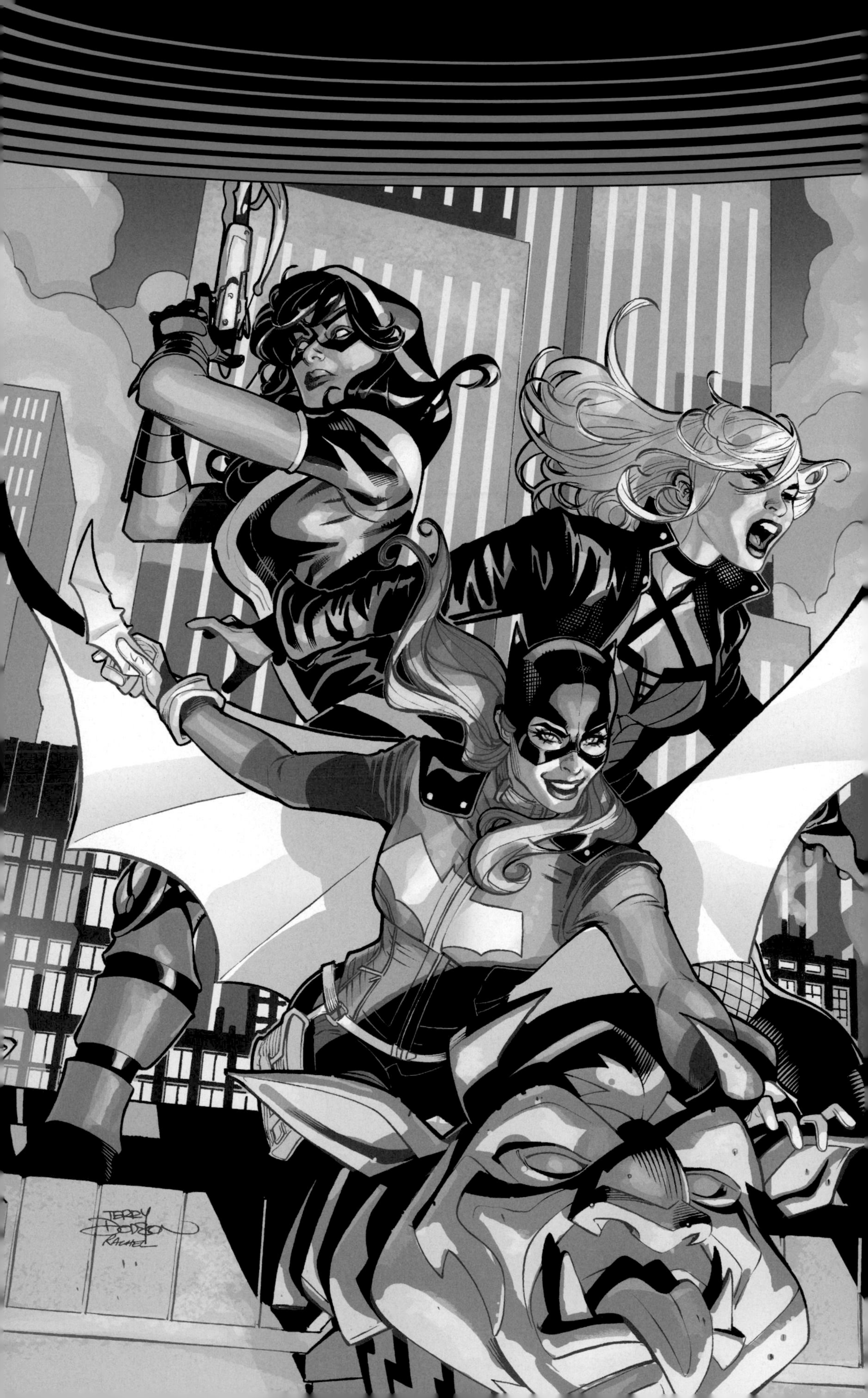
TERRY DODSON RACHEL

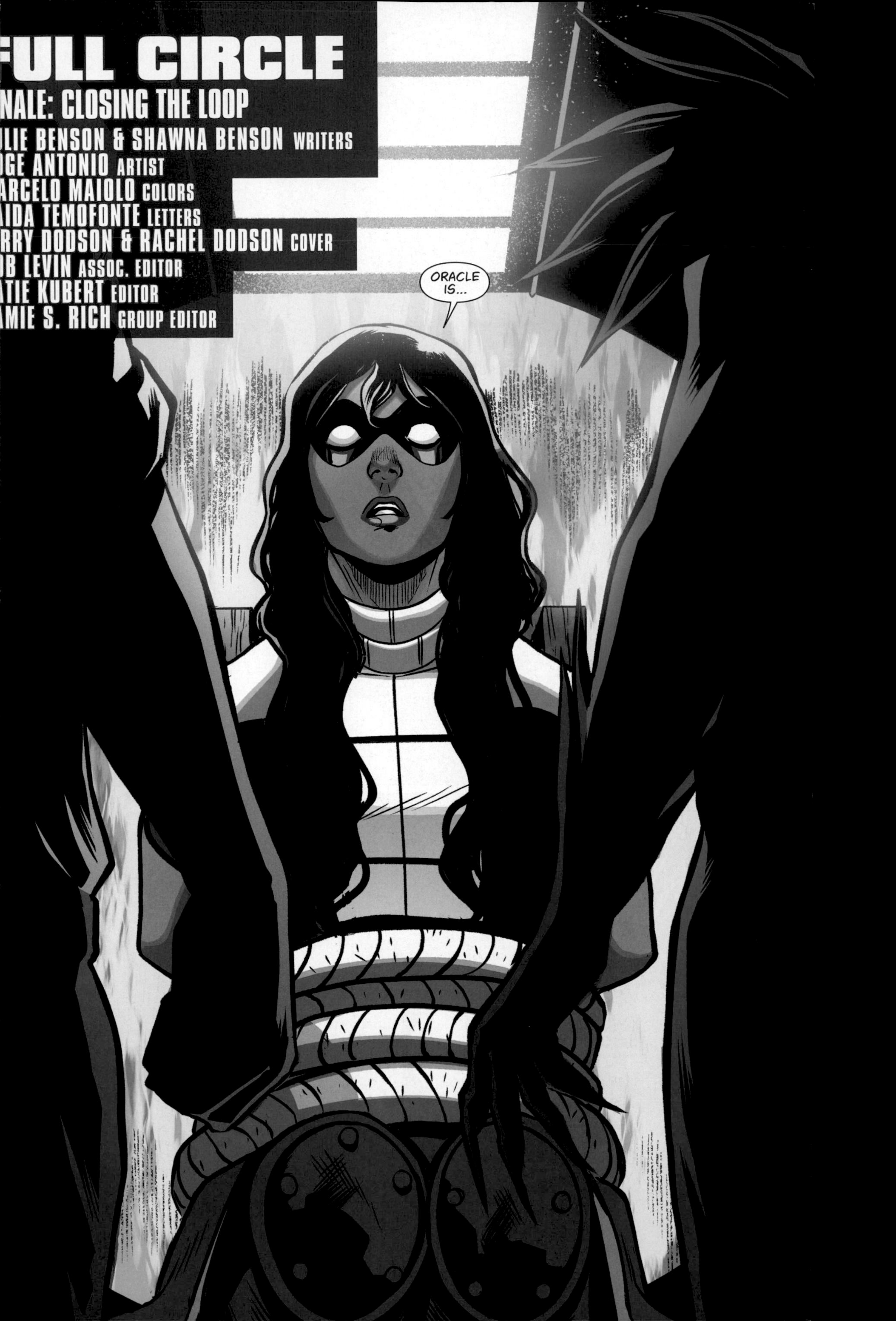
FULL CIRCLE
NALE: CLOSING THE LOOP
ULIE BENSON & SHAWNA BENSON WRITERS
OGE ANTONIO ARTIST
ARCELO MAIOLO COLORS
AIDA TEMOFONTE LETTERS
RRY DODSON & RACHEL DODSON COVER
OB LEVIN ASSOC. EDITOR
ATIE KUBERT EDITOR
AMIE S. RICH GROUP EDITOR
ORACLE IS...

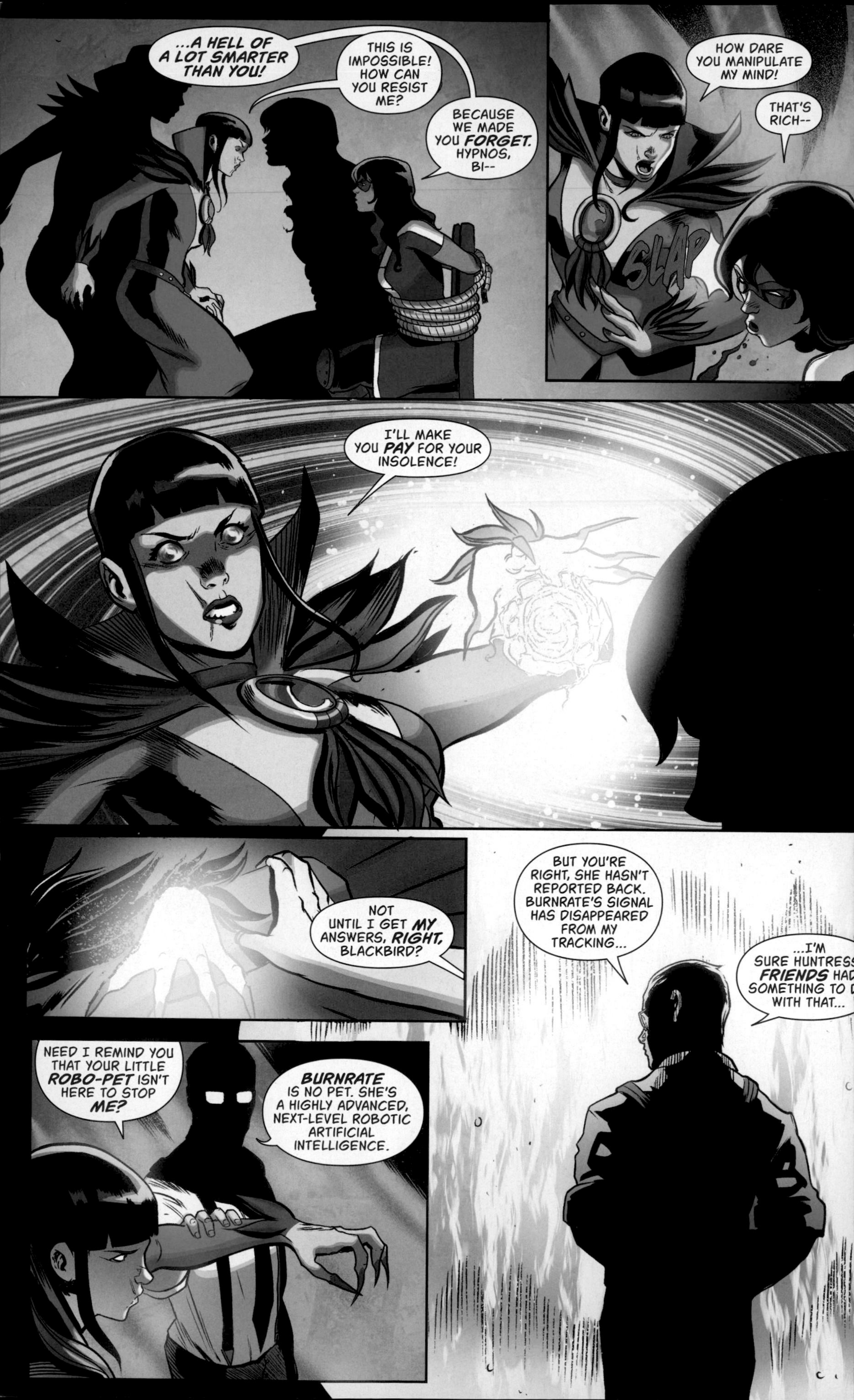
...A HELL OF A LOT SMARTER THAN YOU!
THIS IS IMPOSSIBLE! HOW CAN YOU RESIST ME?
BECAUSE WE MADE YOU FORGET. HYPNOS, BI--
HOW DARE YOU MANIPULATE MY MIND!
THAT'S RICH--
SLAP
I'LL MAKE YOU PAY FOR YOUR INSOLENCE!
NOT UNTIL I GET MY ANSWERS, RIGHT, BLACKBIRD?
NEED I REMIND YOU THAT YOUR LITTLE ROBO-PET ISN'T HERE TO STOP ME?
BURNRATE IS NO PET. SHE'S A HIGHLY ADVANCED, NEXT-LEVEL ROBOTIC ARTIFICIAL INTELLIGENCE.
BUT YOU'RE RIGHT, SHE HASN'T REPORTED BACK. BURNRATE'S SIGNAL HAS DISAPPEARED FROM MY TRACKING...
...I'M SURE HUNTRESS FRIENDS HAD SOMETHING TO D WITH THAT...

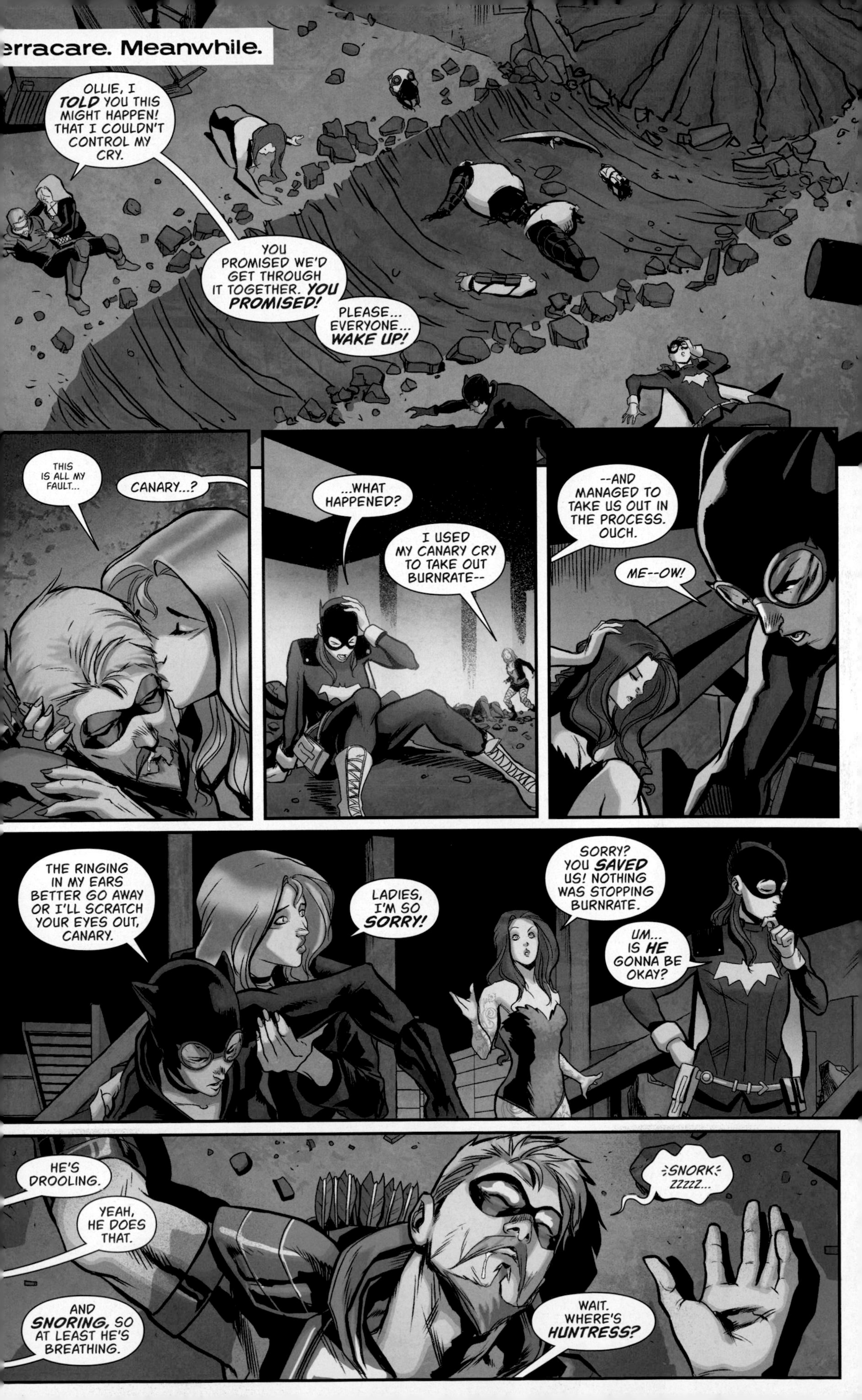

erracare. Meanwhile.
OLLIE, I TOLD YOU THIS MIGHT HAPPEN! THAT I COULDN'T CONTROL MY CRY.
YOU PROMISED WE'D GET THROUGH IT TOGETHER. YOU PROMISED!
PLEASE... EVERYONE... WAKE UP!
THIS IS ALL MY FAULT...
CANARY...?
...WHAT HAPPENED?
I USED MY CANARY CRY TO TAKE OUT BURNRATE--
--AND MANAGED TO TAKE US OUT IN THE PROCESS. OUCH.
ME--OW!
THE RINGING IN MY EARS BETTER GO AWAY OR I'LL SCRATCH YOUR EYES OUT, CANARY.
LADIES, I'M SO SORRY!
SORRY? YOU SAVED US! NOTHING WAS STOPPING BURNRATE.
UM... IS HE GONNA BE OKAY?
HE'S DROOLING.
YEAH, HE DOES THAT.
SNORK ZZZZZ...
AND SNORING, SO AT LEAST HE'S BREATHING.
WAIT. WHERE'S HUNTRESS?

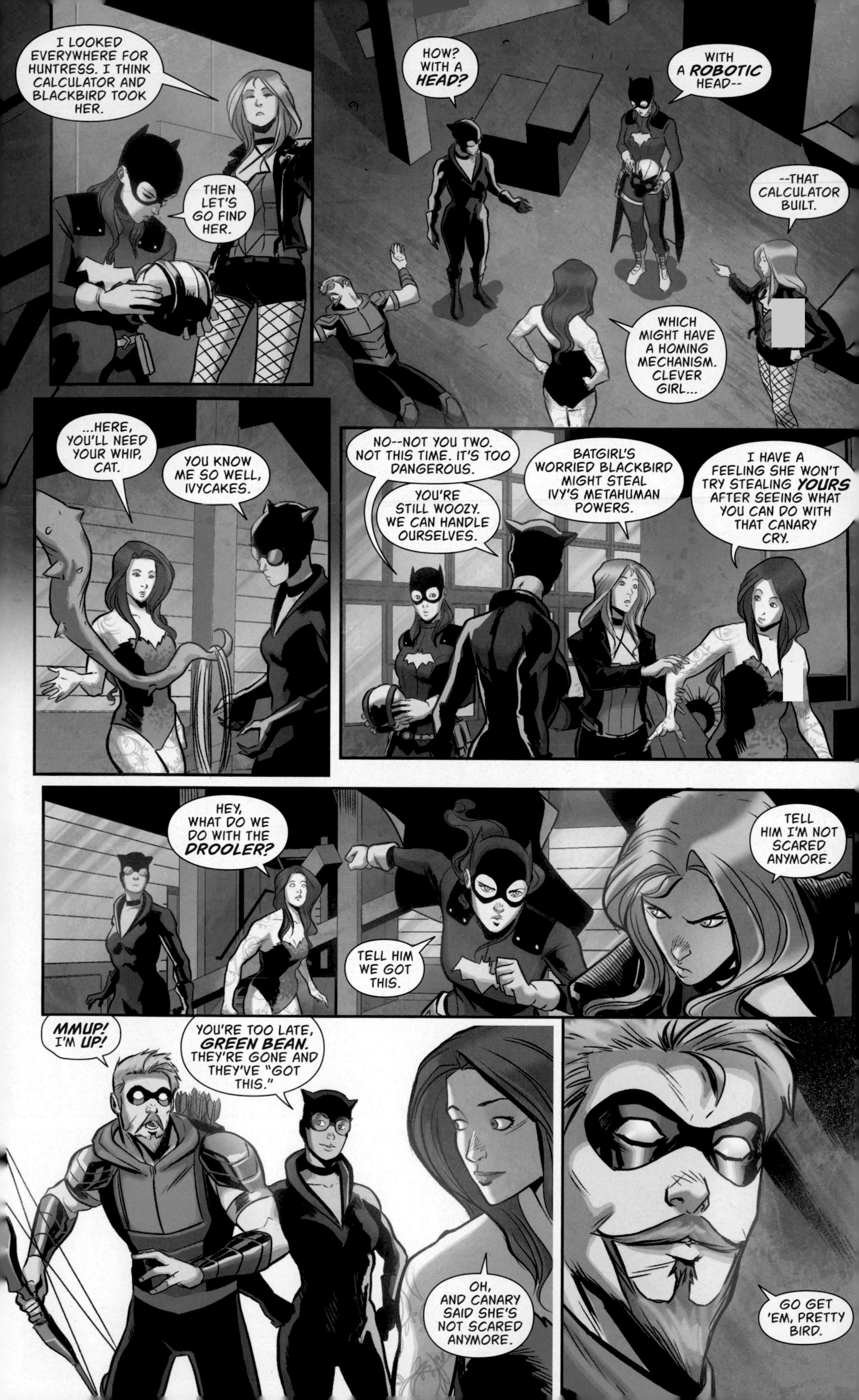
I LOOKED EVERYWHERE FOR HUNTRESS. I THINK CALCULATOR AND BLACKBIRD TOOK HER.
THEN LET'S GO FIND HER.
HOW? WITH A *HEAD?*
WITH A *ROBOTIC* HEAD--
--THAT CALCULATOR BUILT.
WHICH MIGHT HAVE A HOMING MECHANISM. CLEVER GIRL...
...HERE, YOU'LL NEED YOUR WHIP, CAT.
YOU KNOW ME SO WELL, IVYCAKES.
NO--NOT YOU TWO. NOT THIS TIME. IT'S TOO DANGEROUS.
YOU'RE STILL WOOZY. WE CAN HANDLE OURSELVES.
BATGIRL'S WORRIED BLACKBIRD MIGHT STEAL IVY'S METAHUMAN POWERS.
I HAVE A FEELING SHE WON'T TRY STEALING *YOURS* AFTER SEEING WHAT YOU CAN DO WITH THAT CANARY CRY.
HEY, WHAT DO WE DO WITH THE *DROOLER?*
TELL HIM WE GOT THIS.
TELL HIM I'M NOT SCARED ANYMORE.
MMUP! I'M *UP!*
YOU'RE TOO LATE, *GREEN BEAN.* THEY'RE GONE AND THEY'VE "GOT THIS."
OH, AND CANARY SAID SHE'S NOT SCARED ANYMORE.
GO GET 'EM, PRETTY BIRD.

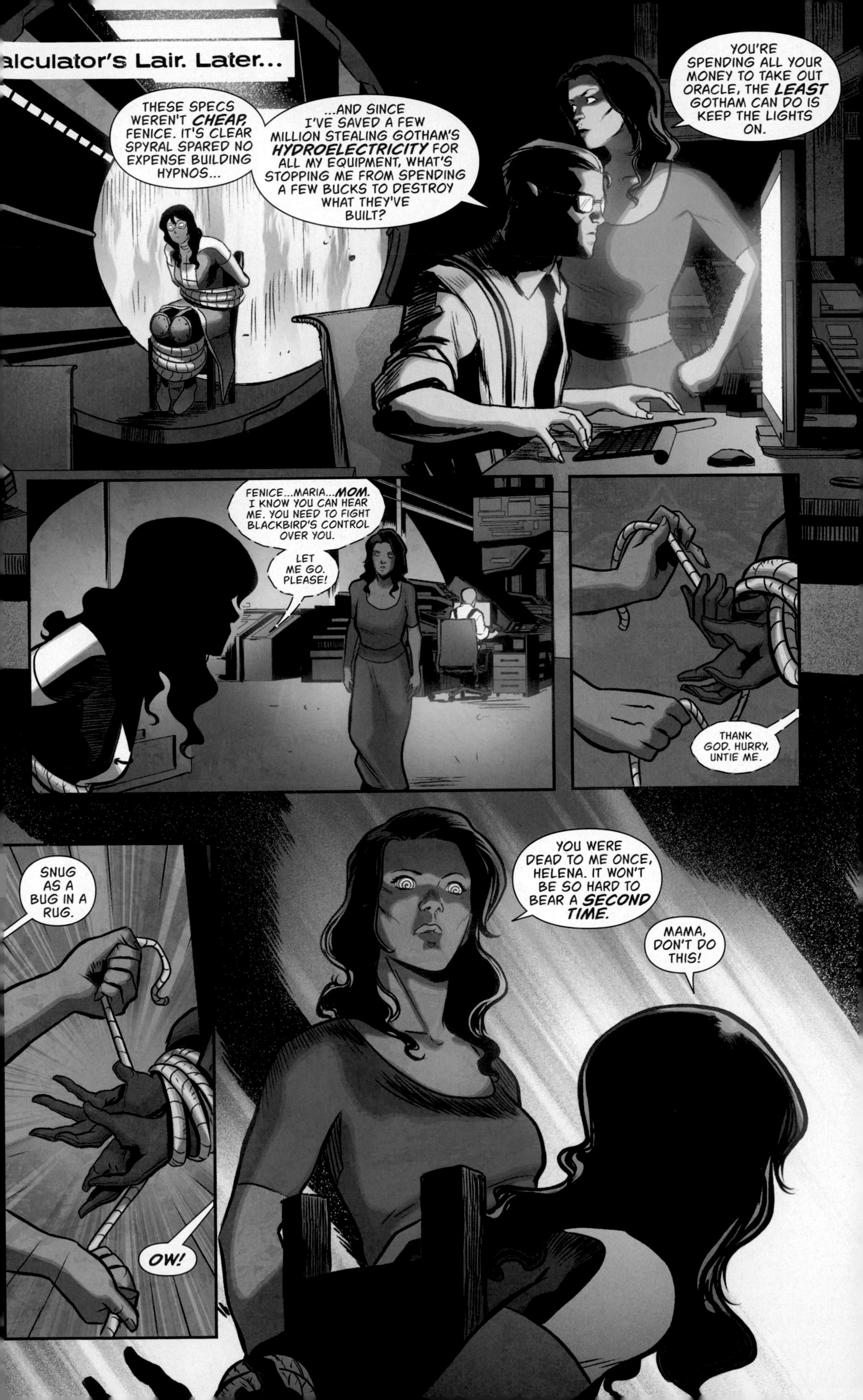
alculator's Lair. Later...
THESE SPECS WEREN'T CHEAP, FENICE. IT'S CLEAR SPYRAL SPARED NO EXPENSE BUILDING HYPNOS...
...AND SINCE I'VE SAVED A FEW MILLION STEALING GOTHAM'S HYDROELECTRICITY FOR ALL MY EQUIPMENT, WHAT'S STOPPING ME FROM SPENDING A FEW BUCKS TO DESTROY WHAT THEY'VE BUILT?
YOU'RE SPENDING ALL YOUR MONEY TO TAKE OUT ORACLE, THE LEAST GOTHAM CAN DO IS KEEP THE LIGHTS ON.
FENICE...MARIA...MOM. I KNOW YOU CAN HEAR ME. YOU NEED TO FIGHT BLACKBIRD'S CONTROL OVER YOU.
LET ME GO. PLEASE!
THANK GOD. HURRY, UNTIE ME.
SNUG AS A BUG IN A RUG.
OW!
YOU WERE DEAD TO ME ONCE, HELENA. IT WON'T BE SO HARD TO BEAR A SECOND TIME.
MAMA, DON'T DO THIS!

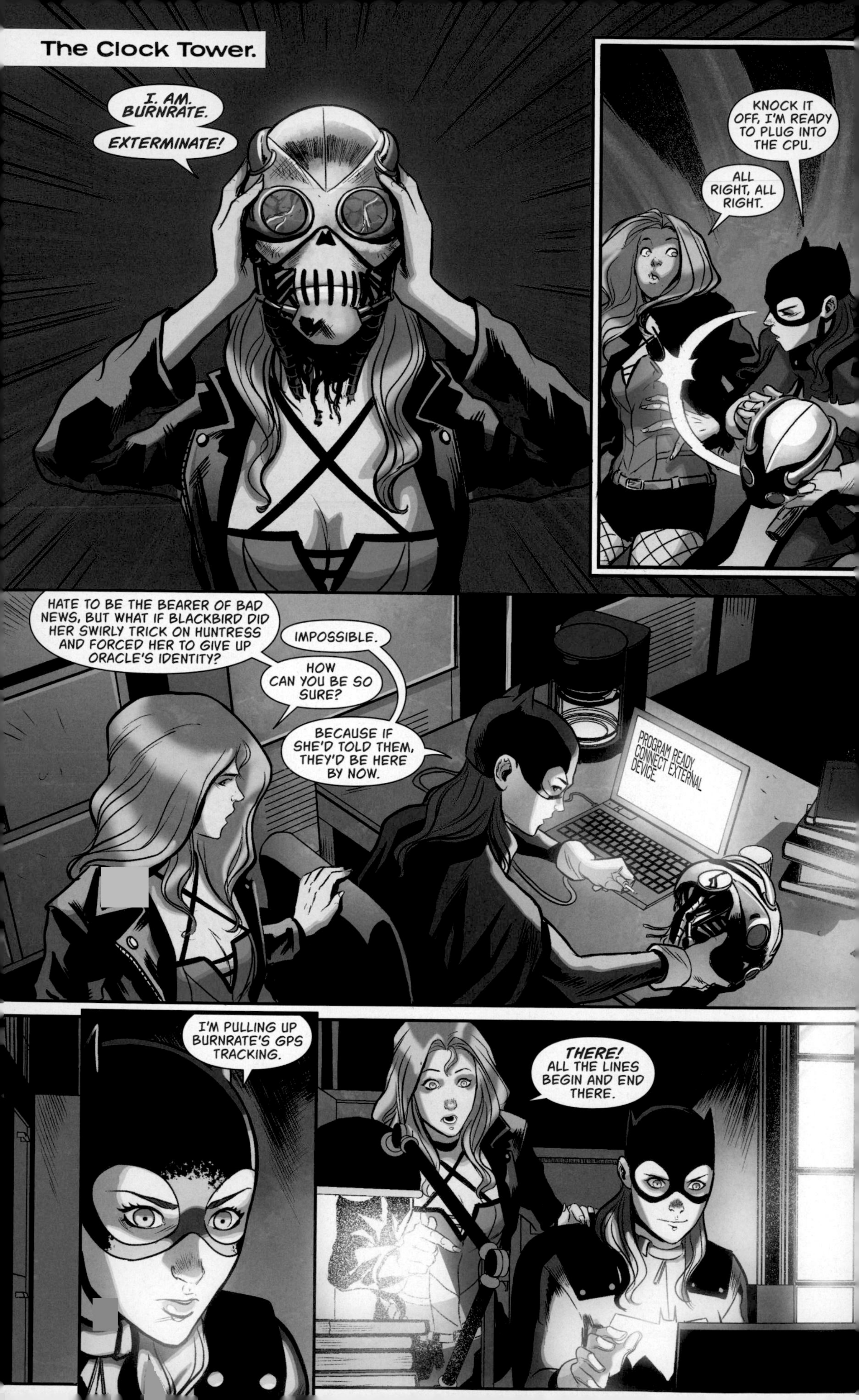
The Clock Tower.
I. AM. BURNRATE.
EXTERMINATE!
KNOCK IT OFF, I'M READY TO PLUG INTO THE CPU.
ALL RIGHT, ALL RIGHT.
HATE TO BE THE BEARER OF BAD NEWS, BUT WHAT IF BLACKBIRD DID HER SWIRLY TRICK ON HUNTRESS AND FORCED HER TO GIVE UP ORACLE'S IDENTITY?
IMPOSSIBLE.
HOW CAN YOU BE SO SURE?
BECAUSE IF SHE'D TOLD THEM, THEY'D BE HERE BY NOW.
PROGRAM READY
CONNECT EXTERNAL
DEVICE.
I'M PULLING UP BURNRATE'S GPS TRACKING.
THERE! ALL THE LINES BEGIN AND END THERE.

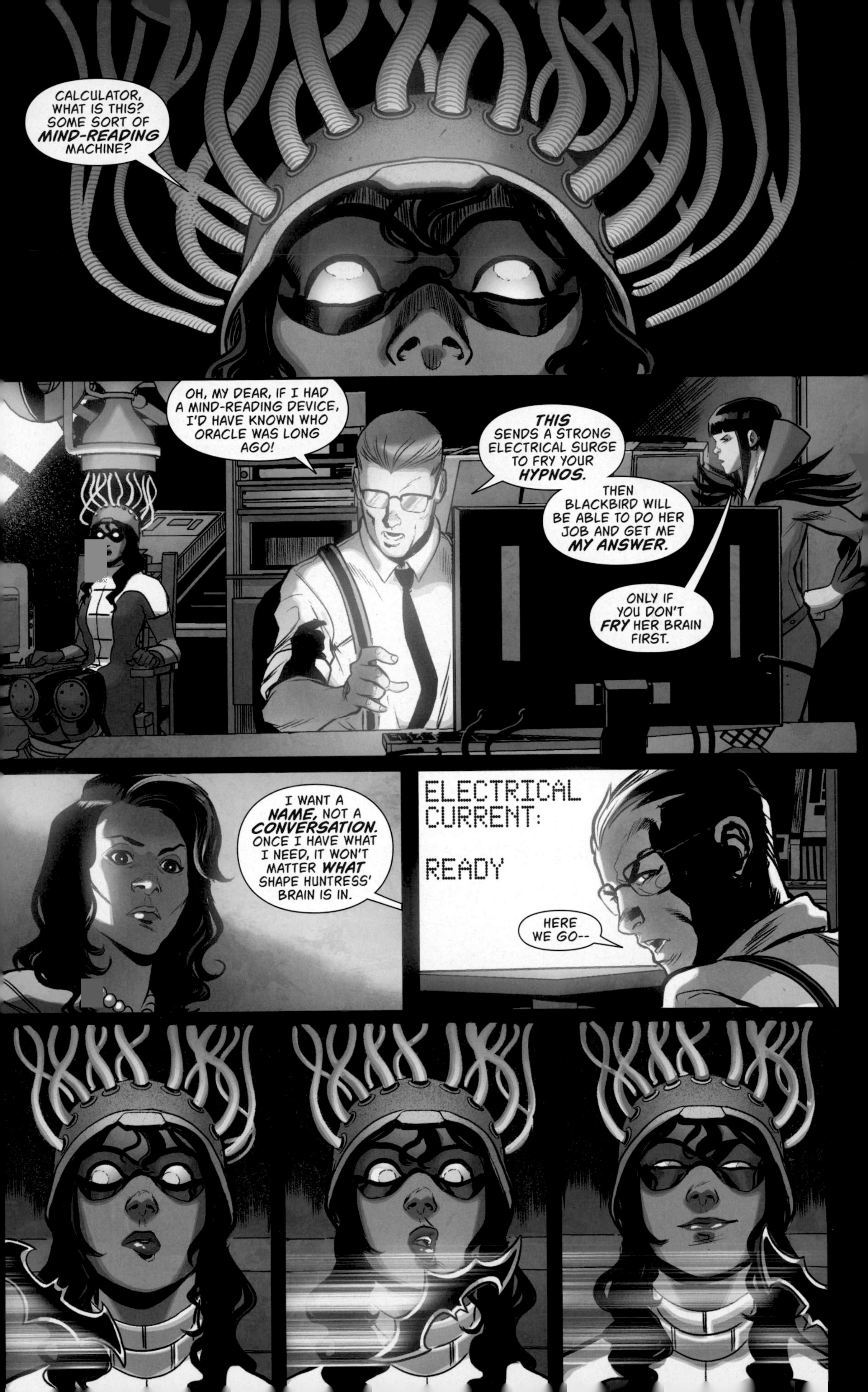
CALCULATOR, WHAT IS THIS? SOME SORT OF MIND-READING MACHINE?
OH, MY DEAR, IF I HAD A MIND-READING DEVICE, I'D HAVE KNOWN WHO ORACLE WAS LONG AGO!
THIS SENDS A STRONG ELECTRICAL SURGE TO FRY YOUR HYPNOS.
THEN BLACKBIRD WILL BE ABLE TO DO HER JOB AND GET ME MY ANSWER.
ONLY IF YOU DON'T FRY HER BRAIN FIRST.
I WANT A NAME, NOT A CONVERSATION. ONCE I HAVE WHAT I NEED, IT WON'T MATTER WHAT SHAPE HUNTRESS' BRAIN IS IN.
ELECTRICAL CURRENT:
READY
HERE WE GO--

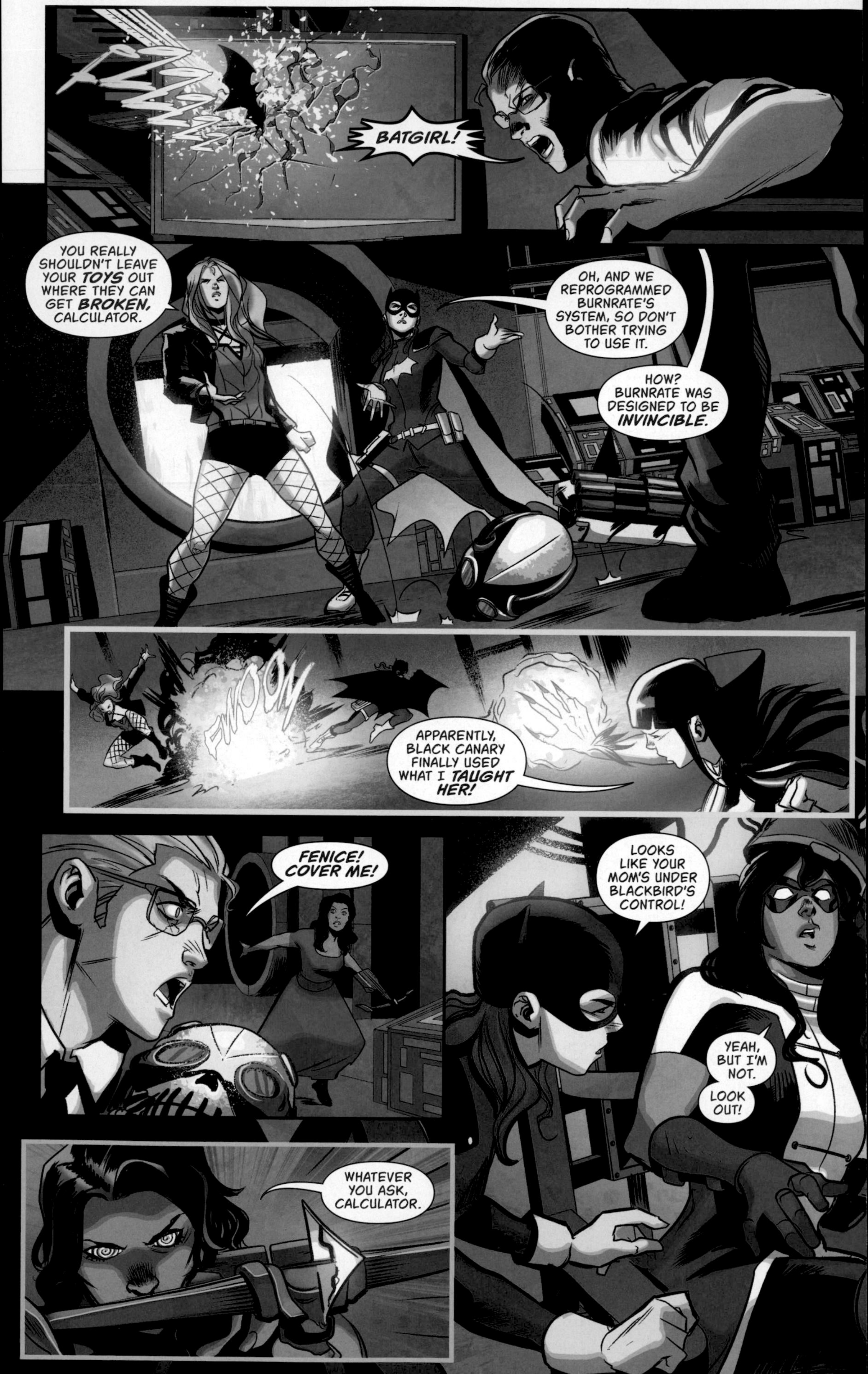
BATGIRL!
YOU REALLY SHOULDN'T LEAVE YOUR TOYS OUT WHERE THEY CAN GET BROKEN, CALCULATOR.
OH, AND WE REPROGRAMMED BURNRATE'S SYSTEM, SO DON'T BOTHER TRYING TO USE IT.
HOW? BURNRATE WAS DESIGNED TO BE INVINCIBLE.
FWOOM
APPARENTLY, BLACK CANARY FINALLY USED WHAT I TAUGHT HER!
FENICE! COVER ME!
LOOKS LIKE YOUR MOM'S UNDER BLACKBIRD'S CONTROL!
YEAH, BUT I'M NOT.
LOOK OUT!
WHATEVER YOU ASK, CALCULATOR.

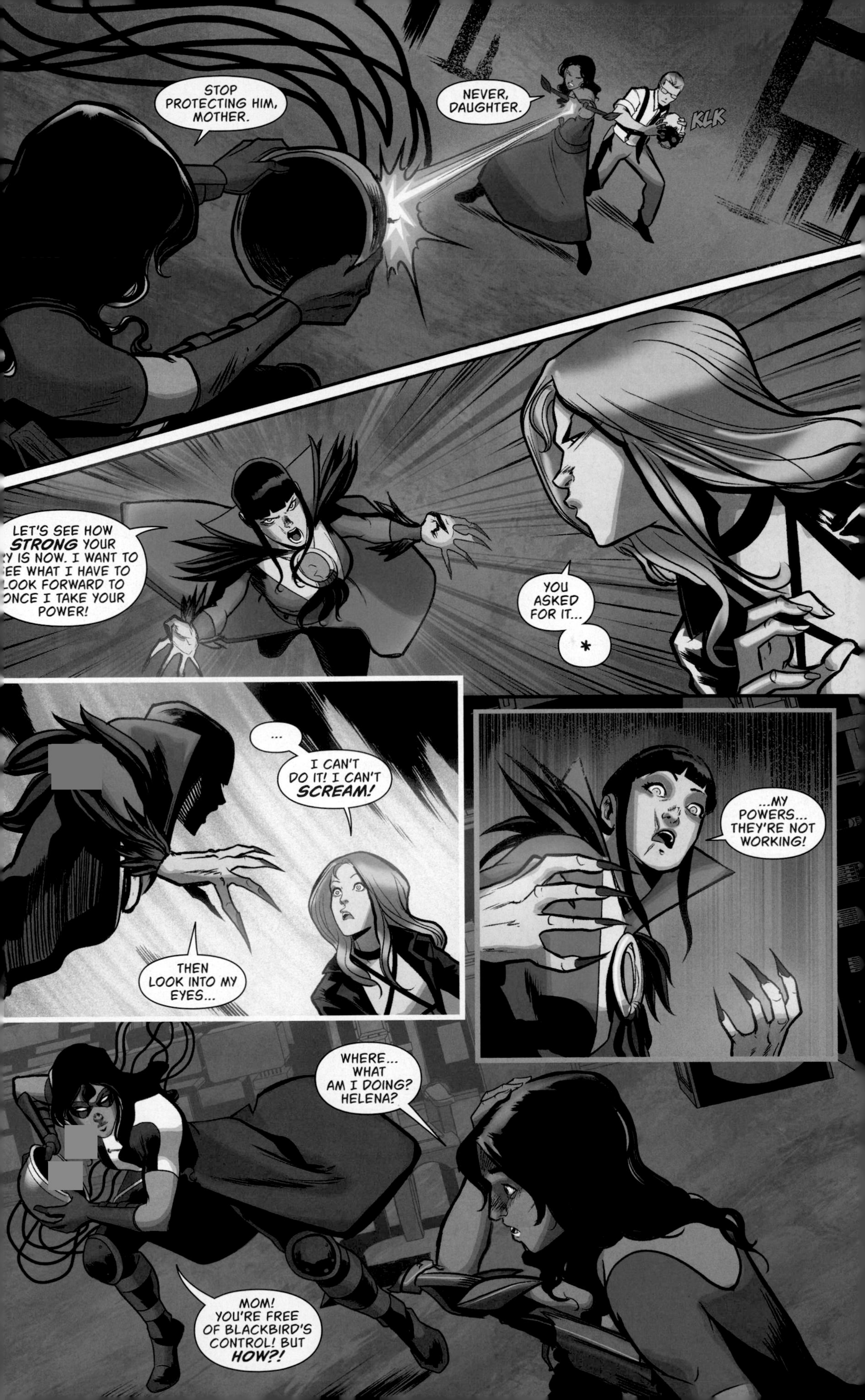
STOP PROTECTING HIM, MOTHER.
NEVER, DAUGHTER.
KLK
LET'S SEE HOW STRONG YOUR Y IS NOW. I WANT TO EE WHAT I HAVE TO OOK FORWARD TO ONCE I TAKE YOUR POWER!
YOU ASKED FOR IT...
*
...
I CAN'T DO IT! I CAN'T SCREAM!
THEN LOOK INTO MY EYES...
...MY POWERS... THEY'RE NOT WORKING!
WHERE... WHAT AM I DOING? HELENA?
MOM! YOU'RE FREE OF BLACKBIRD'S CONTROL! BUT HOW?!

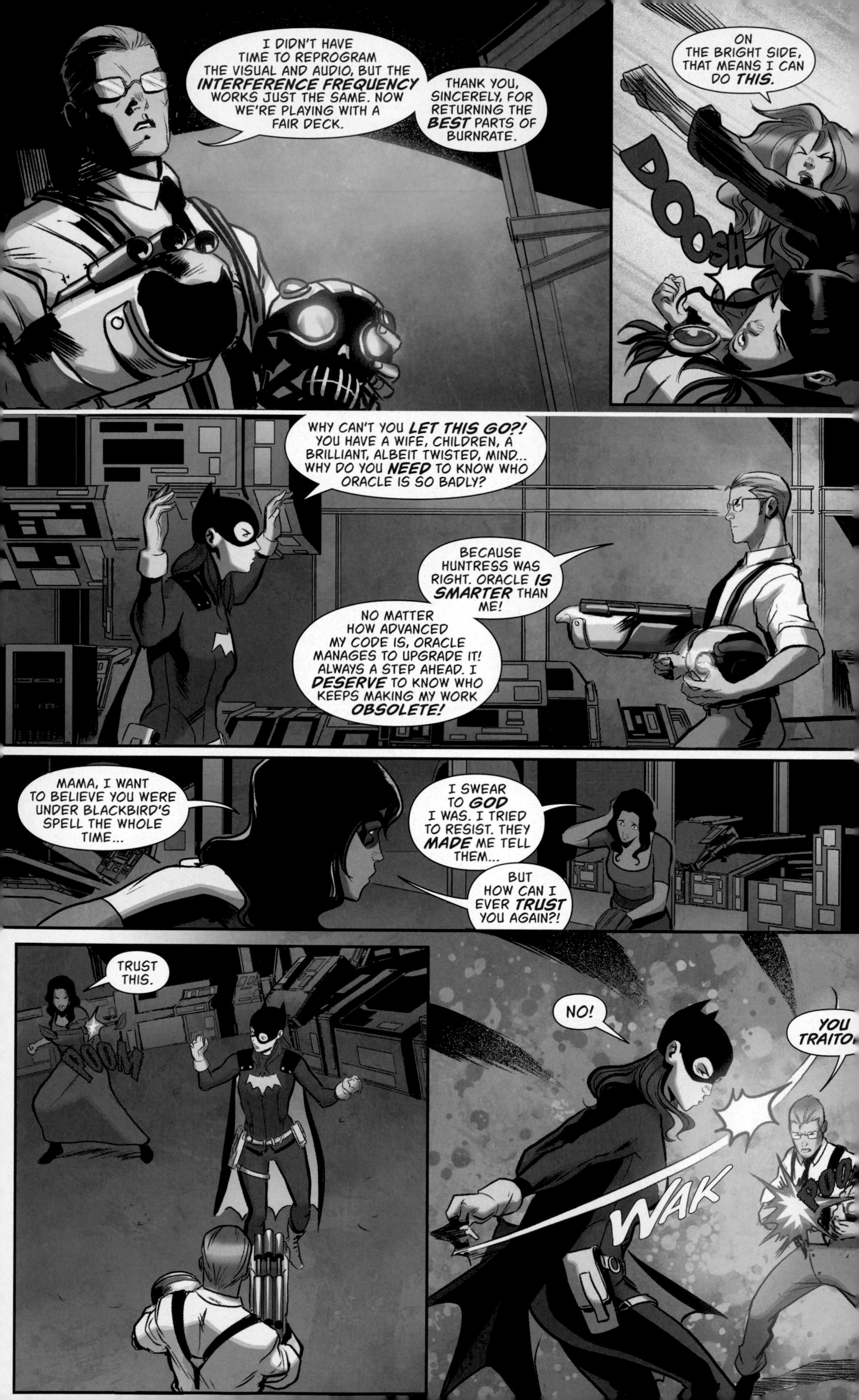
I DIDN'T HAVE TIME TO REPROGRAM THE VISUAL AND AUDIO, BUT THE INTERFERENCE FREQUENCY WORKS JUST THE SAME. NOW WE'RE PLAYING WITH A FAIR DECK.
THANK YOU, SINCERELY, FOR RETURNING THE BEST PARTS OF BURNRATE.
ON THE BRIGHT SIDE, THAT MEANS I CAN DO THIS.
DOOSH
WHY CAN'T YOU LET THIS GO?! YOU HAVE A WIFE, CHILDREN, A BRILLIANT, ALBEIT TWISTED, MIND... WHY DO YOU NEED TO KNOW WHO ORACLE IS SO BADLY?
BECAUSE HUNTRESS WAS RIGHT. ORACLE IS SMARTER THAN ME!
NO MATTER HOW ADVANCED MY CODE IS, ORACLE MANAGES TO UPGRADE IT! ALWAYS A STEP AHEAD. I DESERVE TO KNOW WHO KEEPS MAKING MY WORK OBSOLETE!
MAMA, I WANT TO BELIEVE YOU WERE UNDER BLACKBIRD'S SPELL THE WHOLE TIME...
I SWEAR TO GOD I WAS. I TRIED TO RESIST. THEY MADE ME TELL THEM...
BUT HOW CAN I EVER TRUST YOU AGAIN?!
TRUST THIS.
POOM
NO!
YOU TRAITO
WAK

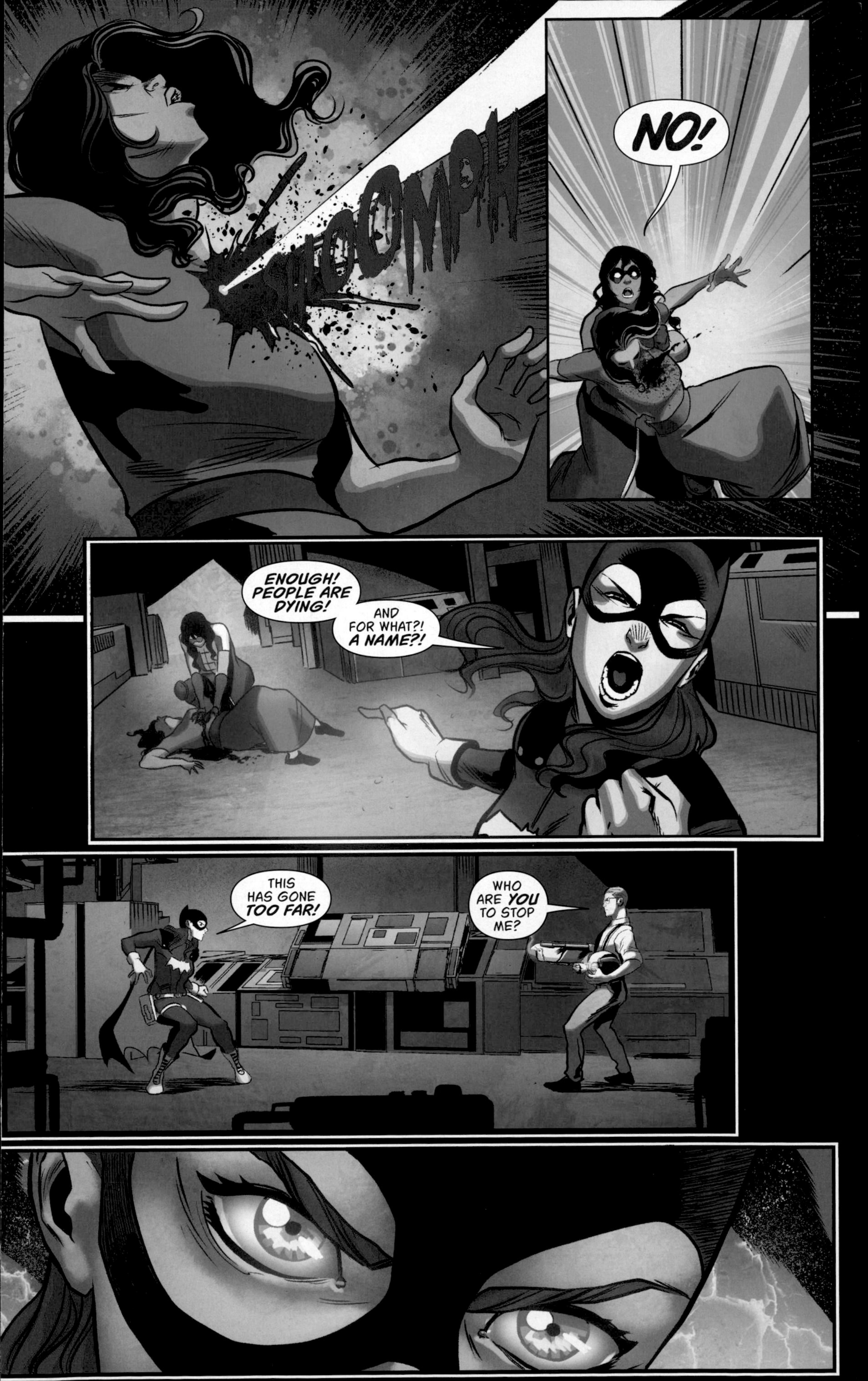
SHOOOMPH
NO!
ENOUGH! PEOPLE ARE DYING!
AND FOR WHAT?! A NAME?!
THIS HAS GONE TOO FAR!
WHO ARE YOU TO STOP ME?

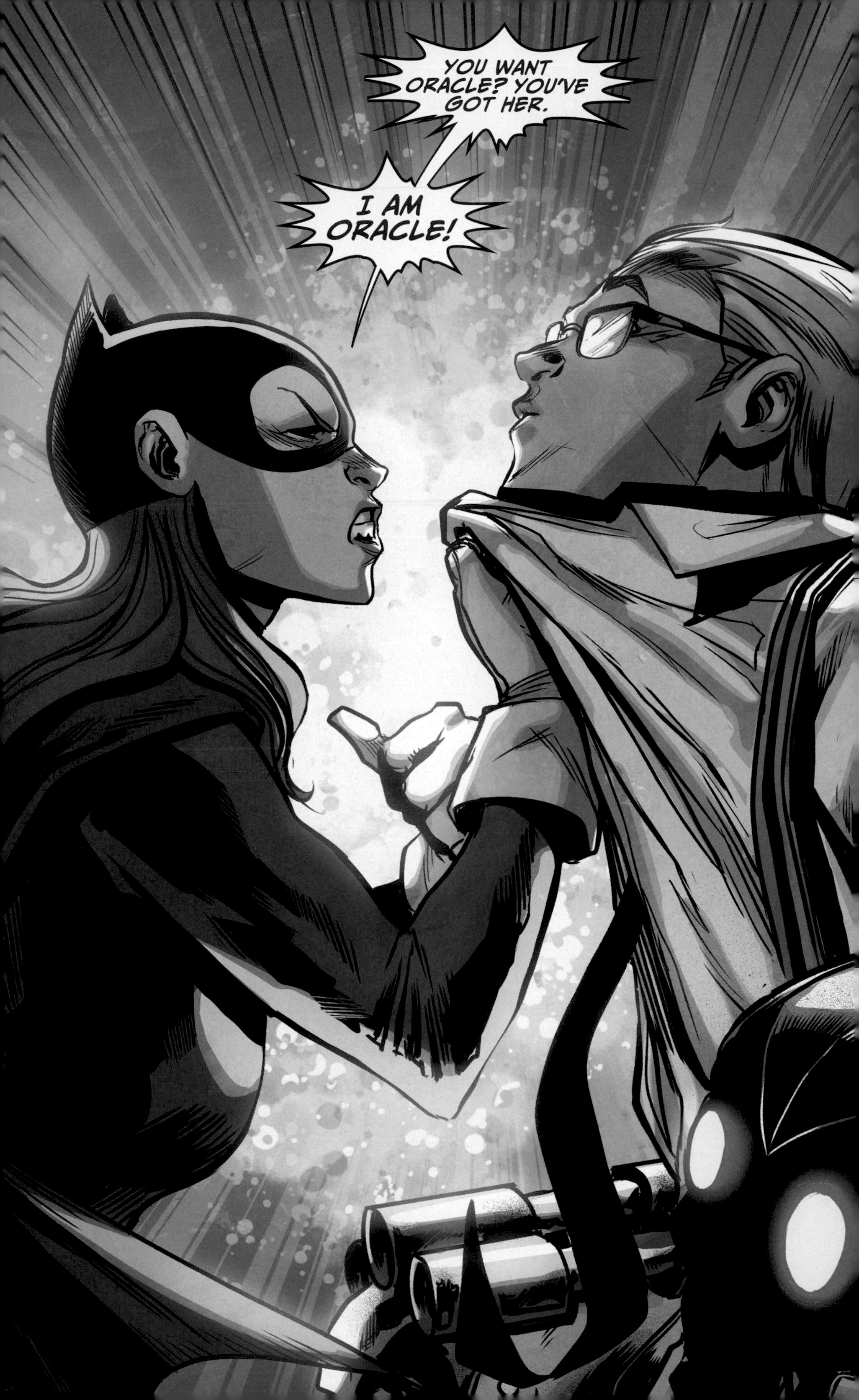
YOU WANT ORACLE? YOU'VE GOT HER.
I AM ORACLE!

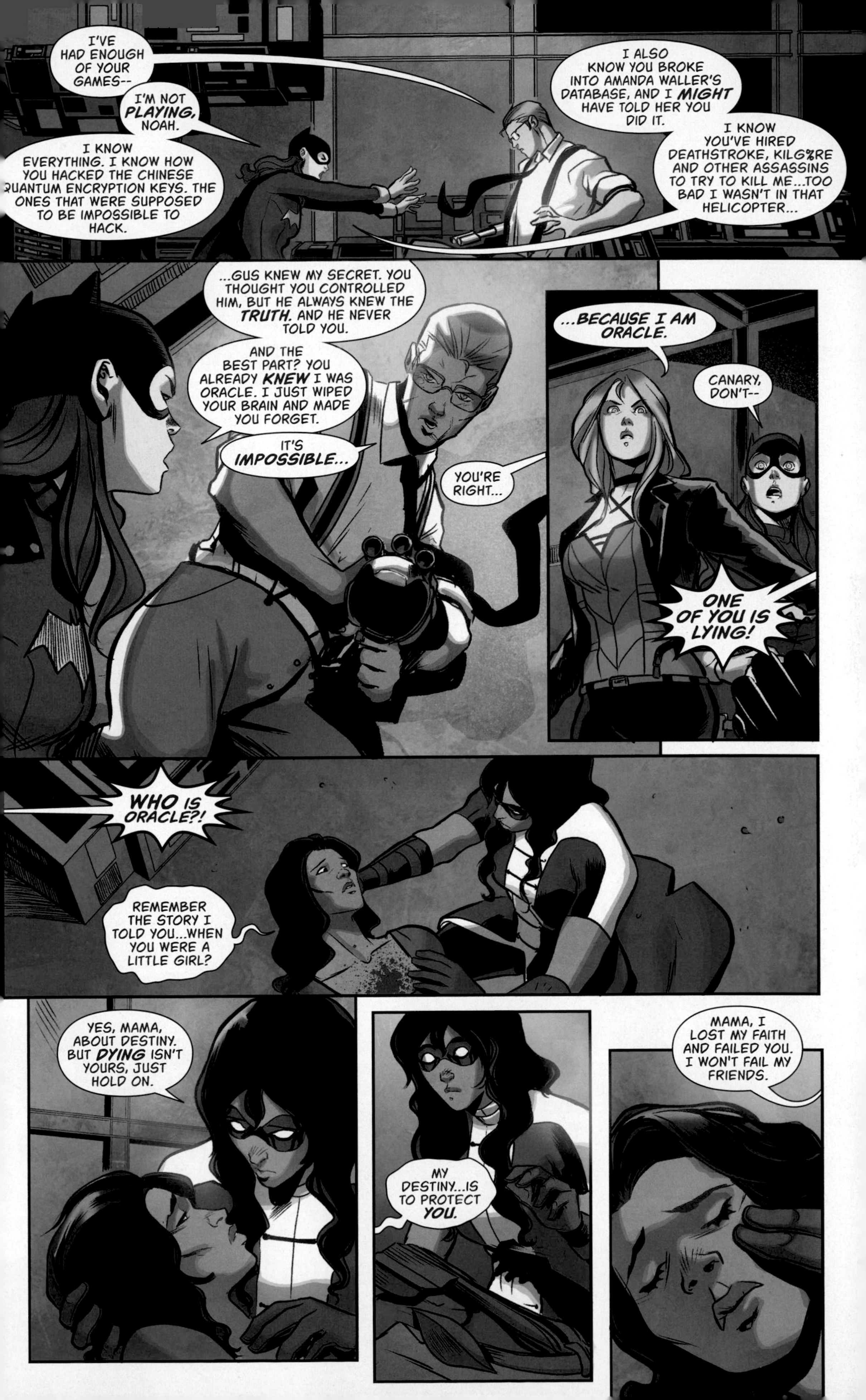
I'VE HAD ENOUGH OF YOUR GAMES--
I'M NOT PLAYING, NOAH.
I KNOW EVERYTHING. I KNOW HOW YOU HACKED THE CHINESE QUANTUM ENCRYPTION KEYS. THE ONES THAT WERE SUPPOSED TO BE IMPOSSIBLE TO HACK.
I ALSO KNOW YOU BROKE INTO AMANDA WALLER'S DATABASE, AND I MIGHT HAVE TOLD HER YOU DID IT.
I KNOW YOU'VE HIRED DEATHSTROKE, KILG%RE AND OTHER ASSASSINS TO TRY TO KILL ME...TOO BAD I WASN'T IN THAT HELICOPTER...
...GUS KNEW MY SECRET. YOU THOUGHT YOU CONTROLLED HIM, BUT HE ALWAYS KNEW THE TRUTH. AND HE NEVER TOLD YOU.
AND THE BEST PART? YOU ALREADY KNEW I WAS ORACLE. I JUST WIPED YOUR BRAIN AND MADE YOU FORGET.
IT'S IMPOSSIBLE...
YOU'RE RIGHT...
...BECAUSE I AM ORACLE.
CANARY, DON'T--
ONE OF YOU IS LYING!
WHO IS ORACLE?!
REMEMBER THE STORY I TOLD YOU...WHEN YOU WERE A LITTLE GIRL?
YES, MAMA, ABOUT DESTINY. BUT DYING ISN'T YOURS, JUST HOLD ON.
MY DESTINY...IS TO PROTECT YOU.
MAMA, I LOST MY FAITH AND FAILED YOU. I WON'T FAIL MY FRIENDS.

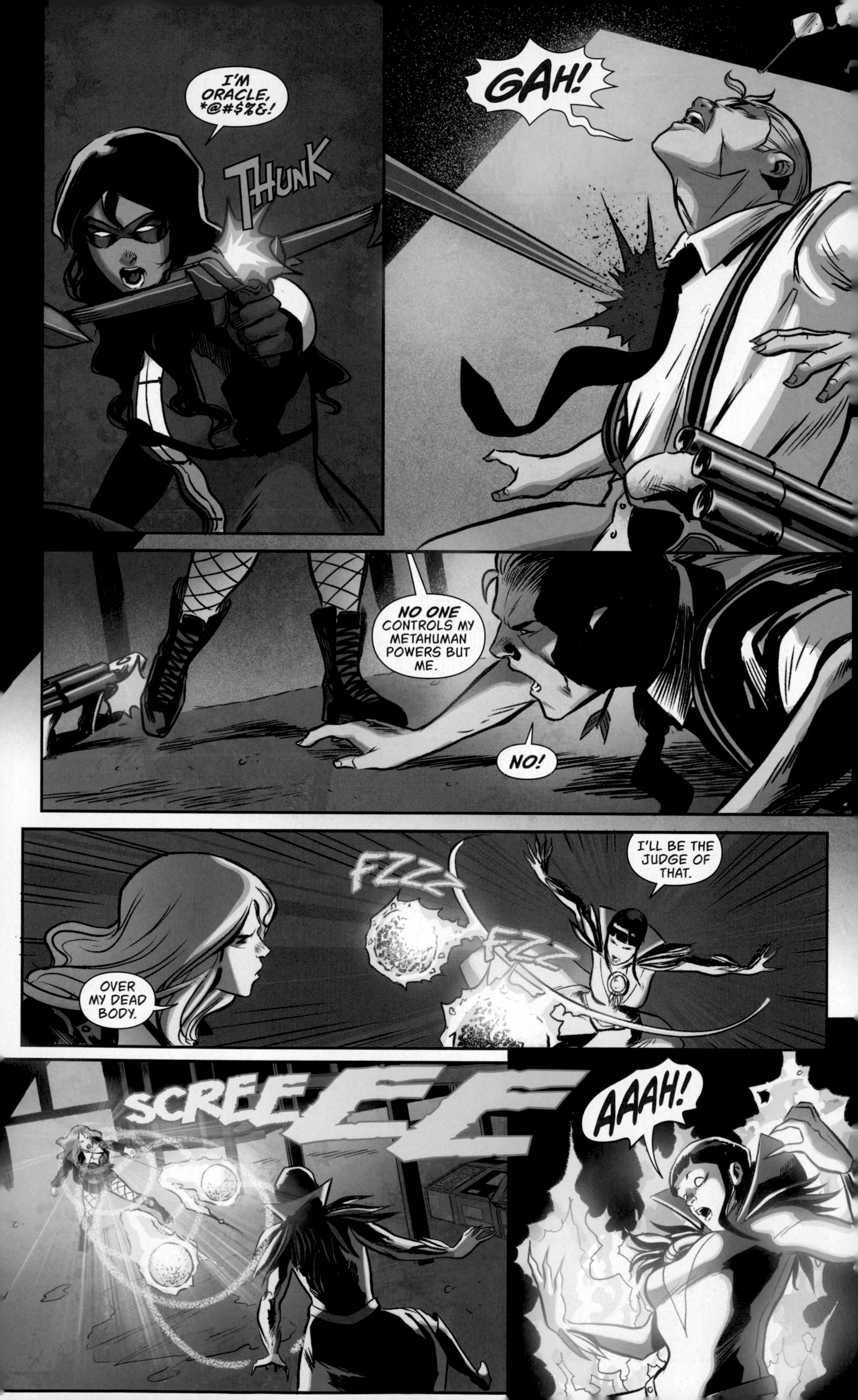
I'M ORACLE, *@#$%&!
THUNK
GAH!
NO ONE CONTROLS MY METAHUMAN POWERS BUT ME.
NO!
OVER MY DEAD BODY.
FZZZ
FZZZ
I'LL BE THE JUDGE OF THAT.
SCREEEE
AAAH!

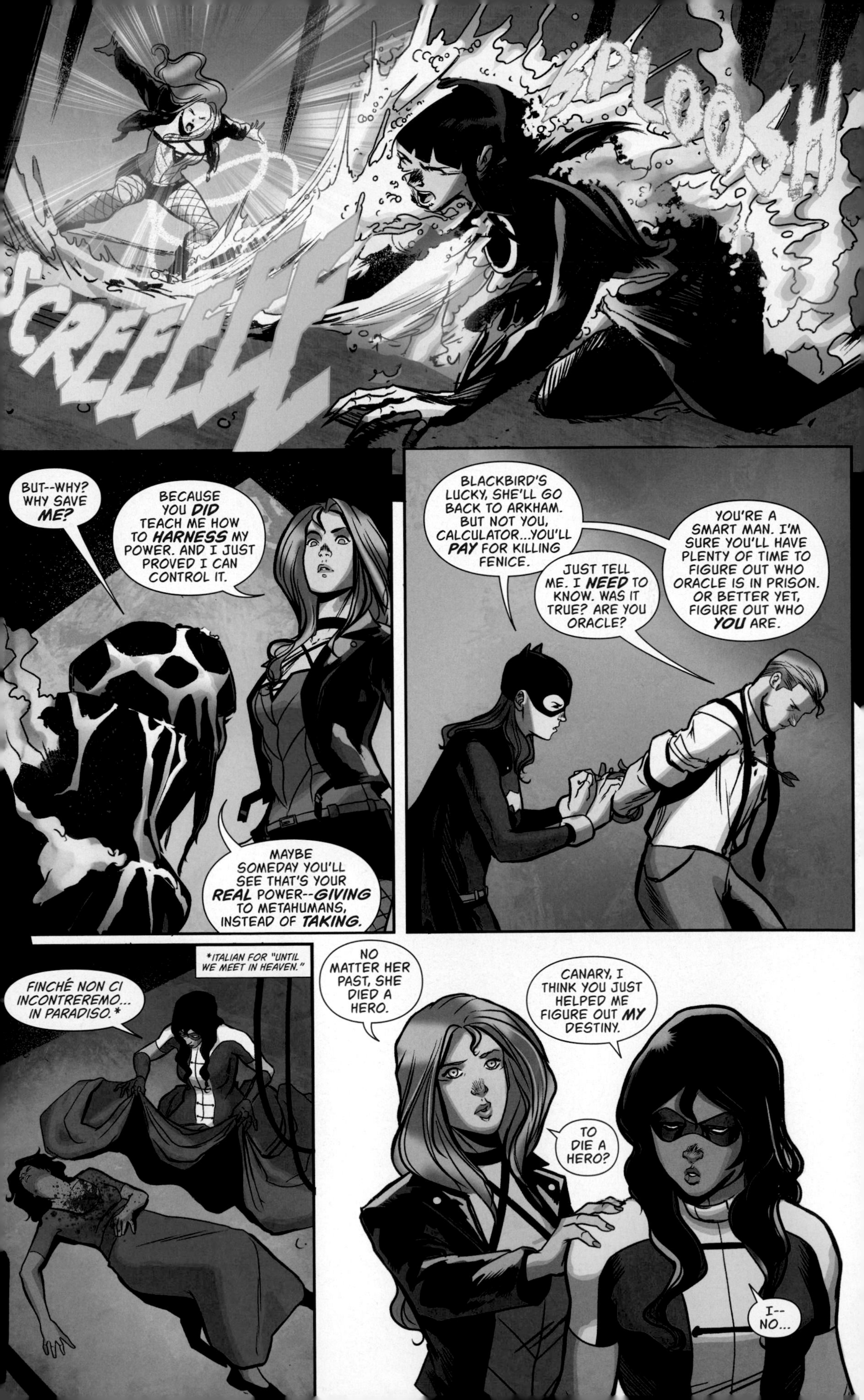
SCREEEE
SPLOOSH
BUT--WHY? WHY SAVE **ME?**
BECAUSE YOU **DID** TEACH ME HOW TO **HARNESS** MY POWER. AND I JUST PROVED I CAN CONTROL IT.
MAYBE SOMEDAY YOU'LL SEE THAT'S YOUR **REAL** POWER--**GIVING** TO METAHUMANS, INSTEAD OF **TAKING.**
BLACKBIRD'S LUCKY, SHE'LL GO BACK TO ARKHAM. BUT NOT YOU, CALCULATOR...YOU'LL **PAY** FOR KILLING FENICE.
JUST TELL ME. I **NEED** TO KNOW. WAS IT TRUE? ARE YOU ORACLE?
YOU'RE A SMART MAN. I'M SURE YOU'LL HAVE PLENTY OF TIME TO FIGURE OUT WHO ORACLE IS IN PRISON. OR BETTER YET, FIGURE OUT WHO **YOU** ARE.
*ITALIAN FOR "UNTIL WE MEET IN HEAVEN."
FINCHÉ NON CI INCONTREREMO... IN PARADISO.*
NO MATTER HER PAST, SHE DIED A HERO.
CANARY, I THINK YOU JUST HELPED ME FIGURE OUT **MY** DESTINY.
TO DIE A HERO?
I-- NO...

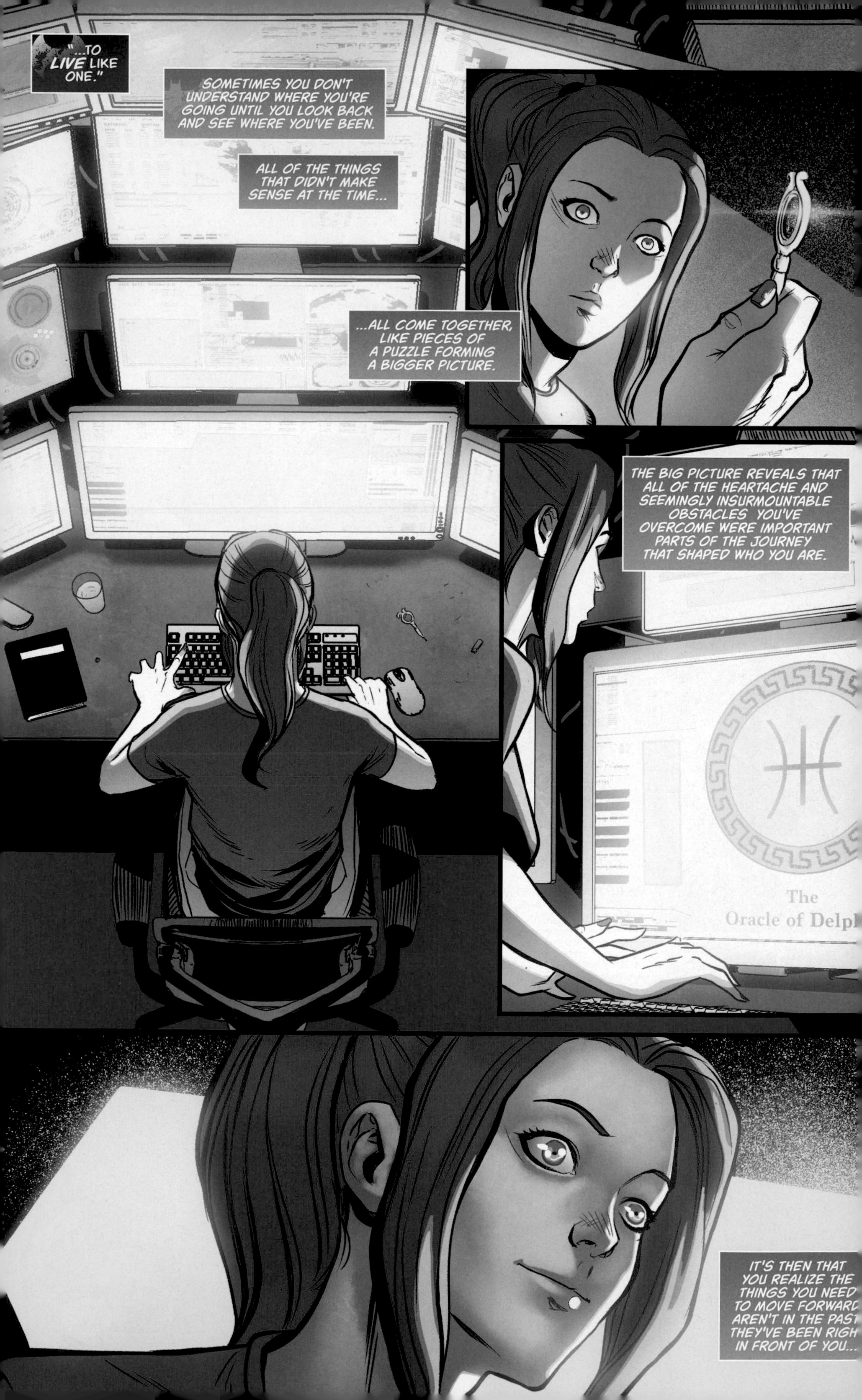
"...TO LIVE LIKE ONE."
SOMETIMES YOU DON'T UNDERSTAND WHERE YOU'RE GOING UNTIL YOU LOOK BACK AND SEE WHERE YOU'VE BEEN.
ALL OF THE THINGS THAT DIDN'T MAKE SENSE AT THE TIME...
...ALL COME TOGETHER, LIKE PIECES OF A PUZZLE FORMING A BIGGER PICTURE.
THE BIG PICTURE REVEALS THAT ALL OF THE HEARTACHE AND SEEMINGLY INSURMOUNTABLE OBSTACLES YOU'VE OVERCOME WERE IMPORTANT PARTS OF THE JOURNEY THAT SHAPED WHO YOU ARE.
The Oracle of Delp
IT'S THEN THAT YOU REALIZE THE THINGS YOU NEED TO MOVE FORWARD AREN'T IN THE PAST THEY'VE BEEN RIGH IN FRONT OF YOU...

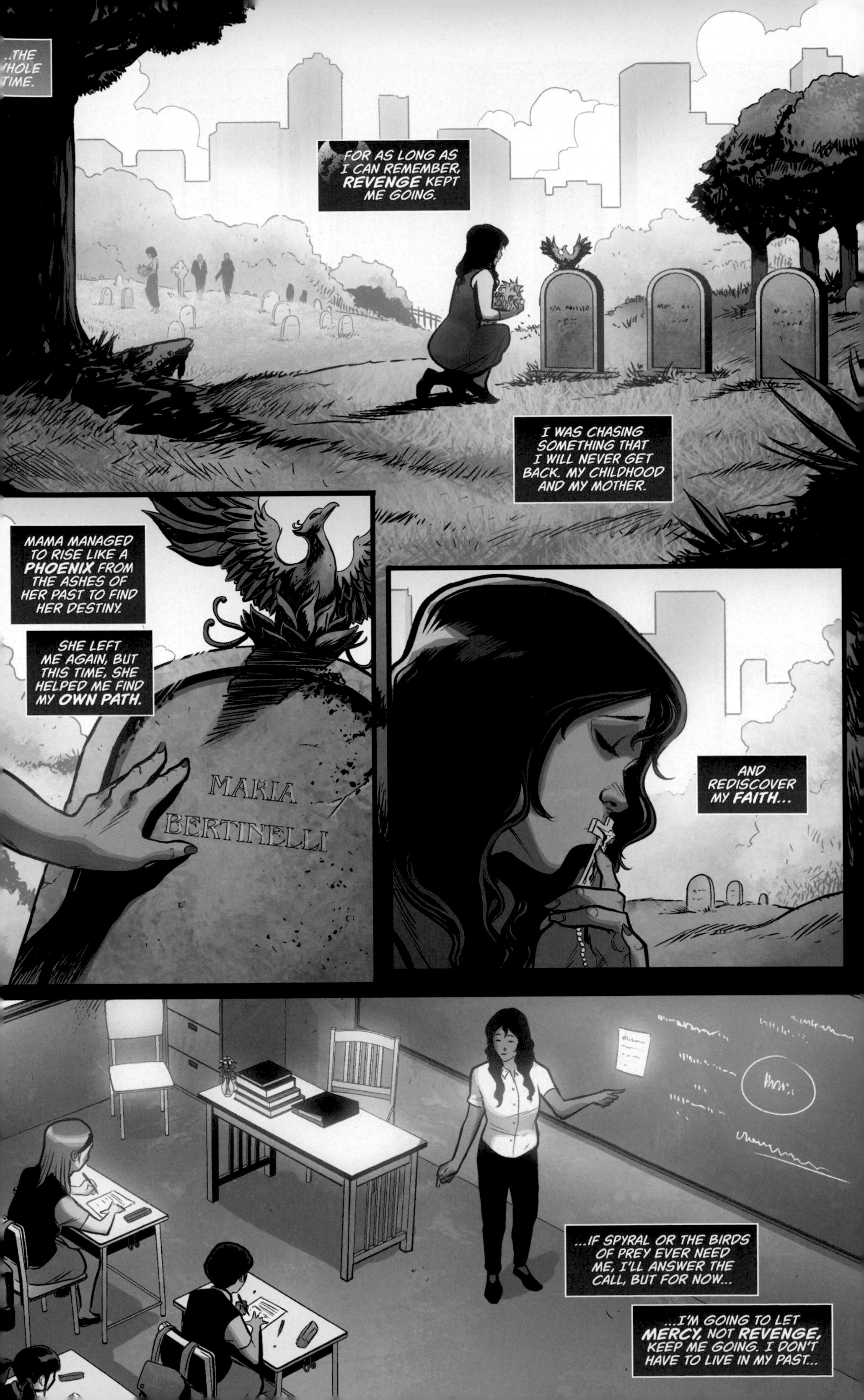
..THE
WHOLE
TIME.
FOR AS LONG AS I CAN REMEMBER, REVENGE KEPT ME GOING.
I WAS CHASING SOMETHING THAT I WILL NEVER GET BACK. MY CHILDHOOD AND MY MOTHER.
MAMA MANAGED TO RISE LIKE A PHOENIX FROM THE ASHES OF HER PAST TO FIND HER DESTINY.
SHE LEFT ME AGAIN, BUT THIS TIME, SHE HELPED ME FIND MY OWN PATH.
MARIA BERTINELLI
AND REDISCOVER MY FAITH...
...IF SPYRAL OR THE BIRDS OF PREY EVER NEED ME, I'LL ANSWER THE CALL, BUT FOR NOW...
...I'M GOING TO LET MERCY, NOT REVENGE, KEEP ME GOING. I DON'T HAVE TO LIVE IN MY PAST...

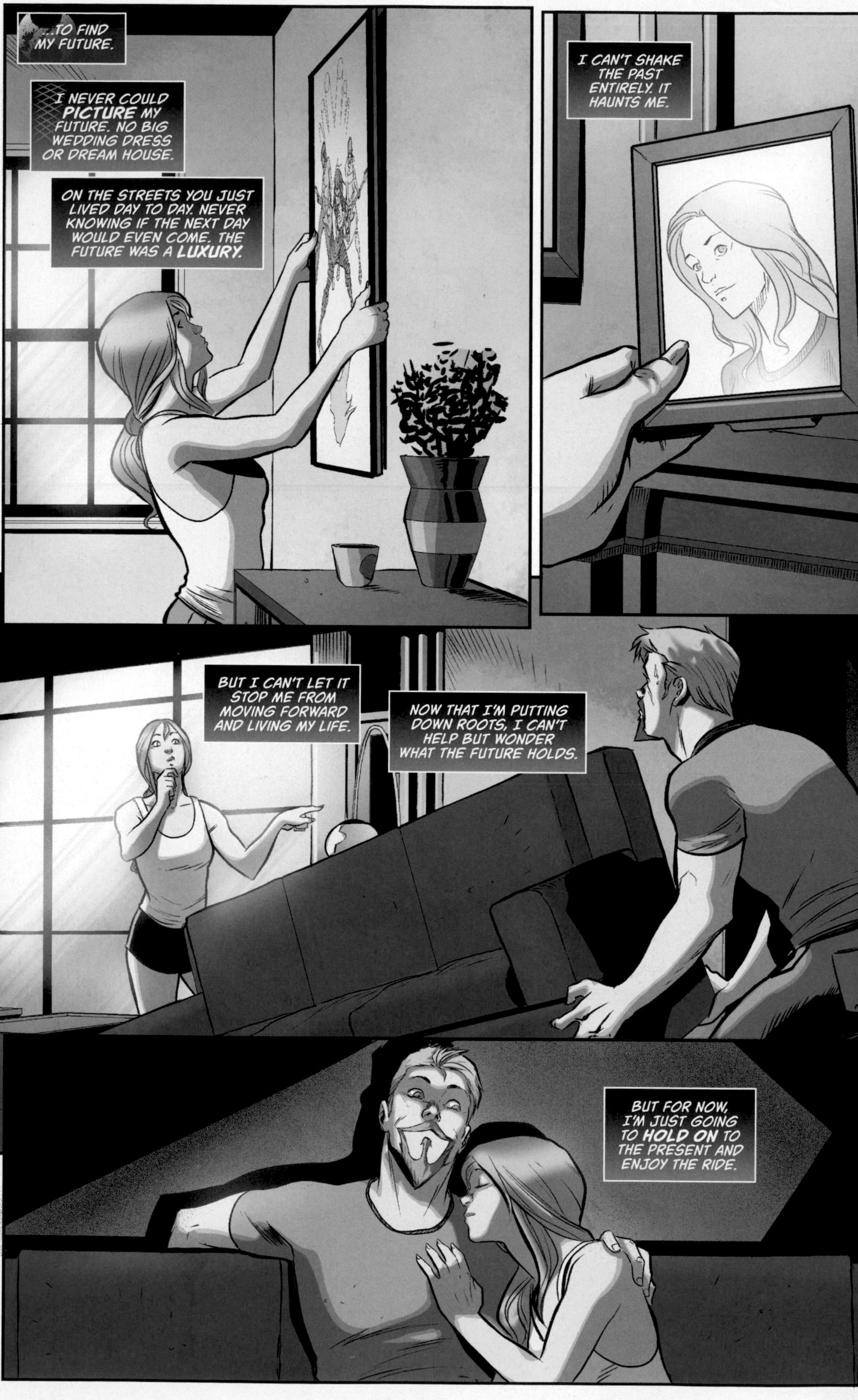
...TO FIND MY FUTURE.
I NEVER COULD PICTURE MY FUTURE. NO BIG WEDDING DRESS OR DREAM HOUSE.
ON THE STREETS YOU JUST LIVED DAY TO DAY. NEVER KNOWING IF THE NEXT DAY WOULD EVEN COME. THE FUTURE WAS A LUXURY.
I CAN'T SHAKE THE PAST ENTIRELY. IT HAUNTS ME.
BUT I CAN'T LET IT STOP ME FROM MOVING FORWARD AND LIVING MY LIFE.
NOW THAT I'M PUTTING DOWN ROOTS, I CAN'T HELP BUT WONDER WHAT THE FUTURE HOLDS.
BUT FOR NOW, I'M JUST GOING TO HOLD ON TO THE PRESENT AND ENJOY THE RIDE.

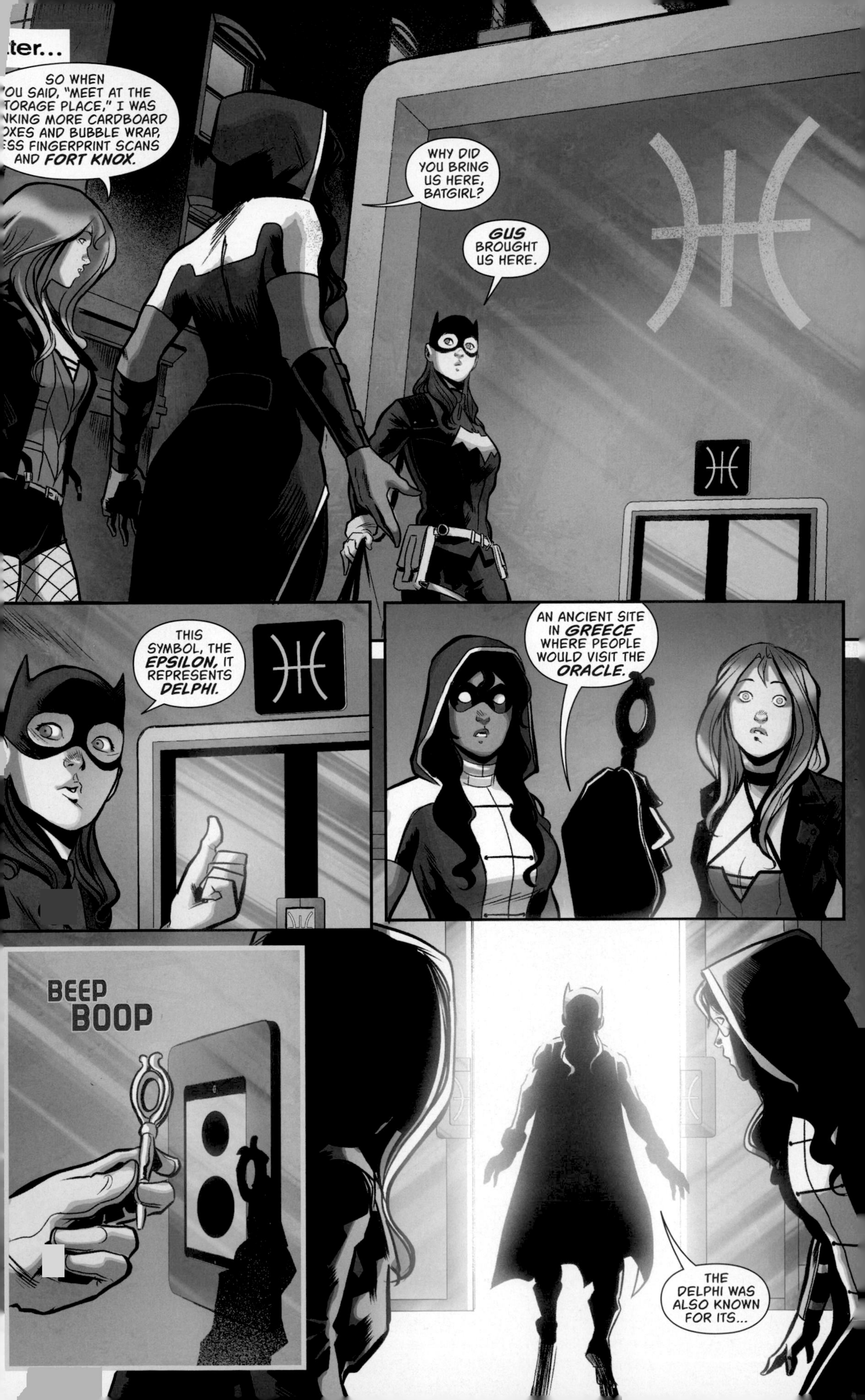

ter...
SO WHEN OU SAID, "MEET AT THE TORAGE PLACE," I WAS NKING MORE CARDBOARD OXES AND BUBBLE WRAP, ESS FINGERPRINT SCANS AND FORT KNOX.
WHY DID YOU BRING US HERE, BATGIRL?
GUS BROUGHT US HERE.
THIS SYMBOL, THE EPSILON, IT REPRESENTS DELPHI.
AN ANCIENT SITE IN GREECE WHERE PEOPLE WOULD VISIT THE ORACLE.
BEEP
BOOP
THE DELPHI WAS ALSO KNOWN FOR ITS...

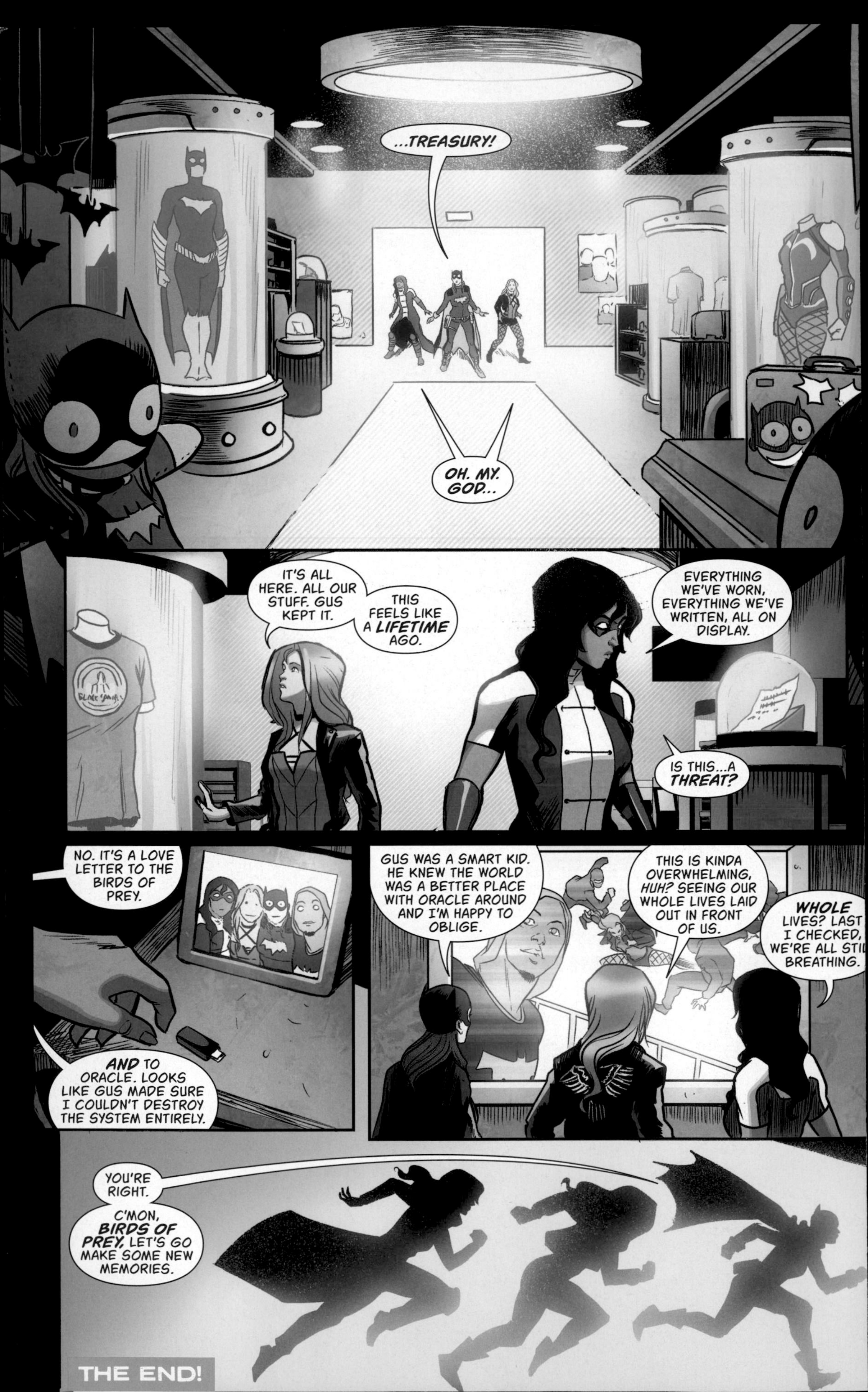

...TREASURY!
OH. MY. GOD...
IT'S ALL HERE. ALL OUR STUFF. GUS KEPT IT.
THIS FEELS LIKE A LIFETIME AGO.
EVERYTHING WE'VE WORN, EVERYTHING WE'VE WRITTEN, ALL ON DISPLAY.
IS THIS...A THREAT?
NO. IT'S A LOVE LETTER TO THE BIRDS OF PREY.
AND TO ORACLE. LOOKS LIKE GUS MADE SURE I COULDN'T DESTROY THE SYSTEM ENTIRELY.
GUS WAS A SMART KID. HE KNEW THE WORLD WAS A BETTER PLACE WITH ORACLE AROUND AND I'M HAPPY TO OBLIGE.
THIS IS KINDA OVERWHELMING, HUH? SEEING OUR WHOLE LIVES LAID OUT IN FRONT OF US.
WHOLE LIVES? LAST I CHECKED, WE'RE ALL STIL BREATHING.
YOU'RE RIGHT.
C'MON, BIRDS OF PREY, LET'S GO MAKE SOME NEW MEMORIES.
THE END!

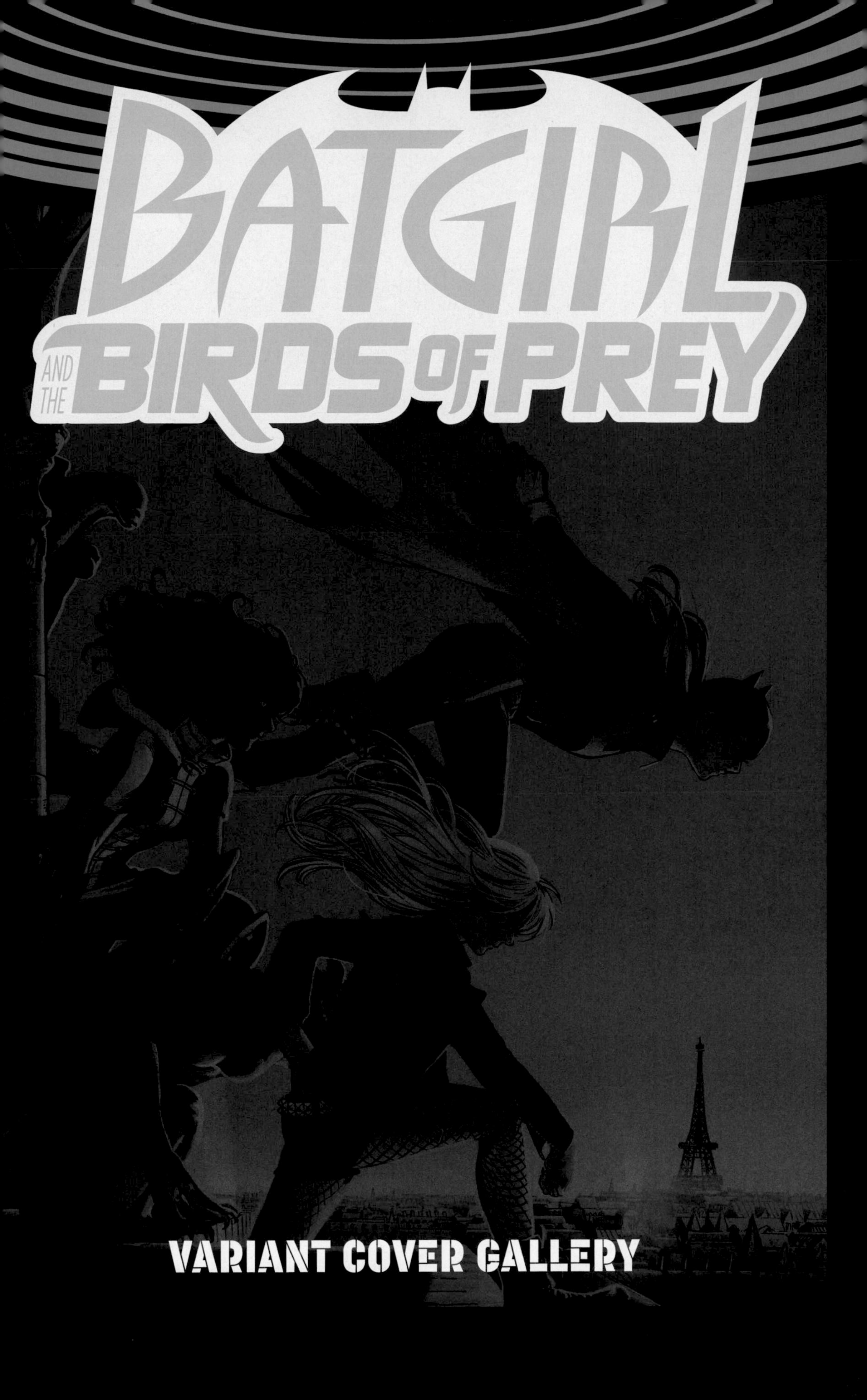
BATGIRL
AND THE BIRDS OF PREY
VARIANT COVER GALLERY

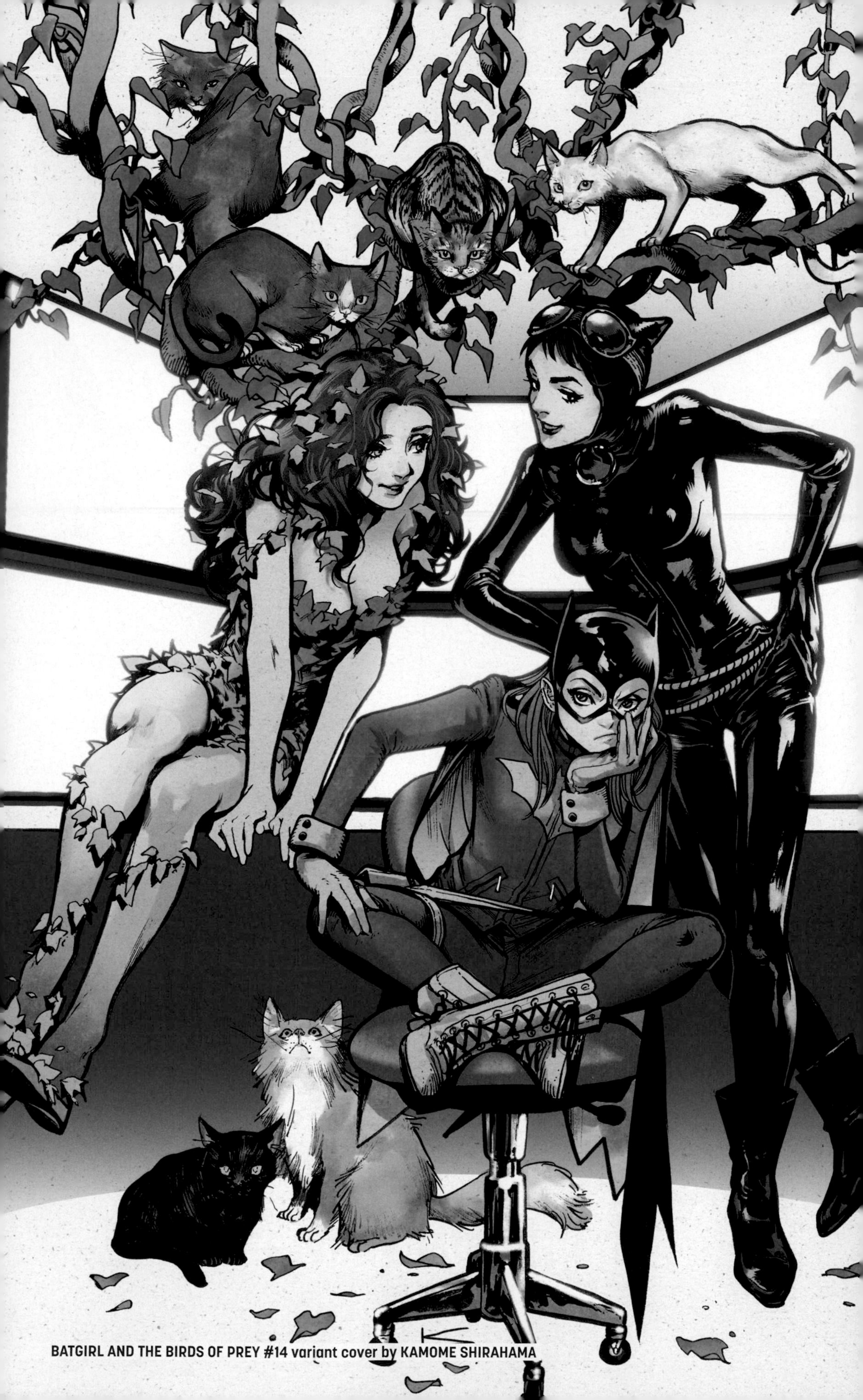

BATGIRL AND THE BIRDS OF PREY #14 variant cover by KAMOME SHIRAHAMA

BATGIRL AND THE BIRDS OF PREY #15 variant cover by KAMOME SHIRAHAMA

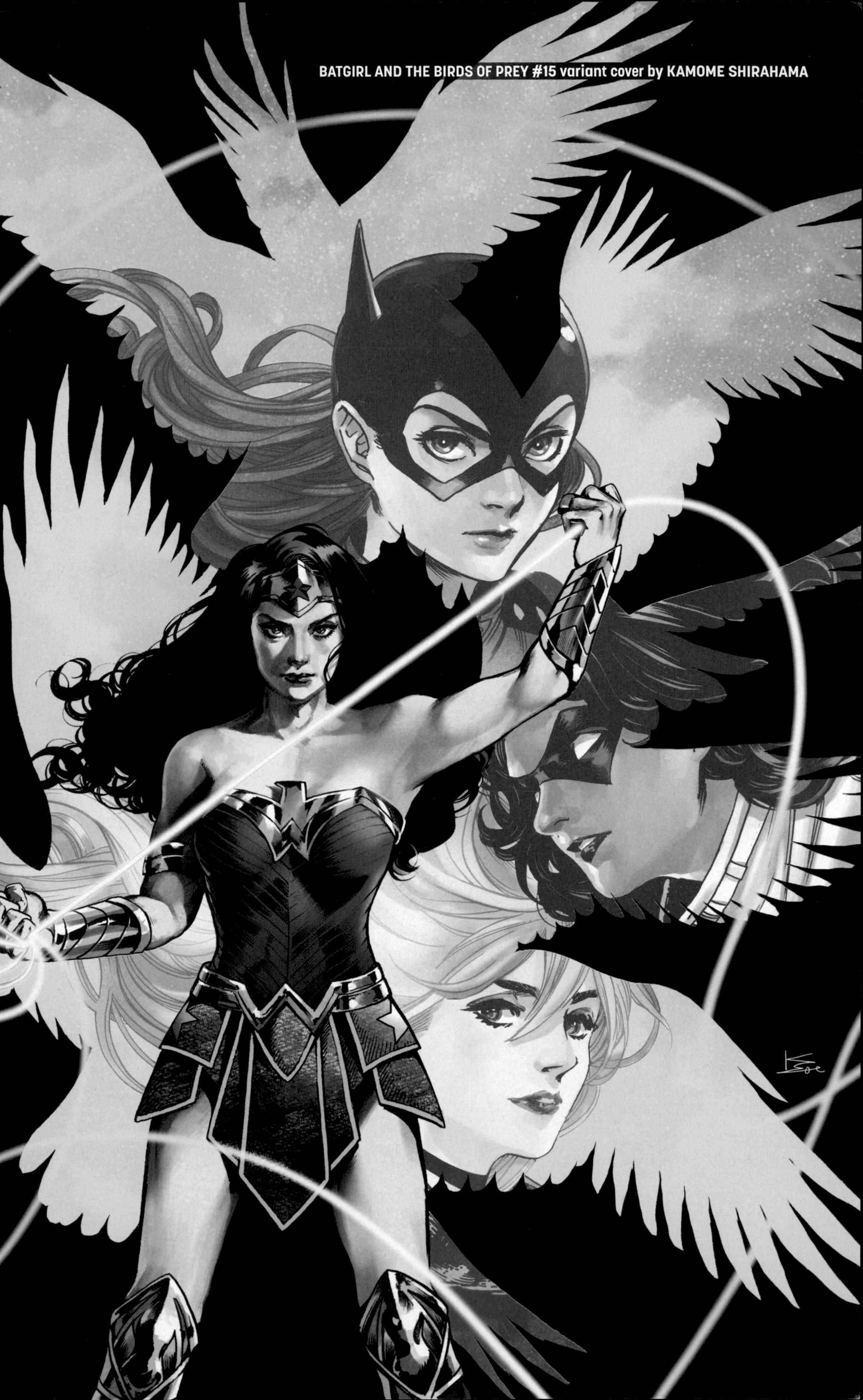

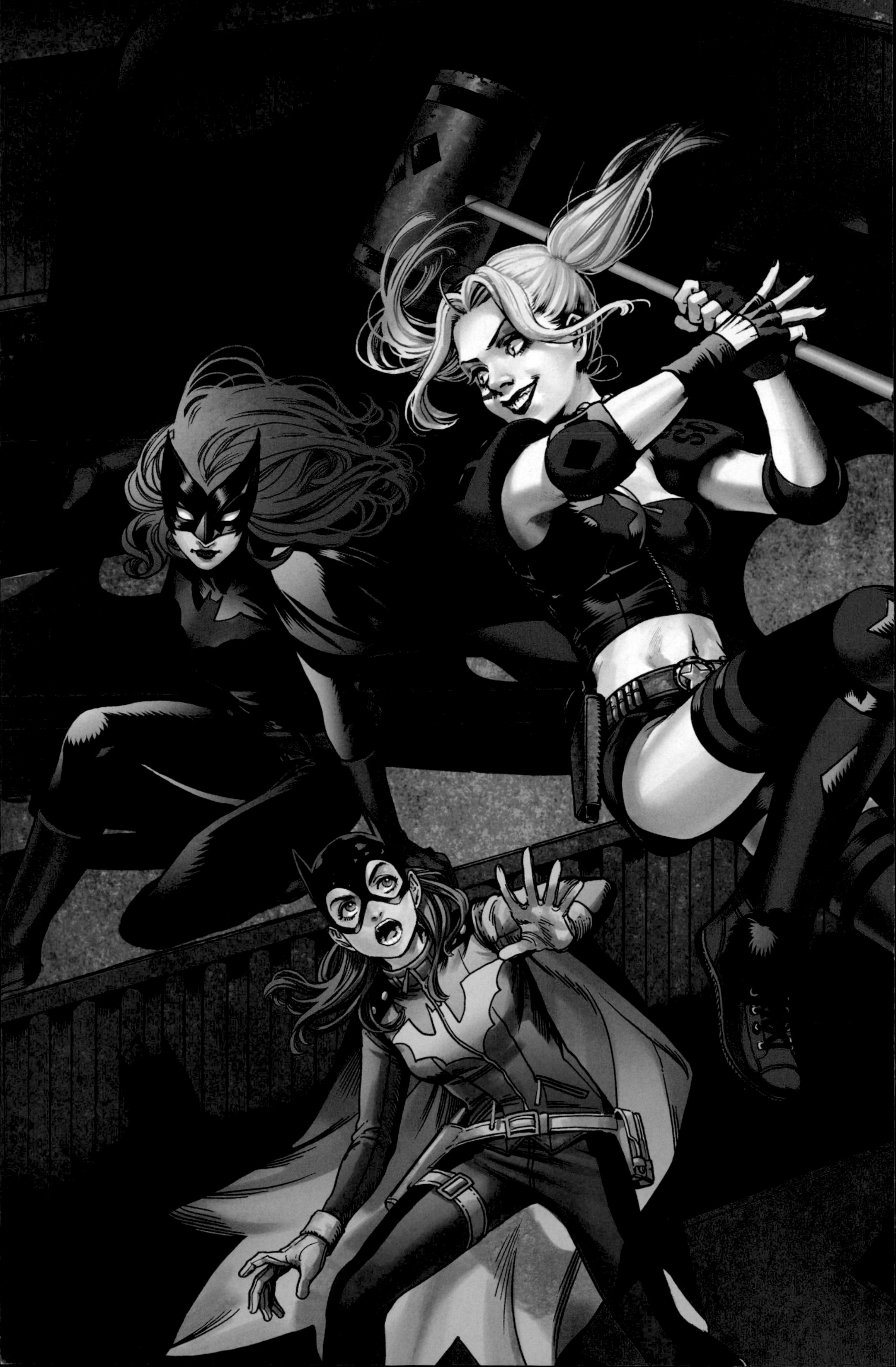

BATGIRL AND THE BIRDS OF PREY #16 variant cover by KAMOME SHIRAHAMA

BATGIRL AND THE BIRDS OF PREY #17 variant cover by KAMOME SHIRAHAMA

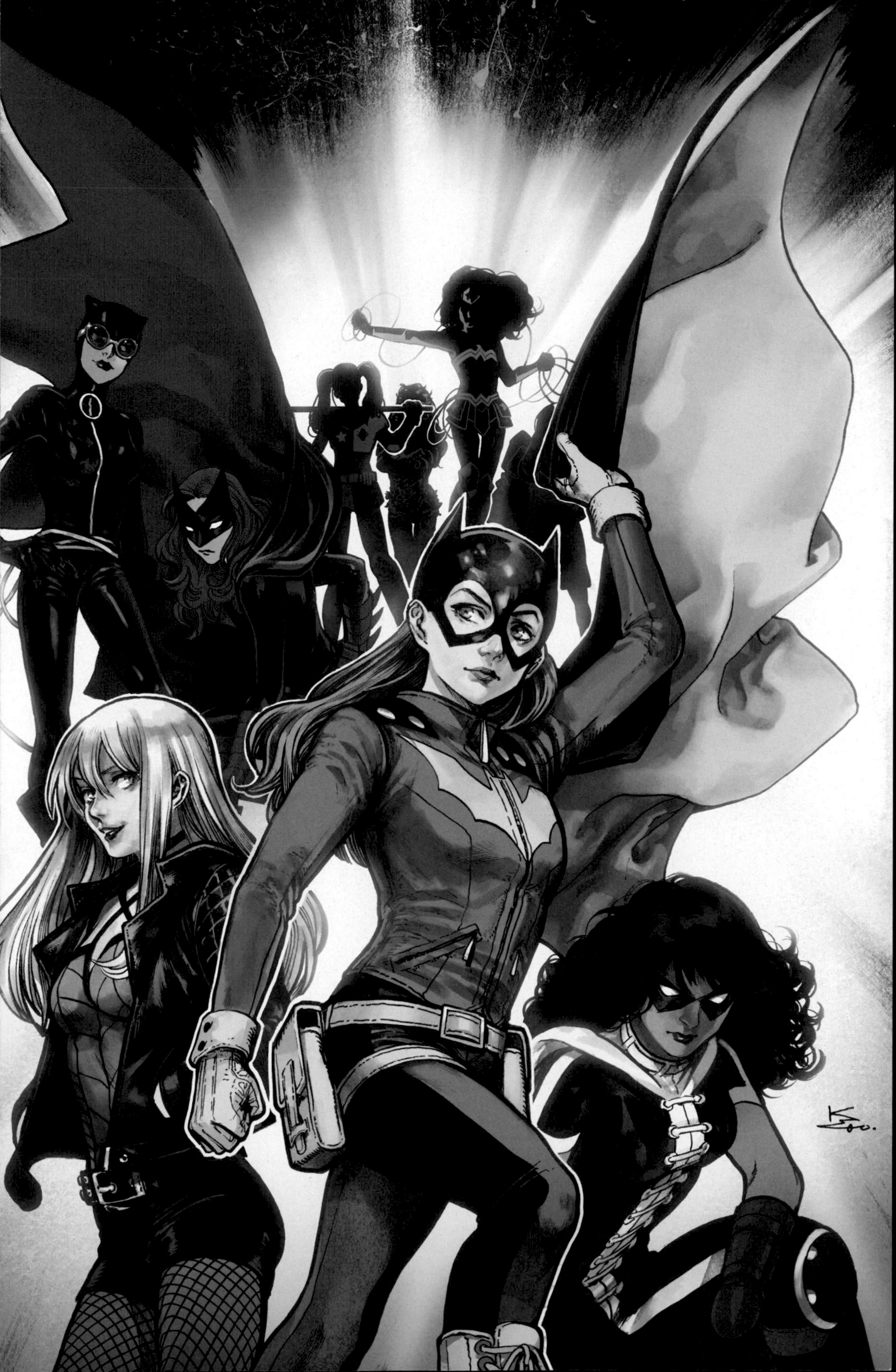

BATGIRL AND THE BIRDS OF PREY #18 variant cover by KAMOME SHIRAHAMA

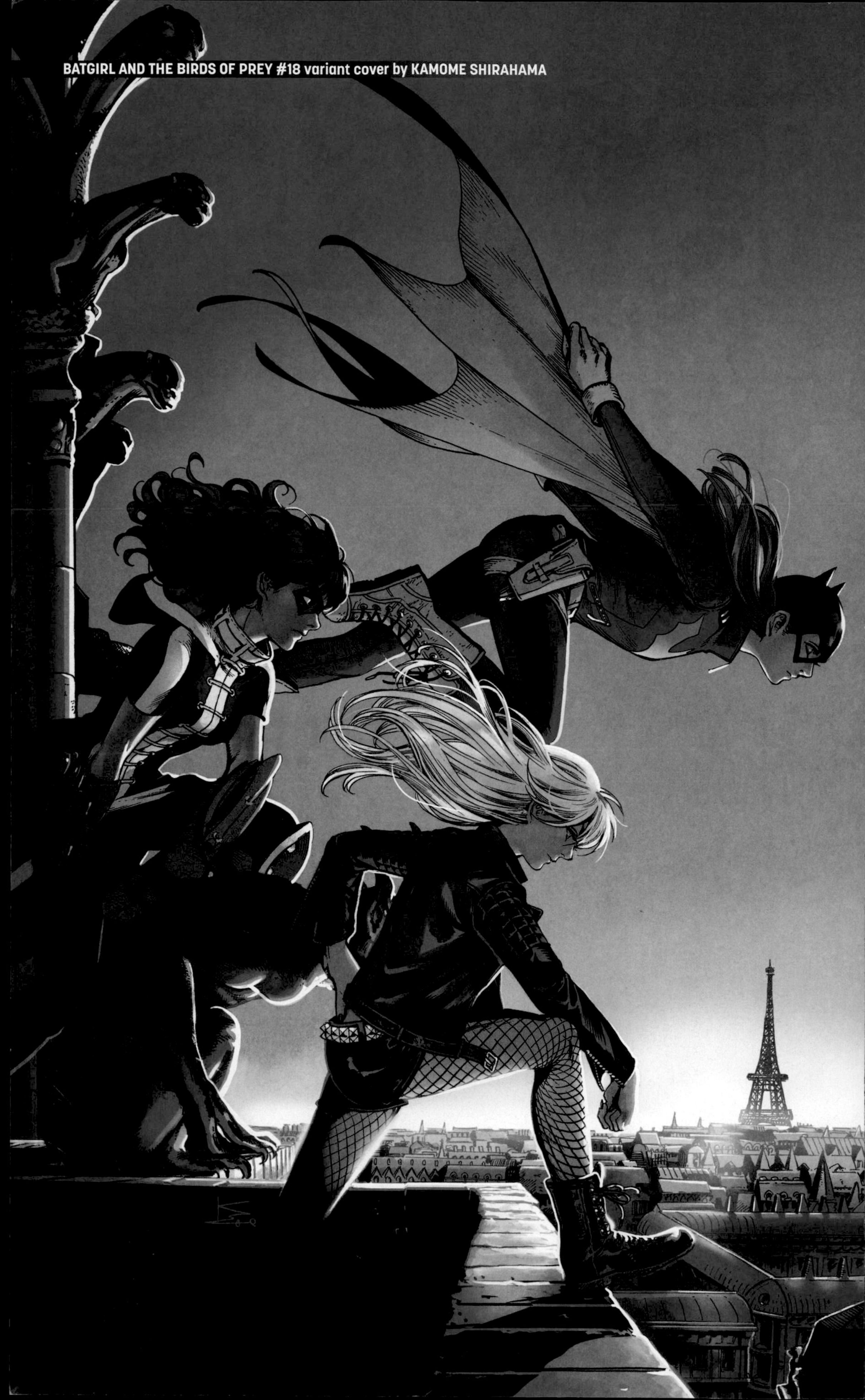

BATGIRL AND THE BIRDS OF PREY #19 variant cover by KAMOME SHIRAHAMA

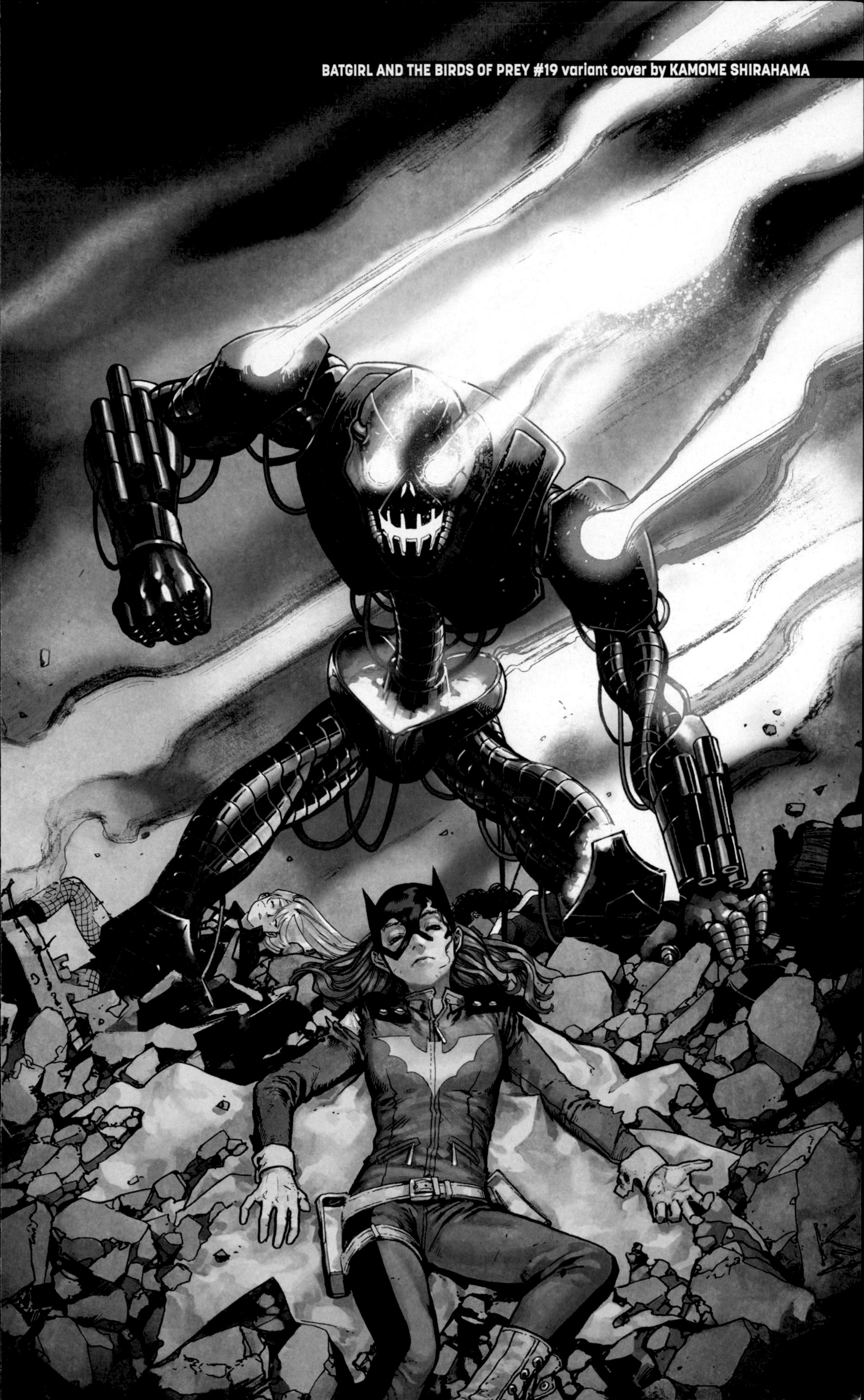

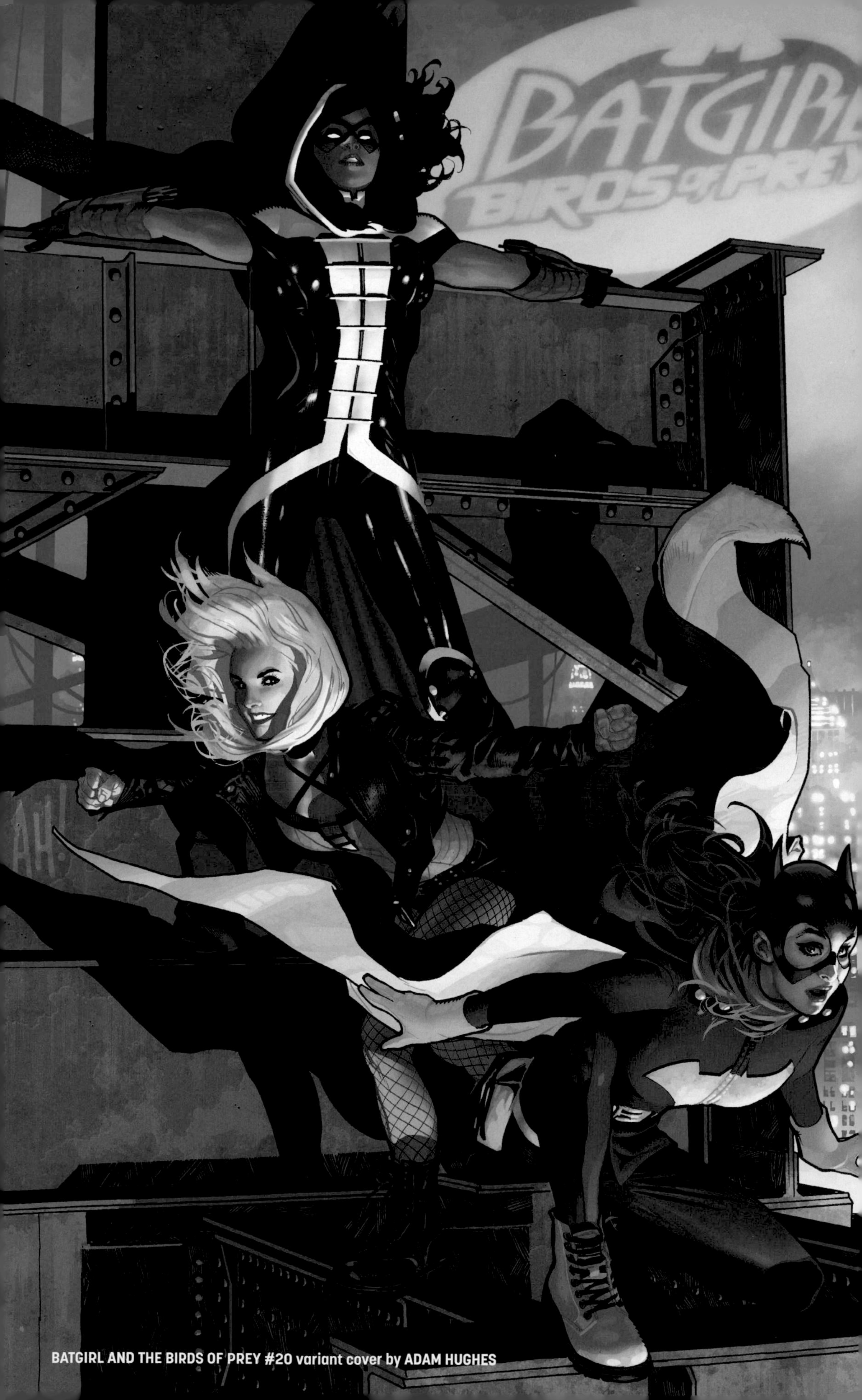

BATGIRL AND THE BIRDS OF PREY #20 variant cover by ADAM HUGHES

BATGIRL AND THE BIRDS OF PREY #21 variant cover by KAMOME SHIRAHAMA

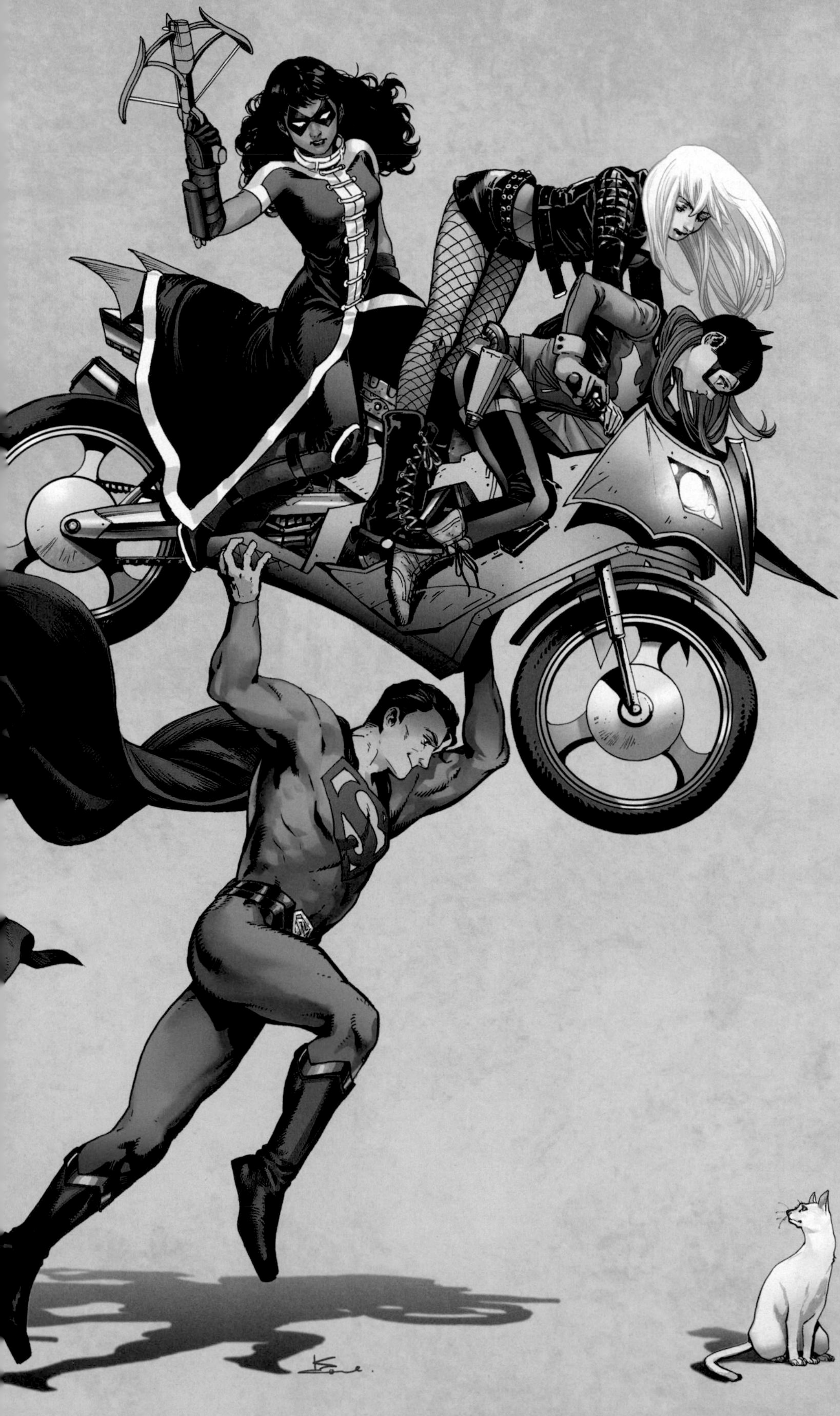

BATGIRL AND THE BIRDS OF PREY #22 variant cover by YASMINE PUTRI

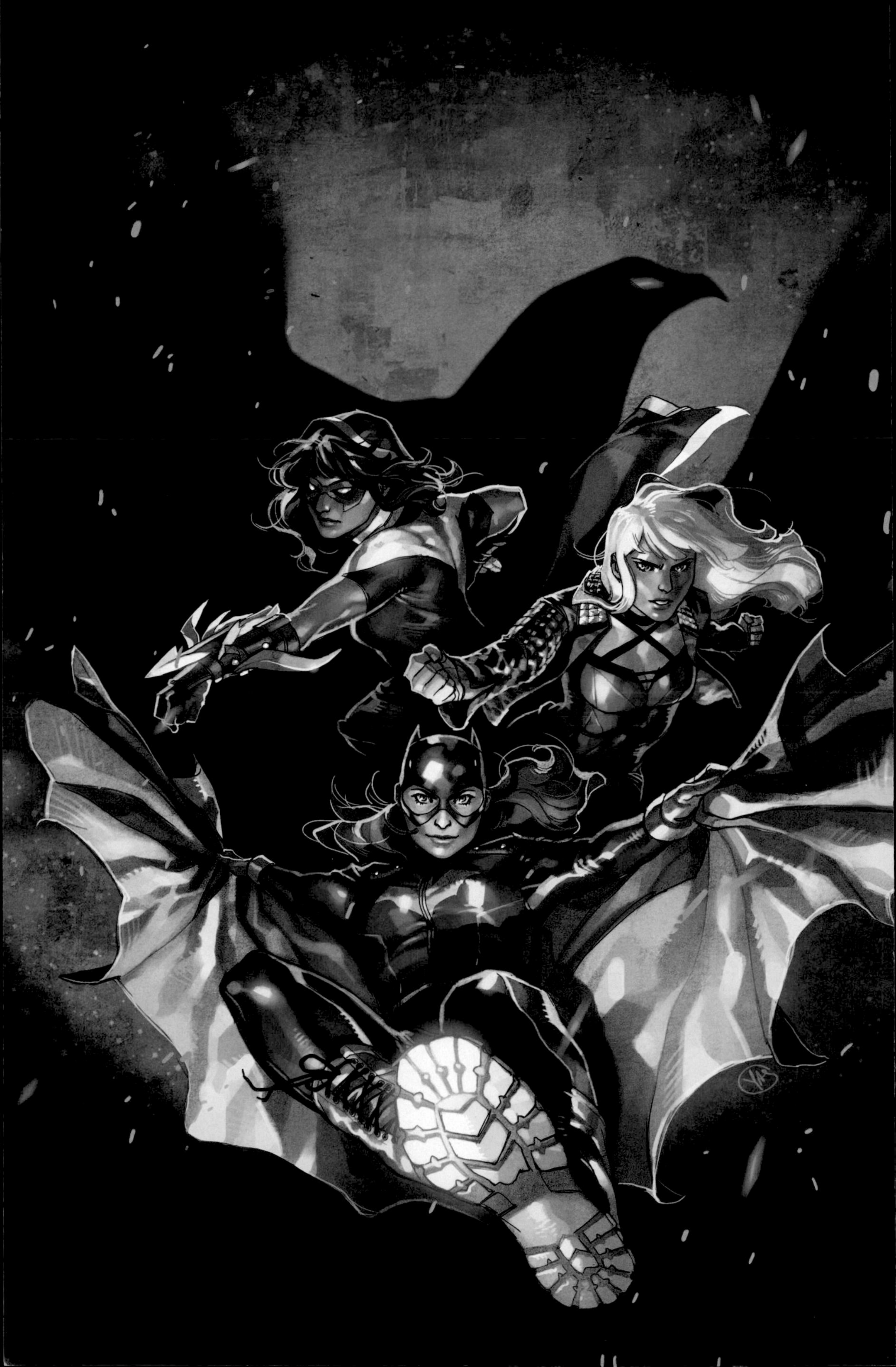

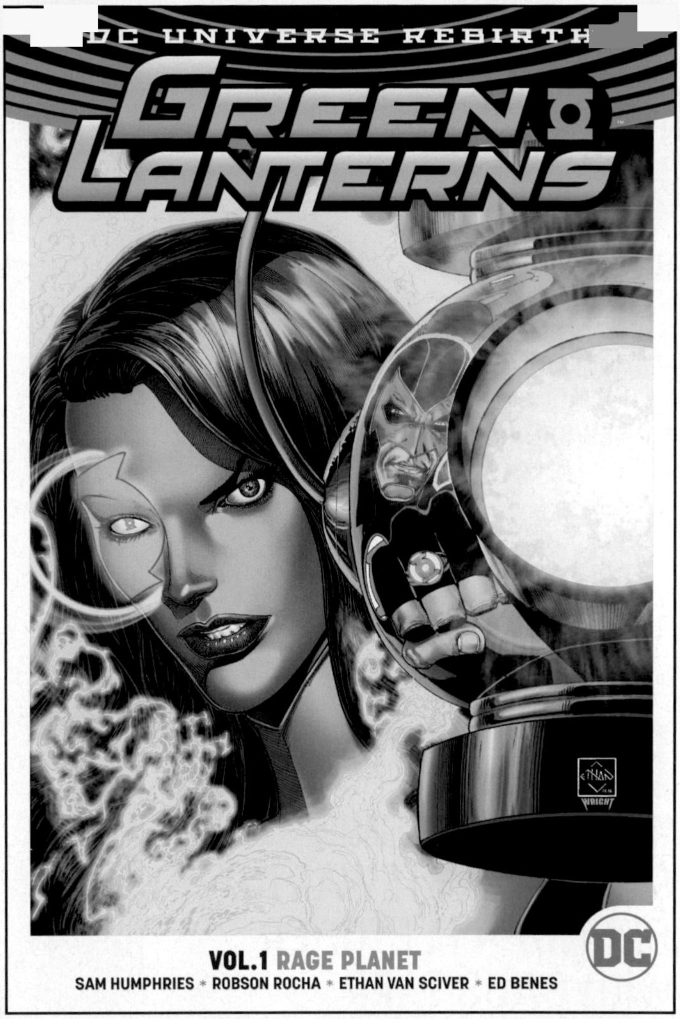
DC UNIVERSE REBIRTH
GREEN LANTERNS
VOL.1 RAGE PLANET
SAM HUMPHRIES • ROBSON ROCHA • ETHAN VAN SCIVER • ED BENES

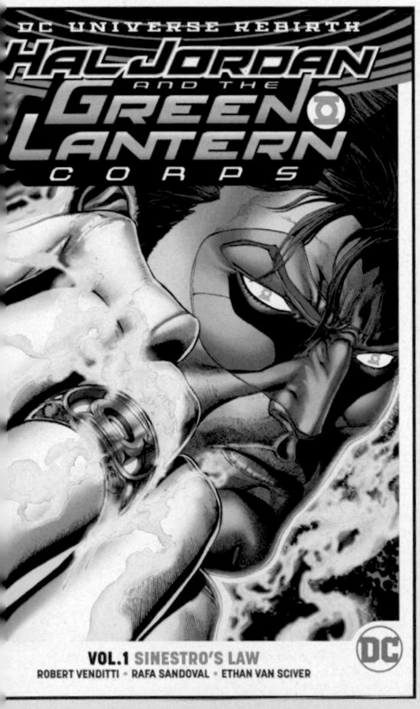
DC UNIVERSE REBIRTH
HAL JORDAN AND THE GREEN LANTERN CORPS
VOL.1 SINESTRO'S LAW
ROBERT VENDITTI • RAFA SANDOVAL • ETHAN VAN SCIVER

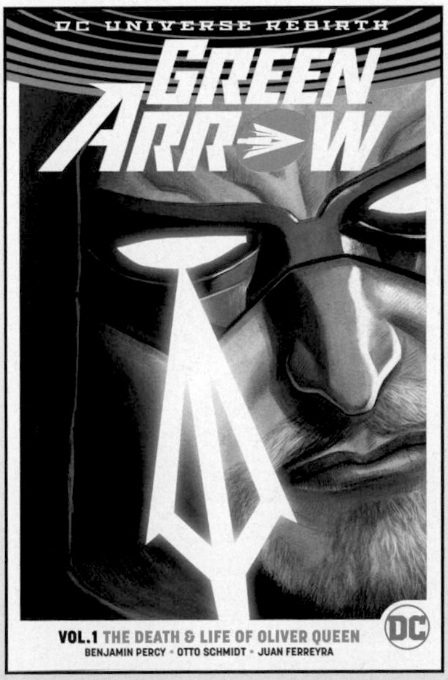
DC UNIVERSE REBIRTH
GREEN ARROW
VOL.1 THE DEATH & LIFE OF OLIVER QUEEN
BENJAMIN PERCY • OTTO SCHMIDT • JUAN FERREYRA

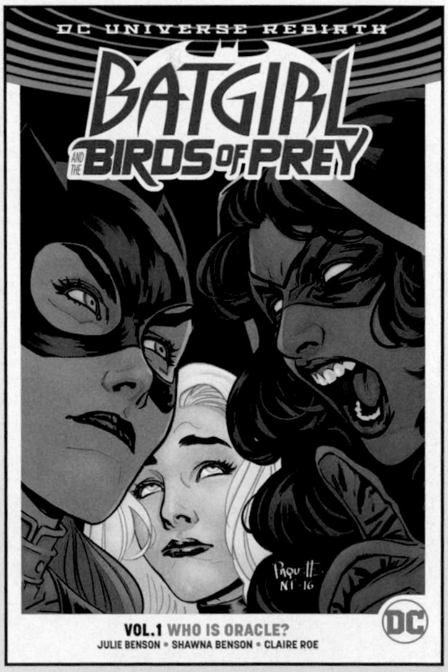
DC UNIVERSE REBIRTH
BATGIRL AND THE BIRDS OF PREY
VOL.1 WHO IS ORACLE?
JULIE BENSON • SHAWNA BENSON • CLAIRE ROE

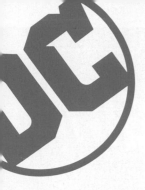

"A brand-new take on a classic, and it looks absolutely, jaw-droppingly fantastic."
– **NEWSARAMA**

"A whole lot of excitement and killer art."
– **COMIC BOOK RESOURCES**

BATGIRL

VOL. 1: BATGIRL OF BURNSIDE
CAMERON STEWART & BRENDEN FLETCHER
with BABS TARR

BATGIRL VOL. 2:
FAMILY BUSINESS

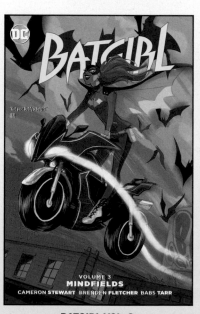

BATGIRL VOL. 3:
MINDFIELDS

WONDER WOMAN
OL. 1: BLOOD
BRIAN AZZARELLO
with CLIFF CHIANG

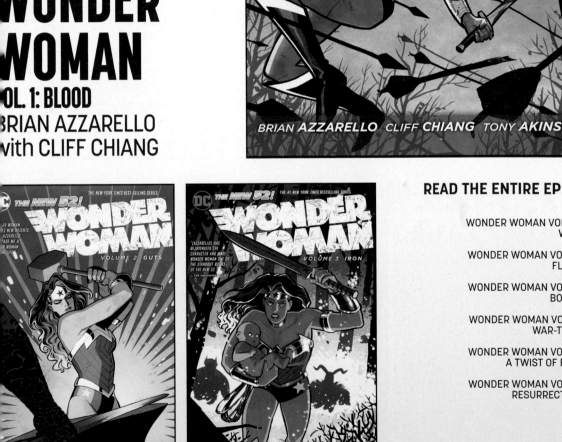

**WONDER WOMAN
VOL. 2: GUTS**

**WONDER WOMAN
VOL. 3: IRON**

DC UNIVERSE REBIRTH

SUICIDE SQUAD

VOL. 1: THE BLACK VAULT

ROB WILLIAMS
with JIM LEE and others

VOL. 1 THE BLACK VAULT

ROB WILLIAMS • JIM LEE • PHILIP TAN • JASON FABOK • IVAN REIS • GARY FRANK

THE HELLBLAZER VOL. 1:
THE POISON TRUTH

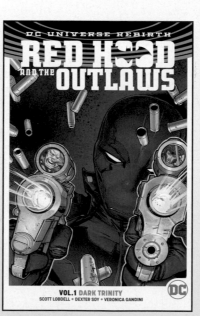

RED HOOD AND THE OUTLAWS VOL. 1:
DARK TRINITY

HARLEY QUINN VOL. 1:
DIE LAUGHING